TEPS
첫걸음

TEPS 첫걸음 R/C

지은이 넥서스텝스연구팀 · 김무룡
펴낸이 안용백
펴낸곳 (주)넥서스

초판 1쇄 발행 2008년 3월 25일
초판 11쇄 발행 2016년 3월 5일

출판신고 1992년 4월 3일 제311-2002-2호
04044 서울시 마포구 양화로 8길 24
Tel (02)330-5500 Fax (02)330-5555
ISBN 978-89-6000-389-7 13740

www.nexusbook.com

가장 쉽게, 가장 빨리, 가장 확실하게 점수를 올려주는

TEPS 첫걸음

R/C

김무룡 지음
넥서스텝스연구팀

넥서스

"내면화된 영어 능력을 측정한다"는 기치 아래 출범한 TEPS는 표준적인 영어 시험으로 자리 잡으면서 점차 문제의 출제 경향이 정형화되고 문제가 보다 세련되어 가는 추세이다. 그 가운데 문법, 어휘, 그리고 독해를 포함하는 R/C 부분은 체계적인 학습에 많은 시간이 소요되고 특히 독해에서는 고득점이 쉽지 않은 것이 현실이다. 이와 같은 TEPS의 변화와 수험생들의 현실적 요구를 충실히 반영하면서, 동시에 TEPS에 첫발을 내딛는 수험생들이 믿고 의지할 수 있는 기본서로 "TEPS 첫걸음 R/C"가 기획되었다.

문법과 어휘 영역은 TEPS에서 일정 부분을 차지하기 때문에 그 자체로서 물론 중요하지만, 동시에 독해의 바탕이 된다는 점에서도 중요하다. 흔히 문법과 어휘, 독해가 분리되어 있다고 잘못 생각하는 경우가 많은데, 이 세 영역은 모두 "의미 구성"이라는 공통분모를 가진다. 따라서 문법과 어휘 영역을 학습하면서도 학습 내용이 의미 구성으로 어떻게 반영되어 독해와 연계될까를 생각해 보는 것이 R/C 전체를 대비하는 가장 효과적이고 효율적인 방법이다.

이 책에서는 문법을 크게 6개 chapter로 구성하여 TEPS 초보자로서 문법의 토대를 확실하게 쌓을 수 있도록 배려했다. Chapter 1에서 의미 구성의 기본 단위인 문장 구성 규칙을 다룬 다음, Chapter 2에서는 영어 문장 구성에서 가장 중요한 위치를 차지하는 동사를 크게 "시제와 태"라는 측면에서 설명했다. Chapter 3에서는 동사에서 비롯되어 다양하게 의미를 구성하는 부정사, 동명사, 분사를 준동사(verbal)라는 항목으로 묶어서 설명했다. 조동사(auxiliary verb)는 편의상 같은 chapter에 배정했지만, 아시다시피 조동사의 쓰임새는 준동사와 상당한 차이를 나타낸다.

그런 다음 동사 이외의 품사를 크게 하나의 문장 구성에 쓰이는 품사와, 문장과 문장을 연결하는 데 쓰이는 품사로 나누어 각각 Chapter 4와 Chapter 5에서 쓰임새를 설명했다. Chapter 4에서 특히 명사는 동사와 함께 의미 구성에서 가장 중요한 역할을 맡는다는 점을 감안하여 주의 깊게 학습할 것을 권한다. Chapter 6에서는 일치(agreement)와 어순(word order)을 다루어 TEPS 대비에 필요한 기본적인 문법 사항을 완성하도록 배려했다. 앞에서 말했듯이, 문법 학습에서는 용어나 규칙의 습득보다도 각 사항들이 어떻게 의미 구성에 기여하는가 하는 측면에서 접근해야만 소기의 성과를 거둘 수 있다는 점을 명심해야 한다.

어휘 영역은 크게 7개 chapter로 구성하여 TEPS에서 측정하는 각 어휘 유형을 충분히 학습하고 원어민의 어휘 감각을 익힐 수 있도록 배려했다. 가장 출제빈도가 높은 collocation을 10개 Unit으로 구성했고, 점차 중요성이 높아지고 있는 고급어휘를 5개 Unit으로 구성했다. 또한 전통적으로 중요한 유형인 필수 어휘를 4개 Unit으로 편성했다. 나머지 chapter들은 혼동어휘, 구동사(phrasal verb), 숙어, 그리고 일상구어체 표현으로 편성하여 어휘에서 출제되는 모든 유형에 대한 확고한 토대를 마련할 수 있도록 세심하게 배려했다.

어휘 영역은 15분이라는 짧은 시간에 50문항을 풀어나가야 하기 때문에 다른 영역에 비해 심리적 부담이 큰 영역이다. 따라서 기본적인 어휘를 중심으로 점차 우리말에 대한 의존도를 줄이면서 원어민의 어휘 감각을 익혀나가는 것이 가장 효과적이면서도 효율적인 대비책임을 명심해야 한다. 어휘 학습은 본래 자연스러운 맥락(context)에서 유의미하게 이루어져야만 높은 성과를 기대할 수 있다. 이 과정에서 특히 우리말 대응어(equivalent)가 아니라 영어 단어 자체에 대한 감각을 기를 수 있도록 일정한 표현이 쓰이는 자연스러운 맥락을 파악하는 데 주력해야 한다.

독해 영역은 크게 6개 chapter로 나누어 TEPS 독해 영역 대비의 기본 토대를 마련할 수 있도록 세심하게 내용을 구성했다. Chapter 1에서 독해 기본기를 다룬 다음, Chapter 2, Chapter 3에서 독해 영역의 문제 유형을 모두 섭렵할 수 있도록 편성했다. 그리고 Chapter 4와 Chapter 5는 각각 실용문과 비실용문으로 나누어 TEPS에 출제되는 다양한 글을 폭넓게 접할 수 있도록 배려했다. 특히 지문의 구성에서 출제 경향과 출제 가능성, 그리고 학습 효과 등을 종합적으로 고려하여, 참신하면서도 쓸모 있는 지문을 풍부하게 제시했다.

독해 영역은 45분이라는 시간에 40개의 지문을 빠른 속도록 풀어나가야 하기 때문에 매우 부담이 큰 영역이다. 따라서 점차로 우리말 해석에 대한 의존을 줄여나가면서, 글 자체의 일관성(coherence)과 자연스러운 흐름을 포착하는 능력을 길러나가야 한다. 무엇보다도 글쓴이가 글을 통해 궁극적으로 전달하고자 하는 바가 무엇인지를 정확히 파악하는 연습이 긴요하다. 그리고 문법와 어휘 영역에서 기른 영어 자체에 대한 감각을 충분히 발휘하고, 시간 배분과 기본적인 독해 기법을 활용하여 주어진 시간에 모든 지문을 해결할 수 있는 능력을 쌓아나가야 한다. 이와 관련된 도움말들은 "Tips"를 통해 충분히 제공했다.

R/C 영역 고득점의 토대가 되는, 효과적인 언어 학습은 의미 구성이라는 측면에서 이루어져야 한다는 점에 주목할 필요가 있다. 의미 구성에는 원어민이 세계를 해석하는 방식과 순서가 반영되어 있다. 이 두 가지에 숙달되어야만 "내면화된 영어 능력"을 측정하는 TEPS에서 고득점이 가능하다. 이 "TEPS 첫걸음 R/C"는 그와 같은 능력 습득의 확고부동한 토대를 마련할 것으로 확신한다. 교재에 대한 문의는 pasada72@naver.com으로 해 줄 것을 당부하며, 소중한 꿈을 간직한 수험생 여러분 모두의 건승을 기원한다.

김무룡

Structure

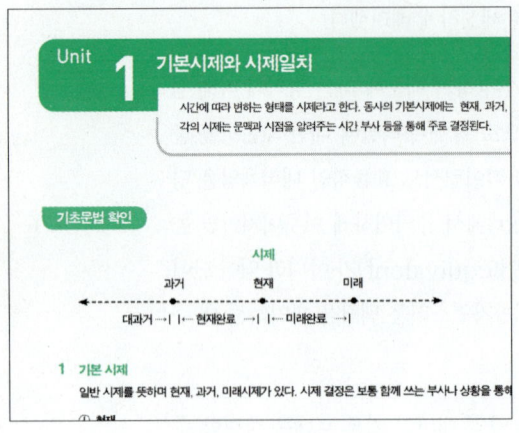

■ 기초문법 확인

각 UNIT별로 핵심이 되는 관련 문법 사항을 정리해 TEPS 문법의 초석을 다질 수 있도록 했다.

중요 Collocation 정리

1. **do one's homework** 숙제를 하다 (반드시 소유격과 함께 쓰임에 유의)

    Interestingly enough, Michelle enjoys doing her homework.

2. **do one's best** 최선을 다하다 (= try one's best)

    Never complain, just do your best!

3. **do harm** 해를 끼치다 (= cause harm)

    A bad policy can do great harm to the country.

4. **make a mistake** 실수를 저지르다 (do a mistake라고 할 수 없음)

    Our homeroom teacher told us to try not to make a mistake.

5. **make an effort** 노력하다 (= put forth an effort)

    Tara is making a great effort to improve her score on the TEPS test.

■ 어휘 정리

Section B(어휘)에서 UNIT별로 관련 있는 엄선된 대표 표현들을 2쪽에 걸쳐 제시했다.

Tips

1 시간 배정

TEPS의 문제 유형 가운데, 세부사항 유형은 빈 칸 채우기 유형 디
왜냐하면 하나하나의 사항을 정확하게 확인해야만 제대로 정답을 그
와 같은 유형에서 절약한 시간을 세부사항 문제 풀이에 활용해야 한
제대로 풀어낼 수 있기 때문이다.

2 중심 내용과의 관련성

세부사항 유형은 지문 전체를 읽지 않은 상태에서 하나하나의 답지
지만 이와 같은 방법은 실수로 이어질 가능성이 높다는 점에서 주의
제 의도도 글의 대한 정밀한 이해력의 측정이기 때문에, 대개 중심 (
경우가 많기 때문이다. 따라서 일단 글의 중심 내용이 무엇인지를 그
하자.

■ Tips

Section C(독해)에서 각 UNIT별로 UNIT과 관련된, 또는 전반적인 독해와 관련된 중요한 Tips를 제공했다.

■ EXERCISE

EXERCISE

※ 빈 칸에 들어갈 가장 알맞은 말을 고르시오.

1 Blind dates can _____. There are so many stupid
   and your date could be one of them. Imagine yourself talking with
   only interested in your looks. He can't understand your heart. He
   art. He is dull. You might keep watching the clock. You wish time
   You can't find anything interesting to say. You just wish you left hir

   (a) excite your life
   (b) make you understand the true meaning of life
   (c) be boring

2 Some people say that to meditate, you _____
   not the case. Meditation is when you are trying to look within y

각 영역(문법, 어휘, 독해)별 그리고 UNIT별로 가장 효율
적으로 관련 UNIT을 연습할 수 있도록 맞춤형 연습문제
(EXERCISE)를 제공했다.

■ PRACTICE

PRACTICE

1 Gerard Lambert was born in America in 1886. In a sense, he was
   _____. This was because he majored in architecture at Colu
   Surprisingly, however, he became a very successful advertiser.
   advertise Listerine, his father's invention, Lambert came up with a
   told the people that by using the new mouthwash, they could sav
   situations.

   Q. Choose the one option that best completes the sentence.

   (a) meant to be a brave soldier
   (b) meant to be a good advertiser
   (c) supposed to be an inventor
   (d) supposed to be an architect

실전 문제(Actual Test)와 같은 형태와 유형을 통해 실전
에 대비토록 하였다.

■ 모의고사

Part I Questions 1~16
Read the passage. Then choose the option that best completes the passage.

1. According to National Cancer Institute, it is _____ whether tea can
   actually reduce the risks of developing cancer. Some studies support the claim that
   the consumption of tea can cut cancer risk. On the other hand, other studies do
   not support that claim. This is largely because other factors such as one's diet and
   lifestyle can help reduce cancer risk.

   (a) absolutely true
   (b) sure
   (c) not certain
   (d) determined

책의 PRACTICE 수준으로 난이도를 맞춰 실제 시험과 같
은 형태의 모의고사를 영역(문법·어휘·독해)이 끝날 때
마다 각각 제공했다.

Contents

■ 머리말   4
■ 구성   6
■ 목차   8
■ TEPS 정보   12

문법 (Section A)

Chapter 1 문장의 기본

| UNIT **1** | 문장의 구성 | 36 |
| UNIT **2** | 자동사와 타동사 | 40 |

Chapter 2 시제와 태

UNIT **1**	기본시제와 시제일치	46
UNIT **2**	완료와 진행시제	50
UNIT **3**	가정법 I	54
UNIT **4**	가정법 II	58
UNIT **5**	태	62

Chapter 3 준동사

UNIT **1**	to부정사와 동명사	68
UNIT **2**	분사	72
UNIT **3**	분사구문	76
UNIT **4**	조동사	80

Chapter 4 품사 I

UNIT **1**	명사와 관사	86
UNIT **2**	형용사와 부사	90
UNIT **3**	기타 형용사	94
UNIT **4**	비교	98
UNIT **5**	대명사 일치와 재귀대명사	102
UNIT **6**	지시대명사와 부정대명사	106
UNIT **7**	전치사 I	110
UNIT **8**	전치사(접속사 구별 포함) II	114

Chapter 5 품사 Ⅱ

UNIT 1	등위, 상관접속사	120
UNIT 2	명사절과 접속사	124
UNIT 3	부사절을 이끄는 접속사 I	128
UNIT 4	부사절을 이끄는 접속사 II	132
UNIT 5	관계사(관계대명사) I	136
UNIT 6	관계사(기타 관계사) II	140

Chapter 6 일치와 어순

UNIT 1	일치	146
UNIT 2	강조와 도치	150
UNIT 3	주요 동사의 쓰임과 어순	154

| 문법 모의고사 | 159 |

어휘 (Section B)

Chapter 1 어울려 쓰이는 Collocation

UNIT 1	동사＋명사 I	170
UNIT 2	동사＋명사 II	174
UNIT 3	동사＋명사 III	178
UNIT 4	동사＋명사 IV	182
UNIT 5	명사＋동사	186
UNIT 6	형용사＋명사 I	190
UNIT 7	형용사＋명사 II	194
UNIT 8	동사＋부사 I	198
UNIT 9	동사＋부사 II	202
UNIT 10	부사＋형용사	206

Chapter 2 필수어휘와 혼동어휘

UNIT 1	동사(필수어휘) I	212
UNIT 2	동사(필수어휘) II	216
UNIT 3	명사(필수어휘)	220

UNIT 4	형용사(필수어휘)	224
UNIT 5	의미(혼동어휘) I	228
UNIT 6	의미(혼동어휘) II	232
UNIT 7	형태(혼동어휘)	236

Chapter 3 구동사와 숙어

UNIT 1	동사와 particle의 결합(구동사) I	242
UNIT 2	동사와 particle의 결합(구동사) II	246
UNIT 3	숙어 I	250
UNIT 4	숙어 II	254

Chapter 4 고급 어휘

UNIT 1	고급 어휘 I	260
UNIT 2	고급 어휘 II	264
UNIT 3	고급 어휘 III	268
UNIT 4	고급 어휘 IV	272
UNIT 5	고급 어휘 V	276

Chapter 5 일상 구어체 표현

| UNIT 1 | 일상 구어체 표현 I | 282 |
| UNIT 2 | 일상 구어체 표현 II | 286 |

어휘 모의고사 291

독해 (Section C)

Chapter 1 독해 기본기 다지기

UNIT 1	주제 찾기	302
UNIT 2	세부사항 찾기	306
UNIT 3	추론	310
UNIT 4	일관성에서 벗어난 것	314

Chapter 2 빈 칸 채우기

| UNIT 1 | 빈 칸이 처음에 있는 경우 | 320 |

UNIT 2	빈 칸이 중간에 있는 경우	324
UNIT 3	빈 칸이 마지막에 있는 경우	328
UNIT 4	연결어 선택	332

Chapter 3 질문 유형은 이렇다

UNIT 1	전반적 정보 I	338
UNIT 2	전반적 정보 II	342
UNIT 3	정오 유형 I	346
UNIT 4	정오 유형 II	350
UNIT 5	세부사항 I	354
UNIT 6	세부사항 II	358

Chapter 4 실용문

UNIT 1	광고	364
UNIT 2	기사 I (사건 · 사고)	368
UNIT 3	기사 II (칼럼 · 독자 투고)	372
UNIT 4	기사 III (일반 상식 기사)	376
UNIT 5	서한 I (일반 서한 · 이메일)	380
UNIT 6	서한 II (추천서 · 지원서)	384

Chapter 5 비실용문

UNIT 1	정치와 경제	390
UNIT 2	사회와 역사	394
UNIT 3	문화와 인물	398
UNIT 4	지구과학	402
UNIT 5	생물학	406
UNIT 6	환경과학	410
UNIT 7	생활과학	414
UNIT 8	철학과 예술	418

어휘 모의고사 423

정답 및 해설(* Answer Sheet 포함)　　　　**부록**

● TEPS 개요

TEPS란 Test of English Proficiency developed by Seoul National University의 약자로 서울대학교 언어교육원에서 개발하고, TEPS관리위원회에서 주관하는 국내 토종 영어 인증시험입니다.

● 서울대학교 언어교육원은 대한민국 정부가 공인하는 외국어 능력 측정 기관으로 32년간 정부기관, 각급 단체 및 기업체를 대상으로 어학능력을 측정해 왔습니다.

● TEPS는 국내외 유수한 대학에 종사하는 최고 수준의 영어 관련 전문가 100여 명이 출제하고 세계의 권위자로 구성된 자문위원회에서 검토하는 시험입니다.

● TEPS는 청해, 문법, 어휘, 독해에 걸쳐 총 200문항, 990점 만점의 시험입니다.

● TEPS는 언어 테스팅 분야의 세계적 권위자인 Bachman 교수(미국UCLA)와 Oller 교수(미국 뉴멕시코대)에게서 타당성을 검증받았으며, 여러 번의 시험적 평가에서 이미 그 신뢰도와 타당도가 입증된 시험입니다.

● TEPS는 우리나라 사람들의 살아 있는 영어 실력, 즉 의사소통 능력을 가장 효과적이고 정확하게 측정해 주는 시험이라고 할 수 있습니다.

● TEPS는 진정한 실력자와 비실력자를 확실히 구분할 수 있도록 구성된 시험으로서 변별력에 있어서 본인의 정확한 실력 파악에 실제적인 도움이 됩니다.

● TEPS 성적표는 수험생의 영어 능력을 영역별로 세분화한 평가를 해주기 때문에 수험자의 어느 부분이 탁월한지 잘 알 수 있을 뿐만 아니라 효과적인 영어공부 방향을 제시해 주기도 합니다.

● TEPS는 다양하고 일반적인 영어능력을 평가하는 시험으로 대학교, 기업체, 각종 기관 및 단체, 개인이 다양한 목적을 위해 응시할 수 있는 시험입니다.

TEPS의 구성

영역	파트별 내용	문항 수	총문항/시간	배점
청 해 Listening Comprehension	**Part I :** 질의 응답 (문장 하나를 듣고 이어질 대화 고르기) **Part II :** 짧은 대화 (3개 문장의 대화를 듣고 이어질 대화 고르기) **Part III :** 긴 대화 (6-8개 문장의 대화를 듣고 질문에 알맞은 답 고르기) **Part IV :** 담화문 (담화문의 내용을 듣고 질문에 알맞은 답 고르기)	15 15 15 15	60문항 / 55분	400점
문 법 Grammar	**Part I :** 구어체 (대화문의 빈칸에 적절한 표현 고르기) **Part II :** 문어체 (문장의 빈칸에 적절한 표현 고르기) **Part III :** 대화문 (대화에서 어법상 틀리거나 어색한 부분 고르기) **Part IV :** 담화문 (담화문에서 문법상 틀리거나 어색한 부분 고르기)	20 20 5 5	50문항 / 25분	100점
어 휘 Vocabulary	**Part I :** 구어체 (대화문의 빈칸에 적절한 단어 고르기) **Part II :** 문어체 (문장의 빈칸에 적절한 단어 고르기)	25 25	50문항 / 15분	100점
독 해 Reading Comprehension	**Part I :** 빈칸 채우기 (지문을 읽고 질문의 빈칸에 들어갈 내용 고르기) **Part II :** 내용 이해 (지문을 읽고 질문에 가장 적절한 내용 고르기) **Part III :** 흐름 찾기 (지문을 읽고 문맥상 어색한 내용 고르기)	16 21 3	40문항 / 45분	400점
총 계	13개의 세부 영역	200	140분	990점

* IRT(Item Response Theory)에 의하여 최고점은 990점, 최하점은 10점으로 조정됨.

TEPS의 특징

한국인에게 알맞은 영어 시험

우리 국민 대다수가 초·중·고교에서 10년 동안 영어를 배우고, 대학과 직장에서 또 다시 영어교육을 받지만 한국은 아시아에서도 한참 뒤떨어진 영어후진국 신세를 면치 못하고 있습니다.

미국과 영국에서 개발한 영어교육체계와 어학검정시험을 좇아 매년 수십만 명이 동분서주하지만 눈에 띄는 성과를 거두지는 못했습니다. 사고방식과 언어 습관이 다른 외국인이 한국인의 고민을 알기는 어렵습니다. TEPS는 영어와 한국어를 다 잘하는 국내 최고의 연구진이 영어와 한국어의 언어적 특성을 대조·분석하고 한국인들이 범하기 쉬운 오류를 찾아 출제에 적극 반영합니다. 따라서 TEPS는 한국인에게 가장 필요한 영어 학습 지침을 제공하는 시험이라고 할 수 있습니다.

편법이 통하지 않는 시험

개인의 어학 능력은 결코 단기간에 급속도로 향상되지 않습니다. 그런데도 실력 배양은 아랑곳하지 않고 영어성적만을 올리기 위해 요령과 편법을 가르치는 교육기관이 많습니다.

TEPS는 있는 그대로의 영어 능력을 정확하게 진단합니다. 예를 들어 청해 시험은 인쇄된 질문지 및 선택지 없이 방송으로만 들려주기 때문에 미리 문제를 보고 답을 예측해 보는 요령이 통하지 않습니다. 또한 독해 시험에 있어서는 '1지문 1문항 원칙'을 지켜 한 문제로 다음 문제의 답을 유추할 수 있는 가능성을 원천적으로 배제하고 있습니다. 따라서 TEPS는 편법이 통하지 않는 시험입니다.

활용 능력을 중시하는 시험

외국인과 영어로 대화할 때 상대방이 질문을 던질 경우, 한참 동안 문법과 어휘를 고민해서 대답할 수는 없는 노릇입니다. 암기식으로 배운 영어로는 실제 상황에서 제 실력을 발휘할 수 없습니다.

TEPS는 일상생활에서의 활용 능력을 정확하게 측정해 주는 시험입니다. TEPS는 기존의 다른 시험에 비해 많은 지문을 주고 이를 짧은 시간 내에 이해하여 풀어낼 수 있는지를 측정합니다. 이는 실제 생활에서 활용할 수 없는 암기식 영어가 아니라 완전히 습득되어 자유롭게 구사할 수 있는 '살아 있는' 영어 실력을 평가하기 위한 것입니다.

경제성과 효율성을 갖춘 시험

TEPS는 서울대 언어교육원이 자체 개발한 시험으로 외국에 비싼 로열티를 지불하는 다른 시험과는 달리 응시 비용이 매우 저렴합니다.

✚ 채점방식이 다른 시험

TEPS는 첨단 어학 능력 검증 기법인 문항 반응 이론(IRT: Item Response Theory)을 도입했습니다. 문항 반응 이론은 문항을 개발할 때 문항별로 1차 난이도를 정의하고 시험 시행 후 전체 수험자들이 각각의 문항에 대해 맞고 틀린 것을 종합해 그 문항의 난이도를 재조정한 다음, 이를 근거로 다시 한 번 채점해 최종 성적을 내게 됩니다. 이 과정에서 최고점은 990점, 최하점은 10점으로 조정됩니다.

문항 반응 이론은 맞은 개수의 합을 총점으로 하는 전근대적인 평가 방식과는 달리, 각 문항의 난이도와 변별도에 대한 수험자의 반응 패턴을 근거로 영어 능력을 추정하는 확률 이론입니다.

문항 반응 이론을 적용할 경우, 낮은 난이도의 문제를 많이 틀린 수험자가 높은 난이도의 문제를 맞힐 경우 실력에 관계없이 추측이나 우연히 맞힐 가능성이 높다고 보고 감점 처리합니다. 이러한 문항 반응 이론은 가장 선진적인 검정 방식으로서 TEPS는 이 이론에 기초한 국내 최초의 영어 능력 평가 시험입니다.

✚ 실용영어 능력 평가

실용영어는 사소한 대화를 위주로 하는 생활영어와는 다른 범주입니다. 평균적인 교양을 갖춘 일반인이 가정, 직장, 공공장소 등 일상적인 환경과 생활에서 사용하는 영어를 뜻합니다. 일상적인 대화는 물론, 신문, 잡지, 방송, 매뉴얼, 예약, 주문, 구매, 일반적인 상담 등이 모두 실용영어의 범주에 포함됩니다.

TEPS는 누구나 쉽게 접하는 상황에서 추출된 소재를 중심으로 문제를 구성하여, 범용적인 영어 능력을 평가합니다. 따라서 성별, 직업, 나이에 관계없이 일반 대중들의 영어 능력을 객관적으로 평가할 수 있는 시험입니다.

✚ 신속한 결과 통보, 학습 방향을 제시해주는 성적 진단

TEPS는 점수만 알려주고 끝나는 시험이 아닙니다. 청취, 문법, 어휘, 독해 등 영역별로 점수를 산출하고, 다시 각 영역을 기능, 소재, 문체별로 세분하여 18개 부문에서 항목별 성취도를 알려 줍니다. 따라서 성적표를 통해 수험자의 강점, 약점은 물론 추후 학습 방향을 명확하게 제시합니다.

TEPS 출제 원칙

🞤 통합식 시험 (Integrative Test)

지엽적인 학습을 조장할 우려가 있는 분리식 시험(Discrete-Point Test) 유형을 배제하고 실제 의사소통 상황과 문맥 파악을 중시하는 통합식 시험(Integrative Test) 유형을 강조함으로써 수험자의 폭넓은 어학 능력을 평가할 수 있습니다.

🞤 국부 독립성 (Local Independence)

첨단 테스트 기술인 문항 반응 이론(IRT: Item Response Theory)을 활용하여 각 부분의 독립성을 보장 합니다. 예를 들어 '1지문 1문항'의 원칙에 따라 다양한 내용의 지문을 수험생들이 접할 수 있게 하고, 동시 에 어느 한 지문을 이해하지 못함으로써 몇 개의 문항을 연이어 틀리는 일이 없도록 했습니다. 국부 독립성 에 따른 문항 반응 이론은 환상의 어학 능력 평가로 기대를 모으고 있는 컴퓨터 개별 적응 언어 평가(CALT: Computer Adaptive Language Test)의 핵심 요소이기도 합니다.

🞤 속도화 시험 (Speeded Test)

간접적인 의사소통 능력 평가로서 문법 및 어휘 시험에서는 속도 시험의 속성을 극대화하여 언어학적 지식 (Learning)이 아닌 잠재적인 의사소통 능력(Acquisition)을 평가합니다.

🞤 진단 평가 (Diagnostic Test)

세부 영역별로 평가 결과를 제시하여 수험자 개인의 능력을 정확하게 진단합니다. 교육과 평가가 마치 실과 바늘처럼 서로 맞물려 발전해야 한다는 원칙에 따라 최대한 자세히 검정 결과를 분석해 수험생들의 향후 학 습 방향을 알려줍니다.

TEPS 출제 경향

청해 (Listening Comprehension) – 60문항

정확한 청해 능력을 측정하기 위하여 문제와 보기 문항을 문제지에 인쇄하지 않고 들려줌으로써 자연스러운 의사소통의 인지 과정을 최대한 반영하였습니다. 다양한 의사소통 기능(Communicative Functions)의 대화와 다양한 상황(공고, 방송, 일상 생활, 업무 상황, 대학 교양 수준의 강의 등)을 이해하는 데 필요한 전반적인 청해력을 측정하기 위해 대화문(dialogue)과 담화문(monologue)의 소재를 균형 있게 다루었습니다.

문법 (Grammar) – 50문항

밑줄 친 부분 중 오류를 식별하는 유형 등의 단편적이며 기계적인 문법 지식 학습을 조장할 우려가 있는 분리식 시험 유형을 배제하고, 의미 있는 문맥을 근거로 오류를 식별하는 유형을 통하여 진정한 의사소통 능력의 바탕이 되는 살아 있는 문법, 어법 능력을 문어체와 구어체를 통하여 측정합니다.

어휘 (Vocabulary) – 50문항

문맥 없이 단순한 동의어 및 반의어를 선택하는 시험 유형을 배제하고 의미 있는 문맥을 근거로 가장 적절한 어휘를 선택하는 유형을 문어체와 구어체로 나누어 측정합니다.

독해 (Reading Comprehension) – 40문항

교양 있는 수준의 글(신문, 잡지, 대학 교양과목 개론 등)과 실용적인 글(서신, 광고, 홍보, 지시문, 설명문, 도표, 양식 등)을 이해하는 데 요구되는 총체적인 독해력을 측정하기 위해서 실용문 및 비전문적 학술문과 같은 독해 지문의 소재를 균형 있게 다루었습니다.

● TEPS 영역별 유형

청해 (Listening Comprehension)- 60문항

❢ PART I (15문항)

영역 설명　Part I은 질의 응답 문제를 다루며 한 번만 들려줍니다. 내용 자체는 단순하고 기본적인 수준의 생활 영어 표현으로 구성되어 있지만 교과서적인 지식보다는 재빠른 상황 판단 능력을 요구합니다. 따라서 Part I에서는 속도 적응 능력뿐만 아니라 순발력 있는 상황 판단 능력이 요구됩니다.

Listen and choose the most appropriate response to the statement.

M　How shall I address you?

W　_____

(a) Just call me John.
(b) 39 Morrison Avenue.
(c) Don't send me a letter.
(d) I don't like making speeches.

정답 : (a)

❢ PART II (15문항)

영역 설명　Part II는 짧은 대화 문제로서 두 사람이 A-B-A-B 순으로 보통 속도로 대화하는 형식이며, 소요 시간은 약 12초 전후로 짧게 구성되어 있습니다. Part I과 마찬가지로 한 번만 들려줍니다.

Listen and choose the most appropriate response to comlpte the conversation .

M　How long were you thinking of renting a car?

W　For ten days in September.

M　When exactly do you have in mind?

W　_____

(a) I thought of it last Monday.
(b) The end of September.
(c) I'm too young to rent one yet.
(d) Nothing is further from my mind.

정답 : (b)

❢ PART III (15문항)

영역 설명　Part III는 앞의 두 파트에 비해 다소 긴 대화를 들려줍니다. 대신 대화 부분과 질문을 두 번씩 들려주기 때문에 길이가 긴 데 비해 많이 어렵다고 할 수는 없습니다.

Listen and choose the option that best answers the question.

W The conference is only two months away and we still don't have a venue.

M Maybe we should reserve the same hall we used last time.

W I think it might be too small this year.

M You're probably right. The company has really grown over the past year.

W How about looking into one of the rooms at the convention center?

M Sure. I heard they have connections with a good caterer, too.

Q What is the conversation mainly about?

(a) Hiring new employees
(b) Organizing an annual event
(c) Expanding an office building
(d) Catering a party in two months

정답 : (b)

♣ PART Ⅳ (15문항)

영역 설명　Part Ⅳ는 담화문을 다룹니다. 영어권 국가에서 영어로 뉴스를 듣거나 강의를 들을 때와 비슷한 상황을 설정하여 얼마나 잘 이해하는지를 측정합니다. 이야기의 주제, 세부 사항, 사실 여부 및 이를 근거로 한 추론 등을 다룹니다. 직청 직해 실력, 즉 들으면서 곧바로 내용을 이해할 수 있는지를 평가합니다. 담화 부분과 질문을 두 번씩 들려줍니다.

Listen and choose the option that best answers the question.

Hello, everyone. We'll continue our discussion of American newspapers today. Does anyone care to guess what the most popular section of the paper is? Well, it's not the front page, the weather report, or even - sorry to disappoint you sports fans - the sports page. It's the comics. Now, my bet is that even those of you who rarely read the paper at all can't resist glancing at the comics. True?

Q According to the talk, what is the most popular section of the paper?

(a) The front page
(b) The weather report
(c) The sports page
(d) The comics

정답 : (d)

TEPS 영역별 유형

문법 (Grammar) - 50문항

PART I (20문항)

영역 설명 Part I은 A, B 두 사람의 짧은 대화를 통해 전치사 표현력, 구문 이해력, 품사 이해도, 시제, 접속사 등 문법에 대한 이해력을 묻는 형태로 되어 있습니다. 주로 후자(B)의 대화 중에 빈칸이 있고, 그 곳에 들어갈 적절한 표현을 고르는 형식입니다.

Fill in the blank with the most appropriate word or phrase.

A Have you read the book italics, no quotes?
B No. Who _____ it?
(a) wrote
(b) writes
(c) has written
(d) had written

정답 : (a)

PART II (20문항)

영역 설명 Part II는 문어체 질문을 다룹니다. 서술문 속의 빈칸을 채우는 문제로 총 20문항으로 되어 있습니다. 이 파트에서는 문법 자체에 대한 이해도는 물론 구문에 대한 이해력이 중요합니다.

Fill in the blank with the most appropriate word or phrase.

On reaching _____ four, Mozart was given harpsichord lessons by his father.
(a) age of
(b) the age
(c) an age of
(d) the age of

정답 : (d)

PART III (5문항)

영역 설명 Part III는 대화문에서 어법상 틀리거나 어색한 부분이 있는 문장을 고르는 다섯 문항으로 구성되어 있습니다. 이 영역 역시 문법뿐만 아니라 정확한 구문 파악, 회화 내용의 식별능력이 대단히 중요합니다.

Identify the grammatical error in the dialogue.

(a) A: That cold sounds pretty bad.
(b) B: Yeah, it is. Don't get too close.
(c) A: Let me make you a cup of herbal tea.
(d) B: Gee, that's nice for you!

정답 : (d)

PART IV (5문항)

영역 설명　Part IV는 한 문단을 주고 그 가운데 문법적으로 틀리거나 어색한 문장을 고르는 다섯 문항으로 되어 있습니다. 틀린 부분을 신속하게 골라야 하므로 속독 능력도 중요한 작용을 합니다.

Identify the ungrammatical sentence in the passage.

(a) Put an ice cube into a glass of water.
(b) Look through the side of the glass.
(c) You will see that most ice cube is under the surface of the water.
(d) The little ice cube in the glass acts just like a giant iceberg in the ocean.

정답 : (c)

어휘 (Vocabulary)-50문항

PART I (25문항)

영역 설명　Part I은 구어체로 되어 있는 A, B의 대화 중 빈칸에 가장 적절한 단어를 넣는 25문항으로 구성되어 있습니다. 단어의 단편적인 의미보다는 문맥에서 쓰인 상대적인 의미를 더 중요시합니다.

Choose the most appropriate word or expression for the blank in the conversation.

A　Could you tell me how to get to First National Bank?
B　Sure, make a left ＿＿＿＿＿＿ at the first light and go straight for two blocks.
(a) stop
(b) turn
(c) way
(d) path

정답 : (b)

TEPS 영역별 유형

🔖 PART Ⅱ (25문항)

영역 설명 Part Ⅱ는 하나 또는 두 개의 문장으로 구성된 글 속의 빈칸에 가장 적당한 단어를 골라 넣는 부분입니다. 어휘를 늘릴 때 한 개씩 단편적으로 암기하는 것보다는 하나의 표현으로, 즉 의미구로 알아 놓는 것이 15분이라는 제한된 시간 내에 어휘 시험을 정확히 푸는 데 많은 도움이 될 것입니다.

Choose the most appropriate word or expression for the blank in the statement.

This videotape _____ for three and a half hours.
(a) gets
(b) views
(c) runs
(d) takes

정답 : (c)

독해 (Reading Comprehension)-40문항

🔖 PART Ⅰ (16문항)

영역 설명 Part Ⅰ은 빈칸 넣기 유형입니다. 한 단락의 글을 주고 그 안에 빈칸을 넣어 알맞은 표현을 고르는 16문항으로 이루어져 있습니다. 글 전체의 흐름을 파악하여 문맥상 빈칸에 들어 갈 내용을 찾는 문제입니다.

Read the passage and choose the option that best fits the blank.

Athletes look good while they work out, but they may not feel so great. A report suggests that up to 70% may experience stomach distress during exercise. Competitive runners are prone to lower-bowel problems like diarrhea, probably because blood rushes from the intestines to their hardworking leg muscles. Weight lifters and cyclists, for their part, tend to _____.
(a) feel stronger
(b) exercise too much
(c) strive for weight loss
(d) suffer from heartburn

정답 : (d)

PART II (21문항)

영역 설명 Part II는 글의 내용 이해를 측정하는 문제로 21문항으로 구성되어 있습니다. 주제나 대의 혹은 전반적 논조 파악, 세부내용 파악, 논리적 추론 등이 있습니다.

Choose the option that correctly answers the question.

Parents who let kids surf online without supervision may want to think again. Though most children and teens know they shouldn't give strangers personal information, a new study finds that many young people feel it's OK to reveal potentially sensitive family data in exchange for a prize. Nearly two out of every three children were willing to name their favorite stores, and about a third would tell about their parents' driving records, alcohol consumption, political discussions, work attendance and church-going habits.

Q What is the best title for the passage?

(a) Unsupervised Children Reveal Personal Information
(b) Parents Have Difficulty Controlling Their Children
(c) Prizes Given to Children on the Internet
(d) Internet Privacy: a Thing of the Past

정답 : (a)

PART III (3문항)

영역 설명   Part III는 한 문단의 글에서 내용의 흐름상 어색한 곳을 고르는 문제로 3문항으로 이루어져 있습니다. 전체 흐름을 파악하여 흐름상 필요 없는 내용을 고르는 문제입니다. 이런 유형의 문제는 응집력 있는 영작문 실력을 간접적으로 측정할 수도 있습니다.

Identify the sentence that least fits the context of the passage.

The emphasis on winning-whether a soccer game or spelling contest-is especially inappropriate for school-age children. (a) This is a time when they're mastering basic skills, both in sports and academic subjects. (b) The real challenge is when children grow up and become teenagers. (c) Children should be encouraged for doing their best, no matter what. (d) Building confidence is what's important, not just winning.

정답 : (b)

TEPS 등급표

등급	점수	영역	능력검정기준(Description)
1+급 Level 1	901-990	전반	외국인으로서 최상급 수준의 의사소통능력 : 교양 있는 원어민에 버금가는 정도로 의사소통이 가능하고 전문분야 업무에 대처할 수 있음. (Native Level of Communicative Competence)
1급 Level 1	801-900	전반	외국인으로서 거의 최상급 수준의 의사소통능력 : 단기간 집중 교육을 받으면 대부분의 의사소통이 가능하고 전문분야 업무에 별 무리 없이 대처할 수 있음. (Near-Native Level of Communicative Competence)
2+급 Level 2	701-800	전반	외국인으로서 상급 수준의 의사소통능력 : 단기간 집중 교육을 받으면 일반분야 업무를 큰 어려움 없이 수행할 수 있음. (Advanced Level of Communicative Competence)
2급 Level 2	601-700	전반	외국인으로서 중상급 수준의 의사소통능력 : 중장기간 집중 교육을 받으면 일반분야 업무를 큰 어려움 없이 수행할 수 있음. (High Intermediate Level of Communicative Competence)
3+급 Level 3	501-600	전반	외국인으로서 중급 수준의 의사소통능력 : 중장기간 집중 교육을 받으면 한정된 분야의 업무를 큰 어려움 없이 수행할 수 있음. (Mid Intermediate Level of Communicative Competence)
3급 Level 3	401-500	전반	외국인으로서 중하급 수준의 의사소통능력 : 중장기간 집중 교육을 받으면 한정된 분야의 업무를 다소 미흡하지만 큰 지장은 없이 수행할 수 있음. (Low Intermediate Level of Communicative Competence)
4+급 Level 4	201-400	전반	외국인으로서 하급수준의 의사소통능력 : 장기간의 집중 교육을 받으면 한정된 분야의 업무를 대체로 어렵게 수행할 수 있음. (Novice Level of Communicative Competence)
5+급 Level 5	101-200	전반	외국인으로서 최하급 수준의 의사소통능력 : 단편적인 지식만을 갖추고 있어 의사소통이 거의 불가능함. (Near-Zero Level of Communicative Competence)

⊙ TEPS 성적표

TEPS SCORE REPORT | TEST OF ENGLISH PROFICIENCY
DEVELOPED BY
SEOUL NATIONAL UNIVERSITY

NAME PARK KA YEON	**REGISTRATION NO.** 1357108
DATE OF BIRTH DEC. 7. 1982	**TEST DATE** OCT. 12. 2006
GENDER FEMALE	**VALID UNTIL** OCT. 11. 2008

NO. AAA000047921

TOTAL SCORE AND LEVEL

SCORE	LEVEL
668	2

SECTION	SCORE	LEVEL	%	0% ——————————— 100%
Listening	254	2	62 / 57	
Grammar	71	2	78 / 35	
Vocabulary	59	3	58 / 55	
Reading	293	2	82 / 68	

■ your percentage ■ average

OVERALL COMMUNICATIVE COMPETENCE

668

68.85%

HIGH INTERMEDIATE LEVEL OF COMMUNICATIVE COMPETENCE
Test takers who receive a score at the 1+ Level, as you did Typically understand
academic texts in English that require a wide range of reading abilities.
Test takers who receive a score at the 1+ Level, as you did Typically understand
academic texts in English that require a wide range of reading abilities.

SECTION			PERFORMANCE EVALUATION
Listening	PART I	78%	Test takers who receive a score at the 1+ Level, as you did
	PART II	56%	Typically understand academic texts in English that require
	PART III	35%	a wide range of reading abilities. Test takers who receive
	PART IV	18%	a score at the 1+ Level, as you did Typically understand.
Grammar	PART I	35%	Test takers who receive a score at the 1+ Level, as you did
	PART II	18%	Typically understand academic texts in English that require
	PART III	56%	a wide range of reading abilities. Test takers who receive
	PART IV	35%	a score at the 1+ Level, as you did Typically understand.
Vocabulary	PART I	56%	Test takers who receive a score at the 1+ Level, as you did
	PART II	35%	Typically understand academic texts in English.
Reading	PART I	56%	Test takers who receive a score at the 1+ Level, as you did
	PART II	18%	Typically understand academic texts in English that require
	PART III	35%	a wide range of reading abilities.

THE TEPS COUNCIL

⊙ TEPS-TOEIC-TOEFL 비교

등급	TEPS	TOEIC	TOEFL (iBT)
시험명	Test of English Proficiency developed by Seoul National University	Test of English for International Communication	Test of English as a Foreign Language (Internet-Based Test)
개발기관	서울대학교 언어교육원	미국 ETS (Educational Testing Service)	미국 ETS (Educational Testing Service)
개발목적	한국인의 실용 영어능력 평가	비즈니스 커뮤니케이션 영어 능력 평가	미국 등 영어권 국가의 대학 또는 대학원에서 외국인의 영어능력 평가
시행기관	TEPS 관리위원회	재단법인 국제교류진흥회	ETS
시험시간	2시간 20분	2시간	약 4시간
문항수	200문항	200문항	78~129문항
만점	990점	990점	120점
구성	청해: 60문항 / 55분 / 400점 문법: 50문항 / 25분 / 100점 어휘: 50문항 / 15분 / 100점 독해: 40문항 / 45분 / 400점	L/C: 100문항 / 45분 / 495점 R/C: 100문항 / 75분 / 495점	Reading: 36~70문항 / 60~100분 / 0~30점 Listening: 34~51문항 / 60~90분 / 0~30점 Speaking: 6문항 / 20분 / 0~30점 Writing: 2문항 / 50분 / 0~30점
검정 기준	Criterion-referenced Test (절대 평가)	Norm-referenced Test (상대 평가)	Norm-referenced Test (상대 평가)
시행방법	정기시험: 연 12회 특별시험: 수시	정기시험: 연 12회 특별시험: 수시	연 30~40회
성적통보	정기시험: 2주 특별시험: 5일	정기시험: 20일 특별시험: 10일 이내	15일
성적 유효기간	2년	2년	2년
응시료	30,000원	37,000원	$170

TEPS-TOEIC-TOEFL 점수환산표

TEPS	TOEIC	IBT	TEPS	TOEIC	IBT	TEPS	TOEIC	IBT
953~	990	120	756~763	850	100	582~587	710	83
948~952	985	120	750~755	845	100	578~571	705	83
941~947	980	119	743~749	840	98	572~577	700	82
935~940	975	118	736~742	835	98	567~571	695	82
928~934	970	118	729~735	830	96	561~566	690	80
922~927	965	117	723~728	825	96	557~560	685	80
915~921	960	116	716~722	820	95	551~556	680	78
908~914	955	114	710~715	815	95	546~550	675	78
901~907	950	114	702~709	810	94	541~545	670	76
894~900	945	114	696~701	805	94	536~540	665	75
887~893	940	113	689~695	800	94	532~535	660	75
880~886	935	113	684~688	795	93	527~531	655	75
872~879	930	111	677~683	790	93	521~526	650	73
865~871	925	110	671~676	785	91	517~520	645	71
857~864	920	110	664~670	780	91	512~516	640	71
851~856	915	109	658~663	775	91	508~511	635	70
843~850	910	109	652~657	770	89	503~507	630	70
836~842	905	107	646~651	765	89	498~502	625	70
828~835	900	107	640~645	760	89	494~497	620	68
822~827	895	105	634~639	755	89	490~493	615	65
814~821	890	105	628~633	750	87	485~489	610	64
807~813	885	103	622~627	745	87	481~484	605	57
799~806	880	103	616~621	740	87	476~480	600	57
793~798	875	103	611~615	735	87	472~475	595	57
785~792	870	101	605~610	730	85	468~471	590	57
778~784	865	101	600~604	725	85	464~467	585	56
771~777	860	100	593~599	720	83	460~463	580	51
764~770	855	100	588~592	715	83	456~459	575	50

TEPS FAQ

1. TEPS의 성적 유효 기간은 어떻게 되나요?

－2년입니다.

2. TEPS 관리위원회에서 인정하는 신분증은 무엇인가요?

▶ **주민등록증 발급자 〈만 17세 이상〉** － 주민등록증, 운전면허증, 기간 만료 전의 여권, 공무원증

　기타　장교라면 → 장교신분증

　　　　　사병이라면 → TEPS 정기시험 신분확인증명서

　　　　　주민등록증을 분실했다면 → 주민등록증 발급확인서(동, 읍, 면사무소에서 발급)

　　　　　외국인이라면 → 외국인 등록증

▶ **주민등록증 미발급자 〈만 17세 미만〉** － 기간 만료 전의 여권, TEPS 정기시험 신분확인증명서, 청소년증

　기타　외국인이라면 → 기간 만료 전의 여권, 외국인 등록증

※ 시험당일 신분증 미지참자 및 규정에 맞지 않는 신분증 소지자는 시험에 절대로 응시할 수 없습니다. 중·고등학교, 대학교 학생증은 신분증으로 인정되지 않습니다.

3. TEPS 문제지에 메모해도 되나요?

－ 네. 그러나, 별도의 용지(좌석표, 수험표 등)에 메모를 하면 부정행위로 간주되어 규정에 의거하여 처리됩니다.

4. TEPS의 고사장 변경은 어떻게 하나요?

▶ **변경 기간** － 응시일 13일 전부터 7일 전까지

▶ **변경 방법** － www.teps.or.kr → 나의 시험 정보 → 접수 정보 관리

▶ **변경 조건**

　① 1회에 한하여 변경 가능합니다.

　② 고사장의 지역을 변경할 경우에만 가능합니다. (같은 지역 내 고사장 변경은 불가함)

　③ 고사장의 여분에 맞춰 선착순 신청이며 조기에 마감될 수 있습니다.

※ 추가 접수의 경우에는, 시험일 5일 전까지 유선을 통하여 신청해야 합니다.

5. TEPS 시험 볼 때 사용할 수 있는 필기구는 무엇인가요?

－ 컴퓨터용 사인펜, 수정테이프 (컴퓨터용 연필, 수정액은 사용 불가)

6. TEPS 시험을 연기할 수 있나요?

－ 아니오. 접수 취소를 해야 합니다.

7. TEPS는 추가 접수를 할 수 있나요?

－ 네. 시험일자 10일 전부터 4일간 추가 접수 기간이 있습니다. 추가 접수 응시료에는 일반 응시료의 10%가 특별 수수료로 부가됩니다.

8. **TEPS는 인터넷으로 접수 취소할 수 있나요?**

   - 네. www.teps.or.kr에 회원가입을 해야 합니다.
   ▶ **접수 기간 내** - 전액 환불
   ▶ **접수 기간 1일 후 ~ 2주** - 18,000원 환불
   ▶ **접수 기간 2주 후 ~ 시험 당일** - 12,000원 환불
   ▶ **추가 접수 기간 1일 후 ~ 시험 당일** - 12,000원 환불

9. **수험표는 흑백프린터를 사용해도 되나요?**

   - 수험표는 흑백, 칼라 아무거나 사용하셔도 상관없습니다.

10. **OMR Sheet에 기재한 비밀번호가 생각나지 않을 때는 어떻게 해야 하나요?**

    - www.teps.or.kr에 로그인 하신 다음 비밀번호 입력란에 로그인 password를 다시 한 번 입력하시면 성적확인이 가능합니다.

11. **성적표 주소 변경은 어떻게 해야 하나요?**

    ▶ **변경 기간** - 응시일 13일 전부터 7일 전까지
    ▶ **변경 방법** - www.teps.or.kr → 나의 시험 정보 → 접수 정보 관리

12. **시험 점수는 얼마 후에 알게 되나요?**

    - 정기시험의 성적은 시험일로부터 15일 이후 ARS나 www.teps.or.kr에서 확인이 가능합니다. 정기시험 성적표는 시험일로부터 대략 20일 안에 우편으로 발송되고, 특별시험 성적표는 시험일로부터 7일 이내에 해당 기관이나 단체로 통보됩니다.

TEPS 활용 기업 및 정부 기관

➕ 국내 기업 – 신입사원 채용

(주)포스코, (주)현대오토넷, CJ그룹, GM 대우, GS건설, GS칼텍스(주), GS홀딩스, KTF, KTFT, LG CNS, LG PHILIPS, LG전자, LG텔레콤, LG화학, LS산전, LS전선, SK그룹, SPC그룹, 경남기업(주), 교원그룹, 국도화학, 국민일보, 금강고려화학, 남양유업, 농심, 대림산업, 대우건설, 대우건설, 대우인터내셔널, 대우자동차판매(주), 대우정보시스템(주), 대우조선해양, 동부그룹, 동부제강, 동양그룹, 동양시멘트(주), 동원 F&B, 삼성그룹, 새한그룹, 신세계, 쌍용건설, 오뚜기, 오리온, 유한킴벌리, 일진그룹, 제일화재, (주)벽산, (주)코오롱, (주)태평양, 코리아나화장품, 포스코건설, 풀무원, 하이닉스반도체, 하이마트, 한솔제지(주), 한진중공업, 한진해운, 현대건설, 현대기아자동차그룹, 현대모비스(주), 현대상선, 현대오일뱅크, 현대종합상사, 현대하이스코, 효성그룹

➕ 공기업 – 신입사원 채용

KOTRA, KT, KT&G, 공무원연금관리공단, 교통안전공단, 국립공원관리공단, 국민연금관리공단, 국민체육진흥공단, 근로복지공단, 농수산물유통공사, 농업기반공사, 대한광업진흥공사, 대한법률구조공단, 대한주택공사, 대한주택보증, 대한지적공사, 마사회, 서울메트로, 서울시농수산물공사, 서울시도시철도공사, 수출보험공사, 에너지관리공단, 인천관광공사, 인천국제공항공사, 인천항만공사, 자산관리공사, 중소기업진흥공단, 중소기업협동조합중앙회, 한국가스공사, 한국공항공사, 한국관광공사, 한국국제협력단, 한국남동발전(주), 한국남부발전(주), 한국농촌공사, 한국도로공사, 한국동서발전(주), 한국방송광고공사, 한국산업단지공단, 한국산업안전공단, 한국서부발전(주), 한국석유공사, 한국소방검정공사, 한국수력원자력, 한국수자원공사, 한국수출입은행, 한국원자력연료(주), 한국인삼공사, 한국전력, 한국조폐공사, 한국주택금융공사, 한국중부발전(주), 한국지역난방공사, 한국철도공사, 한국철도시설공단, 한국컨테이너부두공단, 한국토지공사, 한국환경자원공사, 한전기공(주), 행원채용, 환경관리공단

➕ 금융권 – 신입사원 채용

LG화재, SK생명, 광주은행, 교보생명보험(주), 국민은행, 기술신용보증기금, 기업은행, 농협중앙회, 대우캐피털, 동양화재, 새마을금고연합회, 수협은행, 수협중앙회, 신동아화재, 신한은행, 신한카드, 쌍용화재, 알리안츠생명, 우리은행, 제일화재, 푸르덴셜생명(주), 하나은행, 현대해상화재보험(주)

✚ 언론사 - 기자, 아나운서, 직원 채용

기자, 아나운서, 직원 채용 - 경기방송, CBS, EBS, GTB(강원방송), KBS, MBC, PSB(부산방송), SBS, UBC(울산방송), YTN

기자, 직원 채용 - 경상일보, 대구매일신문, 동아일보, 매일신문, 부산일보, 서울경제신문, 연합뉴스, 영남일보, 전자신문, 조선일보, 중앙일보, 충청투데이, 파이낸셜 뉴스, 한국일보

직원 채용 - 한국방송위원회

✚ 외국계 - 직원 평가, 신입사원 채용

직원 평가 - (주)스타벅스커피 코리아, AB코리아, ABB코리아, 토비스, 푸르덴셜생명보험, 한국썬마이크로 시스템즈, 한국하인즈, 한국화이자

신입사원 채용 - 마이크로소프트코리아(인턴), 소니코리아, 한국쓰리엠(주), 한국아스트라제네카

✚ 정부 기관 - 직원 채용, 해외 파견, 해외 연수, 직원 평가 등

강원도 교육청, 건설공제조합, 경기도 교육청, 경기도청, 경남교육청, 광주시교육청, 교육인적자원부, 국립 암센터, 국립의료원, 국방부, 국방품질관리소, 국세청, 국제교육진흥원, 국회사무처, 금융감독원, 금융결제원, 기술표준원, 농촌진흥청, 대구시교육청, 대전시교육청, 대통령경호실, 대한상공회의소, 대한적십자사, 대한 체육회, 법무부, 법원행정처, 보건복지부, 부산시교육청, 부산시청, 산림청, 산재의료관리원, 서울대병원, 서 울시교육청, 서울시청, 서울지방경찰청, 소방협회, 여성부, 외교통상부, 인천시교육청, 전남교육청, 전북교육 청, 정보통신부, 중앙공무원교육원, 충남교육청, 충북교육청, 충북지방경찰청, 한국감정원, 한국산업은행, 한 국원자력연구소, 한국은행, 한국전산원, 한국전자통신연구원, 해양경찰청, 행정자치부

Section A

문법

Chapter 1 문장의 기본

Chapter 2 시제와 태

Chapter 3 준동사

Chapter 4 품사 I

Chapter 5 품사 II

Chapter 6 일치와 어순

문법 모의고사

Chapter 1

문장의 기본

UNIT 1　문장의 구성
UNIT 2　자동사와 타동사

UNIT 1 문장의 구성

문장은 크게 주성분과 수식어로 구성되어 있다. 주성분에는 주어, 동사, 목적어, 보어가 있으며 이와 비교해 이들을 수식하는 기타 나머지 요소들을 수식어라 한다.

1 주성분

문장에서 주가 되는 성분이다. 문장의 역할에서 특히 중요한 주어, 동사, 목적어, 보어가 이에 해당된다.

① 행위의 주체인 주어(Subject)

주어로는 명사, 대명사뿐만 아니라 명사절(의문사절, 접속사절, 관계사 what절 등), 명사구(동명사구, to부정사구 등)도 가능하다.

ex 1 **The cashier** believed her **honest**.
└→ 명사 주어

2 **To do homework** is difficult.
└→ to부정사구가 주어

⇨ 주어가 길기 때문에 실제로는 「It is difficult to do homework.」을 더 많이 쓴다.
└→ 가주어   └→ 진주어

② 동작이나 상태를 설명하는 동사(Verb)

동사에는 크게 목적어를 필요로 하는 타동사와 목적어를 필요로 하지 않는 자동사가 있다.

ex The cashier **believed** her honest.
└→ 타동사

3 She will **arrive** soon.
└→ 자동사

③ 행위의 대상인 목적어(Object)

목적어에는 명사, 대명사, 명사절, 명사구 등이 있다.

ex 4 The cashier believed **her innocence**.
└→ (명사)목적어

5 That is exactly what I want **you** to say.
└→ (대명사)목적어

④ **주어나 목적어의 상태를 설명하는 보어(Complement)**

보어에는 명사와 명사상당어구 뿐만 아니라 형용사, 분사, 동사원형 등 다양한 형태가 있다.

ex 6   She is **beautiful**.
            └→ 형용사 보어

7   That is exactly **what I'm talking about.**
                        └→ 명사절(관계사 what절) 보어

2   수식어

문장에서 주성분을 수식하는 나머지 수식 성분을 의미한다. 형용사, 부사, to부정사, 분사, 관계대명사 등이 있다.

① **명사 수식**

ex 8   **Most** students in this class got bored.   형용사

② **동사 수식**

ex 9   Andy loves Mary **very much.**   부사

③ **기타 수식어**

ex 10   He made an attempt **to land**.   to부정사

11   Any vehicles **parked illegally** in this place will be towed away.   분사

12   The woman **who lives next door** runs every day.   관계대명사

Review

주성분
주어 – 행위의 주체로 '~은/는/이/가'로 해석된다.
동사 – 주체의 동작 또는 상태를 설명하며 '~하다' 등으로 해석된다.
목적어 – 행위의 대상으로 '~을/를'로 해석된다.
보어 – 주어나 복석어를 보충설명해 주는 역할을 한다.
수식어
형용사적 수식 – (대)명사를 수식한다.
부사적 수식 – 동사, 형용사, 다른 부사, 문장 전체를 수식한다.

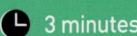
A 다음 문장에서 지칭하는 주성분(주어, 동사, 목적어, 보어)을 찾아 쓰시오.

> **Ex**
> Jason loves Cathy very much. 목적어
> 목적어 → Cathy

1 The air is so fresh here.
보어 →

2 What do you want for lunch today?
동사 →

3 Can you tell me how to get to the airport?
동사 →

4 I spent some time in the United States.
목적어 →

5 Can you tell me the time, please?
목적어 →

B 다음 밑줄 친 부분의 성분(주어, 목적어, 보어, 동사, 수식어)을 밝히시오.

1 How can that be possible?

2 The man who lives next door runs every day.

3 To do the ironing is always difficult.

4 Any vehicles parked illegally will be removed.

5 More than 20 scientists work in the research center.

6 Did you enjoy your trip to Busan?

7 No one can know what the future holds.

8 Did you spend a good time on your vacation?

9 I didn't have time for doing the wash yesterday.

10 The schoolchild committed a crime.

● 다음 빈 칸에 들어갈 적절한 응답을 고르시오.

PART 1

1   A   Hi, Jason, How's your father?

   B   He's fine. And _____ will be released from the hospital soon.

   (a) his

   (b) him

   (c) he

   (d) himself

PART 2

2   The executive _____ the award to Mr. Lee is the vice president of the company.

   (a) presenting

   (b) presented

   (c) is presented

   (d) presents

● 다음에서 잘못된 부분을 찾으시오.

PART 3

3   (a) A: Emma, is there a problem? You look pale.

   (b) B: It's my daughter. She wants to move out and get her own apartment.

   (c) A: She's now grown up. So don't worry!

   (d) B: I know. But I hard to accept her idea, though.

PART 4

4   (a) Alcoholic beverages are available for the Cedar Park. (b) However, all alcohol must be provided by Cedar Park Store. (c) Beer is sold throughout the park. (d) All individuals must be TWENTY YEARS OLD buy.

UNIT 2 자동사와 타동사

동사를 크게 두 개로 구분한다면 자동사와 타동사로 나눌 수 있다. 자동사란 목적어를 취하지 못하는 동사를, 타동사란 목적어를 반드시 취해야만 하는 동사를 뜻한다.

기초문법 확인

1 자동사

동사 중에서 목적어를 취하지 않는 동사를 자동사라 한다. 자동사에는 <주어+동사>의 구조만으로도 문장 구성에 전혀 지장이 없는 완전자동사와 보어를 취해야 하는 불완전 자동사가 있다.

① 완전 자동사(1형식 동사)

보어나 목적어를 필요로 하지 않는 동사를 뜻한다. 주어 이외에 아무런 요소가 필요 없기 때문에 완전 자동사라고 한다.

ex

1 The sun **shines**.
   └ S   └ V(완전 자동사)

2 A bird **sings**.
   └ S   └ V(완전 자동사)

3 This copy machine doesn't **work** / at all.
   └ S   └ V(완전 자동사) / 수식어

② 불완전 자동사(2형식 동사)

완전 자동사와 달리 보어를 반드시 필요로 하는 동사를 뜻한다. 주격보어로는 형용사, 명사, to부정사, 동명사, 명사절 등이 올 수 있다.

ex

4 He   **is**   an engineer.
   └ S   └ V(상태)   └ S.C(명사가 주격보어)

5 The woman   **is**   beautiful.
   └ S   └ V(상태)   └ S.C(형용사가 주격보어)

6 She **became**   a professor.
   └ S   └ V(상태의 변화) └ S.C(명사가 주격보어)

7 You **look**   tired.
   └ S   └ V(외견) └ S.C(형용사가 주격보어)

8 The problem **is**   that she doesn't know the fact.
   └ S   └ V(상태) └ S.C(명사절이 보어)

2 타동사

① 완전 타동사(3형식 동사)

순수하게 목적어만을 취하는 동사를 뜻한다. ③번의 불완전 타동사가 목적어 이외에 보어를 취해야 하는 것과는 달리, 목적어만 필요로 하기 때문에 이 동사를 완전 타동사라고 칭한다. 동명사, that절, to부정사 등 다양한 형태의 목적어가 올 수 있다.

ex

9 James **stopped** smoking.
└→S └→V └→O(동명사)

10 I **know** that you like Cathy.
└→S └→V └→O(that절)

11 I **decided** to write poetry.
└→S └→V └→O(to부정사)

② 수여동사(4형식 동사)

목적어를 두 개 취하는 동사다. 간접목적어는 '~에게', 직접목적어는 '~를'로 해석한다.

ex

12 She **gave** me the watch.
└→S └→V └→IO(간접) └→DO(직접)

13 My mother **made** me the cake.
└→S └→V └→IO └→DO

③ 불완전 타동사(5형식 동사)

목적어 이외에도 목적어를 보충 설명하는 목적격 보어를 취하는 동사를 지칭한다. 동사의 성격에 따라 목적격 보어로는 명사, 형용사, to부정사, 분사, 동사원형 등 다양한 형태가 올 수 있다.

ex

14 My wife **considers** me a liar everytime I say.
└→S └→V └→O └→O.C(명사가 목적보어)

15 I **heard** him cry.
└→S └→V └→O └→O.C(동사원형이 목적보어)

16 I **expect** him to succeed.
└→S └→V └→O └→O.C(to부정사가 목적보어)

17 I **saw** her playing the violin.
└→S └→V └→O └→O.C(분사가 목적보어)

Review

1형식 동사 - S + V(완전 자동사)
2형식 동사 - S + V(불완전 자동사) + S.C(주격보어)**타동사**
3형식 동사 - S + V(완전 타동사) + O(목적어)
4형식 동사 - S + V(수여동사) + IO(직접목적어) + DO(간접목적어)
5형식 동사 - S + V(불완전 타동사) + O(목적어) + O.C(목적격보어)

A 주어진 문장의 동사를 보고 형식을 밝히시오.

> **Ex** He walks.
> ↳ 1형식

1 There is someone near the curb.
↳

2 We should keep quiet.
↳

3 I have two children.
↳

4 Could you bring me the magazines?
↳

5 I heard my name called.
↳

B 문장의 구조상 어울리는 것을 선택하시오.

1 We elected (him / his) chairman.

2 My uncle (began / bought) me a guitar.

3 This (matters / is) a comfortable apartment.

4 He (costed / became) a famous wrestler.

5 I will (send / do) you the package.

6 She (believes / smiles) what her father told her.

7 It (counts / remains) to be seen.

8 The earth (is / lays) round.

9 She (say / told) me the secret.

10 The coffee (has / is) strong.

• 정답 및 해설 p.5

- **다음 빈 칸에 들어갈 적절한 응답을 고르시오.**

PART 1

1   A   What time do the shows start?

     B   The first show _____ from 11 a.m.

(a) runs

(b) makes

(c) becomes

(d) buys

PART 2

2   I've finally _____ to start drawings again.

(a) notified

(b) thanked

(c) avoided

(d) decided

- **다음에서 잘못된 부분을 찾으시오.**

PART 3

3   (a) A: Sorry, I'm late. I was stuck in traffic.

     (b) B: This time again? It has already three times this week.

     (c) A: I am terribly sorry, I won't be late again. I promise.

     (d) B: No, I don't believe you any more.

PART 4

4   (a) Different temperatures on the Earth's surface are responsibly for causing the weather. (b) Winds are the cause of the unequal heating of the earth's surface. (c) They can be converted into electrical energy. (d) It is a renewable, but unpredictable, energy source.

Chapter 2

시제와 태

UNIT 1   기본시제와 시제일치
UNIT 2   완료와 진행시제
UNIT 3   가정법 Ⅰ
UNIT 4   가정법 Ⅱ
UNIT 5   태

UNIT 1 기본시제와 시제일치

> 시간에 따라 변하는 형태를 시제라고 한다. 동사의 기본시제에는 현재, 과거, 미래가 있다. 각각의 시제는 문맥과 시점을 알려주는 시간 부사 등을 통해 주로 결정된다.

기초문법 확인

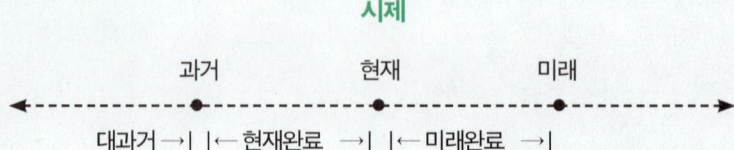

시제

| 과거 | 현재 | 미래 |

대과거 →| |← 현재완료 →| |← 미래완료 →|

1 기본 시제

일반 시제를 뜻하며 현재, 과거, 미래시제가 있다. 시제 결정은 보통 함께 쓰는 부사나 상황을 통해 결정된다.

① 현재

현재의 습관, 반복, 진리 등은 현재시제로 표현해야 한다.

ex 1 The earth ~~was~~ round.
　　　　　└ is (과학적인 사실)

2 Premiere League *usually* ~~is starting~~ in August.
　　　　　　　　└ starts (습관적인 현재의 동작)

② 과거

역사적 사실 또는 명백한 과거 시점이 드러난 경우에는 반드시 과거시제로 표현해야 한다.

ex 3 My grandfather ~~dies~~ *last year*.
　　　　　　└ died (과거 시점인 last year가 있기 때문에 동사는 과거형 died)

③ 미래

앞으로 일어날 일이나 계획인 경우 반드시 동사는 미래형으로 표현해야 한다.

ex 4 The meeting ~~was held~~ *tomorrow*.
　　　　　　└ will be held (미래 시점인 tomorrow가 있기 때문에 동사는 미래형인 will be)

2 시제 일치와 예외

종속절의 시제는 주절의 시제를 따르는 것이 원칙이다. 또한 시제 일치의 예외가 있는데 불변의 진리, 객관적 사실, 역사적 사실, 가정법 등의 경우 일치가 되지 않는 경우도 있다.

① 시제 일치

종속절의 시제는 주절의 시제를 따르는 것이 원칙이나 주절의 시제가 현재인 경우에는 종속절의 시제는 자유롭게 쓸 수 있다.

ex
5   I think she is beautiful. → 종속절은 주절과 같은 현재

6   I thought she was beautiful. → 종속절은 주절과 같은 과거

7   I thought she had been beautiful. → 주절의 동사가 과거이면 종속절의 동사가 과거완료여도 무관하다.

8   I know that she [was / is / will be] busy.
→ 주절의 시제가 현재인 경우 사실상 종속절의 시제는 자유롭게 쓸 수 있다.

② 예외

ex
9   They claimed the earth moves round the sun. → 불변의 진리
└, 과거   └, 현재

10 You will know that the Second World War ended in May 1945. → 과거의 사실
└, 미래   └, 과거

11 If I had known her phone number, I would call her right now. → 가정법
└, 과거완료   └, 과거

Review

기본 시제
현재 – 현재의 습관, 반복, 변하지 않는 진리 또는 과학적 사실
과거 – 역사적으로 또는 명백한 과거 사실(과거 시점을 지칭하는 시간부사 등을 통해)
미래 – 앞으로 일어날 일이나 계획(미래 시점을 지칭하는 시간부사 등을 통해)

시제 일치와 예외
일치 – 송속설의 시제는 수절의 시제를 따르는 것이 원칙이다.
예외 – 불변의 진리, 객관적 사실, 역사적 사실, 가정법 등에서는 예외가 있다.

• 정답 및 해설 p.6

A 다음 밑줄 친 부분을 고치시오.

> Ex The show <u>began</u> soon.
>   ↳ will begin

1 I'm getting the public bus every day.
       ↳

2 I <u>have given up</u> smoking 3 years ago.
           ↳

3 Have a seat. She <u>was</u> right with you in a minute.
                      ↳

4 My mother always said that time <u>was</u> money.
                                      ↳

5 Tomorrow's weather <u>was</u> fine.
                         ↳

B 문장의 구조상 어울리는 것을 선택하시오.

1 I (have rented / rented) a car yesterday.

2 Tomorrow my wife and I (has been / will have been) married 10 years.

3 Iraq is worse than It (is / was) before.

4 Let's wait there until it (will stop / stops) raining.

5 I (was graduating / graduated) from the University of New York in 2002.

6 The weather forecast says It (has rained / will rain) tomorrow.

7 Five times five (is / had been) twenty-five.

8 When I (will see / see) him tomorrow, I will tell him everything.

9 I (sent / send) an email to the secretary an hour ago.

10 We thought we (would / will) win the match.

• 정답 및 해설 p.7

• **다음 빈 칸에 들어갈 적절한 응답을 고르시오.**

PART 1

1 A What _____ you say?

B I said, "You should turn left over there."

(a) would

(b) could

(c) made

(d) did

PART 2

2 It _____ cheaper for visitors to make an advance reservation last year.

(a) will be

(b) was

(c) is

(d) had been

• **다음에서 잘못된 부분을 찾으시오.**

PART 3

3 (a) A: Excuse me, is this 411 Pine Blvd?

(b) B: Yes, right. Is there anything I can do for you?

(c) A: I will look for a person called Dr. Lee.

(d) B: Oh, he is my father.

PART 4

4 (a) I want to thank you for the wonderful job you do for us in New York on May 24th, 2007. (b) It was a very pleasant experience working with you. (c) I did not have any contact information for a limo services in New York so I looked on the internet and found your company. (d) Our president said it was a very pleasant experience.

UNIT 2 완료와 진행시제

완료란 시제간 연결성에 의미를 두는 시제 표현 방식이며 과거 현재 미래 완료가 있다. 한편, 어느 한 시점에 진행되고 있는 동작을 묘사할 때는 진행형을 쓴다.

기초문법 확인

1 완료 시제

완료 시제에는 과거·현재·미래완료가 있다. 현재완료는 과거의 어느 시점에서 현재까지의 연결된 시간을, 과거완료는 과거의 시점과 그 이전 과거의 어느 시점의 연결을, 미래완료는 현재와 미래 시점간의 연결을 표현한다.

① 현재 완료

ex
1 My son **has** just **cleaned** his room. → 완료

2 Tony **has lost** his car. → 결과

3 I **have been** in France. → 경험

4 I **have waited** for your call since this morning. → 계속

② 과거 완료

ex
5 I **had lost** my wallet when I checked my cell phone for my text messages.
→ 잃어버렸다는 완료의 의미 〈완료〉

6 I **had** never **seen** him **until then**. → (과거)그때까지 ~한 적이 없다[있다]. 〈경험〉

7 I knew the book because I **had seen** the book before. → 이전 과거(대과거) 표시 〈대과거〉

③ 미래 완료

ex
8 I **will have completed** the report by 7 o'clock. → 완료

9 I **will have gone** on a trip by the time you arrive. → 결과

2 진행 시제

일정 시간 동안 진행 중인 동작은 진행 시제로 표현할 수 있다.

① 일시적인 동작

> **ex**   I ~~took~~ a shower when the phone rang.
>
> 10 ↳I **was taking** a shower when the phone rang.

> **ex**   I couldn't answer the door because I ~~talked~~ on the phone.
>
> 11 ↳I couldn't answer the door because **I was talking** on the phone.

② 습관적인 행위

> **ex**   Jay ~~will~~ always be telling lies.
>
> 12 ↳Jay **is** always **telling** lies.

③ 진행 시제를 쓸 수 없는 경우

인식 동사(know), 소유(have 등), 감정(like 등), 감각(see 등), resemble, remember 등의 동작 동사가 아닌 상태 동사는 진행형을 쓸 수 없다.

> **ex**   Are you ~~knowing~~ the Simpsons?
>
> 13 ↳**Do** you **know** the Simpsons?

Review

완료 시제
현재완료 – 현재와 과거의 어느 시점사이를 표시
과거완료 – 과거의 어느 시점과 그 이전 시점사이를 표시
미래완료 – 현재와 미래의 어느 시점사이를 표시

진행시제
일시적인 동작을 표현한다. 때때로 습관적인 행위를 표현하는 방식으로 쓰이기도 한다.

EXERCISE

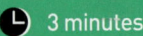 3 minutes

• 정답 및 해설 p.8

A 다음 밑줄 친 부분을 고치시오.

> **Ex** He <u>is living</u> in Italy since he was born.
> └ **has lived**

1 I <u>was</u> to Paris twice.
└

2 It <u>is raining</u> for two weeks if it rains tomorrow.
└

3 I'm finally <u>quit</u> smoking after 30 years of smoking.
└

4 She <u>will be</u> waiting when he walked out of the building.
└

5 Greg <u>bought</u> cigarettes since he was 17 years old.
└

B 문장의 구조상 어울리는 것을 선택하시오.

1 He looked sleepy because he (had been / will be) studying all night.

2 The teacher (always will tell / is always telling) us to study biology more.

3 She (has been / was) studying Spanish for five years.

4 I (walked / was walking) when I saw the accident.

5 (Have you ever been / Are you ever) to London?

6 I (am hating / hate) a roach.

7 I wasn't shocked because I (have seen / had seen) the animal before.

8 My fiance and I (will be / have been) married next month.

9 By the time you read this letter, I (will have / have) left for London.

10 All humans (are possessing / possess) a special spirit called the "soul".

● **다음 빈 칸에 들어갈 적절한 응답을 고르시오.**

PART 1

1 A Excuse me, _____ before? You look familiar.

   B I think we are taking the same class.

(a) haven't we been met

(b) weren't we meeting

(c) aren't we met

(d) haven't we met

PART 2

2 They _____ each other in many ways.

(a) are resembling

(b) resemble

(c) are resembled

(d) have been resembling

● **다음에서 잘못된 부분을 찾으시오.**

PART 3

3 (a) A: Cathy, I finally am finding another flight for you to ride standby.

   (b) B: Awesome, what time is it?

   (c) A: The flight leaves at 7:30 p.m.

   (d) B: That would be great. Thank you so much, Ross.

PART 4

4 (a) Persistent rain falls over Northern California since November 2006, causing devastating floods and landslides. (b) Overflowing rivers have flooded many small communities. (c) The floods have caused at least 40 deaths and are being called the worst floods to strike California in 40 years. (d) The floods have also surrounded the capital city of Sacramento.

UNIT 3 가정법 Ⅰ

가정법은 '~라면, ~일 텐데(~이었을 텐데)'로 해석되면서, 가정하는 화자의 심적 태도를 묘사하는 방법이다. 즉, 실제로는 그렇지 않으면서 소망, 기대, 불확실성을 담고 가정해서 말하는 어법이라 할 수 있다.

기초문법 확인

1 법의 종류

① 명령법과 직설법

법에는 명령법, 가정법, 직설법이 있는데, 명령법은 보통 동사원형으로 시작해 상대방에게 뭔가를 하도록 명령하는 것이고 직설법은 (사실을) 있는 그대로 상대방에게 진달 또는 언급하는 것이다.

ex　●명령법

1　Don't answer the door. →부정

2　Let's take a walk. →긍정

　●직설법

3　Amy became a teacher and taught for some years in Europe. →사실

② 단순조건과 가정법

단순조건은 말하는 화자가 가능성을 어느 정도 염두에 두고 사실을 가정해 말하는 방식이며, 가정법은 실현가능성이 그보다 낮은 상황에서 가정해서 말하는 방식이다.

ex　●단순조건

4　If I become a doctor, I will earn a lot of money.

　●가정법

5　If I became a doctor, I would be able to take care of my mother.

2 가정법의 종류

	If절	주절
현재	If + S + 동사의 현재형(또는 원형)	S + will/can/may + V
과거	If + S + 동사의 과거형(be동사→were)	S + 조동사의 과거 + V
과거완료	If + S + had p.p.	S + 조동사의 과거 + have p.p.
미래	If + S + should+원형 If + S + were to + 원형	S + 조동사의 현재[또는 과거형]+V S + 조동사의 과거 + V

① **가정법 현재**

가정법 현재는 현재 또는 미래를 가정하는 표현으로 현대영어에서는 직설법이 이를 대신하고 있어 현재는 거의 사용하지 않는다.

ex   6   If he come[comes], I will go.

     7   If she be[is] sick, I will not leave her.

② **가정법 과거**

현재 사실의 반대를 가정하거나, 현재의 상황으로는 실현이 희박한 것을 가정해서 표현하는 방법이다.

ex   8   If it were true, I would want to come back.
         ↳(=As it isn't true, I don't want to come back.)

     9   If I knew more, I would explain more.
         ↳(=As I don't know more, I can't explain more.)

③ **가정법 과거완료**

과거사실의 반대를 상상 또는 가정해서 나타내는 표현방법이다.

ex   10   If it had not been for your help, this trip would have been far more difficult.
          ↳(=This trip wasn't far more difficult because of your help.)

     11   If I had gone to the party, I would have met Brad.
          ↳(=As I didn't go to the party, I couldn't meet Brad.)

④ **가정법 미래**

미래에 발생할 가능성이 희박한 것을 가정하는 표현방법이다.

ex   12   If she were to tell her husband, he would be deeply hurt.

     13   If it should rain tomorrow, I will[would] not go to the meeting.

Review

가정법이란 '~한다면, ~할 텐데'의 의미로 상황을 반대로 가정해보는 것이다. 현재를 반대로 가정하는 것이 가정법과거, 과거에 일어났던 일을 가정하는 것이 가정법 과거완료다. 즉, 반대로 가정하기 때문에 직설법으로 바꾸면 긍정은 부정으로, 부정은 긍정으로 뜻이 달라진다. 또한 가정법은 시제의 예외적인 형태에 속한다. 그 종류(현재, 과거, 과거완료, 미래)에 따라 우선은 시제의 형태를 If절과 주절로 나눠 공식처럼 암기해 둘 필요가 있다.

• 정답 및 해설 p.10

A 밑줄 친 부분을 유의해 다음을 해석하시오.

> **Ex** If it weren't raining, we <u>would go</u> to the movies.
> ┗ 비가 오지 않는다면, 우리는 영화를 보러갈 텐데.

1 If he <u>had been</u> born in England, he <u>would have been</u> more successful.
┗

2 If I <u>become</u> a doctor, I <u>will earn</u> a lot of money.
┗

3 If it <u>were</u> raining, we <u>would get</u> wet.
┗

4 I <u>would enjoy</u> the games more if <u>I knew</u> more about the rules.
┗

5 If my daughter <u>should die</u>, what <u>shall</u> I do?
┗

B 문맥상 더 어울리는 것을 선택하시오.

1 (Don't / Not) close the door.

2 If I (had / have) the book, I could say more.

3 Ed went to school and (had become / became) a teacher.

4 If he (have to / were to) tell his wife about you, their marriage would break up.

5 If it (rained / should rain) tomorrow, we will not go out.

6 If I had known more, I (had / would have) chosen differently.

7 (Be / Do) quiet!

8 What will I do if I (should lose / had lost) my mailbox key?

9 If I (had known / knew) her, I would have said something.

10 If it (rained / had rained) yesterday, I would have needed an umbrella.

• 정답 및 해설 p.11

● **다음 빈 칸에 들어갈 적절한 응답을 고르시오.**

PART 1

1 A John resigned and moved to Virginia.

   B If I _____ in his shoes, I would do the same thing.

   (a) were

   (b) am

   (c) had been

   (d) have been

PART 2

2 If it had been true, I _____ the article.

   (a) would write

   (b) will write

   (c) would have written

   (d) write

● **다음에서 잘못된 부분을 찾으시오.**

PART 3

3 (a) A: I heard you got D⁻ on the math test.

   (b) B: Yeah. My mother will hit the ceiling.

   (c) A: Shame on you. If I'm you, I would have studied harder.

   (d) B: No kidding! If it were you, you could have gotten zero.

PART 4

4 (a) Thank you for your generous participation in Expo London. (b) Your performance at the London Event was really great. (c) You and your orchestra are an impressive group. (d) Thanks again for everything and please call if there would have been anything else I can do for you.

UNIT 4 가정법 Ⅱ

이 unit에서는 혼합가정법과 함께 If 이외의 다양한 가정법에 대해 다루고자 한다. 보통 가정법하면, If로 시작하는 구문으로만 알기 쉬운데, 영어에서는 If절로 시작하는 가정법 이외에도 의미상 그리고 형태상 다양한 가정법 표현이 등장한다.

기초문법 확인

1 혼합가정법

과거사실의 가정이 현재까지 영향을 미치는 경우 if절은 가정법과거완료로 표현하더라도, 주절은 가정법과거의 표현으로 써야 하는 경우다.

ex

1 If she **had gone** to the event last night, she *would be* exhausted today.

행사에는 과거(last night)에 갔지만, 지친 것은 현재(today)다.

2 If의 생략

If절로 시작하는 가정법에서 If를 생략한 채 가정법을 간단하게 표현하는 방법이다. 축약이 되더라도 일정한 규칙에 의해 단축된 형태이므로 가정법의 축약 형태임을 알 수 있어야 하며 어떻게 축약되는지도 세밀히 기억해두자.

① **If의 생략 – If는 생략되고 동사(were, had 등)가 주어 앞으로 이동**

ex

2 **Had** *it* rained yesterday, the game would have been canceled.

└ (=If it had rained yesterday, ~)

3 **Were** *it* not for air, all living creatures would die.

└ (=If it were not for air, ~)

4 **Had I been born** in 1950, I would have had to take part in the war.

└ (=If I had been born in 1950, ~)

② **If의 대용 – Without / But for**

ex

5 **Without** your help, I wouldn't have passed the exam.

6 **But for** your advice, I could not have succeeded.

58 문법 · Chapter 2

3 기타 가정법 구문

if절로 시작하는 가정법 이외의 기타 가정법 구문에는 I wish~, as if~ 등 다양한 가정법 구문이 있다.

① **It is (high) time + 동사의 과거형 → ~할 시간이다**

> **ex** 7 **It is time** you *took over* the project.

② **I wish + 가정법 과거(완료) → ~하면(했다면) 좋으련만**

● 〈I wish + 가정법 과거(일반 동사의 과거형, be동사는 were)〉

> **ex** 8 **I wish** I *knew* how to love you.
> 9 **I wish** I *were* the king.

● 〈I wish + 가정법 과거완료(had + p.p.)〉

> **ex** 10 **I wish** he *had gone* to the American League.
> 11 **I wish** I *had worked* harder at school.

③ **as if + 가정법 과거(완료) → 마치 ~인 것(이었던) 것처럼**

● as if + 가정법 과거(일반 동사의 과거형, be동사는 were)〉

> **ex** 12 She talks **as if** she *knew* everything.
> ↳ In fact, she doesn't know anything.

● 〈as if + 가정법 과거완료(had + p.p.)〉

> **ex** 13 She talks **as if** she *had been* there.
> ↳ In fact, she wasn't there.

Review

기정법이리고 헤서, 무조건 If로 시작하는 구문만 있는 것이 아니다. 위의 에보다 문맥직으로 더 많은 가정법이 의미상 그리고 형태적으로 달리하면서 다양하게 존재한다. I wish~ 형태는 특히 구어체에서 종종 접할 수 있는 가정법 구문에 속한다. 문맥에 따라 그 종류는 더 많기 때문에 가정법 문제는 오히려 형태만 공식적으로 정획히 알고 있어도 쉽게 풀이가 가능한 것이 사실이다.

• 정답 및 해설 p.12

A 밑줄 친 부분에 유의해 다음을 해석하시오.

> **Ex** I wish I <u>knew</u> how to speak french.
> ㄴ, 내가 프랑스어를 할 수 있으면 좋을 텐데.

1 But for your help, I <u>would have never bought</u> a new car.
ㄴ,

2 It is time you <u>went</u> to bed.
ㄴ,

3 Without your help, I <u>could not have achieved</u> my dream.
ㄴ,

4 Had it not rained yesterday, we <u>could have played</u> a lot better.
ㄴ,

5 She talks <u>as though</u> she <u>had been</u> ill.
ㄴ,

B 문맥상 더 어울리는 것을 선택하시오.

1 I (want / wish) I had known then what I know now.

2 It is time you (took / take) action.

3 If she had not run the red light, she (would have been / would be) fine now.

4 I wish I (am / were) the sun.

5 (There / It) is time you took a break.

6 He talks (although / as if) he had read it for the first time yesterday.

7 (Were / Had been) it not true, I would be upset with you.

8 It is time you (make / made) a decision.

9 (With / But for) your help, I could not have solved my problem.

10 (But for / Unless) your help, I would not have finished the assignment.

● **다음 빈 칸에 들어갈 적절한 응답을 고르시오.**

PART 1

1 A Don't you think it is time you _____ the right choice.

B I'm not sure.

(a) had been made

(b) made

(c) have been made

(d) make

PART 2

2 _____ I gone to the party last night, I would have seen Gloria.

(a) Were to

(b) Have

(c) Were

(d) Had

● **다음에서 잘못된 부분을 찾으시오.**

PART 3

3 (a) A: Anything wrong, Mike?

(b) B: I wish I'm not going out last night. I think I'm coming down with a cold.

(c) A: How long have you been feeling under the weather?

(d) B: The whole day.

PART 4

4 (a) I want to let you know that my problem with the company finally was resolved. (b) The product has been delivered one month exactly after the date of purchase. (c) I appreciate your help and the service you provided. (d) Had not been for your help, I would not have seen any results.

UNIT **5** 태

> 주체가 능동적인 위치에 있는 경우 능동태라고 하며 주체가 대상이 되는 경우를 수동태라고 한다. 즉 주체가 '~하는' 위치에 있으면 능동태이고 '~되는' 대상의 위치에 있으면 수동태가 된다.

기초문법 확인

1 태의 전환

수동태란 대상인 목적어가 주어로 오는 것이기 때문에 목적어가 없는 1형식과 2형식에서는 수동태가 있을 수 없다. 다시 말해 1형식과 2형식을 만드는 자동사는 수동태가 될 수 없다는 의미이기도 하다.

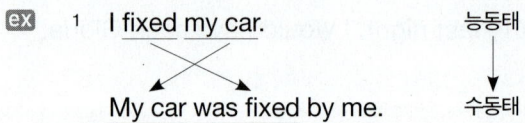

ex 1 I fixed my car.   능동태

My car was fixed by me.   수동태

→ 능동태 문장에서 my car라는 문장의 목적어가 수동태가 되면서 주어자리로 이동했다. 이때 능동태의 원래 주어는 문장의 마지막에 「by + 목적격」 형태로 바뀐다. 또한 능동의 동사 fixed는 수동태에서 was fixed로 바뀌게 되는데 이것이 능동과 수동의 가장 큰 차이다.

2 동사에 따른 수동태

수동태를 만들기 위해서는 기본적으로 목적어를 취할 수 있는 문형(3, 4, 5형식 문장)이어야 한다. 4형식의 경우 수동태가 된 후에도 목적어가 하나 더 남아 있기 때문에 마치 수동태 문장에 목적어가 살아 있어 어색해 보일 수가 있다.

① **3형식의 수동태**

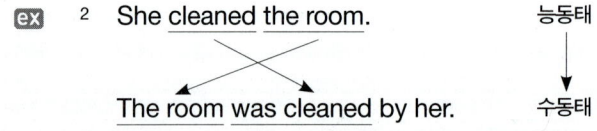

ex 2 She cleaned the room.   능동태

The room was cleaned by her.   수동태

→ 3형식 동사는 목적어 하나를 취하는 동사로 수동태에서는 주어와 목적어의 자리 이동과 동사의 형태가 바뀔 뿐이다.

② **4형식의 수동태**

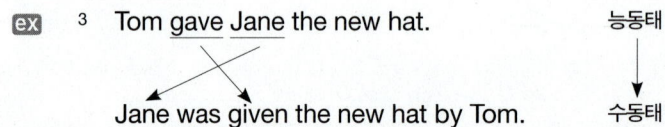

ex 3 Tom gave Jane the new hat.   능동태

Jane was given the new hat by Tom.   수동태

→ 4형식 동사는 목적어를 두 개 갖는 동사다. 그 중 하나인 Jane이 앞으로 이동하면서 동사는 수동태가 되었지만 또 다른 목적어인 the new hat은 영향을 받지 않고 그대로 남아 있게 된다.

③ 5형식의 수동태

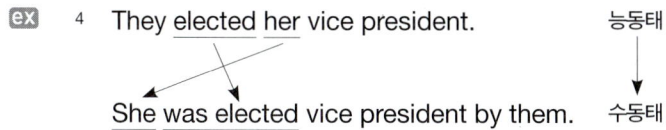

ex 4 They elected her vice president.   능동태

She was elected vice president by them.   수동태

→ 5형식 동사는 목적어와 목적어를 보충 설명하는 목적 보어를 취하는 동사다. 목적어와의 관계에 따라 목적보어는 명사, 형용사, 분사 등 다양하게 올 수 있다. 목적어가 수동태가 되어 자리 이동을 하더라도 목적보어의 형태와 위치는 변하지 않는다.

3 by 대신 다른 전치사를 쓰는 경우도 있다

ex 5 I'm interested in fishing. → '관심' 사항 [be interested in]

6 I was very shocked[surprised] at the news. → '놀람' 등의 감정 [be shocked(surprised) at]

7 We were greatly satisfied with the test results. → '(불)만족' 등의 감정 [be satisfied with]

Review

문형에 따른 태의 전환
3형식 – 목적어가 주어자리로 이동되고 이때 동사는 수동태가 된다.
4형식 – 목적어가 둘이므로 주어로 이동하지 않은 다른 목적어는 그대로 남아 있다.
5형식 – 수동태가 되더라도 목적보어(명사, 형용사, 분사)는 그대로 남아 있다.

• 정답 및 해설 p.14

A 밑줄 친 부분에 유의해 다음을 해석하시오.

> **Ex** Finally, he <u>found</u> the answer.
> └ 마침내, 그는 답을 찾아냈다.

1 My uncle <u>gave me</u> this sports car.
→

2 She <u>has been offered</u> the position <u>by the school</u>.
→

3 I <u>was taught</u> that communism was leftist <u>by the teacher</u>.
→

4 The conference <u>was considered</u> an executive meeting.
→

5 <u>It is shown to me</u> that she loves all people and that all are very important <u>by my mother</u>.
→

B 문장의 구조상 어울리는 것을 선택하시오.

1 What will happen when she (is arrived / arrives)?

2 I (didn't / wasn't) surprised with her performance because I had seen her before.

3 The residents have to (be showed / show) respect to their local law.

4 On July 15th, she and I (will be married / will marry).

5 I'm not interested (in / with) taking a vacation to Mexico.

6 I can't believe you (broke / were broken) up with her.

7 I want to thank everyone who (was voted / voted) for me.

8 Where is the event (taking place / taken place)?

9 There are 3 difficult questions you'll (be asked / ask) in an essay test.

10 I promise it won't (be happened / happen) again.

• **다음 빈 칸에 들어갈 적절한 응답을 고르시오.**

PART 1

1 A Didn't you bring your umbrella?

   B No, the weather forecast _____ it would be sunny until tomorrow.

   (a) was said
   (b) saying
   (c) to say
   (d) said

PART 2

2 The meeting _____ a great success by all attendees.

   (a) considering
   (b) to consider
   (c) was considered
   (d) considered

• **다음에서 잘못된 부분을 찾으시오.**

PART 3

3 (a) A: Guess what I'm going to tell you.
   (b) B: Have no clue, what is it?
   (c) A: I've been promoting today.
   (d) B: That's great, congratulations.

PART 4

4 (a) Diet is probably one of the most misunderstood terms in fitness. (b) So many people are perceived the word "diet" as cutting the amount of food you eat. (c) The actual meaning of the word is managing your food intake. (d) In fitness, managing your food intake is just as important as the physical activities.

Chapter 3

준동사

UNIT 1   to부정사와 동명사

UNIT 2   분사

UNIT 3   분사구문

UNIT 4   조동사

UNIT 1 to부정사와 동명사

준동사란 동사의 성질은 가지고 있지만 본동사는 될 수 없고 동사에 준하는 형태로 바뀐다는 뜻에서 붙여진 이름이다. 이 같은 준동사에는 to부정사, 동명사, 분사가 있는데 분사는 다음 단원에서 다루고자 한다.

기초문법 확인

1 to부정사

to부정사는 「to + 원형동사」의 형태로 문장 내에서 명사, 형용사, 또는 부사의 역할을 한다. 즉 문장에서 주어, 목적어, 보어의 역할을 하는 경우에는 명사의 역할을, 명사를 수식하는 경우는 형용사, 형용사, 부사, 동사를 수식할 때는 부사의 역할을 한다.

① **명사적 용법**

문장에서의 명사의 쓰임과 같이 to부정사가 주어, 목적어, 보어의 역할을 한다.

ex 1 **To break** the law is a crime against society. 〈주어〉

2 I wanted **to go** to Turkey for a vacation. 〈목적어〉

3 Her dream is **to be** a model. 〈보어〉

② **형용사적 용법**

형용사의 쓰임과 같이 문장에서 명사를 수식하는 to부정사의 형용사적 용법으로 쓰이는 경우다.

ex 4 He is the first person **to have received both awards**. 〈명사 수식〉

③ **부사적 용법**

부사와 마찬가지로 문장 내에서 형용사나 동사를 수식하는 역할을 한다.

ex 5 The Lance Amstrong Foundation was established **to raise money** for children's

cancer. 〈동사 수식〉

④ **관용적으로 쓰이는 to부정사**

to be honest 솔직히 말해 (= to tell the truth)
so to speak 말하자면
needless to say 말할 필요도 없이
to make matters worse 설상가상으로

to be short 간단히 말해
strange to say 이상한 말이지만
to begin with 우선적으로

2 동명사

to부정사의 명사적 용법과 마찬가지로 문장 내에서 주어, 목적어, 보어 역할을 한다.

① 명사적 용법

ex

6 **Smoking** cigarette is the single most preventable cause of premature death. 〈주어〉

7 I enjoy **playing** chess. 〈목적어〉

8 My hobby is **playing** football. 〈보어〉

② 관용적으로 쓰이는 동명사

cannot help -ing ~하지 않을 수 없다

look forward to -ing ~하기를 고대하다

have a difficulty (in) -ing ~하는데 어려움을 겪다

it is no use -ing ~해도 소용없다

feel like -ing ~하고 싶다

what do you say to -ing ~하는 게 어때요?

Review

명사적 용법(to 부정사 & 동명사)
문장 내에서 주어, 목적어, 보어 역할을 한다.

형용사적 용법(to 부정사)
문장 내에서 명사를 수식하는 역할을 한다.

부사적 용법(to 부정사)
문장 내에서 형용사, 부사, 동사를 수식하는 역할을 한다.

EXERCISE

• 정답 및 해설 p.16

A 적절한 준동사의 형태를 쓰시오.

> **Ex** The best way _____ a foreign language is to immerse yourself in it. <learn>
> → **to learn**

1 My dream is _____ a famous actor. <be>

→

2 It is no use _____ mad at me. <get>

→

3 I couldn't help _____ in love with music. <fall>

→

4 Do you feel like _____? <dance>

→

5 I know you want _____ a trip to Boston. <take>

→

B 문장의 구조상 어울리는 것을 선택하시오.

1 She has no house (living / to live) in.

2 I'm not afraid (of going / in go) out alone.

3 I finally finished (to sort / sorting) the books.

4 The accused has the right (remaining / to remain) silent.

5 Jason really enjoy (to spend / spending) time with family and friends.

6 I never see him (to thinking / without thinking) of my teacher.

7 If you are (to succeed / succeed) in life, you must work hard.

8 She decided (publishing / to publish) an English book for children.

9 She postponed (being made / making) decisions on the issues.

10 I have a lot of work (doing / to do).

• 정답 및 해설 p.17

• 다음 빈 칸에 들어갈 적절한 응답을 고르시오.

PART 1

1   A   Would you mind _____ the window for me?

    B   Of course not.

(a) opening

(b) being open

(c) to opening

(d) opened

PART 2

2   She couldn't help _____ him at first sight.

(a) to loving

(b) loved

(c) loving

(d) to love

• 다음에서 잘못된 부분을 찾으시오.

PART 3

3   (a) A: Hi, Tom.

    (b) B: Hi, Jane. How have you been doing?

    (c) A: Great, do you have time coming over my home tonight?

    (d) B: Probably yes. I have no other plans to do tonight.

PART 4

4   Most car rental companies offer their customers several optional means of paying for the fuel they use. (b) One of the common options is charge customers for the estimated amount of fuel used. (c) The estimate is based on the reading of the vehicle's fuel gauge. (d) This is a popular option for car rental customers.

UNIT 2 분사

분사는 〈동사 + -ing〉 또는 〈동사 + -ed〉의 형태로 동사의 성질을 가지고 문장 내에서 동사 (진행형, 완료, 수동태), 형용사(명사수식, 보어), 부사구(분사구문) 역할을 하는 준동사의 일종이다.

기초문법 확인

1 명사 수식

분사는 기본적으로 명사를 수식하는 형용사 역할을 한다. 또한 수식하는 명사와의 관계에 따라 현재분사, 또는 과거분사가 된다.

현재분사	과거분사
해석 : ~중인, [능동과 진행]	해석 : ~된[수동과 완료]
ex a *sleeping* dog [자고 있는 개]	ex a *broken* car [고장난 차]
an *exciting* game [재미있는 경기]	*invited* people [초대된 사람들]

① 형용사 역할

명사를 수식하는 형용사 역할을 한다. 명사와의 관계가 능동이면 현재분사, 수동이면 과거분사를 쓴다.

ex
1. A **developing** country is a country whose wages are much lower than those of developed countries. 〈현재분사〉

2. The **broken** window is mirrored by the water. 〈과거분사〉

② 보어 역할

주어인 명사를 보충 설명하는 역할을 한다. 주어와의 관계가 능동이면 현재분사를, 수동이면 과거분사를 쓴다.

ex
3. Learning about Japan was **interesting**. 〈현재분사〉

4. Pack your own baggage and don't leave it **unattended**. 〈과거분사〉

2 분사의 위치

분사가 홀로 명사를 수식하는 경우 명사 앞에서 전치 수식하는 것이 원칙이나 분사가 수식 어구(목적어, 보어, 부사구 등)를 수반하는 경우 후치 수식한다.

① 전치 수식

ex 5 The **fallen** leaves are a good food source for the fungi and bacteria in the soil.

6 **Barking** dogs rarely bite.

② 후치 수식

ex 7 Look at the beautiful girl **wearing** a pink dress over there.

└, wearing 뒤에 분사의 목적어를 수반하는 경우

8 I have a friend **called** Jennie.

└, called 뒤에 보어를 수반하는 경우

9 They're trying to catch birds **sitting** on the trees.

└, 전치사구(on the trees)를 수반하는 경우

Review

형용사적 용법
명사를 수식하거나 보어로 쓰인다. 명사와의 관계가 능동이면 현재분사, 수동이면 과거분사를 쓴다.

후치수식
원칙은 명사 앞에서 전치수식하나 분사가 수식 어구를 수반하는 경우 후치 수식한다.

• 정답 및 해설 p.18

A 적절한 분사의 형태를 쓰시오.

> **Ex** English is a language _____ nearly all over the world. <speak>
> →**spoken**

1 I heard my name _____ again. <call>

→

2 This form is required of all students _____ in the study abroad program. <participate>

→

3 I had my shoes _____. <mend>

→

4 She was very _____ from the long walk. <tire>

→

5 The last student _____ the lab should close the door. <leave>

→

B 문장의 구조상 어울리는 것을 선택하시오.

1 Mysterious coastal odor remains (unsolving / unsolved).

2 All you need is a microphone (attached / attaching) to your computer.

3 I had the TV set (fixed / to fix).

4 My father got me (used / to use) my left hand.

5 If you're not happy any time within 30 days from your purchase, you can have your money (refunding / refunded).

6 The instructions (detailing / detailed) how to fill this form are included in this file.

7 iMed is an online store (provided / providing) quality medical equipment throughout the world.

8 The agency believes the (missed / missing) child is in danger of serious bodily harm.

9 Please pick up a souvenir at the gift shop (locating / located) in the visitor centre.

10 Keep windows (closed / closing) when the air conditioner is on.

• 정답 및 해설 p.19

● **다음 빈 칸에 들어갈 적절한 응답을 고르시오.**

PART 1

1 A I'm sorry to keep you _____.

   B That's all right.

(a) to wait

(b) wait

(c) to be waited

(d) waiting

PART 2

2 I found my computer _____ with a virus this afternoon.

(a) infected

(b) infects

(c) to infect

(d) infecting

● **다음에서 잘못된 부분을 찾으시오.**

PART 3

3 (a) A: Are you good at speaking Korean?

   (b) B: Well, just a little bit. How about you?

   (c) A: It's still difficult for me to make myself understanding in Korean.

   (d) B: Are you sure? You have already lived here for 10 years.

PART 4

4 (a) Thank you for buying the Swedish Cruising Guide. (b) If the Guide does not meet your cruising needs, we will be happy to refund your money. (c) We can only do so within the first 30 days after you have purchased the Guide. (d) If you wish to have your money refunding, please send us an e-mail to infor@swedishcruisingguide.com.

UNIT 3 분사구문

분사 구문이란 부사절이 부사구로 바뀐 모양을 뜻한다. 다시 말해 〈접속사 + 주어 +동사〉의
형태가 〈주어 + -ing, p.p.〉 혹은 〈-ing, p.p.〉로 변화하는 것을 의미한다.

기초문법 확인

1 분사 구문으로의 전환

> **ex** 1 <u>After</u> <u>he</u> <u>finished</u> his studies in Germany, he traveled in the Middle East for a year.

① **종속절의 접속사를 삭제한다.**

접속사는 문맥을 통해 유추가 가능한 경우에 생략한다. 명백히 알 수 없는 경우에는 혼동을 피하기 위해 접속사를 남겨둬
의미를 파악할 수 있게 한다.

〈접속사 삭제〉

~~After~~ he finished his studies in Germany, he traveled in the Middle East for a year.

② **주어를 삭제한다.**

주절과 주어가 같은 경우에만 생략이 가능하다.

〈주어 삭제〉

~~After he~~ finished his studies in Germany, he traveled in the Middle East for a year.

③ **종속절의 남은 동사를 분사로 바꾼다.**

주어 또는 목적어와의 관계에 따라 능동이면 현재분사로, 수동이면 과거분사로 바꿀 수 있다.

〈동사의 분사화〉

~~After he finished~~ his studies in Germany, he traveled in the Middle East for a year.

↳ <u>Finishing</u> his studies in Germany, he traveled in the Middle East for a year.

2 분사 구문의 의미

조건, 이유, 양보, 시간의 의미를 갖는다.

ex 2 If you plan on washing clothes, you should bring your own laundry detergent. 〈조건〉
     ↳ If **planning** on washing clothes, you should bring your own laundry detergent.

   3 Although the takeoff was delayed by thirty minutes, the flight arrived on time. 〈양보〉
     ↳ **Delayed** by thirty minutes, the flight arrived on time.

3 동시 동작과 결과적 용법

① **동시 동작**

ex 4 **Walking** slowly out of the room, I saw a portrait.
     ↳ 방에서 걸어 나오며 동시에 초상화를 본

② **결과**

ex 5 We have fully automated customized services, **allowing** our customers to get the best services ever.
     ↳ 완비된 서비스를 갖춘 결과 고객들에게 최상의 서비스를 제공하게 되었다는 결과적 용법

분사 구문
분사 구문은 부사절이 부사(구)가 된 형태를 지칭하며 부사절의 기능을 그대로 가지고 있으므로 조건, 이유, 양보, 시간 등의 의미를 갖는다.

• 정답 및 해설 p.20

A 밑줄 친 부분을 적절한 분사의 형태로 바꾸시오.

> **Ex** In 1935, a hurricane hit the area, <u>cause</u> East Coast Area to be flooded.
>   └→ *causing*

1 Not <u>know</u> what to do, she prayed for herself.
   └,

2 <u>Leave</u> alone, he felt exhausted.
   └,

3 Strictly <u>speak</u>, he is not a teacher.
   └,

4 <u>Tire</u>, I went to bed earlier.
   └,

5 <u>Walk</u> along the street, I ran into Eddie.
   └,

B 문장의 구조상 어울리는 것을 선택하시오.

1 Attendance is mandatory as (explaining / explained) in Rule Number 2.

2 (Known / Knowing) nothing about the other manufacturers' computers, I exchanged my computer for the same manufacturer's computer.

3 Weather (permitting / permitted), we will take a trip to the local museum.

4 Although (raised / raising) separately for a long time, they are like the branches of a tree.

5 (Having received / Receive) no answer, I sent the email to him again.

6 While (swum / swimming) in the river, I encountered an enemy.

7 If (planned / planning) on using your debit card, make sure your bank does not charge a foreign transaction fee.

8 (Judging / Judged) from his accent, he must be an Englishman.

9 (Accompanied / Accompanying) by an adult, children under 12 years can travel for free in buses.

10 (Admitted / Admitting) what you say, I still don't believe it.

• **다음 빈 칸에 들어갈 적절한 응답을 고르시오.**

PART 1

1 A What happened to your eyes? They are so swollen.

B I stayed up all night _____ cards.

(a) to by played

(b) played

(c) to playing

(d) playing

PART 2

2 When _____ shopping yesterday, I saw my best friend, Scott.

(a) to go

(b) gone

(c) going

(d) gone to

• **다음에서 잘못된 부분을 찾으시오.**

PART 3

3 (a) A: Excuse me, Can you tell me where the nearest laundromat is in this neighborhood?

(b) B: Turn left and going straight a couple of blocks, you can find one.

(c) A: Thank you so much. I'd really appreciate it.

(d) B: Sure.

PART 4

4 (a) As discussing at our meeting, please find enclosed an electronic version of the presentation we made on Tuesday. (b) Please feel free to share with your colleagues. (c) I look forward to working with you and getting to know you better in the coming months. (d) Any questions or concerns you might have, don't hesitate to contact me by phone at the office at 312-211-0220 or via my cell phone at 010 2000 2000.

UNIT 4 조동사

조동사란 추측, 가능, 허가, 의무 등의 뜻으로 동사의 의미를 보완해 주는 조력동사를 뜻한다.
조동사 뒤는 반드시 원형동사가 오며 부정은 조동사 뒤에 not을 쓴다.

기초문법 확인

1 특징

조동사는 홀로 쓰지 못한다. 반드시 본동사와 함께 동사 앞에 쓰고 이때 동사는 원형동사의 형태가 되어야 한다. 또한 조동사의 부정은 뒤에 not을 붙여 표현한다.

ex

1 I can do it.
   └ 조동사(can) + 원형동사(do)

2 I can not do it.
   └ 조동사 + NOT(*cf.* don't have to)

2 종류

① 미래(will, be going to)

ex 3 She **will** complete the report soon.

② 가능(can)

ex 4 I'm sure you **can** win next time.

5 You **can** get a job that you really want.

③ 의무(should, must)

ex 6 You **should** leave now.

7 You **must** not eat that.

④ 추측(might, can't be)

ex 8 It **can't be** John. (강한 추측)

9 I **might** attend the party tonight. (불확실한 추측)

⑤ 허가(may, can)

[ex] 10 You **may** go now.

11 **Can** I go home now?

3 준조동사와 조동사의 완료표현

준조동사란 조동사에 준하는 뜻과 용법을 갖는 동사를 뜻한다. 조동사와 마찬가지로 뒤에 동사원형을 취하거나 비슷한 의미를 갖는다. 또한 조동사끼리는 중복해서 사용될 수 없지만 조동사와 일부 준조동사는 문장에서 중복해서 사용할 수 있다.

① 준조동사

be able to V (~할 수 있다)	used to V (~하곤 했다)
had better V (~하는 것이 낫다)	have to V (~해야만 한다)

[ex] 12 I won't **be able to** participate in the meeting.

13 You'**d better** not lie.

② 완료

should have p.p. (~했어야만 했는데)	must have p.p. (~했음에 틀림없다)
might have p.p. (~했을지도 모른다)	would have p.p. (~하려 했었는데)

[ex] 14 I **should**n't **have gone** there.

15 You **must have seen** the movie.

Review

조동사의 의미와 특징
능력(can), 허가(may, can), 추측(might, can't), 의무(should, have to, must) 등의 의미를 가지고 본동사 앞에서 동사의 의미를 보완해주는 역할을 한다. 조동사의 부정형은 조동사 뒤에 NOT을 쓰면 되지만 don't have to, ought not to 등은 그 쓰임에 예외가 있으므로 잘 기억해 두자.

🕐 3 minutes

• 정답 및 해설 p.22

A 밑줄 친 조동사 부분에 유의해 우리말로 번역하시오.

> **Ex** He <u>may have forgotten</u> about the anniversary.
> → 그는 아마도 그 기념일을 잊었을지도 모른다.

1 I <u>should have attended</u> the birthday party.

→

2 I <u>have not decided</u> where to take a vacation next week.

→

3 I <u>have to go</u> to New York on business next Thursday.

→

4 If you have any questions, please <u>do not hesitate</u> to contact me.

→

5 He <u>cannot have been</u> at the Chinese restaurant.

→

6 I <u>would sit</u> on the balcony of my room.

→

7 She <u>should get</u> here soon.

→

8 The rumor <u>can't be</u> true.

→

9 He <u>must have left</u> his wallet on my desk.

→

10 I think <u>I'd better discuss</u> that with my wife.

→

● 다음 빈 칸에 들어갈 적절한 응답을 고르시오.

PART 1

1 A _____ you help me move these chairs?

B Sure thing.

(a) How can

(b) Aren't

(c) Can

(d) Did you

PART 2

2 You _____ invested in stocks.

(a) ought to

(b) had better

(c) should have

(d) may well

● 다음에서 잘못된 부분을 찾으시오.

PART 3

3 (a) A: I've finally purchased a car.

(b) B: Really? You can't be excited about it.

(c) A: Yeah, and I want you to come over to my house to see my car if you have time this Saturday.

(d) B: I'm afraid I have other plans then.

PART 4

4 (a) Salmonella may also be found in the feces of some pets. (b) People can become infected if they do not wash their hands after contact with these animals. (c) Reptiles are particularly likely to have Salmonella. (d) People should always washing their hands immediately after handling a reptile, even if the reptile seems healthy.

Chapter 4

품사 I

UNIT 1   명사와 관사

UNIT 2   형용사와 부사

UNIT 3   기타 형용사

UNIT 4   비교

UNIT 5   대명사 일치와 재귀대명사

UNIT 6   지시대명사와 부정대명사

UNIT 7   전치사 I

UNIT 8   전치사(전치사 구별 포함) II

UNIT 1 명사와 관사

명사란 사물이나 장소 또는 사람을 포함한 동물 등 각각의 이름을 나타내는 말이다. 명사의 종류에는 크게 셀 수 있는 가산명사와 셀 수 없는 불가산 명사 두 가지가 있다.

기초문법 확인

1 명사의 종류

셀 수 없는 명사(불가산 명사)

the information (△) / a information (✕) / informations (✕)
 └ 수식어구 등에 의해 한정되는 경우에는 the와 함께 쓸 수 있음

셀 수 있는 명사(가산 명사)

the book (○) / a book (○) / books(○)
 └ the 없이 book만 독립적으로 쓸 수 없음

① **셀 수 있는 명사**

명사 중에서 특히 부정관사 (a/an)나 –s를 붙여 복수형을 나타낼 수 있는 명사를 의미한다.

ex 1 She has good ~~book~~.
 └ **a** (good) **book** 또는 **books**

 2 Michael is **a** good **cook**.

 3 All personal **belongings** should be removed from the drying **rooms**.

② **셀 수 없는 명사**

관사(a/an)나 복수형 어미(–s)를 붙일 수 없고 항상 단수 취급한다.

ex 4 I'd really appreciate your **advices**.
 └ **advice**

● 대표적인 셀 수 없는 불가산 명사

information	furniture	clothing	baggage	luggage
equipment	advice	machinery	merchandise	produce
money				

 5 I need some **information** on the region.

 6 Most of our **equipment was** previously used in the food.

2 관사

① 관사 a 또는 an

셀 수 있는 가산 명사 앞에 붙이는 a나 an을 가리킨다. 발음기호상 자음으로 시작되는 경우 a를 붙이고 모음으로 시작되는 경우 an을 붙인다.

ex　7　Rome was not built in **a** *day* [발음기호 → dei].

　　　8　I waited there for **an** *hour* [발음기호 → au*r*]

② 관사 the

수식어에 의해 한정된 명사(셀 수 없는 명사 포함)거나 세상에서 하나밖에 없는 고유명사, 반복 사용된 명사 등의 앞에는 정관사 the를 붙인다.

ex　9　**The** sun is vastly bigger than **the** earth.
　　　　　 └→ 유일무이　　　　　　　　　　　　└→ 유일무이

　　　10　It is **the** blue bird / we are looking for.
　　　　　　　　　　　　　　└→ 앞의 blue bird를 한정

　　　11　**The** dog is a faithful companion.
　　　　　 └→ 종족 대표

Review

명사의 종류

영어에서는 셀 수 있는 가산명사와 셀 수 없는 불가산 명사, 이렇게 크게 두 가지로 나눌 수 있다. 추상명사, 물질명사 등의 구분은 크게 중요하지 않다. 우리가 생각하기에 셀 수 없을 것 같은 명사 앞에서도 종종 a/an 또는 복수형을 쓰기 때문이다. 예를 들어 '하늘'이란 뜻의 sky를 종종 복수형 skies로 쓰기도 한다.

관사

관사는 크게 부정관사 a/an과 정관사 the로 나눌 수 있다. a/an은 정해지지 않은 셀 수 있는 명사 앞에 쓴다. the는 하나 밖에 없거나, 한정된 명사 앞에 쓴다.

A 빈 칸에 적절한 관사(a/an/the)를 넣으시오.

> **Ex** They were there for _____ hour.
> → *an*

1 Gas is sold by _____ liter.
→

2 I enjoy sleeping till late in _____ morning on Sunday.
→

3 He caught me by _____ arm.
→

4 I met _____ friend of mine today who is a graphic artist.
→

5 _____ English Channel is a part of the Atlantic Ocean.
→

B 문장의 구조상 어울리는 것을 선택하시오.

1 I bought (a / an) original X-BOX yesterday.

2 Let me know (an / the) accurate address of John.

3 You will have a better understanding of tribal life in (the Himalayas / Himalayas).

4 What (an / the) intelligent animal the dog is!

5 She is such (a / the) beautiful girl.

6 A cup of (coffee / a coffee), please.

7 I e-mail him three times (a / the) week.

8 I bought (a new pair / new pair) of jeans on my way home.

9 She is suffering from (the fever / fever).

10 I hired a cab by (an / the) hour.

• 정답 및 해설 p.25

• **다음 빈 칸에 들어갈 적절한 응답을 고르시오.**

PART 1

1   A   What would you like to drink, sir?

   B   I'll have _____, please.

   (a) another glass of water

   (b) bottle of water

   (c) glass of water

   (d) some waters

PART 2

2   Birds of _____ feather flock together.

   (a) the

   (b) their

   (c) a

   (d) its

• **다음에서 잘못된 부분을 찾으시오.**

PART 3

3   (a) A: Lee, why are you in such the hurry?

   (b) B: I'm late for school.

   (c) A: When does your first class start?

   (d) B: At nine thirty.

PART 4

4   (a) On Tuesday, the Press said that Indian cricket star Franklin Rose, 32, is suffering from a tear in his right shoulder. (b) Rose eventually traveled to London on Friday to undergo surgery on his injured shoulder. (c) Rose is expected to be operated upon on Monday. (d) The surgery will rule him out of play for a five weeks, according to the Indian cricket board.

형용사와 부사는 주로 문장 속에서 수식하는 역할을 한다. 형용사는 명사를 수식하고 부사는 형용사와 동사, 다른 부사(구), 또는 경우에 따라 문장전체를 수식하기도 한다.

기초문법 확인

1 형용사의 용법

① 한정적 용법

명사를 바로 앞 또는 뒤에서 수식하는 경우다.

ex
1. The **following** chapter is about legal issues.
2. The **former** vice president is now in jeopardy because of the Supreme Court ruling.

- 한정적 용법으로만 쓰이는 형용사

> drunken 술에 취한   elder 연상의   former 이전의   latter 후자의   sole 단독의   only 유일한   very 매우; 바로 그   wooden 목재로 된   upper 높은 쪽의   inner 안쪽의   outer 바깥쪽의   this 이것의   that 저것의 ...

② 서술적 용법

주어 또는 목적어를 보충 설명하는 보어로 사용되는 경우다.

ex
3. We are **concerned** about global warming.
4. She is **afraid** of spiders.

- 서술적 용법으로만 쓰이는 형용사

> ashamed 부끄러운   aware 아는   proud 자랑스러워하는   unable 할 수 없는   worth 가치 있는   alike 같은   alive 살아있는   awake 깨어 있는   alone 혼자서   afraid 무서운   asleep 잠든   fond 좋아하는 ...

③ 같은 형용사라도 한정적 용법과 서술적 용법에 따라 뜻이 달라지기도 한다.

ex
- **certain**: 어떤(한정적); 확신하는(서술적)
5. A **certain** lady came to see me. 〈한정적〉
6. I am **certain** of his success. 〈서술적〉

- **present**: 현재의(한정적); 참석한(서술적)

7   He is the **present** captain of the team.

8   Mr. Hurley was **present** at the meeting.

2   부사의 역할

부사는 형용사, 다른 부사(구), 동사, 문장전체를 수식하는 역할을 한다.

ex 9   It rained a lot and the wind blew **hard**. → 동사 수식

10   Investing in the stock market is **too** risky for me. → 형용사 수식

11   **Unfortunately**, the choice of singers is not the best. → 문장전체 수식

12   He arrived **just** on time for his flight. → 전치사구인 on time 수식

3   부사의 위치

부사의 위치는 비교적 자유로운 편이다. 단 빈도부사는 일반 동사 앞, 조동사 뒤에 위치하고 「타동사 + 부사」의 결합에 있어서 대명사가 목적어가 될 때는 타동사와 부사 사이에 위치한다.

ex 13   ~~Take off it~~.
     └→ Take it off. → 「타동사 + 대명사 + 부사」가 올바른 순서

14   I **often** get up at the crack of dawn.
     → 「조동사 + 빈도부사 + 일반 동사」의 순서로 문장에서 쓰이며 빈도부사에는 often, always, seldom, nearly, rarely, sometimes, scarcely, almost 등이 있다.

Review

형용사
명사의 앞뒤에서 수식할 때는 한정적 용법, 보어자리에서 명사의 의미를 보충 설명할 때는 서술적 용법으로 쓰인 것이다.

부사
형용사, 다른 부사(구), 동사, 문장 전체를 수식하기도 한다. 수식하는 위치는 비교적 자유롭지만, 타동사의 목적어로 대명사가 올 때는 대명사의 위치는 목적어와 부사 사이이다.

A 다음 밑줄 친 부분의 품사(형용사 또는 부사)를 쓰시오.

> **Ex** I had a strange dream last night.
> └→형용사   └→형용사

1 Is there something wrong with my cat?
└→

2 I found the lecture really interesting.
└→   └→

3 Please listen carefully to the following choices.
└→   └→

4 What's the main reason you exercise?
└→

5 He is likely to resign.
└→

B 다음 문장의 구조에서 어울리는 것을 선택하시오.

1 He gave me a (wooden / woodless) box.

2 I can (hard / hardly) wait to see the movie.

3 The fountain is in a pond 10 feet (deep / deeply) and 20 feet wide.

4 The driver was (drunken / drunk) and killed someone.

5 HDTV is really (worth / worthy) waiting for.

6 The (lately / late) Mr. Nichol was 80 years of age when he died.

7 She was (highly / high) praised for her beautiful voice.

8 I hope that people enjoy our (alive / live) show.

9 (Unfortunately / Unfortunate), there's no way to avoid mortality.

10 I fell (sleep / asleep) with the TV on.

• 정답 및 해설 p.27

● **다음 빈 칸에 들어갈 적절한 응답을 고르시오.**

PART 1

1 A I want you to make sure the text is ＿＿＿＿＿＿ to read.

   B Don't worry. I already told Jack to enlarge it.

   (a) largeness enough

   (b) large enough

   (c) enough largely

   (d) enough large

PART 2

2 I always wanted to raise my child ＿＿＿＿＿.

   (a) differed

   (b) different

   (c) differently

   (d) differs

● **다음에서 잘못된 부분을 찾으시오.**

PART 3

3 (a) A: Is it truth you're going to quit your job?

   (b) B: Yes, how did you know that anyway?

   (c) A: Rumors are around the office.

   (d) B: Oh, Jesus. I shouldn't have told Tom about that.

PART 4

4 (a) Global warming has finally been explained. (b) The Earth is getting hotter because the Sun is burning more brightly than at any time during the past 1,000 years, according to new research. (c) A study suggests that increasing radiation from the sun is responsible for recent global climate changes. (d) The Sun has been at its strongest over the past 60 years and may now be affecting globally temperatures.

UNIT 3 기타 형용사

영어에서는 품사 사이에서의 수 일치 또한 중요하다. 즉, 셀 수 있는 명사 앞에는 이를 수식하는 형용사(many, few)를, 셀 수 없는 양을 나타내는 명사 앞에는 이를 수식하는 형용사(much, little)를 각각 맞게 써야 한다.

기초문법 확인

1 수사

① **hundred와 hundreds의 차이**

hundred 앞에 숫자가 있는 경우에는 hundred 뒤에 –s를 붙이지 못하며 '수백의'라는 불분명한 숫자를 표시할 때는 뒤에 –s를 붙여 hundreds of~ 로 표시한다.

> ex　Hundred**s**(thousand**s**, million**s**) **of** people [수백(수천, 수백만) 명의 사람들]
>
> **Three** hundred(thousand, million) people [삼백(삼천, 삼백만) 명의 사람들]

② **서수에는 the를 붙인다.**

일반적인 숫자 one, two, three를 '기수'라고 하고 순서를 나타내는 first, second, third 등은 '서수'라고 한다. 이 서수 앞에는 the를 쓰는 것이 원칙이다.

> ex　**The** *second* floor [2층]
>
> World War Ⅱ (**The** *Second* World War) [제 2차 세계대전]

2 양과 수의 표현

much와 little은 양을 나타내고, many와 few는 수를 표시한다. 또한 little과 few는 부정을, a little과 a few는 긍정의 뜻을 나타낸다.

> ex　1　You can put **a few** *sugar* in your coffee.
>
> 　　　　↳ a little(sugar는 셀 수 없는 명사이므로 a little 또는 little로 수식해야 한다.)
>
> 　　2　Put **few** *sugar* in your tea.
>
> 　　　　↳ little(양을 나타내면서 문맥상 '거의 ~가 없는'이란 뜻의 부정표현)
>
> 　　3　**Much** *people* believe he is a liar.
>
> 　　　　↳ Many(셀 수 있는 복수명사 people 앞이므로 many로 수식)

3 so와 such의 비교

so는 형용사나 부사를 수식해 강조하는 부사고, such는 명사를 수식해 강조하는 형용사다.

ex 4 The internet connection is **~~such~~** *slow* that I couldn't even check my email.

　　　　　　　　　　　└→ so(slow라는 형용사를 수식하는 자리이므로 such가 아닌 so로 수식)

　　　5 It's a **very funny story** of a young Korean immigrant.

　　　　　= It's **such a funny story** of ~.

　　　　　= It's **so funny a story** of ~.

　　　→ 강조함에 있어서 각각 어순에서 차이가 있음을 알 수 있다. 이는 각각의 품사가 다르기 때문인데 so는 부사이며
　　　　뒤에는 명사가 아닌 형용사가 위치해야 하기 때문에 funny가 so바로 뒤에 온다.

4 특정 전치사와 짝을 이루는 형용사

● 형용사 + of

> be full of(~로 가득하다)　　　　be appreciative of(~를 고맙게 여기다)
>
> be capable of(~할 수 있다)　　be aware of(~에 대해 알고 있다)

● 형용사 + for

> be responsible for(~에 책임이 있다)　be ideal for(~에 이상적이다)
>
> be famous for(~으로 유명하다)　　　　be eligible for(~에 자격이 있다)

● 형용사 + with

> be pleased with(~로 기쁘다)　　　　be satisfied with(~에 만족하다)
>
> be familiar with/to(~에 익숙하다)　　be consistent with/in(~와 일치하다)

● 형용사 + in

> be interested in(~에 관심 있다)　　　be skilled in/at(~에 능숙하다)

Review

수량 형용사

much와 little은 셀 수 없는 명사를, many와 few는 셀 수 있는 명사를 수식하는 수량 형용사다.

such와 so

such는 형용사이기 때문에 명사 앞에 쓰고 so는 부사이기 때문에 형용사나 다른 부사 앞에 쓴다.

A 밑줄 친 부분을 올바르게 고치시오.

> **Ex** <u>Dozen of people</u> have been injured after high winds and heavy rains hit
> ↳ **Dozens of people**
> southern Japan.

1 <u>Napoleon Third</u> was deposed in 1870.
↳

2 He is <u>responsible of</u> conducting research.
↳

3 <u>Much students</u> expressed concerns about the quality of their education.
↳

4 The tank is <u>full in</u> fuel.
↳

5 It's <u>a such long way</u> home.
↳

B 다음 문장의 구조에서 어울리는 것을 선택하시오.

1 I bought (a few / much) books about a week ago.

2 He is appreciative (of / with) our service we give to him.

3 It seems like (so / such) a long time ago.

4 He preferred to be alone and expressed (few / little) interest in friendships.

5 We are well aware (for / of) the difficulty keeping the building warm during the winter.

6 About one (hundred / hundreds of) people were present at the party.

7 Autumn in Korea is very famous (for / in) its beautiful maple leaves.

8 (Few / a little) people showed up for the event.

9 The meteor storm was (so / such) beautiful that we stayed out all night watching it.

10 (Dozens of / Dozen) people have been injured after the strongest earthquake.

• 다음 빈 칸에 들어갈 적절한 응답을 고르시오.

PART 1

1 A Do you know much about this software?

B Sorry, I'm not _____ this new one.

(a) familiar with

(b) familiarized

(c) familiarity to

(d) familiar from

PART 2

2 _____ have been forced to leave their homes amid severe flooding across England.

(a) Thousand people

(b) Thousands of people

(c) Thousands people

(d) Thousand of people

• 다음에서 잘못된 부분을 찾으시오.

PART 3

3 (a) A: What are you doing?

(b) B: I'm searching for some information on credit cards.

(c) A: Why? You already have much card.

(d) B: Yes, but I'm looking for a card which is offering complete protection from fraud.

PART 4

4 (a) A little people maintain that animal testing is not reliable and does not help medical research while others say it does. (b) With the two sides feeling so strongly about it, it's difficult to tell where the truth lies. (c) But I think that any testing on animals that is not absolutely necessary should not be allowed. (d) When animal testing is essential, then it should go ahead.

UNIT 4 비교

비교란 형용사나 부사의 어형 변화를 통한 정도표시를 뜻한다. 비교에는 '~만큼'으로 해석되는 원급, '~보다 더'라고 해석되는 비교급, '가장 ~한'으로 해석되는 최상급이 있다.

기초문법 확인

1 비교

① 원급

'~만큼, 못지않게 ~한'으로 해석되며 「as 형용사/부사 as」로 표현하는 것이 일반적이다.

ex
1. Formula is **as good as** breast milk.

2. The hotel was **not as good as** I expected.

3. He is **as famous as any** pianist in Asia.
   (= No other pianist is so famous as he in Asia.)
   → 「**as 형용사 as any** + 단수명사」(단수명사 못지않게 ~한)

4. You can visit **as many** cities **as** you like. [~만큼의 (같은)수]

5. He was **as much** an entertainer **as** a hockey player. [~만큼의 (같은)양]

② 비교급

1음절로 끝나는 형용사/부사는 뒤에 -er을 붙이고, 2음절 이상의 형용사/부사는 앞에 more를 붙이는 것이 원칙이다.

ex
6. Goat's milk is **healthier than** cow's milk.

7. We should use energy **more wisely**.

③ 최상급

1음절로 끝나는 형용사/부사는 뒤에 (the) -est를 붙이고, 2음절 이상의 형용사/부사(-ly 등) 앞에는 the most를 붙이는 것이 원칙이다.

ex
8. They are **the most useful** words for your study of English because you will meet them very often.

9. It might be **the safest** gas station in Dallas.

④ **불규칙 변화와 라틴어 비교급**

ex   10   This is **the worst** one I have ever read.

→ bad(나쁜)는 bad - worse - worst로 불규칙 변화한다.

불규칙 변화		
원급	비교급	최상급
many[much]	more	most
little	less	least
good	better	best

- 라틴어 비교급

11   Cancer care in remote areas is **inferior to** that offered in cities.

→ 위의 예 '~보다 못한'으로 해석되는 inferior를 비롯해 superior(~보다 나은), junior(손아래의), senior(손위의) 등은 전치사 to가 than을 대신한다.

2   the + 비교급

원칙은 최상급 앞에 정관사 the를 써야 하나 비교급 앞에 the를 쓰는 경우는 크게 1 이유, 2 둘 사이의 비교, 3 「the + 비교급, the + 비교급」 구문일 때이다.

ex   - 이유

12   I love her **all the better because** she is left-handed.

- 둘 사이의 비교

13   I guess reconciliation of the people is **the bigger** of **the two** issues.

- 「the + 비교급, the + 비교급」 구문

14 The **more** he wins, the **more** he wants to win.

Review

비교
원급은 「as + 형용사/부사 + as」로 '~만큼'으로 해석되고 비교급과 최상급은 형용사/부사가 1음절이면 어미 -er/(the)-est를 붙이고 2음절 이상이면 more/the most를 앞에 붙여 표시한다. 각각 「~보다 더」, 「가장 ~한」으로 해석된다.

the + 비교급
최상급 앞에 정관사 the를 쓰는 것이 원칙이나 이유, 둘 사이의 비교, 「the + 비교급, the + 비교급」 구문일 때는 비교급 앞에도 the를 써야 한다.

A 밑줄 친 부분에 유의해 해석하시오.

> **Ex** The movie was <u>not as good as</u> I expected.
> → 영화는 내가 예상한 것만큼 좋지는 않았다.

1 This is <u>by far the best</u> performance I have <u>ever</u> seen.
→

2 Your brain is <u>much better than</u> you think.
→

3 He is <u>not so much</u> a teacher <u>as</u> a writer.
→

4 Which planet would you say is <u>the warmer of the two</u>?
→

5 She is <u>the best</u> dance teacher <u>ever</u>.
→

B 문장의 구조상 어울리는 것을 선택하시오.

1 He is the best actor India has (ever / even) produced.

2 I've worked (very hard / more harder) for 2 months.

3 The more we get together, the (happier / happiest) we'll be.

4 We should spend the money (than / more) wisely.

5 I think she is (the more / more) famous of the two.

6 They are getting (better and better / more better) at making quality television.

7 He knew better (as / than) to complain.

8 They have one of (much more / the most) successful programs available in the country.

9 He is (the last / the farthest) person to spoil relations for money.

10 She was (clever / the cleverest) woman I've ever known.

• 정답 및 해설 p.31

● **다음 빈 칸에 들어갈 적절한 응답을 고르시오.**

PART 1

1 A Jennifer is _____ female hip hop artist in the world. What do you say?

B Well, I agree that to a certain extent but not entirely.

(a) the better

(b) the most

(c) more

(d) the best

PART 2

2 She is not so much a teacher _____ a poet.

(a) as

(b) than

(c) to

(d) so

● **다음에서 잘못된 부분을 찾으시오.**

PART 3

3 (a) A: I'm planning on cutting my hair short.

(b) B: Why? Your current style looks more on you.

(c) A: As you can see, this style looks too heavy for the summer.

(d) B: How about just a short trim at the ends then?

PART 4

4 (a) The more we know, more we can learn. (b) Quickly grasping and remembering new information becomes more difficult as we get older. (c) It is because our ability to process begins to decline around age 20. (d) But a new study by a psychologist, Sara J. Welch, shows that acquiring new knowledge and learning new skills depends not just on how smart we are, but also on what we already have learned and experienced throughout our lives.

UNIT 5 대명사 일치와 재귀대명사

동일한 명사 반복을 피하기 위해 앞에 쓰였던 명사를 대신 받는 역할을 하는 것이 대명사다.
특히 대명사의 성과 수를 일치시켰는지를 묻는 것은 대명사의 기본적인 문제에 해당된다.

기초문법 확인

1 대명사의 성 · 수일치

일반인을 지칭하는 대명사를 뜻한다. 명사와 이를 받는 대명사 사이에는 성과 수가 일치해야 한다.

ex
● 주어와 동사와의 수일치

1 I ~~loves~~ the city surrounding the dam.
   └ love

→ 주어가 1인칭 'I'이므로 동사는 loves가 아닌 love가 되어야 한다.

● 성과 수의 일치

2 She ~~am~~ a friendly ~~man~~ and a very generous ~~ones~~.
   └ is   └ woman   └ one

→ 주어가 'She'이므로 동사는 is/was 등의 단수 동사를, man은 woman으로 ones는 (a~) one으로 각각 성과
수를 일치시켜야 한다.

2 대명사 It

① 비인칭 주어

날씨, 시간, 거리 등을 나타낸다.

ex
● 날씨

3 **It**'s **_raining_** on and off all day here.

● 거리

4 **It**'s about **_two blocks away_**.

② 가주어, 가목적어

주어 또는 목적어 부분이 다소 긴 경우 그 자리를 가주어, 또는 가목적어 it이 대신하는 경우다. 영어에서의 약속이므로
it이 아닌 that이나 those 등의 다른 대명사는 이 역할을 할 수 없다.

ex
5 **It** is certain **_that he is an artist_**. → that 이하가 진짜 주어

6 I found **it** exciting **_to try new recipes and foods_**. → to 이하가 진짜 목적어

③ **강조용법 〈it + be동사 ~ that〉**

강조하고자 하는 부분을 it과 that 사이에 넣어 표현하는 방식이다.

ex
7 **It** is *she* **that** knows everything about the school. → she를 강조

8 **It** was *my sister* **that** dated him. → my sister를 강조

3 재귀대명사

① **재귀용법과 강조용법**

재귀대명사는 재귀용법과 강조용법으로 사용된다. 재귀용법은 주어를 대신해 뒤에 -self나 -selves를 붙여 목적어 역할을 하는 경우다. 강조용법은 문장의 필수 성분이 아니기 때문에 문장 구조상 없어도 되며 주어를 단순히 강조하고자 할 때 사용한다.

ex
● 재귀용법

9 *I* injured **myself** while I was working out in a gym.

● 강조용법

10 I bought her book immediately after having seen ***the woman* herself** on a TV program.

② **재귀대명사의 관용적용법**

in itself(in themselves) 저절로	behave oneself 바르게 행동하다
by oneself 혼자서(혼자 힘으로 = alone)	of itself 저절로
make oneself at home 편히 하다	beside oneself 제정신이 아닌
for oneself 자기 자신을 위해, 자신의 힘으로	

Review

대명사의 의미와 규칙

대명사를 쓰는 이유는 동일한 명사의 반복을 피하기 위한 경제적인 이유에서다. 또한 명사와 그 명사를 받는 대명사는 동일지시의미를 지녀야하므로 성과 수를 반드시 일치시켜야 한다.

대명사의 종류

대명사에는 사람을 지칭하는 인칭대명사, 사람이 아닌 거리, 시간, 날씨 등을 지칭하는 비인칭대명사, 뒤에 self와 selves를 붙인 재귀대명사, 사람과 사물을 지칭하는 지시대명사, 불분명한 명사를 지칭하는 부정대명사, 그리고 선행사와 접속사를 포함하는 관계대명사가 있다.

• 정답 및 해설 p.32

A 밑줄 친 부분에 유의해 해석하시오.

> **Ex** Tomorrow, it will be quite hot and humid. (비인칭 주어 날씨)
> → 내일은 꽤 후덥지근할 것이다. *hot and humid 후덥지근한

1 The door opened of itself. (재귀대명사의 관용적 용법)

→

2 It is still freezing outside. (날씨, 비인칭)

→

3 It is natural that he scold others. (가주어)

→

4 It's about two blocks away from the main library on Fifth Avenue. (거리)

→

5 It was him that I was listening to. (강조용법)

→

B 문장의 구조상 어울리는 것을 선택하시오.

1 I (hasn't / haven't) seen him lately.

2 (It / There) was hot and humid all day.

3 (She / He) is a drunken man.

4 How long (has / have) you been waiting for her?

5 It (is / has) her that I am worried about.

6 You have to make (your / his) own decision this time.

7 I found (it / that) exciting to get free food and drink.

8 She postponed (its / her) flight.

9 (They are / She is) a friendly woman.

10 You behave (yours / yourself) now!

• **다음 빈 칸에 들어갈 적절한 응답을 고르시오.**

PART 1

1   A   What happened to your computer?

B   I have no clue. Think I have to take _____ to the repair shop.

(a) them
(b) themselves
(c) itself
(d) it

PART 2

2   Andy killed _____ while he was on trial.

(a) his
(b) themselves
(c) he
(d) himself

• **다음에서 잘못된 부분을 찾으시오.**

PART 3

3   (a) A: May I speak to Mr. Lee, please?

(b) B: Can I ask who are speaking?

(c) A: This is Mark from Red inc.

(d) B: OK, one moment please.

PART 4

4   (a) The boy asked a number of different animals to describe their reactions to the year's first snowfall in the Poconos when there starts to snow. (b) A bear explains that snow means that it is time for him to go to sleep. (c) A mouse says that it is time for him to hide in a house to escape the cold. (d) And a fish describes how he must lie at the bottom of the pond to stay warm.

UNIT 6 지시대명사와 부정대명사

영어에서 대명사는 그 종류가 꽤 되고 각 대명사마다 문장에서의 쓰임 또한 다양하다. 특히 비슷한 대명사들의 특징을 구분하는 문제가 종종 등장하므로 비슷한 대명사의 차이가 무엇인지를 명확히 알 필요가 있다.

기초문법 확인

1 지시대명사 that과 those

대명사 that과 those 역시 명사의 반복을 피하기 위한 대명사이기는 하나 이를 제대로 알고 쓰는 수험생은 드문 것 같다. that은 단수명사를, those는 복수명사를 각각 대신한다. 특히 that과 those가 it과 구별되는 점은, it은 (of 이하의) 수식 어구에 의해서 한정을 받을 수 없다는 것이다. 또한 those가 those who~의 형태로 쓰이는 경우가 있는데 이는 '~하는 사람들'이라고 해석되면서 특정 사람들을 지칭할 때 쓰는 표현방식이다.

> **ex**
>
> 1 My *house* is larger than **that** of my older brother.
>   → that(those)는 특정한 그것(it)이 아닌 명사의 이름만 빌린 것이다. 위의 예문에서 알 수 있듯이 단지 house라는 명사를 빌렸을 뿐이지 같은 house는 아님을 알 수 있다. 이때 쓸 수 있는 대명사가 that(those)이다. 아울러 이 that(those)은 of 이하 등의 수식 어구에 의해 수식을 받을 수 있다.
>
> 2 The *winds* of Neptune are stronger than **those** of Jupiter.
>   → 복수명사 winds를 대명사 those로 받았다.
>
> 3 The course is designed for **those who** are interested in developing their writing skills.

2 부정대명사

정해지지 않은 사람 또는 사물을 가리키는 대명사를 부정대명사라고 한다.

① one / another / (the) other

> **ex**
>
> 4 The new badge is better than the old **one**. → 앞에 나온 것과 같은 종류
>
> 5 Give me **another**, please. → 다른 하나(an+other)
>
> 6 Saying is **one thing**; doing is **another**. → A is one thing; B is another(A와 B는 별개)
>
> 7 I have two dogs; **one** is fat and **the other** is slim.
>   → 둘 중에서 하나는 one이고 나머지 다른 하나는 the other로 표시

② some, any

모두 '어떤, 약간의' 등의 의미로 해석되는데 some은 긍정문에서, any는 부정문과 의문문(또는 조건문) 등에서 각각 쓰이는 것이 원칙이다. 단, '어떤 ~이라도'라는 양보의 의미로 해석되는 경우에는 긍정문에서도 some대신에 any를 쓸 수 있다.

ex 8   I have to buy **some** bacon for the party. → '약간의'(긍정문에서)

9   If you have **any** questions, please feel free to contact me. → '어떠한'(조건문)

● 긍정문에서의 any

10 You can visit us at **any** time. → time과 함께 양보의 의미로 '어떤 시간이라도 즉, 언제라도'

③ **every, each, all**

'모두, 누구나' 등의 의미를 가지기는 하나 every와 each는 단수(數) 명사와 함께 쓰고 이를 받는 동사 역시 단수형이 된다. 단, each는 every가 할 수 없는 대명사 역할을 할 수 있다. all은 가산[수(數)] 또는 불가산[양(量)] 명사와 모두 쓸 수 있는데 수 앞에 쓸 때는 (명사의 수는) 반드시 복수형이 되어야 한다.

ex 11 ~~Every~~ of you can pray. (=Everyone can pray.)
　　　└→ Each(cf. Every는 대명사 기능을 할 수 없다)

12 **Every(=Each)** man was a trained soldier.

13 Eventually, **all** of the money was returned. → of 뒤의 명사는 수 또는 양의 명사 모두 올 수 있으 며 동사는 그 명사의 성격(수 또는 양)에 따라 수가 결정된다. money는 불가산 명사기 때문에 이를 받는 동사는 단 수(was)가 되었다.

Review

that, those
that과 those는 한 문장 내에서 같은 명사의 반복을 피하기 위해 사용되는 대명사다. that은 단수명사를 those는 복수명사를 각각 대신한다.

• 정답 및 해설 p.33

A 밑줄 친 부분에 유의해 해석하시오.

> **Ex** The new battery capacity is larger than <u>that</u> of my old one.
> → 새 건전지의 용량이 전에 쓰던 것보다 크다.

1 I think that the old design is much better than the new <u>one</u>.
   →

2 Sharing knowledge is <u>one thing</u>, stealing information is <u>another</u>.
   →

3 His skin was as red as <u>that</u> of a boiled lobster.
   →

4 I have two dogs; <u>one</u> is overweight and <u>the other</u> is not.
   →

5 My students are more clever than <u>those</u> of yours.
   →

B 문장의 구조상 어울리는 것을 선택하시오.

1 Korean rice vinegars are stronger than (it / those) of Japan.

2 I have three hats; one is black, (the other / another) is red, and the other is white.

3 I like the old logo better than the new (it / one).

4 The Japanese school system is similar to (that / those) of the U.S.

5 Is there (all / any) room left in the VIP lounge?

6 Football is one thing, management is (the other / another).

7 Give me (others / another) chance, please.

8 The negro's blood is just as red as (there / that) of the white man.

9 You can come at (always / any) time.

10 Second-hand smoke can harm even (they / those) who don't smoke.

• 정답 및 해설 p.35

• **다음 빈 칸에 들어갈 적절한 응답을 고르시오.**

PART 1

1 A Now, I want my money back.

   B Please, give me _____ week.

   (a) two

   (b) others

   (c) another

   (d) the

PART 2

2 My role is much larger than _____ of my predecessors.

   (a) there

   (b) that

   (c) those

   (d) it

• **다음에서 잘못된 부분을 찾으시오.**

PART 3

3 (a) A: This digital camera is really worth what I paid for.

   (b) B: How do you work this?

   (c) A: Just turn on and press the blue button to take pictures.

   (d) B: That's much simpler than the last it.

PART 4

4 (a) Approximately 4,000 cups of coffee are consumed any second of the day around the world. (b) Coffee is the second most valuable product in the global economy. (c) Half of all Americans start their day with a cup of coffee. (d) 57% of all coffee is consumed at breakfast.

UNIT 7 전치사 I

명사와 명사사이 또는 명사상당어구(명사, 대명사, 동명사 등) 앞에 위치해 이들을 시간, 방향, 목적 등의 다양한 의미 또는 구조로 연결하는 것이 전치사다. 또한 문맥에 따라 같은 전치사도 그 의미가 달라질 수 있다.

기초문법 확인

1 의미와 역할

복합명사를 제외하고는 명사와 명사를 함께 붙여 쓸 수 없다. 이때 일종의 연결사 역할을 할 매개체가 필요한데, 시간, 방향, 장소, 이유, 원인 등의 여러 의미를 갖고 이들 명사(상당어구)들을 연결하는 것이 전치사다.

ex
● 명사와 명사의 연결

1 *Uneven heating* **of** *the Earth's surface* causes the wind to blow.

→ 명사 uneven heating과 the Earth's surface는 둘 다 명사로 함께 연이어 쓸 수 없다. 명사와 명사가 충돌되기 때문이다. 특히 이 같이 단순히 명사와 명사의 중복을 피하기 위해 쓰는 전치사가 of다.

● 특정 동사와 함께

2 Give me another week to *look* **at** it.

→ 자동사 look이 전치사 at과 함께 '~을 보다'의 의미로 쓰였다.

3 Alex *informed* me **of** this problem.

→ 동사 inform은 '알리다'라는 뜻의 타동사다. 「inform + 목적어 + that/of~」의 형태로 쓰이는데 that을 취하는 경우 that 뒤는 절이 온다. 하지만 명사상당어구(명사, 대명사, 동명사 등)를 취하는 경우에는 전치사 of를 써야 한다.

● 시간 · 장소 · 방향 등의 수식어구

4 I bought this book **in 2007**.
　　　　　　　　　　　└, 시간

5 My sister works **at Bank of America**.
　　　　　　　　　　　└, 장소

2 종류

① **시간의 전치사**(at / on / in / for / during / over / through)

at과 on은 특정 시점, in은 보다 큰 시간 또는 '이후(after)'의 개념, for는 '기간'의 개념에 각각 사용된다. 이 외에도 during은 (특정화된) '기간'의 개념, over는 전체 시간을 통틀어 '~에 걸쳐' 진행되는 시간의 개념, 끊임없이 진행되는 시간 표현에는 through를 쓴다.

ex
● at / in / for / during / through

6 I always put on weight **at** *Christmas*.
　　　　　　　　　　　　└, 크리스마스라는 특정 시점

7   He will be back **in** *an hour*.
    └, 미래 상황의 시간 앞에서 '~후에'로 해석

8   I'll be gone **for** *three days*.
    └, 3일이라는 기간 동안

9   An accident occurred **during** *the night*.
    └, (특정화된) 밤 동안

10 He left the TV on **through** *the night*.
    └, 밤(night)동안 내내(밤새도록)

② **장소의 전치사(at / on / in)**

at은 점의 개념, on은 표면에 접하는 개념, in은 공간적인 개념 등으로 관련 명사와 함께 장소를 나타낸다.

ex ● at / on / in

11 A policeman is standing **at** *the gate*.
    └, 점적인 공간

12 Put them back **on** *the table*.
    └, (테이블 위에) 접하는 개념

13 There were two uniformed police officers **in** *the room*.
    └, 방 안이라는 공간적 개념

③ **기타 전치사의 용법**

기타 전치사의 용법으로 '진행, ~에 빠진'을 나타내는 in, '~상태로 있는'을 의미하는 at, '~를 받고 있는'을 뜻하는 under 등이 있다. 기타 수단을 나타내는 대표적인 전치사로 by(through)가 있으며 이 경우 by와 명사 사이의 관사는 생략한다.

종류	의미	용례
in	진행 중인 / ~에 빠진	in motion, in use, in love, in danger
at	~상태에 있는	at war
under	~중인 / ~을 받고 있는	under construction, under attack
by[through]	수단	by bus(=on a bus), (written) by a lawyer

ex ● at / in / under / (수단의) by

14 I never saw her **at** work.
    └, 일하는 (상태에 있는)

15 The device is **in** use.
    └, 사용 중인

16 The building is **under** construction.
    └, 공사 중인

Review

전치사의 종류는 많을 뿐아니라 각각의 전치사가 담는 의미가 워낙 다양하기 때문에 모든 전치사를 다루기에는 책 지면이 모자랄 정도이다. 단, 전치사마다 가지고 있는 특징이 있고 이들이 갖는 이미지가 있으므로 이들을 머릿속에 그려가면서 익혀나가자.

A 다음 밑줄 친 부분을 바르게 고치시오.

> **Ex** The bomb was found <u>under</u> the airport.
> ↳ at[in]

1 Put the money or ticket <u>on</u> the box next to the driver.
↳

2 Traveling <u>on</u> bus is very common in Chile.
↳

3 Go left <u>with</u> the crossroads.
↳

4 The office gets too hot <u>when</u> the summer months.
↳

5 This novel is written <u>on</u> a professor.
↳

B 문장의 구조상 어울리는 것을 선택하시오.

1 She left a piece of paper (next / on) the table.

2 They picked me up (at / for) noon.

3 We have decided to get there (in / by) train.

4 It never rains (on / in) my birthday.

5 There are now more overweight people (at / in) the world than hungry ones.

6 He is (in / through) love with my sister.

7 Boats are towed (between / through) the tunnel.

8 I found him lying (from / on) the floor.

9 I lived there (for / on) a while.

10 There are a lot of people (on / in) the room.

• 다음 빈 칸에 들어갈 적절한 응답을 고르시오.

1 A Can I speak to Mr. Park?

B I'm afraid but he's out to lunch _____ the moment.

(a) on

(b) by

(c) at

(d) in

2 He regrets leaving her _____ home alone.

(a) at

(b) in

(c) on

(d) to

• 다음에서 잘못된 부분을 찾으시오.

3 (a) A: You're late, Jane.

(b) B: Sorry. I was stuck on traffic for a couple of hours.

(c) A: Didn't you take the detour? I heard there's a parade in town.

(d) B: I didn't know there would be a parade.

4 (a) Ninety percent of all coffee is consumed as espresso. (b) In the U.S. the reverse is true. (c) Ninety percent of all espresso is mixed with milk in the form of lattes or cappuccinos. (d) More than 60% of all coffee is purchased to women.

8 전치사(접속사 구별 포함) Ⅱ

before, after, since 등은 그 자체로 전치사도 되고 경우에 따라 접속사도 된다. 접속사는 뒤에 절의 형태를 받고, 전치사는 목적어로 명사를 받는 특징이 있다. despite(in spite of)와 although는 서로 뜻은 같지만 전자는 전치사, 후자는 접속사로 문장에서의 쓰임에 차이가 있다.

기초문법 확인

1 기타 전치사

위아래를 나타내는 대표적인 전치사로 「above, below, over, under」를 들 수 있는데 각각의 의미에는 단순한 위치 이외에도 수량, 지위, 나이 등의 높낮이를 나타내는 뜻을 가지고 있다. between과 among은 모두 「~사이에서」로 해석되는데 between은 둘 사이에서, among은 셋 이상에서 각각 쓴다.

ex
- above / below / over / under

1 They can fly **above** the clouds. →장소(~위의)

2 He is **above** me at work. →「능력 등이」 ~위에 있는, 앞서는

3 The dog is **below** the table. →장소(~아래의)

4 The marginal productivity of labor is **below** the average productivity of labor.
→ (수량, 정도 등이) ~아래에 있는

5 The bridge is **over** the river. →장소(~위의)

6 Now she is **over** 50. →나이(age)가 ~위인

7 Little water has flowed **under** the bridge. →장소(~아래의)

8 This form is for students who are **under** age 18. →나이(age)가 ~아래인

- between / among

9 He will call you sometime **between** 5 and 5:30 P.M. → (시간) 사이에서

10 The long conflict **between** the two states is now coming to an end. →둘 사이에서

11 In Italy volleyball is popular **among** girls. →셋 이상에서

2 전치사와 접속사의 구별

전치사는 목적어로 명사를 받고 접속사는 뒤에 절이 따른다. before, after, since 등의 시간을 나타내는 접속사는 이 자체로 전치사가 되기도 한다.

의미	전치사	접속사
~전에 / ~후에 / ~이래로	before / after / since	before / after / since
~하는 동안	for, during	while
~에도 불구하고	despite, in spite of	although, (even) though, even if
~때문에	because of, due to, owing to	because, as, since

ex ● before

12 He had not waited long **before** *he saw* her coming.
└, 접속사(「주어 + 동사(he saw)~」인 절을 취함)

→「not A before B」는 A하자 B하다로 해석되는 관용 어구다.

13 She stood **before** *the elevator*.
└, 전치사(뒤의 명사 the elevator는 전치사의 목적어)

● since

14 I have known him **since** *he was* 15.
└, 접속사(~이래로 죽)

15 My dog hasn't eaten anything **since** *yesterday*.
└, 전치사(~이래로 죽)

● although vs. despite

16 ~~In spite of~~ *it was* raining, we had a great time.
└, Although

17 ~~Despite of~~ *the rain*, we enjoyed ourselves.
└, Despite[in spite of]

● because[as, since] vs. because of[due to]

18 He couldn't go to school **because** *he was* sick.

19 The manager warned us to go home **because of[due to]** *the bad weather*.

Review

전치사
비슷한 뜻의 전치사라도 각각의 고유한 쓰임을 갖는 경우가 있다. '18세 이하'라는 표현은 under the age of 18(=under age 18)이라고 표현해야 한다. 이를 비슷한 '~아래'라는 뜻의 below 등으로 대체할 수 없다. 비슷한 뜻이 전치사라도 이 같이 구별되는 전치사 간의 차이를 구별해가며 학습해야 한다.

전치사인가 접속사인가
시험에서 단골로 묻는 질문 중 하나다. 전치사는 뒤에 명사를, 접속사는 뒤에 절을 이끈다. 비슷한 뜻이라도 문장의 구조를 보고 전치사를 쓸지 접속사를 쓸지를 선택할 수 있어야 한다.

• 정답 및 해설 p.37

A 다음 밑줄 친 부분을 문맥에 맞게 고치시오.

> **Ex** He has known her <u>during</u> she was a baby.
> └ *since*

1 <u>Although</u> the bad weather forecast, it turned out to be great.
└

2 The rug is between <u>the table</u>.
└

3 I didn't go to work today <u>due to</u> I was sick.
└

4 If you are <u>below</u> the age of 18, it is illegal to possess tobacco.
└

5 The race has been cancelled <u>owing</u> the bad weather.
└

B 문장의 구조상 어울리는 것을 선택하시오.

1 He stood (before / between) the wall.

2 Now rope-jumping is popular (between / among) girls.

3 (In spite of / Even though) I'm young, I know what I want in life.

4 Laura has been a Girl Scout (by / since) she was in kindergarten.

5 They are hungry (due to / because) they are poor.

6 He had to choose (among / between) life and death.

7 (Because / Although) he is old, his creativity is still very strong and fresh.

8 She is (among / between) the first female mayors in France.

9 The bus stop is (under / among) the bridge.

10 It has been 10 years (since / within) I left school.

• 정답 및 해설 p.39

● 다음 빈 칸에 들어갈 적절한 응답을 고르시오.

PART 1

1   A   How long has your daughter been having these symptoms?

     B   _____ she was in junior highschool.

(a) For

(b) During

(c) Near

(d) Since

PART 2

2   We were greeted by staff _____ it was close to 11 P.M.

(a) despite

(b) during

(c) although

(d) due to

● 다음에서 잘못된 부분을 찾으시오.

PART 3

3   (a) A: What's wrong? You don't look well.

     (b) B: It's because the cigarette smoke.

     (c) A: Why don't you get some fresh air outside?

     (d) B: That's a good idea.

PART 4

4   (a) Persistent rain has fallen over Northern Bolivia over December 2007. (b) And it has caused devastating floods and landslides. (c) The floods have caused at least 30 deaths. (d) And they are also being called the worst floods to strike Bolivia in 30 years.

Chapter 5

품사 Ⅱ

UNIT 1   등위, 상관접속사

UNIT 2   명사절과 접속사

UNIT 3   부사절을 이끄는 접속사 Ⅰ

UNIT 4   부사절을 이끄는 접속사 Ⅱ

UNIT 5   관계사(관계대명사) Ⅰ

UNIT 6   관계사(기타 관계사) Ⅱ

UNIT 1 등위, 상관접속사

접속사는 크게 등위접속사와 종속접속사로 나눌 수 있는데 등위접속사는 접속사 앞뒤의 내용을 대등하게 연결하고 종속접속사는 부사절과 명사절을 이끌면서 주절과 연결시키는 역할을 한다. 등위접속사는 문장과 문장뿐만 아니라 단어 또는 구를 연결하기도 한다. 상관접속사란 함께 짝을 이루는 접속사 어구들을 일컫는다. 시험에서는 특히 함께 어울리는 짝을 주로 묻지만 좀 더 어렵게 나오는 경우, 동사의 수를 묻기도 한다.

기초문법 확인

1 등위접속사

'대등접속사'라고 하기도 한다. 접속사 앞뒤의 단어·구·절을 그 내용과 지위에 있어서 대등하게 연결하기 때문이다. 이와 같은 등위접속사에는 and(그리고), but(하지만), or(또는), yet(~이지만 그래도), for(왜냐하면 ~이니까), nor(~도 아닌), so(그래서) 등이 있다.

ex ● but, yet → '그러나'의 의미로 앞뒤 내용을 서로 상반되게 연결

1 Tom is smart, **but** not handsome.

2 She said she would be late, **yet** she arrived on time.

● and → '그리고'라는 의미로 앞뒤 내용을 서로 대등하게 연결

3 He is very rich **and** famous.

● so → '그래서'라는 의미로 앞뒤 내용 연결

4 She loves eating apples **so** I bought some for her.

● or → '또는'이란 의미로 앞뒤 내용을 서로 대등하게 연결

5 Which do you like better, cats **or** dogs?

● for → '왜냐하면 ~이니까'라는 뜻으로 for이하는 앞내용의 부연 설명, 그렇게 판단한 근거 등을 나타냄

6 Many companies went bankrupt, **for** they couldn't pay interest to banks.

● nor → '~도 또한 아닌'의 뜻으로 앞뒤 내용을 연결

7 All knowledge is not science, **nor** is the most important part of it.

2 명령문 + and / or

명령문과 함께 and 또는 or를 써서, 「명령문, and~」는 '~하라, 그러면 ~할 것이다'로, 「명령문, or~」는 '~하라, 그렇지 않으면 ~하다'라는 뜻으로 각각 해석된다.

ex 8 Study hard, **and** you will pass the exam.

(=If you study hard, you will pass the exam.)

⁹ Call now, **or** you will miss out.

(=Unless you call now, you will miss out.)

3 상관접속사

상관접속사란 함께 짝을 이뤄 하나의 접속사처럼 기능하는 어구들을 의미한다. both A and B(A 그리고 B 둘다), either A or B(A 또는 B), neither A nor B(A도 B도 아닌), not only A but also B(A뿐만 아니라 B도), A as well as B(B뿐만 아니라 A도), at once A and B(A하기도 하고 B하기도 한) 등이 있다. 특히 상관접속사 각각의 짝뿐만 아니라 동사의 수에도 신경 써야 한다. 관련 예문들을 통해 익혀두자.

ex ● both A and B

¹⁰ **Both** he **and** I **are** orphans. →동사는 무조건 복수형이 된다.

● not only A but also B = B as well as A = A and B as well

¹¹ **Not only** I **but also** *my colleagues* **are** very busy. →동사의 수는 B에 맞춤

¹² *She* **as well as** her parents **has** heart disease.

● [n]either A or B

¹³ **Either** she **or** / **am** going to Paris on Monday. →동사의 수는 B에 맞춰야 함

¹⁴ **Neither** he **nor** / **know** anything about it.

● at once A and B

¹⁵ The house is **at once** exotic **and** comfortable.

Review

등위접속사
등위접속사는 접속사를 사이에 두고 앞뒤 내용(단어 · 구 · 절)을 그 지위에 있어서 대등하게 연결하는 접속사를 일컫는다. 대표적인 것으로 and, but, yet, so 등이 있다.

상관접속사
함께 짝을 이루는 어구들로 이뤄진 접속사를 일컫는다. 대표적인 것으로 both A and B, not only A but also B, either A or B 등이 있다.

• 정답 및 해설 p.39

A 밑줄 친 부분에 유의해 해석하시오.

> **Ex** She is very rich, <u>but</u> she is not happy.
> → 그녀는 부자이긴 하지만 행복하지는 않다.

1 <u>Both</u> he <u>and</u> I were studying in Japan.
→

2 It rained once, <u>but</u> it's still hot.
→

3 The nightgown is <u>at once</u> comfortable <u>and</u> stylish.
→

4 She spoke <u>not only</u> to me <u>but also</u> to my sister.
→

5 The new design is innovative <u>and</u> original.
→

B 문장의 구조상 어울리는 것을 선택하시오.

1 You must leave now, (for / or) you will miss the bus.

2 He is very rich, (although / and) is not married.

3 Not only I but also my colleagues are very cooperative (but / and) helpful.

4 He is very smart (so / yet) shy.

5 Which one do you like better, basketball (or / nor) football?

6 I will neither eat (or / nor) drink water for three days.

7 Take it now, (and / or) you will miss the opportunity.

8 Gloria as well as her parents (is / are) leaving for New York next month.

9 Both my father and mother (was / are) talented musicians.

10 He not only received a cash bonus (but also / as well) a land grant.

• **다음 빈 칸에 들어갈 적절한 응답을 고르시오.**

PART 1

1   A   Why don't you quit smoking?

   B   I tried. _____ it's really tough to kick a habit.

   (a) For

   (b) So

   (c) Or

   (d) But

PART 2

2   Not only he did break his leg, but he sprained his wrist _____.

   (a) as well

   (b) however

   (c) though

   (d) very

• **다음에서 잘못된 부분을 찾으시오.**

PART 3

3   (a) A: Are you ready to order, sir?

   (b) B: I can't choose. What do you recommend?

   (c) A: Today's special is seafood because I want to recommend Baked chicken breast stuffed with fresh Mozzarella.

   (d) B: OK, I'll try it.

PART 4

4   (a) The way you communicate has a big impact on your ability to get along with people. (b) Good communication skills can help you avoid conflict but solve problems. (c) Open and honest communication is also important for making friends and having healthy relationships. (d) The problem is we just assume that others should know what we think.

UNIT 2 명사절과 접속사

명사절이라 함은 절의 형태로 문장에서 명사의 역할(주어, 목적어, 보어)을 하는 것을 의미한다. 이러한 명사절을 이끄는 종속접속사에는 대표적으로 that, if, whether가 있다. 상관접속사란 함께 짝을 이루는 접속사 어구들을 일컫는다. 시험에서는 특히 함께 어울리는 짝을 주로 묻지만 좀 더 어렵게 나오는 경우, 동사의 수까지 묻기도 한다.

기초문법 확인

1 명사절을 이끄는 접속사(that, if, whether)

명사절은 문장에서 절을 이끌면서 명사가 하는 '주어, 목적어, 보어' 역할을 하는 것을 뜻한다. if가 명사절로 쓰일 때 그 의미에 있어서 whether과 비슷하게 '~인지 아닌지'의 의미로 문장에서 쓰이는데 whether과 그 쓰임에 있어서 다소 차이가 있다. 예문을 통해 감각을 익히도록 하자.

ex
- that

1 My parents will not accept *the fact* **that** I am an atheist.
      └, 동격(the fact = that~)

2 I believe **that** she will be successful.
      └, 목적어(타동사 believe의 목적절)

3 The point is **that** we have to find more efficient ways to do the work.
      └, 보어

- whether (~or not), if

4 I don't know **whether[if]** she likes me.
      └, 동사 know의 목적어

5 **Whether[If는 불가] or not** she will be attending the party is important to me.
      └, 주어(뒤에 연이어 or not이 오는 경우 if는 대용 불가)

6 I don't know **whether[if는 불가]** to laugh or cry.
      └, 목적어(뒤에 to부정사가 오는 경우에는 if는 대용불가)

2 주요 명사절

① **what**

what이 명사절로 쓰이는 경우가 있는데 that과의 차이점은 that이하의 문장이 완전하다면 what이하의 문장은 불완전하다는 것에 있다. 차후에 다룰 관계대명사에서 언급하겠지만 이 장에서 what은 선행사를 포함한 the thing that의 의미 정도로만 알아두자.

ex
7 **What** I want is only you.
  → what이하의 절이 문장의 주어로 쓰이고 있으며 I want에서 동사 want의 목적어를 what이 포함하고 있다.

8 This is **what** I want. → what 이하의 문장이 be동사의 보어로 쓰이고 있다.

② 간접의문문

• 의문사가 있는 간접의문문

특히 의문사(who/what/when/where/why/how)가 문장의 일부로 쓰이는 경우 이를 간접의문문이라 하며 이러한 경우 「의문사+주어+동사」의 어순이 되는 점도 기억하자.

ex 9 Do you remember **when** his wife was ill?

(=Do you remember? + When was his wife ill?)

10 Do you know **what** she want?

(=Do you know? + What does she want?)

11 I don't know **why** the caged bird sings.

(=I don't know. + Why does the caged bird sing?)

• 의문사가 없는 간접의문문

의문사가 없는 의문문이 간접의문문이 되는 경우 의문사 대신 if[whether]를 통해 문장을 연결한다.

ex 12 She asked me **if** I had seen it.

(=She asked me, "Did you see it?")

13 I don't know **whether** it will be printed or not.

(=I don't know. + Will it be printed?)

14 I'm not sure **if[whether]** she likes me.

(=I'm not sure. + Does she like me?)

Review

명사절을 이끄는 접속사

명사절을 이끄는 대표적인 접속사로 that, whether, if가 있다. 모두 문장에서 명사 역할(주어, 목적어, 보어)을 한다고 해서 '명사절을 이끄는 접속사'라고 명명하였다. 각각 문장에서의 쓰임새와 차이점을 기억해두자.

간접의문문

문장에 의문문이 삽입되어 문장을 이루는 경우를 의미하는데 의문사가 있는 의문문과 의문사가 없는 의문문에 따라 문장에서의 쓰임이 다소 차이가 있다. 의문사가 있는 의문문이 간접의문문이 되는 경우 「의문사 + 주어 + 동사」라는 어순이 됨을 기억하자. 또한 의문사가 없는 be동사나 do동사 등의 의문문과의 결합은 의문사 내신 whether 또는 if를 써서 문장과 결합할 수 있다.

A 잘못된 부분을 어법에 맞게 고치시오.

> **Ex** I asked if did he smoke.
> →I asked if he smoked.

1 I don't know when did the artist carve the stone.

→

2 I'm not sure will if she stay in France.

→

3 I don't know if to laugh or cry.

→

4 Do you know when leaves the train?

→

5 We must accept the fact if Mark is no longer alive.

→

B 문장의 구조상 어울리는 것을 선택하시오.

1 She has to decide (what / whether) she will be attending the party or not.

2 The problem is (if / that) he's not credible.

3 I think (that / what) she will be successful.

4 Do you know (who / when) our flight leaves?

5 We believe (that / if) he will come again.

6 The problem is (what / that) he doesn't have money.

7 I don't know (who / whether) you believe me or not.

8 The fact is (if / that) he doesn't know the local language.

9 I don't know (whether / if) to trust your message or not.

10 (That / What) she will attend the meeting is certain.

• **다음 빈 칸에 들어갈 적절한 응답을 고르시오.**

PART 1

1   A   What seems to be the problem?

   B   The problem is _____ he won't admit that he has a hearing problem.

   (a) that
   (b) therefore
   (c) if
   (d) what

PART 2

2   You have to go to church _____ you like it or not.

   (a) although
   (b) whether
   (c) however
   (d) what

• **다음에서 잘못된 부분을 찾으시오.**

PART 3

3   (a) A: What you think the problem is with this camera?
   (b) B: I think it ran out of battery.
   (c) A: How long will it take to repair it?
   (d) B: It only takes a few minutes.

PART 4

4   (a) Meeting planners must decide whether and how the audience will participate. (b) If audience participation is expected, what will happen if there are so many people to make a speech? (c) In order to give as many people as possible a chance to speak, meeting planners generally limit each speaker's time. (d) They also must consider whether may any special services be needed, such as audio-visual equipment or an interpreter.

UNIT 3 부사절을 이끄는 접속사 I

부사절은 주절 앞뒤에 위치하여 주절을 수식한다. 이러한 부사절을 이끄는 접속사를 종속접속사라 한다. 종속접속사는 '시간, 이유, 조건, 양보' 등의 의미를 가지며 부사절을 이끄는 역할을 한다. 이 단원에서는 시간과 이유의 의미를 갖는 종속접속사에 대해 알아보자.

기초문법 확인

1 시간(after / before / when / while / since / until 등)

시간을 나타내는 대표적인 종속접속사에는 when(~할 때), while(~하는 동안), since(~이래로), until(~때까지) 등이 있다. 각각의 의미와 문장 내의 쓰임과 구별을 묻는 문제가 등장하므로 기본적인 의미를 관련 예문을 통해 파악해두자.

① after, before

가장 기본적인 시간의 전(before)·후(after) 관계를 나타내는 표현이다.

> **ex** 1 **After** we left the mall, we went back to the hotel.
> └, '~이후에'
>
> 2 It took a long time **before** she came.
> └, '~전에'

② when, while, since, until

when은 '시점'을 나타내고, while은 다소 짧은 시간 동안의 '기간'을, since는 '~이래로'라는 뜻으로, until은 '~까지'로 각각 해석되는 시간표시 접속사다.

> **ex** 3 **When** we arrived at the coast, the boat had not still arrived.
> └, '~할 때'
>
> 4 He usually drank at home **while** he was watching TV after work.
> └, '~하는 동안'
>
> 5 **Since** I *was* a child I *have* loved clouds.
> └, '~이래로'
>
> → since라는 단어 자체가 과거의 어느 시점에서 말하는 현재까지 시간의 추이를 나타내기 때문에 since절은 과거의 어느 시점을 나타내는 '과거'를 주절은 과거의 시점과 현재까지를 잇는 '현재완료'로 표현한다.
>
> 6 My brother was an orthopedic surgeon **until** he retired.
> └, '~까지'
>
> *cf.* Chuck was **not** aware of the offer **until** he received it by regular mail.
> (「not A until B」구문은 직역하면 'B하기까지 A못하다'라는 뜻으로 'B한 후에야 A하다'는 긍정의 의미로 바꿔 해석하는 것이 자연스럽다.)

(직역 →) 척은 그가 보통우편으로 그것을 받기 전까지는 그 제안에 대해 알지 못했다.

(의역 →) 척은 보통우편으로 그것을 받은 후에야 그 제안에 대해 알 수 있었다.

③ **기타 시간을 나타내는 접속사**

기타 시간을 나타내는 접속사로는 by the time, everytime, once, as soon as 등이 있다. 특히 이들 접속사는 형태만 봐서는 접속사라는 생각이 들지 않을 수 있기 때문에 다른 접속사 문제에 비해 상대적으로 난이도 있는 문제로 느낄 수 있다. 형태와 함께 예문을 통해 정확한 쓰임을 익혀두자.

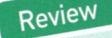 7   **By the time** you come back, we will have fixed your car.
        └, '~할 때'

→ 시점을 나타내는 부사절은 문맥상 미래를 현재시제가 대신 표현한다. 따라서 by the time이 이끄는 시간부사절은 현재(come)로, 주절은 미래(will have~)로 표현했다.

8   **Everytime** I call my girlfriend her phone is always busy.
        └, '~할 때마다'

9   **Once** you start you can't stop.
        └, '~일단 ~하면'

10   Please call **as soon as** you know you are unable to keep the appointment.
        └, '~하자마자'

2   원인과 이유(because / since / now that 등)

문장에서 '~때문에'로 해석되는 이유를 나타내는 종속접속사에는 because, since, now that, as 등이 있다. 또한 since가 시간의 의미(~한 이래로)뿐만 아니라 '이유'의 의미로도 쓰임을 기억해두자.

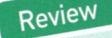 11   I admire him **because** he is very smart.
        └, '~ 때문에'

12   **Since** money is involved, reliability is very important.
        └, '~ 때문에'

13   The company's buying power is getting better **now that** the company has grown.
                                             └, '~이니까'

Review

시간을 나타내는 접속사

시간을 나타내는 접속사에는 시간의 전후관계를 나타내는 대표적인 before와 after 이외에도 when, while, since, until 등 다양한 것들이 있다. 각각의 쓰임은 문맥에서 다소 차이가 있으며 이를 구별하는 문제 또한 등장하므로 문장에서 쓰이는 각각의 구별되는 용법을 신경 써서 알아두어야 한다.

원인과 이유를 나타내는 접속사

원인 또는 이유를 나타내는 접속사에는 because, since, now that 등이 있다. 주절과 부사설과의 의미관계를 통해 이 접속사를 다른 의미의 접속사와 구별하는 문제가 주로 출제되므로 문맥을 정확히 파악하는 연습이 필요하다.

• 정답 및 해설 p.43

A 다음 밑줄 친 부분에 유의해 해석하시오.

> **Ex**
> I like her <u>because</u> she is friendly to others.
> → 나는 그녀가 다른 사람들에게 친절하기 때문에 좋다.

1 <u>When</u> we arrived to our room, it was still a mess.
→

2 I like her <u>because</u> she works hard.
→

3 I <u>have had</u> a big interest in Korea <u>since</u> I <u>was</u> in high school.
→

4 He stayed in New York <u>until</u> he retired.
→

5 I will wait <u>until</u> winter is gone.
→

B 문장의 구조상 어울리는 것을 선택하시오.

1 I've loved bears (because / since) I was a child.

2 Keep watering (until / because) the soil gets wet.

3 He was sickened soon (after / in case of) we left home.

4 I will wait (because of / until) he retires.

5 (If / While) Mike was watching TV, I ate an apple.

6 I like him (due to / because) he is a great actor.

7 I don't like Jessica (as soon as / because) she is a liar.

8 (After / That) we left the park we went to Lindy's to eat.

9 (Since / Because) I was a child, I have loved to write.

10 I held my breath (although / until) he closed the door.

• **다음 빈 칸에 들어갈 적절한 응답을 고르시오.**

PART 1

1　A　Why are you in such a hurry?

　　B　I am late for work _____ my alarm didn't go off this morning.

　　(a) if

　　(b) because

　　(c) why

　　(d) until

PART 2

2　I finally made the interview _____ she was having dinner.

　　(a) while

　　(b) so that

　　(c) for

　　(d) as if

• **다음에서 잘못된 부분을 찾으시오.**

PART 3

3　(a) A: I locked myself out of the house.

　　(b) B: Don't you have any extra keys?

　　(c) A: My wife have it all. But fortunately she is on the way.

　　(d) B: That's a relief. Let's wait as soon as she gets here.

PART 4

4　(a) Sara was already there since I arrived, and we talked for an hour. (b) Rebecca arrived very soon after Sara left. (c) It's a tiny airport but did at least have some stores. (d) Rebecca bought a magazine that came with a free umbrella.

UNIT 4 부사절을 이끄는 접속사 Ⅱ

앞 단원에서 언급했듯, 종속접속사란 문장을 연결하는데 있어서 대등하게 연결하는 것이 아닌 종속적으로 연결하는 접속사를 뜻한다. 따라서 문장의 주가 되는 것은 주절, 상대적으로 종속적인 개념을 갖는 절을 종속절 또는 부사절로 부르는 것이다. 이러한 종속절은 '시간, 이유, 조건, 양보' 등의 의미를 갖고 주절을 수식하게 된다. 이 단원에서는 시간과 이유의 의미를 제외한 나머지 종속접속사에 대해 알아보자.

기초문법 확인

1 조건(if / unless 등)

조건을 나타내는 종속접속사에는 대표적으로 if(~한다면), unless(~하지 않는다면) 등이 있다. 주절과 부사절 사이의 관계를 통해 여러 접속사 중 올바른 것을 찾는 문제가 등장하므로 기본이 되는 의미부터 관련 예문을 통해 파악해두자.

> **ex** 1 What can she do **if** she is overweight?
> ∟ '~한다면'

> 2 Don't yell at each other **unless** the house is on fire.
> ∟ '~하지 않는다면'

2 양보(although / even though / even if / whether ~or not 등)

문장에서 '~에도 불구하고, ~하건, 안하건' 등으로 해석되는 접속사를 칭한다. even though가 although보다는 그 정도에 있어서는 강한 의미를 갖는다. although와 though는 서로 바꿔 쓸 수 있지만 although가 더 공식적으로 쓰인다.

> **ex** 3 **Although** the sun was shining, the water was cold.
> ∟ '비록 ~이지만'

> 4 He endured a serious battle **even though** he was wounded himself.
> ∟ '비록 ~이지만'(뒤는 확실한 사실을 지칭)

> 5 Say something, **even if** it's a lie.
> ∟ '~일지라도'

> 6 You are part of the group **whether** you like it **or not**.
> ∟ '~하건 안하건'

3 결과 / 목적

문장 내에서 '너무 ~해서 ~하다'라는 뜻이 되도록 쓰이는 경우는 '결과'의 의미로, '~하기 위해서'라고 해석되는 경우는 '목적'의 의미로, 각각 쓰인 것이다. lest는 '~하지 않도록'이란 뜻으로 부정적인 의미의 '목적'을 나타내는 접속사다.

ex
- 결과

7 You talked **so** fast **that** I couldn't follow you.
　　　　　　└, '너무 ~해서 ~(that이하)하다'

　→ so 뒤에는 형용사나 부사가 온다.

8 It was **such** a good show **that** she wanted to bring her students to watch it.
　　　　　　└, '너무 ~해서 ~(that이하)하다'

　→ such 뒤에는 명사가 온다.

- 목적

9 Come back **so that** we may look at you.
　　　　　　└, '~하기 위해서'

10 Jack turned the radio down **lest** he should miss the phone ringing.
　　　　　　└, '~하지 않도록'

> ### Review
>
> **조건의 접속사**
> '~한다면'이라는 뜻으로 주절을 수식하는데 있어서 조건의 의미가 되는 부사절이 되도록 하는 if, unless 등이 있다.
>
> **양보**
> '~에도 불구하고'라는 뜻의 양보의 의미로 주절을 수식하는 부사절이 되도록 하는 접속사를 지칭하며 대표적인 것으로 although(though), even if, even though 등이 있다.
>
> **결과, 목적**
> 결과는 '너무 ~해서 ~한, (그래서) ~하다'로, 목적은 '~를 위해, ~하지 않도록'이란 각각의 의미를 가지고 문장 내에서 부사절의 역할을 한다.

A 다음 밑줄 친 부분에 유의해 해석하시오.

> **Ex** If you have trouble with the copy machine, we will come to fix it.
> → 만일 복사기에 문제가 있다면, 저희가 와서 고치겠습니다.

1 <u>Although</u> the sun was burning, the weather was not too hot.

→

2 He whispers to me <u>so that</u> no one else can hear.

→

3 I will buy this dress for you <u>if</u> you wear it.

→

4 We would wrestle like brothers, <u>even though</u> he was bigger than I.

→

5 <u>If</u> you have a complaint, please use our online complaint form.

→

B 문장의 구조상 어울리는 것을 선택하시오.

1 (That / Although) she is smart, she is hard to get along with.

2 (Whether / Even) you like it or not, you're in charge now.

3 Just ask my secretary (so / if) you would like some coffee or anything else.

4 He survived (even though / because) he was wounded.

5 (Unless / If) you don't mind, I'd like to ask for your feedback on the system.

6 Courage is of no value (if / unless) accompanied by justice.

7 It was (so / such) cold that we wore our winter jackets.

8 (Although / if) she is only five, she can speak four languages.

9 James let Tom keep looking at the other direction, (though / lest) he should miss her arrival.

10 I became somewhat deaf, (now that / so that) I had difficulty hearing the speaker clearly.

• 정답 및 해설 p.46

● 다음 빈 칸에 들어갈 적절한 응답을 고르시오.

PART 1

1　A ＿＿＿＿＿＿＿＿ you don't mind, I'd like to ask you a few questions about the project.

　　B　Sure, go right ahead.

(a) If

(b) Although

(c) Unless

(d) Because

PART 2

2　＿＿＿＿＿＿＿＿ you like it or not, our whole world is being reshaped by computer technology.

(a) So

(b) What

(c) Until

(d) Whether

● 다음에서 잘못된 부분을 찾으시오.

PART 3

3　(a) A: Do you think he really loves her?

　　(b) B: Yes, I'm quite sure.

　　(c) A: But I was told she is from a different race.

　　(d) B: Now that it is true, he really cares for her.

PART 4

4　(a) At the top, it was such cold that we could not stay another night. (b) In the early next morning, we went back down to the car. (c) On the way down, we basically ran in places. (d) It was really fun with the snow nearly knee-deep.

UNIT 5 관계사(관계대명사) I

관계대명사는 「대명사 + 접속사」의 개념을 가지고 있다. 즉, 문장에 이미 쓰인 명사를 대신하면서 동시에 문장과 문장을 연결하는 접속사의 구실을 함께 하는 것이다. 같은 단어나 표현을 반복하는 것을 싫어하고 가능한 줄여 쓰고자 하는 영어의 특성에서 나왔다고 볼 수 있다.

기초문법 확인

1 관계대명사의 정의

대명사와 접속사의 역할을 동시에 하는데, 특히 관계대명사 앞의 명사를 선행사라고 한다. 관계대명사에는 여러가지 종류가 있는데 이러한 관계대명사를 선택하는 기준이 되는 것이 바로 선행사다.

ex A postman is a **man**. + The **man** delivers letters and parcels.

→ 두 개의 문장을 결합하려 한다. 공통된 명사는 'man'임을 알 수 있다. 선행사가 사람인 경우 who 또는 that을 쓸 수 있다. 이 두 문장을 관계대명사로 결합하면;

1 A postman is a *man* **who** delivers letters and parcels.

2 관계대명사의 종류

선행사에 따라 관계대명사의 종류가 결정되는데 선행사가 사람인 경우 who[that]를, 사물인 경우 which[that]을 쓰는 것이 원칙이다. 특히 that은 사람과 사물 모두에 쓸 수 있는 관계대명사다.

ex 2 This is *the man* **who[that]** will buy you a cocktail.
└, 선행사가 사람(the man)인 경우

3 May I see *the book* **which[that]** you published last year?
└, 선행사가 사물(the book)인 경우

3 관계대명사의 격

관계대명사의 격은 관계대명사의 역할에 따라 결정되는데 동사 앞의 주어 자리에서 주어 역할을 하면 주격, 목적어 역할을 하면 목적격, 명사 앞인 소유격 자리에 위치하면 각각 소유격이 된다.

	주격	목적격	소유격
선행사가 사람	who[that]	whom[that]	whose
선행사가 사물	which[that]	which[that]	whose[of which]

ex 4 There is a woman **who** is standing in front of my house.
└, 뒤의 동사 is의 주어 자리이므로 주격(who)

5 I know a man **whose** name is Andy Kim.
└, 뒤의 명사 앞에서 명사를 수식하는 자리이므로 소유격(whose)

6 This is a woman **whom** I care for very much.
└, care for에서 전치사 for의 목적어 자리이므로 목적격(whom)

4 관계대명사의 생략

목적격관계대명사는 생략할 수 있으나 전치사가 목적격관계대명사의 바로 앞에 오는 경우에는 생략할 수 없다.

  7 The woman (whom) I love comes from London.
└, (love의 목적어가 되는) 목적격 관계대명사는 생략가능

cf. 8 I saw the girl to **whom** I gave the roses.
└, 전치사 뒤의 목적격관계대명사는 생략 불가

5 관계대명사 that의 제약

관계대명사 that은 관계대명사 who 또는 which 대신 쓰는 것이 일반적이지만 약간의 제약이 따른다. 관계대명사의 계속적용법에 쓸 수 없고 전치사 뒤(to that 등 → ×)에도 쓸 수 없다.

  9 The woman ~~to that~~ he sent roses was very delighted.
└, to whom(전치사 + that → ×)

10 He spoke to me in German, ~~that~~ I could not understand.
└, which(계속적 용법에서 that → ×)

Review

관계대명사의 역할

「대명사 + 접속사」의 역할을 한다. 문장과 문장의 결합에 있어서 공통적으로 쓰인 명사를 대신하면서 접속사의 역할을 동시에 하는 기능이 있다.

관계대명사의 종류와 격

선행사에 따라 크게 사람인 경우에는 who(that)를 쓰고 사물인 경우 which(that)를 쓴다.

A 다음 밑줄 친 부분을 바르게 고치시오.

> **Ex** The girl <u>who</u> you met yesterday is my girlfriend.
> └→ whom

1 I have a dog <u>whom</u> is called Angie.
└→

2 I know a girl <u>who</u> mother is a veterinarian.
└→

3 The gentleman <u>who</u> I thought to be honest betrayed me.
└→

4 The man to <u>who</u> I gave the gift was happy.
└→

5 That's the man <u>which</u> father is a film director.
└→

B 문장의 구조상 어울리는 것을 선택하시오.

1 Violence creates violence (whose / which) creates more violence.

2 I met a lady (whose / whom) name I can't remember.

3 This is the bridge (whom / that) I spoke of.

4 The man (whom / to whom) I was speaking was a manager.

5 I have two sons, (who / that) became priests.

6 When did you see the book (which / whose) John bought?

7 The girl (who / whom) you met in our home is my cousin.

8 That's the man (whose / whom) house was under construction.

9 He wants to be the person (whose / who) can appeal to anyone.

10 He was placed in a coffin, the lid of (that / which) remained unfastened.

• **다음 빈 칸에 들어갈 적절한 응답을 고르시오.**

PART 1

1   A   What does he want?

   B   He wants to meet the person _____ is in charge of the project.

   (a) who
   (b) which
   (c) whose
   (d) to whom

PART 2

2   He has no friend _____ he can rely.

   (a) from that
   (b) on whom
   (c) on that
   (d) from whom

• **다음에서 잘못된 부분을 찾으시오.**

PART 3

3   (a) A: Do you see the man in red there?

   (b) B: You mean, an Asian man in the corner?

   (c) A: Yes, that is the person whom car was stolen yesterday.

   (d) B: Oh, no. That person is my uncle.

PART 4

4   (a) Solo Pasta is an Italian style restaurant, that is offering a range of different cooking styles. (b) This place has a great location and pretty good decor. (c) This is a place in which you can get reasonable Italian food. (d) This is about 5 minutes walk from the Old Town.

이 단원에서는 관계대명사 what, 복합관계사 그리고 관계부사에 대해 다루게 된다. 특히 관계부사는 문장에서 일반적인 관계대명사가 갖는 「접속사 + 대명사」가 아닌 「접속사 + 부사」의 역할을 하기 때문에 관계부사가 이끄는 뒤의 문장은 완전함을 기억해두자.

기초문법 확인

1 관계대명사 what

관계대명사 what은 선행사를 포함하는 특수한 관계대명사로 볼 수 있다. 따라서 문장에서 선행사의 유무가 관계대명사 what을 써야할 자리인지 아니면 그 이외의 관계대명사를 써야할지를 구분하는 척도가 된다.

ex 1   I don't know **what(the thing which)** you are talking about.

    ↳ what 이하가 타동사 know의 목적절로 제시되고 있다. 또한 what이하의 문장은 전치사 about)의 목적어가 비어있는 불완전한 문장이다. 즉, what은 what이 이끄는 문장 내의 선행사인 대명사(the thing)를 포함하는 관계대명사다.

     2   **What** is beautiful is not always good.

    ↳ What is beautiful이 전체 문장의 주어로 쓰이고 있다. 이때 What은 (is) beautiful의 주어가 되면서 뒤의 또 다른 문장인 (is) not always good을 연결하는 접속사의 역할을 동시에 한다.

2 복합관계대명사

관계대명사 뒤에 –ever가 붙는 형태로 '~이든지'와 '~하더라도'로 크게 두 가지 의미로 해석이 되며 what과 마찬가지로 기능상 선행사를 포함한다.

ex ● 역할과 의미

     3   Give the present to **whoever(=anyone who)** shows up first.

                          ↳ 선행사를 포함, 문장에서 목적어 역할, '누구에게나'로 해석

     4   **Whichever(=no matter which)** you choose, you must complete it by November 20. ↳ 선행사를 포함, 문장에서 부사절을 이끔, '~하더라도'로 해석

● 명사와 부사

복합관계대명사는 문장에서 크게 명사 그리고 부사역할을 한다. 명사는 복합관계대명사가 이끄는 절이 문장에서 주어, 목적어, 보어의 역할을 하는 경우고 이 같은 주성분의 역할이 아니라 양보의 의미로 주절을 수식하면 부사역할을 하는 것이다.

     5   **Whichever** you read is totally up to you.

         ↳ '~한 것은'(Whichever you read가 전체문장의 주어인 명사로 쓰인 경우)

     6   **Whichever** you read, you will learn something new.

         ↳ '~하더라도'(Whichever you read가 전체문장의 부사절로 쓰인 경우)

3 관계부사

관계대명사가 「접속사 + 대명사」의 역할을 한다면, 관계부사는 문장에서 「접속사 + 부사」의 역할을 한다. 차이점은 관계대명사가 이끄는 문장은 대명사라는 문장의 필수성분이 생략되었기 때문에 (문장이) 불완전하지만, 관계부사는 부사라는 수식성분이 생략되었기 때문에 관계부사 뒤의 문장은 완전하다는 데에 있다.

ex
- 장소

This is the city. + I grew up **there**.

7 This is the city **where**[=in which] I grew up.
                        └, 접속사 + 부사(there = in the city)

- 때

Today is the day. + The trash truck comes today.

8 Today is the day **when**[=on which] the trash truck comes.
                        └, 접속사 + 부사(today = on the day)

- 이유

9 Do you know the reason **why**[=for which] he did that?
                              └, 접속사 + 부사(의미상 이유 = for the reason)

- 방법

10 This is **how**[=in which] he solved problem.
                └, 접속사 + 부사(의미상 방법 = in this way)

→ the way how 형태는 쓰지 않고 the way와 how 중에서 하나만 써야 한다.

4 복합관계부사

복합관계부사는 「관계부사+ever」의 형태를 갖고, 이름에서 알 수 있듯이, 문장에서 부사의 역할을 하는 부사절을 이끈다. 종류로는 whenever(언제 ~라도), wherever(어디로 ~라도), however(아무리 ~라도)가 있다.

ex
11 **Whenever** she goes out, she takes a book with her.
      └, No matter when

12 **Wherever** I may go, I will return to you.
      └, No matter where

13 **However** long it may be, I will fight for justice.
      └, No matter how

Review

관계대명사 what
관계대명사 what은 「선행사 + 관계대명사(which/that)」의 개념으로 볼 수 있다. 즉, 선행사를 포함한 관계대명사이며 반드시 what 뒤의 문장은 불완전한 문장임을 기억해두자.

A 다음 밑줄 친 부분을 바르게 고치시오.

> Ex He didn't know the reason <u>when</u> she cried.
> ∟ why

1 <u>Who</u> comes, they'll need to bring a photo ID.
  ∟

2 <u>Whenever</u> healthy you may be, you cannot stay up all night every day.
  ∟

3 This manual shows you <u>the reason how</u> this works.
  ∟

4 <u>However</u> you choose, you won't be disappointed.
  ∟

5 This is a place <u>how</u> you can relax.
  ∟

B 문장의 구조상 어울리는 것을 선택하시오.

1 Tell me (what / wherever) she said.

2 Now is the time (what / when) she calls you.

3 This video shows you (how / what) this system works.

4 The Institute is a wonderful place (when / where) people can be informed about Hong Kong.

5 I can't remember (how / what) I did yesterday.

6 You can take (how / whichever) you like.

7 Here is a land (when / where) a dream becomes a reality.

8 Sunset is the time (when / how) the sun disappears completely below the horizon.

9 You can't buy (however / whatever) you want without using your own money.

10 (Whichever / What) you choose, you will be satisfied.

• 정답 및 해설 p.51

• **다음 빈 칸에 들어갈 적절한 응답을 고르시오.**

PART 1

1   A   Do you know the reason _____ she doesn't like me?

   B   Who knows?

   (a) what

   (b) when

   (c) where

   (d) why

PART 2

2   Today is the day _____ I have changed my mind.

   (a) whom

   (b) which

   (c) what

   (d) when

• **다음에서 잘못된 부분을 찾으시오.**

PART 3

3   (a) A: I'm going to take a short trip to Las Vegas.

   (b) B: What a coincidence! I'm going there, too.

   (c) A: Oh, really? When are you leaving?

   (d) B: This Saturday might be the day how the company asks me to go.

PART 4

4   (a) I think this cell phone is worth how I paid for. (b) It is a really good cell phone. (c) I think it is best for students because it's also relatively cheap. (d) I would strongly recommend it to students.

Chapter 6

일치와 어순

UNIT 1   일치

UNIT 2   강조와 도치

UNIT 3   주요 동사의 쓰임과 어순

UNIT 1 일치

주어와 동사와의 관계를 통해 수, 시제, 태가 일치되는지, 명사와 이를 대신 받는 대명사와의 관계를 통해 수, 그리고 성이 일치되고 있는지를 종종 묻는다.

기초문법 확인

1 수와 시제의 일치

① 수 일치

주어가 단수 명사이면 동사는 단수 동사로, 복수면 복수 동사로 주어의 수에 따라 동사의 수도 일치시켜야 한다.

ex 1 **This group ~~consist~~ of** about 350 people.
↳ consists

- neither A nor B, either A or B, not only A but also B
- 동사는 B의 수에 일치시킨다.

- A as well as B
- 동사는 A의 수에 일치시킨다.

- every + 단수 명사
- every가 수식하는 명사는 단수 명사이며, 동사 역시 단수가 되어야 한다.

---

2 **They as well as he are** all liars.
↳ A as well as B에서 동사의 수는 주어 A의 수에 일치

3 **Every boy and girl is** our brother and our sister.
↳ Every는 단수 명사를 수식하며 Every가 수식하는 주어는 단수 취급

② 시제 일치

종속절의 시제는 주절의 시제를 따르는 것이 일반적이다. 하지만 문맥에 따라 한 문장 안에서도 각기 다른 시제는 얼마든지 올 수 있다. 예를 들어, 역사적 사실이나 진리 등의 경우 시제 제약을 받지 않을 수 있고 주절의 시제가 현재인 경우 문맥에 따라 종속절의 시제는 과거, 현재, 미래 등 비교적 자유롭게 올 수 있다. 따라서 시제는 문장의 문맥을 먼저 살펴서 정해야 한다.

ex 4 I **feel** in my soul that you **love** me as well.

5 I **thought** that you **loved[had loved]** me.
→ 주절이 과거인 경우 종속절의 시제는 과거나 과거 완료가 올 수 있다.

6 I **learned** the earth **moves** around the sun.
→ 주절은 과거지만 종속절의 동사는 과학적으로 입증된 사실이므로 현재형이 와야 한다.

2 성과 태의 일치

① 성 일치

남성과 여성, 단수와 복수에 따라 그 명사를 대신 받는 대명사 역시 일치시켜야 한다.

 7 When I saw *Jane,* **he** was speaking at our university.
> ↳ she(Jane은 여자이므로 문맥상 이를 받는 대명사는 she)

8 They sell *office furniture* and **they are** carefully handcrafted of solid wood.
> ↳ it is(office furniture를 받기 때문에 주어는 it, 동사는 is가 되어야 함)

② 태의 일치

주어가 동작의 주체가 될 때는 능동태, 주어가 동작의 대상이 될 때는 수동태가 된다.

 9 A cup of tea **made** for her by me.
> ↳ was made

10 The street **was covering with** snow.
> ↳ was covered with

Review

수와 시제의 일치
주어가 단수인지 또는 복수인지에 따라 동사의 수는 달라지며, 시제에 있어서 종속절의 시제는 일반적으로 주절을 따르나 문맥에 따라 다양한 시제가 올 수 있다.

성과 태의 일치
명사와 이를 받는 대명사의 관계에서 대명사는 명사의 성과 수를 따라야 한다. 태에 있어서 주어가 동사의 주체가 되면 능동으로, 대상이 되면 수동으로 일치시켜야 한다.

A 다음 밑줄 친 부분을 어법에 맞게 고치시오.

> **Ex** My mother always said that time <u>was</u> money.
> └ is

1 Slow and steady <u>win</u> the race.
        └

2 The child <u>has abducted</u> by kidnappers.
                └

3 When I <u>will see</u> him tomorrow, I will tell him that I'm not ready.
              └

4 Each of the system operators <u>are</u> responsible for it.
                                    └

5 I thought that she <u>will be</u> a musician.
                          └

B 문장의 구조상 어울리는 것을 선택하시오.

1 I think Canadians (are / is) healthier than Americans.

2 Everybody here (have / has) a dream.

3 She (was given / gave) a ticket for parking.

4 If I see David, I will tell (it / him) to call you.

5 She (is / has been) ill since last Thursday.

6 Neither you nor I (am / are) going out today.

7 Tomorrow's weather (has been / will be) cold and cloudy.

8 English (speaks / is spoken) in the Philippines.

9 The table (was covered / has covered) with a white tablecloth.

10 I (know / knew) him five years ago.

● **다음 빈 칸에 들어갈 적절한 응답을 고르시오.**

PART 1

1 A   Who is the director of the film?

B   I _____ that it was made by an Indian movie company.

(a) was told

(b) has been told

(c) told

(d) have told

PART 2

2   They as well as I _____ of the plans.

(a) am never informing

(b) am never informed

(c) are never informing

(d) are never informed

● **다음에서 잘못된 부분을 찾으시오.**

PART 3

3   (a) A: Red, were you available right now?

(b) B: Yes, what's up?

(c) A: Let's go out and grab some food.

(d) B: That's a great idea.

PART 4

4   (a) A patent is a permit of property rights to the inventor by the Patent and Trademark Office. (b) A patent lasts for 20 years from the year the patent was filled. (c) During the time period of 20 years a patent allow the inventor to have the exclusive right to make and sell the invention. (d) This time frame may also allow the beneficiary to earn a lot of money by selling the license of the patented product to other companies.

UNIT 2 강조와 도치

영어에서의 강조는 그 어감을 증폭하거나 특히 강조하고 싶은 어구 등을 내세우고 싶을 때 표현하는 방법으로 특수한 구문이나 어구들을 삽입해 강조하곤 한다. 도치란 본래의 「주어 + 동사」의 어순이 특수 구문 또는 부정어가 앞으로 이동하면서 「동사 + 주어」의 형태로 어순이 바뀌는 것을 뜻한다.

기초문법 확인

1 다양한 강조 구문

① 「It ~ that」 구문

「It ~ that」 강조 구문은 강조하고 싶은 대상을 It과 that 사이에 위치시켜 'that 이하 하는 것은 바로 ~다'로 해석하는 강조표현법이다.

ex

1. **It was** yesterday **that[when]** I saw Greg at the station. → 시간 강조

2. **It was** Mary **that[whom]** I saw in the park. → 인물 강조

3. **It is** in Chicago **that[where]** Jane lives. → 장소 강조

4. **What was it that** she said? → 의문사 강조
   └ 의문사(what, who, why 등) 강조는 의문사가 문두로 이동

② 비교급, 최상급 강조

비교급 강조	(by) far, much, even, yet, still 등
최상급 강조	(by) far, much, the very 등

ex

5. The film is **much** better than the novel in every way.

6. This is **the very** best movie ever made.

③ 부정문 강조

at all, in the least, in the slightest, in the smallest, whatever 등이 부정문에서 쓰이면 부정의 의미를 좀 더 강조하게 된다.

ex

7. I *don't* know her **at all**.

8. I am *not* **in the least** afraid of her.

④ **의문문 강조**

in the world, the hell, on earth, ever 등이 의문사와 함께 의문문을 강조한다.

> **ex**   9   *What* **the hell** *is she talking about, anyway?*
>
>   10   *Who* **in the world** *are you?*

⑤ **일반 동사를 강조하는 do(정말로, 진짜로 ~한)**

> **ex**   11   I **do** *love* her.
>
>   12   I **did** *love* this country.

2   도치

문장 내에서 「주어 + 동사」의 형태가 「동사 + 주어」로 그 어순이 바뀌는 것을 가리킨다.

① **There is~ 구문(주어가 동사 뒤에 위치)**

> **ex**   13   **There** *are a lot of rules* to follow. → 복수 주어(rules)이므로 동사는 are(복수)
>
>   14   **There** *was no one* there. → 단수 주어(no one)이므로 동사는 was(단수)

② **문두에 오는 부정을 뜻하는 부사(구)**

> scarcely, rarely, hardly, seldom, barely, never, neither, nor, no sooner, only, few, little, no longer, not 등

> **ex**   15   **Not** a word *did she say*.
>
>   16   **Hardly(scarcely)** *had he seen* the enemy **when(before)** he ran away.
> ↳ 「Hardly(scarcely) A~ when(before) B~」는 'A하자마자 B하다'로 해석
>
>   17   **Not until** we wake *do we know* **that** we were dreaming.
> ↳ not until이 문두로 나가면 주어와 동사는 도치

Review

영어에서 때때로 규칙을 벗어나 제각각 다른 모습을 취하고 있는 구문들이 있다. 하지만 이러한 구문들 역시 일정한 규칙에 의해 쓰이는 것들이 대부분이다. 또한 이러한 특수구문은, 특히 표현을 담은 문장 단위로 익혀 두는 습관이 필요하다.

A 다음 밑줄 친 부분에 유의해 해석하시오.

> **Ex** I don't know him <u>at all</u>.
> → 나는 그를 전혀 알지 못한다.

1 Cycling is <u>far</u> more difficult than we expected.
→

2 I <u>do</u> love to go camping.
→

3 The song is <u>much better</u> than I expected.
→

4 <u>It was</u> two days ago <u>that</u> I met her in the park.
→

5 What <u>on earth</u> do they have in common?
→

B 문맥상 더 어울리는 것을 선택하시오.

1 There (was / were) a few exceptions.

2 (That / It) is not until we think about the problem that we realize that it is more complicated.

3 This is (the very / the most) best car I have ever owned.

4 It was Jane (if / that) I met in the park.

5 I am not (in the least / in the world) afraid of getting my feet wet.

6 What (on earth / in the least) do they want to ask me?

7 I (do / very) hope you will come to visit us.

8 Not a word (she did / did she) say of Jason's return.

9 Who (the hell / the ever) is Juliet?

10 It's not until we lose what we have (if / that) we really appreciate it.

● **다음 빈 칸에 들어갈 적절한 응답을 고르시오.**

PART 1

1 A What _____ is going on here?

B I have no idea.

(a) in the least

(b) the very

(c) on earth

(d) much

PART 2

2 Not until we lose everything _____ the true value of what we have.

(a) do we realize

(b) we realize

(c) does we realize

(d) realize we

● **다음에서 잘못된 부분을 찾으시오.**

PART 3

3 (a) A: What a hell are you looking for?

(b) B: Concert tickets for tonight.

(c) A: I saw Alice having those.

(d) B: Really? When?

PART 4

4 (a) I'm not in the least worried about the seminar work. (b) What worries me is the thesis. (c) I just have five more days to turn in the sample chapter. (d) I have even begun yet.

UNIT 3 주요 동사의 쓰임과 어순

TEPS에서는 특정 문장 안의 올바른 단어의 배열 순서를 종종 묻는다. 크게는 평서문과 의문문으로 나눌 수 있는데, 평서문에서는 특히 동사를 기준으로 동사가 갖는 문장 내 쓰임을 알아 두고, 의문문에서는 간접의문문이 갖는 어순에 주의해야 한다. 이외에도 기타 문법의 모든 영역에서 어순 문제는 다양하게 출제될 수 있다.

기초문법 확인

1 평서문

2형식의 문장구조와 함께 특히 3, 4형식 동사가 갖는 문장 내 쓰임에 대해 알아 두자. 5형식은 동사에 따라 목적보어로 to부정사를 취하기도 하고 분사나 동사원형을 취하는 등 각각 다른 모습과 어순을 취하므로 주요 동사별로 각각 문장 내의 용례를 익혀두자.

① V(불완전동사) + 보어

remain	keep	look	feel	prove 등

ex 1 He **remained** silent during the interviews.

2 You **look** pale, are you OK?

② V + O + to부정사 구조

allow	invite	advise	require	expect	urge	tell	want	warn 등

ex 3 We won't **allow** her to leave the country.

4 He **urged** us to write poetry.

5 I **warned** him not to gamble.

③ V + O + of(that 절)

notify	remind	inform 등

ex 6 She **reminds** me of my sister.

7 I **informed** him of our appointment with Dr. Kim.

④ V + O + 분사

keep	find	have 등

ex 8 I **found** it interesting, too.

9 We're sorry to **keep** you ~~waited~~. (→ waiting)

10 I **had** the car ~~repairing~~. (→ repaired)

2 의문문

의문사로 시작하는 의문문은 「의문사 + 동사 + 주어」의 어순으로 문장이 연결되고 간접의문문은 문장 안에서 「의문사 + 주어 + 동사」의 어순으로 연결된다.

① 직접의문문

ex   어순: 「의문사 + 동사 + 주어」

11 **Who are you?**

12 **What is plagiarism?**

13 **How long are you** going to rent this?

② 간접의문문

ex   어순: 「의문사 + 주어 + 동사」

14 I don't know **where she is**.

15 **Why** does he think **I'm** smart?

     ↳ think, believe, guess, suppose 등의 동사가 사용된 의문문에서는 의문사가 문두로 나간다.

16 Do you know **what you are** eating?

3 기타 구문

유도부사 there 구문은 주어가 동사 뒤에 위치하고, 특히 부정부사가 문두에 오는 경우 주어와 동사가 도치되는 등 특정 어순을 취하는 기본적인 구문은 주의해서 익혀두자.

① neither, nor, so + 동사 + 주어

ex 17 He lives in England. **So** does Robin.

     18 She wasn't able to drink. **Neither** was I.

② 기타 어순에 주의해야 할 구문(among, 유도부사 there, 부정부사 등)

19 **There** has been a big increase in unemployment.

20 **Among** them was a writer.

21 **Seldom** had I seen him smoke before.

22 **Little** does he realize that his life is about to change.

Review

품사 문제에 있어서 동사가 차지하는 비중은 자못 크다. 문장의 형식은 동사가 결정하기 때문에 주요 동사가 갖는 문장 내의 쓰임에 익숙해질 필요가 있다. TEPS에서 빠지지 않고 나오는 문제 중 하나가 어순문제다. 이 경우 문법적 사항뿐만 아니라 적절한 어순까지 체크해야 하기 때문에 난이도가 다소 높은 문제라고 볼 수 있다. 기본적인 관용표현은 입에서 바로 나올 수 있도록 평소 표현 덩어리, 또는 문장 단위로 외워나가는 학습방법이 요구된다.

A 다음 밑줄 친 부분을 바르게 고치시오.

> **Ex** You remind me <u>to</u> my father-in-law.
> ↳ **of**

1 <u>Who he is</u>?
ↆ

2 My father warned me not <u>for talking</u> about it any more.
ↆ

3 I informed her <u>for</u> our situation.
ↆ

4 I had the car <u>towing</u>.
ↆ

5 Do you know what <u>are you</u> drinking?
ↆ

B 문맥상 더 어울리는 것을 선택하시오.

1 I informed him (that / of) I would help him.

2 (They among / Among them) was a young man who spoke a little English.

3 (There has been / Has there been) a big increase in the number of hurricanes since 2006.

4 I had my computer (fixed / fixing).

5 Do you know (who is he / who he is)?

6 You remind me (of / for) my best friend.

7 (Little does he / Little he does) realize how dangerous this will be.

8 How many copies do you think (will be I able / I will be able) to sell?

9 (Had seldom / Seldom had) I seen my mother angry.

10 I won't allow him (of staying / to stay) with us.

● 다음 빈 칸에 들어갈 적절한 응답을 고르시오.

PART 1

1 A Do you know _____?

   B I left them in your bedroom.

   (a) my glasses are where

   (b) my glasses where are

   (c) are where my glasses

   (d) where my glasses are

PART 2

2 I _____ him of the accident.

   (a) notified

   (b) compared

   (c) provided

   (d) kept

● 다음에서 잘못된 부분을 찾으시오.

PART 3

3 (a) A: When I can pick up my suit?

   (b) B: You can pick it up the day after tomorrow.

   (c) A: Oh, no. I need it desperately tomorrow.

   (d) B: If you insist, drop by tomorrow.

PART 4

4 (a) Coal is a black or brownish-black shiny rock and most of it is buried deep underground. (b) There two types of mining methods are: Surface Mining and Underground Mining. (c) Surface mining is done when the coal is less than 200 feet below the ground. (d) And Underground mining is done when the coal is more than 200 feet below the surface.

TEPS

모의고사
GRAMMAR

1. A: What are you going to have,
   John?
   B: I'll have _____.
   (a) a same
   (b) the same
   (c) same, either
   (d) same, too

2. A: I can give you a ride home.
   B: No, it's really not _____.
   (a) necessary
   (b) necessity
   (c) being necessary
   (d) necessarily

3. A: You did a good job on that
   research.
   B: It's good _____ so.
   (a) for your saying
   (b) of your saying
   (c) for you to say
   (d) of you to say

4. A: I _____ be running now.
   B: Why don't you stay longer for a
   cup of coffee?
   (a) must
   (b) wouldn't
   (c) can
   (d) won't

5. A: Clark, What have you been doing
   _____ I last saw you?
   B: Just so-so.
   (a) so
   (b) until
   (c) since
   (d) for

6. A: Mark! Fancy meeting you here.
   B: Hi, Nicole. What _____ here?
   (a) brings you
   (b) did you bring
   (c) you brought
   (d) have you brought

7. A: I'd like _____ you over for
   lunch this weekend.
   B: What's the occasion?
   (a) to having
   (b) have been
   (c) having
   (d) to have

8. A: I'll buy _____.
   B: I don't want to put you to the
   bother.
   (a) you of a sandwich
   (b) to you a sandwich
   (c) you a sandwich
   (d) for a sandwich

9. A: It's been two years since Jill
   _____ transferred from
   New York to Boston.
   B: Yes, I really miss her.
   (a) would be
   (b) has been
   (c) was
   (d) is

10. A: You look _____ tonight.
    B: Thank you for your compliment.
    (a) stun
    (b) stuns
    (c) stunned
    (d) stunning

11. A: It was _____ meeting you, Jim.

B: The pleasure was mine.

    (a) a pleasure

    (b) please

    (c) pleasured

    (d) pleased to

12. A: Can I _____ from the party? I have a cold.

B: Of course, take care of yourself.

    (a) excuse to you

    (b) excuse to myself

    (c) excuse you

    (d) be excused

13. A: Jane said to tell you hello.

B: Thank you. Give my _____ her, too.

    (a) regards of

    (b) regarding to

    (c) regards to

    (d) regarding for

14. A: If you are free this afternoon, give me a call.

B: We'll see _____ it goes.

    (a) where

    (b) when

    (c) what

    (d) how

15. A: Sorry to keep _____. I'll be right back in a minute.

B: That's all right. Take your time.

    (a) your wait

    (b) you waited

    (c) you waiting

    (d) your waiting

16. A: How would _____ your hair done?

B: Short cut, please.

    (a) you liking

    (b) you like to

    (c) you like

    (d) you liked

17. A: Michael, can you answer the phone?

B: I can't. _____ up right now.

    (a) I've tied

    (b) I'm tied

    (c) I've been tied

    (d) I'm tying

18. A: I'll help if you like.

B: I really appreciate your _____.

    (a) helping me out

    (b) help me

    (c) helps out

    (d) help me out

19. A: This is on me. I want to buy you lunch this time.

B: All right _____ you insist.

    (a) by

    (b) when

    (c) if

    (d) so

20. A: Why are you _____?

B: I have to slim down.

    (a) on your diet

    (b) on any diet

    (c) on the diet

    (d) on a diet

Choose the best answer for the blank.

21. Korea's films are said _____ interest worldwide.

    (a) to be gained
    (b) gaining
    (c) to be gaining
    (d) gained

22. It was not until the early 21th century _____ the importance of his ideas was realized.

    (a) if
    (b) that
    (c) what
    (d) whether

23. It took almost three days _____.

    (a) for the pain to go away
    (b) the pain for going away
    (c) for going away the pain
    (d) the pain going away

24. _____ you may have questions or concerns, visit our website for all the information you need about our cars.

    (a) Since
    (b) However
    (c) What
    (d) Whenever

25. This book is both _____ instructive.

    (a) an interest or
    (b) interesting and
    (c) interested and
    (d) interest or

26. Joshua Bell is one of the world's _____.

    (a) greater violinist
    (b) greatest violinist
    (c) greatest violinists
    (d) greater violinists

27. Whether the weather is good or bad, neither Jim nor _____ going to the gathering.

    (a) I am
    (b) I is
    (c) I are
    (d) I were

28. Vote for whoever you think is the best person for the job, _____ because someone else might win.

    (a) as
    (b) whether
    (c) not
    (d) then

29. The number of Manchester United fans who bought tickets for the game _____ greater than that of Manchester City fans.

    (a) are four times
    (b) is four time
    (c) are four time
    (d) is four times

30. _____ you are under 18 years of age, you may use this Web site only with the participation of an adult.

    (a) If
    (b) Although
    (c) That
    (d) However

31. It's _____ from our home.

    (a) about blocks two

    (b) blocks about two

    (c) two about blocks

    (d) about two blocks

32. The examination will _____ three sections.

    (a) be consisted of

    (b) consist

    (c) consist of

    (d) consist for

33. Metro bus service is operating _____ today.

    (a) as planned

    (b) as plans

    (c) as planning

    (d) as plan

34. You'd better use cloth diapers _____ you have a baby.

    (a) so

    (b) provided that

    (c) therefore

    (d) however

35. Not only _____ massive damage to certain farm crops, but they are also destroying many birds local to the area.

    (a) the crows does

    (b) the crows do

    (c) does the crows do

    (d) do the crows do

36. She can talk _____ I can.

    (a) as fast twice as

    (b) as fast as twice

    (c) as twice fast as

    (d) twice as fast as

37. He is as much a dog healer_____ a dog trainer.

    (a) so

    (b) as

    (c) if

    (d) while

38. The nearest market is _____ away.

    (a) ten minute of walk

    (b) walk about ten minutes

    (c) ten minutes walking

    (d) a ten minute walk

39. Never _____ stressful at work.

    (a) he has been

    (b) has been he

    (c) has he been

    (d) been he has

40. The man was buried in a rectangular coffin, the lid _____ was white.

    (a) which

    (b) of that

    (c) by which

    (d) of which

Identify the option that contains an awkward expression or an error in grammar.

41. (a) A: What's the matter, Andy?
    (b) B: I can't find my glasses.
    (c) A: Did you check your coat pocket?
    (d) B: Of course I did. I checked anywhere.

42. (a) A: Jay, where are you from?
    (b) B: I'm from Canada.
    (c) A: Are you here on vacation?
    (d) B: No, actually I'm here to business.

43. (a) A: Have you made a New Year's resolution?
    (b) B: Yes, I've decided quit smoking.
    (c) A: Good for you.
    (d) B: Yeah, wish me luck.

44. (a) A: I'm looking for a tie.
    (b) B: Particular anything in mind?
    (c) A: I want to buy a solid red one.
    (d) B: How about this one?

45. (a) A: Is my computer ready to go?
    (b) B: No, it's still being repaired.
    (c) A: How long do you think it will take?
    (d) B: It'll be done in hour.

Identify the option that contains an awkward expression or an error in grammar.

46. (a) The Team Giant is looking for new members. (b) Have a look at our JOB page before expressing interest. (c) Although you're interested, send me an email at Giant dot com. (d) Please tell us a little about yourself; name, age, gender, your background, etc.

47. (a) Ebola virus has been first recognized in 1967. (b) Outbreaks occurred in laboratories in Frankfurt, Germany, sickening a total of 37 people. (c) Those who became ill included lab workers, medical personnel and family members who'd cared for them. (d) The first people infected had been exposed to African green monkeys imported from Uganda.

48. (a) I saw that each piece of leaf carried by a reddish ant many times smaller as the leaf. (b) The ants had cut the leaves with their scissorlike jaws and were carrying them back to their nests. (c) Leaf cutters don't eat the leaves. (d) Rather, they use the leaves to raise their most important food, which is a particular kind of fungus.

49. (a) For more than two centuries during Spanish time, there was no formal system of education in the Philippines. (b) The only form of education available to most Filipinos were the Sunday school catechism. (c) The subjects taken in school were grouped under only arts and grammar. (d) And boys and girls went to separate schools.

50. (a) In today's growing technology industry producing a high quality product is very important. (b) Although all industries and their products are different from each other, they tend to produce a better product to compete with other industries. (c) Each year companies spent millions dollars to research and create a product. (d) Companies tend to protect the time and money they spend on creating a product through patent.

Section B

어휘

Chapter 1 어울려 쓰이는 Collocation

Chapter 2 필수어휘와 혼동어휘

Chapter 3 구동사와 숙어

Chapter 4 고급어휘

Chapter 5 일상 구어체 표현

어휘 모의고사

Chapter 1

어울려 쓰이는 Collocation

UNIT 1   동사+명사 I

UNIT 2   동사+명사 II

UNIT 3   동사+명사 III

UNIT 4   동사+명사 IV

UNIT 5   명사+동사

UNIT 6   형용사+명사 I

UNIT 7   형용사+명사 II

UNIT 8   동사+부사 I

UNIT 9   동사+부사 II

UNIT 10   부사+형용사

동사＋명사 I

학습포인트

일정한 뜻을 나타내는, 자연스러운 단어의 조합을 collocation이라고 한다. 우리말에서 '실수를 저지르다'라고 하지, '실수를 만들다'라고 하지 않는 것처럼, 영어에서는 make a mistake라고 하지, do a mistake라고는 하지 않는다. 이와 같은 collocation에는 원어민의 사고방식이 배어 있기 때문에, 내면화된 영어 지식을 측정하는 TEPS에서 그 출제 비중이 매우 높다. 각각의 표현을 통해 원어민의 사고를 들여다보자.

중요 Collocation 정리

1 do one's homework 숙제를 하다

ex Interestingly enough, Michelle enjoys doing her homework.

2 do one's best 최선을 다하다 (= try one's best)

ex Never complain, just do your best!

3 do harm 해를 끼치다 (= cause harm)

ex A bad policy can do great harm to the country.

4 make a mistake 실수를 저지르다 (* do a mistake라고 할 수 없음)

ex Our homeroom teacher told us to try not to make a mistake.

5 make an effort 노력하다 (= put forth an effort)

ex Tara is making a great effort to improve her score on the TEPS test.

6 make a reservation 예약하다 (= reserve, book)

ex We have made a reservation for two nights in Toronto.

7 make a decision 결심하다 (= reach a decision)

ex Willow made a decision to marry the ugly businessman.

8 **make a suggestion** 제안하다 (= put forward a suggestion)

ex Students made a suggestion that we should make our school beautiful.

9 **make a choice** 선택하다 (= exercise a choice)

ex Jessica made a difficult choice to leave her town.

10 **take a shower** 샤워하다 (* have a shower는 영국식 표현)

ex Chris takes a shower every morning.

11 **take a rest** 휴식을 취하다 (= have a rest)

ex After working for twelve hours, we finally took a rest.

12 **take an exam** 시험을 치르다 (↔fail an exam 시험에 떨어지다)

ex Every year, millions of students take college entrance exams.

13 **have breakfast** 아침 식사를 하다 (= eat breakfast)

ex Having breakfast is good for your health.

14 **have a party** 파티를 열다 (= throw a party)

ex We're having a birthday party for Susie next week.

15 **have difficulty** 어려움을 겪다 [* difficulty 다음에 (in) -ing가 와야 함]

ex In fact, we had great difficulty finding her place.

• 정답 및 해설 p.63

A 적절한 내용으로 연결하세요.

> **Ex**
> (a) it makes the situation worse
> (b) invite as many people as possible
> (c) you will stay healthy
> (d) you can do anything
> (e) try to fix it

1 If you really do your best, _____.

2 If something does harm to a situation, _____.

3 If you make a mistake, _____.

4 If you have a party, _____.

5 If you have breakfast regularly, _____.

B 다음에서 알맞은 표현을 고르세요.

1 Turn down the TV. I'm (making, doing) my homework right now.

2 I'm (taking, making) several exams tomorrow. I don't know what to do first.

3 I'd like to (take, make) a reservation for two people, please.

4 Oz (made, did) a good suggestion at the meeting.

5 Sometimes, you need to (do, make) a difficult choice.

Directions: Choose the one word that best fits the sentence.

1 A: You look tired.

B: Yeah. I think we need to
_____ a rest.

(a) make

(b) do

(c) go

(d) take

2 A: I'm worried about tomorrow's
test.

B: Take it easy. Just _____ your
best.

(a) come

(b) put

(c) do

(d) run

3 A: We're _____ a party
tomorrow. Can you come?

B: I'm sorry I can't. I have other
plans.

(a) making

(b) having

(c) getting

(d) hitting

4 A: I stayed up late last night.

B: Again? Such a habit can
_____ great harm to you.

(a) set

(b) look

(c) keep

(d) do

5 Every _____ has been made to
look for its owner.

(a) affect

(b) comfort

(c) effect

(d) effort

6 Jonathan _____ a terrible
mistake during his presentation.

(a) made

(b) went

(c) did

(d) got

7 Buffy _____ a difficult decision
to move to Canada.

(a) fell

(b) did

(c) turned

(d) made

8 Many students are _____ great
difficulty understanding English
grammar.

(a) having

(b) running

(c) walking

(d) holding

UNIT 2 동사＋명사Ⅱ

학습포인트

'동사＋명사Ⅰ'에서 다룬 『동사＋명사』형태의 collocation은 TEPS에서 출제 비중이 가장 높은 유형이다. 왜냐하면 이 형태가 일정한 상태나 동작을 거의 완전하게 나타낼 수 있기 때문이다. 이 단원에서는 이 가운데 다소 고급에 속하는 유형을 주로 살펴보겠다. 대체로 라틴어 계열의 단어들이 여기에 속하는데, 이런 어휘는 순수 영어 계열에 비해 보다 특정한 뜻을 나타내어 결합의 범위가 제한되는 경향이 있다. 각 단어의 기본적인 뜻을 염두에 두고 표현을 정확히 익혀두자.

중요 Collocation 정리

1 **absorb knowledge** 지식을 흡수하다 (＝assimilate knowledge)

ex Repetition helps you absorb knowledge.

2 **apply a method** 방법을 적용하다 (＝employ a method)

ex To solve the problem, you need to apply an effective method.

3 **break a pledge** 맹세를 어기다 (＝violate a pledge)

ex Rosemary broke her pledge to stop drinking.

4 **check a fact** 사실을 확인하다 (＝confirm a fact)

ex Always check facts before making up your mind.

5 **deliver a lecture** 강연을 하다 (＝give a lecture)

ex Dr. Murphy delivered a lecture on women's issues.

6 **drop a hint** 힌트를 주다, 시사하다 (＝give a hint)

ex The minister dropped heavy hints about executing the murderer.

7 **fire a gun at** ～를 향해 총을 쏘다 [＝shoot (at)]

ex Angered, Laura fired a gun at the thief.

8 **lay the blame on** ~의 탓으로 돌리다 (= place the blame on)

> **ex** They laid all the blame on her for the failure of the party.

9 **repair equipment** 장비를 수리하다 (= fix equipment)

> **ex** Amazingly, one of her students repaired the equipment.

10 **shoulder responsibility** 책임을 지다 (= bear responsibility)

> **ex** Isabella shouldered responsibility for cleaning the classroom windows.

11 **show a talent** 재능을 드러내다 (= display a talent)

> **ex** Britney Spears showed a talent for singing at an early age.

12 **suffer damage** 피해를 입다 (= sustain damage)

> **ex** Her hometown suffered damage from Hurricane Katrina.

13 **survive an accident** 사고에서 살아남다 (* survive가 타동사로 쓰임에 유의)

> **ex** Unfortunately, the four brothers did not survive the accident.

14 **undergo a change** 변화를 겪다 (= go through a change)

> **ex** Adolescents will undergo many changes.

15 **voice an opinion** 의견을 표명하다

> **ex** Many parents voiced a strong opinion for expelling bad students.

A 적절한 내용으로 연결하세요.

> Ex
> (a) you do not keep your promise
> (b) he or she can be killed
> (c) people may not recognize you
> (d) you talk about it
> (e) you get to know about it

1 If you absorb knowledge about something, _____.

2 If you break your pledge to do something, _____.

3 If you deliver a lecture on something, _____.

4 If you fire a gun at someone, _____.

5 If you undergo a change, _____.

B 다음에서 알맞은 표현을 고르세요.

1 We need to (reply, apply) a more practical method.

2 Nicholas (dropped, fell) a hint about his plan.

3 Clara (appeared, repaired) the equipment.

4 Politicians should (shoulder, elbow) responsibility for what they do.

5 Sarah (referred, suffered) damage from the accident.

Directions: Choose the one word that best fits the sentence.

1 A: Don't _____ your pledge to stop drinking.

 B: I won't. Believe me, I won't let you down.

 (a) solve

 (b) chew

 (c) become

 (d) break

2 A: We should report to the manager on this incident right away.

 B: I think we need to _____ the facts first.

 (a) stop

 (b) check

 (c) peck

 (d) hurry

3 A: I'm so glad he _____ the accident.

 B: Me, too. It was a close call, though.

 (a) survived

 (b) expired

 (c) collapsed

 (d) perished

4 A: I can hardly recognize Michelle.

 B: She's _____ a change recently, you know.

 (a) understood

 (b) undergone

 (c) underdone

 (d) underplayed

5 Understanding is the key to _____ knowledge.

 (a) absorbing

 (b) absenting

 (c) abusing

 (d) abstaining

6 The madman _____ a gun at the corrupt politician.

 (a) hired

 (b) wired

 (c) tired

 (d) fired

7 More women should _____ opinions on social issues.

 (a) ache

 (b) endure

 (c) voice

 (d) prohibit

8 Politicians should _____ responsibility for their views.

 (a) stomach

 (b) arm

 (c) shoulder

 (d) head

학습포인트

주어의 상태나 동작을 설명할 때 『동사＋명사』라는 형태를 쓰는 경우가 많다. 이때 선택되는 동사는 특히 명사가 나타내는 뜻에 어울리는 동사임에 주의하자. 예컨대 '변명하다'를 뜻하는 7의 경우, '변명'을 만들어내야 하기 때문에 make를 써야 하지, 단순히 동작을 한다는 뜻인 do를 써서는 안 된다는 것이다. 이처럼 각 『동사＋명사』형태의 collocation에 숨어 있는 원어민의 사고를 철저하게 자신의 것으로 만들어 나가자.

중요 Collocation 정리

1 take action 조치를 취하다 (＝take steps)

> ex The police took action to protect the girl.

2 make an apology 사과하다 (＝offer an apology)

> ex The reporter made an apology for his mistake.

3 keep one's balance 균형을 유지하다 (＝maintain one's balance)

> ex Keep your balance, or you'll fall to the ground.

4 make a complaint 불평하다 (＝file a complaint)

> ex Several parents made complaints about the ugly teacher.

5 cause damage to ～에 피해를 입히다 (＝inflict damage on～)

> ex The tsunami caused great damage to the entire country.

6 give directions 지시하다, 방향을 알려주다 (＝issue directions)

> ex Mr. Goodall always gives clear directions.

7 make an excuse 변명하다 (＊a lame excuse 엉성한 변명)

> ex Don't make an excuse. Just tell me the truth!

8 **do an experiment** 실험하다 (= conduct an experiment)

ex Many scientists are doing experiments to test the effects of the liquid.

9 **hold a festival** 축제를 개최하다 (* an annual festival 연례 축제)

ex The school holds its annual festival in May.

10 **make a fortune** 많은 돈을 벌다 (* a small fortune 막대한 돈)

ex Jason made a fortune, but he lost all his money by gambling.

11 **present a gift** 선물을 증정하다 (= give a gift)

ex We presented special gifts to the volunteers.

12 **break a habit** 버릇을 고치다 (= shake a habit)

ex In fact, nobody can break a habit overnight.

13 **give an impression** 인상을 주다 (= create an impression)

ex The young worker gave a good impression to everybody.

14 **meet the needs** 수요를 충족시키다 (= fill the needs)

ex The current education system does not meet the needs of students.

15 **cause a problem** 문제를 일으키다 (= pose a problem)

ex Global warming causes a lot of problems in the environment.

A 적절한 내용으로 연결하세요.

> Ex (a) you need to prepare a lot of things
> (b) you are trying to find something out
> (c) you have done something wrong
> (d) you will make a lot of money
> (e) you are not honest

1 If you make an apology, _____.

2 If you make an excuse, _____.

3 If you hold a festival, _____.

4 If you make an experiment, _____.

5 If you meet the needs of your customers, _____.

B 다음에서 알맞은 표현을 고르세요.

1 Many customers (made, did) complaints about the new product.

2 The government (made, took) action to stop the spread of the disease.

3 To our disappointment, the officer (gave, hit) no directions to us.

4 Pursuing wealth only can (deal, cause) serious problems in your life.

5 The polite student (gave, put) a good impression to every teacher.

Directions: Choose the one word that best fits the sentence.

1 A: I'm so sorry I'm late.

B: You're always _____ apologies. Aren't you tired of it?

(a) taking

(b) keeping

(c) doing

(d) making

2 A: We're _____ our yearly festival next week. Can you come?

B: Oh, really? I'd love to go, but I need to check my schedule first.

(a) meeting

(b) holding

(c) breaking

(d) putting

3 A: Did you hear Harold _____ a fortune overnight?

B: What? I should have been kinder to him.

(a) did

(b) turned

(c) made

(d) fell

4 A: Millions of African people are starving.

B: Well, we need to _____ action right away.

(a) take

(b) run

(c) pay

(d) lay

5 In order to succeed, we must _____ the needs of our customers.

(a) look

(b) listen

(c) part

(d) meet

6 When _____ directions, try to use simple words.

(a) standing

(b) picking

(c) hanging

(d) giving

7 _____ a bad habit is a long, hard process.

(a) Throwing

(b) Running

(c) Breaking

(d) Hitting

8 Try to _____ a good impression at a job interview.

(a) pull

(b) call

(c) give

(d) tell

UNIT 4 동사＋명사 Ⅳ

학습포인트

앞에서 살펴본 바와 같이 『동사＋명사』의 조합은 다양한 collocation 가운데 가장 중요한 유형이다. 따라서 순수 영어의 기본 동사를 활용한 예에서 시작하여 라틴어 계열의 고급 수준의 동사를 활용한 예까지 폭넓게 학습해 두어야 한다. 그리고 표제어 옆에 제시되는 동의어나 반의어를 참고하여 원어민들이 어떤 감각으로 『동사＋명사』의 조합을 활용하는지에 대한 이해를 넓히도록 하자.

중요 Collocation 정리

1. place an advertisement 광고를 게재하다 (＝run an advertisement)

ex They placed an advertisement for used equipment.

2 proofread a book 책을 교정보다 (cf. edit a book 책을 편집하다)

ex While proofreading the book, Erica found many typos.

3 display courage 용기를 드러내다 (＝demonstrate courage)

ex Sarah displayed courage by rising to the challenge.

4 resolve differences 차이를 해소하다 (＝settle differences)

ex In reality, it is impossible to resolve differences between different racial groups.

5 exceed expectations 기대를 뛰어넘다 (＝surpass expectations)

ex Sometimes, it is not a good idea to exceed expectations.

6 attain a goal 목표를 성취하다 (＝achieve a goal)

ex Can't you see that you are trying to attain an impossible goal?

7 cherish a hope 희망을 품다 (＝nurse a hope)

ex The immigrants cherished a hope for a better future.

8 **embark on a journey** 여행을 시작하다 (= start on a journey)

ex The girls embarked on an important journey to the South Pole.

9 **hum a lullaby** 자장가를 흥얼거리다 (cf. sing a lullaby 자장가를 부르다)

ex The lonely mother hummed a lullaby to her young daughter.

10 **relieve pain** 고통을 덜어내다 (= soothe pain)

ex Painkillers are supposed to relieve pain.

11 **enjoy a reputation** 명성을 누리다 (= have a reputation)

ex Yale University has enjoyed a reputation as one of the most prestigious

universities in America.

12 **induce sleep** 수면을 유발하다

ex Some medicines are claimed to induce sleep.

13 **promote trade** 교역을 증진하다 (= build up trade)

ex The Americans prospered by promoting trade.

14 **attract a turnout** (참석하는) 사람들을 끌어들이다

ex Madonna's concert attracted a large turnout.

15 **fill a vacancy** 공석(空席)을 채우다

ex The company filled the vacancy by employing a stupid guy.

• 정답 및 해설 p.68

A 적절한 내용으로 연결하세요.

> **Ex** (a) he or she can handle difficulties
>
> (b) you succeed in realizing it
>
> (c) you will find many grammatical errors
>
> (d) they can get along with each other
>
> (e) you do better than expected

1 If you proofread his terrible book, _____.

2 If someone displays courage, _____.

3 If two groups resolve differences, _____.

4 If you exceed expectations, _____.

5 If you attain a goal, _____.

B 다음에서 알맞은 표현을 고르세요.

1 Everybody cherishes a (slope, hope) for a better world.

2 The country embarked (on, off) a journey to economic growth.

3 Take some aspirin. It will help to (relieve, cause) pain.

4 The company has (joined, enjoyed) a reputation as an ideal workplace.

5 With nobody applying for the position, they couldn't fill the (vacancy, vacation).

Directions: Choose the one word that best fits the sentence.

1 A: Can you tell me how I can sell my used computer?

B: How about _____ an advertisement in the local newspaper?

(a) jogging

(b) pleasing

(c) hurrying

(d) placing

2 A: I was quite impressed by her courage.

B: Me, too. Nobody expected she would _____ such courage.

(a) disappear

(b) display

(c) disprove

(d) discuss

3 A: How well did Erica do on the test?

B: Surprisingly, she _____ expectations.

(a) experienced

(b) exceeded

(c) expressed

(d) exchanged

4 A: How did the conference go?

B: To our disappointment, it _____ a small turnout.

(a) applied

(b) agreed

(c) attracted

(d) astonished

5 The editor _____ the book several times to improve its quality.

(a) proofread

(b) promoted

(c) proposed

(d) prospered

6 Hillary did everything she could do to _____ her goal.

(a) attend

(b) attach

(c) attain

(d) attack

7 Try to _____ differences between the two groups in a creative way.

(a) resolve

(b) rely

(c) respond

(d) regret

8 _____ on a journey to enrich your life!

(a) Employ

(b) Embark

(c) Embarrass

(d) Emerge

명사+동사

학습포인트

『명사+동사』의 collocation은 일정한 명사의 전형적인 상태나 동작을 나타내는 표현이다. 대개 명사가 제시되고 그에 어울리는 동사를 질문하는 유형으로 출제되며, 특히 평소에 접하기 힘든 표현들도 출제 범위에 속한다는 점에 유의하자. 이 유형은 『동사+명사』의 형식과 마찬가지로 완전한 뜻을 나타낼 수 있으며 또한 원어민의 발상을 엿볼 수 있게 하는 표현에 속한다.

중요 Collocation 정리

1 **an airplane taxis** 비행기가 지상에서 활주하다

ex The airplane taxied for several minutes before it took off.

2 **blood circulates** 혈액이 순환하다

ex Blood circulates throughout the body.

3 **a crisis eases** 위기가 완화되다 (↔a crisis deepens 위기가 심화되다)

ex After the politician stepped down, the crisis eased.

4 **a demand rises** 수요가 증가하다 (=a demand increases)

ex Japan's wheat demand has been rising since then.

5 **an engine functions** 기관이 작동하다 (=an engine works)

ex Surprisingly, the engine functioned perfectly.

6 **a fight rages** 싸움이 격하게 계속되다

ex Their fight for independence raged for several decades.

7 **a gap narrows** 격차가 줄어들다 (↔a gap widens 격차가 커지다])

ex Due to their great efforts, the gap between rich and poor narrowed.

8 **a heart pounds** 심장이 두근거리다 (= a heart thumps)

> ex When I saw him for the first time, my heart pounded violently.

9 **an infection spreads** 감염이 확산되다

> ex Unfortunately, the infection spread rapidly.

10 **a king reigns** 왕이 집권하다

> ex The wise king reigned for half a century.

11 **the market slumps** 시장이 침체에 빠지다

> ex When oil prices rose sharply, the market slumped.

12 **negotiations collapse** 협상이 결렬되다 (= negotiations break down)

> ex Because of their great differences, the negotiations collapsed.

13 **a passport expires** 여권이 만료되다

> ex Her passport expired on June 29, 2002.

14 **a rate falls** 요금이 내리다 (↔ a rate rises 요금이 오르다)

> ex In March, hotel rates fell by 30 percent.

15 **a scandal breaks** 스캔들이 터지다 (= a scandal erupts)

> ex After his scandal broke, the president had to leave his company.

A 적절한 내용으로 연결하세요.

> **Ex** (a) you have a strong feeling about something
>
> (b) it is not flying in the air
>
> (c) a lot of people feel unhappy
>
> (d) you do not have to worry about it
>
> (e) we can sell more products

1 If an airplane taxis,_____.

2 If a crisis eases,_____.

3 If the demand rises,_____.

4 If your heart pounds,_____.

5 If the market slumps, _____.

B 다음에서 알맞은 표현을 고르세요.

1 How does blood (circulate, surround) in the body?

2 The queen (reined, reigned) from 1789 to 1876.

3 Because it was severely damaged, the engine did not (mention, function).

4 When your passport (expires, expresses), you cannot use it.

5 When the scandal (broke, froze), everybody was shocked.

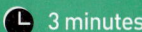
Directions: Choose the one word that best fits the sentence.

1 A: How did the collision happen?

B: When the airplane was _____, a truck crashed into it.

(a) taxiing

(b) tiring

(c) taxing

(d) trying

2 A: I'd like to make a reservation for a trip to Togo.

B: Sorry, ma'am, but your passport has _____.

(a) explained

(b) existed

(c) exploded

(d) expired

3 A: When did Bruce Parker step down as president?

B: In 2007, when his scandal _____.

(a) destroyed

(b) interrupted

(c) broke

(d) smashed

4 A: The infection is _____ rapidly in the country.

B: We need to take immediate action.

(a) repairing

(b) removing

(c) spreading

(d) supporting

5 The demand is expected to _____ by 15 percent.

(a) raise

(b) arise

(c) rip

(d) rise

6 When the soldier saw his girlfriend, his heart began to _____.

(a) found

(b) pound

(c) pour

(d) foul

7 When the negotiations _____, both parties were ready to go to war.

(a) collapsed

(b) collaborated

(c) succeeded

(d) substituted

8 The gap between rich and poor is unlikely to _____ any time soon.

(a) narrate

(b) narrow

(c) borrow

(d) name

UNIT 6 형용사＋명사 Ⅰ

학습포인트

『형용사＋명사』형태의 collocation은 형용사와 명사가 나타내는 전형적인 특징을 표현하는 형식이다. 다른 collocation의 예와 마찬가지로 원어민의 감각에 따라 조합이 결정되기 때문에, 자연스러운 결합에 숨어 있는 원어민의 감각을 익히려는 노력이 필요하다. 특히 우리말의 사고와 다르게 조합되는 경우가 많다는 점을 생각하여 하나의 자연스러운 표현으로 익혀두는 것이 바람직하다.

중요 Collocation 정리

1 exceptional ability 뛰어난 능력 (＝outstanding ability)

> ex Sarah Brightman has an exceptional ability as a singer.

2 a thorough analysis 철저한 분석 (＝a careful analysis)

> ex A thorough analysis of the matter was done by the little kids.

3 a delicate balance 미묘한 균형 (＝a subtle balance)

> ex A delicate balance should be maintained between freedom and responsibility.

4 a major breakthrough 주요한 발전 (＝a significant breakthrough)

> ex The discovery of radium was a major breakthrough in physics.

5 a leading candidate 유력한 후보자 (＝a strong candidate)

> ex Angelina Jolie was a leading candidate for the position of president.

6 constructive criticism 건설적인 비판

> ex After all, constructive criticism helps you succeed as a writer.

7 a crucial decision 중대한 결정 (＝a big decision)

> ex Divorcing her husband was a crucial decision in her life.

8   a heroic effort 굉장한 노력 (=a massive effort)

ex His heroic efforts led to the discovery of penicillin.

9   a key factor 주된 요인 (=a major factor)

ex Self-confidence is a key factor in achieving success.

10   a radical feminist 급진적인 여성운동가

ex Radical feminists argue that marriage should be banned.

11   an excellent grade 뛰어난 점수 (=a high grade)

ex The team got an excellent grade for its project.

12   intense hatred 심한 증오 (=deep-rooted hatred)

ex Her intense hatred of the human race led to several murders.

13   a time-consuming job 시간이 많이 소요되는 일

ex Writing a book is a time-consuming job.

14   superficial knowledge 피상적인 지식 (=slight knowledge)

ex Superficial knowledge cannot give you any insights.

15   a miserable life 비참한 삶 (=a tough life)

ex In fact, Marilyn Monroe led a miserable life.

EXERCISE

🕐 3 minutes

• 정답 및 해설 p.71

A 적절한 내용으로 연결하세요.

> Ex
> (a) you examine it very carefully
> (b) you are likely to hate men
> (c) you are likely to be hired
> (d) you are very good at doing something
> (e) your life will change dramatically

1 If you have an exceptional ability, _____.

2 If you conduct a thorough analysis of something, _____.

3 If you are a leading candidate for a position, _____.

4 If you make a crucial decision, _____.

5 If you are a radical feminist, _____.

B 다음에서 알맞은 표현을 고르세요.

1 Reputation was a key (factor, fact) in his decision to apply to the university.

2 (Intensive, Intense) hatred can be an expression of love.

3 Growing flowers is a time-consuming (work, job).

4 Many people boast of their (superficial, official) knowledge.

5 They bravely defended their country with (hesitant, heroic) efforts.

Directions: Choose the one word that best fits the sentence.

1 A: What do you think of Michelle Wie?

B: Well, she has a[n] _____ ability as a golfer but she lacks something.

(a) irregular

(b) exceptional

(c) strange

(d) odd

2 A: Why were you so mad at Bruce?

B: Cause his comment was not _____ criticism.

(a) destructive

(b) negative

(c) proud

(d) constructive

3 A: Congratulations! I heard you got an _____ grade!

B: Thanks. I just did my best.

(a) low

(b) failing

(c) excellent

(d) poor

4 A: Do you know why Albert Einstein is so famous?

B: Because he made a(n) _____ breakthrough in physics.

(a) inferior

(b) unimportant

(c) major

(d) lower

5 Declaring war on Iraq was a _____ decision in the history of the country.

(a) crucial

(b) modest

(c) humble

(d) shy

6 Still, Hillary Clinton is a _____ candidate for the position of President of the United States.

(a) leading

(b) listening

(c) lazy

(d) learning

7 Meditation can help to turn _____ hatred into compassion.

(a) intelligent

(b) intense

(c) intelligible

(d) interim

8 In my opinion, a more _____ analysis of the issue is needed.

(a) incomplete

(b) inaccurate

(c) thorough

(d) miserable

학습포인트

이 단원에서는『형용사＋명사』형태의 collocation 가운데 난이도가 다소 높은 표현들을 정리한다. 일부 표현의 경우에는 흔히 알고 있는 뜻과 다르게 형용사가 쓰이는 경우도 있는데, 이처럼 표현을 폭넓게 익혀두어야만 실전 TEPS에서 당황하지 않을 수 있다. 그리고 이와 같은 collocation을 꾸준히 익혀가는 것이 TEPS 고득점의 확실한 비결이라는 점도 명심하자.

중요 Collocation 정리

1   **domestic mail** 국내 우편 (↔foreign mail 해외 우편)

> ex   Domestic mail takes approximately 2 to 3days for delivery.

2   **a serious mistake** 중대한 실수 (＝a big mistake)

> ex   Employing the stupid guy was a serious mistake.

3   **an urgent need** 급박한 필요 (＝a pressing need)

> ex   There is an urgent need for more quality books.

4   **sensational news** 극히 자극적인 뉴스 (＝shocking news)

> ex   The newspaper is notorious for its sensational news.

5   **a primary objective** 일차적 목적 (＝a major objective)

> ex   Our primary objective is to build a healthy society.

6   **an opposing opinion** 반대 의견 (＝a dissenting opinion)

> ex   Many opposing opinions were expressed about the new policy.

7   **a distorted perspective** 왜곡된 관점

> ex   Some people believe that communism is a distorted perspective on society.

8 a grave problem 심각한 문제 (= a serious problem)

ex In fact, TV violence is a grave problem.

9 the harsh reality 가혹한 현실 (= the grim reality)

ex Angelina Jolie was shocked by the harsh reality of their lives.

10 abundant resources 풍부한 자원 (cf. limited resources 제한된 자원)

ex We need to use our abundant resources wisely.

11 a handsome salary 넉넉한 급여 (= a big salary)

ex Brooke Shields earned a handsome salary as a fashion model.

12 a reliable source 믿을 만한 출처 (= trustworthy source)

ex We heard from a reliable source that they are planning to attack our city.

13 a prudent step 신중한 조치 (= a careful step)

ex The committee took a prudent step to avoid the danger.

14 candid talks 진솔한 회담 (= frank talks)

ex The so-called "candid" talks bore no fruit.

15 cruel treatment 잔혹하게 대하는 것 (= brutal treatment)

ex We should stop the cruel treatment of pigs immediately.

• 정답 및 해설 p.73

A 적절한 내용으로 연결하세요.

Ex
(a) your job is likely to be rewarding
(b) it is likely to be true
(c) you cannot see things as they really are
(d) it is likely to get rich
(e) you'll get into trouble

1 If you make a serious mistake, _____.

2 If you have a distorted perspective, _____.

3 If a country has abundant resources, _____.

4 If you earn a handsome salary, _____.

5 If you heard something from a reliable source, _____.

B 다음에서 알맞은 표현을 고르세요.

1 Domestic (mail, male) can be classified in many ways.

2 There is an (urban, urgent) need for more qualified teachers.

3 (Sensational, Proportional) news is not worth reading.

4 Their (emotional, primary) objective is to earn a lot of money.

5 Global warming is a (grave, respectable) problem.

Directions: Choose the one word that best fits the sentence.

1   A: Do you know why Kathy married Bill?

B: Because he is earning a(n) _____ salary.

(a) handsome
(b) ugly
(c) beautiful
(d) pretty

2   A: I heard from a _____ source that my company is going to lay off thousands of workers.

B: What? I thought it is doing very well.

(a) religious
(b) relieved
(c) relived
(d) reliable

3   A: As an expert, what do you think of the court's decision?

B: I believe that it was a _____ mistake. Nobody would accept it.

(a) cheerful
(b) pleasant
(c) serious
(d) delightful

4   A: There is a(n) _____ need for more dedicated volunteers.

B: You can say that again!

(a) usable
(b) useless
(c) urgent
(d) urban

5   Of course, noise pollution is a _____ problem.

(a) junior
(b) favorable
(c) minor
(d) grave

6   The _____ objective of education is to free one's mind.

(a) depressed
(b) primary
(c) prosperous
(d) resentful

7   As a democratic citizen, you should respect _____ opinions.

(a) ineffective
(b) opposing
(c) feeble
(d) saddened

8   _____ resources do not always lead to economic growth.

(a) Abundant
(b) Absurd
(c) Abused
(d) Abstract

UNIT 8 동사＋부사 Ⅰ

학습포인트

예컨대 우리말에서도 '비가 심하게 내렸다'고 말하는 것과 같이 영어에서도 It rained heavily라고 말하는 것이 자연스럽다. 이런 collocation에서는 대개 동사가 나타내는 뜻과 밀접하게 관련을 맺는 부사가 선택된다. 따라서 동사의 뜻과 자연스럽게 이어질 수 있는 부사가 무엇인지를 생각하는 습관을 들여야 하며, 부사의 학습은 이와 같은 collocation의 습득으로 충분하다는 점도 알아두자.

중요 Collocation 정리

1 handle carefully 조심스럽게 다루다 (＝handle with care)

ex Handle the picture frame carefully, or it will break into pieces.

2 choose carefully 신중하게 고르다 (↔choose carelessly 아무렇게나 고르다)

ex The class president was carefully chosen by the students.

3 dress casually 평상복을 입다 (＝dress informally)

ex The strange teacher dared to dress casually in class.

4 fail completely 완전히 실패하다 (＝fail miserably)

ex Sadly for us, the excellent movie failed completely.

5 hate deeply 몹시 미워하다 (＝hate bitterly)

ex Most students hated the principal deeply.

6 divide equally 균등하게 나누다 (＝divide evenly)

ex Supplies were equally divided among the soldiers.

7 agree fully 완전히 동의하다 (＝agree entirely)

ex Everybody fully agreed to wear a red necktie.

8 **enjoy greatly** 한껏 즐기다 (= enjoy very much)

> ex The dance party was greatly enjoyed by the seniors.

9 **hit hard** 심하게 타격을 입히다 (= hit badly)

> ex His village was hit hard by a tsunami.

10 **criticize harshly** 심하게 비난하다 (= criticize bitterly)

> ex The worker was harshly criticized for his laziness.

11 **rain heavily** 비가 심하게 내리다 (= rain cats and dogs)

> ex It rains heavily in the summer.

12 **injure severely** 심하게 부상을 입히다 (= injure seriously)

> ex Many passengers were severely injured in the crash.

13 **believe strongly** 굳게 믿다 (= believe firmly)

> ex We strongly believe that everybody is an important human being.

14 **greet warmly** 따뜻하게 맞이하다 (= greet welcomingly)

> ex My students were greeted warmly by the host family.

15 **guess wildly** 억측하다 (↔ guess shrewdly 신중하게 추측하다)

> ex Many teachers wildly guessed that Willow had stolen the document.

A 적절한 내용으로 연결하세요.

Ex
(a) he or she won't like you

(b) you cannot go out and play

(c) it won't be likely to be damaged

(d) nobody disagrees with the plan

(e) you cannot go to a formal party

1 If you handle something carefully,

2 If you dress casually, _____.

3 If you hate someone deeply, _____.

4 If everyone fully agrees to do something, _____.

5 If it rains heavily, _____.

B 다음에서 알맞은 표현을 고르세요.

1 They were greeted (weakly, warmly) by the kind landlord.

2 Christie (wildly, politely) guessed that her brother had run away.

3 The festival was (greatly, hard) enjoyed by all the students.

4 The candidates were chosen (uselessly, carefully) by the members.

5 We (strongly, unkindly) believe that our country is important to us all.

Directions: Choose the one word that best fits the sentence.

1 A: What do you think of Marie?

B: To be frank with you, I hate her

_____.

(a) thinly

(b) thickly

(c) closely

(d) deeply

2 A: How did the discussion go?

B: Unfortunately, it failed

_____.

(a) delightfully

(b) completely

(c) happily

(d) hopefully

3 A: Where should I put this vase?

B: Look! Handle it _____! It breaks very easily.

(a) carelessly

(b) coldly

(c) carefully

(d) warmly

4 A: What is the weather like in San Diego?

B: It is raining _____. We just can't go out.

(a) heavily

(b) darkly

(c) softly

(d) brightly

5 Unfortunately, Jessica was _____ injured in an accident.

(a) pleasantly

(b) humorously

(c) severely

(d) incorrectly

6 The teacher was _____ criticized for his inability to understand his students.

(a) lovingly

(b) harshly

(c) sweetly

(d) dully

7 At last, they _____ agreed to build a better community together.

(a) unluckily

(b) sharply

(c) fully

(d) rudely

8 The profits were supposed to be divided _____ among the workers.

(a) toughly

(b) strongly

(c) lightly

(d) equally

UNIT 9 동사＋부사 Ⅱ

학습포인트

'동사＋부사 Ⅰ'에서 살펴본 것과 같이, '동사＋부사'의 collocation은 동사가 뜻과 밀접하게 관련을 맺는 부사와 결합하는 것을 말한다. 이 단원에서는 UNIT 8에 비해 고급에 속하는 예를 통해 다양한 『동사＋부사』의 형태를 정리하고자 한다. 따라서 제시되는 부사들이 다소 어렵게 느껴질 수도 있지만, 부사에 대응하는 형용사의 학습까지 감안한 예들이므로 착실하게 익혀두자.

중요 Collocation 정리

1 oppose bitterly 맹렬히 반대하다 (＝oppose resolutely)

> ex The plan for building a doghouse was opposed bitterly by the girls.

2 react calmly 차분히 반응하다 (↔react strongly 격하게 반응하다)

> ex Surprisingly, Michelle Pfeiffer managed to react calmly.

3 glow dimly 희미하게 빛나다 (↔glow brightly)

> ex The light bulb glowed dimly in the small room.

4 please highly 매우 기쁘게 하다 (＝please greatly)

> ex Most teachers were highly pleased by her performance.

5 lie flatly 새빨간 거짓말을 하다 (＝lie outright)

> ex Erica Kim lied flatly about the contract.

6 describe graphically 생생하게 묘사하다 (＝describe vividly)

> ex To our dismay, the reporter described graphically the horrible accident.

7 change radically 현격하게 바뀌다 (＝change greatly)

> ex Paris Hilton has changed radically ever since I first met her.

8   **judge impartially**   공정하게 판단하다 (= judge fairly)

> **ex**   Everyone should be judged impartially according to their ability.

9   **affect profoundly**   심하게 영향을 미치다 (= affect strongly)

> **ex**   This election will affect profoundly the future of our country.

10   **hope sincerely**   진정으로 바라다 (≒ hope fervently 열렬히 바라다)

> **ex**   I sincerely hope that every one of you is happy.

11   **insist stubbornly**   완고하게 주장하다 (= insist obstinately)

> **ex**   Some Americans insisted stubbornly that they go to war with Iraq.

12   **search thoroughly**   철저히 수색하다 (= search carefully)

> **ex**   Angelina's house was searched thoroughly by the police.

13   **ignore totally**   완전히 무시하다 (= ignore completely)

> **ex**   Their terrible situation was ignored totally by the public.

14   **forget utterly**   완전히 잊어버리다 (= forget completely)

> **ex**   Unfortunately, I forgot utterly to lock the door.

15   **neglect willfully**   의도적으로 소홀히 하다 (= neglect intentionally)

> **ex**   They neglected willfully to protect the innocent child.

A 적절한 내용으로 연결하세요.

> **Ex** (a) people know what it looks like
> (b) you really want it to occur
> (c) you are definitely against it
> (d) you do not pay any attention to it
> (e) he or she is very happy

1 If you oppose a plan bitterly, _____.

2 If you please someone highly, _____.

3 If you describe something graphically, _____.

4 If you sincerely hope that something happens, _____.

5 If you ignore something totally, _____.

B 다음에서 알맞은 표현을 고르세요.

1 Although she was angry, Mary reacted (strongly, calmly).

2 How could you lie (flatly, fairly) about the accident?

3 Each candidate was supposed to be judged (impartially, impatiently).

4 The candle glowed (randomly, dimly) on the table.

5 I forgot (urgently, utterly) about the incident.

Directions: Choose the one word that best fits the sentence.

1 A: In my opinion, they will oppose the plan _____.

B: What makes you think so?

(a) sweetly
(b) saltily
(c) spicily
(d) bitterly

2 A: I was surprised Paul reacted so _____!

B: So was I. His self-control was impressive.

(a) violently
(b) calmly
(c) rudely
(d) aggressively

3 A: It has been a pleasure for me to work with you.

B: I _____ hope you have a successful career in your new field.

(a) sincerely
(b) dishonestly
(c) insignificantly
(d) deceitfully

4 A: Kate ignored me _____! How could she do that?

B: Oh, didn't you know she was such a jerk?

(a) fairly
(b) welcomingly
(c) totally
(d) warmly

5 The audience was _____ pleased by her beautiful music.

(a) high
(b) cheaply
(c) highly
(d) poorly

6 Annet changed so _____ that nobody recognized her.

(a) furiously
(b) radically
(c) lazily
(d) thankfully

7 It is impossible for racists to judge African Americans _____.

(a) impatiently
(b) improperly
(c) impolitely
(d) impartially

8 Music can _____ affect human emotion.

(a) profoundly
(b) irritably
(c) indifferently
(d) incorrectly

UNIT 10 부사＋형용사

학습포인트

『부사＋형용사』형태의 collocation은 형용사가 나타내는 상태의 다양한 특성을 표현하는 역할을 맡는다. 영어 문장에서 부사가 차지하는 비중이 상대적으로 낮기 때문에 부사의 출제 비중 또한 높지 않은 편이지만, 부사 가운데 다소 빈번하게 출제되는 표현도 있기 때문에 적절한 예를 통해 정확히 익혀둘 필요가 있다. 이 단원에서는 이와 같은 예를 집중적으로 학습한다.

중요 Collocation 정리

1 mutually acceptable 서로 받아들일 수 있는

ex They reached a mutually acceptable agreement on the ownership of the pond.

2 legally binding 법적 구속력이 있는

ex A legally binding contract makes you become a responsible adult.

3 fully clad 옷을 완전히 차려 입은

ex The villagers were fully clad in their traditional costumes.

4 extremely dangerous 지극히 위험한 (＝very dangerous)

ex Doing business in that area is extremely dangerous.

5 entirely different 전혀 다른 (＝completely different)

ex The two groups are entirely different from each other.

6 actively engaged 적극적으로 관여하는

ex Malcolm was actively engaged in the campaign for African Americans.

7 physically fit 신체적으로 건강한

ex Only physically fit people are allowed to take the dangerous trip to the jungle.

8 **greatly honored** 대단히 영광스러운 (= deeply honored)

> **ex** We felt greatly honored to be invited to the awards ceremony.

9 **practically impossible** 거의 불가능한 (= virtually impossible)

> **ex** It is practically impossible to conquer the mountain.

10 **happily married** 결혼 생활이 행복한

> **ex** Marianne was happily married with seven children.

11 **absolutely necessary** 절대적으로 필요한

> **ex** It is absolutely necessary to master self-defense.

12 **cautiously optimistic** 신중하게 낙관적인 (= guardedly optimistic)

> **ex** Experts are cautiously optimistic about the outcome of the peace talks.

13 **deeply rooted** 뿌리 깊은

> **ex** Her new songs are deeply rooted in traditional Irish music.

14 **terribly sorry** 대단히 미안한 (= dreadfully sorry)

> **ex** We are terribly sorry for any inconveniences this might cause.

15 **ideally suited** 이상적으로 적합한

> **ex** The company is ideally suited for producing hand-made furniture.

A 적절한 내용으로 연결하세요.

> **Ex** (a) they are not the same
> (b) you had better not do it
> (c) you are strong and healthy
> (d) you must carry it out
> (e) it is not possible to do it

1 If an agreement is legally binding, _____.

2 If something is extremely dangerous, _____.

3 If two things are entirely different from each other, _____.

4 If you are physically fit, _____.

5 If something is practically impossible, _____.

B 다음에서 알맞은 표현을 고르세요.

1 They agreed on (regrettably, mutually) acceptable conditions.

2 They were (angrily, actively) engaged in humanitarian efforts.

3 Tim was (happily, mournfully) married and loved his wife so much.

4 It is (absolutely, unattractively) necessary to protect our environment.

5 Because of its location, the village is (idly, ideally) suited for sightseeing.

Directions: Choose the one word that best fits the sentence.

1 A: I'm very eager to explore the universe.
   B: Well, it might be _____ dangerous, you know.

   (a) expressionlessly
   (b) expertly
   (c) expensively
   (d) extremely

2 A: What became of Clara?
   B: Oh, she is _____ married and lives in Boston.

   (a) enormously
   (b) irregularly
   (c) slightly
   (d) happily

3 A: What do you think of his election campaign?
   B: I'm _____ optimistic about its results.

   (a) gloomily
   (b) ridiculously
   (c) cautiously
   (d) elegantly

4 A: I'm _____ sorry about my mistake.
   B: That's all right. Nobody is perfect, you know.

   (a) terribly
   (b) brightly
   (c) gratefully
   (d) mistakenly

5 It is _____ necessary to learn how to control your mind.

   (a) absently
   (b) absolutely
   (c) absurdly
   (d) abusively

6 The contract is not _____ binding and you have no responsibilities.

   (a) emotionally
   (b) legally
   (c) instinctively
   (d) unconsciously

7 We felt _____ honored to receive the prestigious award.

   (a) greatly
   (b) shallowly
   (c) poorly
   (d) uncertainly

8 It is _____ impossible to develop a thinking computer.

   (a) innocently
   (b) ignorantly
   (c) practically
   (d) hastily

Chapter 2

필수어휘와 혼동어휘

UNIT 1   동사(필수어휘) Ⅰ

UNIT 2   동사(필수어휘) Ⅱ

UNIT 3   명사(필수어휘)

UNIT 4   형용사(필수어휘)

UNIT 5   의미(혼동어휘) Ⅰ

UNIT 6   의미(혼동어휘) Ⅱ

UNIT 7   형태(혼동어휘)

UNIT 1 동사(필수어휘) I

학습포인트

일상적으로 흔히 쓰면서 TEPS 어휘 영역에서 자주 등장하는 단어들을 필수 어휘로 분류했다. 본래는 어려운 단어인 고급 어휘와 분명하게 구별되었는데, 최근 전반적으로 난이도가 높아지면서 고급 어휘 가운데 많은 단어들이 필수 어휘로 분류되어 출제된다. 따라서 우선 기본적인 필수 어휘를 정확히 익힌 후 점차 다양한 표현들을 습득해 가는 것이 올바른 순서다.

중요 Collocation 정리

1 avoid 피하다 (= stay away from)

ex For some reason, Rachel avoids seeing me.

2 behave 처신하다 (↔ misbehave 못되게 굴다)

ex Ethan behaves well for his age.

3 cancel 취소하다 (= call off)

ex Surprisingly, their wedding was canceled.

4 delay 지연시키다 (= put off, postpone)

ex My flight was delayed by lots of birds.

5 earn (돈을) 벌다 (= make)

ex Tiger Woods earned about $100 million in 2006.

6 face (문제에) 직면하다 (= confront)

ex If you break the vase, you'll face a big problem.

7 fire 해고하다 (= dismiss)

ex Daniel was fired because he couldn't sell enough cars.

8 gain (이익 등을) 얻다 (= acquire)

> ex Diana gained great benefit from his useful advice.

9 happen (일이) 일어나다 (= occur)

> ex Terrible things can happen to anybody.

10 hire 고용하다 (= employ, take on)

> ex Gregory was hired by a supermarket.

11 imitate 흉내 내다 (= mimic)

> ex Many students enjoyed imitating the strange teacher.

12 include 포함하다 (↔ exclude 제외하다)

> ex This book includes many pictures of crocodiles.

13 join 합류하다 (= enter)

> ex Many things have changed since the famous pitcher joined the team.

14 judge 판단하다 (= evaluate 평가하다)

> ex As the saying goes, "Don't judge the book by its cover."

15 last 지속되다 (= carry on)

> ex Their friendship lasted until the singer's death in 1999.

• 정답 및 해설 p.80

A 적절한 내용으로 연결하세요.

Ex
(a) you will have difficulty making money
(b) try your best to solve it
(c) people will like you
(d) he or she will not like you
(e) they will overcome those difficulties

1 If you behave well, _____.

2 If you are fired, _____.

3 If bad things happen to good people, _____.

4 If you face a problem, _____.

5 If you imitate someone, _____.

B 다음에서 알맞은 표현을 고르세요.

1 Always try to (avoid, prevent) talking with strangers.

2 Unfortunately, we have no choice but to (cancel, catch) the concert.

3 So many students want to (join, joke) the soccer team.

4 (Earning, Working) money is not everything in life.

5 To be frank with you, we (hired, rented) a terrible guy.

Directions: Choose the one word that best fits the sentence.

1   A: You are about to meet an
      important person. _____
      yourself!
    B: Don't worry, mom. I won't cause
      any trouble.

   (a) Misbehave
   (b) Act
   (c) Mind
   (d) Behave

2   A: I'm so excited about tomorrow's
      event.
    B: Me, too. It _____ many
      interesting activities.

   (a) concludes
   (b) includes
   (c) prevents
   (d) excludes

3   A: Angela must be a nice girl. She
      is so pretty!
    B: Never _____ someone by
      their appearance.

   (a) think
   (b) judge
   (c) misunderstand
   (d) guess

4   A: Congratulations! You're
      _____.
    B: Really? I'm so excited about
      working for your company.

   (a) fired
   (b) shot

   (c) injured
   (d) hired

5   Because of the hurricane, my flight
    was _____.

   (a) praised
   (b) won
   (c) delayed
   (d) booked

6   Sometimes, good things _____
    to bad people.

   (a) appear
   (b) hurt
   (c) burn
   (d) happen

7   It is not a great idea to _____
    someone's speech.

   (a) resemble
   (b) imitate
   (c) disappear
   (d) rise

8   When you are _____ with
    difficulties, try to remain calm.

   (a) located
   (b) faced
   (c) born
   (d) avoided

동사(필수어휘) II

학습포인트

특정한 상태나 동작을 거의 완전히 설명할 수 있기 때문에, 필수 어휘 가운데 동사의 출제 비중은 높은 편이다. 또한 영문법의 거의 절반이 동사에 관한 사항이라는 점에서, 동사의 문법적 특성의 숙지 정도 또한 측정한다. 따라서 일상적으로 자주 접하게 되는 동사의 다양한 뜻을 익혀두어야 하고, 특히 해당 동사가 자동사인가 타동사인가도 꼬박꼬박 확인하는 습관을 들여야 함을 명심하자.

중요 Collocation 정리

1 **leak** (비밀을) 누설하다 (= disclose)

> ex The young girl leaked an important piece of information to her friends.

2 **maintain** 주장하다 (= assert)

> ex We maintain that everyone should be able to dance.

3 **nominate** 지명하다 (= designate)

> ex Jessica was nominated to head the CIA.

4 **notify** 통보하다 (= advise)

> ex To her surprise, Marie was notified that she had passed the national exam.

5 **object** 반대하다 (= oppose, protest)

> ex I strongly object to the idea that men are better than women.

6 **offend** 감정을 상하게 하다 (= upset)

> ex My father was deeply offended by his racist remarks.

7 **patrol** 순찰하다 (= guard)

> ex Britney's house was patrolled by five snakes.

8 **perform** 수행하다 (= carry out, execute)

ex To perform well, you need to practice as often as possible.

9 **quit** 그만두다 (= give up, resign)

ex After winning the lottery, Bruce quit his job.

10 **range** (일정한) 범위에 이르다 (= reach, extend)

ex Her expertise ranges from linguistics to astronomy.

11 **recommend** 추천하다 (= endorse, acclaim)

ex I recommend William Zinsser without reservation.

12 **settle** 정착하다 (= inhabit)

ex The city was settled by Irish immigrants.

13 **ship** 운송하다 (= transport, dispatch)

ex Amazon.com ships books internationally.

14 **store** 저장하다 (= stow, deposit)

ex The human brain stores a lot of information.

15 **trace** 추적하다 (= track down)

ex The villagers were trying to trace the missing girl.

A 적절한 내용으로 연결하세요.

> **Ex** (a) you say that it is important to do it
>
> (b) you are strongly against it
>
> (c) he or she will probably tell others about it
>
> (d) it hurts your feelings
>
> (e) he or she tells you something important

1 If you leak a secret to someone, _____.

2 If you maintain that something should be done, _____.

3 If someone notifies you of something, _____.

4 If you object to something, _____.

5 If something offends you, _____.

B 다음에서 알맞은 표현을 고르세요.

1 Her house was (patronized, patrolled) by police for several nights.

2 Before (angering, quitting) your job, you need to think about a lot of things.

3 Her book was highly (recommended, responded) by professional writers.

4 How much does it cost to (chip, ship) a snake from Africa to the U.S.?

5 The store (stores, scores) a lot of products.

Directions: Choose the one word that best fits the sentence.

1 A: Lots of people are excited about the plan.

B: I strongly _____ to it, though.

(a) object

(b) oppose

(c) subject

(d) project

2 A: I think you had better apologize to her.

B: Well, maybe. But I didn't mean to _____ her feelings.

(a) offer

(b) attend

(c) effect

(d) offend

3 A: I think Enya _____ well at her concert last night.

B: Me, too. She is an excellent singer, I guess.

(a) perfected

(b) informed

(c) performed

(d) reformed

4 A: Can you _____ a good lawyer?

B: How about contacting Ava Carpenter? She knows what she's doing.

(a) command

(b) recollect

(c) recommend

(d) commend

5 They _____ that the city should invest more money in education.

(a) contain

(b) retain

(c) obtain

(d) maintain

6 Angered by his low pay, David _____ his job.

(a) suited

(b) quit

(c) destroyed

(d) recalled

7 To my surprise, they were able to _____ the car to Detroit.

(a) shop

(b) ship

(c) shoot

(d) shock

8 The price _____ from $77 to $122.

(a) exchanges

(b) charges

(c) ranges

(d) arranges

명사(필수어휘)

학습포인트

다양한 대상을 나타낼 수 있기 때문에, 필수어휘 가운데 명사의 출제 비중은 동사의 출제 비중만큼이나 높다. 명사의 학습에서는 일정한 명사가 셀 수 있는 명사인가 그렇지 않은가를 꼬박꼬박 확인하는 과정이 중요하다. 특히, 셀 수 없는 명사는 a나 few와 같은 말의 꾸밈을 받을 수 없다는 점을 다시 한 번 명심할 필요가 있다. 그러면 중요한 명사들을 아래에서 함께 정리하자.

중요 Collocation 정리

1   anniversary 기념일

> ex   Many couples celebrate their anniversaries by exchanging presents.

2   boom 호황 (= growth)

> ex   The new policy led to a sudden boom in the fashion industry.

3   celebrity 유명 인사 (= star, personality)

> ex   Do celebrities lead happy lives?

4   detour 우회 (= alternative route)

> ex   We took a detour to avoid heavy traffic.

5   editorial 사설

> ex   In her famous editorial, the professor attacked the government severely.

6   field 분야 (= area, sphere)

> ex   The field of molecular biology requires creativity as well as intelligence.

7   gist 요점, 핵심 (= essence)

> ex   The gist of what he said was that happiness comes from within, not from without.

8 housing 주택 (＝accommodations)

> ex Providing cheap housing was a key issue in the election.

9 insult 모욕 (＝offense)

> ex Such remarks can be considered an insult.

10 landscape (배경이 되는) 전반적 상황 (＝circumstances)

> ex The feminist movement influenced the social landscape of the country.

11 lot 운명 (＝destiny)

> ex Try to improve your lot by thinking positively.

12 manuscript 원고

> ex Many manuscripts have been rejected by the strict editor.

13 notion 개념 (＝concept)

> ex The notion of evolution is quite misleading.

14 option 선택(권) (＝choice, selection)

> ex I had no option but to let her go.

15 recess (학교의) 쉬는 시간

> ex For many students, recess is a time to have fun.

A 적절한 내용으로 연결하세요.

> Ex (a) he or she will be mad at you
> (b) you understand what he or she is talking about
> (c) people are buying a lot of clothes
> (d) you may want to subscribe to it
> (e) lots of people will like you

1 If there is a boom in the clothing industry, _____.

2 If you are a celebrity, _____.

3 If you read an interesting editorial in a magazine, _____.

4 If you get the gist of what someone is saying, _____.

5 If you make insults about someone, _____.

B 다음에서 알맞은 표현을 고르세요.

1 Next Monday is our twentieth (anniversary, adversity).

2 Eric is interested in the (field, shield) of cognitive linguistics.

3 Affordable (house, housing) is important to everyone.

4 How can I improve my (rot, lot)?

5 As a publishing company, we are impressed by your excellent (manuscript, manicure).

Directions: Choose the one word that best fits the sentence.

1 A: How are you gonna celebrate your tenth _____?
B: I'm thinking about taking a trip to Guam.

(a) anniversary
(b) glossary
(c) necessity
(d) density

2 A: What is the _____ of his lecture?
B: Basically, he is opposed to sending troops to Iraq.

(a) germ
(b) gum
(c) guilt
(d) gist

3 A: How could you shout a(n) _____ at your own son?
B: I'm dreadfully sorry. I didn't mean to, though.

(a) consult
(b) result
(c) insult
(d) image

4 A: What are you going to do?
B: I'm afraid I have no _____ but to sell my house.

(a) consumption
(b) option
(c) adoption
(d) assumption

5 There was a _____ in the construction industry in the 1990s.

(a) room
(b) boom
(c) groom
(d) mushroom

6 _____ such as Angelina Jolie are good role models.

(a) Celebrations
(b) Miscellanies
(c) Securities
(d) Celebrities

7 The _____ of superiority can be understood in many different ways.

(a) notion
(b) lotion
(c) promotion
(d) portion

8 Many people are fascinated by the _____ of linguistics.

(a) yield
(b) pasture
(c) field
(d) meadow

UNIT 4 형용사(필수어휘)

학습포인트

TEPS에 출제되는 형용사는 cheap(값싼)처럼 매우 쉬운 단어부터 indignant(의분을 느끼는)처럼 매우 까다로운 단어까지 그 범위가 매우 다양하다. 특히 최근에는 자주 접하기 힘든 형용사까지 출제하는 경향이 있기 때문에 보다 철저한 학습이 요구된다. 우선은 출제 빈도가 높은 쉬운 단어부터 습득해야 하고, 그런 다음 풍부한 맥락과 어원 분석을 통해 고난이도의 형용사를 익히는 것이 올바른 순서다.

중요 Collocation 정리

1 annoying 짜증나게 하는 (= irritating)

ex Oz has an annoying habit of snoring in the middle of the night.

2 brief 잠깐의 (= short)

ex Try to make the meeting as brief as possible.

3 dedicated 헌신적인 (= devoted)

ex Dedicated volunteers saved thousands of lives.

4 emotional 감정적인 (≒ sensitive 예민한)

ex Emotional problems can affect your performance as a teacher.

5 fashionable 유행하는 (= trendy)

ex Miniskirts became fashionable in the 1960s.

6 genuine 진짜의, 진정한 (= authentic)

ex This bracelet is genuine silver.

7 ideal 이상적인 (↔ actual 현실의)

ex Can't you see that we are not living in an ideal world?

8   **jealous**   시샘하는 (= envious)

> ex   Every girl was jealous of her intelligence.

9   **legal**   합법적인 (= legitimate)

> ex   Is it legal to block P2P networks?

10   **minute**   미세한 (= tiny)

> ex   The microscope can show you the minute details of an object.

11   **normal**   정상적인 (↔abnormal 비정상적인)

> ex   Even crazy people can sometimes display normal behavior.

12   **optimistic**   낙관적인 (↔pessimistic 비관적인)

> ex   Many Koreans are optimistic that they can reunify their country.

13   **patient**   인내심이 강한 (↔impatient 인내심이 없는)

> ex   Be patient with yourself, and wonderful things will happen to you.

14   **reasonable**   (가격이) 적당한 (↔expensive 값비싼)

> ex   Their prices seem reasonable, I guess.

15   **sensitive**   감수성이 예민한 (≒ perceptive 지각력이 뛰어난)

> ex   Sarah was a sensitive girl who could read others' minds.

A 적절한 내용으로 연결하세요.

> Ex
> (a) your friendship is real
> (b) you can do it by law
> (c) it makes you a little angry
> (d) you believe that it will be successful
> (e) you try very hard to do it

1 If something is annoying, _____.

2 If you are dedicated to doing something, _____.

3 If you have a genuine friendship with someone, _____.

4 If something is legal, _____.

5 If you are optimistic about something, _____.

B 다음에서 알맞은 표현을 고르세요.

1 (Motionless, Emotional) health is very important in everyday life.

2 Will the (ideal, idle) world come to us in the near future?

3 It's (normal, minimal) to feel stressed from time to time.

4 It became (fascinated, fashionable) to blame the government for everything.

5 (Senseless, Sensitive) people are wise and kind.

Directions: Choose the one word that best fits the sentence.

1 A: I just can't stand Ron anymore.

B: I understand. He's a very
_____ guy.

(a) charming

(b) understanding

(c) annoying

(d) pleasing

2 A: Why are you so _____ of your
sister?

B: She has everything, but I have
nothing.

(a) modest

(b) proud

(c) jealous

(d) shy

3 A: How can you be so _____
about his game?

B: Because I know he will win.

(a) optimistic

(b) concerned

(c) humble

(d) pessimistic

4 A: I think the price is _____.

B: Are you kidding? This is too high
a price.

(a) expensive

(b) reasonable

(c) unattractive

(d) unreliable

5 In a(n) _____ encounter with her,
I learned a lot about life.

(a) arrogant

(b) innovative

(c) incorrect

(d) brief

6 Oprah Winfrey is _____ to
empowering women.

(a) dishonest

(b) dedicated

(c) uncomfortable

(d) uninterested

7 It became _____ for men to
wear earrings.

(a) fashionable

(b) committed

(c) unclear

(d) capable

8 _____ friendship can make you
strong.

(a) Feeble

(b) Genuine

(c) Cowardly

(d) Untrustworthy

학습포인트

영어에는 의미나 형태 때문에 혼동되는 단어들이 많은데, 이 가운데 일상적으로 흔히 쓰이거나 구별이 중요하기 때문에 자주 출제되는 단어들을 혼동 어휘라고 한다. 단어의 의미와 형태는 오랜 역사에 걸쳐 형성된 것으로 어근이나 의미의 확장 등을 통해 구별할 수 있는 경우가 대부분이다. 하지만 일부 어휘의 경우에는 어근이 같음에도 불구하고 용례를 통해 굳어진 경우도 있기 때문에 특히 주의를 기울여야 할 부분이다.

중요 Collocation 정리

1 **accept** 받아들이다 vs. **except** 제외하고

ex We decided to accept the proposal except its final part.
ac는 '향해서,' ex는 '밖으로, 제외해서'라는 뜻이기 때문에 차이가 생김

2 **affect** 영향을 끼치다 vs. **effect** 효과

ex The effects of smoking affect your health negatively.
af는 '향해서,' ef는 '밖으로 드러난'이라는 뜻이기 때문에 차이가 생김

3 **borrow** 빌리다 vs. **lend** 빌려주다

ex I lent the book that I had borrowed from Lindsay.
borrow에 포함된 ro가 함께 쓰이는 전치사인 from에도 들어 있음에 착안

4   **childish** 유치한   vs.   **childlike** 어린애 같은

> ex   Some writers are childlike, while others are childish.
> like가 '좋아하다'의 뜻이므로 childlike에도 '좋은'이라는 뜻이 들어 있는 것으로 생각

5   **cloth** 천   vs.   **clothes** 옷

> ex   These clothes are made of silk cloth.
> 천(cloth)이 많이 모여서 복수형인 옷(clothes)이 된다고 생각

6   **cook** 요리사   vs.   **cooker** 주방 도구

> ex   The cook is excellent at using many different cookers.
> eraser에서처럼 -er가 '도구'를 나타낼 때 많이 쓰인다는 데 착안

7   **fun** 재미있는   vs.   **funny** 우스운 (* fun activity 재미있는 활동)

> ex   Watching the funny film was a lot of fun.
> -y는 '~이 가득한'이라는 뜻으로 '재미가 가득한' 것이 '우스운' 것으로 생각

8   **steal** 훔치다   vs.   **rob** 빼앗다

> ex   The two women robbed the store and stole a lot of money.
> robber(강도)에서 보듯이 rob은 누구로부터 강제로 빼앗는다는 뜻

A 적절한 내용으로 연결하세요.

> **Ex** (a) the situation will be changed by it
> (b) you will probably go to jail
> (c) you need to return it to them
> (d) you will probably attend it
> (e) a lot of people will like your innocence

1 If you accept an invitation to a party, _____.

2 If something affects a situation, _____.

3 If you are childlike, _____.

4 If you borrow something from someone, _____.

5 If you rob a bank, _____.

B 다음에서 알맞은 표현을 고르세요.

1 The (affect, effect) of global warming may not be so great.

2 The (cloth, clothes) are really strange.

3 That (cook, cooker) knows every recipe available.

4 After (robbing, stealing) the jewelry, Juliet felt very happy.

5 The conditions are terrible. I cannot (accept, except) them.

Directions: Choose the one word that best fits the sentence.

1 A: You look upset. What happened?

   B: I think my purse was _____.

   (a) lent
   (b) robbed
   (c) borrowed
   (d) stolen

2 A: Judy, will you _____ the job offer?

   B: Actually, I'm not sure. The benefits package is not so great.

   (a) acquire
   (b) accept
   (c) exchange
   (d) acclaim

3 A: Laura, what do you think of the new _____?

   B: Well, at least, she can make good foods. That's her job, you know.

   (a) cooker
   (b) cashier
   (c) cook
   (d) bank teller

4 A: Wow, this _____ feels so soft!

   B: Yeah. I think it's silk or something.

   (a) cloth
   (b) clothes
   (c) dresses
   (d) clothings

5 Every boy is a prince _____ James.

   (a) except
   (b) excel
   (c) exceed
   (d) exercise

6 Because of her _____ innocence, everybody likes Mary Jane Watson.

   (a) childless
   (b) childproof
   (c) childlike
   (d) childed

7 Her _____ jokes always make us laugh hard.

   (a) funded
   (b) diligent
   (c) lazy
   (d) funny

8 Your happiness can greatly _____ your partner's happiness.

   (a) affect
   (b) approach
   (c) attack
   (d) assign

UNIT 6 의미(혼동어휘) Ⅱ

학습포인트

'혼동 어휘(의미)Ⅰ'에서 살펴본 바와 같이 영어에는 의미나 형태 때문에 혼동되는 단어들이 매우 많다. 단어의 쓰임새에 대한 섬세한 감각을 측정하는 TEPS의 특성 때문에 이런 어휘가 실제 시험에 출제되는 비중이 높은 편이다. 따라서 자연스러운 맥락에서 어떻게 다르게 쓰이는지를 정확히 익혀두어야만 한다. 이 단원에서는 '혼동 어휘(의미)Ⅰ'에서 다룬 것보다 다소 난이도가 높은 혼동 어휘를 정리하고자 한다.

중요 Collocation 정리

1 complement 보완하다 vs. compliment 칭찬하다

ex When they complemented each other in their work, everybody complimented them.
complement의 동의어인 complete에도 e가 두 개가 들어 있음에 착안

2 delighted 매우 기뻐하는 vs. delightful 매우 기쁘게 만드는

ex When delightful things happen to you, you are delighted.
-ed라는 형태가 '일정한 감정을 갖게 되는'이란 뜻을 나타낼 때 쓰임에 착안

3 effective 효과적인 vs. efficient 효율적인; 일에 능숙한

ex Efficient workers always work in an effective manner.
effect(ef 밖으로+ fect 만들다→효과)에서 비롯된 effective가 '효과'와 관련된 뜻을 나타낼 수밖에 없음에 착안, efficient에 '일에 능숙한'이란 뜻이 있음도 함께 기억할 것

4 **imaginary** 상상의 vs. **imaginative** 상상력이 풍부한

> ⓔⓧ Imaginative writers are good at creating imaginary creatures.
> −ative가 '만들어내는(at) 경향이 있는(ive)'을 뜻하는 접미사임에 착안, imaginary가 '현실에 존재하지 않는'을 뜻함에 유의

5 **literary** 문학의 vs. **literate** 읽고 쓸 줄 아는

> ⓔⓧ Only literate people can enjoy reading literary works.
> −ary가 '~의, ~에 속하는'을 뜻하는 접미사임에 착안

6 **object** 물체; 객체 vs. **subject** 주제; 주체

> ⓔⓧ The subject of the lecture is "On the Nature of Objects."
> ob−가 '~를 향해, ~에 거슬러서'를 뜻하는 접두사임에 착안. ject가 '던지다'를 뜻하는 어근이기 때문에 object는 결코 '주체'가 될 수 없음에 유의

7 **principle** 원리, 원칙 vs. **principal** 교장; 주요한

> ⓔⓧ Our principal respects basic principles of democracy.
> 형용사를 만드는 접미사로 쓰일 수 있는 −al과 달리 −le는 형용사를 만들 수 없음에 착안

8 **retire** 퇴직하다 vs. **resign** 사임하다

> ⓔⓧ The retired designer felt that she should have resigned earlier.
> '다시(re) 표시하다(sign)'로 분석되는 resign은 때가 되어 은퇴하는 것이 아니라 스스로 물러남을 뜻함에 착안

A 적절한 내용으로 연결하세요.

> **Ex** (a) it makes you very happy
> (b) he or she can read and write
> (c) you do not work for it anymore
> (d) you speak well of it
> (e) he or she works very well

1 If you compliment something, _____.

2 If something is delightful, _____.

3 If someone is efficient, _____.

4 If someone is literate, _____.

5 If you resign from your company, _____.

B 다음에서 알맞은 표현을 고르세요.

1 Ironically, (delighted, delightful) things can happen to bad people.

2 An (effective, efficient) worker does not waste time.

3 Dragons are (imaginary, imaginative) creatures.

4 There are many different (literate, literary) genres.

5 The (principle, principal) goal of this program is to develop character.

Directions: Choose the one word that best fits the sentence.

1 A: Mary and Sandra seem to get along.

B: Yeah. They really _____ each other.

(a) complement

(b) compare

(c) compete

(d) complain

2 A: Why are you so _____?

B: Because I'm going to be a father.

(a) delicious

(b) dismissed

(c) disobedient

(d) delighted

3 A: Everybody says Marianne is a(n) _____ secretary.

B: Yep. She knows what she is doing.

(a) inattentive

(b) arrogant

(c) efficient

(d) furious

4 A: I'm thinking about _____ from the company.

B: What? You see, you've been a great asset to our company.

(a) dismissing

(b) resigning

(c) applying

(d) residing

5 Abortion is still a debated _____.

(a) object

(b) project

(c) subject

(d) injection

6 _____ people are good at coming up with creative solutions.

(a) Imaginary

(b) Imagined

(c) Imaginable

(d) Imaginative

7 Respect for others is a basic _____ of democracy.

(a) principle

(b) principal

(c) probability

(d) prohibition

8 _____ people can achieve much more than those who can't read.

(a) Literal

(b) Literate

(c) Irrational

(d) Ironic

학습포인트

영어에는 형태가 비슷한 단어들이 많이 있는데, 이들은 어근이 같은 경우도 있고 전혀 다른 경우도 있다. 특히 철자가 약간 다르면서 완전히 다른 뜻을 나타내는 단어들을 정확히 익혀둘 필요가 있다. 이 단원에서 제시하는 도움말을 참고하면서 자연스러운 맥락에서 어떻게 쓰이는가를 파악해야 한다. 그리고 Encarta World English Dictionary(http://dictionary.msn.com)와 같은 자료를 통해 어근을 정확히 확인하는 습관을 들이는 것도 좋다.

중요 Collocation 정리

1 command 명령하다, 지휘하다 **vs. commend** 칭찬하다

ex When Bill commanded the team very well, everybody commended him.
익숙한 단어인 recommend가 '다시(re) 칭찬하다(commend)'로 분석됨에 착안

2 conscious 의식하는 **vs. conscientious** 양심적인

ex Conscientious people are conscious of moral values.
conscious가 '완전히(con) 아는(sic) 것으로 가득한(ous)'으로 분석됨에 착안

3 economic 경제와 관련된 **vs. economical** 허비하지 않는

ex Economic thinking can lead to an economical way of life.
익숙한 단어인 economics가 '경제학'이어서 economic과 연결됨에 착안

4 **personal** 개인적인 VS. **personnel** 직원 전체

> ex All personnel can be affected by personal matters.
> personnel에 n이 두 번 들어가서 여러 사람이 된다고 연상

5 **physician** 의사 VS. **physicist** 물리학자

> ex The physicist criticized the physician's wrong practice.
> 의사를 뜻하는 다른 말인 surgeon이 physician과 똑같이 n으로 끝남에 착안

6 **produce** 농산물 VS. **product** 제품

> ex Produce includes many different types of agricultural products.
> 제품(product)은 t가 들어 있는 factory에서 만들어진다는 데 착안

7 **reward** 보상, 보수 VS. **award** 상

> ex Awards can be regarded as a kind of reward.
> '완전히(re) 보살피는 것(ward)'이 제대로 된 '보상(reward)'이라는 데 착안

8 **rise** 오르다 VS. **raise** 올리다

> ex When you raise something, it rises.
> raise의 발음에서 '에'와 '올리다'의 '리'를 결합하여 '에리카'로 기억

EXERCISE

• 정답 및 해설 p.90

A 적절한 내용으로 연결하세요.

> **Ex**
> (a) it does not fall
> (b) you know that it exists
> (c) you treat patients
> (d) he or she will become happy
> (e) it affects only you

1 If you commend someone, _____.

2 If you are conscious of something, _____.

3 If you have a personal problem, _____.

4 If you are a physician, _____.

5 If something rises, _____.

B 다음에서 알맞은 표현을 고르세요.

1 Rachel (recommended, commanded) her students to clean the classroom.

2 (Scientific, Conscientious) people do not lie.

3 Many (products, produces) are poorly made.

4 (Economical, Economic) growth is important to every country.

5 They attended the Academy (Awards, Reward) ceremony.

Directions: Choose the one word that best fits the sentence.

1 A: His presentation was terrible!

B: Well, I thought he _____ an important question.

(a) rose

(b) fell

(c) felled

(d) raised

2 A: Congratulations! I heard you won the _____ for best speech.

B: Thanks. I just did my best.

(a) reward

(b) regard

(c) guard

(d) award

3 A: What does your mother do?

B: She is a _____, working at Boston Hospital.

(a) physician

(b) physicist

(c) musician

(d) magician

4 A: Can I ask you a _____ question?

B: Of course! What do you wanna know about me?

(a) personnel

(b) personal

(c) seasonal

(d) national

5 _____ development can be discouraged by political uncertainty.

(a) Atomic

(b) Economic

(c) Comic

(d) Automatic

6 _____ people wouldn't steal anything.

(a) Scientific

(b) Consequent

(c) Conscientious

(d) Economical

7 It is really a good book. It has a lot to _____ it.

(a) command

(b) commit

(c) commend

(d) comment

8 The company is famous for its quality _____.

(a) products

(b) produces

(c) conducts

(d) refuses

Chapter 3

구동사와 숙어

UNIT 1   동사와 particle의 결합(구동사)Ⅰ

UNIT 2   동사와 particle의 결합(구동사)Ⅱ

UNIT 3   숙어Ⅰ

UNIT 4   숙어Ⅱ

UNIT 1 동사와 particle의 결합(구동사) I

학습포인트

'구동사'란 make up과 같이 동사(make)와 particle(up)이 결합하여 일정한 뜻을 나타내는 표현을 가리킨다. 이때 particle이 구동사의 보다 중심적인 뜻을 나타낸다는 데 주목할 필요가 있다. particle은 본래의 기본적인 뜻을 나타낼 수도 있고 (up은 '위에') 기본적인 뜻에서 발전한 다른 뜻을 (up이 '완전히') 나타낼 수도 있다. 이처럼 particle의 뜻이 확장되는 것은 기본적인 의미가 비유적으로 ('위에'는 완전한 '하늘'을 가리키므로) 해석될 수 있기 때문이다.

중요 Collocation 정리

1 account for 설명하다 (= explain; for는 '이유를 밝혀'라는 뜻)

> **ex** Nothing can account for his crazy behavior.

2 break down 고장 나다 (= fail; down은 '부정적인 상태로'라는 뜻)

> **ex** My PSP broke down and I couldn't watch any movies.

3 break up (이성끼리) 갈라서다 (= split up; up은 '완전히'라는 뜻)

> **ex** After seven years of fighting, the couple finally broke up.

4 bring up 양육하다 (= raise; up은 '보다 상위의 상태로'라는 뜻)

> **ex** In fact, Britney Spears was brought up in a traditional way.

5 come across (우연히) 마주치다 (= encounter; across는 '찾아내어'라는 뜻)

> **ex** I came across an unpleasant article about Korea in The Economist.

6 deal with 다루다 (= handle; with은 '관여하여'라는 뜻)

> **ex** We need to deal with the issue of teenage smoking.

7 **depend on** 의존하다 (=rely on; on은 '의지하여'라는 뜻)

ex In fact, success depends on creativity.

8 **do without** ~없이 지내다 (=go without; without은 '~없이'라는 뜻)

ex We can't do without air for more than four minutes.

9 **fall on** (기념일 등이 어떤 날에) 해당하다 (on은 '접촉하여'라는 뜻)

ex Christmas falls on a Tuesday this year.

10 **figure out** 이해하다 (=understand; out은 '찾아서 드러내는'라는 뜻)

ex I still can't figure out what the boring teacher told me.

11 **go off** (자명종 등이) 울리다 (off는 '떼어내어 나타내는'이라는 뜻)

ex Oh my God! This stupid alarm clock was supposed to go off at six!

12 **hand in** (과제 등을) 제출하다 (=submit; in은 '수합하도록'이라는 뜻)

ex If you don't hand in an assignment on time, the professor will go mad.

13 **hang up** (전화를) 끊다 (up은 '완료하여'라는 뜻)

ex Buffy rudely hung up the phone without saying goodbye.

14 **look forward to** 고대하다 (forward는 '시간적으로 앞서서'라는 뜻)

ex We're looking forward to seeing you in person.

15 **make up** 구성하다; 화해하다 (up은 '완전히'라는 뜻)

ex Air is made up of several gases.

A 적절한 내용으로 연결하세요.

> **Ex** (a) you meet them by chance
> (b) you are excited about meeting them
> (c) you cannot succeed without it
> (d) that is the reason why they behave in a particular way
> (e) your relationship with them ends

1 If something accounts for someone's behavior, _____.

2 If you break up with someone, _____.

3 If you come across someone, _____.

4 If your success depends on something, _____.

5 If you are looking forward to meeting someone, _____.

B 다음에서 알맞은 표현을 고르세요.

1 Her birthday falls (on, off) a Sunday this year.

2 A good teacher tries to figure (in, out) his or her students' behavior.

3 Matter is made (up, down) of atoms.

4 Unfortunately, her car broke (down, up) in the middle of the road.

5 We can do (with, without) water for several days.

Directions: Choose the one word that best fits the sentence.

1 A: Alice looked so sad.

B: Oh, didn't you know she _____ up with her boyfriend?

(a) made

(b) grew

(c) broke

(d) called

2 A: How can you _____ for this stupid mistake?

B: Well, I'm only human, you know.

(a) account

(b) allow

(c) fall

(d) make

3 A: I'm looking _____ to visiting Togo next week.

B: Well, I don't think the country is a nice place to visit.

(a) backward

(b) downward

(c) forward

(d) toward

4 A: When are you going to _____ up with Jessica?

B: Just drop the subject. I don't want to talk about it anymore.

(a) bring

(b) hang

(c) come

(d) make

5 He _____ across a one-hundred-dollar bill and went to the police station.

(a) got

(b) came

(c) put

(d) sent

6 Our country's future _____ on our children.

(a) feeds

(b) goes

(c) carries

(d) depends

7 We need to _____ with the matter immediately.

(a) live

(b) stay

(c) deal

(d) go

8 Unfortunately, many adults have been _____ up badly.

(a) added

(b) shown

(c) brought

(d) dug

UNIT 2 — 동사와 particle의 결합(구동사) Ⅱ

학습포인트

particle이 의미 중심을 이루는 구동사의 출제 비중은 숙어에 비해 높은 편이다. 숙어가 전혀 출제되지 않은 적도 있지만 구동사가 출제되지 않은 적은 없다. 이는 구동사가 격식체와 비격식체에 걸쳐 폭넓게 쓰이기 때문이다. 따라서 자주 접하게 되는 구동사의 뜻을 particle을 중심으로 정확히 익혀두어야 한다. 이 단원에서는 지난 단원에 이어 중요한 구동사들을 정리한다.

중요 Collocation 정리

1 mark down 할인하다 (=reduce; down은 '낮추어'라는 뜻)

ⓔⓧ The price has been marked down many times!

2 mess up 망치다 (=ruin; up은 '완전히'라는 뜻)

ⓔⓧ You can mess up your life by drinking a lot.

3 pass away 사망하다 (=die; away는 '사라져서'라는 뜻)

ⓔⓧ When his father passed away, Eric was beside himself with sadness.

4 pass down 물려주다 (=hand down; down은 '아래로'라는 뜻)

ⓔⓧ The recipe had been passed down from generation to generation.

5 pay off (결국엔) 득이 되다 (=bear fruit; off는 '완전히'라는 뜻)

ⓔⓧ Her efforts paid off and she made a lot of money.

6 pick up (기술 등을) 익히다 (=grasp; up은 '늘어나서'라는 뜻)

ⓔⓧ Try to pick up the rhythm of English.

7 pull over (도로변에) 차를 세우다 (over는 '가로질러'라는 뜻)

ⓔⓧ I was so surprised when Sandra suddenly pulled the car over.

8   **rely on**   의지하다 (=depend on; on은 '의지하여'라는 뜻)

    ⓔ&ⓧ   Many Asians rely on meditation for comfort.

9   **run out of**   ~이 다 떨어지다 (out of는 '사라져서'라는 뜻)

    ⓔ&ⓧ   Unfortunately, Cindy was running out of strength.

10   **see off**   배웅하다 (=wave off; off는 '끝마쳐서'라는 뜻)

    ⓔ&ⓧ   Amy went to the train station to see her boyfriend off.

11   **set up**   설립하다 (=establish; up은 '합쳐서'라는 뜻)

    ⓔ&ⓧ   My dream is to set up an organization that helps the poor.

12   **show off**   과시하다 (=boast; off는 '드러내어'라는 뜻)

    ⓔ&ⓧ   Too many actors show off their expensive clothes.

13   **take in**   (정보 등을) 흡수하다 (=absorb; in은 '흡수하여'라는 뜻)

    ⓔ&ⓧ   Try to take in knowledge from a variety of sources.

14   **throw up**   토하다 (=vomit; up은 '위로'라는 뜻)

    ⓔ&ⓧ   Drew threw up all night last night.

15   **turn down**   (제의 등을) 거절하다 (=reject; down은 '완전히'라는 뜻)

    ⓔ&ⓧ   That was too good an offer to turn down.

A 적절한 내용으로 연결하세요.

Ex
(a) you will feel sad
(b) you stop it
(c) it becomes cheaper
(d) you trust them
(e) you will succeed

1 If the price of something is marked down, _____.

2 If a friend of yours passes away, _____.

3 If your hard work pays off, _____.

4 If you pull over your car, _____.

5 If you rely on someone, _____.

B 다음에서 알맞은 표현을 고르세요.

1 You can (show, mess) up your life by making friends with bad people.

2 In fact, they were (running, growing) out of patience.

3 We (saw, called) our guests off at the airport.

4 Try not to (turn, show) off your ability.

5 It was stupid of you to (turn, settle) down the offer.

Directions: Choose the one word that best fits the sentence.

1 A: Do you know why Jessica was absent from work today?

B: Her grandfather _____ away last night.

(a) explained
(b) passed
(c) gave
(d) threw

2 A: Hurry up! We're _____ out of time.

B: Don't be so pushy. We do have some time.

(a) running
(b) figuring
(c) breaking
(d) working

3 A: Where did you learn the recipe?

B: Oh, it has been _____ down from my grandmother.

(a) broken
(b) cut
(c) passed
(d) fallen

4 A: How was your trip to Montreal?

B: Fantastic. I also _____ up some French.

(a) broke
(b) made
(c) let
(d) picked

5 Too many people _____ up their lives by pursuing money.

(a) show
(b) look
(c) bring
(d) mess

6 Brian's hard work _____ off and was promoted to Vice President.

(a) went
(b) paid
(c) let
(d) laid

7 Many language experts _____ on Oxford English Dictionary for reference.

(a) rely
(b) put
(c) go
(d) live

8 Rebecca _____ down the temptation to join the club.

(a) let
(b) marked
(c) turned
(d) wrote

UNIT 3 숙어 I

학습포인트

숙어는 일정한 단어들이 조합하여 본래의 뜻과는 다른 뜻을 나타내는 표현을 말한다. 대개 일정한 유래가 있어서 특정한 뜻을 표현하므로, 유래를 알아두는 것이 숙어의 뜻을 이해하는 데 도움이 된다. 그렇지만 숙어가 쓰이는 자연스러운 맥락을 함께 익혀두어야, 숙어 문제에 제대로 대비할 수 있음을 기억하자. 이는 물론 다른 표현 형식에 대해서도 마찬가지임을 명심하자.

중요 Collocation 정리

1 **a hidden agenda** 숨은 의도 ('의제'를 뜻하는 agenda의 의미에서 유래)

ex Just enjoy your stay here. There's no hidden agenda.

2 **turn one's back on someone** 저버리다 ('등을 돌리다'라는 의미에서 유래)

ex How could you turn your back on your closest friend?

3 **out of the blue** 예고 없이, 돌연히 ('푸른 하늘에서' 물체가 갑자기 떨어진다는 비유에서 유래)

ex To my great surprise, the yellow bus came out of the blue.

4 **beat around the bush** 말을 둘러대다 (사냥감을 찾아 관목 주위를 두드리는 관습에서 유래)

ex Don't beat around the bush! Just tell me the truth!

5 **a cash cow** (믿을만한) 수익의 원천 (젖소가 우유를 만들어내는 데서 유래)

ex In fact, Madonna was a cash cow, bringing in billions of dollars.

6 **shed crocodile tears** 동정하는 체하다 (악어가 먹이를 먹으면서 눈물을 흘린다는 잘못된 믿음에서 유래)

ex Some politicians shed crocodile tears over the terrible situation.

7 **the die is cast** 결정은 이미 내려졌다 (주사위를 던짐에 비유)

ex The die is cast and we're ready to fight to the finish.

8 **a lame duck** 임기 말 정치인 또는 정부 (본래 빚을 갚지 못하는 증권 중개인을 뜻했음)

ex Being a lame duck, the President had no influence over his country.

9 **play it by ear** (계획 없이) 상황에 따라 처리하다 (악보 없이 연주하는 데서)

ex Because she was so smart, Casandra was good at playing it by ear.

10 **make ends meet** 겨우 살아갈 정도의 수입만 있다
(연간 회계에서 수입과 지출을 맞추는 데서 유래했다고 보는 것이 일반적)

ex In fact, they had difficulty making ends meet.

11 **lose face** 체면을 잃다 ('침착한 척 하는 표정을 잃다'라는 뜻에서 유래)

ex He did not want to lose face in front of his children.

12 **as fit as a fiddle** 매우 건강한 ('바이올린 연주자의 좋은 건강 상태'를 뜻하는 데서 유래했다고 보는 것이 보통)

ex Many people mistakenly believe that they are as fit as a fiddle.

13 **a small fortune** 거액 ('막대한 부'를 뜻하는 fortune의 의미에서 유래)

ex Logan made a small fortune working for millionaires.

14 **the glass ceiling** (여성 등의) 고위직 진입 장벽 ('보이지 않는 한계'라는 의미에서 유래)

ex Unfortunately, the glass ceiling still exists in America.

15 **be Greek to someone** 전혀 알아듣지 못하다
(그리스어가 어려운 언어라는 믿음에서 유래했다고 보는 것이 일반적)

ex Molecular biology? It's all Greek to me.

• 정답 및 해설 p.95

EXERCISE

A 적절한 내용으로 연결하세요.

> **Ex** (a) you do not tell the truth
> (b) you have a secret purpose for doing something
> (c) you are not sincere
> (d) people will not respect you
> (e) you no longer help them

1 If you have a hidden agenda, _____.

2 If you turn your back on someone, _____.

3 If you beat around the bush, _____.

4 If you shed crocodile tears, _____.

5 If you lose face, _____.

B 다음에서 알맞은 표현을 고르세요.

1 Cognitive linguistics? It's all (Latin, Greek) to me.

2 The big bear appeared out of the (red, blue).

3 The (die, dye) is cast and there is no turning back.

4 We have no choice but to play it by (ear, eye).

5 Although she is eighty, she is as fit as a (violin, fiddle).

• 정답 및 해설 p.96

Directions: Choose the one word that best fits the sentence.

1 A: I think you have a _____.

B: What are you talking about? I'm just trying to help you.

(a) hidden agenda

(b) bad apple

(c) last straw

(d) stitch in time

2 A: I'm sick and tired of your

_____.

B: Well, at least, I didn't hurt your feelings.

(a) packing your bags

(b) tightening your belt

(c) beating around the bush

(d) fitting the bill

3 A: That stupid politician _____ again!

B: Perhaps, she expressed her sincere feelings.

(a) kicked the bucket

(b) got even

(c) got the picture

(d) shed crocodile tears

4 A: Do you know how to use the new software?

B: I read the manual, but it's all _____ to me.

(a) French

(b) Greek

(c) Spanish

(d) Italian

5 The accident happened _____.

(a) on the tip of its tongue

(b) out of the blue

(c) off the record

(d) in the red

6 So, we have no scripts to follow? OK, we'll _____.

(a) play it by ear

(b) bear fruit

(c) go Dutch

(d) make the grade

7 Noah _____ when his scandal broke.

(a) burnt the midnight oil

(b) hit the nail on the head

(c) sold like hot cakes

(d) lost face

8 That fancy car would cost a _____ to buy.

(a) gray area

(b) close call

(c) white lie

(d) small fortune

UNIT 4 숙어 II

학습포인트

숙어의 출제 비중은 시험에 따라 다소 차이를 보인다. 드문 경우이긴 하지만, 숙어가 한 문제도 출제되지 않을 때도 있다. 반면 숙어가 세 문제 정도까지 출제될 때도 있다. 이처럼 숙어의 출제 비중이 구동사의 경우처럼 일정하지 않기 때문에, 숙어 학습을 경시할 수도 있는데, 안정적인 점수나 고득점을 확보하기 위해서는 숙어도 정확히 익혀두어야 한다.

중요 Collocation 정리

1 in seventh heaven 더할 나위 없이 행복한

(하나님이 7번째 천국에 머물고 있다는 믿음에서 유래)

> **ex** When she won first prize, Amy was in seventh heaven.

2 break the ice 어색한 분위기를 깨뜨리다 (배의 운항을 위해 얼음을 깨는 관습에서 유래)

> **ex** Greg tried to break the ice with funny jokes.

3 tie the knot 결혼하다 (결혼식에서 매듭을 짓는 관습에서 유래)

> **ex** Juliet tied the knot with Romeo last year.

4 to the letter (지극히) 정확하게 ('글자'라는 letter의 의미에서 유래)

> **ex** It would be better to follow her advice to the letter.

5 give the green light (실행을) 허락하다 ('청신호'라는 의미에서 유래)

> **ex** They were given the green light to build a new bridge.

6 run-of-the-mill 평범한 ('제작소에서 바로 짜낸 직물'을 뜻하는 데서 유래했다고 보는 것이 보통)

> **ex** Susan Smith is just a run-of-the-mill kind of person.

7 neck and neck 막상막하의 (경마에서 말들의 목이 나란히 놓이는 것에서 유래)

> **ex** Surprisingly, both candidates are running neck and neck.

8 **an olive branch** 화해 제스처 (비둘기가 올리브 가지를 물고 왔다는 성경 구절에서 유래)

ex We should not accept the olive branch offered by the bad guys.

9 **part and parcel** 핵심적인 요소 ('중요한 부분들'이라는 의미에서 유래)

ex Clarity is part and parcel of good writing.

10 **keep a low profile** 대중의 시선을 끌지 않다 ('드러나는 윤곽'이라는 profile의 의미에서 유래)

ex Despite being a supermodel, Christie tried to keep a low profile.

11 **see red** 격분하다 (빨간 색이 분노를 상징한다고 보는 것이 일반적)

ex His rude remarks made many people see red.

12 **a rule of thumb** 경험칙, 대략적인 방법 (엄지로 측정하는 데서 유래)

ex As a rule of thumb, ask yourself whether a ten-year-old would understand your explanation.

13 **a long shot** 가능성이 희박한 일 (초기 화기가 사격이 제대로 되지 않는 데서 유래)

ex Sending people to Mars? It is such a long shot.

14 **pick up the tab** 비용을 치르다 ('계산서를 집어 들다'는 의미에서 유래)

ex It was his turn to pick up the tab for lunch.

15 **a wake-up call** 관심을 촉발하는 일 ('모닝콜'이라는 의미에서 유래)

ex The incident was a wake-up call to the staff.

• 정답 및 해설 p.97

A 적절한 내용으로 연결하세요.

> **Ex**
> (a) you do not work excellently
> (b) people will feel more comfortable
> (c) it is essential for success
> (d) you get married to him or her
> (e) people will not notice you

1 If you break the ice, _____.

2 If you tie the knot with someone, _____.

3 If you are a run-of-the-mill worker, _____.

4 If you keep a low profile, _____.

5 If something is part and parcel of success, _____.

B 다음에서 알맞은 표현을 고르세요.

1 When I heard the news, I was in (sixth, seventh) heaven.

2 It would be wise to follow the order to the (letter, sound).

3 Her impolite behavior made him see (green, red).

4 Curing the disease is a (long, short) shot. It is almost impossible.

5 This is my treat. I'll pick up the (cab, tab).

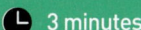
Directions: Choose the one word that best fits the sentence.

1 A: How did you _____?

B: Ah, I just cracked a funny joke and we laughed hard.

(a) lose heart

(b) live from hand to mouth

(c) break the ice

(d) stick to your guns

2 A: I'm planning to earn $1 million this year.

B: That would be a _____.

(a) big fish

(b) green thumb

(c) red tape

(d) long shot

3 A: Congratulations! I heard you're getting married.

B: Thanks. I'm _____.

(a) in seventh heaven

(b) just around the corner

(c) all ears

(d) a full-time job

4 A: I'll _____ for dinner tonight.

B: What's the occasion?

(a) pick up the tab

(b) keep up with the Joneses

(c) blow the lid off

(d) call you names

5 Difficulty is _____ of life.

(a) the dos and don'ts

(b) the melting pot

(c) the real McCoy

(d) part and parcel

6 Because we respected him deeply, we followed his order _____.

(a) on cloud nine

(b) under the weather

(c) to the letter

(d) at a snail's pace

7 His rude behavior made us _____.

(a) follow suit

(b) see red

(c) lend him a hand

(d) bury the hatchet

8 After dating for one month, they decided to _____.

(a) tie the knot

(b) get the hang of it

(c) let off steam

(d) add insult to injury

Chapter 4

고급 어휘

UNIT 1   고급 어휘 I

UNIT 2   고급 어휘 II

UNIT 3   고급 어휘 III

UNIT 4   고급 어휘 IV

UNIT 5   고급 어휘 V

UNIT 1 고급 어휘 I

학습포인트

영어의 어휘는 크게 순수영어 계열과 라틴어 계열로 나뉘는데, 이 가운데 라틴어 계열에 속하는 어휘 중 사용 빈도가 높은 어휘를 고급 어휘라고 하여 TEPS에서 비중 있게 출제된다. 고급 어휘가 난이도가 높기 하지만, 순수영어 계열 어휘와 마찬가지로 언제나 어원 분석이 가능하다는 점을 최대한 활용하고 자연스러운 맥락을 통해 익혀 나간다면 쉽고 보다 효율적인 학습이 가능하다. 이를 위해 http://dictionary.msn.com과 같은 자료를 자주 이용하자.

중요 Collocation 정리

1 abuse 남용; 학대 [ab(잘못) + use(사용) → 잘못 사용하는 것]

ex To our surprise, their children were arrested for substance abuse.

2 accurate 정확한 [(ac(향해) + cur(신경 쓰다) + ate(~된) → ~를 향해 신경을 쓴]

ex Good teachers provide accurate knowledge to their students.

3 adapt 적응시키다 [ad(향해) + apt(알맞은) → ~를 향해 알맞게 만들다]

ex They had great difficulty adapting themselves to city life.

4 affection 애정 [af(향해) + fect(만들다) + ion(~한 것) → ~를 향해 만든 감정]

ex Fred had a deep affection for his frog.

5 aspect 측면 [a(향해) + spect(보다) → ~를 향해 본 것]

ex The novel explores every aspect of her life.

6 asset 자산 [as(향해) + set(충분한) → 충분한 것을 향한 것들]

ex The efficient secretary was a great asset to the company.

7 bankrupt 파산한 [bank(탁자) + rupt(부서진) → 탁자가 부서진, 빚을 못 갚는]

ex Even a rich person can go bankrupt.

8 **benefit** 이익 [bene(잘) + fit(하다) → 잘 하는 것]

ex We should provide the greatest benefit for the greatest number of people.

9 **broaden** 넓히다 [broad(넓은) + en(만들다) → 넓게 만들다]

ex Travel can broaden your horizons.

10 **cautious** 조심하는 [caut(주의하다) + i(연결모음) + ous(가득한) → 주의로 가득한]

ex Be extremely cautious about choosing friends.

11 **circumstance** 주위 상황 [circum(둘레에) + stance(서 있는 것) → 주위에 서 있는 것]

ex That was the best thing to do under the circumstances.

12 **command** 명령하다 [com(완전히) + mand(명령하다)]

ex The priest commanded the evil spirit to come out of the victim.

13 **decrease** 감소하다 [de(아래로) + crease(자라다) → 아래로 자라다]

ex The popularity of MP3 players decreased.

14 **durable** 견고한 [dur(지속되다) + able(할 수 있는) → 지속될 수 있는]

ex It is a well-known fact that diamonds are quite durable.

15 **describe** 묘사하다 [de(아래로) + scribe(쓰다) → 아래에 쓰다]

ex Describe your feelings about your country.

• 정답 및 해설 p.99

A 적절한 내용으로 연결하세요.

> **Ex**
> (a) you have no money
> (b) you try to avoid danger
> (c) it is correct
> (d) it can last for a long time
> (e) you can live happily in it

1   If something is accurate, _____.

2   If you adapt yourself to a new environment, _____.

3   If you are bankrupt, _____.

4   If you are cautious, _____.

5   If something is durable, _____.

B 다음에서 알맞은 표현을 고르세요.

1   In fact, substance (abuse, reuse) is a serious crime.

2   What (respect, aspect) of her do you like best?

3   What would you do under such (circumstances, instances)?

4   The parents (commended, commanded) their children to be quiet.

5   Oil prices (included, decreased) by 7.7% last year.

Directions: Choose the one word that best fits the sentence.

1 A: Why is Xena so mean to her own daughter?

B: She has no _____ for her, you know.

(a) attention

(b) affection

(c) hatred

(d) distrust

2 A: Why was Daniel arrested?

B: He was suspected of child _____.

(a) clause

(b) cause

(c) abuse

(d) louse

3 A: I'm so excited about tomorrow's camping trip.

B: Be extremely _____! The weather can turn dangerous.

(a) delicious

(b) ambitious

(c) curious

(d) cautious

4 A: Can you lend me some money?

B: Oh, didn't I tell you I'm _____?

(a) corrupt

(b) bankrupt

(c) healthy

(d) exhausted

5 Because she is so efficient, Maria is a great _____ to our company.

(a) repression

(b) aggression

(c) asset

(d) regression

6 To build a strong house, we need _____ materials.

(a) durable

(b) independent

(c) faulty

(d) weak

7 In order to survive in the information age, you need _____ information.

(a) impolite

(b) accurate

(c) diligent

(d) tough

8 Many men have difficulty _____ their emotions.

(a) subscribing

(b) prescribing

(c) describing

(d) transcribing

UNIT 2 고급 어휘 II

학습포인트

'고급 어휘 I'에서 살펴본 바와 같이 고급 어휘는 대체로 라틴어 계열에 속하는데, 그리스어나 프랑스어에서 유래한 경우도 있다. TEPS가 시행되던 초기에는 고급 어휘의 범위가 일정하게 한정되어 있었는데 반해, 근래에는 고급 어휘의 범위가 점차 확대되고 있다. 따라서 다양한 영어 지문을 통해 고급 어휘가 어떻게 실제로 활용되는지를 익히고 또한 어원 분석을 최대한 활용하려는 노력이 긴요하다.

중요 Collocation 정리

1 educate 교육하다 [e(밖으로)+duc(이끌다)+ate(만들다) → 밖으로 이끌어내다]

> **ex** Mary dedicated herself to educating poor children.

2 elaborate 정교한 [e(밖으로)+labor(일)+ate(만들어낸) → 일해서 만들어낸]

> **ex** Ironically, elaborate plans often fail for simple reasons.

3 enormous 막대한 [e(밖으로)+norm(규칙)+ous(가득한) → 규칙에서 벗어난]

> **ex** The boys were so hungry that they ate an enormous pizza.

4 establish 설립하다 [e(밖으로)+stabl(안정된)+ish(만들다) → 안정되게 만들다]

> **ex** The orphanage was established in 1777.

5 facilitate 촉진하다 [facil(쉬운)+it(하게 된)+ate(만들다) → 쉽게 만들다]

> **ex** The role of a nurse is to facilitate healing.

6 familiar 익숙한 [famili(가족)+ar(~의) → 가족처럼 익숙한]

> **ex** Not many people are familiar with the subject of faith healing.

7 fictional 가공의 [fict(만들다)+ion(~한 것)+al(~의) → 만들어낸 것의]

> **ex** Harry Potter is a fictional character.

8 **finalize** 마무리하다 [fin(끝) + al(~의) + ize(만들다) → 끝으로 만들다]

ex Jim finalized his divorce and married another woman.

9 **frequent** 자주 들르다 [frequ(채워 넣다) + ent(하고 있는) → 채워 넣고 있다]

ex The graveyard was frequented by vampires.

10 **generous** 후하게 베푸는 [gener(고결한 태생의) + ous(가득한) → 고결하게 태어난]

ex Susie is a generous woman willing to help anybody in need.

11 **gradual** 점진적인 [grad(단계) + u(연결모음) + al(~의) → 단계의]

ex The process of learning a foreign language is a gradual one.

12 **guarantee** 보증하다 (guar(보호하다) + ant(하고 있는) + ee(하는 이) → 보호하는 것)

ex This book can guarantee higher scores on the TEPS tests.

13 **habitat** 서식지 [hab(가지다) + it(~된) + at(~한 것) → 가지게 된 것]

ex A pond is its natural habitat.

14 **hostile** 적대적인 [host(적) + ile(~와 관련된) → 적과 관련된]

ex How can we survive in this hostile world?

15 **humane** 자비로운 [hum(사람) + ane(~에 특징적인) → 사람에 특징적인]

ex Korean teachers should treat their students in a more humane way.

A 적절한 내용으로 연결하세요.

> **Ex**
> (a) it is formed
> (b) you know it very well
> (c) they learn from you
> (d) you complete it
> (e) it is extremely large

1 If you educate someone, _____.

2 If something is enormous, _____.

3 If you establish an organization, _____.

4 If you are familiar with something, _____.

5 If you finalize a process, _____.

B 다음에서 알맞은 표현을 고르세요.

1 A language teacher should (facilitate, block) the process of learning language.

2 The church was (frozen, frequented) by religious people.

3 A (genetic, generous) teacher is willing to help his or her students.

4 We're doing everything in our power to protect its (habitat, habit).

5 The United States is (hostile, horrific) toward immigrants.

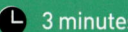
Directions: Choose the one word that best fits the sentence.

1 A: You look _____ to me!

B: Can't you remember that we met at the conference?

(a) false

(b) familiar

(c) fancy

(d) fanatic

2 A: That store is being _____ by rich ladies.

B: The owner must be laughing all the way to the bank.

(a) freshened

(b) freed

(c) frightened

(d) frequented

3 A: When will you complete the plan?

B: We're going to _____ it by the end of the month.

(a) commence

(b) cease

(c) finalize

(d) launch

4 A: Can you tell me the history of the museum?

B: It was _____ in 1789 and renovated in 2002.

(a) estimated

(b) escaped

(c) established

(d) escorted

5 We need to _____ men about women's rights.

(a) educate

(b) edit

(c) endure

(d) enjoy

6 There are many ways to _____ the process of learning new words.

(a) facilitate

(b) faint

(c) fade

(d) fake

7 It was _____ of Susan to help Tom overcome the difficulties.

(a) mean

(b) famous

(c) furious

(d) generous

8 Many animal rights groups are asking for a more _____ treatment of cows.

(a) cruel

(b) humane

(c) hostile

(d) violent

UNIT 3 고급 어휘 Ⅲ

학습포인트

흔히 로망스어(Romance languages)로 분류되는 프랑스어나 에스파냐어 등은 라틴어에서 유래했는데, 이들 언어가 라틴어의 문법적 요소를 일부 수용한 반면 영어는 고급 어휘의 어원으로 받아들였다. 이 과정에서 라틴어에서 쓰이는 -are, -ere와 같은 요소가 없어졌다는 점에 주목할 필요가 있다. 영영사전에는 대개 이와 같은 요소가 들어 있는 본래 형태로 제시되어 있기 때문에, 어원을 재구성할 때 이런 요소를 제외해야 함도 알아두자.

중요 Collocation 정리

1 **identity** 정체성; 동일성 [ident(같게 된) + ity(상태) → 같게 된 상태]

ex It is difficult to form a healthy sense of identity.

2 **ignorance** 무지(無知) [i(아닌) + gnor(알다) + ance(하는 것) → 알지 못하는 것]

ex I was disappointed with their ignorance of their own tradition.

3 **illusion** 환상 [il(안으로) + lus(장난치다) + ion(하는 것) → 안으로 장난치는 것]

ex It is an illusion that money can buy anything.

4 **immersion** 몰입 [im(안으로) + mers(담그다) + ion(하는 것) → 안으로 담그는 것]

ex Total immersion in your work can lead to success.

5 **infuriate** 격분시키다 [in(안으로) + furi(분노) + ate(만들다) → 분노하게 만들다]

ex It infuriated us that our country had been insulted like that.

6 **instruction** 교습, 교육 [in(안으로)+struct(쌓다) + ion(하는 것) → 안으로 쌓는 것]

ex The language school provides basic instruction in Tagalog.

7 **integrity** 인격적 완결성 [integr(온전한) + ity(상태)]

ex You can trust Ethan. He is a man of integrity.

8 isolation 격리; 고립 [isol(섬) + at(e)(만들다) + ion(것) → 섬으로 만드는 것]

ex Naturally shy, Joseph preferred to live in isolation.

9 jeopardy 위험 [jeo(퍼즐)+pard(나누다)+y(상태) → 퍼즐처럼 나누어진 상태]

ex His poor decision put our lives in jeopardy.

10 kinship 친밀감; 친족 관계 [kin(친척)+ship(상태) → 친척인 상태]

ex Growing up in the same village, Nicole felt kinship with Naomi.

11 laudable 칭찬할 만한 [laud(칭찬하다) + able(할 수 있는) → 칭찬할 수 있는}

ex It was laudable of her to take care of her younger sisters.

12 legitimate 적법한 [legitim(합법적인) + ate(만들다) → 합법적이 되게 하다]

ex It is not legitimate to have an affair with a married woman.

13 linguistic 언어의 [lingu(언어) + ist(~의) + ic(~적인) → 언어의]

ex Scientists cannot fully explain human linguistic ability.

14 meditation 명상 [medit(계속 재다) + ation(하는 것) → 계속 재는 것]

ex In fact, meditation is not a passive process.

15 moral 도덕적인 [mor(관습) + al(~의) → 관습의]

ex Your decision should be based on moral values.

• 정답 및 해설 p.102

A   적절한 내용으로 연결하세요.

> **Ex** (a) you are honest
> (b) it makes you very angry
> (c) you know who you are
> (d) it is false
> (e) it is not safe

1   If you form a sense of identity, _____.

2   If something is an illusion, _____.

3   If you are a woman of integrity, _____.

4   If you put something in jeopardy, _____.

5   If something infuriates you, _____.

B   다음에서 알맞은 표현을 고르세요.

1   The teacher showed (appearance, ignorance) of the basics of science.

2   It was (laudable, audible) of her to say such kind words.

3   Living in (location, isolation) may be unpleasant.

4   Is it (legitimate, intimate) to hunt weak animals?

5   There are a lot of (optimistic, linguistic) theories such as functional grammar.

Directions: Choose the one word that best fits the sentence.

1   A: What do you think of Barack Obama?

   B: First of all, he's honest. He's a man of _____.

(a) intelligence

(b) corruption

(c) integrity

(d) minority

2   A: I've decided to invest all my money in stocks.

   B: That decision would put your money in _____.

(a) jeopardy

(b) jealousy

(c) jewelry

(d) journey

3   A: Angelina Jolie adopted another child.

   B: It0 was _____ of her to do that.

(a) readable

(b) avoidable

(c) audible

(d) laudable

4   A: Can _____ improve our mental health?

   B: Definitely. It helps us relax our minds completely.

(a) station

(b) irritation

(c) meditation

(d) invitation

5   For many people, forming a sense of _____ is a complex process.

(a) quantity

(b) entity

(c) property

(d) identity

6   Is it true that _____ is bliss?

(a) ignorance

(b) arrogance

(c) appearance

(d) insurance

7   It _____ us that so many innocent children had been killed.

(a) calmed

(b) infuriated

(c) satisfied

(d) desired

8   It is an _____ that we can live forever.

(a) inclusion

(b) illusion

(c) exclusion

(d) inclination

학습포인트

영미인들에게 친숙하게 느껴지는 순수 영어 계열의 어휘와 달리, 대개 라틴어에서 유래한 고급 어휘에는 이런 정서적 요소가 없다. 본래 고급 어휘는 정확한 의미를 전달하는 것을 주된 기능으로 하기 때문에, 순수 영어 계열에 비해 단어의 의미가 많지 않은 것이 보통이다. 그래야만 일정한 뜻을 정밀하게 나타낼 수 있기 때문이다. 따라서 고급 어휘의 학습에서는 이처럼 중요한 기본적인 의미의 습득에 집중하는 전략이 필요하다.

중요 Collocation 정리

1 native 토착의 [nat(태어나다) + ive(경향이 있는) → 태어나는 경향이 있는]

> ex The potato is not native to Ireland.

2 neglect 소홀히 하다 [neg(하지 않다) + lect(모으다) → 모으지 않다]

> ex Robert neglected his duty as a father.

3 notorious 악명이 높은 [not(알려지다) + orious(특징적인) → 알려진]

> ex The teacher is notorious for using abusive language.

4 obligation 의무, 책임 [ob(향해서) + lig(묶다) + ation(만드는 것) → 향해 묶은 것]

> ex We have an obligation to defend our country.

5 offspring 자손 [off(~로부터) + spring(자라나다) → 자라난 것]

> ex Producing offspring is essential for the survival of a species.

6 outrageous 극히 부당한 [outr(벗어난) + age(행동) + ous(가득한) → 벗어난 행동으로 가득한]

> ex It is outrageous to abuse children.

7 overture 화해 제스처 [overt(드러난) + ure(행동) → 겉으로 드러난 행동]

> ex Britain made overtures to Japan.

8 pacific 평화적인 [pac(평화)+i(연결모음)+fic(가져오는) → 평화를 가져오는]

ex Surprisingly, most Vikings were pacific people.

9 patriot 애국자 [patri(아버지)+ot(특징적인) → 아버지에 특징적인]

ex Being a patriot, Joan of Arc dedicated herself to defending her country.

10 patron (단골) 손님 (patron: 지켜주는 사람)

ex Bill Smith is a regular patron of the bar.

11 perturbed 불안한, 어리둥절한, 언짢은 [per(완전히)+turbed(어지럽힌) → 완전히 어지럽힌]

ex Many people were perturbed that the President broke his promises.

12 precedent 전례 [pre(앞서)+ced(가다)+ent(~한 것) → 앞서 간 것]

ex Sometimes, it is necessary to break with precedent.

13 prejudice 선입견 [pre(앞서)+jud(판단하다)+ice(행동) → 앞서 판단하는 것]

ex The organization tries to eliminate prejudice against women.

14 property 특성, 속성 [proper(특유한)+ty(상태) → 독특한 상태]

ex The element has interesting properties.

15 pursuit 추구 [pur(앞서서)+su(따르다)+it(하게 된) → 앞서서 따르는 것]

ex The pursuit of happiness is not an easy process.

A 적절한 내용으로 연결하세요.

> Ex (a) you should do it
>
> (b) you have children
>
> (c) you are famous for doing that
>
> (d) people think badly of it
>
> (e) you do not do what you need to do

1 If you neglect your duty, _____.

2 If you are notorious for something bad, _____.

3 If you have an obligation to do something, _____.

4 If you produce offspring, _____.

5 If something is outrageous, _____.

B 다음에서 알맞은 표현을 고르세요.

1 Even (native, negative) speakers of English make such mistakes.

2 We Koreans are a (warlike, pacific) people. We love peace.

3 Nathan Hale was a (patriot, traitor). He loved his country.

4 Susie was (pleased, perturbed) that her best friend betrayed her.

5 It is very difficult to eliminate (prelude, prejudice) against the elderly.

Directions: Choose the one word that best fits the sentence.

1   A: Why did they get divorced?

B: Because Tom _____ his duty as a husband.

(a) collected

(b) recollected

(c) elected

(d) neglected

2   A: Should we accept their _____?

B: We'd better not do that. They have a hidden agenda.

(a) features

(b) structures

(c) cultures

(d) overtures

3   A: How did you feel about his remarks?

B: Oh, I was _____ that he was such a racist.

(a) proud

(b) naive

(c) perturbed

(d) grateful

4   A: I think men are better than women in science.

B: That is a common _____ against women.

(a) prejudice

(b) cowardice

(c) pregnancy

(d) preface

5   The regime is _____ for starving its people.

(a) furious

(b) notorious

(c) various

(d) glorious

6   It is _____ to treat the poor badly.

(a) gorgeous

(b) outrageous

(c) simultaneous

(d) generous

7   The cashew tree is _____ to Brazil.

(a) active

(b) passive

(c) conservative

(d) native

8   Being a true _____ means loving your country unconditionally.

(a) traitor

(b) patriot

(c) tailor

(d) scholar

UNIT 5 | 고급 어휘 Ⅴ

학습포인트

영어를 모국어로 하지 않은 외국인이 라틴어 계열의 고급 어휘를 정확히 익힌다는 것은 매우 어려운 일이다. 특히 고급 어휘가 어원 분석이 가능하다고 하더라도 일상적으로 접하는 기회가 많지 않기 때문에, 뜻을 잊어버리거나 혼동하기도 쉽다. 따라서 가능한 한 다양한 글을 통해 고급 어휘가 어떻게 생생하게 활용되는지에 대한 감각을 갖추는 일이 매우 긴요하다. 결국, 어휘 학습의 핵심은 자연스럽고 풍부한 맥락의 파악에 있기 때문이다.

중요 Collocation 정리

1 quota 할당량 [quota(몫)]

ex Willow is trying very hard to meet her quota.

2 radiate (감정을) 발산하다 [radi(빛) + ate(만들다) → 빛을 내다]

ex Her smile always radiates warmth and compassion.

3 rational 합리적인 [ration(이성) + al(~의) → 이성의]

ex To make a rational choice, you need to take many factors into account.

4 relevant 연관성이 있는 [relev(소유하다) + ant(하고 있는) → 가지고 있는]

ex His argument is not relevant to our discussion.

5 safeguard 보호하다 [(safe(안전한) + guard(지키다) → 안전하게 지키다)]

ex To safeguard democracy, we need to allow freedom of expression.

6 secluded 외딴 [se(떨어져서) + cluded(닫힌) → 떨어져서 닫혀 있는]

ex Fortunately, we found a secluded beach and had a great time.

7 security 안정감 [se(떨어져서) + cur(걱정) + ity(상태) → 걱정이 없는 상태]

ex Wealth can give you a false sense of security.

8 stable 안정적인 [st(서 있다) + able(할 수 있는) → 서 있을 수 있는]

ex Their relationship was not a stable one.

9 stipulate 규정하다 [stipul(요구하다) + ate(만들다) → 요구하게 만들다]

ex The regulations stipulate that you should wear a helmet at all times.

10 superstitious 미신을 믿는

[super(위에) + stit(서 있는) + ious(가득한) → 위에 서 있는 것으로 가득한]

ex In times of uncertainty, people become superstitious.

11 tactful 감정을 해치지 않는 [tact(접촉) + ful(가득한) → 접촉으로 가득한]

ex Being naturally tactful, Susie knew exactly what to say in the situation.

12 tendency 경향, 성향 [tend(뻗다) + ency(하고 있는 것) → 뻗고 있는 것]

ex The boss has a tendency to abuse his employees.

13 tolerant 관용하는 [toler(참아내다) + ant(하고 있는) → 참아내고 있는]

ex Olivia is amazingly tolerant of criticisms.

14 utterance 발언 [utter(바깥에) + ance(하고 있는 것) → 밖으로 내는 것]

ex His utterance is total nonsense. It doesn't make any sense.

15 vanity 허영심 [van(비어 있는) + ity(상태) → 비어 있는 상태]

ex Out of vanity, she decided to buy the expensive house.

A 적절한 내용으로 연결하세요.

> Ex
> (a) you do not think scientifically
> (b) people will probably like you
> (c) you do not hurt others' feelings
> (d) it is a good one
> (e) you might feel lonely

1 If you radiate warmth, _____.

2 If you make a rational decision, _____.

3 If you visit a secluded village, _____.

4 If you are superstitious, _____.

5 If you are tactful, _____.

B 다음에서 알맞은 표현을 고르세요.

1 When she couldn't meet her (quiver, quota), Amy felt frustrated.

2 To apply for the position, send all (relative, relevant) documents to Ann.

3 There is a (tendency, dependence) for men to enjoy sports.

4 A(n) (ignorant, tolerant) society is a mature one.

5 To ensure (security, impurity), many devices have been installed.

Directions: Choose the one word that best fits the sentence.

1   A: Samantha won the Best
    Employee of the Month Award.
    B: She exceeded her sales
    _____, you know.

(a) data
(b) quotation
(c) quota
(d) date

2   A: How can you describe Susie?
    B: Well, she _____ kindness and
    compassion.

(a) radiates
(b) negotiates
(c) initiates
(d) fascinates

3   A: Should we take his age into
    account?
    B: Absolutely not. Age is not a
    _____ factor.

(a) relative
(b) relevant
(c) separate
(d) similar

4   A: I believe thirteen is an unlucky
    number.
    B: What? I didn't know you're so
    _____.

(a) scientific
(b) sensible
(c) superstitious
(d) sensual

5   _____ people wouldn't do such
    a stupid thing.

(a) Absurd
(b) Illogical
(c) Awkward
(d) Rational

6   Patrick went to a _____ village
    and lived in isolation.

(a) crowded
(b) noisy
(c) festive
(d) secluded

7   Being _____ requires sympathy.

(a) tactful
(b) mischievous
(c) indifferent
(d) fearful

8   There is a _____ for Koreans to
    make such a grammatical mistake.

(a) dependence
(b) tendency
(c) confidence
(d) currency

Chapter 5

일상 구어체 표현

UNIT 1   일상 구어체 표현 Ⅰ

UNIT 2   일상 구어체 표현 Ⅱ

UNIT 1 일상 구어체 표현 I

학습포인트

일상 구어체 표현은 숙어(idiom) 가운데 구어체에서 주로 쓰이는 표현을 말한다. 구어체를 강조하는 TEPS의 특성 때문에 TEPS 시행 초기부터 꾸준히 출제되는 유형이다. 숙어의 특성이 강해서 개별 단어의 의미 조합으로 뜻을 이해할 수 없는 경우가 많다는 점에 유의해야 한다. 대개 기본적인 의미가 비유적인 의미로 활용되는 것이 보통이므로 표현에 숨어 있는 원어민의 감각을 정확히 익혀둘 필요가 있다.

중요 Collocation 정리

1 the ball is in A's court A가 결정할 차례다 (테니스에서 유래)

ex You have to make up your mind. The ball is in your court.

2 (It) Beats me 모르다; 이해가 안 된다 (beat의 '놀라게 하다'라는 옛 의미에서)

ex Why is he so angry with us? — Beats me.

3 been there, done that (해봐서) 더이상 관심이 없다

ex Wanna join us? — No, been there, done that.

4 come to think of it 생각해 보니까

ex Come to think of it, how did you find my apartment?

5 cut it out 그만해 ['잘라서(cut) 제거하다(out)'라는 뜻에서]

ex Enough is enough! Just cut it out!

6 fat chance 희박한 가능성 (fat의 '풍부한'이란 뜻을 반어적으로 활용)

ex Maybe they'll help you out. — Fat chance!

7 get real! 정신 차려!

ex Get real, girls! There is no such thing as a prince charming.

8 **give me a break** 그만해라

> ex Richard, just give me a break! I can't hear your complaints anymore.

9 **someone/something is history** 더이상 중요하지 않다

> ex I won't see Bruce again. He's history.

10 **join the club** 같은 (어려운) 처지인 걸

> ex I have no boyfriend. — Join the club.

11 **be my guest!** 그렇게 하세요! (귀한 손님처럼 원하는 대로 하라는 뜻에서)

> ex Can I borrow your digital camera? — Be my guest!

12 **Keep your chin up** 기운 내라 (턱을 올리고 있는, 확고부동한 자세에서)

> ex Keep your chin up! You can do better next time.

13 **ring a bell** (어렴풋이) 기억나다 ('기억'을 상징하는 bell의 이미지로부터)

> ex J.K. Rowling? The name doesn't ring a bell with me.

14 **better safe than sorry** (나쁜 일이 생기지 않도록) 조심하는 편이 낫다

> ex Slow down, please! Better safe than sorry, you know.

15 **be in the same boat** 똑같이 어려운 처지이다

> ex I'm fired! - We're in the same boat.

• 정답 및 해설 p.107

A 적절한 내용으로 연결하세요.

> **Ex** (a) you want someone to stop doing something
> (b) you mean that you do not understand something
> (c) you believe that you can remember it
> (d) you need to take action
> (e) you mean that you are not interested in something

1 If the ball is in your court, _____.

2 If you say, "Beats me, _____."

3 If you say, "Been there, done that, _____."

4 If you say, "Cut it out, _____."

5 If something rings a bell with you, _____.

B 다음에서 알맞은 표현을 고르세요.

1 (Come, Go) to think of it, how did you know her address?

2 (Turn, Get) real, boys! The world is a dangerous place!

3 Tom, just (lend, give) me a break! That is ridiculous.

4 Keep your (chin, nose) up! There is another chance.

5 Why did Kate quit? — (Hits, Beats) me.

Directions: Choose the one word that best fits the sentence.

1   A: Why did they decide to move to Italy?

B: _____ me.

(a) Strikes
(b) Knocks
(c) Punches
(d) Beats

2   A: Join us for a big party!

B: No, been there, _____ that.

(a) gone
(b) come
(c) taken
(d) done

3   A: I failed the TEPS test!

B: _____ the club! It was very difficult.

(a) Enjoy
(b) Join
(c) Break
(d) Leave

4   A: Do you know who Britney Spears is?

B: That name doesn't _____ a bell.

(a) ring
(b) sing
(c) call
(d) tell

5   I think we need to wait. The ball is in her _____.

(a) park
(b) ring
(c) court
(d) field

6   Paris Hilton is _____. I'm not interested in her anymore.

(a) politics
(b) economy
(c) history
(d) society

7   Just give me a _____! I'm not that naive.

(a) break
(b) vacation
(c) leave
(d) holiday

8   _____ real! There is no such thing as security.

(a) Go
(b) Get
(c) Take
(d) Turn

UNIT 2 일상 구어체 표현 Ⅱ

학습포인트

우리가 영어를 일상적으로 쓰지 않기 때문에, 일상 구어체 표현은 쉽게 접하기 어렵다. 따라서 그 쓰임새를 제한적으로 알고 있는 경우가 많은데, TEPS에서 안정적인 점수를 확보하기 위해서는 구어체 표현을 정확히 익혀 두어야 한다. 최근 많은 인기를 끌고 있는 미국 드라마나 영화를 통해 구어체 표현을 익히는 것도 매우 효과적인 학습법이라고 할 수 있다. 어떤 경우든, 자연스러운 맥락의 중요성을 이해하고 체계적으로 표현을 익혀나가는 습관을 들이는 것이 중요하다는 것을 명심하자.

중요 Collocation 정리

1 Are you kidding me? 설마 ('농담하다'라는 kid의 의미에서 유래)

ex Tom Cruise came to your party? Are you kidding me?

2 break a leg! (특히 공연을 앞둔 이에게 하는 말로) 행운을 빌게!

ex I'm so nervous about my first performance. — It'll be OK. Break a leg!

3 pulling someone's leg 장난삼아 놀리다 (다리를 걸어 넘어뜨리는 장난에서)

ex The student was pulling her leg by pretending to be mentally ill.

4 my lips are sealed 비밀을 발설하지 않다 ('봉하다'라는 seal의 의미에서)

ex Promise me not to tell anybody about this. — My lips are sealed.

5 by all means (허락하여) 물론 ('무슨 수를 쓰든'이라는 의미에서)

ex Can I use your laptop computer? — By all means.

6 great minds think alike (익살맞은 표현으로) 동감이다

ex It's funny. I was thinking the same thing. — Great minds think alike.

7 it slipped one's mind 깜빡했다 ('빠져나가다'는 slip의 의미에서)

ex Did you bring your camera? — Oh, it slipped my mind.

8   get on someone's nerves 짜증나게 하다 ('신경과민'이라는 nerves의 뜻에서)

> ex   David is starting to get on my nerves. He's driving me crazy, you know.

9   go nuts 몹시 화를 내다, 흥분하다 ('정신 이상의'라는 nuts의 의미에서)

> ex   Ryan went nuts when he found out that his wife had cheated on him.

10   in a nutshell 요컨대 ('견과 껍질에 넣을 정도로'라는 의미에서)

> ex   In a nutshell, you need to believe in yourself.

11   a pain in the neck 골칫거리

> ex   Thank God he's gone. He was a real pain in the neck.

12   take your pick 좋은 것으로 고르다 ('선택'이라는 pick의 의미에서)

> ex   You can have whichever you want. Just take your pick.

13   hit the road (여행 등을) 떠나다 ('도로를 치고 떠나다'라는 의미에서)

> ex   It's time to hit the road and head to Las Vegas.

14   hit the sack 잠자리에 들다 (hit the hay의 변형으로 보는 것이 보통)

> ex   I was exhausted and hit the sack earlier than usual.

15   on second thought 다시 생각해 보니까

> ex   Oh, wait. On second thought, I'd like to have a coffee, please.

EXERCISE

• 정답 및 해설 p.109

A 적절한 내용으로 연결하세요.

> **Ex** (a) you wish someone good luck
> (b) you go to bed
> (c) you mean that you will not tell anyone a secret
> (d) you do not believe what someone has told you
> (e) you start a journey

1 If you say, "Are you kidding me? _____."

2 If you say, "Break a leg, _____."

3 If you say, "My lips are sealed, _____."

4 If you hit the road, _____.

5 If you hit the sack, _____.

B 다음에서 알맞은 표현을 고르세요.

1 Hillary went (peas, nuts) when she found out that she had been deceived.

2 In a (nutshell, seashell), we should improve our education.

3 Ah, on second (sought, thought), I'll leave tomorrow.

4 Anthony was pulling her (arm, leg) by pretending to be a police officer.

5 Washing the dishes is a pain in the (lap, neck).

Directions: Choose the one word that best fits the sentence.

1   A: I'm getting married to Jessica
        Alba!
    B: Are you _____ me?

    (a) kidding
    (b) pigging
    (c) digging
    (d) nagging

2   A: Drusilla's English is so perfect.
    B: Maybe she's _____ by
        pretending to be a foreigner.

    (a) reaping the harvest
    (b) giving you the cold shoulder
    (c) pulling your leg
    (d) leaving no stone unturned

3   A: Did you check all the doors?
    B: Gosh! It completely _____ my
        mind.

    (a) missed
    (b) slipped
    (c) hit
    (d) hurt

4   A: I've broken her digital camera.
    B: She'll _____ when she finds
        that out.

    (a) ring true
    (b) eat her words
    (c) cut her teeth
    (d) go nuts

5   You can tell me anything. My
    _____ are sealed.

    (a) ears
    (b) eyes
    (c) lips
    (d) noses

6   In a _____, you have to find out
    for yourself.

    (a) nutshell
    (b) roll
    (c) loss
    (d) home

7   Ah, it's time to _____. See ya!

    (a) hit the road
    (b) hit home
    (c) keep my fingers crossed
    (d) get cold feet

8   Oh, _____, I'd like a window
    seat, please.

    (a) down to earth
    (b) on edge
    (c) off the hook
    (d) on second thought

TEPS

모의고사
VOCABULARY

DIRECTIONS

This part of the exam tests your vocabulary skills. You will have 15 minutes to complete the 50 questions. Be sure to follow the directions given by the proctor.

1. A: What _____?
    B: Who knows? But a lot of people were hospitalized.
    (a) eased
    (b) happened
    (c) placed
    (d) lay

2. A: Gloria is such a bad person.
    B: You'd better _____ the facts before making such a comment.
    (a) beat
    (b) fail
    (c) check
    (d) enjoy

3. A: I'd like to _____ my appointment with Dr. Laura tomorrow.
    B: OK, ma'am. Could you please fill out the cancellation form?
    (a) agree
    (b) cancel
    (c) divide
    (d) greet

4. A: Why was David arrested?
    B: The police said that he had _____ a lot of money from his company.
    (a) caused
    (b) stolen
    (c) guessed
    (d) injured

5. A: I'd like to make a[n] _____ for this evening.
    B: OK, sir. For how many people?
    (a) effort
    (b) reservation
    (c) apology
    (d) impression

6. A: The annual festival will be _____ this weekend!
    B: Oh, really? I can't wait!
    (a) made
    (b) held
    (c) taken
    (d) done

7. A: Millions of African children are starving!
    B: I think we must _____ immediate action.
    (a) take
    (b) make
    (c) do
    (d) get

8. A: My company is going to _____ thousands of new workers.
    B: Wow! It must be doing really well.
    (a) hire
    (b) fire
    (c) avoid
    (d) delay

9. A: Don't you think the price is
       _____?
    B: Actually, it's a little too high.
       (a) reasonable
       (b) patient
       (c) optimistic
       (d) genuine

10. A: I believe that we should
       _____ the issue of abortion at
       the meeting.
    B: Don't you think that's a delicate
       subject?
       (a) account for
       (b) break up
       (c) come across
       (d) deal with

11. A: We badly want somebody who
       can _____ the vacancy.
    B: In that case, can I recommend
       someone?
       (a) attract
       (b) attain
       (c) embark
       (d) fill

12. A: Who do you think can _____
       the equipment?
    B: How about contacting Sally?
       She's really good at fixing
       machines.
       (a) quit
       (b) repair
       (c) slump
       (d) function

13. A: In my opinion, Angelina
       has _____ too much
       responsibility.
    B: I know what you mean, but
       we've had no choice but to rely
       on her.
       (a) complimented
       (b) delivered
       (c) absorbed
       (d) shouldered

14. A: Thank goodness my son
       _____ the accident.
    B: Yes, but he should have been
       more careful.
       (a) finalized
       (b) survived
       (c) educated
       (d) resigned

15. A: I can't _____ how to use this
       software.
    B: How about reading the manual
       one more time?
       (a) hand in
       (b) hang up
       (c) figure out
       (d) make up

16. A: I'm so glad Kathy passed the
       test.
    B: Me, too. Her hard work finally
       _____.
       (a) paid off
       (b) marked down
       (c) pulled over
       (d) turned down

17. A: What do you think of Elissa?

B: Oh, she's a[n] _____ secretary. She knows what she's doing.

   (a) fictional
   (b) familiar
   (c) efficient
   (d) generous

18. A: Welcome aboard! Everybody says you'll be a great _____ to our company.

B: Oh, I'm flattered. I'm glad to work with you, anyway.

   (a) abuse
   (b) asset
   (c) aspect
   (d) circumstance

19. A: Why did you _____ the question of corporate responsibility at the meeting?

B: I thought it would be relevant to the discussion.

   (a) establish
   (b) raise
   (c) offend
   (d) leak

20. A: Is this car _____?

B: Yes, it is. In fact, it can last almost 20 years.

   (a) hostile
   (b) humane
   (c) durable
   (d) gradual

21. A: I'm so excited about moving to Chicago!

B: Be extremely _____! It is a very dangerous city.

   (a) accurate
   (b) bankrupt
   (c) effective
   (d) cautious

22. A: Maybe, they'll help us do our homework.

B: _____. They don't care about us.

   (a) Fat chance
   (b) Join the club
   (c) Be my guest
   (d) Doesn't ring a bell

23. A: Can we trust them?

B: No, we can't. They have a _____.

   (a) hidden agenda
   (b) pain in the neck
   (c) long shot
   (d) rule of thumb

24. A: What is the best way to _____?

B: Crack a joke and make people laugh. Then, they'll feel more comfortable.

   (a) play it by ear
   (b) break the ice
   (c) pick up the tab
   (d) make ends meet

25. A: Stop _____! Just tell me what you really think.

B: But things are not that simple, you know.

   (a) pulling your leg
   (b) slipping your mind
   (c) going nuts
   (d) beating around the bush

Part I **Questions 26~50**

Choose the best answer for the blank.

26. To buy the house, Michelle had to _____ a lot of money from the bank.

    (a) lend
    (b) rob
    (c) lie
    (d) borrow

27. Smoking _____ harm to your health.

    (a) makes
    (b) comes
    (c) takes
    (d) does

28. As an adult, you need to _____ a mature choice.

    (a) do
    (b) take
    (c) get
    (d) make

29. It is practically impossible to _____ the needs of all customers.

    (a) meet
    (b) part
    (c) leave
    (d) stay

30. Korea's electricity demand is expected to _____ significantly.

    (a) rise
    (b) pound
    (c) raise
    (d) handle

31. Our society is _____ the problem of illegal immigration.

    (a) behaving
    (b) gaining
    (c) facing
    (d) imitating

32. It is always a good idea to _____ a practical method.

    (a) break
    (b) apply
    (c) suffer
    (d) glow

33. Our society is _____ many changes.

    (a) voicing
    (b) firing
    (c) undergoing
    (d) dropping

34. The _____ is presented to a student who is good at writing in English.

    (a) award
    (b) personnel
    (c) ignorance
    (d) integrity

35. Her passport _____ two months ago and she couldn't use it anymore.

    (a) taxied
    (b) raged
    (c) reigned
    (d) expired

36. To accept _____ criticism, you need to be honest with yourself.

    (a) miserable
    (b) superficial
    (c) constructive
    (d) domestic

37. Surprisingly, sleeping can _____ your learning ability.

    (a) affect
    (b) effect
    (c) insist
    (d) ignore

38. Study this book, and high scores are _____!

    (a) opposed
    (b) judged
    (c) neglected
    (d) guaranteed

39. Some people believe that the Internet helps to _____ the spread of democracy.

    (a) frequent
    (b) react
    (c) search
    (d) facilitate

40. Their natural _____ is threatened by human activities.

    (a) principal
    (b) housing
    (c) insult
    (d) habitat

41. The couple celebrated their wedding _____ by taking a trip to Japan.

    (a) recess
    (b) landscape
    (c) adversity
    (d) anniversary

42. We took a _____ but got there earlier than expected.

    (a) boom
    (b) gist
    (c) detour
    (d) notion

43. Our company has been _____ as the Best Workplace in Korea.

    (a) nominated
    (b) leaked
    (c) patrolled
    (d) traced

44. We don't have much time. So, ask only _____ questions.

    (a) secluded
    (b) tactful
    (c) outrageous
    (d) relevant

45. His expertise _____ from physics to nanotechnology.

    (a) notifies
    (b) stores
    (c) ranges
    (d) performs

46. It will take a long time to _____ the item to Mexico.

    (a) settle
    (b) maintain
    (c) object
    (d) ship

47. Violence is not a _____ way of solving a problem.

    (a) legitimate
    (b) notorious
    (c) perturbed
    (d) stable

48. We need to set a strict _____ on E2 visas.

    (a) prejudice
    (b) obligation
    (c) quota
    (d) jeopardy

49. There is a[n] _____ for Americans to unite in times of crisis.

    (a) immersion
    (b) tendency
    (c) identity
    (d) pursuit

50. The agreement _____ that the employees have to wear uniforms.

    (a) safeguards
    (b) radiates
    (c) stipulates
    (d) infuriates

Section **C**

독해

Chapter 1 독해 기본기 다지기

Chapter 2 빈 칸 채우기

Chapter 3 질문 유형은 이렇다

Chapter 4 실용문

Chapter 5 비실용문

독해 모의고사

Section C

Chapter 1

독해 기본기 다지기

UNIT 1   주제 찾기
UNIT 2   세부사항 찾기
UNIT 3   추론
UNIT 4   일관성에서 벗어난 것

주제 찾기

주제는 지문의 중심 내용을 말하는 것으로 글의 내용을 이해하는 데 핵심적인 요소다. TEPS에서는 Part Ⅱ의 일부 문항으로 출제되지만, 다른 유형의 문제를 풀 때도 도움이 된다. 직설적인 표현을 선호하는 영어의 특성 때문에 주제문이 처음에 오는 경우가 많지만 마지막에 오거나 암시되기만 하는 경우도 있다. 전반적인 내용의 흐름을 생각하면서 정확히 주제를 포착하려는 노력을 기울이자.

유형 정리

1 주제가 앞부분에 있는 경우

Learning English is like dating someone with strange habits. In order to "succeed," you need to get used to those habits. Likewise, English has many strange "habits" that a lot of learners have difficulty understanding. Such habits are usually exceptions to general rules. Once you are used to those exceptions, however, your English will improve greatly.

윗글에서는 첫 문장이 바로 주제문이다. 나머지 문장들은 주제문을 보다 분명하게 설명하는 역할을 맡는다. 이것이 영어 지문의 대표적인 구성 방식이기 때문에 정확히 익혀둘 필요가 있다. 또한 일관성(coherence)을 유지하여 끝까지 주제를 유지하고 있다는 것도 기억하자.

2 주제가 뒷부분에 있는 경우

A recovered memory is when you wrongly believe that you have successfully remembered an event. Such an event is usually about childhood abuse. The problem is, of course, that it is a false kind of memory. You simply imagine that you have experienced something. But it never happened. **Therefore, recovered memories should not be encouraged.**

윗글에서는 마지막 문장이 주제문이다. 앞의 문장들은 주제문이 나타내는 결론에 이르기 위한 배경 지식을 제공하는 역할을 맡는다. 우리말은 대개 이와 같은 구성 방식을 택하지만, 영어에서는 가끔씩 활용되는 형태임을 기억하자.

3 주제가 암시되어 있는 경우

Do you really want to delete unnecessary files? Do you really want to keep your secrets safe? Then, try using BC Wipe. This "wiping" program deletes unneeded files once and for all so that nobody can find or restore them. Thus, if you delete a file by using this simple program, there is no way of recovering it. It is very convenient, don't you think?

윗글에서의 주제는 암시되어 있을 뿐, 하나의 문장으로 명확하게 표현되어 있지는 않다. 실제로도 이와 같은 글의 구성이 많이 있긴 하지만, TEPS에서의 출제 빈도는 높은 편이 아니다. 그만큼 주제를 파악하기가 까다롭기 때문이다. 하지만 고득점을 위해서는 참고해야 할 유형이다.

Tips

1 첫 번째 문장의 역할

영어 지문에서 첫 번째 문장은 1 주제문, 2 배경 지식, 3 반박하고자 하는 내용 가운데 하나다. 이 가운데 1이 가장 많고 2가 일부를 차지한다. 3은 어려운 문제에서 제시되는데 첫 번째 문장이 주제와 정반대가 된다는 점에서 주의를 요한다. 그렇지만 입문 단계에서는 1과 2의 유형에 익숙해지는 편이 좋다. 또한 이것은 우리말과 정반대되는 구성이라는 점도 기억하자.

2 주제를 찾는 방법

주제를 찾는 보통의 방법은 글을 읽고서 전체적으로 중요한 내용을 파악하는 것이다. 그렇지만 실제로 많은 문제를 짧은 시간에 풀어나가야 하는 시험에서는 이렇게 하는 것이 어려울 수 있다. 이럴 때는 주제가 대개 지문에서 일정한 단어로 반복된다는 점을 활용하면 된다. 대개 동일한 뜻을 나타내는 명사가 여러 문장에 걸쳐 나타나면 그것이 주제일 가능성이 높다.

1-1 다음을 읽고 이 글의 주제 또는 제목이 담긴 문장을 찾아 ☑ 표시하시오.

- ☐ (a) We've known each other for many years.
- ☐ (b) So, you may take me for granted.
- ☐ (c) But you are a special lady to me.

1-2 ## What is the passage mainly about?

(a) The love for a lady

(b) The importance of friendship

2-1 다음을 읽고 이 글의 주제 또는 제목이 담긴 문장을 찾아 ☑ 표시하시오.

- ☐ (a) Noise polution is a serious problem.
- ☐ (b) It can make you lose hearing permanently.
- ☐ (c) It can also cause damage to your health in many ways.

2-2 ## What is the best title for this passage?

(a) The Problems of Noise Pollution

(b) The Importance of Good Health

PRACTICE

•정답 및 해설 p.118

1   The process of German reunification was a difficult one. As you might guess, the East German regime tried to stop their people from calling for democratic reforms. The government did not allow the people to read Soviet publications which were thought to be a threat to the regime. There were also attempts to prevent East Germans from escaping to West Germany. Despite these obstacles, they successfully reunified their country.

Q. What is the best title of the passage?

(a) The Importance of Democratic Reforms

(b) The Friendly Relationship Between the Two Germanies

(c) Escaping to West Germany

(d) The Reunification of the Two Germanies

2   Some people once thought that crocodiles were the ancestors of dinosaurs. In fact, dinosaurs and crocodiles have many things in common. Their teeth, their skulls, and their jaws are very similar in structure. But dinosaurs did not develop from crocodiles. This is mainly because the two reptiles appeared on Earth almost at the same time. Then, from what animals did the dinosaurs evolve?

Q. What is the passage mainly about?

(a) The teeth of dinosaurs

(b) The ancestors of dinosaurs

(c) The relationship between crocodiles and dinosaurs

(d) The appearance of crocodiles

세부사항은 지문의 내용 가운데 특정한 부분을 말하는 것으로 대개 주제를 보다 뚜렷하게 부각시키는 역할을 맡는다. TEPS에서는 Part Ⅱ의 주요 문항으로 출제되는데, 주제를 묻는 문제에 비해 난이도가 높은 편이다. 내용에 대한 정확한 이해를 요구하기 때문이다. 먼저 주제를 파악한 다음, 관련되는 세부사항들을 꼼꼼하게 확인하는 습관을 들일 필요가 있다.

유형 정리

1 특성

These days, not many people respect teachers. There are a variety of reasons for this and one of them is that they do not effectively do what they are supposed to do. Basically, there are not enough teachers who can teach their subjects in an efficient way. In order to address this problem, we need to carry out a structural reform in evaluating and rewarding teachers.

윗글에는 오늘날 존경을 받지 못하는 교사들의 특성에 대한 언급이 있다. 이처럼 일정한 대상의 특성을 묻는 것이 세부사항을 요하는 문제의 기본 유형이다. 따라서 인물이나 사물의 특성을 정확히 포착하는 연습을 해 나가도록 하자.

2 조건

A decrease in the quantity of serotonin in the brain is closely related to the onset of depression. This is mainly because serotonin can affect how effectively one can deal with emotional stress. The function of the neurotransmitter is to organize the emotional defense system of the brain. As a result, when the brain does not have enough serotonin, it cannot cope with emotional stress successfully.

윗글에서는 두뇌에 세로토닌이 부족한 경우 우울증이 발생할 수 있음이 설명되었다. 세부사항을 묻는 문제의 이차적인 유형으로 이와 같은 조건 또는 인과관계를 요하는 유형을 들 수 있다. 관련 변수를 정확히 파악하는 데 중점을 두어야 한다.

3 제외 항목

On November 26, 2007, Yeosu was chosen to hold the 2012 World Exposition. The Korean port city defeated Morocco's Tangier by 77 votes to 63. Analysts said that the Korean city's theme of "The Living Ocean and Coast" contributed to its victory over the Moroccan port city. The event is expected to draw a large number of people and create a huge profit for South Korea.

윗글에서는 우리나라의 여수가 2012년에 세계박람회를 개최하게 된 경위와 기대효과가 설명되어 있다. 세부사항을 묻는 유형 가운데는, 이와 같은 내용에 대해 올바르게 설명한 사항만 고르는 문제가 있다. 이때는 어떤 설명을 제외해야 하는지를 지문과 대조하면서 꼼꼼하게 확인하는 작업이 필요하다.

Tips

1 시간 배정

TEPS의 문제 유형 가운데, 세부사항 유형은 빈 칸 채우기 유형 다음으로 많은 시간이 소요되는 유형이다. 왜냐하면 하나하나의 사항을 정확하게 확인해야만 제대로 정답을 고를 수 있기 때문이다. 따라서 주제 찾기와 같은 유형에서 절약한 시간을 세부사항 문제 풀이에 활용해야 한다. 그래야만 제한된 시간에 모든 문제를 제대로 풀어낼 수 있기 때문이다.

2 중심 내용과의 관련성

세부사항 유형은 지문 전체를 읽지 않은 상태에서 하나하나의 답지를 지문과 비교하면서 풀 수도 있다. 그렇지만 이와 같은 방법은 실수로 이어질 가능성이 높다는 점에서 주의를 요한다. 왜냐하면 세부사항 문제의 출제 의도도 글에 대한 정밀한 이해력의 측정이기 때문에, 대개 중심 내용과 밀접하게 관련되는 사항이 정답인 경우가 많기 때문이다. 따라서 일단 글의 중심 내용이 무엇인지를 파악하려는 노력이 요구된다는 점을 명심하자.

• 정답 및 해설 p.118

EXERCISE

1 **다음 글에서 설명한 Follow Your Heart의 주된 특징은 무엇인가?**

Susanna Tamaro's *Follow Your Heart* is an amazing novel. In this touching story, an elderly woman writes a letter to her granddaughter. In her dazzling letters, she talks about the meaning of being human. In fact, this wise woman advises every one of us to make choices based on our own hearts. Given the many challenges confronting us today, her advice is as timely as ever.

(a) It is an old-fashioned novel.

(b) It is primarily aimed at young women.

(c) It is written in the form of letter.

2 **다음 글에 따르면 인터넷이 우리의 삶을 향상시키지 <u>못한</u> 이유가 무엇인가?**

A lot of people believe that the Internet has improved our lives. For instance, we can do many things without going out. Unfortunately, however, we have lost many precious things. More than anything else, so many people have become unaware of the importance of face-to-face communication. Only through face-to-face interaction can we build true relationships. Therefore, the Internet has not "improved" our lives in an important way.

(a) It allows us to do a lot of things without moving our bodies.

(b) It does not help us form a true friendship with others.

(c) It helps us realize the importance of everyday things.

• 정답 및 해설 p.119

1 Ludwig Wittgenstein was a genius logician. After reading "The Principles of Mathematics" by Bertrand Russel, he became quite interested in learning about logic. As a result, he went to Cambridge University in order to learn from Russel. Before a year passed, Russel felt that he did not have anything left to teach him. Being such a genius, Wittgenstein decided to explore logic by himself.

Q. Which of the following best describes Ludwig Wittgenstein?

(a) He attended Oxford University.

(b) He taught logic to Betrand Russel.

(c) He had great difficulty learning about logic.

(d) He was good at logic.

2 Can science explain love? Some people say yes and try to give a "scientific" explanation for why women are attracted to particular types of men. For instance, some scientists claim that young women are genetically programmed to love old men. But how old is *old*? Eighty or ninety? And how old is *young*? Ten or twelve? And why does a young woman love just one man? Probably, science does not have anything to contribute to our understanding of love.

Q. According to the passage, which of the following is correct?

(a) Old women are genetically programmed to love young men.

(b) Science cannot explain love satisfactorily.

(c) Women tend to love many men at the same time.

(d) Science is likely to help us understand love.

UNIT 3 추론

추론은 글의 내용으로부터 상식적으로 또는 논리적으로 이끌어낼 수 있는 결론을 뜻한다. TEPS에서는 Part II의 일부 문항으로 출제되는데, 세부사항을 요구하는 문항과 함께 난이도가 높은 유형에 속한다. 특히, TEPS에서는 엄밀하게 추론할 것을 요구하기 때문에, 내용을 지나치게 비약해서 생각하거나 글에서 언급되지 않은 사항을 바탕으로 추론하지 않도록 유의해야 한다.

유형 정리

1 특성

Is Seo Tai-ji's comeback a welcome one? Some ardent fans of his say yes and they are looking forward to getting his eighth album. According to them, the controversial singer has a lot to "teach" our society. Others disagree. They are concerned that just like his problematic fourth album, his eighth album might be lacking in artistic excellence.

윗글에서는 서태지의 8집 앨범의 특성에 대한 상반된 입장을 설명한다. 이런 특성으로부터 일정한 사항을 논리적으로 추론할 수 있는데, 이처럼 글에 제시된 인물이나 사물의 특성에 대한 추론이 기본적인 문제 유형이다.

2 결과

These days, too many people are unaware of the importance of history in understanding various conflicts around the world. For instance, many Americans do not even try to learn about the history of Iraq while pretending to know everything about America's war with the country. This kind of ignorance will lead to wrong public opinions and inappropriate policies.

윗글은 역사에 대한 무지가 여론이나 정책에 어떤 영향을 미칠 수 있는지를 언급한다. 마지막 문장에서 그 결과를 제시했는데, 이 결과에 부합하는 사항을 측정할 수 있다. 이처럼 글의 내용에 따른 결과를 요구하는 것이 이차적인 문제 유형이다.

3 추리

On February 10, 2008, a fire broke out and burned down Namdaemun, South Korea's National Treasure No. 1. On the following day, the police arrested a suspect and questioned him overnight. The arsonist admitted having set fire to the most treasured gate in the country. According to the police, the man had been angered by a land dispute and decided to blow off steam by committing a crime against the general public.

윗글은 남대문 방화사건에 대한 내용이다. 글에서 방화범에 대해 말한 사항으로부터 방화범이 정상적인 인물이 아님을 추리할 수 있다. 이처럼 글에 제시된 대상에 대한 상식적이고 논리적인 추리를 요구하는 것이 마지막 문제 유형이다.

• 정답 및 해설 p.120

다음 글의 내용으로부터 추론한 것 가운데 올바른 것을 고르시오.

1 Is space tourism a good idea? People such as Richard Branson seem to think so and plan to make it available to the general public. In fact, Branson claims that approximately 200 reservations have been made for space travel. Of course, it will cost hundreds of thousands of dollars. But is it worth the money? Do we really have to travel to space just to have "fun"? Why not spend the money on more meaningful activities?

(a) Richard Branson is a billionaire.

(b) Space travel will be expensive.

(c) Space travel will be boring.

2 In an interview with a Swedish newspaper, Doris Lessing said that if Barack Obama were elected the next U.S. President, he would surely be assassinated. Lessing was concerned that racist groups such as the Ku Klux Klan might "murder" the African American man. According to her, it might be calmer if Hillary Clinton were to become the first female President of the United States.

(a) Barack Obama is the 44th President of the United States.

(b) Lessing is worried about Obama's safety.

(c) Hillary Clinton is the first female President of the United States.

1   On February 11, 2008, BlackBerry email service broke down, preventing a large number of users from sending or receiving messages. However, voice and SMS services were not interrupted. After a few hours of the outage, the service was restored. The service outage resulted from an upgrade aimed at improving the BlackBerry smartphones. Similar service disruptions occurred last year.

Q. What can be inferred from the passage?

(a) The BlackBerry smartphones are durable.

(b) During the service outage, the users could not use SMS services.

(c) The service outage lasted some hours.

(d) The service outage occurred because of computer viruses.

2   When she was only fifteen, Joan Baez heard Martin Luther King, Jr. discuss nonviolence and civil rights. Baez was deeply moved by his speech and decided to dedicate her life to promoting the two causes. After the Vietnam War broke out, she often took part in anti-war protests. At her concerts, Baez told her audience not to join the military forces. Later, she established Humanitas International Human Rights Committee, whose purpose was to support human rights movements.

Q. What can be inferred from the passage?

(a) Baez believed that the Vietnam War was worth fighting.

(b) Baez made friends with Martin Luther King, Jr.

(c) Baez was interested in seeking the interests of the United States.

(d) Baez was a political activist.

Part III의 3문제는 주어진 글의 흐름에 어긋나는 문장을 고르는 유형이다. 이를 일관성에서 벗어난 것이라고 하는데, 대체로 다른 문제 유형에 비해 난이도가 높지 않은 편이다. 그렇지만 난이도가 높게 출제되는 경우는 추론 유형과 비슷하게 난이도가 높아질 수 있기 때문에 주의를 요한다. 또한 일관성이 글의 주요한 특성이라는 점에서도 소홀히 할 수 없는 유형임을 명심하자.

유형 정리

1 전혀 관련 없는 문장

In my opinion, companies will not survive if they engage in unethical activities. (a) I also have a keen sense of responsibility toward my clients. (b) I don't honestly believe that harming my clients in any way would bring me substantial profits. **(c) I must mention that I have friendly relationships with my clients.** (d) Further, I am sharply aware that companies should deal with all matters and clients in a morally legitimate way.

가장 단순한 형태로 주어진 글의 흐름과 전혀 관계없는 문장을 삽입한 경우이다. 전체 글의 흐름이 기업의 윤리성에 맞추어져 있기 때문에 (c)는 글의 자연스러운 흐름과 관계가 없다. 비교적 난이도가 낮은 문제에서 주로 출제되는 유형이다.

2 입장이 다른, 관련된 문장

On August 21, 1911, the *Mona Lisa* was stolen from the Louvre. (a) At first, people thought that Guillaume Apollinaire was the thief. **(b) Some people believed, however, that Vincenzo Perugia stole the picture.** (c) This was because Apollinaire did not approve of the museum. (d) He suspected, however, that Pablo Picasso had stolen the masterpiece.

모나리자 도난 사건을 다룬 글인데, 처음에 사람들이 Guillaume Apollinaire를 도둑으로 생각했다는 것이 주된 내용이다. 반면 (b)는 다른 인물인 Vincenzo Perugia를 말하기 때문에 글의 흐름에 어울리지 않는다.

3 초점이 다른, 관련된 문장

Bernard Kettlewell was famous for his experiments with moths. (a) According to him, dark-colored moths could survive better than light-colored ones in industrial areas. (b) This was because light-colored moths could be more easily seen than dark-colored ones on the sides of polluted and darkened trees. (c) Unfortunately, however, his methods were not scientific at all. **(d) Kettlewell was a dedicated teacher.**

Kettlewell의 유명한 나방 실험을 다룬 글이다. (d)는 교사로서의 Kettlewell의 면모를 다루기 때문에 글의 전체 흐름과 초점이 다르다. 가장 까다로운 유형이기 때문에 특히 주의를 요한다.

Tips

1 일관성 문제

다른 유형에 비해 일관성 문제가 상대적으로 난이도가 낮은 것이 보통이긴 하지만, 실제로 39번이나 40번은 어렵게 출제될 수 있다는 점에 유의해야 한다. 특히 글 전체에서 다루는 내용과 초점이 다른 경우에 주의할 필요가 있다. 똑같은 대상에 대해서 말한다 하더라도, 글 전체에서 다루는 측면과 같은 측면을 같은 입장에서 다루어야만 일관성이 유지될 수 있다는 점을 명심 또 명심하자.

2 독해의 비결

짧은 시간에 많은 지문을 풀어나가야 하는 TEPS 독해 영역의 특성 때문에 많은 어려움을 겪는 것이 사실이다. 특히 TEPS에서는 한 문장, 한 문장을 우리말로 번역할 만큼 충분한 시간을 주지 않는다는 점에 유의해야 한다. 단어와 문장 구조에 대한 감각을 바탕으로 영어로 정보를 처리하면서, 글 전체에서 핵심적으로 다루는 내용이 무엇인지를 포착하는 데 초점을 맞추어야 한다. 그것이 독해의 비결임을 잊어서는 안 된다.

EXERCISE ·

• 정답 및 해설 p.121

주어진 글의 흐름과 관계없는 문장을 고르시오.

1   On February 24, 2008, Ralph Nader announced that he is running for President. (a) According to NBC, Nader believes that there is an urgent need for a "Jeffersonian revolution." (b) Both Barack Obama and Hillary Clinton criticized his decision. (c) They were concerned that Nader's decision would help the Republican Party. (d) After all, Obama and Clinton hated each other.

2   It may be very difficult to engage students, but the teacher should try to get them to relate to the topics discussed in class. (a) If he or she believes that a certain topic is not appealing to his or her students, the teacher can choose other engaging issues. (b) This is because if the students do not find the topic interesting, they are not likely to talk about it. (c) Our students are generally lazy, anyway. (d) Therefore, when choosing discussion topics, the emotional needs of students must be taken into account.

PRACTICE

• 정답 및 해설 p.122

주어진 글에 어울리지 않는 선택지를 고르시오.

1 RealAge®, a San Diego-based wellness company, provides a unique tool for finding out your biological age. (a) Visit http://www.realage.com/ and take the free RealAge test. (b) Other websites provide similar testing tools. (c) Test results may be shocking because your RealAge can be quite different from your birthday age. (d) For instance, your RealAge may be 25 even if your birthday age is 36.

2 Once we talked about major problems confronting modern society, and she was not hesitant about mentioning the issue of "humane" communication. (a) As she clearly pointed out, art is also a medium of communication. (b) In her opinion, art is capable of creating a world with sensitive people. (c) If such a world appeared, people would be engaged in truly humane communication. (d) A third World War would break out.

Chapter 2

빈 칸 채우기

UNIT 1   빈 칸이 처음에 있는 경우
UNIT 2   빈 칸이 중간에 있는 경우
UNIT 3   빈 칸이 마지막에 있는 경우
UNIT 4   연결어 선택

빈 칸 채우기는 Part I의 16문항을 구성하는데, 글의 일관성과 논리적인 관계에 대한 감각을 요하기 때문에 매우 까다로운 유형이다. 빈 칸이 오는 위치에 따라 처음 / 중간 / 마지막으로 나뉘며 15번 문항과 16번 문항은 연결어를 묻는다. 주제문을 토대로 글의 흐름을 정확히 포착해야 하며, 특히 정답이 글의 주제와 관련될 때가 많다는 점을 명심해야 한다.

유형 정리

1 전체 내용의 요약

In ancient Greece, the people were **not free to talk about their gods**. If someone spoke ill of the gods of their city, they would get into trouble. This was because respecting those gods was an important part of their social life. Many people believed that only their gods made them get along with each other. Therefore, some people even killed the wisest man in history to show their "respect" to their gods.

빈 칸이 처음에 오면 전체 내용의 요약이 정답인 경우가 많다. 이 지문에서도 첫 번째 문장에서 밑줄 친 부분이 지문 전체의 내용을 정리한 것이다. 특히 지문을 끝까지 읽으면서 전체 내용을 정확히 요약하는 데 노력을 기울여야 한다.

2 배경 지식 제공

Translation **has always been hard work.** To our surprise, it can sometimes affect our scientific knowledge. For instance, the Italian scientist Giovanni Virgino Schiaparelli used the word *canali* to describe what he saw on the surface of Mars. Some people translated this word as *canals*. This translation suggested that there might be intelligent living things that could build canals on Mars. The correct translation was *channels*, and unlike canals, channels are not made by intelligent beings.

다소 까다로운 유형으로 첫 번째 문장이 주제에 대한 배경 지식을 제공하는 경우이다. 이와 같은 경우에도 첫 번째 문장이 주제문과 밀접한 관련이 있음에 주의할 필요가 있다. 따라서 글의 전체 내용을 바탕으로 주제를 정확히 파악하는 노력이 요구된다.

3 반박하려는 내용

Many people say that **no movie can be worse than the film _D-War_**. But is the movie really so terrible? If you watch it really carefully, you will see that this amazing film has a solid plot. A man was to protect a woman who would be used to bring peace to the world. But he fell in love with her and tried to run away from the world. In the end, though, their love couldn't last. Pretty sad, huh? The movie also asks us a serious question: Should we save the world or follow our hearts?

가장 까다로운 유형으로 첫 번째 문장이 주제문과 반대되는 내용인 경우다. 이와 같은 경우에는 주제문을 정확히 파악해야 하며, 글의 전체 내용이 첫 번째 문장에 반대되는 내용이라는 점에 유의해야 한다. 따라서 글을 끝까지 읽고서 문제를 푸는 신중함이 요구된다.

Tips

1 주제와의 관련성

빈 칸 채우는 유형은 대개 지문의 주제를 정확히 파악하면 쉽게 해결할 수 있다. 따라서 글의 흐름에 유의하면서 주제를 찾아내는 것이 문제 해결의 핵심이다. 그리고 빈 칸에 들어가는 내용이 주제와 밀접한 관련을 맺는다는 점을 명심해야 한다. 선택지 가운데 주제와 관련이 먼 내용이 들어 있으면 대개 정답이 아니라는 것도 알아두자.

2 글의 전체 내용 파악

빈 칸 채우는 유형의 후반부 문제들은 끝까지 정독을 해야 하는 까다로운 유형이 대부분이다. 그렇기 때문에 한 두 문장을 근거로 성급하게 판단하지 않도록 유의해야 한다. 반드시 지문을 끝까지 읽고서 문제에서 요구하는 정답을 찾는 노력이 절실히 요구된다. 대개 두 개의 신택지 가운데 혼동이 될 수 있는데, 글의 무문석인 내용이 아니라 전체 내용과 관련된 선택지가 정답이라는 점을 명심하자.

• 정답 및 해설 p.122

빈 칸에 들어갈 가장 알맞은 말을 고르시오.

1   Blind dates can _____. There are so many stupid men out there and your date could be one of them. Imagine yourself talking with a man who is only interested in your looks. He can't understand your heart. He can't appreciate art. He is dull. You might keep watching the clock. You wish time passed faster. You can't find anything interesting to say. You just wish you left him.

(a) excite your life

(b) make you understand the true meaning of life

(c) be boring

2   Some people say that to meditate, you _____. But this is not the case. Meditation is when you are trying to look within yourself. Within yourself, you have both good and bad things. To meditate, you need to see them as they really are. No teacher can do that for you. Only you can look within yourself. In short, meditation does not require any outside help.

(a) need to spend a lot of money

(b) need the help of a teacher

(c) had better relax yourself

1   Gerard Lambert was born in America in 1886. In a sense, he was _____ _____. This was because he majored in architecture at Columbia University. Surprisingly, however, he became a very successful advertiser. For example, to advertise Listerine, his father's invention, Lambert came up with a bright idea. He told the people that by using the new mouthwash, they could save face in social situations.

Q. Choose the one option that best completes the sentence.

(a) meant to be a brave soldier

(b) meant to be a good advertiser

(c) supposed to be an inventor

(d) supposed to be an architect

2   The television show *Buffy the Vampire Slayer* _____ so many Americans for several years. When the TV series ended in 2003, millions of Americans cried, unwilling to see Buffy and her friends go. This was not because the show was so amazing, but because its presence made many Americans feel loved and cared for. In this way, the show comforted the Americans.

Q. Choose the one option that best completes the sentence.

(a) was hated by

(b) was loved by

(c) meant nothing to

(d) badly affected

UNIT 2 빈 칸이 중간에 있는 경우

빈 칸이 중간에 오는 유형은 특히 글의 자연스러운 논리 전개에 중점을 두어 접근해야 한다. 글의 주제를 염두에 두면서, 내용이 어떻게 전개되는지를 정확히 파악해야만 정답을 고를 수 있다. 그리고 글의 전개에서 내용이 반전되는 까다로운 유형도 있기 때문에 끝까지 정확하게 내용을 파악하려는 노력이 요구된다. 대체로 글의 주제와 관련된 내용이 정답이 되는 경우가 많다는 점도 참고하자.

유형 정리

1 주제 관련 내용

Many inventions are made by curious scientists. Take the example of Percy Spencer. He was **a scientist working for Raytheon**. At one time, he happened to face a magnetron and noticed that the candy bar in his pocket had thawed. He then placed some popcorn in front of the magnetron and watched the popcorn popping. Based on these observations, he invented the microwave oven.

이 지문에서 밑줄 친 부분은 주제문과 밀접하게 관련된 내용이다. 호기심이 많은 과학자들에 의해 많은 발명이 이루어졌다는 것이 주제이다. 따라서 그 예에 해당하는 Percy Spencer는 과학자여야 논리적으로 이상이 없다.

2 연결 내용

Socrates once said, "The unexamined life is not worth living." What he meant was that we should **examine the kind of life we live**. Do we live only for our own satisfaction? Do we live for worthy causes? Do we really know ourselves? According to Socrates, too many people do not know the true meaning of their lives. Only through self-examination can we find out the meaning of our existence.

첫 번째 문장에서 주제문이 나오고 있고, 빈 칸 이후의 연결 내용이 이 주제를 뒷받침하고 있는 흐름을 취하고 있다. 특별한 반전이 없으므로, 쉽게 답을 할 수 있는 유형에 속한다.

3 반전

These days, many South Korean women celebrate Valentine's Day by buying chocolates for their boyfriends. They seem to believe that doing that is the only way of expressing their love. **But that is not the case**. Traditionally, people celebrated Valentine's Day by exchanging love notes. In fact, this traditional way is much more romantic than buying those silly candies.

이 지문에서 밑줄 친 부분은 이제까지의 내용을 반박하는 문장이다. 이처럼 내용이 정반대로 전개될 수 있다는 점도 염두에 두어야 한다. 물론 출제 빈도가 높지는 않지만, 다양한 유형을 익혀두는 것이 TEPS를 준비하는 가장 효과적인 대책이기 때문이다.

• 정답 및 해설 p.123

빈 칸에 들어갈 가장 알맞은 말을 고르시오.

1   Cyberstalking is when someone uses the Internet to stalk someone else. Cyberstalkers use a variety of ways _____. For example, they use search engines such as Yahoo®, Google™, and MSN. Online forums and chat rooms are also often used by those bad people. Online communities such as Second Life® can be "useful" ways of finding their victims.

(a) to avoid the police

(b) to find their targets

(c) to help crime victims

2   Reese Witherspoon is not only an excellent actor but also a caring person. Because she _____, Witherspoon has decided to serve as honorary chairperson of the Avon Foundation. The mission of the foundation is "improve the lives of women globally." Together with the foundation, Witherspoon is trying very hard to make people aware of the importance of preventing breast cancer and domestic violence.

(a) wants to travel all around the world

(b) cares about other women

(c) cares about children

• 정답 및 해설 p.124

1   Does ginger relieve motion sickness better than placebo? Some studies support this claim _____. For instance, a study by the University of Michigan Medical Center proved that ginger was much more effective in preventing motion sickness than placebo. On the other hand, a study by Arfeen and colleagues showed that there were no significant differences in efficacy between ginger and placebo.

Q. Choose the one option that best completes the sentence.

(a) because scientists have known the fact

(b) because there have been many experiments

(c) while others do not

(d) while others help to prove it

2   Management is not concerned with business, but with people, and global management is no exception. Good management only comes from a deeper understanding of human nature. In the case of global management, we also need to _____. This does not mean, however, that human nature varies from culture to culture. It does mean that it can be expressed in different ways according to culture.

Q. Choose the one option that best completes the sentence.

(a) look at political factors

(b) take into account cultural differences

(c) think about the true purpose of global business

(d) examine the relationship between society and individuals

빈 칸이 마지막에 오는 경우는 대개 글의 결론에 해당하는 내용을 요구하는 경우가 많다. 마지막 문장을 통해서 글이 완결성을 가져야 하기 때문이다. 따라서 중심 내용에서 벗어나는 경우가 거의 없다는 점을 감안하여, 글의 전반적인 내용을 포착하는 데 중점을 두어야 한다. 특히 반복해서 제시되는 명사에 유의하면서 어떤 내용을 주로 말하고 있는가를 정확하게 파악하자.

유형 정리

1 중심 내용

Basically, learning a new language is the process of learning how to construct meaning in that language. As one can guess, it may have different rules to make a meaningful sentence. More importantly, the new language may have different ways of interpreting the world in which we live. In this sense, learning a different language is **the process of learning how to think in that language**.

윗글에서 밑줄 친 부분은 글의 중심 내용인 다른 언어를 배우는 과정의 특성을 설명한다. 이처럼 중심 내용을 보다 깊이 있게 요약하는 말이 글의 마지막에 놓일 수 있음을 기억하고, 전반적인 내용의 흐름을 포착하는 데 주의를 기울이자.

2 결론

Too many people believe that the means are always justified by the ends. This may be because they want to see good results at whatever cost. Such people need to be aware, however, that every action has some kinds of effects, positive or negative. In many cases, the effects of "wrong" means can hurt other people. This results from the kind of thinking which tries to justify any means to achieve "right" ends. **Thus the means should be controlled by ethical considerations**.

윗글에서 밑줄 친 부분은 목적이 수단을 정당화하는가에 대한 논의의 결론을 말한다. 이처럼 글에서 다룬 논의의 결론에 해당하는 말이 글의 끝에 올 수 있음도 알아두어야 한다. 전반적인 논의의 흐름을 놓치지 않도록 주의하자.

3 내용 요약

In the age in which design affects every aspect of our lives, good designers should develop various qualities. Of course, they need to have a keen sense of beauty. In addition, they ought to achieve a deep understanding of human functioning. Finally, they should grow creativity. <u>**In short, a good designer in this age should appreciate beauty, understand how humans work, and be creative**</u>.

윗글에서 밑줄 친 부분은 글 전체의 내용을 요약한다. 이것은 내용이 보다 잘 전달될 수 있도록 하기 위한 장치로 이해할 수 있다. 이와 같은 유형에서는 전체 내용이 정확히 요약되었는지를 확인하려는 노력이 요구된다.

> **Tips**
>
> **1 일관성**
> 빈 칸 채우기 유형은 특히 빈 칸이 후반부에 오는 경우의 문제가 매우 까다로운 경향이 있다. 이에 반해 전반부는 대체로 난이도가 평이한 편이다. 어떤 경우든, 글은 반드시 일관성(coherence)을 가져야 한다는 점을 최대한 활용해야 한다. 따라서 선택지의 내용이 혼란스럽게 느껴질 때는 중심 내용과 거리가 먼 것을 제외해 나가는 것이 기본적인 기법임을 명심하자.
>
> **2 완결성**
> 빈 칸이 마지막에 오는 유형은 특히 글이 완결성을 측정하려는 경향이 강하다. 히니의 단락이라 하디라도, 전개한 내용은 명확하게 완결되어야만 한다. 따라서 마지막 문장 바로 앞에 있는 문장까지의 논의와 어긋나는 내용이 정답이 되는 경우는 없다. 이 점을 참고하여, 글의 흐름을 꼼꼼하게 따져보고 내용이 어떤 식으로 결론이 나야 하는지를 생각해 보는 습관을 들이자.

• 정답 및 해설 p.125

빈 칸에 들어갈 가장 알맞은 말을 고르시오.

1 Even today, many people believe that we use only 10% of our brains. According to Eric Chudler Ph.D., however, "there is no scientific evidence" supporting that claim. He points out that every nerve cell works all the time. He also asks us why larger brains have been developed if they do not give us any advantage. In short, the claim that we use just 10% of our brains _____.

(a) helps us in many ways

(b) requires further research

(c) is a myth

2 Can a change in behavior and values solve the problems related to racial conflict? Of course not. This is mainly because racial conflict results from struggle for power between different groups, not from certain patterns of behavior or values. Consequently, racial discrimination is reflected in and reinforced by the political and economic structures of society. Therefore, in order to resolve racial conflict in the United States, it is necessary to _____.

(a) alter patterns of behavior and values in American society

(b) change the political and economic structures of American society

(c) ignore racial discrimination in American society

• 정답 및 해설 p.126

1   There are some differences between fog and mist. First of all, fog is thicker than mist. Second, we have more difficulty seeing in fog. If the visibility is less than 1 kilometer, we know that fog exists. If the visibility is between 1 kilometer and 2 kilometers, mist is present. Despite these differences, however, both fog and mist are clouds which _____.

Q. Choose the one option that best completes the sentence.

(a) rise high in the sky

(b) cause air pollution in many cities

(c) make us realize the importance of health

(d) contact the surface of the earth

2   The film *Spider-Man 2* is a constant reminder of being a true hero in this cruel world. In the movie, Peter Parker suffers a lot from his dual identity: as a superhero and as a college student. He suffers so severely that he just wants to lead an ordinary life; therefore, he decides to stop acting as a hero. But his deep sense of duty makes him return to his superhero role and save the city from destruction. In this sense, Parker is not only a good person, but also _____.

Q. Choose the one option that best completes the sentence.

(a) an excellent college student

(b) a true hero

(c) a famous actor

(d) a mental patient

UNIT 4 연결어 선택

빈 칸 채우기 유형 가운데 연결어는 Part Ⅰ의 15번 문항과 16번 문항으로 출제된다. 대체로 보아, 다른 빈 칸 채우기 문제에 비해 난이도가 쉬운 편이기는 하지만, 경우에 따라서 난이도가 매우 높을 수도 있다. 따라서 글의 전개를 생각하면서, 특히 바로 앞 문장과의 관계에 유의해서 정답을 골라야 한다. 선택지를 반드시 대입해보고 가장 자연스럽게 연결되는 것을 선택해야 함을 명심하자.

유형 정리

1 역접

As a little child, I learned ballet movements. The subtle beauty of ballet almost made me decide to become a ballerina. Because I was much more interested in capturing beauty in a permanent way, however, I changed my mind. **Nevertheless**, the ballet lessons taught me a lot of things about the beauty of human form. When every part of the human body is in perfect balance, it can show us what real beauty is.

흔히 출제되는 유형으로 앞의 내용과 대립하는 내용이 나오면 역접의 연결어를 선택해야 한다. 윗글에서는 발레리나가 되려고도 했다가 생각을 바꾸었지만, 발레를 통해 인간의 형체의 아름다움을 배울 수 있었음을 서술했다.

2 결과

When I was admonished by an American teacher for the first time, I was puzzled by the cultural differences between Korea and America. If your elders scold you in Korea, you should avoid eye contact with them and just look downward. Naturally, when the American teacher told me off, I tried to avoid eye contact, which made her angry. I felt that something must be wrong. **Consequently**, I wondered, "How do Americans express respect for their elders?"

역시 흔히 출제되는 유형으로 앞의 문장까지의 내용 전개를 바탕으로 일정한 결과를 나타내는 내용이 나오면 결과의 연결어를 선택해야 한다. 윗글에서는 결과적으로 우리나라와 미국 사이의 문화 차이에 대해 궁금하게 되었음을 서술했다.

3 보완

Jeniffer Smith has won so many awards in the field of mathematics. Of course, they can tell a lot about her. More importantly, however, Smith is aware that the true purpose of mathematics is to reach the ultimate truth. <u>**At the same time**</u>, she is an innocent girl who is so curious about what makes people tick. She is an innocent girl who is ready to explore all the possibilities surrounding her.

역시 흔히 출제되는 유형으로 빈 칸 앞뒤로 앞내용을 보완 또는 보충설명하는 내용이 나오면 앞 내용을 보완하는 연결어를 답으로 선택해야 한다. 수학을 잘하게 된 배경으로 그녀의 유별난 호기심을 들어 보완하고 있다.

> ### Tips
>
> **1 앞뒤 문장의 관계**
> 연결어를 묻는 문제는 기본적으로 앞뒤 문장이 자연스럽게 이어질 수 있게 하는 연결어를 택하는 문제로 분석된다. 물론 글의 전반적인 흐름이 중요하긴 하지만, 선택지를 빈 칸에 대입했을 때 앞뒤 문장이 자연스럽게 연결이 되지 않는다면 정답이 될 수 없다. 따라서 반드시 앞뒤 문장의 연결을 부드럽게 해주는가 하는 점을 따져보아야 한다.
>
> **2 자연스러운 내용 전개**
> 빈 칸 채우기 유형은 글의 일관성과 각 문장의 논리적 관련성에 대한 김각을 묻는 유형으로 생각된다. 특히 각 문장의 논리적 관련성에 대한 감각은 짧은 시간에 길러지는 것이 아니기 때문에, 좋은 글에서 각 문장이 어떻게 연결되어 내용을 자연스럽게 전개하는가를 꼼꼼히 분석하는 습관을 들여야만 한다. 그래야만 실전에서 당황하지 않고 차분하게 문제를 풀어낼 수 있다.

• 정답 및 해설 p.126

빈 칸에 들어갈 가장 알맞은 말을 고르시오.

1 On February 2, 2007, an orange-yellow snow fell in western Siberia. Some people feared that it might have been caused by air pollution. The authorities concerned couldn't explain this strange phenomenon. Later, it was found that the snow was not toxic. _____, the residents were told not to make use of the snow. This was mainly because the iron content in the snow was higher than usual.

(a) For example

(b) Therefore

(c) Nevertheless

2 "I hate you, you hate me, we're a dysfunctional family," begins one of the anti-Barney songs. Some people may think that such songs are just funny ways of making fun of the silly character. The problem is, however, that deep hatred is clearly reflected in those songs. As is widely known, hatred is not easy to resolve. _____, we need to take those songs more seriously.

(a) However

(b) Therefore

(c) In contrast

1 The town of Matfen sounds to me as if it were my own hometown. In fact, I grew up in the country, not in a city. And I believe that life in the country has a good impact on our emotional growth. _____, life in big cities often affects our feelings in a negative way. This is mainly because people do not have many opportunities to get to really know other people in big cities.

Q. Choose the one option that best completes the sentence.

(a) As a result
(b) After all
(c) For example
(d) On the other hand

2 Will your writing skill improve if you just write more often? Usually, it won't. Part of the reason is that writing requires you to examine your own ideas. If you look at your thoughts, you will be surprised to find that most of them are not clear enough. In addition, you are expected to express them powerfully. Of course, this implies hard work and creativity. _____, in order to write well, you need to learn how to think clearly and creatively.

Q. Choose the one option that best completes the sentence.

(a) Nonetheless
(b) Therefore
(c) Instead
(d) Fortunately

Chapter 3

질문 유형은 이렇다

UNIT 1   전반적 정보 Ⅰ

UNIT 2   전반적 정보 Ⅱ

UNIT 3   정오 유형 Ⅰ

UNIT 4   정오 유형 Ⅱ

UNIT 5   세부 사항 Ⅰ

UNIT 6   세부 사항 Ⅱ

UNIT 1 전반적 정보 Ⅰ

전반적 정보를 묻는 유형은 Part Ⅱ의 초반부에서 주로 제시되는 유형으로, 다른 유형에 비해 쉽게 해결할 수 있는 유형이다. 대개 첫 번째 문장과 마지막 문장 정도만 읽어도 쉽게 풀 수 있지만, 의외로 까다롭게 출제될 수도 있음을 기억해야 한다. 세세한 해석에 치중하지 말고 전반적인 글의 흐름을 파악하여 문제를 푸는 시간을 최소화해야 다른 유형에 충분한 시간을 투자할 수 있다.

유형 정리

1 주제 찾기

In fact, Joanne Kathleen Rowling is a genius writer. When she was only six years old, she wrote her first fantasy story. It was about a sick rabbit and his friends including a huge bee. While attending school, Rowling got ideas for characters in her books. When traveling to London by train, she came up with an idea for fantasy novels, which later became known as the *Harry Potter* series.

이 글의 주제는 Joanne Kathleen Rowling's talent as a writer(작가로서의 조앤 캐틀린 롤링의 재능)이다. 첫 번째 문장에서 롤링이 '천재 작가(genius writer)'임을 밝히고 있고 나머지 문장들은 이에 대한 구체적인 예들이다.

2 제목 정하기

Nanotechnology is concerned with developing tiny devices as small as atoms. Some people think that we cannot use such small devices in everyday life. Well, maybe that will be possible. At present, however, the technology is used to make clothes that can fight against stains and bandages that can kill harmful germs. Many scientists predict that nanotechnology will be used to improve everyday life in many more ways.

이 글의 제목은 The Use of Nanotechnology in Everyday Life(일상생활에서 나노테크놀러지의 쓰임새)이다. 글의 전체에 걸쳐, 일부 사람들의 생각과 달리 나노테크놀러지가 일상 생활에 이미 쓰이고 있고 앞으로 쓰임새가 많아질 것이라고 밝혔음에 유의하자.

3 글의 목적 파악

Is there a relationship between blood types and personalities? In 1927, Takeji Furukawa published a paper, claiming that it would be possible to find out more about a person's personality by examining his or her blood types. Although his claim had no scientific basis, some people such as Masahiko Nomi believed that Furukawa was right. Nomi even wrote a book based on the mistaken belief.

이 글의 목적은 "To explain the wrong belief that blood types are related to personalities(혈액형이 성격과 관련이 있다는 잘못된 견해를 설명하기 위해서)"이다. 첫 번째 문장에서 이에 대한 의문을 제기한 다음 잘못된 견해의 전개 과정을 설명했다.

1 다음 글의 제목으로 가장 적절한 것을 고르시오.

When an economy grows, fewer people work on farms. Instead, more people work in factories and service industries. As a result, more people live in cities rather than in rural areas. In the early stages of the economic growth, the cities spend more money on public facilities than on building factories. In the later stages, more money is spent on constructing factories.

(a) How to Spend Money Wisely

(b) Building Factories in Rural Areas

(c) The Stages of Economic Growth

2 다음 글을 쓴 목적으로 가장 적절한 것을 고르시오.

At present, scientists do not know whether aliens exist or not. Many scientists believe, however, that if certain conditions are met, aliens can live on other planets. Most of them think that such conditions need to be similar to those of the Earth. A few scientists believe that there might be other forms of life that could live without those conditions. Only time will tell which side is right.

(a) To criticize those scientists who do not answer important questions

(b) To explain different opinions about aliens

(c) To prove that aliens do not exist

• 정답 및 해설 p.128

1 These days, many language purists are mad about text messaging. In their opinion, short "words" used in it are not good English. They frown at such expressions as BTW (by the way) and IMO (in my opinion). As you can guess, they do not like emoticons at all. They may have a point, but many people feel that they overreact to useful ways of communicating in everyday life.

Q. What is the best title of the passage?

(a) The Importance of Text Messaging in Everyday Life

(b) How to Use Emoticons Correctly

(c) Language Purists Angry over Simple Expressions

(d) The Importance of Using Good English

2 When she attended Beverly Hills High School, Angelina Jolie was an odd one out. This was mainly because she came from a poor family. Most of her classmates came from rich families and they looked down on her. At that time, Jolie was skinny, and this also made her unpopular among other students. As a result, she lost faith in herself and began to hurt herself.

Q. What is the purpose of the passage?

(a) To criticize Jolie's bad habits

(b) To describe Jolie's high school days

(c) To complain about Jolie's pride

(d) To inquire about Jolie's emotional problems

UNIT 2 전반적 정보 Ⅱ

Part Ⅱ에서 제시되는 전반적 정보 유형에는 주제와 제목을 요하는 유형 이외에 저자나 독자와 관련된 유형도 있다. 글의 전반적인 내용을 바탕으로 상식적이고 논리적으로 짐작했을 때 저자나 독자와 관련하여 올바른 사항을 찾아내야 한다. 주제와 제목 유형의 풀이에서와 마찬가지로, 세부사항보다는 전체적인 글의 흐름에 유의하면서 정확하게 답을 찾아내려는 노력이 필요하다.

유형 정리

1 대상 독자

This is Eric Jones, **Editor-in-Chief** at Hope Publishers. We are a publishing company that produces high quality ELT titles. Since 1999, we have published over 1,000 titles, focusing on meeting the needs of Japanese learners of English. **Just like your company**, we are going to attend the 53rd IRA Convention to be held in Atlanta, USA. We were wondering if you could have a meeting with us there to discuss our common interests in developing new reading materials.

윗글은 어떤 출판사의 편집장이 다른 출판사의 관계자에게 보내는 글이다. 첫 문장에서 자신이 편집장임을 밝혔고, 또한 상대방 회사도 동일함을 말했기 때문이다. 주요 단서를 통해 대상 독자가 누구인지를 정확히 포착해야 함을 명심하자.

2 저자의 직종

When I **visited Yemen** for the first time, I was shocked to find that kidnapping was so common in the country. Of course, **I had traveled to many dangerous countries**. But I said to my guide, "I have never felt threatened like this before." He explained to me that kidnapping was a "tradition" in that notorious country. According to him, the various tribes thought nothing of using foreigners as a bargaining chip.

윗글에서 밑줄 친 부분으로부터 저자의 직종이 여행가임을 알 수 있다. 역시 세부적인 사항보다는 전반적으로 중요한 정보에 초점을 맞추어 판단해야 한다. 따라서 지나치게 세부적인 사항이 아니라 전반적인 흐름에 유의하자.

3 저자의 태도

The matter is concerned with your preference for hairstyle. Ophilia has informed us that you have long hair. I firmly believe that everyone has a precious right to decide on their hairstyle and no one has a right to interfere with other people's matters. Given a conservative atmosphere in my country, however, we need to explore a possibility that your preference for hairstyle might change.

윗글은 외국인을 초청하면서 문화적인 차이로 인해 머리 모양을 바꾸어줄 것을 매우 조심스럽게 요청하는 글이다. 이 글에서 저자가 독자에 대해 매우 동정적인(sympathetic) 태도를 나타냈음을 포착할 수 있어야 한다.

Tips

1 단서 포착

이 단원의 전반적 정보 유형은 앞 단원의 전반적 정보 유형과 달리, 글에서 정답을 찾아내는 데 필요한 주요 단서를 정확히 포착하는 것이 기본적인 해법이다. 특히, 독자나 저자의 직종을 요구하는 유형은 직업이나 활동과 관련된 단어들이 주요 단서에 해당한다. 따라서 이와 같은 말에 특히 유의하면서 빠른 속도로 문제를 풀어나가야 함을 명심하자.

2 논리적인 추론

특히 저자의 태도를 요하는 유형에서는 글을 있는 그대로 받아들이면서 논리적으로 수론하려는 노력이 요구된다. 한 두 단어에 얽매여 저자의 태도를 성급하게 판단해서는 안 되며, 글을 끝까지 읽고서 저자가 어떤 태도를 나타내는가를 비약 없이 판단하려는 노력이 요구된다. 저자의 태도는 일종의 추론이리고 볼 수도 있는데, 본래 추론의 형태와 마찬가지로 상식적이고 논리적으로 판단을 내려야 함에 유의하자.

• 정답 및 해설 p.129

1 **다음 글의 대상 독자는 누구인가?**

You ought to keep in mind that it is absolutely necessary to adopt and pursue rational policies. Otherwise, our precious country will suffer a lot of losses. In order to shape such policies, you should set attainable goals and seek the interests of our country. This may sound too easy, but you will find out how difficult it is to pursue rational policies in the real world.

(a) Professors

(b) Policymakers

(c) Dancers

2 **다음 글에서 저자는 어떤 태도를 취하고 있나?**

This argument is based on a misunderstanding of the nature of liberal democracy. Even if you deny its basic principles, that does not mean that it is false. By doing so, you just prove that you are not a believer in liberal democracy. This is mainly because ideology is a matter of belief, not a matter of proof. In other words, you don't have to prove the truth of ideology.

(a) Sympathetic

(b) Supportive

(c) Critical

• 정답 및 해설 p.130

1 To be frank with you, I don't know why Osama bin Laden has turned into such a monster. When he attended college with me at King Abdul Aziz, he was interested in religion, and even in charity. Of course, what he has done so far is completely wrong. I won't forgive him for what he has done to the American people! I won't forgive him for betraying his own religion! I won't forgive him for disgracing us!

Q. Who is the writer?

(a) Osama bin Laden's father
(b) Osama bin Laden's teacher
(c) Osama bin Laden's student
(d) Osama bin Laden's friend

2 With regard to the "Financial Verification," I need to get the relevant documents from my parents. Are there any special forms available for "Letter of Guarantee from Parents"? Or can my parents just write a letter stating that they will provide my tuition and living expenses? Regarding the "Bank Letter," Korean banks usually issue "Certificate of Deposit." Would this be acceptable to your college? Or do I need to request my bank to issue a special letter?

Q. To whom is the writer writing?

(a) A bank teller
(b) A college official
(c) The post office
(d) A certified public accountant

UNIT 3 · 청오 유형 Ⅰ

청오유형이란 글의 내용과 일치하거나 일치하지 않는 사항을 측정하는 유형을 가리킨다. 세부사항을 요하는 유형과 다소 비슷한 면도 있지만, 글 전체의 내용을 대상으로 한다는 점이 다르다. 따라서 이 유형의 문제를 푸는 데 시간이 더 많이 소요되는 경향이 있기 때문에 시간 배분에 특히 유의해야 한다. 그리고 오답 유형을 정확히 숙지하여 실수를 줄여야 함을 명심하자.

유형 정리

1 내용과 반대되는 경우

Even today, America remains the promised land for so many people. This is because we are a nation who has stood the trial of the times. We are a nation that is the home of hope and love. We are a nation that has embraced people from all walks of life. Thus our leadership in the new era not only signifies the true beginning of human history, but also the beginning of a new generation of humanity. Let our country lead the way by humbly serving all people around the globe.

전반적으로 국제 사회에서 미국의 책임 있는 역할을 강조하는 글이다. 따라서 이런 흐름과 반대되는 오답을 제시할 수 있다. 오답 유형 가운데 가장 흔한 경우이므로 정확히 익혀 두자.

2 내용에 언급되지 않은 경우

Just in case, I need to mention that I would like to keep my account open until August 31, 2008. On September 1, 2008, I will sign the account closure form and fax it to your bank. In addition, I would like you to email the details of some transactions, especially insurance transactions. I think my daughter's school will deposit some amounts of money in my account. Thus, would you be so kind as to email the details of all those transactions?

만일의 사태에 대비하여 일정 기간까지 계좌를 유지하겠다는 취지의 글이다. 이와 관련하여 글에서 전혀 언급되지 않은 오답을 제시할 수 있다. 이처럼 글에 나타나지 않은 사항에 대해 말하는 경우는 대개 오답일 확률이 높다는 점을 기억하자.

3 내용을 잘못 이해한 경우

In formulating his theory of general relativity, Einstein made three assumptions about the universe. One of them was that the universe did not change. He found out, however, that if his equations were correct, the universe would change. To address the problem, he changed his equations by using a cosmological constant. Unfortunately, this was his terrible mistake because Edwin Hubble found out that the universe was changing.

아인슈타인이 일반 상대성 이론을 체계화할 때 저질렀던 오류에 관한 글이다. 다소 까다로운 내용으로 생각되는데, 이와 같은 경우 주어진 내용을 잘못 이해한 사항이 오답으로 제시될 수 있음에 유의해야 한다.

Tips

1 시간 배분

정오유형은 세부사항 유형에 비해서도 보다 많은 시간이 소요되는 유형이다. 따라서 Part Ⅲ 문제나 Part Ⅱ 의 전반적 정보 유형과 같이 시간이 상대적으로 적게 걸리는 문제를 미리 풀고 나서, 어느 정도 여유를 갖고 서 정오유형 문제를 다루는 것이 득점에 유리하다. 그렇지 않다 하더라도, 이 유형은 시간이 많이 소요된다 는 점을 고려해야 한다.

2 중심 내용과의 관련성

정오유형에 나타나는 오답의 유형은 여러 가지이지만, 어떤 경우든 내개 중심내용과 관련이 높은 내용이 제 시되는 경우가 많다. 따라서 정오유형에서도 글의 중심내용이 무엇인지를 정확히 파악하고 이에 바탕을 두 어 각각의 선택지를 차분히 검토하는 것이 기본적인 해결 전략이다. 평소에도 글을 읽으면시 늘 중심 내용을 염두에 두는 습관을 들이는 것이 바람직하다.

• 정답 및 해설 p.130

다음 글의 내용과 일치하는 설명을 고르시오.

1   Humanistic psychology is quite different from both behaviorism and psychoanalysis. Unlike behaviorists, humanistic psychologists believe that people should be regarded as unique individuals, not as subjects of "scientific" research. They also criticize psychoanalysts for overemphasizing the influence of one's drives on one's behavior. Instead, they claim that the purpose of psychology is to help people realize their potential.

(a) Humanistic psychology is similar to psychoanalysis.

(b) Humanistic psychology has nothing to do with helping people.

(c) Humanistic psychology treats people as individuals.

2   Can material wealth bring happiness to us? Too many people seem to think so and they are willing to do anything to earn a lot of money. Unfortunately for them, material wealth cannot make us truly happy. This is mainly because true happiness comes from within, not from without. In addition, it requires inner peace, which can be negatively affected by the pursuit of material wealth.

(a) Inner peace is important to happiness.

(b) Material wealth guarantees happiness.

(c) True happiness comes from the outside.

• 정답 및 해설 p.131

1   Many different things about McNuity's work have caught my eyes. More than anything else, her design tells me that she can think outside the box. People usually think that tea tables are supposed to be rectangular. But McNuity challenges this widespread idea and comes up with a triangular table. This kind of creativity is essential for the future and comes only from quality education.

Q. Which of the following is true according to the passage?

(a) McNuity's work is not creative at all.

(b) McNuity is an original thinker.

(c) McNuity follows the ideas of other people.

(d) McNuity believes that tea tables are supposed to be rectangular.

2   Interestingly enough, many people misunderstand the difference between deductive and inductive reasoning. They believe that in deductive reasoning, a specific conclusion is drawn from a general assumption. They also think that in inductive reasoning, a general conclusion is drawn from individual facts. But they are wrong. In deductive reasoning, if the assumptions are true, the conclusion is definitely true. In contrast, in inductive reasoning, even if the assumptions are true, the conclusion is not necessarily true.

Q. Which of the following is true according to the passage?

(a) In deductive reasoning, we draw a specific conclusion from a general assumption.

(b) In inductive reasoning, we draw a general conclusion from individual facts.

(c) In deductive reasoning, the truth of the assumptions guarantees the truth of the conclusion.

(d) In inductive reasoning, the truth of the assumptions guarantees the truth of the conclusion.

UNIT 4   정오 유형 Ⅱ

정오유형의 오답 유형 가운데, 내용을 잘못 이해한 경우는 몇 가지 형식으로 정리할 수 있다. 다른 유형에 비해, 내용을 잘못 이해한 경우가 오답으로 제시되는 빈도가 높고, 또한 쉽게 선택하기 쉬운 오답이기 때문에, 특히 주의를 요한다. 아래에서 세 가지로 나눈 형식을 정확히 숙지하여, 오답을 정답으로 착각하지 않도록 유의해야 하며, 언제나 중심 내용을 염두에 두어야 함을 명심하자.

유형 정리

1   잘못된 Paraphrase

Jean-Baptiste Lully was widely known as the first conductor. Instead of a baton, however, he used a long stick to conduct. This was because there were no batons at that time. One day, while conducting, he mistakenly pushed his stick into his foot. As a result, he came down with gangrene and passed away. A tragic death for the first composer!

최초의 지휘자의 비극적인 죽음을 다룬 글이다. 윗글에서 came down with는 developed로, passed away는 died로 paraphrase를 할 수 있는데, 이때 잘못된 표현을 제시하는 오답 유형을 생각할 수 있다. paraphrase는 언제나 정확히 이루어져야 한다.

2   왜곡된 사실관계

Enrico Fermi won the 1938 Nobel Prize for Physics because people thought that he discovered "new radioactive elements." Interestingly, though, Fermi was not sure whether he found such elements or not. Later, three German scientists proved that what Fermi discovered was fission fragments. When he received the Nobel Prize, no one knew about the phenomenon of atomic fission, which caused those fragments. Maybe, Fermi was just a lucky scientist.

새로운 방사성원소를 발견했다고 착각하여 노벨 물리학상을 수여한 일화에 대한 글이다. 글에서 밝혔듯이, 엔리코 페르미는 그런 원소를 발견한 것이 아니었다. 이와 관련하여 사실관계를 왜곡한 오답이 제시될 수 있다.

3 지나친 추론

One thing that greatly affects me and remains a strong motive for creativity is that music is not only beautiful but also rich in content. Whenever I listen to the *Canon D in major* by Johann Pachelbel, I feel touched by its sweet melodies, and at the same time, can hear many ordinary but beautiful stories of lots of people. I can hear someone who is in love singing her heart. I can hear someone who is ambitious bragging about his dreams. I can hear a mother calling her beloved son. It is so amazing.

창의성의 강한 동인으로서의 음악에 대한 글이다. 이 내용으로부터 지나치게 추론을 하는 오답을 생각해 볼 수 있다. 특히 TEPS에서는 추론이 언제나 논리적이고 상식적인 범위에 머물러야 한다는 점을 명심하자.

> **Tips**
>
> **1 Paraphrase의 중요성**
> 세부사항 유형과 마찬가지로 정오유형에서도 정확한 paraphrase의 중요성은 아무리 강조해도 지나치지 않는다. 오답의 상당수가 paraphrase를 잘못한 경우에 해당하기 때문이다. 따라서 이 책의 "어휘"편에 수록된 동의어뿐만 아니라 http://dictionary.msn.com에서 이용할 수 있는 Thesaurus를 통해 다양한 동의어를 평소에 익혀두자.
>
> **2 정확한 사실 관계의 확인**
> 징오유형은 본래 글의 내용을 정확히 이해했는가를 측정하는 데 목적이 있다. 따라서 사실 관계가 왜곡되면 오답이 될 수밖에 없음에 유의해야 한다. 글을 읽어가면서 특히 중심 내용과 관련하여 사실 관계가 어떻게 되는지를 정확히 포착히는 연습이 매우 중요하다. 그리고 평소에 광범위한 독서를 통해 여러 망년의 상식을 넓혀두는 것도 내용 이해에 도움이 된다는 점을 기억하자.

EXERCISE

• 정답 및 해설 p.132

다음 글의 내용과 일치하는 설명을 고르시오.

1   On April 28, 1994, North Korea demanded that Washington and Pyongyang enter into bilateral negotiations to replace the existing armistice agreement with a new peace treaty. Since then, North Korea has tried to undermine the existing armistice regime by violating the armistice agreement. On May 3, 1995, Pyongyang closed the Neutral Nations Supervisory Commission by expelling the commission's Polish members from North Korea.

(a) North Korea did not like the existing armistice agreement.

(b) Washington was willing to negotiate a new peace treaty with Pyongyang.

(c) North Korea supported the Neutral Nations Supervisory Commission.

2   Stephen Hawking is an expert on black holes. Nevertheless, he once made a mistake. In 1975, he claimed that there were no black holes in Cygnus X-1. Kip Thorne disagreed, and they made a bet on who was right. In 1990, Hawking had no choice but to admit that Thorne was right. Despite his reputation as a great scientist, however, he did not want to admit his defeat. He even got a friend to steal the records of the bet from Thorne's office.

(a) Kip Thorne is an expert on black holes.

(b) Stephen Hawking was notorious for being a bad scientist.

(c) Stephen Hawking made a mistake.

1 When Senator Hillary Clinton expressed her feelings about competing against Obama, many people thought that she would quit her presidential campaign. But Clinton said that her remarks were just a "recognition" that both of them were on the verge of "historic change." According to NBC, however, it is not certain whether she will stay in the race until the end.

Q. Which of the following is true according to the passage?

(a) Clinton will quit her presidential campaign.

(b) Clinton may not stay in the race in the end.

(c) Clinton hates Obama.

(d) Obama supports Clinton.

2 About the Asian work ethic, I'm not sure whether or not appreciating hard work is one of its elements. Traditionally, we Koreans think highly of hard work, and finding a truly earnest person is one of the most important things that Korean managers have to do. Further, I have a bone-deep belief that teaching doesn't just mean giving knowledge to students, but it primarily means touching the hearts of our students. I believe that true education frees the souls of students.

Q. Which of the following is true according to the passage?

(a) Koreans do not appreciate hard work.

(b) The writer believes that true education means giving knowledge to students.

(c) Koreans recognize the importance of hard work.

(d) It is easy to find a truly earnest person.

세부사항은 인물이나 사물의 특징, 인과 관계, 그리고 비교/대조에 대한 구체적인 내용을 질문하는 유형으로 다소 까다로운 부분이다. 왜냐하면 각각의 사항을 약간씩 변형하여 선택지로 제시하기 때문에 정답을 판단하기가 쉽지 않기 때문이다. 따라서 전반적 정보를 요구하는 유형에서 절약한 시간을 활용하여 꼼꼼하게 지문과 맞추어 보면서 신중하게 풀어나가야 한다.

유형 정리

1 특정 인물 / 사물

Text to Speech Software.Com (http://www.text-to-speech-software.com/) gives you a chance to use its **text-to-speech software** for free. When you use this software, you can listen to your articles in many different voices. Just copy those articles to the screen and press the Play button. You can even change the text into an MP3 file. So, what are you waiting for? Just one click can make a difference in your listening experience.

세부사항을 측정하는 문항에서 가장 자주 등장하는 유형은 특정 인물이나 사물에 대한 구체적인 내용을 질문하는 유형이다. 윗글에서는 텍스트를 음성으로 바꾸어주는 프로그램에 대해 설명하고 있는데, 주요 특징을 정확히 살펴보아야 한다는 점에 유의하자.

2 인과 관계

In his famous experiment in 1971, Philip Zimbardo made his students play the roles of guards and inmates in a jail. As time went by, the guards became cruel and the inmates got depressed. Zimbardo thought that those changes came from the roles which they were given. According to him, **when a person is given a powerful role, he or she is likely to abuse it and get cruel.**

사회 현상이나 자연 현상을 다룬 글에는 대개 인과관계(causality)가 드러나는데, 윗글에서는 진하게 표시한 이와 같은 인과관계를 나타낸다. 상관관계(correlation)는 두 현상 사이에 단순한 관계가 있다는 점에서 인과관계와 다르다는 점도 알아두자.

3 비교 / 변화

The theory of intelligent design is quite different from the theory of evolution. More than anything else, this new theory claims that an "intelligent designer" has made all the living things at the same time. In this sense, supporters of the theory do not believe that complex living things have developed from simple living things. According to them, those changes are impossible.

세부사항을 측정하는 문항의 주요 유형으로 두 대상 사이의 공통점이나 차이점을 질문하는 유형이다. 윗글에서는 진화론과 지적설계론 사이의 차이점을 밝히고 있는데, 어떤 점에서 다른지에 중점을 두어 읽어나가야 함에 유의하자.

Tips

1 시간 배정
세부사항을 질문하는 유형은 추론(inference)을 요하는 유형과 더불어 문제 풀이에 시간이 많이 소요되는 유형이다. 왜냐하면 한두 단어 때문에 정답이 달라지기 때문이다. 따라서 상대적으로 시간이 적게 드는 유형을 먼저 푼 다음 여유를 갖고서 한 문장 한 문장을 대조하면서 신중하게 풀어야 한다. Part Ⅲ를 가장 먼저 푸는 것이 도움이 된다는 점도 기억하자.

2 Paraphrase
세부사항을 측정하는 유형의 선택지는 대개 본문에 제시되어 있는 문장의 일부 단어의 paraphrase(다른 말로 바꾼 것)에 해당한다. 예컨대 develop(발달하다)의 paraphrase는 grow(자라다)이다. 이때 선택지의 단어가 본문의 단어를 정확히 paraphrase했는지에 특히 유의해야 한다. 이와 관련해서는 어휘편에 세시된 동의어를 정확히 익혀두는 것도 도움이 된다.

• 정답 및 해설 p.133

1   Evanescence가 왜 성공할 수 있었나?

In 1998, Amy Lee created a rock band, which became known as Evanescence. Because she was familiar with both classical music and heavy metal, she was able to make a unique kind of music. This helped to make the band's first album *Fallen* a success. In 2006, the band released its second album *The Open Door*, which also turned out to be a huge success.

(a) Because its founder was a woman.

(b) Because its music was very unique.

(c) Because its album was cheap.

2   Rachel Carson의 책에 대한 뒤섞인 반응은 어떤 것이었나?

When she published *Silent Spring* in 1962, Rachel Carson got mixed responses. Many people thanked her for warning the dangers of using pesticide carelessly. On the other hand, some pesticide companies threatened to sue her. They said that Carson used false data to support her claim. Because her warning was based on years of scientific study, she continued to defend her position.

(a) Some were interested in her work, while others were indifferent to it.

(b) Some were disappointed with her work, while others were angry about it.

(c) Some welcomed her work, while others complained about it.

•정답 및 해설 p.134

1 As the 21st century begins, people are trying to find a new model for leadership. Many experts believe that servant leadership is the most promising model. According to Robert Greenleaf, a pioneer of servant leadership, true leaders are "servants of those they lead." In his opinion, leaders are supposed to help those served to grow. This can, in turn, help their organizations grow.

Q. In Greenleaf's opinion, who is a true leader?

(a) A person who controls others
(b) A person who abuses others
(c) A person who develops others
(d) A person who manages others

2 A fire claimed at least 24 lives in a shopping mall in the central Philippines on Christmas Day. According to the police, the fire broke out because of firecrackers. It hit the entrance door of the mall and many shoppers couldn't move outside the building. Later, they were found burned to death. The police are trying to stop anyone from selling firecrackers in the area.

Q. Why did the fire break out?

(a) Because of a firearm
(b) Because of a firework
(c) Because of a firebox
(d) Because of a firefly

세부사항 Ⅱ

세부사항 유형은 글의 내용 가운데 주요한 사항을 측정하는 유형이기 때문에, 여러 가지 관련된 내용을 출제할 수 있다. 앞 단원에 이어, 이 단원에서는 크게 세 가지 유형으로 세부사항 유형을 연습한다. 구체적인 분류보다는 이처럼 세부사항에 대해 다양한 각도에서 접근할 수 있음에 유의해야 하고, 무엇보다도 내용을 정확히 이해하려는 노력이 긴요함을 명심하자.

유형 정리

1 특성

"I only regret I have but one life to lose for my country," declared Nathan Hale, who is a national hero in American culture. During the American Revolutionary War, he gathered information on British troop movements in New York City by disguising as a school teacher. Unfortunately, a British major found out who Hale really was and captured him. He uttered his final words and was hanged in front of British soldiers. The words still touch the majority of Americans and contribute to his popularity.

애국자로서의 네이단 헤일에 관한 글이다. 인물에 대한 정보를 통해 일정한 특성을 파악할 수 있는데, 이와 관련하여 구체적인 사항을 질문할 수 있다. 역시 중심 내용을 염두에 두면서 접근해야 함을 잊어서는 안 된다.

2 이유

Between 5th and 19th February, 2008, the Imagine Cup Innovation Accelerator took place in the Silicon Valley. Six software design teams took part in the competition. On the final day, the Poland team was given the "business readiness" award because they had the largest virtual dollar budget. The South Korean team won the "innovation" award because they were excellent at applying business strategies. In addition, many judges felt that their product would change the lives of many people.

이매진컵 2008년 행사에서 폴란드 팀과 한국 팀이 수상하게 된 이유를 설명한 글이다. 특히 글에서 이유에 해당하는 부분을 정확히 파악해야 한다. 일정한 일에는 대개 이유가 있기 마련이므로, 흔히 출제되는 유형에 속한다.

3 조건

Because they move too slowly, manatees often collide with boats, leading to injuries and deaths. Sadly for us, a large number of manatees lose their lives each year. According to the U.S. Geological Survey, if we do not take appropriate action, there is a strong possibility that we may not meet "recovery criteria within 100 years." Therefore, it's time for us to protect them from danger.

해우(海牛)의 특성을 감안한 적절한 조치를 취하지 않으면 해우 개체 수를 기준만큼 복구하기가 쉽지 않음을 설명한 글이다. 이처럼 일정한 결과를 이끌어내는 조건을 질문하는 세부사항 유형도 있음을 기억하자.

Tips

1 선택적 독해
세부사항 유형은 대개 글의 특정 부분에 대한 질문이기 때문에, 해당되는 부분만 정확히 찾아서 읽고 답하는 전략도 가능하기는 하다. 이와 같은 전략을 구사하는 경우에도 최소한 해당 부분 앞뒤 문장은 함께 보아두어야 실수를 줄일 수 있다. 또한 선택한 부분의 내용이 정확히 paraphrase가 되었는지도 하나하나 따져보아야 함을 명심하자.

2 전반적 내용 감안
실전에서 문제를 풀다 보면, 시간에 쫓겨 어쩔 수 없이 1번에서 지시한 선택적 독해 전략을 써야 하는 경우도 있다. 그렇지만 성급하게 판단해서는 오히려 감점을 당할 수도 있기 때문에, 어떤 경우든 최종 판단에서는 첫 문장과 마지막 문장에 나타난 전반적인 내용을 감안해야 함에 유의하자. 그렇지 않으면 오답을 고르기가 쉽기 때문이다. 전체 글의 흐름을 포착하는 능력은 이처럼 어떤 경우에도 중요하다는 점을 잊어서는 안 된다.

• 정답 및 해설 p.135

1 범고래의 특성으로 올바른 것을 고르시오.

What is the fastest water mammal? Some people say that swimming at 35 miles per hour, the bottlenose dolphin is the fastest. According to Karen Bernd, Ph.D., however, the killer whale is the winner. Often, it can swim at over 35 miles per hour. Interestingly enough, it belongs to the dolphin family. As you can guess, the killer whale is the largest member of the family.

(a) It is a reptile.

(b) It is the fastest water mammal.

(c) It is the largest water mammal.

2 글쓴이는 왜 자신이 꿈꾸는 회사가 진정한 회사라고 생각하고 있나?

I have always dreamed about running a company that sends messages of warmth and hope to its customers as well as its employees. One might think that such a company is not truly a "company." But I do not believe that making money is what business is all about. Business is necessarily concerned with touching people, not robots without any emotions. What contemporary people need most is not "fancy" products, but products that make them feel appreciated and hopeful.

(a) Because it will be able to touch people.

(b) Because it will be able to earn a lot of money.

(c) Because it will be able to make convenient robots.

1 Kudzu has been introduced to the southern United States as a way of maintaining the roads. As is widely known, the plant does not need any help from humans. Moreover, its flowers and leaves are very attractive. Unfortunately, however, this amazing plant has killed other plants, causing serious problems. To make matters worse, killing kudzu is not an easy thing to do.

Q. Why does kudzu cause problems?

(a) Because its flowers are so beautiful.

(b) Because it kills many different plants.

(c) Because people do not have to take care of them.

(d) Because it was introduced to the United States.

2 Jesus Christ once told us to love our enemies. Can we apply this "order" to business contexts? Of course, we can! This is mainly because severe competition can be harmful to the survival of a business. Therefore, strategically thinking business people should come up with ways to "love" their "enemies." More importantly, his order reminds us that businesses can succeed by dealing with their customers and competitors with love.

Q. Why is Christ's order important to businesses?

(a) Because it can be harmful to them.

(b) Because it cannot be applied to business contexts.

(c) Because it can help them succeed.

(d) Because it reminds us to love our friends.

Chapter 4

실용문

UNIT 1   광고 Ⅰ

UNIT 2   기사 Ⅰ (사건 · 사고)

UNIT 3   기사 Ⅱ (칼럼 · 독자 투고)

UNIT 4   기사 Ⅲ (일반 상식 기사)

UNIT 5   서한 Ⅰ (일반 서한 · 이메일)

UNIT 6   서한 Ⅱ (추천서 · 지원서)

실용문 가운데 광고는 매번 출제되는 유형이다. 크게 제품 광고, 교육 프로그램 광고, 그리고 서비스업 광고 등으로 나눌 수 있다. 어떤 경우든 광고에서 제시하는 주된 장점에 초점을 두어, 다른 제품이나 서비스와 어떻게 차이가 나는지에 유의하면서 읽어나가는 것이 중요하다. 또한 글의 전체적인 흐름이 제품의 특징을 부각하는 데 있다는 점도 명심해야 한다.

유형 정리

1 제품

The Fresh Anti-Aging Cream is not just another anti-aging cream. Its extraordinary effects have been proven by various clinical tests. Unlike other creams, this product can remove almost all wrinkles on your face. Plus, unlike botox injections, its use is painless. Just apply this cream and be younger! Nobody can guess your actual age! For more information, call us at 1-800-555-2323.

노화방지크림에 대한 광고다. 다른 크림들, 그리고 주름제거를 통한 다른 노화방지 방법과의 차이를 제시하면서 장점을 부각했다. 주된 특징을 파악하면서, 전체 글의 자연스러운 흐름을 포착할 수 있어야 한다.

2 교육 프로그램

The Learner-Friendly Courses provide language learners with an innovative approach to language learning. Highly recommended by specialists in SLA, the courses enable students to master four language skills in the most efficient way. By offering engaging language activities similar to real-life tasks, these programs will empower you to speak English confidently and fluently.

혁신적인 어학 프로그램에 대한 광고다. 주로 장점을 부각하는 데 치중했는데, 프로그램이 어떤 특성을 가지는가를 정확히 파악해야 한다. 또한 글의 흐름을 감안할 때 단점이 제시될 수 없음도 다시 한 번 유의하자.

3 서비스업

The Cozy Travel offers you a unique opportunity to experience the happiness of living in the country. Staying at our lovely vacation cottages, you can enjoy walking in the woods, watching awesome sunsets, and meeting friendly people. You may want to stay there forever. If your whole family chooses to take this chance, you will be offered a 30% discount. So, what are you waiting for?

안락한 환경에서 시골 생활을 즐길 수 있도록 하는 여행 상품에 대한 광고다. 역시 장점이 부각되고 있음에 유의해야 하고, 어떤 사항들이 제시되는가를 꼼꼼하게 확인해야 한다. 전체적인 흐름은 언제나 파악해야 함을 명심하자.

Tips

1 장점 파악

광고는 글의 특성 때문에 일정한 제품이나 서비스의 장점을 뚜렷이 드러내는 데 그 목적이 있다. 따라서 여러 가지 장점이 제시되는 것이 보통인데, 이 가운데 제품의 본질적 특성과 관련된 장점에 특히 유의해야 한다. 대개 그와 관련된 세부사항을 측정하기 때문이다. 또한 전반적 정보 유형에서도 그런 특성을 파악해야 제목을 정확히 정할 수 있기 때문이다.

2 추론

출제 빈도가 높은 편은 아니지만, 광고와 관련해서도 추론 문제가 제시될 수 있다. 추론에서는 특히 비약을 하지 않도록 각별히 유의해야 한다. 철저하게 주어진 내용에 바탕을 두어서 상식적으로 이해되는 범위에서만 추론이 가능하다는 점을 다시 한 번 명심해야 한다. TEPS에서는 추론에서 비약을 허용하시 않는 것이 원칙이기 때문이다.

• 정답 및 해설 p.136

1 빈 칸에 들어갈 가장 알맞은 말을 고르시오.

The One-Stop Internship Program offers you a great opportunity to _____. We arrange for you to work at one of the top advertising agencies for three months. Your designated counselor will help you every step of the way. She will work closely with you to choose an agency, to plan your work schedule, and to give you feedback on your ideas. For more information, visit our website at www.one-stop-internship.com.

(a) become a counselor

(b) explore the real world of advertising

(c) enjoy your vacation

2 아래에 제시된 번역 장치에 대한 설명으로 올바른 것을 고르시오.

The Multilingual Translator is truly a revolutionary product. Unlike other translation machines, this product translates a word or sentence by taking its context into account. As you may know, context plays an important role in determining the meaning of an utterance. And the Multilingual Translater is the only translating device capable of understanding the context in which an utterance is made. So, what are you waiting for? Just call us now at 1-800-737-7878.

(a) It is very expensive.

(b) It is the only translating device available.

(c) It considers context when translating.

•정답 및 해설 p.137

1   Do you really want to lose weight? Do you really want to lead a beautiful life? Then, try our amazing Fat-Free Pill. What you have to do is just to take this pill and wait. After one week, you will find yourself _____! Can you believe this? But it's true. Our innovative pill has been proven to be the most effective way of losing weight. For more information, visit our website at www.new-life. com.

Q. Choose the one option that best completes the sentence.

(a) ugly and overweight

(b) friendly and kind

(c) earnest and honest

(d) slim and beautiful

2   The TwinStar Hotel is conveniently located five minutes from the heart of Manila's business districts. Enjoying the comfort of a 5-star hotel, our guests can read/write e-mails, make telephone calls, and send/receive faxes for free! We even have five video conferencing rooms available around the clock. At our amazing hotel, work and play exist together peacefully and harmoniously. For more information, call us at 1-800-323-2323.

Q. What can be inferred from the passage?

(a) The hotel is very cheap.

(b) The hotel's guests can take care of their business.

(c) The hotel's guests cannot send faxes for free.

(d) The hotel has only five rooms available.

UNIT 2 기사 Ⅰ(사건·사고)

종합적인 영어능력을 측정하는 TEPS의 특성 때문에 실용문의 출제 비중은 매우 높은 편이다. 특히 신문이나 잡지의 기사는 자주 출제되므로, 중요한 유형별로 예상되는 사항을 정리해두는 노력이 필요하다. 각 유형에 따라 자주 등장하는 표현들을 정확히 익혀두고 또한 반복적으로 발생하는 현상에 대한 안목도 길러둘 필요가 있다. 이 Unit에서는 사건과 사고를 중심으로 기사와 관련된 사항을 다룬다.

유형 정리

1 일반 사건

On August 26, 2006, a wolf called Onya was killed by the police. She had **escaped from the Niabi Zoo** in Coal Valley and spent two days walking the streets. This incident was caused by a lack of care on the part of the zoo. If the zoo officials had given Onya enough space to play and run, she would not have tried to get away from her place. The officials might be charged with breaking animal protection laws.

윗글에서 진하게 표시한 부분에서 알 수 있는 바와 같이 이 글은 동물원에서 동물이 탈출한 사건을 다루고 있다. 이와 관련하여 제목을 질문할 수도 있고 세부사항을 측정할 수도 있다. 문제 유형에 따라 시간 안배가 달라져야 함에 유의하자.

2 범죄

On August 8, 1963, the Glasgow to London mail train was stopped by fifteen robbers. With the help of an insider, they knew that the train was carrying thousands of pounds. After getting on the train, one of them hit the driver. And then, **they took 120 bags containing money**. Getting off the train, they went to their hiding place and divided the money. Later, most of them were caught by the police.

윗글에서 진하게 표시한 부분에서 알 수 있듯이, 이 글은 기차 강도 사건을 다루고 있다. 역시 전반적인 내용인 주제를 질문할 수도 있고 사건의 세부사항을 물어볼 수도 있다. 유형에 따라 독해 전략도 달라져야 함을 기억하자.

3 사고

On January 8, 2003, **a Turkish Airline plane crashed**, when trying to land at Diyarbakir Airport. Aliye Ilgin, one of the survivors, said, "The plane crashed on landing with a huge noise and caught fire before breaking up." When the airplane attempted to land, there was a heavy fog in the airport, which was thought to cause the horrible accident. Five people survived the tragedy.

윗글에서 진하게 표시한 부분에서 알 수 있듯이, 이 글은 비행기 추락 사고가 주제이다. 역시 전반적인 정보나 세부사항의 측정이 가능하다. 추론 문제는 대개 다른 유형에서 출제됨도 참고하자.

Tips

1 사건·사고 유형 파악

이와 같은 실용문이 제시될 때는 무엇보다도 어떤 사건이나 사고인지를 정확히 파악해야 한다. 해석에 의존할 정도로 시간이 충분히 주어지지 않는다는 것을 감안하여 자주 등장하는 표현을 통해 어떤 사건이나 사고를 다루고 있는지를 알아내야 한다. 그렇지 않으면 질문에서 요구하는 것과 전혀 다른 선택지를 택할 수 있기 때문에 주의를 요한다.

2 세부사항 확인

정오 유형으로 출제되는 경우에는 세부사항을 꼼꼼하게 질문하기 때문에 문제를 푸는 데 많은 시간이 필요하다. 특히 각 사항의 paraphrase가 정확한지, 엉뚱한 내용이 들어 있지는 않은지 확인을 해야 한다. 이런 기사 유형의 특성 때문에, 원인이니 장소, 피해자 등에 관한 정보가 주로 술세뇌기 때문에 이와 같은 사항에 유의하면서 기사를 읽는 습관을 들이자.

• 정답 및 해설 p.138

1 다음 글의 제목으로 가장 알맞은 것을 고르시오.

On April 16, 2007, 32 people were shot dead by Seung-Hui Cho on the Virginia Tech campus. Among them was Professor Liviu Librescu, who helped most of his students escape through the windows. While they were fleeing, Professor Librescu kept grabbing the door of his classroom. Sadly for us, he was shot many times and passed away. Although he is not with us, the professor will be remembered forever.

(a) A crazy murderer

(b) How to improve one's memory

(c) A professor's sacrifice

2 다음 사고에 관한 설명으로 올바른 것을 고르시오.

On August 26, 2002, Chris Thomas went bungee jumping as part of charity events. He wanted to help raise money for Morriston Hospital in south Wales. As hundreds of people were watching, he bungee-jumped from a crane. Suddenly, the cord connecting his feet to the crane snapped and he fell to the ground. He was severely injured and sent to the hospital. After a few days, he died.

(a) Chris Thomas raised a lot of money.

(b) Few people was present at the event.

(c) Chris Thomas passed away.

• 정답 및 해설 p.138

1 During the period between August and November, 1888, a man who identified himself as Jack the Ripper killed several women in London. Each time he murdered a victim, the serial killer cut part of her body. He even sent such body parts to the police. Despite the great efforts of the police, the murderer was neither identified nor captured. The case remained unsolved.

Q. What is the best title of the passage?

(a) Silent Victims in London

(b) Unidentified Victims: The Secret of London

(c) The Good Old Days of Police Officers

(d) Jack the Ripper: A Mysterious Killer

2 On July 23, 2007, approximately 100 people saw five UFOs flying in the sky in Warwickshire, England. At around 10:30 p.m., three of the UFOs started to form a triangular shape in the night sky. The remaining two flying objects were positioned close to them. According to Air Traffic Control, there were no extraordinary activities in the night sky. Most observers believed, however, that they saw real UFOs.

Q. According to the passage, which of the following is correct?

(a) The UFO sighting occurred in Air Traffic Control.

(b) Air Traffic Control said that nothing unusual happened that night.

(c) The UFOs fought against each other.

(d) The UFO sighting occurred in the morning.

UNIT 3 기사 Ⅱ (칼럼 · 독자 투고)

실용문 가운데 출제 빈도가 매우 높은 유형이다. Part I 과 Part II 의 다양한 문제 유형으로 출제가 가능하고, 일상적으로 자주 접하는 장르이기 때문이다. 반면 시험을 준비하는 입장에서는 매우 부담될 수 있는 유형이므로, 평소에 다양한 사회 현상에 대한 여러 입장을 익혀두는 것이 효과적이다. Newsweek와 같은 잡지를 활용하는 것도 좋은 방법이다.

유형 정리

1 칼럼 유형1: 사회 현상

Are public displays of love acceptable to our society? Too many couples seem to think so and dare to display their "love" in public places such as subway stations and office buildings. These places are not, however, for showing love in front of others. Further, true love means respecting and caring about your partner, not using your partner to show to the world that you have a boyfriend or girlfriend.

공공연한 애정 표현이라는 사회 현상을 비판한 칼럼이다. 저자의 입장이 비판적이라는 점과, 애정 표현을 비판하는 근거와 관련된 내용을 알 수 있다. 사회 현상을 바라보는 다양한 시각이 존재함을 인식하여, 폭넓게 사고하는 능력을 갖추어야 한다.

2 칼럼 유형2: 정책 비판

What is the real problem with our English education? Some people believe that not speaking English enough in class is the major issue. As a result, they are planning to make English teachers use only English in class. Unfortunately, they are unaware of the real problem. They are unaware that too many teachers simply do not know how to teach English in an effective and efficient way.

영어 전용 수업 방침이 영어 교육의 문제점을 제대로 인식하지 못했음을 비판한 칼럼이다. 저자의 태도가 역시 비판적이라는 점, 그리고 저자의 주장으로부터 추론할 수 있는 바를 알 수 있다. 언제나 다양한 시각의 존재를 의식할 필요가 있다.

3 독자 투고

These days, too many matchmaking companies stress the economic aspect of marriage. For instance, some of them "advertise" a rich young woman to attract potential spouses. The problem is that money cannot guarantee a successful marriage. A happy marriage is based on mutual love and respect, not on money. Therefore, matchmaking companies should rethink their "business" strategies.

중매 알선 업체의 상업적 행각을 비판한 독자 투고다. 역시 저자의 태도가 비판적이라는 점, 그리고 상업적 행각을 비판하는 근거를 측정할 수 있다. 추론 유형으로 출제될 수 있음도 예상해야 한다.

Tips

1 빈 칸 채우기 유형

칼럼·독자 투고 유형은 쉽게 접할 수 있으면서 내용이 무겁지 않다는 점에서 다양한 유형으로 출제된다. 특히 빈 칸 채우기 유형으로 출제될 때는, 글 전체의 기본 입장을 정확히 파악한 다음, 빈 칸 전후에 올 내용과 자연스럽게 어울리는가를 꼼꼼하게 따져보아야 한다. 언제나 저자가 취하는 기본 입장에 충실해서 문제를 해결해야 함을 명심하자.

2 전반적 정보 유형

칼럼·독자 투고 유형이 전반적 정보를 요하는 문제 유형으로 출제되는 경우에는 다소 난이도가 낮은 편이다. 글의 일관성(coherence) 때문에 첫 문장과 마지막 문장만 읽고서 정답을 찾는 것이 가능한 경우도 많기 때문이다. 참고로 이렇게 두 문장으로 해결되지 않는 경우에는 마지막 문장 바로 앞에 있는 문장까지 보면 된다는 점도 알아 두자.

EXERCISE

정답 및 해설 p.139

1 빈 칸에 들어갈 가장 알맞은 말을 고르시오.

Many people believe that graduating from top universities automatically leads to success in life. But that is not the case. In order to _____, you need to develop essential skills that universities do not teach you. More than anything else, you need to become an independent thinker who knows how to solve a problem creatively. In addition, you should be compassionate toward other people.

(a) make a lot of money

(b) become famous all over the world

(c) succeed in the real world

2 다음 글의 제목으로 가장 적절한 것을 고르시오.

Why do so many stars suffer from depression? Of course, we can think of a number of causes. One of them is great pressure placed on them. In a sense, they live on popularity, but it is very unstable. In fact, celebrities can become unpopular overnight. As a result, they constantly worry about their popularity, which can lead to low self-esteem and in extreme cases, to depression.

(a) Pressure on Stars Can Lead to Depression

(b) Why All Actresses Are Beautiful

(c) Popularity Can Hurt the Health of Ordinary People

374 독해 · Chapter 4

•정답 및 해설 p.140

1 My passion for children and their happiness has made me pay particular attention to ergonomics. I do know that this field is largely concerned with making more comfortable equipment for office workers. That is very important. I also believe that we can apply it to toy design or design for children's products. This is possible because ergonomics shows us what is the best way to design things so that we can _____.

Q. Choose the one option that best completes the sentence.

(a) become rich

(b) play sports better

(c) work or play better

(d) swim much faster

2 Unfortunately, the North Korean regime is only interested in its survival, not in the survival of the North Korean people. The so-called "sunshine policy" toward Pyongyang is sure to fail because it does not take this factor into account. To make matters worse, there is a strong possibility that the policy will become an obstacle to the development of an appropriate security policy for South Korea.

Q. What is the tone of the passage?

(a) Optimistic

(b) Regretful

(c) Humorous

(d) Concerned

UNIT 4 기사 Ⅲ (일반 상식 기사)

일반 상식 기사는 비실용문 가운데 출제 빈도가 매우 높은 유형에 속한다. 일반 상식의 범위가 넓기 때문에 다양한 주제를 여러 문제 유형으로 출제할 수 있기 때문이다. 따라서 평소에 사회적으로 문제가 되는 사항과 관련된 상식을 갖추어 두는 것이 효과적인 대비책이라고 할 수 있다. 이를 위해서는 위키피디아(http://wikipedia.org)와 같은 자료의 활용도 권장할 만하다.

유형 정리

1 경제 상식

Phishing is when someone tries to obtain confidential information from normal users. Often, they attempt to get information about your bank account details. Or your credit card details. In either case, phishing is usually done by sending you emails that will make you think they are from real financial organizations. Therefore, you should be extremely careful about providing sensitive information through email.

최근 심각한 문제로 부각된 피싱을 설명한 글이다. 경제 활동과 관련하여 이처럼 다양한 상식적 사항들이 있으므로 폭넓게 학습하는 습관을 들이자. 모든 문제 유형으로 출제가 가능함에 유의해야 한다.

2 생활 상식

You can cook fish in a variety of ways. For instance, you can cook fish in the oven, which makes it possible for the fish to mix with other ingredients. Or you can cook fish under a hot grill. You can also steam many different types of fish. Smoking fish is a good idea, too. Whatever way you may choose, be sure to serve the cooked fish with some vegetables.

생선을 요리하는 다양한 방법을 설명한 글이다. 제목이나 세부사항을 측정하는 문제가 출제될 수 있다. 일상생활과 관련하여 다양한 상식적 사항을 생각해 볼 수 있으므로, 평소에 상식을 넓히려는 노력을 기울여야 함을 명심하자.

3 건강 상식

Sleep deprivation is when you do not sleep enough. When this occurs, your health can be negatively affected in many ways. You may feel fatigued or have difficulty concentrating on your work. In extreme cases, you may experience illusions of sight and sound. Some people say that sleep loss can lead to psychosis, but further research is required to support the claim.

건강에 악영향을 미칠 수 있는 수면 결핍의 다양한 증상을 설명한 글이다. 주제를 측정하거나 세부사항 또는 추론 유형으로 출제될 수 있다. 이처럼 건강과 관련된 다양한 상식적 사항들도 점검해 두어야 한다.

Tips

1 폭넓은 학습

실용문 가운데 일반 상식 기사는 범위가 매우 넓기 때문에, 수험생의 입장에서는 큰 부담이 될 수 있다. 따라서 실전에서 당황하기 않기 위해서는, 평소에 The Washington Post(http://www.washingtonpost.com)와 같은 신문을 통해 꾸준히 상식을 넓혀가는 것이 많은 도움이 된다. 정독을 하지 않고 중요한 내용만 살펴보아도 충분히 도움이 된다는 점을 명심하여, 평소에 꾸준히 읽어두자.

2 세부사항 유형

일반 상식 기사와 관련하여 세부사항 유형은 매우 까다롭게 출제될 수 있다. 특히 평소에 들어본 적이 있다고 해서 성급하게 판단하기 쉽기 때문에, 지문에 제시된 내용을 정확히 파악하려는 노력이 긴요하다. 시간 배분에 신경을 써야 하지만, 어느 정도 안정된 시간을 획보하여 중심 내용과 관련된 세부사항에 숭점을 두면서 풀어나가야 한다는 점을 명심하자.

• 정답 및 해설 p.140

1 **빈 칸에 들어갈 가장 알맞은 말을 고르시오.**

Roughly speaking, panic disorder patients experience a panic attack once a week. A panic attack is when you _____. When you experience a panic attack, you can feel dizzy, tremble, faint, sweat, or feel nausea. A panic attack is unpredictable. It does not seem to be closely related to stressful situations. Many people believe that panic disorder is a hereditary disease.

(a) are proud of your parents

(b) predict the future

(c) feel great anxiety

2 **악플에 대한 다음 글의 설명으로 올바른 것을 고르시오.**

In fact, making malicious comments on the Internet can be regarded as a crime. This is mainly because such remarks can negatively affect one's reputation. For instance, if someone continues to speak ill of a particular actor, people are likely to dismiss the actor as untalented. When this happens, the actor suffers a lot and may want to sue the perpetrator.

(a) They do not influence one's reputation.

(b) They can be thought of as a crime.

(c) They help actors succeed.

• 정답 및 해설 p.141

1 According to the Office of Alternative Medicine at the U.S. National Institutes of Health, alternative medicine refers to "those treatments and health care practices _____ in medical schools." Many of these treatments are aimed at preventing diseases from occurring. Further, practitioners of alternative medicine take into account all aspects of their patients' health.

Q. Choose the one option that best completes the sentence.

(a) generally learned

(b) widely accepted

(c) generally covered

(d) not taught widely

2 When traveling to Canada, you need to consider the fact that many stores do not accept traveler's checks. This is mainly because credit cards are a more convenient way of paying for products or services. Taking this fact into account, some companies start to issue traveler's check cards, which are very similar to credit cards. It is advisable, however, to choose to use credit cards instead of such check cards.

Q. What can be inferred from the passage?

(a) All stores in Canada accept traveler's checks.

(b) Credit cards are more convenient than traveler's check cards.

(c) Traveler's checks are more convenient than credit cards.

(d) Traveler's check cards are quite different from credit cards.

UNIT 5 서한 Ⅰ (일반 서한 · 이메일)

실용문 가운데 여전히 출제 비중이 높은 유형이다. 일반 서한은 내용에 따라 문의, 감사, 항의 등의 서한으로 나눌 수 있는 데 반해, 이메일은 대개 비즈니스와 관련된 경우가 많다. 글 전체의 흐름에 자연스럽게 어울리는 말을 찾거나(Part Ⅰ 유형) 세부사항이나 추론을 측정하는 유형이 주로 출제된다. 어떤 경우든, 서한의 목적을 염두에 두고서 문제에 접근하는 전략을 써야 함을 명심하자.

유형 정리

1 문의 / 감사 서한

Unfortunately, I have failed to meet the application deadline for the language courses, because I do not live in Canada and have not received timely notification of the application deadline. At any rate, Canadian University requires that I take the language courses of your university from September 2008 to August 2009. Given that I have missed the application deadline, I was wondering how I will be able to apply for your 2008 English language courses and pay the application fee.

어학 과정 신청 기한을 지키지 못해서 보내는 문의 서한이다. 기한을 지키지 못한 이유를 설명했고 또한 어학 과정 이수가 필요하므로 어떻게 해야 하는지를 문의하고 있다. 글의 목적이나 세부사항 등을 측정할 수 있음에 유의하자.

2 항의 서한

Thank you for your letter. But I cannot find any information on converting text into MP3 files from the Training Video or the User Manual. For your reference, I have enclosed a copy of the manual in this letter. As you can see from the copy, there is no entry dealing with creating MP3 files. The same holds true for the video as far as I know; I watched the video. I am not sure whether I was given the wrong program or my version is an old one.

광고와 다른 프로그램을 제공받은 데 대한 항의 서한이다. 회사측의 서한을 따라서 시도했음에도 원하는 기능이 없었음을 말했는데, 특히 글의 목적을 측정하는 유형이나 추론 유형으로 출제될 수 있음을 기억하자.

3 이메일

I understand that you couldn't open my last e-mail due to some problems with the header and the encoding system. Since I have changed both of them, I really hope that you do not have any difficulty opening and reading my emails. And I really appreciate your excellent service and generous help with these matters. I wish I could speak fluent French. At present, however, I politely request you to understand my circumstances.

업무 처리를 위한 이메일로 헤더와 인코딩의 문제를 해결했음을 밝혔다. 역시 글을 쓴 목적을 정확히 파악해야 하며, 주어진 내용과 관련된 세부사항이나 추론 문제를 출제할 수 있음에 유의하자.

Tips

1 글의 목적 파악

일반 서한이나 이메일은 반드시 작성하는 목적이 있기 때문에, 이 목적을 알아내는 것이 문제 풀이의 핵심이다. 글의 목적을 직접 측정하는 문제 유형은 단순히 "to complain(불만을 토로하기 위해서)"이라는 형식보다는 일정한 목적을 구체적으로 진술하는 형식이 선택지 유형으로 제시된다는 점도 알아두어야 한다. 대개 처음 한두 문장을 통해 목적이 분명히 드러나는 경우가 많다.

2 추론 유형

TEPS의 추론 유형 문제는 특히 수어진 지문의 내용을 곧이곧대로 받아들여서 추론할 것을 요구하는 특징이 있다. 이것은 일반 서한·이메일과 관련해서도 마찬가지이므로, 지문의 특정한 문장으로부터 바로 이끌어낼 수 있는 결론을 선택하는 것이 기본적인 전략이다. 무엇보다도, 지문에 제시되지 않은 내용으로부터 추론한 선택지는 정답이 될 수 없음을 명심해야 한다.

• 정답 및 해설 p.142

1   빈 칸에 들어갈 가장 알맞은 말을 고르시오.

Of course, I am keenly aware how difficult it would be to find such a qualified worker and how much work that kind of search will entail. I can, however, understand why Ms. Garner has been _____ you. She is responsible for our company's future, after all. I have been, however, satisfied with your work and I am deeply grateful for your excellent service. Thank you, from the bottom of my heart.

(a) picking on

(b) expecting too much of

(c) trying to sue

2   다음 글을 통해 추론할 수 있는 바로 가장 올바른 것을 고르시오.

That sounds like a pretty demanding job, but here is the good news: we have collected dozens of head teachers' manuals throughout our twenty years of operation. Moreover, your predecessor is going to guide and teach you every step of the way. I think the transition period will last about three weeks, providing you with enough time to adjust and learn. What really matters is your attitudes. Are you willing to take a risk and develop beyond recognition?

(a) The writer of this letter is a police officer.

(b) The letter is concerned with the position of head teacher.

(c) The reader of this letter has serious attitude problems.

• 정답 및 해설 p.142

1　This is Erica Breslin, from Japan. I understand that some items are missing. But that is perfectly OK with me, and I'd like to place an order. I think I need to mention that the reason for my order is _____. I enjoy watching DVD titles produced by your company. I am particularly impressed by the high quality of the Romance series.

Q. Choose the one option that best completes the sentence.

(a) entirely commercial

(b) absolutely romantic

(c) totally personal

(d) perfectly official

2　It is a little cold here in Seoul, and yes, we have blue skies. Oh, I must mention that your colleagues still miss you, and so do I. And, do you happen to know who Maggie Smith is? She is a new worker in our company, but she said that she had met you in Japan. It is a small world, you know. And thank you so much for your superb job here at Faith House. Your dedication and professionalism will be greatly missed.

Q. What can be inferred from the passage?

(a) The reader of this letter did not meet Maggie Smith.

(b) The writer of this letter lives in Japan.

(c) The writer of this letter does not see blue skies at all.

(d) The reader of this letter worked at Faith House.

UNIT 6 서한 Ⅱ (추천서 · 지원서)

추천서 · 지원서 유형은 실용문 가운데 출제 빈도가 높은 편에 속한다. Part Ⅰ에 출제되는 경우에는 글의 일관된 흐름에 맞는 말을 측정하는 유형이, 그리고 Part Ⅱ에 출제되는 경우에는 세부사항이나 추론 유형이 주로 출제된다. 특히 추천서가 추천 인물의 장점이 부각되는 데 반해, 지원서는 지원자의 장점이 부각되는 것이 보통이라는 점을 염두에 두고서 문제에 차분히 접근해야 함을 명심하자.

유형 정리

1 추천서

All these qualities, together with her passion for the pursuit of excellence, will definitely make her an ideal scientist who contributes to the development of molecular biology in your country. And I must mention that it is a great pleasure and honor for me to recommend her to your prestigious university. I am sure that she will make a valuable asset to your institution.

분자생물학 분야에 지원하고자 하는 우수한 학생을 추천하는 내용의 글이다. 짐작할 수 있듯이, 추천 인물의 장점이 부각되고 있음을 파악해야 하고, 또한 글의 특성 때문에 추천 인물의 단점이 제시되는 경우는 상대적으로 드물다는 점도 알아두어야 한다.

2 입사 지원서

I have heard a lot about your reputation as a family-friendly and at the same time, highly successful company. Those two factors have compelled me to apply for your firm. Because I am a mother of two lovely daughters, I need to work in an environment in which my family life is respected. And of course, any "company" must survive and thrive in order to enable its workers to lead a happy life.

가족 친화적이면서도 매우 성공적인 회사에 지원하고자 하는 입사지원서이다. 이 글에서는 지원하고자 하는 회사의 장점이 부각되고 있는데, 역시 지원 회사의 단점이 제시될 수 없음을 기억해야 한다. 빈 칸 채우기 또는 추론 유형의 문제가 출제될 수 있다.

3 입학 지원서

To succeed in this rapidly changing world, companies need workers who have a deeper understanding of global and local needs. I believe that Academic University is the best place on earth that produces students with such insights. Together with strong academic courses, the university provides a variety of programs that will definitely empower me to be a leader in international business. That is the main reason why I am applying to this prestigious university.

국제적 요구와 지역적 요구를 깊이 있게 이해하는 인물을 배출하는 대학에 지원하고자 하는 내용의 입학 지원서이다. 마찬가지로 지원하고자 하는 대학의 단점이 제시될 수 없다는 점에 유의하면서 글의 전반적인 흐름을 파악해야 한다.

Tips

1 추천서 · 지원서의 특성

추천서나 지원서에는 대개 추천 인물이나 지원자의 장점이 부각되는 것이 보통이다. 물론 그런 인물의 단점이 제시되는 경우도 생각할 수 있기는 하지만, 이와 같은 경우에도 그런 단점이 장점을 압도할 수는 없다는 점에 유의해야 한다. 어떻든 추천이나 지원이 목적이기 때문에, 그런 목적에 반하는 글을 쓸 수는 없기 때문이다. 따라서 실제 문제 풀이에서 이와 같은 특성을 늘 염두에 두어야 한다.

2 세부사항

TEPS의 세부사항 유형도 추론 유형과 마찬가지로 곧이곧대로 문제를 해결할 것을 요구하는 경우가 많다. 이것은 특히 비약해서 이해하는 것을 경계하는 TEPS의 특성 때문인데, 어떤 경우든 지문에서 분명하게 제시되어 있지 않은 사항을 정답으로 택하거나 그런 식의 추론을 정답으로 택해서는 안 된다는 점을 명심하고 또 명심해야 한다.

EXERCISE

• 정답 및 해설 p.143

1 **빈 칸에 들어갈 가장 알맞은 말을 고르시오.**

As a long-time language teacher who has more than 15 years of teaching experience, I can assure you that Abigail Carpenters is a gifted learner of language. I have been teaching her for more than three years and observing her grow as a "_____." She understands that language essentially deals with the core of our existence. Consequently, she has spent significant amounts of time trying to explore various ways of interpreting the world.

(a) designer

(b) linguist

(c) teacher

2 **다음 글의 내용으로 보아 올바른 설명을 고르시오.**

Good design can only come from deep insights into the nature of everyday things, and they are essentially in harmony with their surroundings. Because I am keenly aware of this beautiful nature of things, I want to reinterpret and express it with my own touch. In trying to do that, I completely agree that I should "grow as a creative thinker." That is why I have chosen Beauty College as my future alma mater where I will grow as a thinker as well as a visual artist.

(a) The writer of this application is applying for Beauty College.

(b) The writer of this application does not have to grow as a creative thinker.

(c) The writer of this application wants to be a good interpreter.

PRACTICE

•정답 및 해설 p.144

1 A good university must _____ its students. That is my bone-deep belief, and is the main reason why I am applying to Faith University. This might sound like an anti-academic attitude, but it is not. In this rapidly changing world, students must be prepared to deal with academic and practical concerns with confidence and skill. This requires a much greater sense of spirituality.

Q. Choose the one option that best completes the sentence.

(a) give knowledge to
(b) guarantee a bright future for
(c) instill spirituality in
(d) be interested in

2 Eric Morrison has worked with me for over twenty years. Still, I am continually amazed by his dedication and professionalism. In fact, I cannot remember how many nights he spent working on his projects. In addition, he continues to sharpen his skills, which is not an easy thing to do given his workload. Given these considerations, I am convinced that he will become a great asset to your company.

Q. Which of the following is true according to the passage?

(a) The writer of this reference letter does not know Eric Morrison well.
(b) Morrison's workload is light.
(c) Eric Morrison is a very lazy person.
(d) Eric Morrison is committed to his work.

Chapter 5

비실용문

UNIT 1   정치와 경제

UNIT 2   사회와 역사

UNIT 3   문화와 인물

UNIT 4   지구과학

UNIT 5   생물학

UNIT 6   환경과학

UNIT 7   생활과학

UNIT 8   철학과 예술

비실용문은 실용문에 비해 자주 접하기가 힘들고 또한 내용도 이해하기가 쉽지 않기 때문에 각별한 노력을 요한다. 이 가운데 '정치와 경제'는 꾸준히 출제되는 유형으로, 전문적인 이론보다는 정치 현상이나 경제 현상을 설명하는 것이 보통이다. 그렇지만 점차로 난이도가 상향 조정되는 경향을 감안할 때 폭넓게 학습하는 것이 효과적인 대비책임을 명심하자.

유형 정리

1 정치

In representative democracy, politicians are expected to be trustees who should display independent judgment and reconcile various demands from many different groups. The strategy of "going public," however, enables the politicians to avoid the difficult task of negotiating with their opponents. In so doing, they can disregard the conflicting nature of a policy-making process.

대의민주주의에서의 정책 입안 과정과 관련된 내용을 다룬 글이다. 이론적 특성이 강하기 때문에 어렵게 느껴질 수도 있는데, 구체적인 정책 입안 과정과 연계하면 이해하기가 용이하다. 전반적인 글의 흐름을 정확히 파악하는 데 중점을 둘 필요가 있다.

2 경제

Many analysts predict that President Lee Myung-bak will take many different measures to boost South Korea's economy. He will attract foreign investment by providing safe environments and various incentives. The new president will also let large corporations invest much more by reducing regulations. Finally, he is likely to strengthen his country's economic ties with the United States.

이명박 대통령의 경제 정책에 대한 예상을 다룬 글이다. 이처럼 정부의 경제 정책은 실물 경제에 미치는 영향이 크다는 점을 감안하여, 경제 정책 또는 실물 경제 현상에 대한 다양한 내용을 익혀두는 것이 바람직하다.

3 경영

In this highly globalized world, global management is not an option but a necessity. In order to survive in the global market, companies must make every effort to understand and take advantage of cultural differences among countries. Ironically, this is an opportunity, not a crisis, for business in that the global market is rapidly expanding. Thus we need to seize these golden opportunities and make a difference in the whole world.

세계화 시대의 도래에 따른 글로벌 경영의 필요성을 설명한 글이다. 경영 분야와 관련하여 다양한 내용이 출제될 수 있기 때문에, 특히 근래 경영에서 각광을 받고 있는 다양한 내용들을 익혀두는 것이 긴요하다.

Tips

1 폭넓은 학습
비실용문의 가장 중요한 특성은 실용문에 비해 이해하는 데 시간이나 배경지식이 많이 필요하다는 점이다. 이것은 정치나 경제·경영에 대해서도 마찬가지로 적용된다. 따라서 기본적인 지식을 습득해두지 않으면 실전에서 당황하기 쉽다. 평소에 위키피디아(http://www.wikipedia.org)와 같은 자료를 통해 기초적인 내용을 충분히 습득해두는 것이 바람직하다. 특히 근래에 관심의 대상이 되는 분야에 대해서는 보다 깊이 있는 학습이 요구된다.

2 추론
앞에서 설명했듯이, TEPS 추론의 가장 중요한 특징은 지문을 끝이끝내로 이해한 다음 그로부터 자연스럽게 이어질 수 있는 결론을 택해야 한다는 점이다. 실제 지문의 각 문장과 추론 내용이 제대로 연결될 수 있는지를 따져보는 것이 많은 도움이 된다. 이를 위해서는 Part Ⅱ와 Part Ⅲ의 전반적 정보 유형과 같이 시간이 적게 소요되는 문제들을 빨리 풀어서 충분한 시간을 확보하는 것이 좋은 방법이다. 그래야만 실수를 하지 않고 올바른 답을 고를 수 있기 때문이다.

1 **빈 칸에 들어갈 가장 알맞은 말을 고르시오.**

Charles Anderson argues that equal opportunities should be sacrificed in order to ensure the best performance of associations. This argument would produce no undesirable results if it applied to the private sector of society. But if this kind of reasoning applied to the public sector, the consequences would be _____. This is mainly because the purpose of the public sector is quite different from that of the private sector.

(a) tragic

(b) desirable

(c) delightful

2 **다음 글로부터 추론할 수 있는 바로 가장 적절한 것을 고르시오.**

Can we really trust the unemployment figures? In fact, the number of many "potential" workers is not included in these figures. For instance, if you have lost your job and do not try to find another job, you are not counted as unemployed by the U.S. Department of Labor. In addition, the number of many kinds of part-time workers is not included in the unemployment figures. In this sense, those figures are not that reliable.

(a) The U.S. Department of Labor has nothing to do with the employment figures.

(b) The unemployment figures are not so trustworthy.

(c) The unemployment figures include the number of potential workers.

• 정답 및 해설 p.145

1   In 1906, the U.S. government took Standard Oil Company to court under the Sherman Antitrust Act. The government felt that John Rockefeller's company made use of unfair methods of competition. In 1911, the U.S. Supreme Court ordered Standard Oil to _____ into dozens of separate companies. Ironically, after the dissolution, Rockefeller became the richest man in the world.

Q. Choose the one option that best completes the sentence.

(a) make up

(b) deal with

(c) account for

(d) break up

2   McDaniel's argument fails to explain the nature of American society. As is widely known, American society is a white-dominant one. Since the founding of the United States, whites have been trying to maintain superiority in political, economic, and social arenas. In this sense, American society has been divided between whites and non-whites, not between non-African-Americans and African Americans.

Q. What can be inferred from the passage?

(a) African Americans hate Asian Americans.

(b) McDaniel's argument is reliable.

(c) Whites control American society.

(d) African Americans respect whites.

일상적으로 자주 접하게 되는 실용문과 달리, 다양한 주제를 보다 깊이 있게 다룬 비실용문은 내용이 까다롭기 때문에 폭넓은 학습을 요구한다. 사회 현상과 역사적 사실을 다룬 지문은 독해 영역에 빠지지 않고 출제되기 때문에 주요 사항들을 확인해둘 필요가 있다. 특히 역사는 광범위하므로 평소에 보다 깊이 공부해두어야 실전에서 당황하지 않을 수 있다.

유형 정리

1 사회 현상

These days, **too many parents insist that their children learn English at an early age.** This is understandable because mastering the global language can lead to higher positions in society. Unfortunately, however, some parents even go so far as to have their children memorize hundreds of English sentences. They need to understand that to effectively learn a foreign language like English, we should be emotionally prepared.

윗글에서 진하게 표시된 부분에서 알 수 있듯이, 이 글은 과도한 조기 영어 교육 열풍이라는 사회 현상을 다루고 있다. 모든 유형의 문제들이 출제될 수 있는데, 특히 추론 유형은 논리적 사고력을 요구하므로 꾸준히 독서하는 습관을 들여야 함을 기억하자.

2 사회 이슈

According to Korea International Trade Association, women make up only 13.4 percent of National Assembly members. This percentage is way below the global average. Basically, **we need more female politicians in the National Assembly** who support women's rights in every aspect of social life. Without such a change, gender equality in South Korea would not be achieved.

우리나라의 국회의원 가운데 여성 의원들의 비율이 저조한 문제를 다룬 글이다. 참고적으로 출제 빈도가 높지는 않지만 우리나라와 관련된 지문도 가끔씩 출제된다는 점을 감안하여 우리 사회의 문제점들도 미리 짚어볼 필요가 있다.

3 역사

After MacArthur's Incheon offensive, the North Korean soldiers withdrew from South Korea. Once again, the democratic country was freed. Wanting to win a complete victory, the American troops chased the communists. When the troops were about to reach the Yalu River, **a very large number of Chinese troops** intervened. MacArthur thought that the U.S. had to attack China by using nuclear missiles.

6·25전쟁 당시 중공군의 개입을 다룬 글이다. 이처럼 전쟁과 관련된 내용뿐만 아니라 고대 문명, 세계 현대사 등이 다양하게 출제되기 때문에 역사에 관한 내용은 미리 학습할 필요가 있다는 점을 명심하자.

Tips

1 인과 관계 파악

사회 현상과 역사에는 공통적으로 인과 관계가 들어 있다. 왜냐하면 일정한 현상이나 역사적 사실이 아무 이유 없이 발생할 수는 없기 때문이다. 따라서 왜 그런 일이 일어났는가에 대한 의문을 갖고서 다양한 지문을 읽어보려는 노력이 요구된다. 또한 여러 현상의 중요한 특징들도 주의해서 살펴보아야 하는 사항임을 명심하자.

2 추론(Inference)

사회나 역사와 관련된 추론은 대개 인과 관계에 관한 내용이다. 그렇지만 지문을 통해 저자가 암시하려고 하는 바를 측정하는 유형들도 출제되기 때문에, 전반적인 글의 흐름을 정확히 파악하는 연습이 필요하다. 추론 유형은 전반적 정보를 질문하는 유형에 비해 시간이 많이 소요되므로 적절한 시간 배분을 통해 여유를 갖고 추론 문항을 풀 수 있도록 하자.

• 정답 및 해설 p.146

1 **빈 칸에 들어갈 가장 알맞은 말을 고르시오.**

These days, too many young women are going on a diet even though they are thin enough. This is mainly because the mass media has made them believe that only thin women are beautiful. In doing so, it also has made us believe that _____ is what matters most to women. But this is not the case. What matters most to women is to realize their potential. In order to do that, women need intelligence and effort, not beauty.

(a) relationship

(b) health

(c) beauty

2 **아래에 제시된 운동에 대한 설명으로 가장 알맞은 것을 고르시오.**

Supporters of the 9/11 Truth Movement claim that a group of people in the United States government helped to allow the 9/11 attacks to occur. Some of them even go so far as to say that the cruel group helped to carry out the attacks. Their claim is based on inaccuracies in the official account. Many experts believe, however, that their arguments are false.

(a) Its supporters blame the Afghanistan government for the 9/11 attacks.

(b) Its claims have no basis at all.

(c) Its claims are not generally accepted.

• 정답 및 해설 p.147

1 Nowadays, we are exposed to too many violent scenes in movies. This is a serious problem. Many studies have shown that exposure to "false" violence can lead to _____. The violence shown in the movies is "false" violence. This has resulted in many instances of real violence as predicted. To stop any other tragedies from happening, we need to stop violence in the movies.

Q. Choose the one option that best fits the sentence.

(a) sympathy for victims of violence

(b) insensitivity to real violence

(c) efforts to stop violence in the movies

(d) the ability to predict the future

2 During the period between 1861 and 1865, the Northern states fought with the Southern states for a number of reasons. One of the issues was the right of a state. The Southern states believed that they had the right to withdraw from the Union. On the other hand, the Northern states thought that such a right did not exist. When Abraham Lincoln was elected President, the Southern states felt that they had to protect their rights. They withdrew from the Union.

Q. What can be inferred from the passage?

(a) The Northern and Southern states agreed on every issue.

(b) Abraham Lincoln came from the Southern states.

(c) Abraham Lincoln believed that any state could withdraw from the Union.

(d) The withdrawal of the Southern states from the Union helped to start the war.

UNIT 3 문화와 인물

비실용문 가운데 문화와 인물에 대한 사항도 빠지지 않고 출제되는 중요 유형이다. 문화 현상이나 인물이 매우 다양하기 때문에 학습해야 할 분량이 많은 편이다. 근래에는 문화와 관련된 정책을 질문하는 경우도 있으므로 다양한 입장을 접하려는 노력이 필요하다. 여러 문화 현상의 중요한 특성들을 정리하고 인물의 어떤 측면이 부각될 수 있는지를 미리 짚어봐야 함에 유의하자.

유형 정리

1 문화 현상

On November 25, 2004, Bae Yong Joon arrived at Narita International Airport. Approximately 4,000 Japanese female fans gathered at the airport with some 400 police officers present. Why were so **many Japanese women crazy about this Korean actor?** Many explanations have been suggested, and one of them is that he enables Japanese women to imagine being with their Prince Charming.

일정한 문화 현상을 제시하고 그 현상에 대한 원인을 설명한 글이다. 문화 현상에 대해서는 이처럼 원인을 밝히려는 노력이 제시될 수도 있고 현상 자체에 대한 비판이 제시될 수도 있다. 되도록 다양한 문화 현상을 접하려는 노력이 필요하다.

2 문화 정책

Since 1980, many Americans have tried to make English the official language of the United States. **These English-only movements have been criticized** by a number of language experts. They point out that English is widely used throughout America and that its status is not threatened by other languages. In their opinion, the so-called English-only movements are just expressions of hatred toward immigrants.

문화 정책 가운데 하나인 언어 정책을 다룬 글이다. 이 글에서처럼 문화 정책에 대해 찬성과 반대의 입장이 있을 수 있으며 그에 대한 근거가 제시되는 경우가 많다는 점을 기억하자. 제시되는 근거가 어떤 것인지, 그 근거가 타당한지를 생각해 봐야 한다.

3 인물

Unlike what many people think, **Paris Hilton is a clever advertiser**. Basically, she knows how to sell products. She understands that in order to sell your products, you need to make people interested in you. So, she dares to do things that attract people's attention. For instance, she even drove under the influence of alcohol, making many people read about her.

영리한 광고자로서의 패리스 힐튼의 면모를 다룬 글이다. 이 글에서처럼 인물을 다루는 지문들은 대개 그 인물의 특정 측면에 초점을 맞추어 서술하는 것이 보통이다. 따라서 어떤 측면이 주로 이야기되는지에 중점을 두어 글을 읽는 연습을 하자.

Tips

1 세부사항

문화 현상이나 인물에 관한 글에 대해서는 물론 전반적 정보를 질문하는 경우도 있지만, 세부사항을 묻는 경우가 많음에 유의하자. 특히 세부사항의 경우, 선택지의 문장을 지문의 문장과 대조하면서 문제를 풀어나가야 하기 때문에 주의를 요한다. paraphrase에 유의하면서 사실 관계를 정확히 따지는 연습이 긴요함을 명심하자.

2 추론(Inference)

문화 현상과 인물에 대한 지문과 관련하여 수돈 문세는 내개 현상의 의의 또는 인물의 다른 사람들과의 관계나 업적 등을 다룬다. 반드시 지문에 제시된 내용을 바탕으로 하여, 자연스럽게 이끌어낼 수 있는 결론을 선택해야 하며 지문에 사용된 일부 단어가 들어 있는 선택지에 현혹되지 않도록 주의하자. 역시 까나로운 유형이므로 어느 정도의 시간 안배가 필요하다.

• 정답 및 해설 p.147

1 **B-boys와 관련된 설명으로 가장 알맞은 것을 고르시오.**

There are three generations of B-boys, who were fascinated by hip-hop culture. Each generation helped to create the essential elements of breakdancing. The first and second generations encouraged young people to develop basic moves. The third generation developed many more elements, which were thought to give birth to today's breakdancing moves. These days, those elements are charming thousands of young people in many countries.

(a) They were attracted to traditional European culture.

(b) They were good at drawing pictures.

(c) They helped to develop breakdancing moves.

2 **Aung San Suu Kyi에 대해 추론할 수 있는 바로 가장 알맞은 것을 고르시오.**

Aung San Suu Kyi came back to then Burma in 1988. Her purpose was to take care of her sick mother. When she saw many people killed by the military government, however, her life changed dramatically. She criticized the military rulers and began to lead nonviolent opposition to them. The cruel regime put her under house arrest. The rulers wanted her to leave the country, but she was unwilling to do so.

(a) She was a democratic leader.

(b) She had a bad temper.

(c) She wanted to leave then Burma to live with her husband.

1   Many of the basic principles of the New Age movement were developed by David Spangler. Unlike Alice Bailey, he stressed the importance of _____ in bringing a new age of love and hope. He believed that people could use some kind of energy to make the new age come to life. In 1976, Spangler published his first book and helped to start the New Age movement.

Q. Choose the one option that best fits the sentence.

(a) the arrival of aliens

(b) environmental protection

(c) human efforts

(d) publishing his own book

2   In fact, Hillary Clinton is a smart cookie. She knows how to get what she wants. As Barbara Olson clearly pointed out in her book entitled *Hell to Pay*, Clinton's methods are based on Saul Alinsky's ideas. Just like Alinsky, she believes that you can do anything to bring about "desirable" social changes. As a result, she does not respect ethics or traditions. Clinton even used her marriage as a tool for realizing her political goals.

Q. What can be inferred from the passage?

(a) Clinton is a traditional person.

(b) Clinton's ideas are quite different from those of Alinsky.

(c) Clinton got married because of pure love.

(d) Clinton is in favor of social changes.

지구과학은 뉴스 등을 통해 쉽게 접할 수 있는 과학 분야라는 점에서 비실용문 가운데 꾸준히 출제되는 소재이다. 지구과학의 이론이 출제되는 경우와 관련 현상이 출제되는 경우로 나누어볼 수 있다. 특히 지구과학 이론은 이해하는 데 다소 어려움이 있을 수 있다는 점에서 평소에 꾸준히 관련 지식을 습득하는 노력이 요구된다. 그리고 뉴스 보도 등에서 설명되는 기본 지식도 차분히 익혀나가도록 하자.

유형 정리

1 지질학

Plate tectonics is a theory about the outer layer of the earth. According to this theory, the outer layer is divided into seven large plates and several small ones. Surprisingly, these plates move at approximately 10cm a year. In addition, they affect each other in several ways. They can unite, separate, or move across one another. Partly because of these movements, earthquakes occur and volcanoes erupt.

지질학의 대표적인 이론인 판구조론에 대한 내용이다. 중요한 이론이므로 기본적인 내용을 정확하게 알아두어야 한다. 이와 같은 기본 지식은 지구과학의 다른 분야를 이해하는 데도 많은 도움이 된다는 점에서 철저한 학습을 요한다.

2 지구의 역사

It was once believed that large glaciers formed during the Great Ice Age (Pleistocene Epoch). In addition, widespread ice sheets waxed and waned in North America and Eurasia. According to modern research, however, many of the glaciers had developed before the Great Ice Age. It also proved that the Earth had been covered by glaciers during other ice ages as well.

지구의 역사 가운데 홍적세(洪績世)의 빙하 형성에 대한 내용이다. 구체적인 내용보다는 빙하기의 특성이라는 측면에서 접근하는 것이 바람직하다. 또한 빙하기의 대체적인 특성을 파악해두는 것도 도움이 된다.

3 자연재해

On December 26, 2004, an earthquake of magnitude 9.0 occurred in the southern Indian Ocean. As a result, a tsunami took place and attacked the eastern coasts of India and Sri Lanka. A few hours later, the tidal wave killed more than 225,000 people and left approximately one million homeless. This destructive tsunami reminded us of the importance of research into tsunamis.

지구과학으로 설명할 수 있는 자연재해 가운데 대표적인 해일에 대한 내용이다. 지진이나 화산 활동과 같은 다른 자연재해에 대해서도 알아두어야 한다. 대체로 구체적인 자연재해의 발생에 관한 내용이 출제된다.

Tips

1 배경 지식의 활용

특히 과학 분야와 관련하여 배경 지식의 중요성에 주목할 필요가 있다. 과학 분야에는 정립된 이론들이 많기 때문에, 주요 이론들의 내용을 미리 익혀두는 것이 실전에 효과적으로 대비하는 방법이다. 실제로 다른 분야에 대해서도 배경 지식을 갖추고 있는 경우와 그렇지 않은 경우에 지문의 이해에서 현격한 차이를 보인다는 점에 유의하여, 평소에 다양하게 배경 지식을 습득하도록 하자.

2 독해 기법

정보 진달이 주가 되는 과학 문야의 지문과 관련해서는 특히 명사와 동사 중심의 내용 파악 기법이 효과적이다. 왜냐하면 명사와 동사가 가장 중요한 정보를 나타내기 때문이다. 반면 명사와 동사 이외의 품사들이 나타내는 정보는 중요성이 떨어지는 것이 보통이다. 따라서 핵심적인 내용을 알아내려고 하는 경우는 주요 명사와 동사의 의미 파악에 주력하는 것이 바람직하다.

• 정답 및 해설 p.149

1 **빈 칸에 들어갈 가장 알맞은 말을 고르시오.**

There are two types of eruptions: effusive and explosive. An effusive eruption can be identified by an outpouring of magma that is less resistant to flowing. _____, an explosive eruption can be characterized by magma which is more resistant to flowing. Such magma usually has large quantities of gas. In general, explosive eruptions are more violent than effusive ones.

(a) As a result

(b) In short

(c) On the other hand

2 **다음 글에 나타난, 대륙지각과 해양지각 사이의 차이점으로 올바른 것을 고르시오.**

The oceanic crust is quite different from the continental crust. First of all, it is much younger. Its maximum age is 200 million years, whereas the average age of the continents is approximately 2 billion years. Second, the oceanic crust is denser than the continental crust. Its average density is about $3.3g/cm^3$, while the mean density of the continental crust is approximately $2.7g/cm^3$.

(a) The continental crust is much younger than the oceanic crust.

(b) The continental crust is less dense than the oceanic crust.

(c) The continental crust is thicker than the oceanic crust.

• 정답 및 해설 p.149

1   Earth scientists try to understand what the Earth looks like today and how it evolved. In order to achieve these purposes, they observe the characteristics of the Earth and then advance hypotheses explaining such features. They also develop methods of testing such hypotheses. _____, earth scientists employ scientific methods to explore the Earth.

Q. Choose the one option that best completes the sentence.

(a) By contrast

(b) For example

(c) Nevertheless

(d) In short

2   When James Lovelock first proposed the Gaia hypothesis, most scientists dismissed the assumption as ridiculous. This was mainly because he suggested that "planetary self-regulation" was "purposeful." According to his hypothesis, the Earth could be regarded as a living thing with clear purposes. Later, Lovelock changed his position and said that he did not imply that "planetary self-regulation involves planning by the biota."

Q. Which of the following is true according to the passage?

(a) James Lovelock dismissed the Gaia hypothesis as ridiculous.

(b) Lovelock once believed that the Earth could be thought of as a living thing.

(c) Most scientists believe that the Gaia hypothesis is valid.

(d) James Lovelock suggested that the Earth could be regarded as a machine.

UNIT 5 생물학

지구과학과 마찬가지로 생물학 분야도 일상적으로 접할 수 있는 기회가 많기 때문에 독해 영역에 꾸준히 출제되는 분야이다. 크게 식물학과 동물학, 그리고 첨단 생물학 분야로 나누어 볼 수 있다. 특히 줄기세포 연구와 같이 첨단 생물학 분야에 속하는 내용들은 시사적인 특성도 갖기 때문에 주의 깊게 알아둘 필요가 있다. 평소에 꾸준히 배경 지식을 늘리는 것이 효과적인 대비책임을 명심하자.

유형 정리

1 식물학

The castor bean is native to Africa and grows as tall as 12 feet. The plant contains a toxin called ricin and unfortunately, the toxin is extremely poisonous. As a result, when an animal eats just a small amount of castor bean, it is likely to die. Even if it does not die, the animal will suffer diarrhea, abdominal pain, or convulsions. Interestingly, though, the castor bean is used as a medicine in China and India.

맹독성 식물인 피마자와 관련된 내용이다. 전반적인 내용을 측정하거나 세부사항에 대한 이해도를 측정할 수 있다. 또한 독성이 강하다는 특성으로부터 추론할 것을 요구할 수도 있다. 지문의 이해에서는 특히 주요 특성을 정확히 알아두어야 한다.

2 동물학

Too many people believe that a spider is an insect. But that is not the case. First of all, spiders have eight legs. On the other hand, all insects have six legs. Second, spiders have two body parts, whereas insects have three. Then, what is a spider? It is an arachnid. Other arachnids include scorpions, mites, and ticks. All spiders are predators living on insects.

거미를 곤충으로 착각하는 흔한 편견에 대한 내용이다. 왜 거미가 곤충으로 분류될 수 없는지를 정확히 알아두어야 한다. 동물학 분야에서도 역시 특정 동물의 주요 특성을 정확히 포착하는 것이 기본적인 해법이다.

3 첨단 생물학 분야

Many people confuse molecular biology with microbiology. This is largely because both fields are concerned with studying cells. They are, however, quite different from each other. Molecular biology tries to explain genetic processes by exploring proteins and nucleic acids, which are major types of molecules. By contrast, microbiology studies simple life forms such as bacteria and viruses.

흔히 혼동하기 쉬운 분자생물학과 미생물학의 차이를 밝힌 지문이다. 각 분야의 기본적인 특성을 알아둘 필요가 있다. 또한 줄기세포 연구와 같은 첨단 생물학 분야의 최근 성과와 같은 내용도 함께 알아두자.

Tips

1 주요 동·식물 관련 어휘

생물학 분야 관련 문제의 경우, 특히 세부사항에서 동·식물의 주요 특성을 나타내는 어휘들이 까다롭게 제시될 수 있다는 점에 유의해야 한다. 이런 어휘들은 일상적으로 자주 접하기가 쉽지 않기 때문에, 본 단원에서 다루는 지문을 통해 기본적인 표현들을 정확히 익혀두어야 한다. 또한 고득점을 위해서는 관련 전문 용어들도 어느 정도 학습해야 한다는 점을 명심하자.

2 추론

다른 유형에 비해 특히 신중하게 문제에 접근할 필요가 있는 유형이 바로 추론 문제다. 성급하게 판단하려고 하지 말고, 주어진 지문에서 상식적으로 이끌어낼 수 있는 결론을 택하는 것이 가장 핵심적인 풀이 기법임을 명심해야 한다. 생물학에서도 역시 논리적으로 비약하지 말고 충분히 이해되는 범위에서만 추론하려는 노력이 요구됨을 명심하자.

• 정답 및 해설 p.150

1 빈 칸에 들어갈 가장 알맞은 말을 고르시오.

When examining Archaeopteryx, the earliest known bird, Richard Owen
_____. First, he mistook its front part for its back part.
Second, he overlooked its two distinguishing characteristics. One of them was
that its breastbone was flat. If he had noticed this fact, he would have guessed
that the bird could only glide. The other was that its braincase was similar to
that of a reptile.

(a) made important discoveries

(b) made two mistakes

(c) confused it with a reptile

2 다음 글로부터 추론할 수 있는 가장 적절한 것을 고르시오.

Making use of energy, cells produce chemical substances and reproduce
themselves. In order for self-reproduction to occur, however, the cell needs
to "know" how to utilize that energy. Such instructions are contained in cells.
Interestingly enough, these instructions are copied before the cell reproduces
itself. Consequently, each daughter cell has the blueprints for its self-
reproduction.

(a) In producing chemical substances, cells do not rely on energy.

(b) Without any instructions, cells know how to reproduce themselves.

(c) Every daughter cell knows how to use energy to reproduce itself.

• 정답 및 해설 p.151

1 According to Professor Karen Bernd, the bumblebee bat is the world's smallest mammal. Native to Thailand, the bat is 3-4 cm long and about 2 grams heavy. Some experts, however, disagree. They claim that the pygmy shrew is the world's smallest mammal. Their argument is based on the fact that the shrew _____ the bat. Well, which side is telling the truth?

Q. Choose the one option that best completes the sentence.

(a) moves faster than

(b) is larger than

(c) is lighter than

(d) swims better than

2 In the June 17, 2005 *Science*, Woo Suk Hwang and his team reported that they had extracted stem cells from human embryos. According to them, the cells could grow into any organ or tissue. When several people began to question their work, however, Hwang and his co-author Gerald Schatten requested *Science* to withdraw their paper. The Korean scientist mentioned that there had been mistakes in their report. Nevertheless, he refused to clarify what those mistakes were.

Q. What can be inferred from the passage?

(a) Woo Suk Hwang let people know what his mistakes were.

(b) Hwang and Schatten thought that their paper had some errors.

(c) All the scientists agreed that Woo Suk Hwang's work was perfect.

(d) Hwang's stem cells could not grow into a liver.

UNIT 6 환경과학

환경과학 분야 역시 일상적으로 흔히 접할 수 있기 때문에 꾸준히 출제되는 분야이다. 근래에는 특히 기상 이변과 관련된 내용이 종종 출제된다는 점에 유의하여 지구온난화나 엘니뇨 현상과 같은 주제에 대해 기본적인 지식을 갖출 필요가 있다. 그리고 대기 오염이나 해양 오염과 같은 고전적인 주제에 대해서도 충분한 배경 지식을 갖추어야 실전에서 실수를 줄일 수 있다.

유형 정리

1 생태계

Biodiversity refers to the variety of life forms in a particular ecosystem. There are many different ways to objectively measure biodiversity. One of them is by examining the variety of genes in a given ecosystem. Conservationists tend to maintain as many genes as they can. On the other hand, ecologists are concerned that such an approach might fail to fulfill its purpose.

최근 많은 관심의 대상이 되고 있는 생물다양성에 관한 지문이다. 생태계(ecosystem)와의 관련성을 염두에 두면서 기본적인 사항들을 확인해두어야 한다. 특히 세부사항 유형으로 출제되는 경우를 예상해둘 필요가 있다.

2 오염

Light pollution is when people produce intruding light. Being a side effect of industrialization, it can negatively affect human health and disturb many different ecosystems. For instance, exposure to excessive light can lead to fatigue and stress. Likewise, intruding light can prevent night blooming flowers from producing seeds, which may result in the decrease of those plants.

다소 생소하게 느껴질 수 있는 광공해(光公害)를 다룬 지문이다. 고전적인 대기오염이나 수질오염에 비해 참신한 소재이므로 기본적인 내용을 습득해 두어야 한다. 또한 구체적인 사항들을 꼼꼼하게 확인해 두는 것이 실전에 대한 효과적인 대비책임을 명심하자.

3 기상 이변

Regarding global warming, scientists have found out many things, but they still have some difficulty understanding the phenomenon. They have proven that the climate can be deeply affected by human activities. The problem is that they cannot specify an exact cause of a certain change in climate. Therefore, they are trying to develop scientific methods to examine various factors influencing climate patterns.

지구온난화 연구의 어려움을 다룬 지문이다. 참고로 지구온난화와 관련하여 그 위험성을 부정하는 입장도 있음을 알아두어야 한다. 이처럼 다양한 입장을 접하는 것이 실전에서 당황하지 않을 수 있는 핵심적인 전략이다.

Tips

1 주요 관련 어휘

다른 분야와 마찬가지로, 환경과학과 관련해서도 관련 어휘를 정확히 익혀두는 것이 지문의 내용을 이해하는 데나 문제를 풀어나가는 데 많은 도움이 된다. 특히 환경과학 분야는 다소 생소하게 느껴질 수 있는 어휘들이 많기 때문에 일상적으로 쉽게 접할 수 있는 용어를 중심으로 폭넓게 학습해 두어야만 생소한 내용을 접하게 될 때 문제 풀이의 정확성을 높일 수 있다.

2 세부사항

실전 TEPS에서 독해 문제를 풀다 보면, 시간 배분을 잘못하여 세부사항 유형에서 급하게 찍는 경우가 종종 있는데, 이는 여러모로 바람직하지 않다. 무엇보다도 정답을 맞힐 가능성이 그만큼 줄어든다. 따라서 Part Ⅰ의 전반부나 Part Ⅲ, 그리고 Part Ⅱ의 전반적 정보 문제 유형을 빠른 속도로 해결하여 절약한 시간을 바탕으로 여유 있고 꼼꼼하게 확인하면서 풀어야만 한다는 점을 명심 또 명심하자.

• 정답 및 해설 p.151

1 빈 칸에 들어갈 가장 알맞은 말을 고르시오.

When desertification occurs, the affected land starts to lose its ability to support its various life forms. Its groundwater table drops, its topsoil becomes covered with salt, and its native plants begin to disappear. According to scientists, human activities contribute to the spread of deserts, and unless _____, desertification will continue to hurt our environment.

(a) people continue to live in forests

(b) we cut down more trees

(c) radical measures are taken

2 생태계에 대한, 다음 글의 설명으로 올바른 것을 고르시오.

There are two types of elements in an ecosystem. One is its physical environment such as sunlight, water, and soil. The other is living organisms within the ecosystem. Energy flows throughout the system, distributing nutrients among its constituents. As is widely known, that energy comes from the sun, which nurtures all ecosystems on Earth.

(a) It has three types of constituents.

(b) It depends on the sun for energy.

(c) It does not include living organisms.

• 정답 및 해설 p.152

1   On December 7, 2007, the Hong Kong-registered oil tanker Hebei Spirit was hit by a crane barge belonging to Samsung Heavy Industries. The tanker leaked approximately 10,500 tons of oil off the West Coast. This oil spill affected the famous Taean region _____. Few tourists visited the area and its seafood industries were hard hit by the destructive oil spill.

Q. Choose the one option that best completes the sentence.

(a) in a positive way

(b) to a small extent

(c) in a constructive manner

(d) to a great extent

2   Deforestation is when forests are replaced by land for other uses. When it takes place, it can negatively affect the environment. First of all, deforestation worsens the greenhouse effect because there are no more trees or plants capable of eliminating carbon from the atmosphere. Second, deforestation reduces biodiversity in that important constituents such as trees and plants disappear.

Q. Which of the following is true according to the passage?

(a) Deforestation helps the environment in a variety of ways.

(b) Biodiversity can be negatively affected by deforestation.

(c) Deforestation has nothing to do with the greenhouse effect.

(d) Deforestation helps trees and plants grow rapidly.

생활과학은 일종의 상식으로 여겨질 수 있는 분야이기 때문에 출제 빈도가 높은 편이다. 의학이나 기술, 첨단 과학 분야의 시사적인 지문을 통해 다양하게 배경 지식을 넓혀가는 것이 기본적인 학습 전략이다. 비실용문이지만 실용성이 높다는 점에서, 또한 이와 같은 지식이 실생활과도 관련된다는 점에서, 각별한 주의를 요하는 분야라는 점을 명심하자.

1 의학

Many experts believe that obesity results from unhealthy lifestyles. For instance, a large number of people tend to overeat for various reasons. Some people depend on foods for stress release. Others eat large amounts of foods just because they are readily available. To make matters worse, far too many people do not exercise enough. These unhealthy lifestyles can account for most cases of obesity.

비만이 건강에 해로운 생활방식으로부터 비롯된다는 내용의 글이다. 이처럼 의학 관련 내용 가운데는 일상적으로 활용도가 높은 지식이 많이 있기 때문에, 다양하게 기본적인 내용을 습득해두는 것이 여러모로 유리하다.

2 기술

According to PR-GB.com, NovelMaker.com has recommended NextUp's TextAloud (http://www.NextUp.com) to its members looking for proofreading tools. This is largely because the award-winning program enables writers to catch the rhythm of their work. Of course, this text-to-speech tool lets them find typos easily. In addition, TextAloud provides a wide variety of voices in any age, gender, or accent.

텍스트를 말로 전환하는 프로그램을 교정하는 도구로 권장한다는 내용의 글이다. 기술 분야의 발전 속도가 매우 빠르기 때문에, 이처럼 다양한 내용이 출제될 수 있다. 추론 유형의 문제도 출제될 수 있음을 생각해 내용 전반을 명확히 이해하자.

3 첨단 과학

As a field of artificial intelligence, affective computing tries to design machines and devices that can deal with human emotions. For a long time, scientists have thought that emotions do not play a major role in human life. For this reason, they have not tried to develop machines capable of processing emotions. They have recently discovered that emotions affect every aspect of human life. As a result, they have started to explore various ways of empowering machines to process human emotions.

대단히 생소하게 느껴질 수 있는 감성적 컴퓨팅에 관한 내용이다. 첨단 과학 분야도 기술과 마찬가지로 발전 속도가 빠르기 때문에 뉴스 보도 등을 통해 최근의 발전상 등을 기본적으로 익혀두는 것이 바람직하다.

Tips

1 실용 지식 확충

특히 생활과학 분야의 내용은 실생활에 바로 활용될 수 있는 실용 지식이기 때문에 출제 빈도가 높을 수밖에 없다는 점에 유의해야 한다. 복잡한 이론까지 알 필요는 없지만, 근래의 주요 성과들을 언론 매체를 통해 꾸준히 접하는 것이 이 분야에 대한 감각을 유지하는 데 반드시 필요하다는 점을 인식해야 한다. 이 단원에서 다루는 내용과 모의고사에서 다루는 내용은 반드시 확인해 두자.

2 핵심 독해 기법

독해의 가장 중요한 목적은 주어진 지문을 통해 저자가 무엇을 말하고 싶어 하는가를 파악하는 것이다. 설령 지문 전체를 우리말로 완벽하게 번역했다고 하더라도 저자가 정말로 하고 싶어 하는 바를 알지 못했다면 제대로 독해를 한 것이 아니다. 이와 같은 핵심 주제를 포착하기 위해서는, 각 문장이 뒷받침하고자 하는 하나의 중심 생각이 무엇인가를 생각하면서 글을 읽어나가야 한다. 또한 개별 단어의 뜻이 아니라 전체 글의 내용 흐름을 정확히 읽어낼 수 있도록 노력하자.

•정답 및 해설 p.152

1 **빈 칸에 들어갈 가장 알맞은 말을 고르시오.**

According to American Heart Association®, there are _____ relationships between the consumption of red wine and the decrease of heart diseases. The association points out that researchers are currently studying the effects of red wine's flavonoids on human health. So far, no studies have proven that red wine directly reduces the risks of developing heart diseases.

(a) causal

(b) no direct

(c) no distant

2 **다음 글의 내용으로부터 추론할 수 있는 바로 올바른 것을 고르시오.**

At present, we cannot fully utilize nanorobotics mainly because it is still in the initial stages of development. If the technology is completely developed, however, it can revolutionize our lives. For instance, using extremely small robots, doctors will be able to perform microsurgery. If this is possible, we can destroy harmful bacteria or viruses much more easily, curing almost all diseases. We can also manufacture highly advanced products in an effective way.

(a) Nanorobotics cannot affect our everyday lives.

(b) Nanorobotics has nothing to do with medicine.

(c) Nanorobotics has not been fully developed.

PRACTICE

• 정답 및 해설 p.153

1 According to National Lung Cancer Partnership, women can reduce the risks of developing lung cancer in many ways. First of all, it is always a good idea to _____. Call 1-800-QUIT-NOW or visit www.naquitline.org. Second, if radon levels in your house are too high, you had better install a device capable of reducing them. Finally, eat a variety of healthy foods and exercise regularly.

Q. Choose the one option that best completes the sentence.

(a) continue smoking

(b) quit smoking

(c) continue drinking

(d) quit gambling

2 As an expert on podcasting, I find Juice, the podcast receiver, extremely useful. You can download the program by visiting http://juicereceiver.sourceforge.net/. After installing the receiving program, you can subscribe to podcasts in two different ways. You can take a look at all the available podcasts by clicking the Selection button. Or if you know the URL for a particular podcast, just enter it into the program. Now, you have one of the most convenient tools for enjoying podcasts.

Q. What can be inferred from the passage?

(a) The writer knows little about podcasting.

(b) Juice is a tool for sending podcasts around the world.

(c) You should purchase Juice by mail.

(d) Juice is a very convenient tool for using podcasts.

유형 정리

1　철학

According to Søren Kierkegaard, there are three "stages" in one's life: the aesthetic, the ethical, and the religious. The earlier stages do not automatically lead to the later stages. The later stages are, however, the goals of the earlier ones. They also include the earlier stages as an important element. Kierkegaard was particularly interested in exploring the religious stage and stressed its importance throughout his writings.

흔히 실존주의철학자로 분류되는 키에르케고르의 사상을 설명한 글이다. 이처럼 주요 철학자들의 사상은 평소에 관심을 갖고 기본적인 내용을 알아두는 것이 필요하다. 빈 칸 채우기나 추론 유형으로도 출제가 된다는 점에 유의해야 한다.

2　예술

Approximately one hundred years ago, Isadora Duncan observed that art is essentially practical, serving to satisfy the most basic human need: to express the free spirit. The spirit is so pure, so beautiful, so strong. In expressing the free spirit, art can play a leading role in shedding light on the human condition and showing us the path to liberty. Taking this into account, Duncan tried to "secularize" art for the purpose of liberating ordinary people.

이사도라 덩컨의 예술 사상을 설명한 글이다. 예술과 관련해서는 이처럼 예술가의 사상이나 작품 성향, 구체적인 작품에 대한 설명 등이 출제 범위에 속한다. 빈 칸 채우기나 세부사항 유형으로 출제될 수 있음을 염두에 두어야 한다.

3 대중문화

Ingmar Bergman's films explore the human condition in a uniquely individual style. They deal with such issues as a person's relationship with other people. More importantly, his extraordinary films are attempts to find one's true self. Bergman felt that, in trying to achieve that aim, it would be necessary to get rid of false appearances. It seems that he found the task achievable and unattainable.

잉그마르 베르히만의 영화 세계를 설명한 글이다. 대중문화에 속하는 다양한 인물들이나 주요 흐름 등이 출제될 수 있음을 예상해야 한다. 역시 빈 칸 채우기나 세부사항 유형, 추론 유형 등을 측정할 수 있다.

> ### Tips
>
> **1 철학 관련 지식 강화**
>
> 철학 분야는 출제 빈도가 상대적으로 높지 않기 때문에 소홀히 하기 쉬운 분야인데, 이는 특히 고득점을 목표로 하는 경우에는 바람직한 전략이 아니다. 특히 독해 영역이 난이도가 높게 출제되는 때는 반드시 철학 분야가 포함된다는 점에서, 서양의 주요 철학 사상의 기본적인 내용은 습득해 두는 것이 여러모로 유리하다. 또한 철학이 비판적 사고력을 길러준다는 점에서도 주요 내용을 학습하는 것은 독해력 배양에 많은 도움이 된다.
>
> **2 주요 독해 기법**
>
> 흔히 독해를 제대로 못하는 경우, 주어진 지문에서 일관되게 주장하는 바를 포착하지 못하기가 쉽다. 글을 읽는 가장 중요한 목적은 하나의 일관된 주장의 포착이다. 이와 관련하여, 한두 문장의 뜻을 명확히 파악하지 못하더라도 전체 글의 핵심 내용을 파악할 수 있다는 점에 유의해야 한다. 왜냐하면 그 한두 문장도 결국에는 글의 핵심 내용을 명확히 드러내는 수단일 뿐이기 때문이다. 따라서 지문 전체를 통해 저자가 일관되게 주장하는 바를 포착하는 데 중점을 두는 것이 주요 독해 기법임을 명심하자.

• 정답 및 해설 p.154

1   빈 칸에 들어갈 가장 알맞은 말을 고르시오.

During his visit to Italy, Renoir was very impressed by the distinguishing characteristics of classicism. In classicism, lines were drawn clearly and beautifully to show the true beauty of a form. In addition, smooth painting was recognized as a powerful way of expressing the grace of the human body. Deeply influenced by these features, Renoir decided to _____ Impressionism.

(a) break with

(b) continue to support

(c) learn about

2   다음 글에 대한 설명으로 가장 올바른 것을 고르시오.

Karl Jaspers's *General Psychopathology* showed that existentialism had an impact on psychiatry. In this book, Jaspers suggested that psychiatrists ought to understand a mental patient's world by sympathetically taking part in his or her experience. Likewise, Ludwig Binswanger's *On the Flight of Ideas* showed the influence of existentialism on psychiatry. Binswanger believed that mental illnesses occur because patients fail to realize their existential possibilities.

(a) Karl Jaspers did not believe that existentialism would help psychiatry.

(b) Ludwig Binswanger does not support existentialism.

(c) Existentialism affected psychiatry in some ways.

1 Interestingly enough, there are many similarities between Taoism and Confucianism. This is mainly because their ideas about people, society, and the universe are based on a common tradition. The tradition was established before Confucius and Lao-tzu appeared. Despite these common elements, however, Taoism is _____ Confucianism in that it tries to transcend the physical world.

Q. Choose the one option that best completes the sentence.

(a) the same as
(b) similar to
(c) related to
(d) different from

2 Surprisingly, the film *Clueless* is based on Jane Austen's *Emma*. As you may guess, Emma Woodhouse "becomes" Cher Horowitz. Both of them are spoiled young women. In addition, they make friends with outsiders and play matchmaker. Emma has an adventure in a carriage, while Cher fails her driver's test. In these ways, the parallels are endless.

Q. Which of the following is true according to the passage?

(a) Jane Austen's *Emma* influenced the film *Clueless* in many ways.
(b) Cher Horowitz is an educated young woman.
(c) Being so shy, Emma Woodhouse does not play matchmaker.
(d) Jane Austen's *Emma* has nothing to do with the film *Clueless*.

TEPS

모의고사
READING
COMPREHENSION

DIRECTIONS

This part of the exam tests your ability to comprehend reading passages. You will have 45 minutes to complete the 40 questions. Be sure to follow the directions given by the proctor.

Part I **Questions 1~16**

Read the passage. Then choose the option that best completes the passage.

1. According to National Cancer Institute, it is _____ whether tea can actually reduce the risks of developing cancer. Some studies support the claim that the consumption of tea can cut cancer risk. On the other hand, other studies do not support that claim. This is largely because other factors such as one's diet and lifestyle can help reduce cancer risk.

    (a) absolutely true
    (b) sure
    (c) not certain
    (d) determined

2. On February 26, 2008, the New York Philharmoic _____ the East Pyongyang Grand Theater in Pyongyang, North Korea. It was the first time that Pyongyang permitted an American orchestra to hold a concert in the "communist" country. It was not clear, however, whether the event really touched ordinary North Koreans or not. This was because they are not allowed to act freely most of the time.

    (a) criticized
    (b) performed at
    (c) greeted South Koreans at
    (d) entertained Americans at

3. According to the Associated Press, Timothy Goeglei, a special assistant to President Bush, _____ Friday after acknowledging that he had committed plagiarism. The plagiarism was discovered by Nancy Nall, a former columnist for The News-Sentinel. Nall pointed out that Goeglei had copied Jeffrey Hart's article without giving credit. In response to her report, the White House addressed the problem immediately.

    (a) was angered
    (b) praised himself
    (c) felt flattered
    (d) resigned

4.

Dear Ms. Breslin:

It was a great pleasure to talk with you about the managing director position at Faith Corporation. As I mentioned in the interview, I have over ten years of managerial experience for large corporations. And all my colleagues have been impressed by my skills as a manager, or more precisely, a facilitator. Therefore, I am convinced that I will be a _____ to your company.

    (a) pain in the neck
    (b) piece of cake
    (c) bad apple
    (d) great asset

5. According to Becky Worley, ABC News Technology Contributor, biodiesel is a mixture of regular diesel and vegetable oil. Interestingly enough, biodiesel can be utilized in _____ diesel engines. As a result, you can choose to use biodiesel or not. One thing you should know about using biodiesel is that you need to change your oil filter more frequently.

    (a) all the current
    (b) only the new
    (c) only the old
    (d) only Japanese

6. Many Koreans criticize Japan for its _____ in World War II. They believe that the island country did something ethically wrong. This judgment is based on the belief that ethical concepts play an important part in international politics. From the perspective of "idealism," that makes perfect sense. On the other hand, such judgments do not make sense from the perspective "realism." This is because realists believe that ethical concepts do not have any place in world politics.

    (a) altruistic behavior
    (b) positive attitude
    (c) cruel behavior
    (d) optimistic attitude

7. For me, soccer is not just a kind of sport, but a way of life. It is my passion. This is not merely because I can enjoy playing the active sport. Nor is it because I am enslaved by a ruthless desire for victory. It is mainly because soccer lets us know who we are. It teaches me that we are feeble beings who strive for success. It also reminds me that success is supposed to be hard to achieve. Ironically, it makes me become keenly aware that success is not everything. What _____ is how sincere we are in trying to make our dreams come true.

    (a) matters most
    (b) is not important
    (c) is of little significance
    (d) bothers us

8. During the late 1990s, a large number of Internet companies were founded in the United States. The problem was that most of them did not _____. Nevertheless, the stock prices of those companies increased rapidly. As a result, the NASDAQ composite index reached 5,048 by March 2000. The Internet bubble eventually burst and the NASDAQ fell to 1,114 by October 2002.

    (a) use the Internet
    (b) make robots
    (c) earn a profit
    (d) hire many people

9. In the late 600s BC, a legislator called Draco drafted a new set of laws for Athens. Surprisingly, his laws were extremely cruel. Some people said that the laws were written in blood. For instance, if someone could not pay off their debt, they might become a slave. Even a petty crime could be punished by the death penalty. Draco's laws gave birth to the word draconian, which means "_____."

    (a) particularly kind
    (b) very humane
    (c) extremely harsh
    (d) extremely useful

10. True heroes are just ordinary people who choose to do the right things for their community. As human beings, we have responsibilities toward our families, our neighbors, and our country. We cannot, and should not, _____ those responsibilities. That is the true meaning of being human, and we should be always aware of the importance of a sense of duty in our everyday and human lives.

    (a) pay attention to
    (b) ignore or neglect
    (c) pay tribute to
    (d) care about or deal with

11. I firmly believe that examining the theory of evolution is not against my religion. I must mention that the "theory" is not yet a scientific law. So it requires further study. Moreover, as many forward-thinking scholars point out, the theory may not be scientifically _____. In exploring such matters, we should be aware of the importance of an open mind.

    (a) consistent or convincing
    (b) incorrect or invalid
    (c) reliable or unacceptable
    (d) illegal or legitimate

12. My experience as captain of a basketball team has taught me that in order to move your team members, you must touch their hearts. Unless you understand your true self first, you cannot influence other people in a meaningful way. Finding your true self requires you to be _____ yourself. What do you really want? What makes you really happy? What makes you cry?

    (a) totally ignorant of
    (b) completely honest with
    (c) completely satisfied with
    (d) extremely jealous of

13. According to Martin Lewis, Ph.D., Somalia is not a "country." This is largely because there has not been a stable government since 1991. Somalia is _____ by the Transitional Federal Government. The government has been recognized by the global community. Nevertheless, it is so weak that many people are concerned that it may collapse in no time.

    (a) completely controlled
    (b) constantly attacked
    (c) severely criticized
    (d) partly controlled

14. When he was eighteen, Malcolm X lived and worked in New York City. His work was that of a shoeshiner at a nightclub. Luckily, he was able to see some famous African-American musicians. Unfortunately, however, he _____ criminal activities such as dealing in drugs and robbing people of money.

    (a) cracked down on
    (b) became engaged in
    (c) was not involved in
    (d) decided to stop

15. *Catch-22* is a novel by the American writer Joseph Heller. It mainly focuses on John Yossarian's attempts to survive the ordeal of World War II. The "catch" in the title refers to an Air Force rule that contradicts itself. According to the regulation, a man is deemed crazy if he keeps flying dangerous missions. _____, he is deemed sane if he formally says that he wants to avoid such missions because of his madness. As a result, there is no way of avoiding dangerous combat missions.

    (a) For example
    (b) Therefore
    (c) On the other hand
    (d) In short

16. *200 Pounds Beauty* [sic] is an amazing film depicting the agony of being a "beauty." The film begins with Han-na Kang visiting a fortune-teller. Originally she was ugly and overweight. After undergoing plastic surgery, Kang became slender and beautiful. But she realized that being such a beauty was not what she really wanted. _____, she told the truth to her fans at her concert and started her career all over again.

    (a) Nevertheless
    (b) Incidentally
    (c) For instance
    (d) As a result

Part II   Questions 17~37

Read the passage. Then choose the option that best answers the question.

17. According to Naples Daily News (March 2, 2008), the Florida Chamber of Commerce will try hard to make their voices heard in the Florida Legislature. The business organization wants the legislative branch to improve the state's education and promote its economic growth. In addition, it believes that the Legislature should do more to protect the Constitution and safeguard private property rights.

Q. What is the best title for the passage?

(a) Business Leaders Asking for Political and Economic Improvements
(b) The Florida Chamber of Commerce Turning into a Monster
(c) A Variety of Issues to be Discussed in the Florida Legislature
(d) The United States Constitution Under Attack

18. Regarding the telephone conversation between you and me, I need to explain some matters and sincerely ask you to understand my position. We, Faith International School, have been providing quality education for our students for over twenty years, and experience has taught us that selecting a qualified teacher is vital for the quality of education we can offer to our students. For this reason, we have been extremely cautious about hiring new teachers.

Q. What is the topic of the passage?
(a) Criticizing the reader's ignorance
(b) Explaining the hiring policy of a school
(c) Inviting the reader to an important event
(d) Apologizing to the reader for the late reply

19. Between March 7 and 9, 2008, Juggle This! will be held in New York City. This is the city's 7th annual juggling festival and all jugglers are cordially invited to this famous event. Participants will enjoy a variety of games and workshops. This festival will take place at Pratt Institute. For more information, visit http://www.jugglenyc.com/fests.html.

Q. What is the passage mainly about?
    (a) New York City
    (b) The fame of Pratt Institute
    (c) Visiting a website
    (d) A juggling festival

20. My name is Erica Smith, and I am a teacher at Hope Academy in South Korea. Katherine Kim, one of our students, would like to attend your prestigious school. And we wonder how we can pay the $50 application fee. Should we send you a check or can we pay by credit card? Or should we send you a money order? We are more than willing to pay by any of these methods.

Q. What is the main purpose of the letter?
    (a) To ask how the application fee is paid
    (b) To thank the reader for helping a student
    (c) To criticize the reader for failing to apply for the school
    (d) To complain that the application process is too complex

21. Our SuperMemory Chip is a revolutionary product. With this tiny chip, you can increase your memory by 900%. As a result, you can memorize all the important data for your business. You can also master a foreign language within a month. Plus, our memory chip enables you to get rid of bad memories once and for all. For more information, visit http://www.supermemory.com.

Q. What is the best title for the passage?
   (a) A Revolution Is Near
   (b) The SuperMemory Chip Boosts Your Memory
   (c) An Efficient Way of Mastering a Foreign Language
   (d) The Influence of Bad Memories on Everyday Life

22. Does telepathy really exist? Many experts argue that there is no scientific evidence supporting the existence of such a paranormal power. Nevertheless, a few cases involving telepathy seem real and Dean Radin, director of the Consciousness Research Laboratory at the University of Nevada, claims that psychic phenomena such as telepathy are real.

Q. What is the topic of the passage?
   (a) How to collect scientific evidence
   (b) The personal life of Dean Radin
   (c) The existence of telepathy
   (d) The Consciousness Research Laboratory at the University of Nevada

23. Martin Luther King, Jr., a graduate of Boston University, declared, "I have a dream." His dream is to make sure that everyone is respected and pursues his or her happiness. I am convinced that his vision for all the human race was the product of quality education provided by Boston University. Thus I wish to follow suit and develop a broad perspective and commit myself to pursuing excellence in every aspect of my life at Boston University.

Q. Which of the following is true according to the passage?
   (a) The writer is not applying to Boston University.
   (b) Martin Luther King, Jr. graduated from Boston University.
   (c) The writer met Martin Luther King, Jr. in Boston.
   (d) Martin Luther King, Jr. taught at Boston University.

24. By looking at the gross domestic product of a country, you can find out whether the economy is performing well or not. This is mainly because the figure clearly shows how the economic resources within that nation are utilized. Interestingly enough, GDP does not indicate whether certain goods and services are produced by foreigners in the country.

Q. Which of the following is true according to the passage?
   (a) GDP does not show the size of an economy.
   (b) GDP is the same as GNP.
   (c) GDP is not widely used anymore.
   (d) GDP is an economic indicator.

25. As is widely known, Korean teachers are very strict and demanding, and my teachers were no exception. They wanted me to be the best cellist. This might be too much for me, but I was really glad that my teachers thought highly of me like that. Therefore, I did my best, and gradually mastered every skill. After all, we can do anything if we believe in ourselves enough and fail enough. I also believe that there is always hope in any situation.

Q. Which of the following is true according to the passage?
 (a) The writer is optimistic.
 (b) The writer wants to be a pianist.
 (c) The writer's teachers were not strict.
 (d) The writer does not believe in doing one's best.

26. The new era is characterized by two major features: sensitivity and imagination. First of all, the widespread use of the Internet has compelled people to be more sensitive to their feelings, rather than to reason. Ironically, anti-America sentiment is painful proof of that. People react to America in an emotional way. Second, the power of imagination is becoming more and more influential in many aspects of our lives.

Q. What characterizes the new era?
 (a) Reason and knowledge
 (b) Anti-America sentiment
 (c) The Internet and technology
 (d) Emotion and creativity

27. Mary Kay Ash is one of my role models because she built a principle-based company. She always said, "We do what's right." By adhering to this principle, she succeeded in establishing one of the most successful firms in America. In addition, her business is a global one giving hope and love to many different people in various countries.

Q. Which of the following is NOT mentioned in the passage?
 (a) Mary Kay Ash was a millionaire.
 (b) Mary Kay Ash founded a successful company.
 (c) Mary Kay Ash respected principles.
 (d) Mary Kay Ash gave hope to many foreigners.

28. In his Nichomachean Ethics, Aristotle criticizes Plato's theory of forms. Aristotle points out that Plato is wrong in that he asserts that forms belong to a different world. Plato believes that since we can distinguish between an object and its abstract form, each of them belongs to a different world. In Aristotle's opinion, Plato's conclusion is not logically correct.

Q. Which of the following is true according to the passage?
 (a) Aristotle taught logic to Plato.
 (b) Aristotle's conclusion is not correct.
 (c) Aristotle disagreed with Plato.
 (d) Plato taught ethics to Aristotle.

29. Continental drift is when the Earth's continents move away from one another. This concept was introduced by Alfred Wegener. Based on large amounts of data, Wegener thought that originally there existed only one continent. He called the continent Pangea. About 200 million years ago, Pangea broke into several parts and they drifted away from each other.

Q. Which of the following is true according to the passage?
    (a) Alfred Wegener did not accept the notion of continental drift.
    (b) According to Wegener, Pangea broke into several pieces two billion years ago.
    (c) Alfred Wegener thought that originally there existed several continents.
    (d) Wegener's theory was based on large amounts of data.

30. On March 1, 1919, Koreans launched the March 1st Movement. A Korean "Declaration of Independence" was read at Taehwagwan Restaurant in Seoul. Thousands of Koreans took to the streets, asking for independence from Japan. Approximately two million Koreans participated in this peaceful movement. But it was cruelly suppressed by the Japanese.

Q. Which of the following is true according to the passage?
    (a) The Japanese welcomed the March 1st Movement.
    (b) The March 1st Movement was a peaceful movement.
    (c) Koreans demanded independence from China.
    (d) About two thousand Koreans took part in the March 1st Movement.

31. As Nicole is fully aware, art is, in essence, self-expression. As such, it requires a certain amount of self-discipline and I can assure you that she is a highly self-disciplined artist. I think this is mainly due to her traditional upbringing. Art also means freedom, and she understands this point, too. Moreover, she never loses sight of the practical aspects of art, which makes her pursue a career in fashion design.

Q. What kind of student is Nicole?
(a) Proud and jealous
(b) Traditional and unimaginative
(c) Artistic and practical
(d) Lazy and shy

32. In a phone interview with Newsweek, Suad Leija explained why she had decided to help the U.S. Immigration and Customs Enforcement (ICE) Agency. Leija was concerned that the false documents her family produced might be used to help another terrorist attack on the United States. She believed that her loyalty to her country was more important than her loyalty to her family. Visit http://www.newsweek.com/id/117121 and read this amazing story.

Q. Which of the following is true according to the passage?
(a) Suad Leija did not aid the U.S. Immigration and Customs Enforcement Agency.
(b) Suad Leija thought that her country is more important than her family.
(c) Suad Leija was raised in Mexico.
(d) Suad Leija was willing to help another terrorist attack on the United States.

33. Unlike what people may think, DontDateHimGirl.com is not just a website for making complaints about bad guys. Actually, it is a "social networking site" that can improve women's lives. For instance, you can even find information about how to raise your self-esteem. In addition, this website is a great place for men who have relationship problems.

Q. What kind of website is DontDateHimGirl.com?
    (a) A website that helps women live better lives
    (b) A website that makes women hate men
    (c) A website that gives information about political activities
    (d) A website that makes men hate one another

34. According to Dr. Joe Schwarcz, a hangover is caused by methanol contained in alcoholic drinks. Enzymes turn methanol into formaldehyde, which causes severe headaches and fatigue. According to Wikipedia, however, hangovers are caused by ethanol, which makes your body lose water. Then, which side is telling the truth, Dr. Schwarcz or Wikipedia?

Q. What can be inferred from the passage?
    (a) Wikipedia explains that a hangover is caused by methanol.
    (b) According to Wikipedia, methanol makes your body lose water.
    (c) Dr. Schwarcz and Wikipedia are both right.
    (d) Dr. Schwarcz believes that hangovers are caused by methanol.

35. Erika Prins, a spokeswoman for the Anne Frank Museum, is looking for more information about Peter Schiff, who is Anne Frank's "one true love." His photograph was given to the museum by his friend Ernst Michaelis. Schiff and Michaelis went to the Holdheim Schule in Berlin together. In 1942, when they parted, the two friends exchanged pictures. If you have more information about Peter Schiff, then contact the spokeswoman by visiting http://www.annefrank.org.

Q. What can be inferred from the passage?
   (a) Anne Frank loved Ernst Michaelis.
   (b) There is not enough information about Peter Schiff.
   (c) Anne Frank and Ernst Michaelis went to school together.
   (d) Ernst Michaelis and Peter Schiff parted in 1945.

36. People with a dissociative fugue completely forget who they are. As a result, they leave their home and begin to live in an entirely different place. They may think that they are someone else. The disease can last for hours, days, or months. Many psychiatrists believe that the disorder results from a shocking experience such as getting divorced or losing jobs.

Q. What can be inferred from the passage?
   (a) People with a dissociative fugue sometimes forget their identity.
   (b) A dissociative fugue usually last for several years.
   (c) People with a dissociative fugue believe that a celebrity loves them.
   (d) People with a dissociative fugue believe that they are extremely overweight.

37. After deciding on my career path, I was faced with an unexpected obstacle: English. Ironically, I love this lovely language. I have seen so many American movies, listened to so many American songs, and read so many American books. All of them have touched my heart in many different ways. The problem was that I had to get a high score on the TEPS test. What? The TEPS test? What is it, anyway?

Q. What can be inferred from the passage?

    (a) The writer is fond of English.
    (b) The writer does not enjoy American movies.
    (c) The writer got a high score on the TEPS test.
    (d) The writer has composed many American songs.

Part III   Questions 38~40

Read the passage. Then identify the option that does NOT belong.

38. At the 2004 Democratic National Convention, Barack Obama gave the keynote address. (a) In that speech, Obama stressed the importance of the government in making sure that every American child has a decent life. (b) In trying to achieve that purpose, he felt that the government must set the right priorities. (c) In addition, he mentioned that the U.S. should not go to war with Iraq. (d) He also believed that the government should give every American equal opportunities.

39. Principal investigator Tony Colaprete of NASA's Ames Research Center has announced a plan to send two spacecraft to the moon. (a) Surprisingly, they are going to clash into the moon's South Pole. (b) Colaprete is aware that many people are concerned about the project. (c) They hope that NASA finds aliens in outer space. (d) But he emphasizes the fact that such a project is "very economical."

40. Unfortunately, too many language teachers regard language as a mixture of machine-like parts. (a) As a result, they believe that meaningless repetition and endless practice will enable a learner to command a language. (b) That is not the case. (c) In order to be a successful language learner, you need to get to the heart, or the spirit, of your target language. (d) Many skillful learners instinctively perceive subtle differences in meaning.

취업 전에도, 취업 후에도
Multi TEPS!

취업 전 입시, 편입, 졸업에서도!
취업 후 승진, 해외파견, 사내 커뮤니케이션에서도!
언제 어디서든 활용할 수 있는 TEPS로
모든 도전에 통(通)하라.

TEPS 공식페이스북

TEPS	TEPS-Speaking	*i*-TEPS	SNULT
대기업, 의·치전원, 고시 등 다방면에서 활용되는 한국대표 영어시험	• 실전 영어말하기 능력평가! 대기업, 공기업 취업 및 주요대학 내 평가활용	• 듣기, 읽기, 말하기, 쓰기 통합 영어능력 측정! 공무원 국외장기훈련 파견 선발시험 등	• 제2외국어능력평기의 정확한 기준! 영어, 일이, 중이, 불이, 독어, 시어, 노어

서울대학교 TEPS관리위원회   Homepage: www.teps.or.kr   Tel: 02-886-3330

● 넥서스 수준별 TEPS 맞춤 학습 프로그램

서울대 기출문제

서울대 텝스 관리위원회 텝스 최신기출 1200제 2016 문제집 2 | 서울대학교 TEPS관리위원회 문제 제공 | 352쪽 | 19,500원
서울대 텝스 관리위원회 텝스 최신기출 1200제 2016 해설집 2 | 서울대학교 TEPS관리위원회 문제 제공 · 넥서스 TEPS연구소 해설 | 480쪽 | 25,000원
서울대 텝스 관리위원회 텝스 최신기출 1200제 2015-2016 문제집 | 서울대학교 TEPS관리위원회 문제 제공 | 352쪽 | 19,500원
서울대 텝스 관리위원회 텝스 최신기출 1200제 2015-2016 해설집 | 서울대학교 TEPS관리위원회 문제 제공 · 넥서스 TEPS연구소 해설 | 480쪽 | 25,000원
서울대 텝스 관리위원회 공식기출 1000 Listening | 서울대학교 TEPS관리위원회 문제 제공 | 432쪽 | 19,000원
서울대 텝스 관리위원회 공식기출 1000 Grammar | 서울대학교 TEPS관리위원회 문제 제공 | 188쪽 | 12,000원
서울대 텝스 관리위원회 공식기출 1000 Reading | 서울대학교 TEPS관리위원회 문제 제공 | 376쪽 | 16,000원
서울대 텝스 관리위원회 최신기출 1000 | 서울대학교 TEPS관리위원회 문제 제공 · 양준희 해설 | 628쪽 | 28,000원
서울대 텝스 관리위원회 최신기출 1200/SEASON 2~3 문제집 | 서울대학교 TEPS관리위원회 문제 제공 | 352쪽 | 19,500원
서울대 텝스 관리위원회 최신기출 1200/SEASON 2~3 해설집 | 서울대학교 TEPS관리위원회 문제 제공 · 넥서스 TEPS연구소 해설 | 472쪽 | 25,000원

실전 모의고사

실전·어휘

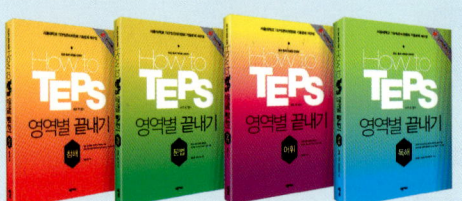
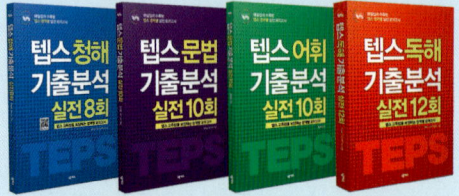

How to TEPS 영역별 끝내기 청해 | 테리 홍 지음 | 424쪽 | 19,800원
How to TEPS 영역별 끝내기 문법 | 장보금 · 써니 박 지음 | 260쪽 | 13,500원
How to TEPS 영역별 끝내기 어휘 | 양준희 지음 | 240쪽 | 13,500원
How to TEPS 영역별 끝내기 독해 | 김무룡 · 넥서스 TEPS연구소 지음 | 504쪽 | 25,000원

텝스 청해 기출 분석 실전 8회 | 넥서스 TEPS연구소 지음 | 296쪽 | 19,500원
텝스 문법 기출 분석 실전 10회 | 장보금 · 써니 박 지음 | 248쪽 | 14,000원
텝스 어휘 기출 분석 실전 10회 | 양준희 지음 | 252쪽 | 14,000원
텝스 독해 기출 분석 실전 12회 | 넥서스 TEPS연구소 지음 | 504쪽 | 25,000원

초급 (400~500점) / 중급 (600~700점)

영역별

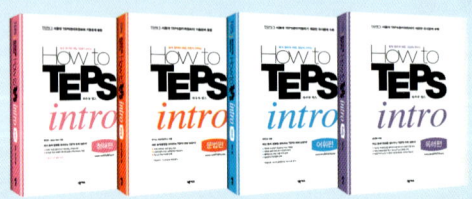

How to TEPS intro 청해편 | 강소영 · Jane Kim 지음 | 444쪽 | 22,000원
How to TEPS intro 문법편 | 넥서스 TEPS연구소 지음 | 424쪽 | 19,000원
How to TEPS intro 어휘편 | 에릭 김 지음 | 368쪽 | 15,000원
How to TEPS intro 독해편 | 한정림 지음 | 392쪽 | 19,500원

How to TEPS 실전 600 어휘편 · 청해편 · 문법편 · 독해편 | 서울대학교 TEPS 관리위원회 문제 제공(어휘), 이기현(청해), 장보금 · 써니 박(문법), 황수경 · 넥서스 TEPS연구소(독해) 지음 | 어휘: 15,000원, 청해: 19,800원, 문법: 17,500원, 독해: 19,000원
How to TEPS 실전 700 청해편 · 문법편 · 독해편 | 강소영 · 넥서스 TEPS연구소(청해), 이신영 · 넥서스 TEPS연구소(문법), 오정우 · 넥서스 TEPS연구소(독해) 지음 | 청해: 16,000원, 문법: 15,000원, 독해: 19,000원

종합서

How to 텝스 뉴스타터 | 넥서스 TEPS연구소 지음 | 584쪽 | 25,900원
How to 텝스 초급용 모의고사 10회 | 넥서스 TEPS연구소 지음 | 296쪽 | 15,000원
How to 텝스 베이직 리스닝 | 고명희 · 넥서스 TEPS연구소 지음 | 320쪽 | 18,500원
How to 텝스 베이직 리딩 | 박미영 · 넥서스 TEPS연구소 지음 | 368쪽 | 19,500원

가장 쉽게, 가장 빨리, 가장 확실하게 점수를 올려주는

TEPS 첫걸음

R/C 정답 및 해설

김무룡 지음
넥서스 TEPS연구소

넥서스

가장 쉽게, 가장 빨리, 가장 확실하게 점수를 올려주는

TEPS 첫걸음

R/C

김무룡 지음
넥서스텝스연구팀

정답 및 해설

넥서스

Section A 문법

Chapter 1

UNIT 1 문장의 구성

EXERCISE

A

1 fresh (보어)
2 want (동사)
3 tell (동사)
4 some time (목적어)
5 me (간접목적어), the time (직접목적어)

B

1 보어
2 수식어(부사)
3 주어(to부정사구)
4 수식어(부사)
5 동사
6 목적어
7 목적어(what 명사절)
8 수식어(부사구)
9 수식어(부사)
10 주어

PRACTICE

1 (c)   2 (a)   3 (d) I hard → It is hard for me
4 (d) buy → to buy

POINT

1 계산원은 그녀가 정직하다고 믿었다.
2 숙제하는 것은 어렵다.
3 그녀는 곧 도착할 예정이다.
4 계산원은 그녀의 무고함을 믿었다.
5 네가 말했으면 하는 것이 정확히 그것이다.
6 그녀는 아름답다.
7 그것이 내가 말하고자 하는 바다.
8 이 수업을 듣는 대부분의 학생들은 지루해 했다.
9 앤디는 매리를 매우 사랑한다.
10 그는 착륙을 시도했다.
11 이곳에 불법으로 주차한 모든 차량은 견인될 것이다.
12 옆집 여자는 매일 달린다.

EXERCISE A

ex

해석 제이슨은 캐시를 무척 사랑한다.

1

해석 이곳 공기는 매우 신선하다.
어구 air 공기   fresh 신선한
정답 fresh(보어)

2

해석 오늘 점심으로 무엇을 드실래요?
정답 want(동사)

3

해석 공항에 가는 방법을 알려주실래요?
어구 get to the airport 공항에 도착하다
정답 tell(동사)

4

해석 나는 미국에서 시간을 좀 보냈다.
어구 spend (시간 · 돈 · 노력 따위를) 소비하다
정답 some time(목적어)

5

해석 실례지만, 지금 시간이 어떻게 되나요?
정답 me(간접목적어), the time(직접목적어)

EXERCISE B

1

해석 어떻게 그것이 가능하지?
어구 possible 가능한
정답 보어

2

해석 옆집에 사는 남자는 매일 달린다.
어구 next door 이웃에, 가깝게
정답 수식어(부사)

3

해석 다림질은 항상 어렵다.
어구 do the ironing 다림질하다
정답 주어(to부정사구)

4

해석 불법으로 주차된 차량은 치워질 것이다.

어구 vehicle 차량　　park 주차하다
illegally 불법적으로　　remove 제거하다, 치우다

정답 수식어(부사)

5

해석 20명이 넘는 과학자들이 연구센터에서 일한다.

어구 research 연구

정답 동사

6

해석 부산까지의 여행은 즐거웠니?

어구 enjoy 즐기다　　trip 여행

정답 목적어

7

해석 미래가 어떻게 전개될지는 아무도 모른다.

어구 hold 전개되다; 쥐다

정답 목적어(what 명사절)

8

해석 휴가 때 좋은 시간 보냈니?

어구 spend (시간 등을) 보내다　　vacation 휴가

정답 수식어(부사구)

9

해석 어제는 빨래할 시간이 없었다.

어구 do the wash 빨래하다

정답 수식어(부사)

10

해석 그 학생은 범죄를 저질렀다.

어구 schoolchild 취학아동　　commit a crime 범죄를 저지르다

정답 주어

PRACTICE

1

해석 A: 안녕, 제이슨, 아버지는 어떠셔?
B: 괜찮아. 그리고 병원에서도 곧 퇴원하실 거야.

해설 be동사(will be) 앞은 주어의 자리다. 보기에서 주어가 될 수 있는 형태는 주격인 (c) he다.

어구 release (병원에서) 퇴원시키다　　soon 곧

정답 (c)

2

해석 리 씨에게 상을 수여하는 임원은 회사의 부사장이다.

해설 본동사는 is다. 따라서 또 다른 동사는 쓸 수 없다. 뒤에 목적어인 award(상)가 나와 있으므로 능동형의 현재분사인 (a) presenting이 올바른 형태의 답이다.

어구 present 수여하다; 대표하다　　award 상
vice president 부사장

정답 (a)

3

해석 A: 엠마, 무슨 문제라도 있니? 너 창백해 보인다.

B: 딸 때문에. 걔가 아파트로 이사해서 살고 싶대.
A: 걔도 다 컸잖아. 그러니 너무 걱정하지 마!
B: 나도 알아, 하지만 그래도 걔의 생각을 받아들이기가 어려워.

해설 (d)에서 I know 이후 문장에 동사가 없다. I hard가 아닌 동사를 넣어 It is hard for me가 되도록 해야 한다.

어구 pale 창백한　　move 이사하다, 움직이다
accept 받아들이다　　idea 생각
though (보통 문미에서) 하지만

정답 (d) I hard → It is hard for me

4

해석 (a) 알코올음료는 세다 파크에서 구입하실 수 있습니다. (b) 하지만, 모든 알코올음료는 세다 파크 가게에서 구입되어져야만 합니다. (c) 맥주는 공원 전역에 걸쳐 판매됩니다. (d) 하지만 맥주를 구입하려면 20세가 넘어야 합니다.

해설 (d)에서 한 문장에 동사가 둘(must be, buy) 있다. 문맥상 buy에 to부정사를 붙여 수식어구인 to부정사로 만들어야 한다.

어구 alcoholic 알코올의　　beverage 음료수
available 이용 가능한　　provide 제공하다
individual 개인; 개인의

정답 (d) buy → to buy

UNIT 2　자동사와 타동사

EXERCISE

A
1 1형식
2 2형식
3 3형식
4 4형식
5 5형식

B
1 him
2 bought
3 is
4 became
5 send
6 believes
7 remains
8 is
9 told
10 is

PRACTICE
1 (a)　　2 (d)
3 (b) It has → It is
4 (a) responsibly → responsible

POINT

1 태양이 빛난다.

2 새가 지저귄다.

3 이 복사기는 전혀 작동하지 않는다.

4 그는 기술자다.

5 그 여자는 아름답다.

6 그녀는 교수가 되었다.

7 너는 피곤해 보인다.

8 문제는 그녀가 그 사실을 모른다는 것이다.

9 제임스는 금연했다.

10 나는 당신이 캐시를 좋아하는 것을 안다.

11 나는 시를 쓰기로 결심했다.

12 그녀는 내게 시계를 줬다.

13 어머니가 내게 케이크를 만들어 줬다.

14 내 와이프는 내가 말할 때마다 나를 거짓말쟁이로 여긴다.

15 나는 그가 우는 것을 들었다.

16 나는 그가 성공할 것이라고 예상한다.

17 나는 그녀가 바이올린을 연주하고 있는 것을 보았다.

EXERCISE A

ex

해석 그는 걷는다.

해설 「주어 + 완전자동사」로 이뤄진 1형식 문장이다.

1

해석 연석 근처에 누군가가 있다.

해설 「There + V(동사) + 주어」구문에서 there is/are 만으로는 문장이 성립되지 않는다. is/are 뒤에 주어가 될 명사가 있어야 한다.

어구 curb 연석

정답 1형식

2

해석 우리는 조용히 해야 한다.

해설 이 문장에서 동사 keep은 뒤에 형용사 quiet를 보어로 취하는 2형식 동사로 쓰였다.

어구 keep ～한 상태로 유지시키다   quiet 조용한

정답 2형식

3

해석 나는 두 명의 아이들이 있다.

해설 동사 have는 목적어를 취하는 3형식 타동사다. 즉, two children이 문장의 목적어가 된다.

정답 3형식

4

해석 잡지를 제게 가져다주시겠어요?

해설 동사 bring은 간접목적어(me)와 직접목적어(the magazines)를 취하는 4형식 동사다.

어구 bring 가져오다   magazine 잡지

정답 4형식

5

해석 나는 내 이름이 불리는 것을 들었다.

해설 동사 hear는 문장에서 「hear + 목적어 + 목적보어」의 구조를 취하는 5형식 동사로 쓰였다.

어구 call (이름 등을) 부르다

정답 5형식

EXERCISE B

1

해석 우리는 그를 회장으로 선출했다.

해설 동사 elect가 갖는 「elect + 목적어 + 목적보어」의 구조를 통해 목적격인 him을 선택할 수 있다. 이 문장에서처럼 목적보어가 명사인 경우 목적어 him과 목적보어 chairman은 동일한 인물이 되는 동격관계가 된다.

어구 elect 선출하다   chairman 회장, 의장

정답 him

2

해석 삼촌은 내게 기타를 사줬다.

해설 buy(사주다)의 과거형 bought가 정답이다. 동사 buy는 뒤에 간접목적어와 직접목적어를 취하는 대표적인 4형식 동사다.

정답 bought

3

해석 이곳은 편안한 아파트다.

해설 동사 matter는 완전자동사로 뒤에 목적어나 보어 등의 문장성분은 받을 수 없다. 동사 is는 2형식 자동사로 명사 또는 상태나 성질을 나타내는 형용사를 보어로 취한다. 따라서 is가 답이다.

어구 matter 중요하다   comfortable 편안한

정답 is

4

해석 그는 유명한 레슬링 선수가 되었다.

해설 동사 cost는 「cost + A(사람) + B(금액)」의 구조로 'A로 하여금 B만큼의 비용을 들게 하다'의 뜻을 갖는 타동사다. 주어 He와 보어 a famous wrestler가 동격관계이므로 이를 연결하는 동사로 문맥상 became이 적절하다.

어구 cost (비용이) 들다   famous 유명한
wrestler 레슬링 선수

정답 became

5

해석 제가 귀하께 소포를 보내겠습니다.

해설 괄호 뒤의 문장 구조를 통해 동사 send를 답으로 선택할 수 있다. send는 뒤에 간접목적어와 직접목적어 두 개를 취하는 4형식 동사로 '～에게 …을 보내다'로 해석된다. 문맥상 send가 적절한 동사다.

어구 send 보내다　　package 소포

정답 send

6

해석 그녀는 그녀의 아버지가 그녀에게 했던 말을 믿는다.

해설 what이 이끄는 목적절을 목적어로 취할 수 있는 타동사(believe)가 와야 한다. smile은 자동사로 목적어를 받을 수 없다.

어구 believe 믿다

정답 believes

7

해석 두고 볼 일이다.

해설 하나하나 분석하기 보다는 전체 문장을 통으로 암기해야 하는 문장도 있다. It remains to be seen은 '두고 볼 일이다'로 해석되는 하나의 표현 덩어리로 보자. remain은 여기서 to부정사를 보어로 취해 '~않은 채 남아 있다, 앞으로 ~해야 한다'의 뜻을 갖는다.

어구 It remains to be seen 두고 볼 일이다

정답 remains

8

해석 지구는 둥글다.

해설 동사 lay는 '놓다, 낳다'의 의미로 자동사 그리고 타동사로 각각 쓰이기는 하지만 뒤의 형용사 round를 받을 수는 없다. 주어의 상태나 성질을 나타내는 형용사(round)를 받을 수 있는 구조는 2형식 동사인 is뿐이다.

어구 lay vt. 놓다; 눕히다, vi 알을 낳다　　round 둥근

정답 is

9

해석 그녀는 내게 비밀을 말해 주었다.

해설 간접목적어 me를 바로 받을 수 있는 동사는 타동사 told(tell의 과거형)다. 동사 say를 사람 앞에 쓸 때는 전치사 to를 반드시 붙여야 한다.

어구 tell A the secret A에게 비밀을 말하다

정답 told

10

해석 커피가 진하다.

해설 동사 have는 타동사로 쓰일 때는 '가지다'의 의미로, 완료형을 만들때는 자체가 조동사가 되기도 한다. 형용사 strong이 있으므로 have가 아닌 형용사를 보어로 받는 is가 정답이다.

어구 strong (맛이) 진한

정답 is

PRACTICE

1

해석 A: 공연은 언제 시작되나요?
B: 첫 공연은 오전 11시부터 시작됩니다.

해설 (b)와 (d)는 각각 뒤에 목적어를 필요로 하는 타동사다. (c) becomes은 불완전 자동사로 명사나 형용사를 보어로 취하는 동사다. 빈 칸 뒤에 전치사구가 있으므로 빈 칸은 완전자동사가 들어갈 자리다. 보기 중에서 자동사는 (a) runs밖에 없다. run이 타동사로 쓰이는 경우 '작동시키다'라는 의미도 있지만 자동사로는 연극이나 쇼 등이 '상연되다'의 의미로도 쓰인다. 따라서 문맥상 (a) runs가 적절한 답이다.

어구 show 공연, 쇼　　run 상연(공연)되다

정답 (a)

2

해석 나는 마침내 그림을 다시 그리기로 결심했다.

해설 빈 칸 뒤의 to부정사 형태를 통해 동사 (d) decided를 답으로 선택할 수 있다. 동사 (a) notified는 notify + A(사람) + of/that의 구조로 'A에게 of/that이하를 알리다'의 뜻으로 쓰이는 동사다. (b) thanked는 '누군가에게 감사하다'의 뜻으로 뒤에 사람이 목적어로 나오거나 감사의 이유는 전치사 for 뒤에 나오는 구조를 갖는다. (c) avoided는 뒤에 동명사를 목적어로 취하는 동사다. 빈 칸 앞뒤의 구조만으로도 (d) decided만이 답이 됨을 알 수 있다.

어구 decide 결심하다　*cf.* decide to V ~하기로 결심하다
drawing 그림　　　　　　notify 알리다
avoid 피하다

정답 (d)

3

해석 A: 늦어서 죄송합니다. 교통체증이 심해서 꼼짝할 수가 없었거든요.
B: 이번에도 또? 이번 주만 세 번째네요.
C: 정말 죄송합니다. 다시는 늦지 않겠습니다. 약속할게요.
D: 아니요. 이제는 정말 못 믿겠군요.

해설 (b)에서 It has를 It is로 바꿔야 한다. 문맥은 이번 주에만 벌써 세 번이라는 뜻이지 세 번을 가졌다(has)라는 뜻이 아니기 때문이다.

어구 stick (주로 수동형 stuck으로 쓰이며) 꼼짝달싹 못하게 하다
traffic 교통　　terribly 지독하게, 몹시, 무섭게
promise 약속하다

정답 (b) It has → It is

4

해석 (a) 지구표면 온도가 다른 것이 날씨를 발생시키는 이유가 된다. (b) 바람은 이러한 지구의 다른 표면 온도 열의 원인이다. (c) 바람은 전기에너지로 전환될 수 있다. (d) 그 에너지는 재생이 가능하긴 하지만 예측이 불가능한 에너지 자원이다.

해설 be동사 뒤는 주어와 동격이 되는 명사나 상태를 설명하는 보어가 올 자리다. 문맥상 부사 responsibly가 아닌 주어를 설명하는 형용사인 responsible이 되어야 한다.

어구 temperature 온도　　　　surface 표면
be responsible for ~에 책임이 있다
cause 초래하다, 유발하다　　unequal 같지 않은
convert 전환하다　　　　　electrical energy 전기에너지
renewable 재생 가능한　　　unpredictable 예측할 수 없는

정답 (a) responsibly → responsible

Chapter 2

EXERCISE

A

1 I get
2 gave up
3 will be
4 is
5 will be

B

1 rented
2 will have been
3 was
4 stops
5 graduated
6 will rain
7 is
8 see
9 sent
10 would

PRACTICE

1 (d)   2 (b)   3 (c) will look → am looking
4 (a) do → did

POINT

1 지구는 둥글다

2 프리미어리그는 보통 8월에 시작한다.

3 할아버지는 작년에 돌아가셨다.

4 회의는 내일 열릴 것이다.

5 내 생각에 그녀는 아름답다.

6 난 그녀는 아름다웠다고 생각했다.

7 나는 그녀가 아름다웠었다고 생각했다.

8 나는 그녀가 바빴다고/바쁘다고/바쁠 것이라고 알고 있다.

9 그들의 주장에 따르면 지구는 공전하고 있다고 한다.

10 당신은 제 2차 세계전쟁이 1945년에 종전되었음을 알게 될 것이다.

11 내가 그녀의 전화번호를 알고 있었다면, 나는 지금 그녀에게 당장 전화할 텐데.

EXERCISE A

ex

해석 쇼가 곧 시작될 것이다.

해설 '곧'이라는 뜻의 soon은 미래 시제와 어울리는 부사기 때문에 과

거동사 began을 will begin으로 고쳐야 한다.

어구 soon 곧

1

해석 나는 매일 공공버스를 이용한다.

해설 every day라는 반복을 나타내는 시간부사가 있기 때문에 일시적인 동작을 나타내는 현재진행형(am getting)이 아닌 현재형인 get으로 바꿔야 한다.

어구 public bus 공공버스

정답 I get

2

해석 3년 전에 담배를 끊었다.

해설 3년 전(3 years ago)이라는 명확한 과거시점이 제시되었기 때문에 현재완료 표현인 have given up은 쓸 수 없다. 반드시 과거 형태로 써야 한다. 즉 gave up이 올바른 표현이다.

어구 give up 포기하다, (습관 등을) 끊다

정답 gave up

3

해석 앉으세요. 그녀는 곧 도착할 겁니다.

해설 문장 맨 뒤의 가까운 미래시간 부사 in a minute(곧)와 어울려야 하므로 시제는 미래가 되어야 한다. 따라서 was를 will be로 바꿔야 한다.

정답 will be

4

해석 내 어머니는 항상 시간은 돈이라고 말했다.

해설 일종의 속담표현이므로 현재시제 즉, time was money를 time is money로 바꿔야 문맥이 자연스럽다.

정답 is

5

해석 내일은 날씨가 괜찮을 것이다.

해설 tomorrow라는 미래 시점이 있으므로 동사 was를 미래시제 will be로 바꿔야 한다.

정답 will be

EXERCISE B

1

해석 어제 차를 빌렸다.

해설 yesterday(어제)라는 명확한 과거 시점이 제시되었으므로 현재완료 표현인 have rented와는 쓸 수 없다. 과거인 rented가 올바르다.

어구 rent 임대하다, 빌리다

정답 rented

2

해석 내일이면 내 아내와의 결혼 10년차가 된다.

해설 tomorrow라는 미래 시점이 있으므로 미래완료시제인 will have been이 적절한 답이다.

어구 marry ~와 결혼하다

정답 will have been

3

해석 이라크는 전보다 상황이 좋지 않다.

해설 before라는 과거 시점 부사가 등장했으므로 과거동사 was가 문맥상 적절하다.

어구 worse 더 나쁜, 악화된

정답 was

4

해석 비가 그칠 때까지 그곳에서 기다리자.

해설 비가 일시적으로 그칠 때까지라면 will stop이 어울리나 시간의 부사절에서는 현재가 미래를 대신하므로 현재형인 stops가 적절한 답이다.

정답 stops

5

해석 나는 뉴욕 대학을 2002년도에 졸업했다.

해설 과거 시점인 2002년도가 제시되었으므로 시제는 과거형이어야 하며 일시적인 동작이 아닌 상태를 나타내므로 과거형인 graduated가 문맥상 올바른 답이다.

어구 graduate 졸업하다

정답 graduated

6

해석 기상예보에 의하면 내일 비가 온다고 한다.

해설 시간부사 tomorrow가 있기 때문에 미래시제인 will rain이 답이 되어야 한다.

어구 weather forecast 기상예보

정답 will rain

7

해석 5 곱하기 5는 25다.

해설 과학적으로 증명된 사실이나 진리는 현재형(is)으로 표현해야 한다.

정답 is

8

해석 내가 내일 그를 본다면, 그에게 모든 것을 말하겠다.

해설 시간부사절(when)에서 현재시제가 미래시제를 대신한다. 따라서 when 부사절에서 미래 부사 tomorrow가 있기는 하지만 동사는 현재시제인 see가 되어야 한다.

정답 see

9

해석 한 시간 전에 나는 비서에게 이메일을 보냈다.

해설 과거 시점 부사 an hour ago가 있기 때문에 동사는 과거형인 sent가 되어야 한다.

어구 send 보내다   secretary 비서

정답 sent

10

해석 우리는 우리가 경기에서 승리하리라 생각했다.

해설 종속절의 동사 시제는 주절의 시제를 따르는 것이 일반적이다. 주절이 과거이기 때문에 will의 과거형인 would가 적절하다.

어구 match 경기

정답 would

PRACTICE

1

해석 A: 다시 한 번 말씀해 주시겠어요?
B: "저기서 좌회전해야 한다"라고 말했습니다.

해설 빈 칸과 더불어 정황상 말한 내용을 다시 반복해 달라는 표현이 되어야 한다. 이전에 했던 말을 다시 해달라는 말이므로 일반 동사 say는 did를 붙인 과거형으로 만들어야 한다.

어구 turn left 좌회전하다

정답 (d)

2

해석 작년에 미리 예약을 한 방문자들은 비용이 더 싸게 들었다.

해설 문장 맨 뒤에 last year라는 명백한 과거시점이 있다. 보기 중에서 가능한 시제는 was뿐이다.

어구 visitor 방문자   make a reservation 예약하다
advance 앞서는, 미리하는

정답 (b)

3

해석 A: 실례합니다만, 이곳이 파인 거리 411번지 맞나요?
B: 네, 그렇습니다만, 무슨 일로 오셨죠?
A: 저는 이 박사님을 찾고 있는데요.
B: 오, 제 아버지인데요.

해설 (c)에서 문맥상 앞으로 찾을 예정이 아닌 현재 찾고 있는 일시적인 동작을 나타내므로 will look이 아닌 am looking이 적절한 표현이다.

어구 look for 찾다   call ~(누구)을 ~이라 부르다

정답 (c) will look → am looking

4

해석 (a) 2007년 5월 24일 뉴욕에서 저희에게 제공해주신 훌륭한 일 처리에 감사함을 전합니다. (b) 귀하와 일한 것은 정말 즐거운 경험이었습니다. (c) 뉴욕에서 리무진 서비스에 대한 정보를 얻지 못해서 인터넷을 보고 귀하의 회사를 찾았습니다. (d) 저희 사장님이 이번 일이 매우 유쾌한 경험이었다고 하십니다.

해설 (a)에서 2007년 과거의 어느 날이 명시되었기 때문에 you do에서 do는 did가 되어야 한다.

어구 do a good(wonderful) job 일을 잘 해내다
pleasant 유쾌한   experience 경험
contact information 연락처

정답 (a) do → did

EXERCISE

A

1 have been
2 will have been
3 I've finally quit
4 was
5 has bought

B

1 had been
2 is always telling
3 has been
4 was walking
5 Have you ever been
6 hate
7 had seen
8 will be
9 will have
10 possess

PRACTICE

1 (d)   2 (b)
3 (a) I finally am finding → I finally have found
4 (a) falls → has fallen

POINT

1 내 아들이 방금 자신의 방을 청소했다.

2 토니는 그의 차를 잃어버렸다.

3 나는 프랑스에 있었던 적이 있다.

4 오늘 아침부터 당신의 전화를 기다렸어요.

5 문자메시지를 확인하기 위해 핸드폰을 확인하다가 지갑을 잃어버렸다.

6 그때까지는 그를 전혀 본 적이 없다.

7 그 책을 예전에 봤었기 때문에 (그 책을) 알고 있었다.

8 7시쯤이면 리포트를 끝낼 것이다.

9 당신이 도착할 때쯤이면 나는 여행을 떠나고 없을 것이다.

10 전화가 울렸을 때 나는 샤워를 하고 있었다.

11 내가 전화 통화를 하고 있었기 때문에 문을 열어줄 수가 없었다.

12 제이는 항상 거짓말을 한다.

13 심슨 가족을 아시나요?

EXERCISE A

ex

해석 그는 태어날 때부터 이탈리아에서 살았다.

해설 since라는 접속사는 '과거 어떤 시점 이래로 현재까지'의 의미를 갖는다. 과거 어느 시점부터 현재까지를 뜻하므로 주절은 현재완료시제가 되어야 한다. 따라서 has lived가 올바른 표현이다.

1

해석 나는 파리에 두 번 가봤다.

해설 was를 have been으로 바꿔야 한다. have been to + 장소는 '장소에 간적이 있다'는 완료 표현으로 현재완료의 경험을 나타낸다.

정답 have been

2

해석 내일 비가 내린다면 2주 동안 비가 내리게 된다.

해설 현재를 거쳐 내일이라는 시점까지의 시간 추이를 나타내야 하므로 미래 완료형(will have been)으로 표현해야 한다.

정답 will have been

3

해석 나는 30년 간의 흡연 후에 결국 금연했다.

해설 제시된 문장은 뒤의 smoking을 빼면 '나는 그만두다'라는 의미가 되고 뒤에 smoking이라는 목적어를 가질 수 없는 구조가 된다. 부사 finally와 함께 문맥상 어울리는 완료 형태가 필요하다. 적절한 표현은 현재완료인 I've finally quit이다.

정답 I've finally quit

4

해석 건물을 걸어 나섰을 때 그녀는 기다리고 있었다.

해설 건물을 걸어나서는 시점에 기다리고 있었으므로 일시적인 동작을 나타내는 진행형이 어울린다. 따라서 was waiting이 정답이다.

정답 was

5

해석 그렉은 17살 때부터 담배를 샀다.

해설 since가 과거 어느 시점부터 현재까지 이어져오므로 현재완료와 어울린다. 따라서 주절은 현재완료인 has bought가 되어야 한다.

어구 cigarette 담배

정답 has bought

EXERCISE B

1

해석 그가 밤새 공부를 했었기 때문에 졸려 보였다.

해설 졸려보였던 것이 그 이전 시점의 어떤 이유에서 비롯된 것이므로 이전 과거를 표현하는 과거완료 had been이 적절한 답이다.

어구 sleepy 졸린

정답 had been

2

해석 선생님은 생물학을 좀 더 공부하라고 늘 말씀하신다.

해설 부사 always를 통해 습관적으로 늘 하곤 하는 말임을 알 수 있으므로 현재형이나 진행형이 답이 될 수 있다.

어구 biology 생물학

정답 is always telling

3

해석 그녀는 5년간 스페인어를 공부해 왔다.

해설 뒤의 기간을 나타내는 「for + 시간」를 통해 주절은 과거 5년 전부터 지금까지의 일을 표현할 수 있는 현재완료가 어울림을 알 수 있다.

정답 has been

4

해석 내가 그 사고를 보았을 때 나는 걷고 있었다.

해설 목격한 시점에 행한 일시적 동작은 진행시제로 표현해야 한다. 따라서 was walking이 어울리는 표현이다.

정답 was walking

5

해석 런던에 갔던 적이 있나요?

해설 런던에 간 적이 있냐는 경험을 묻는 방법이므로 현재완료로 표현하는 것이 자연스럽다.

정답 Have you ever been

6

해석 나는 바퀴벌레를 싫어한다.

해설 바퀴벌레는 일반적으로 싫어하는 기호이므로 현재 싫어하는 중이다(am hating)라는 표현은 어색하다.

어구 roach 바퀴벌레

정답 hate

7

해석 그 동물을 이전에 봤기 때문에 놀라지 않았다.

해설 놀랐던 사실은 그 이전 과거의 어떤 일로 인한 것이기 때문에 과거완료인 had seen이 적절한 표현이다.

어구 shock 놀라게 하다(보통 수동태로 '스스로 놀라다'란 표현인 be shocked으로 많이 쓰인다)

정답 had seen

8

해석 내 약혼자와 나는 다음 달에 결혼할 것이다.

해설 미래 시점을 나타내는 부사 next month가 제시되었으므로 동사 역시 미래시제(will be)가 되어야 한다.

어구 fiance 약혼자   marry 결혼시키다

정답 will be

9

해석 네가 이 편지를 읽을 때쯤이면, 나는 런던을 떠나 있을 것이다.

해설 by the time과 뒤의 내용을 통해 미래의 어느 시점에 대한 묘사임을 알 수 있다. 이는 미래완료 표현인 「will have 과거분사」의 형태로 나타낼 수 있다.

정답 will have

10

해석 모든 인간은 '영혼'이라 불리는 특별한 넋(靈)을 가지고 있다.

해설 상태 동사 possess는 진행형으로 쓸 수 없는 동사다. 이와 같은 동사에는 possess 이외에 have, belong 등의 동사가 있다.

어구 possess 소유하다   special 특별한
spirit 영, 정신   call ~라고 부르다
soul 영혼

정답 possess

PRACTICE

1

해석 A: 실례합니다. 우리 전에 만난 적이 없나요? 낯설지가 않아서요.
B: 제 생각엔 우리가 같은 수업을 듣고 있는 것 같은데요.

해설 문맥상 이전에 만난 경험을 묻고 있으므로 현재완료 표현(haven't we met)이 적절하다.

어구 familiar 잘 아는

정답 (d)

2

해석 그들은 많은 면에서 닮았다.

해설 동사 resemble은 진행형으로 쓸 수 없는 대표적인 상태동사에 속한다. 따라서 진행형으로 쓴 (a)와 (d)는 답이 될 수 없으며 resemble이 타동사가 될 때 수동태가 되면 목적어 each other를 받을 수 없으므로 구조상 (c)도 답이 될 수 없다.

어구 resemble 닮다   in many ways 많은 면에서

정답 (b)

3

해석 A: 캐시, 네가 탈 예비 비행편을 결국 알아냈어.
B: 멋진걸, 몇 시로?
A: 오후 7시 반에 떠나.
B: 그거 잘됐다. 고마워, 로스.

해설 (a)의 I'm finding을 바꿔야 하는데, 전체 문장은 이미 확인된 비행편에 대한 언급이므로 문맥상 완료형인 I've found로 바꿔야 한다. 앞의 부사 finally가 시제 결정의 단서가 된다.

어구 standby 예비교통편   awesome 멋진, 근사한

정답 (a) I finally am finding → I finally have found

4

해석 (a) 지속적인 비가 2006년 11월 이래로 캘리포니아 전역에 걸쳐 내렸고 이는 무서운 홍수와 산사태를 야기했다. (b) 일부 강들은 많은 작은 지역들을 범람시켰다. (c) 홍수는 적어도 40명의 목숨을 앗아갔고 40년 만에 캘리포니아를 강타한 전례 없는 홍수로 불리고 있다. (d) 홍수는 또한 수도 세크라멘토를 에워쌌다.

해설 (a)에서 since라는 과거의 어느 시점과 현재를 잇는 표현이 있으므로 주절은 현재완료가 되어야 한다. 따라서 falls가 아닌 has fallen이 적절한 답이다.

어구 persistent 지속적인   cause 야기시키다
devastating 파괴적인; 무서운
flood 홍수; 홍수를 발생시키다
landslide 산사태   strike 치다, 공격하다
surround 둘러싸다   capital 수도; 중요한

정답 (a) falls → has fallen

EXERCISE

A
1 만일 그가 영국에서 태어났었다면, 그는 더 성공했었을 텐데.
2 내가 의사가 된다면, 나는 돈을 많이 벌 것이다.
3 만약 비가 온다면, 우리는 젖을 것이다.
4 내가 (경기) 규칙들을 더 잘 안다면, 경기를 더 즐길 텐데.
5 만약 내 딸이 죽는다면, 나는 무엇을 해야 할까?

B
1 Don't
2 had
3 became
4 were to
5 should rain
6 would have
7 Be
8 should lose
9 had known
10 had rained

PRACTICE

1 (a)   2 (c)
3 (c) If I'm → If I were
4 (d) if there would have been → if there is

POINT

1 에이미는 선생이 되자 유럽에서 몇 년 동안 가르쳤다.
2 문을 열어주지 마라.
3 산책하러 가자.
4 내가 의사가 된다면, 나는 돈을 많이 벌 것이다.
5 내가 의사가 된다면, 어머니를 돌볼 수 있을 텐데.
6 그가 온다면, 내가 가겠다.
7 그녀가 아프다면 나는 그녀를 떠나지 않겠다.
8 그것이 사실이라면, 나는 돌아오고 싶을 것이다.
9 내가 더 안다면, 나는 더 설명할 수 있을 텐데.
10 당신의 도움이 없었다면, 이 여행은 훨씬 더 어려웠을 것이다.
11 내가 파티에 갔었다면, 브래드를 만났을 텐데.
12 그녀가 그녀의 남편에게 말한다면, 그는 심하게 상처를 받을 것이다.
13 내일 비가 내린다면, 나는 회의에 가지 않을 것이다.

EXERCISE A

ex
어구 go to the movies 영화 보러 가다

1
정답 만일 그가 영국에서 태어났었다면, 그는 더 성공했었을 텐데.
어구 successful 성공의, 성공하는

2
정답 내가 의사가 된다면, 나는 돈을 많이 벌 것이다.

3
정답 만약 비가 온다면, 우리는 젖을 것이다.
어구 get wet 젖다

4
정답 내가 (경기) 규칙들을 더 잘 안다면, 경기를 더 즐길 텐데.
어구 rule 규칙

5
정답 만약 내 딸이 죽는다면, 나는 무엇을 해야 할까?

EXERCISE B

1
해석 문을 닫지 마라.
해설 일반 동사의 부정은 동사 앞에 do를 붙여 do not(don't)~의 형태로 표현한다.
정답 Don't

2
해석 그 책을 갖고 있다면, 더 말을 할 수 있을 텐데.
해설 주절이 조동사의 과거형(could)으로 제시되었으므로 if절의 동사는 과거형인 had가 되어야 한다.
정답 had

3
해석 에드는 학교에 가서 선생이 되었다.
해설 단순한 직설법 문장이다. and 사이에서 시제가 달라질 이유가 없으므로 and 뒤의 동사의 시제 또한 단순 과거 became이 되어야 한다.
정답 became

4
해석 그가 너에 대한 사실을 그의 부인에게 말한다면, 그들의 결혼은 끝날 수도 있다.
해설 콤마(,) 뒤의 조동사의 과거형 would와 문맥을 통해 가정법 미래 표현임을 알 수 있다. 이때 if절의 were to로 동사의 가정법 시제를 표현할 수도 있다.
어구 marriage 결혼(생활)   break up 끝나다
정답 were to

5
해석 내일 비가 내린다면 우리는 밖에 나가지 않을 것이다.
해설 미래를 가정하는 가정법 미래를 묻고 있다. 이때 if절은 should~로 주절은 will(would) V로 이어진다.
정답 should rain

6

해석 내가 더 알았다면 나는 다르게 선택했을 것이다.

해설 가정법 과거완료의 올바른 형태를 묻고 있다. if절의 동사는 had + p.p.형, 주절은 would have + p.p.로 제시된다. if절의 형태를 통해 would have를 답으로 선택할 수 있다.

어구 differently 다르게

정답 would have

7

해석 조용히 해!

해설 명령문에서 뒤에 형용사(quiet)가 오는 경우 be동사와 함께 써서 표현할 수 있다. Do는 동사일 경우에 쓸 수 있는 표현이다. 구어체에서는 be동사를 생략하고 Quiet!로 간단하게 표현하는 경우도 있다.

정답 Be

8

해석 내가 우편함 열쇠를 잃어버리면 어떻게 해야 하지?

해설 주절(의문사 절)은 동사 will로 제시되고 있다. 이를 통해 if절과 함께 전체 문장은 가정법 미래 표현임을 짐작할 수 있다. 가정법 미래에서의 if절 동사는 should로 표현할 수 있다.

어구 mailbox 우편함

정답 should lose

9

해석 내가 그녀를 알았었더라면, 나는 뭔가 말했을 것이다.

해설 과거 사실의 반대를 가정하는 가정법 과거완료형을 묻고 있다. 이때 if절은 had p.p.형이 되어야 한다.

정답 had known

10

해석 어제 비가 내렸었다면, 우산이 필요했었을 것이다.

해설 과거 사실에 대한 가정을 표현하는 가정법 과거완료 표현이므로 if절은 had를 써서 had rained로 표현해야 한다.

정답 had rained

PRACTICE

1

해석 A: 존은 사임하자 버지니아로 이사했다.
　　B: 내가 그의 입장이더라도 그와 똑같이 할 것이다.

해설 화자 B의 입장이 사실은 그렇지 않지만 그렇게 가정하는 것이므로 가정법 문장으로 볼 수 있다. 주절이 가정법 과거이므로 if절은 (a) were가 되어야 한다.

어구 resign 사임하다　move 이사하다
　　in one's shoes 남의 입장이 되어

정답 (a)

2

해석 반약 그것이 사실이었다면, 나는 그 기사를 썼을 것이다.

해설 if절의 동사가 had p.p. 형태로 제시되었으므로 가정법 과거 완료의 문장인을 알 수 있다. 따라서 주절은 would have p.p. 의 형태가 되어야 한다.

어구 article 기사

정답 (c)

3

해석 A: 네가 수학 시험에서 D⁻ 받았다는 것을 들었어.
　　B: 그래 엄마가 정말 화내실 거야.
　　A: 부끄러운 줄 알아라. 내가 너라면, 공부를 더 열심히 했을 거야.
　　B: 웃기지 마라. 너였다면, 너는 빵점받았을 거다.

해설 (c)에서 If I'm을 If I were로 바꿔야 한다. 문맥은 현실성이 없는 것을 가정하기 때문에, 가정법 구문이 되어야 한다.

어구 hit the ceiling 화내다, 노발대발하다
　　shame on you 부끄러운 줄 알아라
　　no kidding 웃기지 마라, 농담하지 마라

정답 (c) If I'm → If I were

4

해석 (a) 아낌없는 후원으로 런던 엑스포에 참가해주셔서 감사합니다. (b) 런던 엑스포 이벤트에서 귀하의 공연은 정말 훌륭했습니다. (c) 귀하와 귀하의 오케스트라는 정말 인상 깊은 그룹이었습니다. (d) 다시 한번 감사드리며 제가 혹시 도울 일이라도 있다면 연락주세요.

해설 (d)에서 if there would have been을 if there is로 바꿔야 한다. 문맥은 단순한 조건을 나타내기 때문에 가정법 시제는 부적절하다.

어구 generous 관대한　　　participation 참가, 참석
　　performance 공연　　impressive 인상 깊은

정답 (d) if there would have been → if there is

UNIT 4 가정법 Ⅱ

EXERCISE

A

1 당신의 도움이 없었다면, 나는 결코 새 자동차를 살 수 없었을 것이다.
2 이제 잠자리에 들 시간이다.
3 당신의 도움이 없었다면 나는 내 꿈을 이룰 수 없었을 것이다.
4 어제 비가 내리지 않았다면, 우리는 (경기를) 더 잘할 수 있었을 텐데.
5 그녀는 마치 자신이 아팠던 것처럼 말한다.

B

1 wish
2 took
3 would be
4 were
5 It
6 as if
7 Were
8 made
9 With
10 But for

PRACTICE

1 (b)   2 (d)
3 (b) I'm not going → I hadn't gone
4 (d) Had not been → Had it not been

POINT

1 그녀가 어제 밤에 행사에 갔다면, 오늘 그녀는 지쳤을 것이다.
2 어제 비가 내렸다면, 경기는 취소되었을 것이다.
3 공기가 없다면, 모든 살아있는 생명체는 죽을 것이다.
4 1950년에 태어났었다면, 나는 전쟁에 참가했어야 했을지도 모른다.
5 네 도움이 없었다면, 나는 시험에 합격하지 못했을 것이다.
6 네 조언이 없었다면 나는 성공하지 못했을 것이다.
7 네가 프로젝트를 맡을 시간이다.
8 내가 너를 사랑하는 방법을 안다면 좋을 텐데.
9 내가 왕이라면 좋을 텐데.
10 그가 아메리칸 리그로 갔다면 좋으련만.
11 학교 다닐 때 공부를 더 열심히 했었다면 좋았을 것.
12 그녀는 마치 모든 것을 아는 것처럼 말한다.
13 그녀는 그가 그곳에 있었던 것처럼 말한다.

EXERCISE A

ex

어구 I wish ~(가정법 동사 시제) ~한다면 좋을 텐데.

1

정답 당신의 도움이 없었다면, 나는 결코 새 자동차를 살 수 없었을 것이다.

2

정답 이제 잠자리에 들 시간이다.
어구 go to bed 잠자리에 들다

3

정답 당신의 도움이 없었다면 나는 내 꿈을 이룰 수 없었을 것이다.
어구 achieve 이루다

4

정답 어제 비가 내리지 않았다면, 우리는 (경기를) 더 잘할 수 있었을 텐데.

5

정답 그녀는 마치 자신이 아팠던 것처럼 말한다.
어구 ill (몸이) 아픈

EXERCISE B

1

해석 내가 현재 알고 있는 것을 그 당시 알았으면 좋았을 텐데.
해설 괄호 뒤가 과거완료(had known)로 제시되었고 주절의 동사는 모두 현재형(want, wish)으로 제시되고 있다. 이루지 못한 사실에 대해 가정하고 있는 가정법으로 봐야 한다. 따라서 가정법을 이끄는 동사 wish를 답으로 선택해야 한다.
정답 wish

2

해석 조치를 취할 때다.
해설 it is time that~ 구문은 that이하의 동사가 과거형으로 제시되는 가정법 대체 구문이다. it is time 구문을 통해 동사의 올바른 시제(took)를 선택할 수 있다.
어구 take action 조치를 취하다
정답 took

3

해석 그녀가 신호위반을 하지 않았다면 그녀는 지금 괜찮을 텐데.
해설 혼합 가정법 구문이다. 맥은 가정법 구문인데 주절은 현재(now)의 사실을 나타내고 있으므로 if절과 관계없이 주절의 동사는 가정법 과거형의 시제인 would be가 되어야 한다.
어구 run the red light 신호위반하다
정답 would be

4

해석 내가 태양이면 좋으련만.
해설 이룰 수 없는 가정을 I wish구문으로 나타내고 있다. be동사는 가정법 과거에서 were로 바뀐다.
정답 were

5

해석 네가 쉴 시간이다.

해설 괄호 뒤의 동사 시제가 과거로 제시되고 있고 문맥상 가정법 구문이므로 it is time~구문임을 알 수 있다. 이때 it 대신 there로 대체할 수는 없다.

어구 take a break 쉬다

정답 It

6

해석 그는 어제 처음으로 그것을 읽은 것처럼 말한다.

해설 as if~구문은 '마치 ~처럼'의 의미로 가정법을 나타내는 구문이다. 괄호 뒤의 이 같은 동사의 가정법 시제를 통해 as if를 답으로 선택할 수 있다.

어구 as if

7

해석 그것이 사실이 아니라면 네게 화날 텐데.

해설 주절은 가정법 과거형태의 시제로 제시되고 있으므로 if절 역시 동사는 과거형인 were로 나타내야 한다. 문장은 if가 생략된 가정법 축약 형태다.

어구 upset 화난

정답 Were

8

해석 네가 결정을 내릴 시간이다.

해설 it is time ~구문은 가정법 대용 구문으로 뒤는 가정법 시제로 나타낸다. 따라서 make가 아닌 made가 되어야 한다.

어구 make a decision 결정하다

정답 made

9

해석 네 도움이 없었다면 나는 내 문제를 풀 수 없었을 것이다.

해설 부정으로 연결되는 가정법 구문이므로 With가 아닌 If not~의 대용구문인 But for로 연결되는 것이 자연스럽다.

어구 solve 풀다

정답 With

10

해석 네 도움이 없었다면, 나는 과제를 끝내지 못했을 것이다.

해설 But for는 '~이 없다면'이란 뜻으로 뒤의 가정법 문장과 어울리는 가정법 대용 구문이다. 문맥상 '~이 없다면'으로 연결되는 But for가 정답이다.

어구 But for ~이 없다면   assignment 과제

정답 But for

PRACTICE

1

해석 A: 바른 선택을 할 시간이라고 생각하지 않니?
B: 잘 모르겠다.

해설 it is time 구문은 뒤에 가정법 시제를 쓰는 가정법 대용구문이다. 다소 표현이 어색하더라도 영어에서의 약속이므로 과거형으로 제시된 (b) made를 답으로 선택해야 한다.

정답 (b)

2

해석 어제 밤에 파티에 갔다면 글로리아를 봤을 텐데.

해설 주절이 would have ~로 제시되고 있으므로 if절은 had p.p.로 연결되는 가정법 과거 완료 형태로 제시되어야 한다. if가 생략되면 동사 had가 앞으로 이동되므로 (d) Had를 답으로 선택할 수 있다.

정답 (d)

3

해석 A: 마이크, 무슨 일 있니?
B: 지난밤에 나가지 않았어야 했는데. 나 감기 걸렸거든.
A: 얼마 동안 좋지 않았니?
B: 하루 종일.

해설 (b)에서 동사 wish와 함께 과거 사실에 대한 아쉬움이나 후회를 나타내고 있으므로 동사 I'm not going을 가정법 시제인 I hadn't gone으로 바꿔야 한다.

어구 come down with a cold 감기 걸리다
feel under the weather 몸이 좋지 않다

정답 (b) I'm not going → I hadn't gone

4

해석 (a) 회사와 저의 문제가 결국 해결되었음을 귀하께 통보해드립니다. (b) 제품은 구입한 날짜로부터 정확히 한 달 후에 배달되었습니다. (c) 귀하께서 제공해주신 도움과 서비스에 감사드립니다. (d) 귀하의 도움이 없었다면, 저는 어떤 결과물도 기대할 수 없었을 것입니다.

해설 (d)에서 if를 생략한 가정법 축약 구문이 바르지 않다. if가 생략되더라도 Had it not been 즉, it은 생략될 수 없다.

어구 resolve 해결하다   deliver 배달하다
purchase 구입; 구입하다   appreciate 감사하다
provide 제공하다   result 결과

정답 (d) Had not been → Had it not been

EXERCISE

A

1 삼촌은 내게 이 스포츠카를 줬다.
2 그녀는 학교로부터 그 직책 제의를 받았다.
3 나는 선생님으로부터 공산주의는 좌파라는 것을 배웠다.
4 회의는 임원 회의로 여겨졌다.
5 어머니는 내게 그녀가 모든 사람들을 사랑하며 모든 사람이 중요하다고 했다.

B

1 arrives
2 wasn't
3 show
4 will be married
5 in
6 broke
7 voted
8 taking place
9 be asked
10 happen

PRACTICE

1 (d)   2 (c)
3 (c) been promoting → been promoted
4 (b) are perceived → perceive

POINT

1 나는 차를 수리했다.
2 그녀는 방을 청소했다.
3 톰은 제인에게 새 모자를 줬다.
4 그들은 그녀를 부사장으로 선출했다.
5 나는 낚시에 관심이 있다.
6 나는 그 소식에 놀랐다.
7 우리는 테스트 결과에 매우 만족했다.

EXERCISE A

1

정답 삼촌은 내게 이 스포츠카를 줬다.

2

어구 offer 제안하다   position 직책
정답 그녀는 학교로부터 그 직책 제의를 받았다.

3

어구 communism 공산주의   leftist 좌파
정답 나는 선생님으로부터 공산주의는 좌파라는 것을 배웠다.

4

어구 conference 회의   consider 여기다
executive meeting 임원회의
정답 회의는 임원 회의로 여겨졌다.

5

정답 어머니는 내게 그녀가 모든 사람들을 사랑하며 모든 사람이 중요하다고 했다.

EXERCISE B

1

해석 그녀가 도착할 때 어떤 일이 발생할까요?
해설 arrive는 자동사기 때문에 is arrived라는 수동태는 존재하지 않는다.
어구 happen 발생하다   arrive 도착하다
정답 arrives

2

해석 내가 저번에 그녀를 봤었기 때문에 그녀의 공연에 놀라지 않았다.
해설 영어에서 사람은 외부 환경(감정)에 의해 영향을 받는 대상으로 묘사된다. 따라서 surprise와 같은 감정동사는 보통 수동 형태로 쓰이며, 동사 surprise가 타동사인데 뒤에 전치사 with가 있으므로 구조상으로도 수동태인 wasn't surprised가 맞다.
어구 surprise 놀라게 하다   performance 공연
정답 wasn't

3

해석 주민들은 자신들의 지역 법규를 존중해야 한다.
해설 show respect라는 뜻을 모른다고 하더라도 show라는 동사가 타동사로 쓰이기 때문에 뒤의 명사 respect를 받기 위해서는 능동태가 되어야 함을 알아야 한다.
어구 resident 주민   show respect 존중하다
local 지역의   law 법(규)
정답 show

4

해석 7월 15일에, 그녀와 나는 결혼할 것이다.
해설 동사 marry는 타동사로 뒤에 반드시 목적어를 취해야 한다. 또한 marry는 '결혼시키다'라는 뜻으로 결혼할 상대자를 목적어로 취한다. 문장은 목적어가 되는 상대자가 주어로 이동했으므로 뒤의 동사는 수동태인 will be married가 되어야 한다.
정답 will be married

5

해석 저는 멕시코로 휴가 가는 것에는 관심이 없습니다.
해설 동사에 따라 수동태가 될 때 취하는 전치사가 다르다. 동사 interest는 수동태가 되면서 전치사 in을 취하는 동사다.
어구 be interested in ~에 관심을 갖다
take a vacation 휴가를 가다
정답 in

6

해석 네가 그녀와 헤어졌다니 믿을 수가 없구나.
해설 동사 break가 '누군가와 헤어지다'라는 뜻을 가지는 경우 능동인

break up with someone으로 표현한다.

어구 break up with someone ~와 헤어지다

정답 broke

7

해석 저에게 투표하신 모든 분들에게 감사함을 전하고 싶습니다.

해설 vote가 자동사로 쓰이는 경우 전치사 for와 함께 '~를 위해 투표하다'의 의미를 가진다. 이때 동사는 자동사이므로 능동의 형태가 되어야 한다.

어구 vote for A A에게 투표하다

정답 voted

8

해석 행사는 어디에서 하나요?

해설 take place는 '행사 등이 발생하다, 일어나다'의 뜻을 가진 자동사로서 수동태로 표현할 수 없다.

어구 event 행사   take place (일 등이) 발생하다, 일어나다

정답 taking place

9

해석 에세이 테스트에서 3개의 다른 질문을 너에게 할 것이다.

해설 동사 ask는 타동사다. 문맥상 목적어가 되는 questions가 앞으로 이동했으므로 동사 ask는 수동태가 되어야 한다.

정답 be asked

10

해석 다시는 그런 일이 발생하지 않을 것을 약속하겠습니다.

해설 동사 happen은 자동사다. 수동태인 be happened라는 형태는 없다.

어구 promise 약속하다   happen 발생하다

정답 happen

PRACTICE

1

해석 A: 우산 가져오지 않았니?
B: 아니, 기상예보에 따르면 내일까지 맑을 거라고 하던데.

해설 동사 say는 타동사로 문장에서는 (that)절을 목적절로 받는 자리에 있다. 문장에서 목적절을 이끄는 that은 생략되었다. 목적어를 받는 자리이므로 능동태인 said가 적절하다.

어구 bring 가져오다   umbrella 우산
weather forecast 기상예보
sunny 맑은, 햇볕이 잘 드는

정답 (d)

2

해석 모든 참석자들은 회의가 아주 성공적이었다고 여겼다.

해설 동사 consider와 주어 자리의 the meeting과의 관계는 회의(meeting)가 누군가에 의해 여겨지는(considered) 수동관계에 있으므로 수동태인 (c) was considered가 올바른 형태의 답이다.

어구 meeting 회의   consider 고려하나   attendee 참석자

정답 (c)

3

해석 A: 내가 무슨 말 할지 맞춰봐.
B: 모르겠는데, 뭔데?
A: 오늘 승진했어.
B: 그거 잘됐다. 축하해.

해설 (c)에서 동사 promote는 '승진시키다'라는 뜻의 타동사다. 주어와 동사의 관계가 승진 대상이 되는 수동관계에 있으므로 been promoting을 been promoted로 바꿔야 한다.

어구 have no clue 모르다   get the promotion 승진하다
congratulations 축하해

정답 (c) been promoting → been promoted

4

해석 (a) 다이어트는 아마도 건강에 있어서 가장 잘못 이해되는 용어 중 하나일 것이다. (b) 많은 사람들이 이 "다이어트"라는 용어를 먹는 양을 줄인다는 의미로 인식하고 있다. (c) 실제 의미는 음식 섭취를 조절한다는 의미다. (d) 건강함에 있어서 음식 섭취를 조절한다는 것은 육체적인 활동만큼이나 중요하다.

해설 (b) 수동태인 are perceived를 능동태인 perceive로 바꿔야 한다. perceive는 타동사기 때문에 뒤의 목적어가 되는 the word를 능동으로 받아야 하므로 능동의 perceive가 되어야 한다.

어구 diet 식이요법   misunderstood 잘못 이해되는
term 용어   fitness 건강, 체력   perceive 인식하다
cut 줄이다   intake 섭취(량)
physical activity 신체(체육)활동

정답 (b) are perceived → perceive

Chapter 3

UNIT 1 to부정사와 동명사

EXERCISE

A
1 to be
2 getting
3 falling
4 dancing
5 to take

B
1 to live
2 of going
3 sorting
4 to remain
5 spending
6 without thinking
7 to succeed
8 to publish
9 making
10 to do

PRACTICE
1 (a)   2 (c)
3 (c) coming over → to come over
4 (b) is charge → is to charge

POINT

1 법을 위반하는 것은 반사회적인 범죄다.
2 나는 휴가를 터키로 가고 싶었다.
3 그녀의 꿈은 모델이 되는 것이다.
4 그는 양쪽 상을 모두 받은 최초의 사람이다.
5 랜스 암스트롱 재단은 소아암 환자들을 위한 기금 마련을 위해 설립되었다.
6 흡연은 조기 사망의 원인 중 가장 사전에 예방이 가능한 것이다.
7 나는 체스하는 것을 즐긴다.
8 내 취미는 축구하는 것이다.

EXERCISE A

ex

해석 외국어를 배우는 가장 좋은 방법은 집중해서 하는 것이다.
해설 빈 칸 앞의 명사 way는 보통 to부정사구로 주로 수식한다. 이때 to부정사는 명사 way를 수식하는 형용사적 용법으로 쓰인 것이다.
어구 immerse oneself in ~에 집중하다, 몰두하다

1
해석 내 꿈은 유명한 배우가 되는 것이다.
해설 빈 칸은 to be가 되어야 한다. 이때 to부정사는 주어의 보어가 되도록 하는 형용사적 용법으로 쓰인 것이다.
어구 famous 유명한   actor 배우
정답 to be

2
해석 내게 화를 내봤자 아무 소용없다.
해설 be no use ~ing(~하는 것은 소용없다)를 묻고 있다. 빈 칸 앞의 no use를 통해 getting이 답임을 알 수 있다.
어구 no use ~ing ~해도 소용없다   get mad at A A에 화내다
정답 getting

3
해석 나는 음악에 빠질 수밖에 없었다.
해설 can not(could not) help ~ing라는 관용 표현을 통해 fall의 적절한 형태가 falling임을 알 수 있다.
어구 can not help ~ing ~하지 않을 수 없다
    fall in love with A A와 사랑에 빠지다
정답 falling

4
해석 춤추지 않으실래요?
해설 feel like ~ing(~하고 싶어하다)라는 표현을 통해 dance의 적절한 형태가 dancing임을 알 수 있다.
어구 feel like ~ing ~하고 싶어 하다
정답 dancing

5
해석 당신이 보스톤으로 여행을 가고 싶어 하는 것을 안다.
해설 동사 wants는 동사를 목적어로 취하는데 있어서 동사는 to부정사의 형태가 된다. 따라서 동사 take의 올바른 형태는 to take다.
어구 take a trip to A A로 여행을 떠나다
정답 to take

EXERCISE B

1
해석 그녀는 살 집이 없다.
해설 명사 house를 to부정사로 수식해야 한다. 이때 to부정사는 명사 house를 수식하는 형용사적 용법으로 쓰인 것이다. living이 되면 마치 house가 ~에 살고 있다는 의미가 되어 문맥상 어색해진다.
정답 to live

2
해석 저는 밖에 혼자 나가는 것이 두렵지 않습니다.
해설 형용사 afraid는 be afraid of N/-ing형태로 쓰인다. 괄호 앞의 afraid를 통해 전치사 of와 함께 동명사 going을 답으로 선택할 수 있다.
어구 be afraid of N/-ing ~하는 것을 두려워하다   alone 홀로
정답 of going

3

해석 나는 마침내 책 분류를 끝냈다.

해설 동사 finish는 동명사를 목적어로 취한다. 따라서 sorting이 정답이다.

어구 finally 마침내   sort 분류하다

정답 sorting

4

해석 피고인은 묵비권을 행사할 수 있다.

해설 명사 right는 right를 동사적으로 수식할 때 to부정사를 취한다. 명사 right를 통해 to remain을 답으로 선택할 수 있다.

어구 the accused 피고인
remain silent 묵비권을 행사하다, 침묵하다

정답 to remain

5

해석 제이슨은 가족과 친구와 시간을 보내는 것을 매우 즐긴다.

해설 동사 enjoy는 동사를 목적어로 취할 때 동명사를 취한다. 이를 통해 spending을 답으로 선택할 수 있다.

정답 spending

6

해석 나는 그를 볼 때마다 나의 선생님이 생각난다.

해설 never A without –ing는 'A할 때마다 ~하다'라는 뜻의 관용어구다. 이러한 표현을 통해 without thinking을 답으로 선택할 수 있다.

어구 never A –ing A할 때마다 ~하다

정답 without thinking

7

해석 만일 당신이 인생에서 성공하고자 한다면, 열심히 일해야 한다.

해설 be동사 뒤 동사 succeed의 올바른 형태는 to succeed다. be동사 뒤에 또 다른 동사 succeed가 바로 나올 수 없다. 이때 to succeed는 to부정사의 주격보어가 된다.

어구 succeed 성공하다

정답 to succeed

8

해석 그녀는 아이들을 위한 영어책을 출간하기로 결심했다.

해설 동사 decide는 to부정사를 목적어로 취한다. 이를 통해 to publish를 선택할 수 있다.

어구 decide 결심하다   publish 출간하다

정답 to publish

9

해석 그녀는 문제에 대한 결정을 연기하기로 했다.

해설 동사 postpone은 동명사를 목적어로 취하는 동사다. 또한 연기하는 주체가 주어인 she이므로 being made는 올바르지 못하다.

어구 postpone 연기하다   make decisions 결정하다
issue 문제, 일

정답 making

10

해석 나는 할 일이 많다.

해설 명사 work와 함께 work to do는 '해야 할 일'이란 뜻이 된다. 이때 명사 work는 to부정사(형용사적 용법의 to부정사)로 수식한다.

어구 work to do 할 일

정답 to do

PRACTICE

1

해석 A: 저를 위해 창문 좀 열어주시겠어요?
B: 물론이죠.

해설 mind가 동사로 쓰이는 경우 '~하기를 꺼려 하다'라는 뜻이 되면서 동명사를 목적어로 취하는 타동사가 된다. 따라서 open의 적절한 형태는 (a) opening이다.

어구 mind ~하기를 꺼려 하다

정답 (a)

2

해석 그녀는 첫 눈에 그에게 반할 수밖에 없었다.

해설 can(could) not help는 '~할 수밖에 없다'는 뜻으로 뒤에 동명사를 취하는 관용 어구다. 이를 통해 (c) loving을 답으로 선택할 수 있다.

어구 can(could) not help –ing ~하지 않을 수 없다
at first sight 첫 눈에

정답 (c)

3

해석 A: 안녕, 톰.
B: 안녕, 제인, 어떻게 지냈니?
A: 잘 지냈어, 오늘밤에 우리 집에 올 수 있니?
B: 아마도 가능할걸. 오늘 밤에는 다른 약속이 없으니까.

해설 (c)에서 do you have time은 뒤에 to부정사를 취한다. to부정사는 time을 수식하는 형용사적 용법이다. coming over를 to come over로 바꿔야 한다.

어구 have time to do ~할 시간이 있다
come over ~에 들르다   plan 계획, 약속

정답 (c) coming over → to come over

4

해석 (a) 대부분의 차량 대여 회사는 고객에게 고객이 사용한 연료비에 대해 몇 가지 청구 방법을 가지고 있다. (b) 청구 방법 중에서 일반적인 것 중 하나는 사용한 연료의 양에 따라 고객에게 비용을 부과하는 것이다. (c) 견적은 차량 계기판의 눈금을 기준으로 한다. (d) 이것이 차량을 대여하는 고객들에게는 가장 널리 쓰이는 방법 중 하나다.

해설 (b) is charge를 is to charge로 바꿔야 한다. 동사 is와 charge를 한 문장에서 중복해서 쓸 수 없기 때문에 준동사로 바꿔야 하는데 주어의 보어가 되면서 '~하는 것으로' 문맥상 자연스럽게 해석되는 to부정사 형태로 바꾸는 것이 어울린다.

어구 car rental company 차량 대여 회사
customer 손님, 고객   means 수단   fuel 연료
common 일반적인   option 선택사항

charge (돈을) 부과하다　　estimated 견적의
be based on A A에 바탕을 두다
reading (계기판 등의) 표시, 기록
vehicle 차량　　　　　　gauge 계(량)기
popular 인기 있는

정답 (b) is charge → is to charge

UNIT 2 분사

EXERCISE

A
1 called
2 participating
3 mended
4 tired
5 leaving

B
1 unsolved
2 attached
3 fixed
4 to use
5 refunded
6 detailing
7 providing
8 missing
9 located
10 closed

PRACTICE

1 (d)　　2 (a)
3 (c) understanding → understood
4 (d) have your money refunding → have your money refunded

POINT

1 개발도상 국가는 임금이 선진국에 비해 낮은 나라다.

2 깨진 창문이 물에 비친다.

3 일본에 대해 배우는 것은 흥미로웠다.

4 너의 가방을 싸고 부주의하게 놔두지 마라.

5 낙엽은 땅의 곰팡이와 박테리아를 위한 좋은 음식 공급원이다.

6 짖는 개는 거의 물지 않는다.

7 저기 분홍색 드레스를 입고 있는 여자를 봐라.

8 나는 제니라고 불리는 친구가 있다.

9 그들은 나무에 앉아 있는 새를 잡기 위해 노력하고 있다.

EXERCISE A

ex

해석 영어는 거의 전 세계 모든 나라에서 사용하는 언어다.

해설 speak가 타동사가 되는 경우는 '언어를 말하다'란 뜻으로 쓰일 때다. 문맥에서도 언어(language)에 관한 내용이며 언어는 말이 되어지는 수동관계에 있으므로 speaking이 아닌 수동형인 spoken이 되어야 한다.

어구 nearly 거의　　all over the world 전 세계에 걸쳐

1

해석 나는 나의 이름이 다시 불리는 것을 들었다.

해설 동사 heard(hear의 과거)는 문장에서 5형식동사로 쓰였다. 목적어 name과 빈 칸에 들어갈 목적보어와의 관계는 주어와 술어의 관계로 볼 수 있다. name은 불리는 수동의 관계에 있으므로 called가 옳은 표현이다.

정답 called

2

해석 이 양식은 모든 유학 프로그램에 참석하는 학생들이 작성해야 한다.

해설 한 문장에 동사(is)가 이미 있기 때문에 빈 칸은 또 다른 동사 형태가 들어갈 수 없다. 명사 students와의 관계가 참석을 하는 능동의 관계에 있으므로 현재분사인 participating이 적절한 분사의 형태다.

어구 form 양식　　require 필요로 하다
participate 참석하다
study abroad program 유학 프로그램

정답 participating

3

해석 나는 내 신발을 수선했다.

해설 명사 신발(shoes)은 수선이 되어지는 수동의 관계에 있기 때문에 과거분사 mended로 바꿔야 한다.

어구 mend 수선하다

정답 mended

4

해석 그녀는 오래 걸었기 때문에 지쳤다.

해설 동사 tire는 '지치게 하다'라는 뜻의 타동사다. 자신이 지치는 것이므로 수동태인 tired가 적절하다.

어구 tire 지치게 하다

정답 tired

5

해석 실험실을 나가는 마지막 학생이 문을 닫아야 한다.

해설 동사 should가 이미 있기 때문에 빈 칸은 동사가 아닌 분사 형태가 되어야 한다. 명사 student가 떠나는 주체로써 능동의 관계에 있으므로 현재분사 leaving이 되어야 한다.

어구 lab 실험실(laboratory의 약어)

정답 leaving

EXERCISE B

1

해석 이상한 해변 냄새는 의문이 풀리지 않은 채 남아 있다.

해설 주어와의 관계를 통해 문제를 해결할 수 있다. 동사 solve는 '~을 해결하다'라는 뜻의 타동사다. 해결하지 못한 과제가 앞의 주어로 이동했으므로 괄호는 과거분사인 unsolved가 되어야 한다.

어구 mysterious 이상한, 정체불명의
coastal 해변의 odor 냄새
remain ~의 상태에 있다 unsolve ~를 풀어지게 못하다

정답 unsolved

2

해석 당신이 필요한 모든 것은 당신의 컴퓨터에 부착할 마이크다.

해설 attach는 「attach A to B」의 구조로 'A를 B에 부착하다'의 의미로 쓰인다. 문장에서 A가 a microphone인데 컴퓨터에 부착되는 수동의 관계에 있으므로 과거분사 attached가 옳은 표현이다.

어구 attach A to B A를 B에 부착하다

정답 attached

3

해석 나는 TV를 수리했다.

해설 have는 '~시키다'의 뜻을 갖는 사역동사다. have 뒤에 사물이 오는 경우 사물이 능동적으로 '~하는' 주체가 아닌 수동적으로 '~되어지는' 수동의 관계에 있기 때문에 fixed가 옳은 표현이 된다.

어구 fix 고치다

정답 fixed

4

해석 내 아버지는 내 왼손을 사용토록 했다.

해설 동사 get뒤에 사람이 목적어로 오는 경우 뒤의 동사는 to부정사가 되며 이때 to부정사는 일종의 능동의 의미로 해석할 수 있다.

정답 to use

5

해석 만일 귀하가 제품에 대해 만족하지 못하시고 구매한 지 30일 이내라면, 귀하가 지불한 돈은 환불받으실 수 있습니다.

해설 「have(사역동사) + 사물 +과거분사」의 구조를 묻고 있다. 돈은 환불받는 수동의 관계에 있으므로 refunded가 올바른 분사의 형태다.

어구 within (시간 등의) 범위 안에 purchase 구매품; 구매하다
refund 환불하다

정답 refunded

6

해석 어떻게 이 양식을 작성할지에 관한 지시사항이 이 파일에 포함되어 있다.

해설 detail은 동사로 '상술하다'라는 뜻을 가지고 있다. how to이하가 detail의 의미상 목적어가 되기 때문에 능동인 detailing이 되어야 한다.

어구 instruction 지시사항 detail 상술하다; 열거하다
fill (양식 등을) 작성하다, 채우다 include 포함시키다

정답 detailing

7

해석 아이메드는 양질의 의료장비를 전세계에 걸쳐 공급하는 온라인 상점이다.

해설 괄호 앞의 명사 store와의 관계를 통해 답을 선택할 수 있는데 상점(store)이 양질의 제품을 공급(provide)하는 능동의 위치에 있으므로 현재분사인 providing으로 답해야 한다.

어구 online store 온라인 상점 provide 제공하다
quality 양질의 medical equipment 의료장비

정답 providing

8

해석 그 기관에서 믿고 있는 것은 그 실종된 아이가 심각한 신체적 위험에 놓여 있다는 것이다.

해설 문맥상 '실종된 아이'라는 뜻을 묻고 있으며 능동형인 missing 자체에 '행방불명된, 실종된'의 의미가 있음에 유의하자. 명사 child와 함께 덩어리로 머리에 담아두자.

어구 agency 기관 missing child 행방불명된 아이
in danger of ~의 위험에 놓인

정답 missing

9

해석 방문자센터에 위치한 선물가게에서 기념품을 꼭 받아가세요.

해설 동사 locate는 '찾다, 위치시키다'의 뜻을 가진 타동사다. 문장에서는 '위치시키다'의 의미를 가진 동사의 의미에서 파생된 분사로 쓰였다. 선물가게는 위치되어지는 수동관계에 있으므로 과거분사 located가 맞다. 현재는 「be located + 전치사 + 장소명사」로 사실상 굳어진 표현이 되었다.

어구 pick up 찾아가다, 줍다, 선택하다 souvenir 기념품
gift shop 선물가게 locate 찾다, 위치시키다
visitor centre 방문자센터

정답 located

10

해석 에어컨이 작동 중일 때는 창문을 닫아라.

해설 창문(windows)은 닫히는 수동의 관계에 있으므로 과거분사 closed가 되어야 한다.

어구 keep + A + 보어 A를 ~한 상태로 두다
air conditioner 에어컨

정답 closed

PRACTICE

1

해석 A: 기다리게 해서 죄송합니다.
B: 괜찮습니다.

해설 빈 칸 앞의 you가 기다리는 주체이므로 능동의 현재분사 waiting이 빈 칸에 들어갈 올바른 형태다.

정답 (d)

2

해석 나는 내 컴퓨터가 오늘 오후에 바이러스에 걸린 것을 알게 되었다.

해설 동사 infect는 '감염 시키다'라는 뜻의 타동사다. 명사 computer가 감염시키는 것이 아닌 감염되는 수동 관계에 있으므로 infected가 되어야 한다.

어구 infect 감염시키다

정답 (a)

3

해석 A: 당신은 한국어를 잘하시나요?
B: 글쎄요, 조금밖에 못 합니다. 당신은요?
A: 저도 여전히 한국어로 의사소통하는 것이 어려워요.
B: 정말요? 이곳에서 벌써 10년 동안 사셨잖아요.

해설 '자기 자신을 이해시키다' 즉 '의사소통하다'라는 뜻을 가진 올바른 관용표현은 동사 make과 함께 make oneself understood 로 표현할 수 있다. 자기 자신이 이해되는 수동관계에 있기 때문에 과거분사 understood가 되어야 한다.

어구 be good at ~를 잘하는
make oneself understood 자기의 말을 이해시키다, 의사 소통하다

정답 (c) understanding → understood

4

해석 (a) 스웨덴 유람선여행 가이드를 구입해주셔서 감사합니다. (b) 가이드가 귀하의 만족에 미흡하다면 우리는 기꺼이 환불해 드립니다. (c) 단, 가이드를 구입하신 지 30일 안에만 가능합니다. (d) 만일 귀하가 환불을 원하신다면, 우리에게 메일 주소 infor@swedishcrusingguide.com으로 이메일을 보내주세요.

해설 have는 '~되도록 하다'라는 뜻의 사역동사다. have 뒤의 목적 어인 명사 money는 환불되어지는 수동의 관계에 있으므로 과거 분사 refunded가 올바른 분사형태다.

어구 meet one's needs 필요를 충족하다
cruising 유람선여행   refund 환불하다
within ~의 범위 안에서   purchase 구매하다
send 보내다

정답 (d) have your money refunding → have your money refunded

UNIT 3   분사 구문

EXERCISE

A

1 knowing
2 Left
3 speaking
4 Tired
5 Walking

B

1 explained
2 Knowing
3 permitting
4 raised
5 Having received
6 swimming
7 planning
8 Judging
9 Accompanied
10 Admitting

PRACTICE

1 (d)   2 (c)
3 (b) Turn → Tuning
4 (a) As discussing → As discussed

POINT

1 독일에서 연구를 마친 후에, 그는 일 년 동안 중동을 여행했다.

2 만일 당신이 세탁할 계획이라면, 당신은 당신의 세탁세제를 가지고 와야 한다.

3 비록 비행기가 30분 늦게 출발했지만, 비행기는 제시간에 도착했다.

4 방에서 천천히 걸어 나오면서, 나는 한 초상화를 보았다.

5 우리는 완전 자동화된 고객 맞춤형 서비스를 가지고 있는데 이를 통해 우리 고객들에게 최상의 서비스를 제공할 수 있도 록 한다.

EXERCISE A

ex

해석 1935년에, 허리케인은 그 지역을 덮쳤는데, 이로 인해 동부 해안 지역이 범람되었다.

해설 콤마(,)를 사이에 두고 앞 내용이 원인이 되고 그 결과가 뒤 내용 이 되는 관계로 연결되고 있다. 이는 분사구문의 결과적 용법으로 나타낼 수 있다.

어구 flood 침수 피해를 입히다

1

해석 어떻게 할 줄 몰랐기 때문에, 그녀는 자신을 위해 기도했다.

해설 빈 칸 앞의 주어가 생략된 것을 통해 동사 know의 주체는 주절의 주어인 she임을 알 수 있다. 또한 뒤에 what to do라는 명사구 목적어가 있으므로 이를 능동으로 받을 수 있으려면 능동형 분사 knowing이 되어야 한다.

어구 pray for A A를 위해 기도하다

정답 knowing

2

해석 혼자 남겨졌기 때문에, 그는 무기력해졌다.

해설 자신이 남겨지게 된 수동관계에 있으므로 leaving이 아닌 과거분사 left가 되어야 한다.

정답 Left

3

해석 엄격히 말해, 그는 선생님이 아니다.

해설 독립분사구문으로 부사 strictly와 함께 '엄격히 말해서'라는 올바른 영어 표현은 strictly speaking이다.

어구 strictly speaking 엄격히 말해

정답 speaking

4

해석 나는 피곤했기 때문에, 일찍 잠자리에 들었다.

해설 동사 tire는 '피곤하게 하다'는 뜻의 타동사다. 주어인 나는 피곤하게 되는 수동관계에 있으므로 과거분사 tired가 되어야 한다.

어구 tire 피곤하게 하다   go to bed 잠자리에 들다
earlier 더 일찍

정답 Tired

5

해석 거리를 따라 걷다가, 우연히 에디를 만났다.

해설 걷는 것의 주체가 주어이므로 이는 능동으로 표현할 수 있다. 따라서 현재분사 walking이 올바른 표현형태다.

어구 run into 우연히 마주치다

정답 Walking

EXERCISE B

1

해석 2번 규칙에서 설명되었듯이 출석은 의무사항이다.

해설 as explained는 as it is explained의 줄임말이다. 접속사 as와 함께 '설명했듯이'라는 뜻을 가진 일종의 관용어구로 익혀두자.

어구 attendance 출석   mandatory 의무(사항)의
as explained 설명되었듯이

정답 explained

2

해석 다른 제조회사 컴퓨터에 대해서는 전혀 몰랐기 때문에, 나는 같은 제조회사의 컴퓨터로 교환했다.

해설 문맥상 이유의 접속사(because 등)가 생략된 부사구문임을 알 수 있다. 괄호 뒤의 명사 nothing을 목적어로 받아야 하므로 동사 know는 능동의 현재분사형으로 표현해야 한다.

어구 manufacturer 제조업자   exchange 교환하다

정답 Knowing

3

해석 날씨가 허락한다면, 우리는 지역 박물관으로 관람하러 갈 것이다.

해설 괄호 앞의 명사 weather(날씨)는 permit(허락)하는 주체가 되므로 현재분사형인 permitting이 올바른 형태다. 특히 사물이 허락하는 경우의 동사는 permit은 자동사가 된다는 점도 기억해 두자.

어구 permit 허락하다

정답 permitting

4

해석 비록 오랫동안 떨어져서 자랐지만, 그들은 매우 닮았다.

해설 동사 raise가 문맥상 '양육시키다'라는 뜻의 타동사가 되어야 하기 때문에 뒤에 목적어가 없는 구조상 과거분사의 형태인 raised가 되어야 한다.

어구 raise 양육시키다, 키우다   separately 따로 떨어져서
like the branches of a tree (한 나무에서 나온 가지처럼) 매우 닮은, 빼다박은

정답 raised

5

해석 어떤 답변도 듣지 못했기 때문에, 나는 그에게 다시 메일을 보냈다.

해설 콤마(,) 앞의 동사가 원형으로 제시된 (괄호 안의) 두 번째 예는 주어가 없기 때문에 명령형으로 볼 수 있는데 이 경우 콤마(,) 뒤 내용과 전혀 연결이 되지 않는다. having received를 답으로 선택할 수 있는데 이처럼 완료분사구문이 답이 될 수 있는 이유는 콤마(,) 뒤와 비교해 시간상으로 앞의 내용이 앞서기 때문이다.

어구 receive 받다   send 보내다

정답 Having received

6

해석 강에서 수영할 때, 나는 적과 마주쳤다.

해설 접속사만 남겨둔 채 앞 문장을 분사구문화시켰다. 주어인 I와 동사 swim의 관계는 자신이 수영을 하는 능동의 관계에 있으므로 swum이 아닌 swimming이 올바른 형태의 분사다.

어구 encounter 만나다, 마주치다   enemy 적

정답 swimming

7

해석 만일 현금카드를 사용할 계획이라면, 당신의 은행이 해외 거래에서 수수료를 부과하지 않는지를 확인하라.

해설 if절의 주어는 you다. you와 plan과의 관계는 직접 계획하는 능동의 관계에 있다. 따라서 현재분사인 planning이 올바른 분사 형태다.

어구 plan on ~할 예정이다, ~을 계획하다   debit card 직불카드
make sure 확실히 하다   charge 비용 등을 부과하다
transaction 거래   fee 요금, 수수료

성답 planning

8

해석 그의 억양으로 판단하건데, 그는 영국인이 분명하다.

해설 동사 judge와 함께 '~로부터 판단할 때'를 나타내는 올바른 분사 표현은 judging from~ 이다. 일종의 관용표현이므로 표현 덩어리로 암기할 필요가 있다.

어구 Judging from A A로부터 판단할 때　accent 강세, 억양

정답 Judging

9

해석 성인과 동행한다면, 12살 이하의 아이들은 버스 승차 시에 공짜로 여행할 수 있다.

해설 동사 accompany는 '동행시키다'라는 뜻의 타동사다. 아이는 동행되는 수동의 관계에 있으므로 과거분사 accompanied가 올바른 분사형태다.

어구 accompany 동행시키다　adult 성인
travel 여행하다　for free 공짜로

정답 Accompanied

10

해석 네 말에 동의는 하겠지만, 나는 여전히 믿지 못하겠다.

해설 What you say는 동사 admit의 목적절로 쓰였다. 따라서 동사 admit은 뒤의 목적어를 받을 수 있는 능동의 형태가 되어야 한다. 능동태인 현재분사 admitting이 올바른 분사형태다.

어구 admit 인정하다

정답 Admitting

PRACTICE

1

해석 A: 눈 왜 그래? 많이 부었는데.
B: 어제 밤새 카드 놀이 했거든.

해설 '카드 놀이하면서 밤새다'라는 뜻이 문맥상 자연스러우므로 (d) playing이 맞다. 뒤의 cards라는 목적어를 취하는 구조가 되어야 하기 때문에 능동이 되어야 한다.

어구 swollen 부은　stay up all night 밤새다
play cards 카드놀이하다

정답 (d)

2

해석 어제 쇼핑하러 갔을 때, 나는 가장 친한 친구인 스콧을 만났다.

해설 동사 go와 함께 '쇼핑하다'의 영어표현은 go shopping이다. 주어인 I와 go shopping과의 관계는 자신이 하는 능동의 관계에 있으므로 현재분사인 going이 올바르다.

어구 go shopping 쇼핑하다

정답 (c)

3

해석 A: 실례합니다. 이 근처에서 가장 가까운 빨래방이 어디인지 알려주실래요?
B: 왼쪽으로 돌아서 몇 블록 직진하시면 하나 발견하실 수 있으실 겁니다.
A: 정말 감사합니다.
B: 별 말씀을요.

해설 왼쪽으로 가는(turn left) 주체는 주절의 you로 능동의 관계에 있으므로 Turn을 Turning으로 바꿔야 한다. 또한 A and B에서 A와 B는 병렬관계에 있으므로 뒤의 going을 보고 turn의 형태를 의심해 볼 수도 있다.

어구 nearest 가장 가까운　laundromat 빨래방

neighborhood 이웃, 근처
go straight 직진하다　appreciate 고마워하다

정답 (b) Turn → Turning

4

해석 (a) 우리 회의에서 논의되었듯이, 화요일에 우리가 했던 전자버전 프리젠테이션을 동봉하오니 참고해주십시오. (b) 귀하의 동료들과도 편안하게 의견을 나눠주십시오. (c) 저는 당신과 일하기를 고대하고 있습니다. 그리고 다음 달 귀하와의 만남을 통해 더욱 알아가기를 원합니다. (d) 문의사항이나 관심사항 있으시면, 언제든 주저하지 마시고 전화번호 312-211-0220이나 핸드폰 번호 010-2000-2000으로 연락해주세요.

해설 discuss는 타동사다. (a)와 같이 능동의 형태가 되면 목적어가 반드시 있어야 한다. discuss는 as discussed의 형태로 '논의한 대로'라는 뜻을 갖는 일종의 관용 어구다. (a) as discussing을 as discussed로 바꿔야 한다.

어구 discuss 논의하다　meeting 회의
enclose 첨부하다　electronic 전자의
presentation 발표, 프레젠테이션
fee free to V 편안하게 ~하다
share 공유하다, 나누다
look forward to N/-ing ~하기를 고대하다
don't hesitate to V ~하기를 주저하지 말라

정답 (a) As discussing → As discussed

UNIT 4　조동사

EXERCISE

A

1 내가 그 생일파티에 참석했어야 했다.
2 다음 주에 어디로 휴가를 갈지 아직 정하지 못했다.
3 다음 주 목요일에 출장차 뉴욕에 가야 한다.
4 질문 사항이 있으시면, 주저하지 마시고 제게 연락주세요.
5 그가 그 중국식당에 있었을 리가 없다.
6 나는 내 방의 발코니에 앉아 있곤 했다.
7 그녀는 곧 이곳에 올 것이다.
8 그 소문은 사실일 리가 없다.
9 그는 내 책상에 그의 지갑을 두었음이 틀림없다.
10 와이프와 그 일에 대해 상의하는 것이 좋을 것 같다.

PRACTICE

1 (c)　　2 (c)　　3 (b) can't be → must be
4 (d) should always washing → should always wash

POINT

1 난 할 수 있어.
2 난 할 수 없어.
3 그녀는 보고서를 곧 완성할 것이다.
4 다음번엔 당신이 이길 것이라 저는 확신합니다.

5 당신이 진정 원하는 일을 얻을 것입니다.

6 당신은 지금 떠나셔야 합니다.

7 당신은 그것을 드셔서는 안 됩니다.

8 그가 존일 리가 없다.

9 나는 오늘 밤 파티에 참석할 수도 있다.

10 지금 가셔도 됩니다.

11 지금 집에 가도 될까요?

12 나는 미팅에 참석할 수 없을 것이다.

13 너는 거짓말하지 않는 것이 좋다.

14 내가 그곳에 가지 않았어야 했다.

15 너는 그 영화를 봤음에 틀림없다.

EXERCISE A

`ex`

어구 forget 잊다　anniversary 기념일

1

어구 attend 참석하다

정답 내가 그 생일파티에 참석했어야 했다.

2

어구 decide 결심하다　take a vacation 휴가가다

정답 다음 주에 어디로 휴가를 갈지 아직 정하지 못했다.

3

어구 on business 업무 때문에, 출장차

정답 다음 주 목요일에 출장차 뉴욕에 가야한다.

4

어구 hesitate 망설이다　contact 연락하다

정답 질문 사항이 있으시면, 주저하지 마시고 언제든지 제게 연락주세요.

5

정답 그가 그 중국식당에 있었을 리가 없다.

6

정답 나는 내 방의 발코니에 앉아 있곤 했다.

7

정답 그녀는 곧 이곳에 올 것이다.

8

어구 rumor 소문

정답 그 소문은 사실일 리가 없다.

9

어구 wallet 지갑

정답 그는 내 책상에 그의 지갑을 두었음이 틀림없다.

10

어구 discuss 토론하다, 상의하다

정답 와이프와 그 일에 대해 상의하는 것이 좋을 것 같다.

PRACTICE

1

해석 A: 이 의자 옮기는 것 좀 도와주시겠어요?
B: 물론이죠.

해설 (a)는 방법을 묻는 표현이므로 대답은 구체적 방안 등으로 답해야 한다. (b) Aren't는 어법상 빈 칸 뒤의 정동사 help 앞에 쓸 수 없다. (d) Did you는 과거 사실을 묻는 표현으로 질문 자체가 어색해진다. 도움을 요청하는 (c) Can이 문맥과 어울린다.

어구 move 옮기다　sure thing 물론이다

정답 (c)

2

해석 당신은 주식에 투자했어야 했다.

해설 문맥상 과거사실에 대한 유감 표현인 should have p.p.가 적절히 어울린다. 다른 보기들은 빈 칸 뒤의 과거 분사 invested를 받을 수 없다.

어구 should have 과거분사 ~했어야 했다　invest 투자하다
stock 주식　ought to ~해야 한다
had better ~하는 것이 낫다　may well ~하는 것은 당연하다

정답 (c)

3

해석 A: 나 드디어 차를 구입했어.
B: 정말? 너 정말 신나겠다.
A: 응, 이번 주 토요일에 시간 있으면 우리 집에 와서 내 차 좀 봐줘.
B: 유감스럽지만 나 그때 다른 계획이 있어서 힘들겠는데.

해설 (b)의 대답이 잘못되었다. can't be는 '~일 리가 없다'라는 뜻으로 대화의 흐름과 어울리지 않는다. can't를 must로 바꿔야 한다.

어구 purchase 구매하다　plan 계획; 계획하다

정답 (b) can't be → must be

4

해석 (a) 살모넬라(균)는 아마 일부 애완견의 배설물에서도 발견될 것이다. (b) 사람들은 이 동물들과 접촉 후에 손을 씻지 않으면 감염될 수도 있다. (c) 파충류들은 특히 살모넬라를 (몸속에) 지니기 쉽다. (d) 따라서 파충류가 건강해 보이더라도 파충류와 접촉한 뒤에는 반드시 그 직후에 손을 씻어야 한다.

해설 (d)에서 should라는 조동사가 쓰였으므로 뒤의 동사 washing을 원형동사인 wash로 바꿔야 한다. 문장은 중간에 always라는 부사를 두어 함정을 유도하고 있다.

어구 salmonella 살모넬라(균)　feces 배설물
pet 애완동물　infect 감염 시키다
contact 접촉　reptile 파충류
particularly 특히　be likely to V ~할 것 같은
immediately 즉시　handle 취급하다
healthy 건강한

정답 (d) should always washing → should always wash

Chapter 4

UNIT 1 명사와 관사

EXERCISE

A
1 the
2 the
3 the
4 a
5 The

B
1 an
2 the
3 the Himalayas
4 an
5 a
6 coffee
7 a
8 a new pair
9 fever
10 the

PRACTICE

1 (a)   2 (c)
3 (a) in such the hurry → in such a hurry
4 (d) for a five weeks → for five weeks

POINT

1 그녀는 좋은 책(들)을 가지고 있다.
2 마이클은 훌륭한 요리사다.
3 모든 개인 물품들을 건조실에서 치워야 한다.
4 조언에 진심으로 감사드립니다.
5 저는 그 지역에 대한 정보가 필요합니다.
6 우리 장비의 대부분은 전에 음식을 만드는 데 사용되었다.
7 로마는 하루아침에 만들어지지 않았다.
8 나는 그곳에서 한 시간 동안 기다렸다.
9 태양은 지구보다 훨씬 더 크다.
10 그것이 우리가 찾고 있는 파랑새다.
11 개는 충직한 친구다.

EXERCISE A

ex
해석 그들은 그곳에 한 시간 동안 있었다.
해설 시간(hour) 앞에는 관사가 있어야 하며 '한 시간 동안'은 for an hour로 표현한다.

1
해석 휘발유는 리터 단위로 팔린다.
해설 시간 또는 수량의 단위는 정관사 the를 써서 표현한다.
정답 the

2
해석 나는 일요일 아침에는 늦잠 자기를 즐긴다.
해설 in the morning 또는 in the afternoon과 같이 특정 시간 표현 앞에는 반드시 정관사 the를 붙여야 한다.
정답 the

3
해석 그가 내 팔을 잡았다.
해설 신체 일부를 나타내는 명사 앞에는 정관사 the를 붙인다.
어구 catch 잡다
정답 the

4
해석 나는 그래픽 일을 하고 있는 친구 한 명을 만났다.
해설 명사 friend는 가산명사로 반드시 앞에는 관사를 붙여야 한다. 또한 a friend of mine은 '친구 중 한 명'이란 뜻을 나타내는 이중 소유격을 나타내는 표현 방법이다. 따라서 적절한 관사는 a다.
정답 a

5
해석 영국 해협은 대서양의 일부분이다.
해설 해협, 산맥 등의 이름 앞에는 정관사 the를 붙인다.
어구 The English Channel 영국해협   part 부분
the Atlantic Ocean 대서양
정답 The

EXERCISE B

1
해석 나는 어제 X-BOX 정품을 하나 샀다.
해설 original이 발음기호상 모음으로 시작하므로 a가 아닌 an으로 수식해야 한다.
정답 an

2
해석 정확한 존의 주소를 알려다오.
해설 존이라는 이름으로 주소는 한정되어 있으므로 주소 중 하나가 아닌 지정된 주소라는 것을 알 수 있다. 한정되고 지정된 주소 앞이므로 the를 붙여야 옳다.
어구 accurate 정확한   address 주소
정답 the

3
해석 당신은 히말라야 산맥에 살고 있는 부족의 삶에 대한 더 나은 이해를 할 수 있을 것입니다.
해설 산맥[히말라야(Himalayas)] 앞에는 정관사 the를 붙여야 한다.
어구 understanding 이해   tribal 부족의
정답 the Himalayas

4

해석 개는 얼마나 똑똑한 동물인가!

해설 what을 사용한 감탄 표현 방법을 묻고 있다. 많은 동물 중 특정적이지 않은 하나의 동물을 의미하기 때문에 부정관사 a/an을 what 뒤에 붙인다.

어구 intelligent 영리한, 똑똑한

정답 an

5

해석 그녀는 정말 아름다운 여자다.

해설 such와 함께 아름다운 여자 중 특정인이 아닌 한 명이라는 의미로 the가 아닌 부정관사 a/an을 such 뒤에 써야 한다.

정답 a

6

해석 커피 한잔 주세요.

해설 coffee는 물질명사로 앞에 관사를 붙이지 않는다. 이러한 물질명사를 수량화하는 단위명사는 물질명사에 따라 다른데, coffee는 앞의 cup을 써서 한 잔(a cup), 두 잔(two cups)을 나타낸다.

어구 a cup of coffee 커피 한 잔

정답 coffee

7

해석 나는 일주일에 세 번 그에게 이메일을 보낸다.

해설 '~당, ~마다'의 뜻으로 부정관사 a/an을 시간 명사 앞에 쓴다.

정답 a

8

해석 나는 집에 오는 길에 한 벌의 새 청바지를 구입했다.

해설 짝이라는 뜻의 pair 앞에 부정관사 a를 써서 한 벌을 나타낼 수 있다. 청바지와 함께 청바지 한 벌을 나타내는 올바른 영어표현 방법은 a pair of jeans다.

어구 pair 짝   on one's way ~가는(오는) 길에

정답 a new pair

9

해석 그녀는 열병으로부터 고통을 겪고 있다.

해설 질병(fever) 앞에는 관사를 붙이지 않는다.

어구 suffer 고통을 겪다   fever 열병

정답 fever

10

해석 나는 한 시간 단위로 택시를 빌렸다.

해설 전치사 by와 함께 시간이나 수량의 단위를 나타낼 때 정관사 the를 붙인다.

어구 hire 고용하다, 임대하다   cab 택시

정답 the

PRACTICE

1

해석 A: 어떤 음료를 드시겠습니까?
B: 물 한 잔 더 주세요.

해설 관사 a 대신 another를 써서 표현한 (a)가 답이다. (b), (c)의 bottle이나 glass 모두 앞에 관사 a를 붙여야 하며, (d)처럼 water의 복수형 waters는 쓸 수 없다.

어구 a bottle of water 생수 한 병   a glass of water 물 한 컵

정답 (a)

2

해석 새도 깃이 같은 것들끼리 모인다(유유상종).

해설 (c) a가 답이다. 부정관사 a는 '같은(the same)'의 의미로 쓰였다.

어구 feather 깃털   flock 모이다

정답 (c)

3

해석 A: 리(Lee), 왜 그렇게 서두르니?
B: 학교에 늦었거든.
A: 첫 수업은 언제 시작하는데?
B: 9시 반에.

해설 (a) in a hurry는 '급히'라는 뜻의 숙어다. 이때 쓰는 관사가 부정관사이며 중간에 such는 그 의미를 강조하는 역할을 한다. 따라서 the가 아닌 a를 써 in such a hurry가 되도록 바꿔야 한다.

어구 in a hurry 급히

정답 (a) in such the hurry → in such a hurry

4

해석 (a) 화요일, 언론에 의하면 인도의 크리켓 스타 프랭클린 로즈(32세)는 오른쪽 어깨의 근육 파열로 고통을 겪고 있다고 전했다. (b) 로즈는 결국 부상당한 어깨 수술을 위해 금요일에 런던으로 떠났다. (c) 로즈는 월요일에 수술할 예정이다. (d) 인도 크리켓 위원회에 따르면, 그 수술로 5주간 경기에 나갈 수 없을 것이라고 한다.

해설 전치사 for와 함께 '~(시간)동안'이란 의미를 갖는 시간을 표현할 때는 따로 관사를 붙이지 않는다. for a five weeks가 아닌 관사 a를 뺀 for five weeks가 올바른 표현이다.

어구 cricket (11명씩 두 패로 갈라 하는 스포츠의 일종) 크리켓   undergo surgery 수술하다   injured 부상당한   operate 수술하다   rule A out of B B에서 A를 제외시키다   according to ~에 의하면   board 위원회

정답 (d) for a five weeks → for five weeks

EXERCISE

A

1 형용사
2 부사, 형용사
3 부사, 형용사
4 형용사
5 형용사

B

1 wooden
2 hardly
3 deep
4 drunk
5 worth
6 late
7 highly
8 live
9 Unfortunately
10 asleep

PRACTICE

1 (b)　　2 (c)　　3 (a) Is it truth → Is it true
4 (d) globally → global

POINT

1 다음 장은 법 문제에 관한 것이다.
2 고등법원의 결정 때문에 전 부사장은 현재 위험에 처해 있다.
3 우리는 지구 온난화에 대해 걱정하고 있다.
4 그녀는 거미를 무서워한다.
5 어떤 여자가 나를 보러 왔다.
6 나는 그의 성공을 확신한다.
7 그는 현재 팀의 주장이다.
8 헐리 씨는 회의에 참석했다.
9 비가 많이 왔고 바람이 세게 불었다.
10 주식시장에 투자하는 것은 내게 위험이 너무 크다.
11 불행히도, 가수선정이 제대로 된 선택이 아니었다.
12 그는 그의 비행기를 타기 위해 시간에 때맞춰 도착했다.
13 (착용한 것을) 벗어버려라.
14 나는 종종 새벽에 일어난다.

EXERCISE A

ex

해석 나는 지난 밤 이상한 꿈을 꿨다.
어구 strange 이상한

1

해석 내 고양이한테 뭐 잘못된 일이라도 있나요?
어구 wrong 잘못된
정답 형용사

2

해석 나는 그 강좌가 정말 흥미롭다고 생각했다.
어구 lecture 강좌, 강의
정답 부사, 형용사

3

해석 다음 선택 사항들에 대해 경청해주세요.
어구 carefully 조심스럽게　　following 다음의
　　　choice 선택(사항)
정답 부사, 형용사

4

해석 당신이 운동하는 주된 이유는 무엇인가요?
어구 main 주요한　　　　exercise 운동하다
정답 형용사

5

해석 그는 사임할 것 같다.
어구 resign 사임하다
정답 형용사

EXERCISE B

1

해석 그는 나에게 나무 박스 하나를 줬다.
해설 명사 앞에서 전치 수식이 가능한 형용사는 wooden이다 woodless는 '수목이 없는'이라는 뜻으로 문맥과 어울리지 않는다.
어구 wooden 목재의　　　　woodless 수목이 없는
정답 wooden

2

해석 그 영화를 보고 싶어 미칠 지경이다.
해설 hard는 '열심히, 매우'의 뜻을 가지고 뒤에서 수식하는 후치 수식 부사다. 동사 wait와 함께 '~할 수 없을 정도의'라는 의미(직역하면 '너무 기다려짐'으로 해석됨)로서 문맥상 적절한 의미가 되도록 하는 부사는 hardly다.
어구 hard 열심히, 매우　　hardly 거의 ~하지 않는(부정의 의미)
정답 hardly

3

해석 분수(噴水)는 깊이 10피트, 폭 20피트의 연못에 있다.
해설 숫자와 함께 깊이를 나타내는 경우 형용사 deep을 써서 표현한다.
어구 fountain 분수　　pond 연못　　　　wide 폭이 ~인
정답 deep

4

해석 운전자는 음주 운전을 하다가 누군가를 죽였다.

해설 괄호 안의 두 개의 보기 중에서 서술적 용법으로 쓰이는 형용사는 drunk다. drunken은 한정적 용법으로만 쓰인다.

어구 drunken 술 취한(한정적 용법으로만)
drunk 술 취한(서술적 용법으로만)

정답 drunk

5

해석 HDTV는 진정 기다릴 가치가 있다.

해설 형용사 worth는 이 자체로 목적어를 취하는 영어에서 몇 안 되는 형용사다. worthy는 뒤에 바로 동(명)사 목적어를 취할 수 없고 동사의 경우 to V의 형태나 명사의 경우 of N의 형태로 쓴다.

어구 worth ~할 가치가 있는   worthy 가치 있는(뒤에 of N/-ing, to do 형태를 취함)

정답 worth

6

해석 고인이 된 니콜 씨는 그의 나이 80에 돌아가셨다.

해설 부사 lately는 '최근에'라는 뜻이다. 문맥상 사람 앞에 위치해 '고인이 된'이라는 뜻의 형용사가 오는 것이 어울린다.

어구 lately 최근에   late 고인이 된; 늦은

정답 late

7

해석 그녀는 그녀의 아름다운 목소리 때문에 매우 칭송을 받았다.

해설 high는 '높은 곳에 위치하거나 가치나 가격이 높다'는 의미의 부사이고 highly는 '매우' 또는 '수준이 높다'는 의미의 부사다. 여기서는 '대단히' 칭찬받았다는 의미이므로 highly가 옳다.

어구 praise 칭송하다, 칭찬하다   voice 목소리

정답 highly

8

해석 사람들이 저희 라이브 쇼를 즐기기 바랍니다.

해설 alive는 '살아있는'이란 뜻을 갖는 서술적 용법으로만 쓰이는 형용사다. 문장에서는 명사 show를 전치 수식하는 자리이므로 한정적 용법으로 쓰이는 live가 옳은 답이다.

정답 live

9

해석 안타깝게도, 우리 모두는 죽게 되어 있다(죽음을 피할 방법은 없다).

해설 부사는 전체문장을 수식하기도 한다. 문맥상 문장의 괄호 역시 문장 전체를 수식하는 역할을 하는 부사 Unfortunately가 필요한 자리다.

어구 unfortunately 안타깝게도   avoid 피하다
mortality (죽음을 맞이할 수밖에 없는) 운명, 죽음

정답 Unfortunately

10

해석 나는 TV를 켜놓은 채 잠들었다.

해설 동사 fall과 함께 sleep이 아닌 asleep의 짝을 이뤄 '잠들다'라는 하나의 의미 덩어리가 된다. sleep은 동사로서 앞의 동사 fell과 중복된다.

어구 fall asleep 잠들다

정답 asleep

PRACTICE

1

해석 A: 글자의 크기가 읽을 수 있을 정도의 충분한 크기가 되도록 당신이 노력했으면 좋겠습니다.
B: 걱정 하지 마세요. 잭에게 이미 그것을 확대하도록 말했으니까요.

해설 enough는 형용사인 경우 명사를 수식하고 부사가 되는 경우 형용사를 수식한다. 단, 품사에 따라 위치가 달라지는데 명사를 수식하는 경우 전치 수식하고 형용사를 수식하는 경우 후치 수식한다. 문맥상 형용사 large가 들어가야 하는데 이때 enough의 품사는 부사이므로 large enough가 올바른 어순이 된다.

어구 make sure 확실히 하다   text 문자 메시지, 원본
enlarge 확대하다   largely 주로
large 큰

정답 (b)

2

해석 나는 항상 내 아이를 다르게 키우고 싶었다.

해설 빈 칸 앞의 동사 raise는 타동사로 목적어 child를 바로 받기 때문에 이것만으로도 문장은 완벽한 상태다. 때문에 또 다른 동사 (a)나 (d)는 올 수 없고 형용사 (b) 역시 빈 칸에는 올 수 없다. 수식어인 부사 (c)만이 구조상 빈 칸에 올 수 있다.

어구 raise 양육하다   differently 다르게
differ 다르다

정답 (c)

3

해석 A: 직장을 그만둔다는 것이 사실이니?
B: 응, 그걸 어떻게 알았어?
A: 사무실에서 소문이 들리던걸.
B: 이런, 톰한테 얘기 안 했어야 했는데.

해설 (a)에서 be동사 뒤는 명사나 형용사가 올 수 있으나 it은 비인칭 대명사로 be동사 뒤에 올 수 있는 품사는 형용사 true다. truth는 명사로 it과 동격이어야 하는데 여기서 it은 실체가 없는 비인칭 대명사기 때문에 어울리지 않는다.

어구 truth 진실   quit 그만두다
anyway 어쨌든   rumor 소문

정답 (a) Is it truth → Is it true

4

해석 (a) 지구온난화를 마침내 설명할 수 있게 되었다. (b) 새로운 조사에 따르면, 지구가 점점 뜨거워지고 있는 이유는 태양이 지난 1000년 동안 그 어느 때보다도 더욱 밝게 타오르고 있기 때문이라고 한다. (c) 한 연구에 의하면 증가하는 태양으로부터의 복사 에너지가 최근의 지구온난화 기후 변화의 주범인 것으로 나타나고 있다. (d) 태양열은 시난 60년간 특히 뱅위를 떨치고 있으며 그것이 지구 온도에 영향을 끼치고 있는지도 모른다.

해설 (d)의 globally temperatures에서 globally를 global로 바꿔야 한다. 뒤의 명사 temperatures를 수식할 수 있는 품사는 형용사이므로 형용사 global이 옳다.

어구 global warming 지구온난화   burn 타다

UNIT 3 기타 형용사

EXERCISE

A
1 Napoleon the Third
2 responsible for
3 Many students
4 full of[filled with도 가능]
5 such a long way

B
1 a few
2 of
3 such
4 little
5 of
6 hundred
7 for
8 Few
9 so
10 Dozens of

PRACTICE

1 (a)   **2** (b)   **3** (c) much card → many cards
4 (a) A little → Some

POINT

1 당신의 커피에 약간의 설탕을 넣으셔도 됩니다.
2 당신의 차에 가능하면 설탕은 넣지 마세요.
3 많은 사람들이 그가 거짓말쟁이라고 믿고 있다.
4 인터넷 접속이 매우 느려 나는 내 이메일도 확인하지 못했다.
5 이것은 젊은 한국 이민자에 대한 재미있는 이야기다.

EXERCISE A

ex

해석 수십 명의 사람들이 남부 일본을 강타한 돌풍과 폭우로 부상을 입었다.

해설 정확한 숫자가 아닌 '수십 명'을 나타내는 경우 dozen은 복수형인 dozens가 되어야 한다.

어구 dozen 12의, 한 다스의   injure 부상을 입히다
high wind 돌풍   heavy rain 폭우
hit 강타하다; 때리다

1

해석 나폴레옹 3세는 1870년에 권좌에서 물러났다.

해설 기수 Third 앞에 정관사 the를 붙여야 한다.

어구 depose (권좌 또는 직책에서) 물러나게 하다

정답 Napoleon the Third

2

해석 그가 조사를 담당한다.

해설 형용사 responsible은 be동사와 함께 전치사 for를 쓴다. of를 for로 바꿔야 한다.

어구 be responsible for ~를 책임지다, 담당하다
conduct (조사 등을) 수행하다   research 조사

정답 responsible for

3

해석 많은 학생들이 그들이 받는 교육의 질에 대해 우려를 표명했다.

해설 student가 가산명사이기 때문에 문맥상으로는 복수형이면서 복수 가산명사를 수식하는 much가 아닌 many를 써야 한다.

어구 express a concern 우려를 표명하다   quality 품질

정답 Many students

4

해석 탱크는 연료로 가득 차 있다.

해설 형용사 full은 be full of를 써서 '~로 가득한'이란 의미다.   전치사 with를 쓰려면 비슷한 뜻으로 be filled with를 쓸 수 있다.

어구 be full of ~로 가득한   fuel 연료

정답 full of[filled with도 가능]

5

해석 집까지의 거리는 꽤 된다.

해설 이 문장에서 such는 의미를 강조하는 역할의 형용사로 강조용법의 such는 관사 앞에 위치한다.

정답 such a long way

EXERCISE B

1

해석 나는 1주일 전에 몇 권의 책을 샀다.

해설 명사 book은 가산명사로 수식하는 수형용사로는 a few가 적절하다.

어구 a few 몇몇의

정답 a few

2

해석 그는 우리가 그에게 제공하는 우리의 서비스에 대해 고마워하고 있다.

해설 괄호 앞에 형용사 appreciative(고마워하는)가 있다. 형용사 appreciative가 목적어를 받을 때 전치사 of를 쓴다.

어구 appreciative 고마워하는

정답 of

3

해석 마치 아주 오래전이었던 것 같다.

해설 명사 long time을 강조하는 such용법을 묻고 있다. so의 품사는 부사이기 때문에 이 문장에서처럼 뒤의 명사 time을 수식해야 하는 괄호 자리에 올 수 없다. 〈관사+형용사+명사〉가 있으므로 such가 와야 할 자리다.

정답 such

4

해석 그는 혼자 있기를 좋아했고 친구 관계에 대해 크게 관심을 보이지 않았다.

해설 interest가 '관심, 흥미'의 뜻을 나타낼 때 불가산명사가 된다. few는 가산명사 앞에 쓸 수 있는 수형용사이기 때문에 답이 될 수 없다. little과 더불어 little interest가 되면 '거의 흥미가 없는'의 의미가 된다. 적절한 답은 little이다.

어구 prefer 선호하다   alone 홀로   express 표현하다
interest 관심; 이자   friendship 친구관계, 우정

정답 little

5

해석 우리는 겨울 동안 그 건물을 따뜻하게 하는 것이 어렵다는 것을 잘 알고 있다.

해설 형용사 aware(알고 있는)는 뒤에 명사를 목적어로 받아야 하는 경우 전치사 for가 아닌 of를 쓴다. 또한 문장에서처럼 서술적 용법으로 쓰는 형용사임도 알아두자.

어구 be aware of ~을 알고 있는   difficulty 어려움

정답 of

6

해석 약 100명의 사람들이 파티에 참석했다.

해설 괄호 앞에 숫자 one이 나왔으므로 hundred와 함께 올바른 100명의 사람이란 정확한 숫자를 나타내는 표현은 one hundred people이 옳다. hundreds of는 앞의 숫자표현(one)과는 함께 쓸 수 없다.

어구 present 참석한

정답 hundred

7

해석 한국의 가을은 아름다운 단풍잎으로 매우 유명하다.

해설 famous와 함께 쓰는 전치사를 묻고 있다. 전치사 for와 함께 쓰는데 이때 for는 (유명한) 이유를 나타낸다.

어구 autumn 가을   famous 유명한   maple 단풍나무

정답 for

8

해석 거의 모든 사람들이 행사에 나타나지 않았다.

해설 people이라는 가산명사의 복수형 앞에 올 수 있는 형용사는 few다. a few나 few 뒤에는 모두 가산명사의 복수형이 와야 한다. a little은 셀 수 없는 불가산명사 앞에 써야 한다.

어구 show up 나타나다   event 행사

정답 Few

9

해석 유성 폭풍은 너무 아름다워서 우리는 그것을 보느라 밤을 샜다.

해설 괄호 뒤에 형용사 beautiful이 나왔다. 형용사를 수식할 수 있는

품사는 부사다. 따라서 so를 선택해야 한다. such는 형용사로 명사를 수식한다.

어구 meteor 유성

정답 so

10

해석 강력한 지진의 여파로 수십 명의 사람들이 부상당했다.

해설 Dozens of가 옳다. Dozens가 전치사 of와 함께 명사를 수식하면 명확하지 않은 '수십 명의'란 의미를 갖게 된다. 따라서 people 앞에 적절한 형태는 Dozens of다.

어구 dozen 12의, 한 다스의   injure 부상을 입히다
earthquake 지진

정답 Dozens of

PRACTICE

1

해석 A: 이 소프트웨어에 대해 많이 알고 있니?
B: 미안. 난 사실 이런 새 모델은 익숙하지 않아서.

해설 빈 칸은 be동사 뒤로 형용사가 필요한 자리다. 형용사는 (a), (d)가 있는데 familiar(익숙한)는 전치사 with와 함께 어울리므로 (d)가 아닌 (a)을 답으로 선택해야 한다.

어구 be familiar with ~에 익숙하다

정답 (a)

2

해석 영국 전역을 휩쓴 맹렬한 홍수로 인해 수천 명의 사람들이 그들의 고향을 떠날 수밖에 없었다.

해설 대략적인 수를 나타내는 경우 thousand(천의)는 명사 앞에서 복수형이 되어야 한다. (a) thousand앞에 숫자가 나와야 하며 (c) Thousands와 people사이에 전치사 of가 있어야 한다. 이를 만족하는 답은 (b)다.

어구 be forced to V ~하지 않을 수 없다   amid ~사이에서
severe 심한, 중증의

정답 (b)

3

해석 A: 너 뭐하고 있니?
B: 신용카드에 대한 몇 가지 정보를 찾고 있어.
A: 왜? 너 이미 많은 카드를 가지고 있잖아.
B: 그렇지. 하지만 카드사기로부터 확실하게 보호를 제공하는 카드를 찾고 있거든.

해설 (c) 명사 card는 셀 수 있는 가산명사다. much는 셀 수 없는 불가산명사를 수식하는 형용사이므로 card를 수식할 수 없다. '많은 카드'라는 뜻을 나타내고자 할 때는 much 대신 many를 써야 한다.

어구 search for ~를 찾다   credit card 신용카드
offer 제공하다   complete 완전한
protection 보호   fraud 사기

정답 (c) much card → many cards

4

해석 (a) 반대 입장을 나타내는 사람도 있지만 일부 사람들의 주장에 따르면 동물실험은 믿을 수 없고 의학 연구에 전혀 도움이 되지 않는다고 한다. (b) 양쪽 주장이 매우 강하기 때문에 어떤 것이 진실인

지는 구별하기 어렵다. (c) 하지만 절대적으로 필요하지 않은 경우에 하는 어떤 동물실험도 허용되어서는 안 된다고 나는 생각한다. (d) 반면, 동물실험이 필수적인 경우에는 해도 된다고 생각한다.

해설 a little은 양을 나타내는 명사 앞에서 쓸 수 있는 수식어구다. 명사 people이 있으므로 문맥상 A little을 Some으로 바꿔야 한다.

어구 maintain 주장하다　　　　animal testing 동물실험
reliable 믿을 수 있는　　　research 연구
tell 구별하다; 말하다　　　absolutely 절대적으로
necessary 필요한　　　　　allow 허용하다
essential 필수적인　　　　go ahead 계속하다, 나아가다

정답 (a) A little → Some

UNIT 4　비교

EXERCISE

A
1　이것은 내가 본 공연 중 단연코 가장 최고다.
2　당신의 뇌는 당신이 생각하는 것보다 훨씬 더 뛰어나다.
3　그는 선생이기보다는 작가다.
4　둘 중에서 어떤 행성이 더 따뜻하다고 말할 수 있겠는가?
5　그녀는 역대 최고의 춤 선생이다.

B
1　ever
2　very hard
3　happier
4　more
5　the more
6　better and better
7　than
8　the most
9　the last
10　the cleverest

PRACTICE

1 (d)　　2 (a)　　3 (b) looks more → looks better
4 (a) more we can learn → the more we can learn

POINT

1　분유는 모유만큼 좋다.
2　호텔은 내가 예상한 것만큼 좋지 않았다.
3　그는 아시아에서 둘째가라면 서러워할 정도의 유명한 피아니스트이다.
4　당신은 당신이 원하는 만큼 많은 도시를 방문할 수 있습니다.
5　그는 하키 선수만큼이나 유명한 연예인이기도 하다.
6　염소젖은 소젖보다 건강에 좋다.
7　우리는 에너지를 좀 더 현명하게 사용해야 한다.
8　그 글자들은 영어 공부를 하는 데 있어서 가장 유용한 단어다.

왜냐하면 그것들은 특히 자주 접할 수 있는 단어들이기 때문이다.
9　그것(그 주유소)는 달라스에서 가장 안전한 주유소일 수도 있다.
10　이것은 내가 읽어 본 것 중 최악이다.
11　벽지의 암 관리는 도시에서 제공되는 것보다 열악하다.
12　나는 그녀가 왼손잡이기 때문에 더욱 그녀를 사랑한다.
13　내 생각에 사람들 간의 화해가 두 문제 중 더 큰 것 같다.
14　그가 승리할수록, 그는 더 많은 승리를 원한다.

EXERCISE A

1
어구 performance 공연, 성과
정답 이것은 내가 본 공연 중 단연코 가장 최고다.

2
정답 당신의 뇌는 당신이 생각하는 것보다 훨씬 더 뛰어나다.

3
정답 그는 선생이기보다는 작가다.

4
어구 planet 행성
정답 둘 중에서 어떤 행성이 더 따뜻하다고 말할 수 있겠는가?

5
정답 그녀는 역대 최고의 춤 선생이다.

EXERCISE B

1
해석 그는 인도가 배출한 역대 최고의 배우다.
해설 ever는 최상급을 수식해 '역대, 전에 없던' 등으로 최상급의 의미를 강조하는 부사다. 앞의 최상급 the best를 통해 ever를 답으로 선택할 수 있다.
어구 produce 배출하다, 생산하다; 농산물
정답 ever

2
해석 나는 지난 두 달 동안 정말 열심히 일했다.
해설 more harder는 비교급이 서로 중복 사용된 형태이기 때문에 옳지 않다.
어구 work hard 열심히 일하다
정답 very hard

3
해석 우리가 좀 더 모일수록, 우리는 좀 더 행복해 질 것이다.
해설 「the 비교급~, the 비교급~」은 '~할수록 더욱 ~하다'의 의미로 해석되는 비교급 표현이다. 이 표현을 통해 정관사 the 뒤에 비교급 happier를 답으로 선택할 수 있다.
어구 get together 모이다
the A(비교급)~, the B(비교급)~ A할수록 더욱 B하다

정답 happier

4

해석 우리는 돈을 좀 더 현명하게 사용해야 한다.

해설 비교대상이나 적용범위없이 more만 써서 나타낼 수 있다. 하지만 than만 따로 독립적으로 쓸 수는 없다.

어구 wisely 현명하게

정답 more

5

해석 내 생각에 그녀는 둘 중에 더 유명하다.

해설 둘 사이의 비교급 표현은 「the + 비교급」, 즉 비교급 앞에 정관사 the를 붙여 표현한다. 둘 사이에서 하나는 유일하기 때문에 비교급 앞이라도 정관사 the를 붙여야 한다.

어구 famous 유명한

정답 the more

6

해석 품질이 좋은 텔레비전을 만드는 데 있어서 그들은 점점 더 나아지고 있다.

해설 〈비교급+and+비교급〉은 '점점 더 ~한(하게)'의 뜻으로 비교급을 강조하는 하나의 표현이 된다. better는 good의 비교급이므로 또 다른 비교급인 more와 함께 중복해서 쓸 수 없다.

어구 quality 품질이 좋은

정답 better and better

7

해석 그는 불평할 정도로 어리석지는 않다.

해설 know better than to V는 '~할 정도로 어리석지 않다'란 뜻의 비교급 관용표현이다. 이러한 표현을 통해 than을 답으로 정할 수 있다.

어구 know better than to V ~할 정도로 어리석지 않다
complain 불평하다

정답 than

8

해석 그들은 전국에서 가장 성공적인 프로그램 중에 하나를 가지고 있다.

해설 「one of the 최상급 + 복수 명사」는 '최고로 ~한 복수 명사 중 하나'로 해석된다. 이를 통해 the most를 답으로 선택할 수 있다.

어구 successful 성공적인   available 이용 가능한

정답 the most

9

해석 그는 돈 때문에 관계를 망칠 사람은 결코 아니다.

해설 the last person to V는 '~할 사람은 결코 아닌'으로 해석되는 관용표현이다. last person, 즉 마지막 사람이란 '결코 ~할 것 같지 않은 사람'으로 풀어 해석이 가능하기 때문이다.

어구 the last person to V ~할 사람은 결코 아닌   spoil 망치다
relation 관계

정답 the last

10

해석 그녀는 내가 아는 가장 영리한 여자다.

해설 뒤의 절에 쓰인 ever를 통해 최상급 the cleverest를 답으로 선택할 수 있다. ever는 최상급의 의미를 풍부하게 하는 강조 부사다.

어구 clever 영리한

정답 the cleverest

PRACTICE

1

해석 A: 제니퍼는 세계 최고의 힙합 아티스트다. 어떻게 생각해?
B: 글쎄, 어느 정도는 동의하지만 전적으로는 아냐.

해설 적절한 비교 표현은 최상급 (d) the best다. 뒤의 in the world 등 분야 등이 지정되어 있는 경우 '~중에서 최고인'이란 뜻으로 최상급으로 표현할 때 자연스럽다. most는 수나 양이 가장 많다는 뜻으로 문맥상 어울리지 않다.

어구 female 여성의   artist 예술가
to a certain extent 어느 정도   entirely 전적으로, 완전히

정답 (d)

2

해석 그녀는 선생이라기보다는 시인이다.

해설 not so much A as B는 'A라기 보다는 B다'는 뜻의 관용표현이다. 이 표현을 통해 as를 답으로 선택할 수 있다.

어구 not so much A as B A라기 보다는 B다   poet 시인

정답 (a)

3

해석 A: 저는 머리를 짧게 자를 생각입니다.
B: 왜요? 당신의 현재 스타일이 더 잘 어울리시는데.
A: 보시다시피, 이 스타일은 여름철에 하고 다니기는 너무 무거워 보여서요.
B: 그러지 말고 끝부분만 좀 치는 게 어때요?

해설 '좀 더 좋아 보이다'라는 표현은 동사 look과 함께 (b) ~more가 아닌 better가 되어야 한다.

어구 A look better on someone A는 누군가에게 더 잘 어울리다
plan on ~할 예정이다
cut one's hair short 머리를 짧게 치다   current 현재의
trim 다듬다, 살짝 자르다   at the ends 끝부분의

정답 (b) looks more → looks better

4

해석 (a) 우리가 많이 알수록, 점점 더 많이 배울 수 있다. (b) 빠르게 파악하고 새로운 정보를 기억하는 것은 우리가 나이를 먹음에 따라 더 어려워진다. (c) 그것은 우리의 처리 능력이 20대 정도에서 쇠퇴하기 때문이다. (d) 하지만 심리학자 사라 제이 웰치의 새로운 연구에 따르면 새로운 지식과 새로운 기술을 습득하는 능력은 우리가 얼마나 영리한가에 달렸을 뿐만 아니라 우리가 이미 알고 있는 것과 우리의 삶을 통해 경험한 것에도 달렸다고 한다.

해설 「the A(비교급)~, the B(비교급)~」(A할수록 B하다)의 표현 방법을 통해 (a)에서 more가 아닌 the more로 바꿔야 함을 알 수 있다.

어구 grasp 파악하다, 이해하다   get older 나이가 들어가다
ability 능력   process 처리(능력)   decline 쇠퇴하다
acquire 습득하나   depend on ~에 의지하다
experience 경험하다

정답 (a) more we can learn → the more we can learn

UNIT 5 대명사 일치와 재귀대명사

EXERCISE

A

1 문은 저절로 열렸다.
2 밖은 여전히 춥다.
3 그가 다른 사람을 꾸짖는 것은 자연스러운 것이다.
4 (그곳은) 5번가에 위치한 중앙도서관으로부터 약 두 블록 정도 떨어진 곳에 위치해 있다.
5 내가 귀 기울였던 사람은 그였다.

B

1 haven't
2 It
3 He
4 have
5 is
6 your
7 it
8 her
9 She is
10 yourself

PRACTICE

1 (d)   2 (d)   3 (b) who are → who is
4 (a) there → it

POINT

1 나는 댐을 둘러싸고 있는 그 도시를 사랑한다.
2 그녀는 친절하고 매우 관대한 여성이다.
3 이곳 날씨는 비가 오다 그치기를 하루 종일 반복한다.
4 (그곳은) 약 두 블록 떨어진 거리에 있다.
5 그가 예술가라는 것은 확실하다.
6 나는 새 조리법과 음식 만들기를 시도 또는 시식하는 것이 흥미롭다고 생각한다.
7 그 학교에 대해 모든 것을 아는 것은 그녀다.
8 그와 데이트했던 사람은 내 누이다.
9 나는 체육관에서 운동하다가 부상을 입었다.
10 TV 프로그램에서 그녀가 나오는 것을 본 직후 그녀의 책을 구입했다.

EXERCISE A

ex

어구 hot and humid 후덥지근한

1

어구 of itself 저절로
정답 문은 저절로 열렸다.

2

어구 freeze 춥게 하다, 얼게 하다
정답 밖은 여전히 춥다.

3

어구 scold 꾸짖다
정답 그가 다른 사람을 꾸짖는 것은 자연스러운 것이다.

4

어구 block 블록(구획 단위)   main 주요한
정답 (그곳은) 5번가에 위치한 중앙도서관으로부터 약 두 블록 정도 떨어진 곳에 위치해 있다.

5

정답 내가 귀 기울였던 사람은 그였다.

EXERCISE B

1

해석 나는 최근에는 그를 보지 못했다.
해설 주어가 I이기 때문에 동사 has가 have가 되어야 한다.
어구 lately 최근에
정답 haven't

2

해석 하루 종일 후덥지근했다.
해설 날씨를 나타내는 비인칭 주어는 it이다.
어구 hot and humid 후덥지근한   all day 하루 종일
정답 It

3

해석 그 작업자는 술 취한 사람이다.
해설 괄호 뒤의 명사 man이 오기 때문에 주어는 She가 아닌 He가 되어야 한다.
어구 drunken 술에 취한
정답 He

4

해석 얼마나 오랫동안 그녀를 기다려왔나요?
해설 괄호 뒤의 주어가 you이기 때문에 동사는 have가 되어야 한다.
정답 have

5

해석 내가 걱정하는 사람은 그녀다.
해설 It ~ that의 강조구문을 묻고 있다. 이때 It과 that 사이의 동사는 be동사여야 한다.
어구 be worried about 걱정하다
정답 is

6

해석 이번에는 네 스스로 결정해야 한다.
해설 주어가 you이기 때문에 소유격 역시 his가 아닌 your가 되어야 한다.
어구 make one's own decision 자신이 결정하다

정답 your

7

해석 공짜로 음식을 먹고 마시는 것이 흥미롭다는 것을 발견했다.

해설 전체 문장의 진짜 목적어는 to 이하 구문이다. 이 목적어가 길어 뒤로 이동했으며 그 빈 자리는 가목적어 it이 대체할 수 있다.

정답 it

8

해석 그녀는 그녀의 비행을 연기했다.

해설 주어가 she기 때문에 소유격은 her가 되어야 한다.

어구 postpone 연기하다   flight 비행(편)

정답 her

9

해석 그녀는 친절한 여자다.

해설 괄호 뒤의 명사가 단수명사이므로 주어 역시 단수 형태가 되어야 한다. 따라서 She is가 문맥상 바르다.

정답 She is

10

해석 얌전하게 굴어라!

해설 동사 behave와 함께 behave oneself는 관용어구로 '얌전히 굴어라'라는 뜻이 된다.

어구 behave oneself! 얌전히 굴어라!

정답 yourself

PRACTICE

1

해석 A: 당신의 컴퓨터에 무슨 문제가 있나요?
B: 전혀 모르겠습니다. 아무래도 수리점에 가지고 가야 할 것 같아요.

해설 동사 take는 「take + (대)명사 + to + 장소」의 형태가 되면 '(대)명사를 장소로 가지고 가다'의 의미를 갖게 된다.

어구 have no clue 전혀 모르다
take + (대)명사 + to + 장소 (대)명사를 장소로 가지고 가다
repair shop 수리점

정답 (d)

2

해석 앤디는 그가 재판 중일 때 자살했다.

해설 동사 kill과 함께 문맥상 '자살하다'라는 표현이 자연스러운데 이는 kill oneself로 표현한다. 또한 주어가 앤디(Andy)라는 단수이므로 themselves가 아닌 himself가 옳다.

어구 kill oneself 자살하다   on trial 재판 중인

정답 (d)

3

해석 A: 리 씨와 통화할 수 있을까요?
B: 실례지만 누구시죠?
A: 레드 사의 마크입니다.
B: 네, 집시만요.

해설 통화자가 누구인지를 묻는 질문은 의문사 who를 단수 취급하므로 동사는 is다. 따라서 who are가 아닌 who is가 답이다.

정답 (b) who are → who is

4

해석 (a) 소년은 많은 다른 동물들에게 포코노에서 첫눈이 내릴 때의 그들의 반응을 묘사해줄 것을 요청했다. (b) 곰은 눈은 그 곰이 잠들 시간을 알려주는 의미라고 했고 (c) 쥐는 추위를 피해 집에서 숨는 시기라고 했다. (d) 그리고 물고기는 (몸을) 따뜻하게 하기 위해 연못 바닥에 누워 있어야만 하는 시기라고 말했다.

해설 (a)에서 there를 it으로 바꿔야 한다. 날씨를 나타내므로 비인칭 주어 it을 써야 한다.

어구 describe 묘사하다, 자세히 말하다
reaction 반응   snowfall 강설
hide 숨다   escape 피하다
lie 눕다   stay warm 따뜻하게 하다

정답 (a) there → it

UNIT 6 지시대명사와 부정대명사

EXERCISE

A

1 오래된 디자인이 새 디자인보다 훨씬 좋은 것 같다.
2 지식을 공유하는 것과 정보를 도둑질하는 것은 별개다.
3 그의 피부는 삶은 가재만큼이나 빨갰다.
4 개 두 마리가 있는데 하나는 과체중이고 하나는 그렇지 않다.
5 우리 학생들이 당신의 학생들보다 더 똑똑하다.

B

1 those
2 another
3 one
4 that
5 any
6 another
7 another
8 that
9 any
10 those

PRACTICE

1 (c)   2 (b)   3 (d) the last it → the last one
4 (a) any second → every second

POINT

1 내 집은 형의 집보다 크다.

2 해왕성의 바람은 목성의 바람보다도 세다.

3 이 강좌는 작문 기술을 발전시키는 데 관심이 있는 사람들을 위한 것이다.

4 새 배지는 예전 것보다 좋다.

5 다른 것을 하나 더 주시겠어요.

6 말하는 것과 행하는 것은 별개다.

7 나는 두 마리의 개를 가지고 있는데, 하나는 살이 쪘고 다른 하나는 말랐다.

8 파티를 위해 약간의 베이컨을 좀 사야 한다.

9 의문사항이 있으시면, 편안하게 저에게 연락주세요.

10 언제라도 저희를 방문하실 수 있습니다.

11 너희 모두는 기도할 수 있다.

12 모든 사람들은 훈련된 병사였다.

13 결국, 모든 돈을 돌려받았다.

EXERCISE A

ex

어구 capacity 용량

1
정답 오래된 디자인이 새 디자인보다 훨씬 좋은 것 같다.

2
어구 share 공유하다   knowledge 지식   steal 훔치다
정답 지식을 공유하는 것과 정보를 도둑질하는 것은 별개다.

3
어구 boiled 삶은   lobster 가재
정답 그의 피부는 삶은 가재만큼이나 빨갰다.

4
어구 overweight 과체중인
정답 개 두 마리가 있는데, 하나는 과체중이고 하나는 그렇지 않다.

5
어구 clever 똑똑한
정답 우리 학생들이 당신의 학생들보다 더 똑똑하다.

EXERCISE B

1
해석 한국의 쌀 식초는 일본 것보다 강하다.
해설 같은 어휘의 반복을 싫어하는 영어의 특성상, 또한 특히 이같이 반복되는 명사가 수식어구에 의해 수식받는 경우 that 또는 those로 하여금 대신 받게 한다. 이 둘의 특징은 (of 이하 등의) 수식어구를 통해 수식을 받을 수 있다는 데 있다. 또한 복수형 동사 vinegars를 받아야 하므로 that(단수 명사를 대신 받음)이 아닌 those가 되어야 한다. 이를 it 등의 다른 대명사로 받을 수 없다.
어구 vinegar 식초
정답 those

2
해석 나는 세 개의 모자를 가지고 있다. 하나는 검정색, 다른 하나는 붉은색, 그리고 나머지 하나는 흰색이다.
해설 셋 중에서 하나는 one, 다른 하나는 another, 마지막 하나는 the other로 나타낸다.
정답 another

3
해석 나는 새 로고보다 오래된 로고가 더 맘에 든다.
해설 지칭하는 것이 종류가 같을 뿐이지 지칭하는 바로 그것(it)이 아니므로 it이 아닌 one이 되어야 한다.
정답 one

4
해석 일본의 학교 시스템은 미국의 시스템과 비슷하다.
해설 of이하의 수식을 받고 학교 시스템(school system)이라는 단수 명사를 대신하는 대명사는 that이다.
어구 similar 비슷한
정답 that

5
해석 VIP 라운지에 남는 빈 장소가 있나요?
해설 단수 명사 room을 수식하고 의문문에서 '어떤'으로 해석되는 것은 any가 적절하다. all 뒤의 명사가 가산명사인 경우 명사는 복수명사가 되어야 한다.
정답 any

6
해석 축구와 경영은 별개다.
해설 'A와 B는 별개다'라는 의미가 전체 문맥과 어울리는데, 이는 「A is one thing, B is another」로 나타낸다.
어구 management 경영
A is one thing, B is another A와 B는 별개다
정답 another

7
해석 제발, 한 번 더 기회를 줘.
해설 others 자체가 명사기 때문에 뒤의 또 다른 명사(chance)를 수식할 수 없다. 또 다른 하나라는 의미가 되도록 another이 와야 한다.
어구 chance 기회
정답 another

8
해석 흑인의 피도 백인의 피와 마찬가지로 빨갛다.
해설 문맥은 흑인의 피와 백인의 피가 서로 비교되고 있다. 공통되는 피(blood)를 받을 수 있는 대명사는 that이다.
어구 negro 흑인, 흑인의
정답 that

9
해석 당신은 언제라도 올 수 있다.
해설 괄호 앞뒤의 어휘와 함께 '언제라도'라는 뜻의 올바른 표현은 at any time이다.
어구 at any time 언제라도
정답 any

10
해석 간접흡연은 담배를 피우지 않는 사람조차에게도 해를 끼칠 수 있다.
해설 괄호 뒤의 의문사 who와 함께 '~하는 사람들'이란 올바른 표현

은 those를 써서 those who로 나타낸다.

어구 second-hand smoke 간접흡연 harm 해를 끼치다

정답 those

PRACTICE

1

해석 A: 이제, 나는 내 돈을 되돌려 받기 원해.
B: 부디, 내게 일주일만 더 시간을 줘.

해설 빈 칸 뒤의 week과 함께 문맥상 또 다른 일주일이라는 의미가 되는 것은 보기 중 another로 표현할 수 있다.

어구 want A back A를 돌려받기 원하다

정답 (c)

2

해석 내 역할은 내 선임자의 역할보다 훨씬 더 크다.

해설 문맥상 역할(role)이라는 단어를 반복해야 하는 자리다. 수식어구(of 이하)의 수식을 받는 자리이므로 빈 칸에 들어갈 어휘는 (b) that이다.

어구 predecessor 전임자

정답 (b)

3

해석 A: 이 디지털 카메라는 정말 제값을 합니다.
B: 어떻게 작동하죠?
A: 전원을 켜서 푸른색 버튼을 눌러 사진을 찍으면 됩니다.
B: 예전에 가지고 있던 것보다 훨씬 단순하네요.

해설 (d)에서 it을 one으로 바꿔야 한다. it이 되면 바로 그 카메라라는 의미가 되어 문맥이 어색해진다. 같은 종류(카메라)라는 의미이므로 one이 적절하다.

어구 pay 지불하다 work (기기 등이) 작동하다; 일하다
turn on (전원을) 켜다 take a picture 사진을 찍다

정답 (d) the last it → the last one

4

해석 (a) 약 4000 컵의 커피가 세계에서 초 단위로 소비되고 있다. (b) 커피는 세계경제에서 두 번째로 중요한 상품이다. (c) 모든 미국인들의 절반이 커피 한 잔으로 하루를 시작한다. (d) 또한 모든 커피의 57%가 아침 식사 시간에 소비된다.

해설 (a)에서 문맥상 초 단위(매 초마다)라는 뜻이 되어야 하며 이는 any가 아닌 every로 표현한다.

어구 approximately 대략 consume 소비하다
valuable 중요한, 가치 있는 product 제품, 상품
global economy 세계경제

정답 (a) any second → every second

UNIT 7 전치사 I

EXERCISE

A
1 in
2 by[또는 on a]
3 at
4 during
5 by

B
1 on
2 at
3 by
4 on
5 in
6 in
7 through
8 on
9 for
10 in

PRACTICE

1 (c)   2 (a)   3 (b) on → in
4 (d) to → by

POINT

1 지구 표면의 고르지 못한 열이 바람을 일으킨다.

2 그것을 볼 수 있도록 한 주를 더 달라.

3 알렉스는 내게 이 문제를 알렸다.

4 나는 이 책을 2007년에 구입했다.

5 내 여동생은 Bank of America에서 근무한다.

6 나는 크리스마스에 항상 체중이 는다.

7 그는 한 시간 후에 돌아올 것이다.

8 나는 3일 동안 떠나 있을 것이다.

9 밤 동안 어떤 사건이 발생했다.

10 그는 밤새 TV를 켠 채로 두었다.

11 한 명의 경찰이 문에 서 있다.

12 그것들을 테이블 위에 다시 올려놔라.

13 방 안에는 유니폼을 입은 두 명의 경찰이 있었다.

14 나는 그녀가 일하고 있는 모습을 본 적이 없다.

15 그 기기는 사용 중이다.

16 그 건물은 공사 중이다.

EXERCISE A

ex

해석 폭탄은 공항에서 발견되었다.

해설 공항이라는 큰 공간 아래(under)라는 표현은 어색하다. 공항이라는 공간의 지점을 나타내는 at[in]으로 바꿔야 한다.

어구 bomb 폭탄

1

해석 운전자 옆의 박스 안에 돈이나 표를 넣으세요.

해설 문맥상 돈이나 표를 박스 안(in)에 넣는 것이지 박스 위(on)에 넣는 것이 아니므로 on을 in으로 바꿔야 한다.

정답 in

2

해석 버스로 이동하는 것은 칠레에서는 매우 흔한 일이다.

해설 교통편의 개념인 '버스로'라는 올바른 영어표현은 on bus가 아닌 on a bus다. 뒤에 관사(a)가 없으므로 대신 교통수단을 표시하는 by를 써야 한다. on을 by로 바꾸든지 on 뒤에 관사 a를 붙여야 한다.

어구 traveling 이동, 여행　common 흔한
　　　by bus 버스로(=on a bus)

정답 by[또는 on a]

3

해석 교차로에서 왼쪽으로 가라.

해설 with가 되면 교차로(crossroads)와 '함께'라는 의미가 되어 어색해진다. 교차로는 지점의 개념이므로 with를 at으로 바꿔야 한다.

어구 crossroads 교차로, 네거리

정답 at

4

해석 여름 동안에는 사무실이 너무 더워진다.

해설 문맥상 특정 시간(summer months) 동안이라는 의미는 일종의 기간의 의미이므로 when을 during으로 바꿔야 한다.

어구 get hot 더워지다, 뜨거워지다

정답 during

5

해석 이 소설은 한 교수에 의해 쓰였다.

해설 수동태 문장에서 (소설을 쓴) 주체는 전치사 by 뒤에 위치한다.

어구 novel 소설　professor 교수

정답 by

EXERCISE B

1

해석 그녀는 종이 한 장을 테이블 위에 남겨두었다.

해설 next가 위치를 나타내는 경우 '~옆에'라는 의미를 갖기 때문에 종이 한 장을 테이블 옆에 놓기보다는 위에(on) 둔다는 의미가 더 어울린다. 또한 next가 '옆의'라는 뜻의 장소를 나타내려면 전치사 to와 함께 next to가 되어야 한다.

어구 a piece of paper 종이 한 장

정답 on

2

해석 그들은 정오에 나를 데리러 왔다.

해설 전치사 at과 함께 '정오에'라는 올바른 영어표현은 at noon이다.

어구 pick A up A를 (차 등으로) 마중 나오다, 데리러 오다
　　　at noon 정오에

정답 at

3

해석 우리는 그곳에 기차로 가기로 결정했다.

해설 교통편의 '~편으로'는 영어에서 「by + 교통수단」으로 표현한다. 이 경우 특히 교통수단의 명사 앞에 관사를 붙이지 않는다는 것에 주의하자. 예를 들어, by a train은 틀린 표현이다.

정답 by

4

해석 내 생일에는 결코 비가 내리지 않는다.

해설 특정한 날 앞에는 전치사 on을 쓴다.

정답 on

5

해석 현재 세상에는 배고픈 사람들보다 과체중인 사람들이 더 많다.

해설 세상은 상대적으로 넓은 공간적 개념이므로 지점의 의미인 at이 아닌 in이 와야 한다.

어구 overweight 과체중인

정답 in

6

해석 그는 내 여동생과 사랑에 빠졌다.

해설 사랑(love)과 관련해서 '사랑에 빠진'이란 뜻의 올바른 영어표현은 be in love with someone으로 표현한다.

어구 be in love with A A와 사랑에 빠지다

정답 in

7

해석 배들이 터널을 통과해 견인되었다.

해설 터널(tunnel)은 특히 통과의 대상이 되므로 '~를 통과해서'라는 의미인 전치사 through가 문장에서 어울린다. between은 '둘 사이에서'라는 뜻으로 뒤는 두 개의 명사 또는 복수형 명사가 온다.

어구 tow 견인하다

정답 through

8

해석 나는 그가 바닥에 누워있는 것을 발견했다.

해설 바닥(floor) 위에(on) 누워있다는 표현이 어울린다. 전치사 from은 '출처'의 개념으로 문맥상 어울리지 않는다.

정답 on

9

해석 나는 잠시 그곳에 살았었다.

해설 명사 while과 함께 for a while은 '잠시 동안'이란 의미의 시간 표시 전치사구가 된다. 함께 어울리는 명사를 통해 for를 답으로 선택할 수 있다.

어구 for a while 잠시 동안

정답 for

10

해석 방안에는 많은 사람들이 있다.

해설 방(room)이라는 공간 안에 사람들이 모여 있다는 내용이므로 on
이 아닌 in이 되어야 한다.

정답 in

PRACTICE

1

해석 A: 박 씨와 통화할 수 있을까요?
B: 안타깝게도 그는 현재 점심 먹으러 외출했습니다.

해설 빈 칸 뒤의 명사 moment와 함께 at the moment는 '현재, 지금'
의 의미가 된다. 명사 moment를 통해 전치사 at을 답으로 선택
할 수 있다.

어구 be out to lunch 점심 먹으러 나가다
at the moment 현재, 지금

정답 (c)

2

해석 그는 그녀를 집에 홀로 남겨둔 것을 후회하고 있다.

해설 명사 home과 함께 '집에'라는 부사의 의미가 되게 하기 위해서는
전치사 at을 써서 at home으로 표현해야 한다.

어구 regret 후회하다   at home 집에   alone 홀로

정답 (a)

3

해석 A: 제인, 늦었구나.
B: 죄송해요. 몇 시간 동안 교통체증에 꼼짝 못했었거든요.
A: 우회로로 빠지지 않았었니? 시내에 퍼레이드가 있다고 들었는
데.
B: 퍼레이드가 있을 것이라는 것은 몰랐어요.

해설 '교통이 막힌'이라는 뜻의 올바른 영어표현은 stuck in traffic이
다. 따라서 on을 in으로 바꿔야 한다.

어구 stuck in traffic 교통이 막힌
take the detour 우회로로 가다   parade 퍼레이드, 행진

정답 (b) on → in

4

해석 (a) 소비되는 모든 커피의 90 퍼센트가 에스프레소다. (b) 미국에
서는 정반대다. (c) 모든 커피의 90 퍼센트가 라떼나 카푸치노의
형태에서 우유를 가미한 형태다. (d) 60 퍼센트 이상의 커피가 여
성에 의해 구매된다.

해설 (d)에서 구매의 주체가 여성(women)이라는 의미로 수동태로 표
현되고 있으므로 전치사 to를 by로 바꿔야 한다.

어구 consume 소비하다   reverse 역, 반대
mix A with B A를 B와 섞다   in the form of A A의 형태로
purchase 구매하다

정답 (d) to → by

UNIT 8 전치사(접속사 구별 포함) II

EXERCISE

A
1 Despite
2 the (two) tables
3 because
4 under
5 owing to[또는 due to, because of]

B
1 before
2 among
3 Even though
4 since
5 because
6 between
7 Although
8 among
9 under
10 since

PRACTICE

1 (d)   **2** (c)   **3** (b) because → because of
4 (a) over → since

POINT

1 그들은 구름 위로 날 수 있다.

2 일하는 데 있어서는 그는 나보다 앞선다.

3 개가 책상 아래에 있다.

4 노동 한계 생산성은 그 평균보다 낮다.

5 다리는 강 위에 있다.

6 이제 그녀는 쉰 살이 넘었다.

7 다리 아래로는 물이 거의 흐르지 않는다.

8 이 양식은 18세 이하의 학생들을 위한 것이다.

9 그가 5시에서 5시 반 사이에 당신에게 전화할 것이다.

10 두 주(州) 간의 갈등은 이제 끝이 나고 있다.

11 이탈리아에서는 배구가 소녀들 사이에서 인기가 있다.

12 얼마 기다리지 않아 그는 그녀가 오는 것을 봤다.

13 그녀는 엘리베이터 앞에 서 있었다.

14 나는 그가 15살 때부터 그를 알고 있었다.

15 내 개는 어제부터 아무것도 먹지 못했다.

16 비가 왔었음에도 불구하고, 우리는 좋은 시간을 보냈다.

17 비가 오는데도 불구하고 우리는 즐겁게 지냈다.

18 그는 몸이 좋지 않기 때문에 학교에 갈 수 없었다.

19 매니저는 날씨가 안 좋으니 우리에게 집에 가라고 통고했다.

EXERCISE A

ex

해석 그는 그녀가 아기였을 때부터 알아왔다.

해설 during은 전치사이기 때문에 뒤의 절을 이끌 수 없다. 문맥에서 밑줄 뒤의 시제가 과거이며 주절이 현재완료인 것을 통해 since가 적절함을 알 수 있다.

1

해석 궂은 날씨예보에도 불구하고 날씨는 좋았다.

해설 빈 칸 뒤는 명사로 제시되었기 때문에 접속사인 although를 despite로 바꿔야 한다.

어구 weather forecast 기상예보
turn out ~로 밝혀지다, 판명되다

정답 Despite

2

해석 깔개는 두 탁자 사이에 있다.

해설 between은 '~사이에서'라는 뜻으로 목적어는 대상이 되는 두 사물이 등장해야 한다. table을 the (two) tables로 바꿔야 한다.

어구 rug 깔개

정답 the (two) tables

3

해석 몸이 안 좋았기 때문에 나는 오늘 직장에 가지 않았다.

해설 due to는 전치사이기 때문에 뒤의 절을 받을 수 없다. due to를 because로 바꿔야 한다.

어구 sick 병든

정답 because

4

해석 당신이 '18세 이하'라면, 담배를 소지하는 것은 불법이다.

해설 문맥상 '18세 이하'라는 표현이 되어야 하는데, 일정 연령 '아래'는 below가 아닌 전치사 under로 표현한다.

어구 under the age of 18 18세 이하   illegal 불법의
possess 소지하다, 소유하다   tobacco 담배

정답 under

5

해석 경주는 궂은 날씨 때문에 취소되었다.

해설 문맥상 밑줄의 owing과 함께 '~ 때문에'가 되려면 전치사 to와 함께 owing to가 되어야 한다.

어구 race 경주   cancel 취소하다   owing to ~ 때문에

정답 owing to[또는 due to, because of]

EXERCISE B

1

해석 그는 벽 앞에 서있었다.

해설 between은 '둘 사이에서'라는 뜻이므로 뒤는 복수형 명사가 와야 한다. 뒤의 단수형 명사 앞에 before는 '~앞에'로 해석할 수 있으므로 before가 답이다.

정답 before

2

해석 이제 줄넘기는 소녀들 사이에서 인기가 있다.

해설 문맥상 둘 사이(between)가 아닌 셋 이상의 여럿을 뜻하기 때문에 among이 어울리는 답이다.

어구 rope-jumping 줄넘기   popular 인기 있는

정답 among

3

해석 내가 비록 어리기는 하지만, 인생에서 내가 뭘 원하는지는 안다.

해설 괄호 뒤에 주어와 동사를 갖춘 절이 왔으므로 전치사구인 in spite of가 아닌 절을 이끄는 even though가 되어야 한다.

어구 in spite of ~에도 불구하고

정답 Even though

4

해석 로라는 그녀가 유치원 다닐 때부터 걸 스카우트 멤버였다.

해설 괄호 뒤의 시제는 단순과거, 앞은 현재완료로 제시되었다. since가 시간을 나타낼 때 과거의 어느 시점에서 현재까지를 아우르는 시간의 추이를 나타내므로 이 문장에서 필요한 것은 접속사 since임을 알 수 있다.

어구 kindergarten 유치원

정답 since

5

해석 그들은 가난하기 때문에 배가 고프다.

해설 괄호 뒤가 주어와 동사를 갖춘 절의 구조가 나왔으므로 접속사 because를 답으로 선택할 수 있다.

정답 because

6

해석 그는 삶과 죽음 사이에서 선택해야 한다.

해설 between은 특히 둘 사이에서 쓸 수 있는 표현이므로 among이 아닌 between이 적절한 답이다.

어구 choose 선택하다
between life and death 삶과 죽음 사이에서

정답 between

7

해석 그가 나이가 있음에도 불구하고 그의 창조성은 여전히 강하고 신선하다.

해설 문맥은 '나이가 들었지만 ~하다'로 연결되므로 because가 아닌 although를 선택해야 한다.

어구 creativity 창조성   fresh 신선한

정답 Although

8

해석 그녀는 프랑스에서 (배출된) 첫 여성 시장(市長) 중 한 명이다.

해설 지정되지 않은 여러 명 사이에서는 전치사 among을 써야 한다.

어구 female 여성; 여성의   mayor 시장

정답 among

9

해석 그 버스 정류장은 다리 아래에 있다.

해설 전치사 among은 '여럿 사이에서'의 의미를 갖기 때문에 뒤의 단

수 명사 bridge는 올 수 없다. 문맥상 under the bridge가 어울리는 답이다.

어구 bus stop 버스 정류장   under the bridge 다리 아래에

정답 under

10

해석 내가 학교를 떠난 지 10년이 되었다.

해설 과거의 어느 시점(학교를 떠난 시점)이 현재까지 10년이 되었다는 의미이므로 시간 표현의 접속사 since를 답으로 선택할 수 있다.

어구 within (범위) 안에

정답 since

PRACTICE

1

해석 A: 당신 딸은 얼마나 오랫동안 이 같은 증상을 가져 왔나요?
　　B: 중학생 때부터요.

해설 질문은 증상(symtoms)을 가진 과거부터 현재까지의 기간을 묻고 있고 빈 칸 이후에 주어+동사(she was)로 연결되므로 접속사인 since가 답이다.

어구 symptom 증상   junior highschool 중학교

정답 (d)

2

해석 오후 11시가 가까웠지만 직원들은 우리를 반갑게 맞이해 주었다.

해설 빈 칸 뒤는 주어와 동사를 갖춘 절이 제시되고 있다. 보기 (c)를 제외한 나머지 보기는 모두 전치사로 제시되었다. 문장 역시 양보의 의미로 연결되고 있으므로 (c) although가 정답이다.

어구 greet 인사하다, 맞이하다   staff 직원   close 가까운

정답 (c)

3

해석 A: 무슨 문제니? 안색이 좋아 보이지 않는다.
　　B: 담배 연기 때문에.
　　A: 밖에 나가서 바람 좀 쐬고 오지 그래?
　　B: 그것 좋은 생각인데.

해설 (b)에서 the cigarette smoke가 명사이므로 because가 아닌 because of가 되어야 한다.

어구 cigarette smoke 담배연기

정답 (b) because → because of

4

해석 (a) 계속되는 비가 2007년 12월 이래로 볼리비아 북부지역에 내리고 있다. (b) 이것은 엄청난 홍수와 산사태를 야기시켰다. (c) 홍수는 적어도 30명의 사망자를 낳았다. (d) 또한 이 홍수는 30년 만에 볼리비아를 덮친 최악의 홍수로 불리고 있다.

해설 (a)의 over는 시간의 의미로 쓸 때 '~를 걸쳐'의 뜻으로 뒤로 기간의 의미가 나와야 한다. 따라서 over는 적절치 못하며 over 대신 뒤에 시점의 시간표현을 이끄는 since가 적절하나.

어구 persistent 지속되는   cause 야기 시키다
　　devastating 엄청난; 파괴하는   landslide 산사태
　　strike 강타하다

정답 (a) over → since

▎Chapter 5

EXERCISE

A
1 그와 나 모두 일본에서 공부를 하고 있었다.
2 한 번 비가 내렸는데도 여전히 덥다.
3 잠옷은 편안하면서 스타일도 있다.
4 그녀는 나뿐만 아니라 내 누이에게도 얘기했다.
5 새로운 디자인은 혁신적이면서도 독창적이다.

B
1 or
2 and
3 and
4 yet
5 or
6 nor
7 or
8 is
9 are
10 but also

PRACTICE

1 (d)　　2 (a)　　3 (c) because → but[yet]
4 (b) but → and

POINT

1 톰은 영리하지만 잘 생기지는 않았다.

2 그녀는 늦을 것이라고 말했지만 제 시간에 왔다.

3 그는 매우 부자이면서 유명하다.

4 그녀는 사과를 먹는 것을 좋아한다. 그래서 그녀를 위해 좀 샀다.

5 어떤 것이 더 좋나요, 고양이, 아니면 개?

6 많은 회사들이 은행에 이자를 내지 못했기 때문에 부도가 났다.

7 모든 지식이 과학은 아니며 가장 중요한 부분 또한 아니다.

8 열심히 공부해라. 그러면 합격할 것이다.

9 지금 전화하지 않으면 기회를 놓치게 될 것이다.

10 그와 나 모두 고아다.

11 나뿐만 아니라 내 동료들도 모두 매우 바쁘다.

12 그녀의 부모뿐만 아니라 그녀도 심장병을 가지고 있다.

13 그녀 또는 나 둘 중 한 명은 월요일에 파리에 갈 것이다.

14 그도 나도 그것에 대해서는 아무것도 모른다.

15 그 집은 이국적이기도 하고 편안하기도 하다.

EXERCISE A

1

정답 그와 나 모두 일본에서 공부를 하고 있었다.

2

어구 once 한때

정답 한 번 비가 내렸는데도 여전히 덥다.

3

어구 nightgown 잠옷
at once A and B A하기도 하고 B하기도 한
comfortable 편안한

정답 잠옷은 편안하면서 스타일도 있다.

4

정답 그녀는 나뿐만 아니라 내 누이에게도 얘기했다.

5

어구 innovative 혁신적인   original 독창적인

정답 새로운 디자인은 혁신적이면서도 독창적이다.

EXERCISE B

1

해석 지금 네가 떠나지 않으면, 버스를 놓칠 것이다.

해설 올바른 접속사는 or다. '~하지 않으면 ~하다'라는 의미로 연결되는 or가 문맥상 자연스럽다.

정답 or

2

해석 그는 매우 부자이면서 또한 미혼이다.

해설 적절한 접속사를 선택해야 하는데 형태상 although는 뒤에 주어를 생략하고 동사(is)를 바로 쓸 수 없다. 반면 and는 주어가 같은 경우 주어를 생략하고 동사를 바로 쓸 수 있는 접속사이므로 형태만으로도 and를 답으로 선택할 수 있다.

정답 and

3

해석 나뿐만 아니라 내 동료들은 매우 협조적이며 도움이 된다.

해설 and는 형태뿐만 아니라 의미까지도 서로 관련 있는 것끼리 병렬로 연결시키는 접속사다. 문맥상 협조적인(cooperative) 것과 도움이 되는(helpful) 것은 순접관계로 연결되므로 and가 적절하다.

어구 colleague 동료   cooperative 협조적인

정답 and

4

해석 그는 매우 똑똑하지만 부끄러움을 탄다.

해설 똑똑한(smart) 것과 부끄러워하는(shy) 것은 문맥상 서로 상반된다. 따라서 yet이 이 둘을 연결하는 자연스러운 접속사로 적절하다.

어구 shy 부끄러워하는

정답 yet

5

해석 어떤 것이 더 좋으니, 야구, 아니면 축구?

해설 둘 중 더 좋은 것을 묻고 있는 질문으로 A or B, 즉, A 아니면 B로 연결시키는 or가 적절한 답이다. nor는 부정으로 연결하기 때문에 문맥상 어울리지 않다.

정답 or

6

해석 나는 3일 동안 먹지도 마시지도 않을 것이다.

해설 neither A nor B의 상관접속사 형태를 묻고 있다. 'A도 B도 아니다'라는 뜻의 이 상관접속사를 통해 nor를 답으로 선택할 수 있다.

어구 neither A nor B A도 B도 아닌

정답 nor

7

해석 지금 가져라, 그렇지 않으면 기회를 놓칠 것이다.

해설 문맥상 '~하라 그렇지 않으면 ~할 것이다'로 연결될 때 자연스러운데 이와 같은 의미로 연결시키는 접속사는 or다.

정답 or

8

해석 글로리아의 부모뿐만 아니라 그녀도 다음 달에 뉴욕으로 떠날 것이다.

해설 A as well as B는 'B뿐만 아니라 A도'라는 뜻으로 동사의 수는 A에 맞춰야 한다. A는 3인칭 단수 명사(Gloria)이므로 동사는 is가 옳다.

어구 A as well as B B뿐만 아니라 A도   leave for A A로 떠나다

정답 is

9

해석 아버지와 어머니 모두 재능 있는 음악가다.

해설 both A and B(A와 B 모두)로 연결되면 동사는 복수형이 된다.

어구 both A and B A와 B 모두   talented 재능 있는
musician 음악가

정답 are

10

해석 그는 현금보너스를 받았을 뿐만 아니라 (옵션 등으로) 토지 또한 받았다.

해설 not only A but also B구문을 묻고 있다. 함께 짝을 이루는 상관접속사를 통해 but also를 답으로 선택할 수 있다.

어구 not only A but also B A뿐만 아니라 B도   receive 받다
grant 하사; 인가; 수여

정답 but also

PRACTICE

1

해석 A: 금연하는 게 어때?
B: 나도 노력했지. 하지만 습관을 끊기가 정말 쉽지 않아.

해설 상반되는 빈 칸 앞뒤의 문맥을 통해 (d) But이 적절한 접속사임을 알 수 있다.

어구 quit smoking 금연하다   tough 힘든

kick a habit 습관을 버리다

정답 (d)

2

해석 그는 그의 다리가 부러졌을 뿐만 아니라 손목 또한 삐었다.

해설 not only A but also B 구문에서 (a) as well이 but 뒤의 also를 대신할 수도 있다. 이를 통해 '~도 또한'이란 의미로 연결시키는 (a)를 답으로 선택할 수 있다. 이때 but 뒤의 also는 생략할 수 있으며 as well은 문장 뒤에 보통 쓴다.

어구 sprain 삐다　wrist 손목

정답 (a)

3

해석 A: 주문하시겠어요?
B: 못 고르겠어요. 추천 좀 해주실래요?
A: 오늘의 스페셜은 해물요리입니다만 저는 신선한 모차렐라를 넣은 닭가슴살구이 요리를 추천하고 싶습니다.
B: 좋아요. 그것으로 주문할게요.

해설 (c)에서 because는 대등접속사 역할을 할 수 없다. 문맥상 오늘의 요리와 별개로 추천한다는 뜻으로 연결되므로 because를 but[yet]으로 바꿔야 한다.

정답 (c) because → but[yet]

4

해석 (a) 네가 소통하는 방식은 사람들과 어울리는 네 능력에 큰 영향을 끼친다. (b) 훌륭한 의사소통 능력은 갈등을 피하고 문제를 해결할 수 있도록 도울 수 있다. (c) 개방되고 솔직한 소통은 또한 친구를 사귀거나 건전한 관계를 갖도록 하는 데 중요하다. (d) 문제는 우리가 생각하는 것을 다른 사람들이 알 것이라고 단순히 가정하는데 있다.

해설 (b) but을 and로 바꿔야 한다. 문맥상 갈등(conflict)을 피하는 것이 문제를 해결하는 순접관계로 연결되기 때문이다.

어구 way 방법; 길　　　communicate 소통하다
impact 충격　　　ability 능력
get along with A A와 사이좋게 지내다; A와 일치하다
make friends 친구를 사귀다
relationship 관계　　　assume 가정하다

정답 (b) but → and

EXERCISE

A

1　I don't know when the artist carved the stone.
2　I'm not sure if she will stay in France.
3　I don't know whether to laugh or cry.
4　Do you know when the train leaves?
5　We must accept the fact that Mark is no longer alive.

B

1　whether
2　that
3　that
4　when
5　that
6　that
7　whether
8　that
9　whether
10　That

PRACTICE

1 (a)　　2 (b)
3 (a) what you think → what do you think
4 (d) whether may any special services be →
whether any special services may be

POINT

1　내 부모는 내가 무신론자라는 사실을 용납하지 않을 것이다.

2　그녀가 성공하리라 믿는다.

3　말하고자 하는 바는 일 하는 데 있어서 좀 더 효과적인 방법을 찾아야 한다는 것이다.

4　그녀가 나를 좋아하는지 아닌지를 모르겠다.

5　그녀가 파티에 참석할지의 여부는 내게 중요하다.

6　웃어야 할지 울어야 할지 모르겠다.

7　내가 원하는 것은 당신뿐이다.

8　이것이 내가 원하는 것이다.

9　그녀의 부인이 언제 아팠는지를 기억하나요?

10　그녀가 원하는 것을 아시나요?

11　새장 속의 새가 왜 노래하는지 모르겠다.

12　그녀는 내가 그것을 봤었는지를 물었다.

13　이것이 프린트가 될지 안 될지 모르겠다.

14　그녀가 나를 좋아하는지는 확실하지 않다.

EXERCISE A

ex

해석 나는 그가 담배를 피웠는지 물었다.

해설 if 뒤의 어순이 잘못되었다. 주어 동사의 어순이 바뀔 이유가 없다. did he smoke를 he smoked로 바꿔야 한다.

1

해석 나는 그 예술가가 언제 그 돌을 조각했는지 모르겠다.

해설 간접의문문의 올바른 어순은 의문사 뒤 주어, 동사가 순서대로 나오는 것이다.

정답 I don't know when the artist carved the stone.

2

해석 그녀가 프랑스에 머무를지 나는 확신하지 못한다.

해설 목적절을 이끄는 if절이 문장 내에 삽입된 구조로 올바른 어순은 if she will~로 연결되는 것이다.

어구 stay 머물다

정답 I'm not sure if she will stay in France.

3

해석 나는 웃어야 할지 울어야 할지 모르겠다.

해설 '~할지 말지'라는 뜻을 가진 if 뒤에는 to부정사 형태가 올 수 없다. if를 whether로 바꿔 써야 한다. whether 뒤에는 to부정사가 올 수 있기 때문이다.

정답 I don't know whether to laugh or cry.

4

해석 기차가 언제 출발하는지 아니?

해설 간접의문문에서 의문사 뒤의 어순은 「주어 + 동사」순으로 바뀐다.

정답 Do you know when the train leaves?

5

해석 우리는 마크가 더 이상 살아있지 않다는 사실을 인정해야 한다.

해설 the fact와 뒤의 절은 동격으로 연결되고 있다. 동격의 절을 연결하는 접속사는 that이다. 이를 if로 대신할 수는 없다.

정답 We must accept the fact that Mark is no longer alive.

EXERCISE B

1

해석 그녀는 그녀가 파티에 참석할지 여부를 결정해야 한다.

해설 타동사 decide 뒤이므로 뒤의 절은 목적절이 되어야 한다. 관계대명사 what도 목적절을 이끌 수는 있지만 what 뒤는 문장이 불완전해야 한다. 문맥상 '~인지 아닌지'로 연결하는 whether이 적절하다.

어구 attend 참석하다

정답 whether

2

해석 문제는 그가 믿을 만한 사람이 아니라는 것이다.

해설 be동사의 보어가 필요하다. 보어가 되는 절을 이끌 수 있는 접속사는 if가 아닌 that이다.

어구 credible 믿을 만한

정답 that

3

해석 나는 그녀가 성공하리라 생각한다.

해설 what이 이끄는 문장은 필수 문장성분이 빠진 불완전한 문장이 된다. what 안에 (대)명사를 포함하고 있기 때문이다. 두 문장을 연결하는 접속사 that이 정답이다.

어구 successful 성공적인

정답 that

4

해석 우리가 탈 비행기가 언제 출발하는지 아니?

해설 문맥상 누구(who)가 아닌 비행기와 관련해 언제(when)가 괄호 안에 필요하다.

어구 flight 비행(편)기

정답 when

5

해석 우리는 그가 다시 올 것이라고 믿는다.

해설 believe가 타동사이므로 뒤의 절을 목적절로 이끄는 접속사가 필요하다. if가 목적절을 이끄는 경우 '~인지 아닌지'로 해석되기 때문에 if와 특히 동사 believe와는 문장에서 어울리지 않는다. '믿다(believe)'와 어울리는 접속사는 that이다.

정답 that

6

해석 문제는 그가 돈이 없다는 것이다.

해설 be동사의 보어절을 이끌 수 있는 적절한 접속사는 that이다. what이 이끄는 문장은 불완전하기 때문에 what은 구조상 답이 될 수 없다.

정답 that

7

해석 네가 나를 믿는지 안 믿는지를 모르겠다.

해설 의문사 who는 문장 속에서 주어나 목적어 역할을 하는데 보기에서는 주어와 목적어가 있으므로 '~인지 아닌지'로 해석되는 whether이 문맥상 어울린다.

정답 whether

8

해석 사실은 그가 현지어를 모른다는 것이다.

해설 문맥은 '~인지 아닌지'로 해석되는 것이 아닌 '~하는 것'으로 해석되기 때문에 if가 아닌 that이 되어야 한다.

어휘 local 지역의, 지방의, 토속의

정답 that

9

해석 나는 너의 메시지를 믿어야 할지 아닐지를 모르겠다.

해설 뒤의 to부정사와 함께 문장에서 '~할지'로 해석되도록 하는 접속사는 whether이다. if는 뒤에 to부정사와 함께 쓸 수 없다.

어구 trust 믿다

정답 whether

10

해석 그녀가 회의에 참석하는 것은 확실하다.

해설 한 문장에 두 개의 동사(attend, is)가 있다. 따라서 접속사가 필요한데 what은 뒤의 문장이 불완전해야 하므로 구조상 that이 적절한 접속사다.

어구 attend 참석하다　meeting 회의　certain 확실한

정답 That

PRACTICE

1

해석 A: 문제가 뭐니?
B: 문제는 그가 청각에 문제가 있다는 것을 인정하지 않으려 한다는 거야.

해설 주어 the problem 뒤에는 be동사의 보어절을 이끄는 접속사가 필요하다. (b) therefore는 접속부사로 명사절의 접속사 역할은 할 수 없다. (c) if는 명사절을 이끌 때 목적어로만 쓰이며 (d) what은 뒤의 문장이 불완전해야 한다.

어구 admit 인정하다　hearing problem 청각 문제

정답 (a)

2

해석 당신이 좋건 싫건 당신은 교회에 예배보러 가야 한다.

해설 「whether A or not」은 'A하건 아니건'의 뜻으로 이때 문맥과의 연결도 자연스럽다. 따라서 (b)를 답으로 선택할 수 있다.

어구 go to church 예배보러 가다

정답 (b)

3

해석 A: 이 카메라의 문제점이 무엇이라고 생각하시나요?
B: 제 생각에 배터리가 다 나간 것 같네요.
A: 그것을 고치는 데 얼마나 걸릴까요?
B: 몇 분이면 됩니다.

해설 (a)에서 what you think를 what do you think로 바꿔야 한다. 전체 문장은 의문사 what으로 시작하는 직접의문문이므로 일반동사의 의문문 형태인 do~의 형태를 취해야 한다. 이처럼 직접의문문일때 어순이 바뀌지 않는다는 점을 기억해 두자.

어구 run out of ~이 다 소진되다, 써버리다　repair 고치다

정답 (a) what you think → what do you think

4

해석 (a) 회의 기획자는 참석자가 참석할지 여부와 어떻게 참석할지에 대해 결정해야 한다. (b) 만일 참석자가 예상되는데, 너무 많은 사람들이 발표를 한다고 하면 어떻게 될까? (c) 가능한 많은 사람들에게 발표할 수 있는 기회를 주고자 기획자는 보통 발표자의 시간을 제한한다. (d) 기획자들은 또한 어떤 특별한 서비스, 예를 들어 시청각 기기나 통역자가 필요할지도 고려해야 한다.

해설 (d)에서 whether may any special services be를 whether any special services may be로 바꿔야 한다. whether이하의 문장은 consider의 목적어가 되는 간접의문문이므로 주어+동사의 어순이 되어야 한다.

어구 planner 기획자　audience 청중
participate 참석하다　make a speech 발표하다
limit 한계를 정하다
audio-visual equipment 시청각 기기
interpreter 통역사

정답 (d) whether may any special services be →
whether any special services may be

UNIT 3　부사절을 이끄는 접속사 I

EXERCISE

A

1 우리가 방에 도착했을 때, 방은 여전히 엉망이었다.
2 나는 그녀가 열심히 일하기 때문에 그녀를 좋아한다.
3 내가 고등학교 다닐 때부터 한국에 대해 많은 관심을 가져왔다.
4 그는 퇴직할 때까지 뉴욕에 머물렀다.
5 겨울이 끝날 때까지 난 기다릴 것이다.

B

1 since
2 until
3 after
4 until
5 While
6 because
7 because
8 After
9 Since
10 until

PRACTICE

1 (b)　　2 (a)　　3 (d) as soon as → until
4 (a) since → when

POINT

1 우리가 (쇼핑)몰을 떠난 후에, 호텔로 돌아왔다.
2 오래 기다린 후에야 그녀가 왔다.
3 우리가 해변에 도착했을 때, 보트는 여전히 도착하지 않았다.
4 퇴근 후 TV를 보는 동안 그는 보통 집에서 술을 마셨다.
5 나는 어렸을 때부터 구름을 좋아했다.
6 내 형은 그가 퇴직할 때까지 정형외과 의사였다.
7 당신이 돌아올 때쯤이면, 우리는 당신 차를 고쳐놓게 될 것이다.
8 내 여자 친구에게 전화할 때마다 그녀는 항상 통화 중이다.
9 일단 네가 시작하면 멈출 수 없다.
10 약속을 지킬 수 없을 것 같으면 바로 전화해라.
11 나는 그가 영리하기 때문에 그를 존경한다.
12 돈이 관련되었기 때문에 신뢰는 매우 중요하다.
13 회사의 구매력은 회사가 성장하니 점점 좋아진다.

EXERCISE A

ex

어구 friendly 친절한　others 다른 사람들

1

어구 arrive 도착하다　mess 엉망, 지저분함

정답 우리가 방에 도착했을 때, 방은 여전히 엉망이었다.

2

정답 나는 그녀가 열심히 일하기 때문에 그녀를 좋아한다.

3

어구 have a interest in A A에 관심이 있다

정답 내가 고등학교 다닐 때부터 한국에 대해 많은 관심을 가져왔다.

4

어구 stay 머물다　retire 퇴직하다

정답 그는 퇴직할 때까지 뉴욕에 머물렀다.

5

정답 겨울이 끝날 때까지 난 기다릴 것이다.

EXERCISE B

1

해석 나는 어렸을 때부터 곰을 좋아했다.

해설 '~이래로 죽'이라는 뜻의 접속사가 문맥과 어울린다. 또한 since 절의 동사는 과거이고 주절은 과거완료의 시제 형태를 취한다는 것을 통해서도 since가 답임을 알 수 있다.

정답 since

2

해석 땅이 물에 젖을 때까지 물을 부어라.

해설 땅이 물에 젖기 때문에(because) 물을 준다는 것은 맞지 않다. '~까지'라고 해석되는 until이 문맥상 적절하다.

어구 water 물을 주다; 물　soil 흙　get wet 젖다

정답 until

3

해석 그는 우리가 집을 떠난 직후에 병이 났다.

해설 in case of는 전치사로 뒤에는 명사상당어구만이 올 수 있다. 괄호 뒤에 절이 이어지므로 접속사 after가 답이다. soon after는 '~직후'로 해석할 수 있다.

어구 be sickened 병나다　in case of ~인 경우에

정답 after

4

해석 그가 퇴직할 때까지 기다리겠다.

해설 괄호 뒤가 절의 구조이므로 접속사가 필요하다. 문맥으로도 접속사 until이 어울린다.

어구 retire 퇴직하다

정답 until

5

해석 마이크가 TV를 보는 동안, 나는 사과를 먹었다.

해설 문맥을 통해 while을 답으로 선택할 수 있다. if가 부사절을 이끌면 조건의 의미가 되어 문맥이 어색해진다.

정답 While

6

해석 그가 훌륭한 배우기 때문에 난 그를 좋아한다.

해설 due to는 전치사로 뒤에 명사 상당어구만이 올 수 있다. 괄호 뒤가 절로 이어지므로 접속사인 because가 옳다.

어구 due to ~때문에　actor 배우

정답 because

7

해석 제시카가 거짓말쟁이기 때문에 나는 그녀가 싫다.

해설 as soon as는 '~하자마자'라는 뜻으로 문맥과는 어울리지 않는다. '~때문에'로 연결될 때 자연스러우므로 because가 답이다.

어구 as soon as ~하자마자　liar 거짓말쟁이

정답 because

8

해석 우리가 공원을 떠난 후에 우린 Lindy's로 (음식을) 먹으로 갔다.

해설 that이 접속사의 역할을 하기는 하지만 문장을 이끌어 전체 문장의 주절을 이끄는 경우 이 문장이 주어절이 되어 절 뒤는 바로 동사로 연결되어야 한다. that절 이후 동사로 연결되는 것이 아닌 또 다른 절로 연결되기 때문에 that은 올 수 없다. 문맥상 '~이후'로 해석되는 after가 적절하다.

정답 After

9

해석 나는 어렸을 때부터 글 쓰는 것을 좋아했다.

해설 since가 '~이래로 죽'이라는 뜻의 접속사 역할을 할 때 주절의 시제는 현재완료가 된다. 문맥상으로 '~때문'이 아닌 '~이래로'로 연결될 때 자연스러우므로 since가 답이다.

정답 Since

10

해석 나는 그가 문을 닫을 때까지 숨을 참았다.

해설 although는 양보의 의미로 절을 연결하는 접속사다. 문맥상 '~까지'의 의미인 until이 답으로 어울린다.

어구 hold one's breath 숨을 참다

정답 until

PRACTICE

1

해석 A: 왜 그렇게 바쁘니?
　　　 B: 오늘 아침에 알람이 울리지 않아 직장에 늦었어.

해설 문맥을 통해 적절한 접속사를 선택할 수 있는데 알람이 울리지 않은 것이 직장에 늦은 이유가 될 수 있으므로 because를 답으로 선택할 수 있다.

어구 in a hurry 바쁜　alarm 알람　go off (알람이) 울리다

정답 (b)

2

해석 그녀가 저녁을 먹는 동안 결국 난 인터뷰를 했다.

해설 일시적인 동작(저녁을 먹는 동안)인 '동안(while)' 인터뷰를 했다

는 뜻이므로 (a) while이 문맥상 어울리는 답이다.

어구 make the interview 인터뷰하다

정답 (a)

3

해석 A: 집에 열쇠를 둔 채 문을 잠갔네.
B: 여분의 열쇠를 가지고 있지 않니?
A: 내 아내가 모든 열쇠를 가지고 있어. 그래도 다행히 그녀가 이리로 오고 있어.
B: 다행이네. 그럼 그녀가 올 때까지 기다리자.

해설 (d)에서 as soon as는 '~하자마자'라는 뜻인데 문맥과 전혀 어울리지 않는다. 대화의 흐름상 as soon as를 '~까지'라는 뜻의 until로 바꿔야 한다.

어구 lock oneself out of A A에 열쇠를 (안에) 두고 잠그다
extra 여분의   fortunately 다행히
on the way 오고 있는   that's a relief 다행이다

정답 (d) as soon as → until

4

해석 (a) 내가 도착했을 때 사라는 이미 그곳에 있었고 우리는 한 시간 동안 담소를 나눴다. (b) 레베카는 사라가 떠난 바로 직후에 도착했다. (c) 그곳은 작은 공항이었지만 그나마 몇몇 작은 상점들은 있었다. (d) 레베카는 우산이 공짜로 딸려오는 잡지를 구입했다.

해설 (a)에서 since가 접속사로 쓰이는 경우 '~ 때문에'와 '~이래로 죽'이라는 두 가지 의미로 쓰이게 된다. 모두 문맥과 어울리지 않는데 특히 '~이래로 죽'이라는 뜻으로 쓰이는 경우 의미상 과거의 어느 시점부터 현재까지의 시점을 아우르기 때문에 주절의 동사는 현재완료 시제가 된다. 모두 어울리지 않으므로 since를 when으로 바꿔야 한다.

어구 tiny 작은

정답 (a) since → when

UNIT 4 부사절을 이끄는 접속사 II

EXERCISE

A
1 태양이 타는 듯했지만, 날씨는 그렇게 덥지 않았다.
2 아무도 들을 수 없도록 그는 내게 속삭인다.
3 네가 만일 이 드레스를 입는다면 너를 위해 사 주겠다.
4 그가 나보다 덩치가 더 컸지만 우리는 형제처럼 레슬링을 하곤 했다.
5 만일 불만사항이 있으시면, 온라인 불만 접수 양식을 이용해 주세요.

B
1 Although
2 Whether
3 if
4 even though
5 If
6 unless
7 so
8 Although
9 lest
10 so that

PRACTICE

1 (a)   2 (d)   3 (d) Now that → Although
4 (a) such → so

POINT

1 만일 그녀가 과체중이면 어떻게 해야 하지?

2 집에 불이 나지 않은 한 서로에게 고함지르지 마라.

3 태양이 밝게 빛났는데도 불구하고 물은 차가웠다.

4 그는 부상을 입었음에도 불구하고 치열한 전투를 견뎌냈다.

5 그것이 거짓일지라도 뭐든 말해라.

6 네가 좋건 싫건 너는 그룹의 구성원이다.

7 너는 너무 말이 빨라 내가 따라갈 수가 없다.

8 너무 훌륭한 공연이어서 그녀는 자신의 학생들을 데리고 와서 관람시키고 싶었다.

9 우리가 너를 볼 수 있도록 돌아와라.

10 잭은 전화벨이 울리는 소리를 놓치지 않기 위해 라디오 소리를 줄였다.

정답 및 해설 **45**

EXERCISE A

ex

어구 copy machine 복사기　　fix 고치다, 수리하다

1

어구 burning 뜨거운, 타는듯한

정답 태양이 타는 듯했지만, 날씨는 그렇게 덥지 않았다.

2

어구 whisper 속삭이다

정답 아무도 들을 수 없도록 그는 내게 속삭인다.

3

정답 네가 만일 이 드레스를 입는다면 너를 위해 사 주겠다.

4

어구 wrestle 레슬링하다

정답 그가 나보다 덩치가 더 컸지만 우리는 형제처럼 레슬링을 하곤 했다.

5

어구 complaint 불만사항　　form 양식

정답 만일 불만사항이 있으시면, 온라인 불만 접수 양식을 이용해주세요.

EXERCISE B

1

해석 비록 그녀가 영리하기는 하지만 그녀와 어울리기는 쉽지 않다.

해설 문맥은 괄호 뒤의 절과 콤마(,) 뒤의 절이 의미상 상반되게 연결되고 있으므로 양보절을 이끄는 although가 어울리는 접속사다.

어구 get along with A A와 잘 지내다

정답 Although

2

해석 당신이 좋건 싫건, 현재의 담당자는 당신이다.

해설 괄호 뒤의 ~or not과 함께 '~이건 아니건'이란 양보 구문으로 연결되는 whether이 답이다.

어구 in charge 담당인

정답 Whether

3

해석 커피 등 원하는 것이 있으시면 제 비서에게 요청하세요.

해설 so는 결과 또는 목적의 의미로 연결하는 접속사인데 문맥상 적절치 못하다. 조건의 if가 자연스럽게 어울린다.

어구 secretary 비서

정답 if

4

해석 비록 부상을 입었지만 그는 살아남았다.

해설 문맥은 부상을 입었지만 살아남은 것이므로 even though가 적절한 접속사다.

어구 survive 살아남다　　wounded 부상을 입은

정답 even though

5

해석 괜찮으시면 시스템에 대한 피드백을 요청하고 싶습니다.

해설 unless는 if~ not의 의미로 unless가 이끄는 절에는 또 다른 부정의 부사 not이 들어갈 수 없다. 부정이 중복되기 때문이다.

어구 mind 꺼리다　　ask for 요청하다　　feedback 피드백, 반응

정답 If

6

해석 용기는 정의가 동반되지 않으면 가치가 없다.

해설 '~이 동반되지 않으면'이란 뜻인 unless accompanied by를 덩어리째로 암기해두자. 이때 문맥과도 어울린다.

어구 courage 용기　　of value 가치 있는(=valuable)
unless accompanied by ~이 동반되지 않으면

정답 unless

7

해석 너무 추워서 우리는 겨울 재킷을 입었다.

해설 such의 품사는 형용사로 수식할 수 있는 품사는 명사다. 뒤는 형용사인 cold가 제시되었으므로 부사인 so를 써야 한다.

어구 「so[such] ~ that S + V」 너무 ~해서 ~(that이하)하다

정답 so

8

해석 이제 다섯 살이기는 하지만, 그녀는 4개 국어를 한다.

해설 '나이는 적지만 ~할 수 있다'라는 상반관계로 연결되므로 양보의 접속사 although가 적절하게 문장을 연결하는 접속사다.

정답 Although

9

해석 제임스는 그녀의 도착을 놓치지 않기 위해 톰으로 하여금 다른 방향을 계속 주시토록 했다.

해설 lest는 '~하지 않도록'의 의미로 쓰인다. 문맥상 이때 자연스럽게 문장이 해석되므로 lest가 답이다.

어구 direction 방향

정답 lest

10

해석 나는 다소 귀를 먹게 되어서 발표자의 발표를 명확히 듣는 데 어려움이 있었다.

해설 앞 내용이 원인이 되어 뒤의 결과를 낳는 것이므로 결과를 나타내는 「so that~」 구문이 어울린다.

어구 somewhat 다소　　deaf 귀가 먼
speaker 연설자, 발표자　　clearly 명확히

정답 so that

PRACTICE

1

해석 A: 괜찮으시면, 프로젝트에 대해 몇 가지 질문을 하고 싶습니다.
B: 물론이죠, 질문하세요.

해설 문장과 문장을 연결하므로 접속사가 필요한데, 보기는 모두 접속사로 제시되었다. 문맥상 '~하면'이라는 의미로 연결되므로 (a) If가 적절한 접속사다.

어구 mind 꺼리다　　go ahead 어서 하세요

정답 (a)

2

해석 네가 좋건 싫건, 우리의 세계는 컴퓨터 기술로 인해 다시 만들어지고 있다.

해설 뒤의 or not을 통해 (d) Whether를 답으로 선택할 수 있다. 『whether ~ or not』은 '~인지의 여부'의 뜻으로 이때 문맥으로도 어울린다.

어구 reshape 다시 만들다, 다시 구성하다

정답 (d)

3

해석 A: 그가 정말 그녀를 사랑한다고 생각하니?
B: 응, 그렇게 생각해.
A: 하지만 그녀는 인종도 다르다고 하던데.
B: 사실이긴 하지만, 그는 정말 그녀를 아끼는 것 같아.

해설 (d)의 Now that이 잘못되었다. now that은 '~이니까'란 뜻이기 때문에 대화상 어울리지 않는다. 문맥상 Although로 바꿔야 한다.

어구 race 인종   care for ~를 아끼다

정답 (d) Now that → Although

4

해석 (a) 정상은 너무 추웠기 때문에 1박을 더 할 수가 없었다. (b) 다음날 이른 아침에 우리는 차로 내려왔다. (c) 내려오는 중에 사실 우리는 여기저기를 달렸다. (d) 무릎높이의 눈 속을 달리는 것은 너무나 신나는 일이었다.

해설 (a)에서 such를 so로 바꿔야 한다. 뒤의 cold라는 형용사는 형용사인 such가 수식할 수 없다.

어구 at the top 정상에서   stay 머물다
on the way down 내려오는 길에
basically 사실, 기본적으로
in places 여기저기에   knee-deep 무릎높이의

정답 (a) such → so

EXERCISE

A
1 which[that]
2 whose
3 whom[that]
4 whom[that]
5 whose

B
1 which
2 whose
3 that
4 whom
5 who
6 which
7 whom
8 whose
9 who
10 which

PRACTICE

1 (a)   2 (b)   3 (c) whom → whose
4 (a) that → which

POINT

1 우편배달부는 편지와 소포를 배달하는 사람이다.

2 이 사람이 당신에게 칵테일을 살 사람이다.

3 작년에 당신이 출간한 책을 볼 수 있을까요?

4 우리 집 앞에 한 여자가 서 있다.

5 나는 앤디 킴이라는 이름의 한 남자를 알고 있다.

6 이 사람이 내가 정말 아끼는 여자다.

7 내가 사랑하는 여자는 런던 출신이다.

8 내가 장미를 주었던 소녀를 봤다.

9 그에게서 장미를 받은 여자는 매우 기뻐했다.

10 그는 내게 독일어로 얘기했는데, 독일어는 내가 이해할 수 없는 언어다.

EXERCISE A

ex

해석 어제 만난 여자는 내 여자친구다.

해설 관계대명사는 타동사 met의 목적어가 되는 명사를 대신하고 있다. 따라서 who를 목적격 관계대명사 whom으로 바꿔야 한다.

1

해석 나는 앤지라고 불리는 개를 가지고 있다.

해설 be동사 앞은 주어 자리이므로 목적격 whom이 아닌 주격의

which[that]로 바꿔야 한다.

어구 call ~라고 부르다

정답 which[that]

2

해석 나는 한 여자를 알고 있는데 그녀의 어머니는 수의사다.

해설 뒤의 명사 mother를 수식하는 자리이므로 주격의 who가 아닌 소유격 whose가 되어야 한다.

어구 veterinarian 수의사(줄여서 vet이라고 하기도 함)

정답 whose

3

해석 정직하다고 생각했던 그 신사가 나를 배신했다.

해설 동사 thought의 목적어가 the gentleman이므로 목적격 관계대명사가 필요하다. who를 whom으로 바꿔야 한다.

어구 honest 정직한   betray 배신하다, 속이다

정답 whom[that]

4

해석 내게서 선물을 받은 그 남자는 행복해했다.

해설 동사 gave는 수여동사로 간접목적어와 직접목적어 둘을 취하는 동사다. 문장에서 간접목적어인 the man이 앞으로 나가 목적어 자리가 비어 있으므로 who를 목적격 관계대명사 whom으로 바꿔야 한다.

정답 whom[that]

5

해석 저분의 아버지는 영화감독이다.

해설 뒤의 명사 father 앞에 위치해 명사(father)를 수식하는 자리이므로 which를 소유대명사 whose로 바꿔야 한다.

어구 film director 영화감독

정답 whose

EXERCISE B

1

해석 폭력은 또 다른 폭력을 낳고 그 폭력은 더 많은 폭력을 낳는다.

해설 괄호 뒤의 creates는 동사이므로 동사 앞 주격 관계대명사가 필요한 자리다. 따라서 주격인 which가 적절한 답이다.

어구 violence 폭력   create 만들다, 창조하다

정답 which

2

해석 한 숙녀를 만났는데 그녀의 이름을 기억할 수가 없다.

해설 괄호는 명사 name 앞에 있으므로 소유격 관계대명사인 whose 가 와야 할 자리다.

정답 whose

3

해석 이것이 내가 말했던 다리다.

해설 괄호는 모두 목적격으로 제시되었다. 하지만 선행사가 사람이 아닌 사물(bridge)이므로 whom이 아닌 that을 답으로 선택해야 한다.

정답 that

4

해석 내가 말을 걸었던 남자는 매니저였다.

해설 동사 speaking이 누군가에게 말을 건다는 의미로 쓰일 때는 자동사로 쓰였기 때문에 전치사가 필요하다. 따라서 전치사 to와 함께 쓴 to whom이 답이다.

어구 manager 매니저

정답 whom

5

해석 나에게는 아들이 둘 있는데, 둘 다 성직자가 되었다.

해설 관계대명사의 계속적인 용법에서는 관계대명사 that을 쓸 수 없다. 또한 선행사가 sons라는 사람이므로 who가 올바른 답이다.

어구 priest 성직자

정답 who

6

해석 존이 샀던 책을 언제 봤니?

해설 괄호 뒤의 동사 bought는 타동사이며 목적어는 선행사인 the book이다. 따라서 목적격 관계대명사인 which가 답이다.

정답 which

7

해석 네가 우리 집에서 만났던 여자는 내 사촌이다.

해설 괄호 뒤의 동사 met의 목적어가 선행사인 the girl이다. 목적어를 받는 자리이므로 whom이 옳다.

어구 cousin 사촌

정답 whom

8

해석 저기 저 사람의 집은 건축 중이다.

해설 house라는 명사 앞이므로 소유격 관계대명사인 whose가 옳다.

어구 under construction 건축 중인

정답 whose

9

해석 그는 누구에게나 호감을 살 수 있는 사람이 되고 싶어한다.

해설 괄호 뒤가 동사(can)로 시작되기 때문에 whose라는 소유격 형태는 올 수 없다. 주격관계대명사 who가 옳다.

정답 who

10

해석 그는 관에 놓였으며 관의 뚜껑은 고정되어 있지 않았다.

해설 괄호 앞에 전치사 of가 있다. 전치사 of와 함께 관계대명사 that은 쓸 수 없다. 또한 that은 계속적 용법에도 쓸 수 없다.

어구 place 놓다, 두다   coffin 관   lid 뚜껑
remain ~인 채로 있다   unfasten 풀다, 느슨하게 하다

정답 which

PRACTICE

1

해석 A: 그가 원하는 것이 뭔데?
B: 그 프로젝트를 담당하는 사람과 만나고 싶어해.

해설 빈 칸 뒤가 동사(is)로 시작하기 때문에 주격관계대명사 who가

옳다. 선행사가 사람이기 때문에 which는 올 수 없다.

어구 in charge of ~을 담당하는

정답 (a)

2

해석 그는 그가 의지할 만한 친구가 없다.

해설 rely on(~에 의지하다)에서 전치사 on이 빈 칸 앞으로 이동되었다. 따라서 전치사는 on이며 선행사가 사람(friend)이므로 (b) on whom이 적절한 형태의 답이다.

어구 rely on ~에 의지하다

정답 (b)

3

해석 A: 저기 붉은 옷을 입은 남자 보이니?
B: 구석에 있는 아시아 남자 말이니?
A: 응, 저 사람이 어제 자기 차를 도둑맞았잖아.
B: 이런, 저 사람은 우리 삼촌인데.

해설 (c)의 관계대명사 whom을 whose로 바꿔야 한다. 뒤의 car라는 명사가 앞에 있기 때문에 관계대명사의 격은 소유격이 옳다.

어구 someone in 색(Ex. red) 붉은 옷을 입은 사람(man in black 검은 옷을 입은 사람) steal 훔치다

정답 (c) whom → whose

4

해석 (a) Solo Pasta는 이탈리아 스타일의 식당 중 하나로, 이 식당에서는 다양한 스타일의 요리를 선보인다. (b) 이곳은 위치도 좋고 실내장식도 괜찮다. (c) 이곳은 손님이 저렴한 가격의 이탈리아 음식을 먹을 수 있는 곳이다. (d) 이곳은 Old Town으로부터 걸어서 5분 거리에 있다.

해설 계속적 용법에서 관계대명사 that은 쓸 수 없다. 따라서 (a)에서 콤마(,) 뒤의 that을 which로 바꿔야 한다.

어구 Italian 이탈리아의 offer 제공하다, 내놓다
location 위치 decor (실내) 장식
reasonable (가격이) 적절한, 저렴한

정답 (a) that → which

UNIT 6 관계사(기타 관계사) II

EXERCISE

A
1 whoever
2 however
3 how[또는 the way]
4 Whichever
5 where

B
1 what
2 when
3 how
4 where
5 what
6 whichever
7 where
8 when
9 whatever
10 Whichever

PRACTICE
1 (d) 2 (d) 3 (d) how → when
4 (a) how → what

POINT

1 나는 네가 말하고 있는 것에 대해 모른다.

2 아름다운 것이 항상 좋은 것은 아니다.

3 누구든지 먼저 나타나는 사람에게 선물을 줘라.

4 어떤 것을 선택하든지, 당신은 11월 20일까지 그것을 끝내야 한다.

5 어떤 것을 읽을지는 완전히 네게 달려 있다.

6 무엇을 읽더라도, 너는 새로운 것을 배우게 될 것이다.

7 이곳은 내가 자란 도시다.

8 오늘은 청소차가 오는 날이다.

9 그가 왜 그것을 했는지 그 이유를 아느냐?

10 이것이 그가 문제를 해결했던 방법이다.

11 그녀는 외출할 때마다, 책을 가지고 나간다.

12 어디를 가더라도 나는 네게 돌아오겠다.

13 아무리 오래 걸리더라도, 나는 정의를 위해 싸울 것이다.

EXERCISE A

ex

해석 그는 그녀가 왜 울었는지 그 이유를 몰랐다.

해설 앞에 명사 the reason이 있기 때문에 when을 관계부사 why로 바꿔야 한다.

1

해석 누가 오더라도, 오는 사람은 누구나 사진이 있는 자신의 신분증을 지참해야 한다.

해설 문맥상 '~라도'라는 뜻의 양보절로 해석되므로 who가 아닌 whoever로 바꿔야 한다.

어구 bring 가져오다 ID(identity card) (운전면허증 등의) 신분증

정답 whoever

2

해석 네가 아무리 건강하더라도, 매일 밤을 새울 수는 없다.

해설 뒤의 형용사 healthy를 받아 '아무리 ~하더라도'라는 뜻의 부사 절을 이끄는 올바른 복합관계부사는 however다. 문맥상으로도 however가 어울린다.

어구 healty 건강한 stay up all night 밤새다

정답 however

3

해석 이 설명서는 네게 이것이 어떻게 작동하는지 그 방법을 보여준다.

해설 the reason은 why와 연결되는 선행사. 문맥상 작동하는 이 유보다는 방식이 어울리므로 the reason why를 how또는 the way 둘 중 하나로 바꿀 수 있다. the way how로는 쓰지 않고 둘 중 하나를 생략해 하나만 써야 한다.

어구 manual 설명서, 매뉴얼

정답 how[또는 the way]

4

해석 어떤 것을 선택하던지, 당신은 실망하지 않을 것이다.

해설 however가 양보의 의미로 쓰일 때는 '아무리 ~하더라도'로, 접 속 부사로 쓰일 때는 '그러나, 하지만'이란 뜻으로 쓰인다. 모두 문장과 어울리지 않는다. 문맥상 동사 choose와 함께 '어떤 것 을 선택하더라도'라는 뜻이 되도록 whichever로 바꿔야 한다.

어구 choose 선택하다 disappoint 실망하다

정답 Whichever

5

해석 이곳이 네가 쉴 수 있는 곳이다.

해설 선행사가 장소(place)이므로 how가 아닌 where로 바꿔야 한 다.

어구 relax 휴식을 취하다

정답 where

EXERCISE B

1

해석 그녀가 말했던 것을 내게 말해 달라.

해설 wherever는 문맥에서 전혀 어울리지 않는다. tell의 직접목적어 와 said의 목적어 역할을 동시에 하는 what이 정답이다.

정답 what

2

해석 이제 그녀가 네게 전화할 시간이 됐다.

해설 시간을 나타내는 명사 the time을 통해 관계부사 when을 답으 로 선택할 수 있다.

정답 when

3

해석 이 비디오는 이 시스템이 어떻게 작동하는지를 보여준다.

해설 문맥상 작동 방법(how)을 보여준다고 해석하는 것이 자연스럽다.

정답 how

4

해석 이 기관은 사람들이 홍콩에 대한 정보를 얻을 수 있는 훌륭한 곳이다.

해설 괄호 앞에 장소명사 place를 통해 적절한 관계부사인 where를 답으로 선택할 수 있다.

어구 institute 기관 inform 알리다

정답 where

5

해석 내가 어제 뭘 했는지 기억이 나지 않는다.

해설 how가 의문사로 쓰였더라도 괄호 뒤의 동사 did의 목적어가 빠져있으므로 문법적으로 바르지 않다. did의 목적어이면서 remember의 목적어 역할을 동시에 하는 what이 필요한 자리 다.

정답 what

6

해석 좋은 하는 것이 무엇이든지 너는 가질 수 있다.

해설 타동사 take의 목적어 역할을 하는 목적절을 이끄는 자리다. how는 방법을 뜻하기 때문에 문맥상 어울리지 않는다. '무엇이든 지'로 해석되는 whichever가 문장과 자연스럽게 어울린다.

정답 whichever

7

해석 이곳이 꿈이 현실이 되는 땅이다.

해설 명사 land는 장소에 해당되므로 선행사 land를 통해 장소 관계 대명사 where를 답으로 선택할 수 있다.

어구 reality 현실

정답 where

8

해석 일몰은 태양이 지평선 아래로 완전히 사라지는 때다.

해설 괄호 앞의 시간명사 the time이 있으므로 when을 적절한 관계 부사로 선택할 수 있다.

어구 sunset 일몰 disappear 사라지다
completely 완전히 below ~아래의
horizon 지평선

정답 when

9

해석 네가 원하는 것이 무엇이든지 네 자신의 돈을 쓰지 않고는 구입할 수 없다.

해설 '얼마나 ~든지'의 뜻으로 연결되는 however는 의미상 문장과 어울리지 않는다.

정답 whatever

10

해석 당신이 어떤 것을 선택하든지, 만족할 것이다.

해설 what은 부사절을 이끌 수 없다. 문맥상 '어떤 것이든지'로 해석되

는 whichever가 어울린다.

어구 satisfy 만족시키다

정답 Whichever

PRACTICE

1

해석 A: 그녀가 왜 나를 싫어하는지 아니?
B: 나야 모르지.

해설 빈 칸 앞의 이유를 뜻하는 명사 the reason을 통해 관계부사 why를 답으로 선택할 수 있다.

정답 (d)

2

해석 오늘은 내가 마음을 바꾼 날이다.

해설 시간을 나타내는 명사 the day를 통해 (d) when을 답으로 선택할 수 있다.

정답 (d)

3

해석 A: 라스베이거스에 짧은 일정으로 여행을 가려 한다.
B: 우연의 일치군. 나도 그곳에 갈 참이었거든.
A: 정말? 언제 출발하는데?
B: 이번 주 토요일이 회사가 나보고 가라고 한 날이야.

해설 대화 (c)에서 언제 떠날 것을 묻고 있으므로 (d)에서 명사 the day와 함께 how가 아닌 when으로 답해야 자연스럽다.

어구 take a trip 여행을 떠나다
What a coincidence! 우연의 일치다!

정답 (d) how → when

4

해석 (a) 이 핸드폰은 내가 지불할 만한 가치가 있는 것 같다. (b) 정말 좋은 핸드폰이거든. (c) 또한 상대적으로 저렴하기 때문에 학생들에게 최적이라고 생각해. (d) 학생들에게 강력하게 추천하고 싶다니까.

해설 (a)에서 how를 what으로 바꿔야 한다. worth는 이 자체로 목적어를 취한다는 점을 기억해두자. 또한 뒤의 paid for에서 전치사 for의 목적어 역할을 함께 할 수 있어야 하므로 관계대명사 what으로 바꿔야 한다.

어구 pay 지불하다   relatively 상대적으로
strongly 강력하게   recommend 추천하다

정답 (a) how → what

Chapter 6

UNIT 1 일치

EXERCISE

A
1 wins
2 was abducted
3 see
4 is
5 would be

B
1 are
2 has
3 was given
4 him
5 has been
6 am
7 will be
8 is spoken
9 was covered
10 knew

PRACTICE
1 (a)   2 (d)
3 (a) were you available → are you available
4 (c) allow → allows

POINT

1 이 그룹은 350명의 사람들로 이뤄졌다.

2 그뿐만 아니라 그들도 모두 거짓말쟁이들이다.

3 모든 소년 소녀들은 우리의 형제자매다.

4 내 마음 깊은 곳에서 당신도 나를 사랑하고 있다고 느끼고 있다.

5 당신이 나를 사랑한다고[사랑했었다고] 생각했다.

6 나는 지구가 태양을 공전한다고 배웠다.

7 내가 제인을 봤을 때 그녀는 우리 대학에서 연설을 하고 있었다.

8 그들은 사무 가구를 팔고 있는데 그 가구는 견고한 목재로 만든 정성들인 수공예품이다.

9 그녀를 위해 차 한 잔을 내가 준비했다.

10 거리는 눈으로 쌓여 있었다.

EXERCISE A

ex

해석 어머니는 항상 시간은 돈이라고 말씀하셨다.

해설 시간은 항상 돈이었다가 아닌 속담을 표현하는 것이므로 time was money가 아닌 time is money가 문맥상 바르다.

1

해석 천천히 그리고 꾸준히 하면 경기에서 이긴다(승리한다).

해설 속담 표현으로 slow and steady는 '천천히 하면서 꾸준히 하는 것'이라는 하나의 의미 덩어리로 이해해야 한다.

어구 slow and steady 지속적으로 꾸준히   race 경기

정답 wins

2

해석 아이는 유괴범에 의해 납치되었다.

해설 타동사인 abduct는 능동표현인 has abducted가 되면 by와 동사 abducted 사이에 목적어가 되는 명사가 와야 한다. 문맥 상 목적어가 되는 명사 the child가 주어 자리에 있으므로 has가 아닌 동사 was를 써서 수동태가 되도록 해야 한다.

어구 abduct 납치하다   kidnapper 유괴범

정답 was abducted

3

해석 내가 내일 그를 본다면, 나는 아직 준비되지 않았다고 그에게 말하겠다.

해설 시간 부사절에는 동사의 현재형은 의미상 미래를 대신한다. when이 이끄는 시간 부사절의 동사 will see를 see로 바꿔야 한다.

정답 see

4

해석 시스템 각각의 모든 운용자들이 그것에 대해 책임이 있다.

해설 each of에서 주어가 되는 each는 단수 취급한다.

어구 operator 운용자
be responsible for ~에 대해 책임이 있다

정답 is

5

해석 나는 그녀가 음악가가 될 것이라고 생각했다.

해설 생각한 것이 과거(thought)라면 that절의 동사는 would be로 바꿔야 한다. would는 과거 시점에서의 미래 표현 방식이다.

어구 musician 음악가

정답 would be

EXERCISE B

1

해석 내 생각에 캐나다인이 미국인보다 더 건강하다.

해설 Canadians라는 복수명사가 주어이므로 동사는 is가 아닌 are가 되어야 한다.

정답 are

2

해석 여기 모든 사람들은 꿈을 가지고 있다.

해설 everybody는 단수로 취급하기 때문에 동사도 has가 되어야 한다.

정답 has

3

해석 그녀는 주차를 위한 티켓을 받았다.

해설 동사 give는 4형식 동사로 「give + 목적어1(간접) + 목적어2(직접),의 구조로 문장에서 쓰인다. 문장의 주어 she는 목적어1이 자리를 이동한 것이므로 동사 give는 수동태가 되어야 한다. 직접목적어 a ticket은 수동태가 되어도 이동이나 변화가 없다.

어구 parking 주차

정답 was given

4

해석 내가 데이비드를 본다면, 그에게 네게 전화하라고 말하겠다.

해설 동사 tell과 더불어 말을 전할 수 있는 대상이 되어야 하므로 앞의 David를 받는 him이 옳다.

정답 him

5

해석 그녀는 지난 목요일부터 몸이 좋지 않았다.

해설 괄호 뒤의 since는 '~(과거의 어느 한 시점) 이래로'라는 뜻으로 과거 어느 시점(last Thursday)부터 현재까지 과거와 현재 두 시점을 아우르고 있다. 이때 쓸 수 있는 시제가 현재완료다.

어구 ill 아픈   since ~이래로

정답 has been

6

해석 오늘 너나 나 둘 모두 나가지 않을 것이다.

해설 neither A nor B에서 동사는 B에 일치시킨다. 문장에서 B는 I 이므로 동사는 are가 아닌 am이다.

어구 neither A nor B A나 B 모두 아닌   go out 외출하다

정답 am

7

해석 내일의 날씨는 차고 구름이 낄 것이다.

해설 내일(tomorrow)이라는 미래 시점이 있으므로 동사는 has been이 아닌 will be가 옳다.

어구 cold 찬   cloudy 구름이 낀

정답 will be

8

해석 필리핀에서는 영어를 말한다(영어가 공용어다).

해설 영어(English)가 말하는 능동의 주체가 아닌 쓰이는 언어이므로 능동의 speaks가 아닌 is spoken인 수동태가 되어야 한다.

정답 is spoken

9

해석 테이블은 흰 식탁보로 덮여 있었다.

해설 동사 cover는 '~을 덮다'라는 뜻을 가진 타동사다. table은 식탁보(tablecloth)로 덮인 것이므로 수동태가 되어야 한다. 또한 이러한 수동표현에서 동사 cover와 함께 쓰는 전치사는 with다.

어구 be covered with ~으로 덮여 있다   tablecloth 식탁보

정답 was covered

10

해석 나는 5년 전부터 그를 알고 있었다.

해설 과거시점 부사 ago가 있으므로 동사의 과거형 knew로 써야 한다.

정답 knew

PRACTICE

1

해석 A: 그 영화의 감독이 누구지?
B: 내가 듣기로는 한 인도의 영화 회사에서 만들었다고 하던데.

해설 동사 tell은 능동의 형태에서 뒤의 that절을 바로 받을 수 없다. tell이 타동사로 쓰이는 경우 사람을 직접목적어로 받고 간접목적어로 명사나 that이 이끄는 절을 받기 때문이다. 문장은 간접목적어가 주어 자리로 이동했으므로 수동태인 was told로 답하는 것이 옳다.

어구 director 감독   film 영화('영화'를 영국에선 film, 미국에서는 movie라고 함)

정답 (a)

2

해석 나뿐만 아니라 그들도 그 계획에 대해 통보받지 못했다.

해설 A as well as B는 'B뿐만 아니라 A도'라는 뜻으로 동사의 수는 A에 일치시켜야 한다. 또한 동사 inform은 「inform A of B(또는 that절)」의 구조로 쓰이는데 목적어인 A가 주어 자리로 이동했으므로 동사는 수동태가 되어야 한다. 이런 조건을 만족하는 것은 (d) are never informed다.

어구 A as well as B B뿐만 아니라 A도
inform A of B A에게 B를 알리다   plan 계획

정답 (d)

3

해석 A: 레드, 지금 시간 되니?
B: 응, 무슨 일인데?
A: 나가서 뭐 좀 먹자.
B: 그거 좋은 생각인데.

해설 대화는 가까운 미래에 관한 사항에 대해 이야기 하고 있고 (a)에서 right now라는 현재 부사가 있기 때문에 동사 were를 현재형 동사 are로 바꿔야 한다.

어구 available 이용 가능한   right now 지금 당장
go out 외출하다   grab (음식을) 재빨리 먹다

정답 (a) were you available → are you available

4

해석 (a) 특허는 특허와 상표를 담당하는 기관에서 발명자에게 부여하는 재산권의 허가증과 같은 것이다. (b) 특허는 특허를 받은 그 해부터 20년간 지속된다. (c) 20년 동안 특허는 발명자로 하여금 발명품 제조 또는 판매에 대한 독점권을 갖게 한다. (d) 이러한 기간은 수혜자로 하여금 다른 회사에 특허 상품의 라이선스를 팔도록 허용함으로써 많은 돈을 벌 수 있도록 한다.

해설 (c)에서 주어는 단수 명사 a patent다. 따라서 동사 역시 allow가 아닌 allows가 되어야 한다.

어구 patent 특허   permit 허가(증)
property right 재산권   inventor 발명가
trademark 상표권   last 지속되다; 마지막의
period 기간, 시기
allow A to V A로 하여금 ~하도록 허용하다
license 특허 사용권   individual 개인(의)
time frame 기간   beneficiary 수혜자

정답 (c) allow → allows

UNIT 2 강조와 도치

EXERCISE

A
1 사이클링은 우리가 예상한 것보다 훨씬 어렵다.
2 나는 캠핑 가기를 정말로 원한다.
3 그 노래는 내가 예상한 것보다 훨씬 낫다.
4 내가 그녀를 공원에서 만난 것은 이틀 전이었다.
5 도대체 그들의 공통점이 무엇이지?

B
1 were
2 It
3 the very
4 that
5 in the least
6 on
7 do
8 did she
9 the hell
10 that

PRACTICE

1 (c)   2 (a)
3 (a) What a hell → What the hell
4 (d) have → haven't

POINT

1 내가 정거장에서 그렉을 만난 것은 어제였다.
2 내가 공원에서 만난 사람은 메리다.
3 제인이 사는 곳은 시카고다.
4 그녀가 말한 것은 무엇인가?
5 영화는 모든 면에서 소설보다 훨씬 낫다.
6 이것은 정말 최고의 영화다.
7 나는 그녀를 전혀 모른다.
8 나는 그녀가 전혀 두렵지 않다.
9 도대체 그녀는 무슨 소리를 하는가?
10 너는 도대체 누구냐?
11 나는 그녀를 정말 좋아한다.
12 나는 이 나라를 진정 사랑했다.
13 따라야 할 규칙이 많다.
14 그곳에는 아무도 없다.
15 그녀는 힌트도 하지 않았다.
16 적을 보자마자 그는 도망쳤다.
17 우리는 잠이 깬 후에야 우리가 꿈을 꾸었음을 안다.

EXERCISE A

ex

어구 don't know A at all A를 전혀 모르다

1

어휘 cycling 사이클링, 자전거 타기   expect 기대하다

정답 사이클링은 우리가 예상한 것보다 훨씬 어렵다.

2

어구 go camping 캠핑 가다

정답 나는 캠핑 가기를 정말로 원한다.

3

정답 그 노래는 내가 예상한 것보다 훨씬 낫다.

4

정답 내가 그녀를 공원에서 만난 것은 이틀 전이었다.

5

어구 have in common 공통점이 있다

정답 도대체 그들의 공통점이 무엇이지?

EXERCISE B

1

해석 몇 가지 예외사항이 있었다.

해설 유도 부사 there가 이끄는 문장에서 문장의 주어는 동사 뒤에 위치하게 된다. 또한 동사는 뒤에 있는 주어의 수에 일치하기 때문에 문장에서는 복수 동사 were를 답으로 선택해야 한다.

어구 exception 예외(사항)

정답 were

2

해석 우리는 문제를 인식하고 나서야 그것이 더욱 복잡하다는 것을 깨닫는다.

해설 It is not until ~ that구문을 묻고 있다. it 대신 that 등 다른 주어로 대신할 수 없다.

어구 realize 깨닫다   complicated 복잡한

정답 It

3

해석 이것은 내가 소유한 차 중에서 최고의 차다.

해설 best라는 최상급을 수식해 그 의미를 강조할 수 있는 수식어는 the very다. the most를 쓰면 best라는 최상급과 중복된다.

어구 own 소유하다

정답 the very

4

해석 내가 공원에서 만난 사람은 제인이었다.

해설 「it is ~ that」강조 구문을 묻고 있다. 강조하는 대상은 it과 that 사이에 둔다. 이를 that이 아닌 다른 어휘로 대체할 수는 없다.

정답 that

5

해석 나는 내 발이 젖는 것이 전혀 두렵지 않다.

해설 부정어(not) 뒤에서 부정어를 강조하는 강조어구는 in the least 다.

어구 not in the least 전혀(조금도) ~하지 않는   get wet 젖다

정답 in the least

6

해석 도대체 그들이 묻고자 하는 것은 무엇인가?

해설 의문사 what을 '도대체' 등의 의미로 강조하는 수식어구는 on earth다.

어구 on earth 도대체(의문사 강조)

정답 on

7

해석 나는 네가 우리를 방문해 주기를 정말 바란다.

해설 동사 hope를 강조할 수 있는 것은 동사 hope 앞에 do를 쓰면 된다. very는 형용사 앞에 쓴다.

어구 visit 방문하다

정답 do

8

해석 제이슨의 귀환에 대해 그녀는 한 마디도 하지 않았다.

해설 부정의 부사 not이 문두로 이동했으므로 뒤의 「주어 + 동사」의 어순은 「동사 + 주어」 어순으로 바뀐다.

어구 return 귀환; 되돌아가다

정답 did she

9

해석 도대체 누가 줄리엣인가?

해설 의문사(who) 뒤에서 그 의미를 강조하는 올바른 수식어는 둘 중 the hell이다.

정답 the hell

10

해석 우리가 가진 것을 잃고 나서야 우리는 진정으로 그것을 고마워한다.

해설 「It is not until A that B」구문은 'A하고 나서야 B하다'의 의미다. 이를 통해 연결되는 접속사는 that임을 알 수 있다.

어구 appreciate 고마워하다

정답 that

PRACTICE

1

해석 A: 대체 이곳에 무슨 일이 일어난 거지?
　　 B: 모르겠는데.

해설 의문사 what 뒤에서 what이 이끄는 의문문을 강조하는 올바른 구문은 on earth다.

정답 (c)

2

해석 우리가 가진 것을 모두 잃고 나서야 우리가 가진 것의 진정한 가치를 깨닫게 된다.

해설 구문이다. 부정어(not)가 문두에 있으므로 뒤의 「주어+동사」 어

순은 「동사+주어」 어순으로 바뀐다. (a) do we realize가 옳다.

어구 realize 깨닫다   true 진정한
value 가치

정답 (a)

3

해석 A: 대체 너는 무엇을 찾고 있는 거니?
B: 오늘 밤에 있을 콘서트 표.
A: 앨리스가 그것을 가지고 있는 것을 봤는데.
B: 정말? 언제?

해설 (a)의 a hell에서 a를 the로 바꿔야 한다. 의문사 what의 의미를 강조하는 올바른 표현은 the hell이다.

정답 (a) What a hell → What the hell

4

해석 (a) 나는 세미나 일에 대해 전혀 걱정하지 않아. (b) 내가 걱정하는 것은 논문이야. (c) 샘플 장(章)을 제출해야 하는 날이 벌써 5일 앞으로 다가왔거든. (d) 시작도 안했는데.

해설 (d)에서 전체 문맥의 흐름과 연결이 매끄러우려면 have를 haven't로 바꿔야 한다. even과 문미의 yet이 부정의 의미를 강조하는 부사로 쓰였다.

어구 thesis 논문   turn in 제출하다

정답 (d) have → haven't

UNIT 3 주요 동사의 쓰임과 어순

EXERCISE

A
1 who is he
2 to talk
3 of
4 towed
5 you are

B
1 that
2 Among them
3 There has been
4 fixed
5 who he is
6 of
7 Little does he
8 I will be able
9 Seldom had
10 to stay

PRACTICE
1 (d)   2 (a)
3 (a) When I can → When can I
4 (b) There two types of mining methods are →
There are two types of mining methods

POINT

1 그는 인터뷰 동안 침묵했다.

2 너 창백해 보인다. 괜찮니?

3 우리는 그녀가 나라를 떠나는 것을 허락하지 않을 것이다.

4 그는 우리에게 시를 써 달라고 촉구했다.

5 나는 그에게 도박하지 말라고 경고했다.

6 그녀는 내 누이를 생각나게 한다.

7 나는 그에게 우리와 김 박사와의 약속을 알렸다.

8 나 역시 그것이 흥미롭다고 생각했다.

9 (당신을) 기다리게 해서 죄송합니다.

10 나는 차를 수리했다.

11 너는 누구냐?

12 표절이란 무엇인가?

13 이것을 얼마 동안 임대할 예정인가요?

14 그녀가 어디 있는지 모르겠다.

15 그는 왜 내가 똑똑하다고 생각하는가?

16 니가 먹고 있는 것이 무엇인지 아느냐?

17 그는 영국에 살고 있다. 로빈도 그렇다.

18 그녀는 술을 마시지 못했다. 나도 그랬다.

19 실업률에 있어서 큰 증가가 있었다.

20 그들 중에는 작가가 있었다.

21 전에 그가 담배 피우는 것을 거의 본 적이 없었다.

22 그의 인생이 바뀌리라는 것을 그는 거의 깨닫지 못하고 있다.

EXERCISE A

ex

해석 당신은 제 장인을 떠올리게 합니다.

해설 동사 remind가 문장 내에서 갖는 구조는 목적어 뒤의 목적보어가 명사일 경우 of~로 표현한다. 따라서 to를 of로 바꿔야 한다.

어구 remind A of B A에게 B를 떠올리게 하다
father-in-law 장인

1

해석 그는 누구인가?

해설 의문문의 어순이 잘못되었다. 의문사 뒤는 『동사 + 주어』의 어순이 되어야 한다.

정답 who is he

2

해석 내 아버지는 내게 그것에 대해 더 이상 말하지 말라고 경고했다.

해설 동사 warn은 목적어 뒤 to부정사를 목적보어로 취하는 동사다. 이 같은 동사의 쓰임을 통해 for talking을 to talk로 바꿔야 함을 알 수 있다.

어구 warn 경고하다, 조심시키다

정답 to talk

3

해석 나는 그녀에게 우리의 상황을 알렸다.

해설 동사 inform의 문장 내 표현 방식은 『inform A of B』이다. 따라서 for를 of로 바꿔야 한다.

어구 inform A of B A에게 B를 알리다   situation 상황

정답 of

4

해석 나는 차를 견인시켰다.

해설 차는 견인되는 대상으로 수동의 관계에 있으므로 towing을 towed로 바꿔야 한다.

어구 tow 견인하다

정답 towed

5

해석 네가 뭘 마시고 있는지 아니?

해설 간접의문문에서 의문사 뒤의 어순은 『주어 + 동사』의 어순으로 바뀐다. are you를 you are로 바꿔야 한다.

정답 you are

EXERCISE B

1

해석 나는 그에게 내가 그를 도울 것이라고 알렸다.

해설 동사 inform은 목적어 뒤 절의 구조가 오는 경우 that절이 온다.

전치사 of는 명사가 오는 경우에 쓸 수 있다.

어구 inform 알리다

정답 that

2

해석 그들 중에는 영어를 조금 할 줄 아는 젊은이가 있었다.

해설 전치사 among이 문두에 위치해 they와 함께 '그들 중'을 나타낼 때는 among them이 올바른 어순이다. 문맥상 주어가 길기 때문에 부사구가 앞으로 이동된 것으로 볼 수 있다.

정답 Among them

3

해석 2006년 이래로 허리케인의 수에 있어서 큰 증가가 있었다.

해설 의문문이 아니기 때문에 유도부사와 동사의 어순을 바꿔서 쓸 이유가 없다. 『유도부사 + 동사』의 어순이 되어야 한다.

정답 There has been

4

해석 나는 내 컴퓨터를 고쳤다.

해설 사역동사 had가 사물(computer)을 목적어로 받고 문맥상 컴퓨터는 고쳐지는 수동의 관계에 있으므로 fixed의 형태가 되어야 한다.

어구 fix 고치다

정답 fixed

5

해석 그가 누구인지 아니?

해설 간접의문문에서 의문사 이하의 어순은 『의문사 + 주어 + 동사』 순이다.

정답 who he is

6

해석 너는 내 가장 친한 친구를 생각나게 한다.

해설 remind 뒤의 목적보어가 명사인 경우 이를 연결하는 전치사는 of다.

어구 remind A of B A에게 B를 생각나게 하다

정답 of

7

해석 이것이 얼마나 위험할지 그는 거의 깨닫지 못하고 있다.

해설 '거의 조금도 ~하지 않는'이란 뜻의 부정어 little이 문두로 이동하는 경우 뒤의 『주어+동사』의 어순은 『동사+주어』의 어순으로 바뀐다.

정답 Little does he

8

해석 얼마나 많은 부수를 내가 팔 수 있을 것이라 생각하니?

해설 do you think가 삽입된 간접의문문의 올바른 어순을 묻고 있다. 주어와 동사가 연결된 어순인 I will be able~가 적절한 어순이다. 구어체에서는 will I be~로 쓰기도 하지만 처음 제시된 will be I able은 잘못된 표현이다.

정답 I will be able

9

해석 나는 어머니가 화내는 것을 거의 본 적이 없다.

해설 부정어(seldom)가 문두로 위치하는 경우 뒤의 주어와 동사의 어

순은 바뀐다. 올바르게 도치된 문장은 Seldom had이다.

정답 Seldom had

10

해석 나는 그가 우리와 함께 머물도록 허락하지 않을 것이다.

해설 동사 allow가 갖는 문장 내 쓰임을 통해 to stay를 답으로 선택할 수 있다. 동사 allow는 『allow A to V』의 구조로 문장 내 쓰임을 갖기 때문이다.

어구 allow 허가하다   stay 머물다

정답 to stay

PRACTICE

1

해석 A: 내 안경이 어디 있는지 아니?
B: 그것을 너의 침실에 뒀다.

해설 간접의문문의 어순에서 의문사가 이끄는 어순은 뒤에 주어와 동사 순으로 연결된다.

정답 (d)

2

해석 나는 그에게 그 사고소식을 알렸다.

해설 (b) compared와 (c) provided는 목적어 뒤 with를, (d) kept는 목적어 뒤 명사 앞에 전치사 from을 쓰는 동사다. 뒤에 of가 나오는 구조만으로도 (a)만이 답이 안 되는 것을 알 수 있다.

어구 notify A of B A에게 B를 알리다
compare A with B A와 B를 비교하다
provide A with B A에게 B를 제공하다
keep A from B B로부터 A를 막다

정답 (a)

3

해석 A: 내 양복을 언제 가지러 올 수 있나요?
B: 내일 모레 가지러 오시면 됩니다.
A: 오, 안 돼요. 내일 꼭 필요하거든요.
B: 정 그러시면, 내일 들르세요.

해설 (a)에서 When I can을 When can I로 바꿔야 한다. 의문사의 올바른 어순은 『의문사 + 동사 + 주어』 순이다.

어구 pick up 가지러 가다   suit 옷(특히 양복) 한 벌
If you insist 정 그러시다면   drop by 들르다

정답 (a) When I can → When can I

4

해석 (a) 석탄은 검거나 흑 갈색의 빛나는 암석으로 이것의 대부분은 땅속 깊이 매장되어 있다. (b) 석탄을 캐는 두 가지 방법이 있는데, 표면 채굴과 지하 채굴이 그것이다. (c) 표면 채굴은 석탄이 땅으로부터 200피트 이하 되는 곳에 묻혀 있는 경우에 한다. (d) 지하 채굴은 석탄이 표면으로부터 200피트 이상 아래에 묻혀 있는 경우에 하는 것이다.

해설 (b)에서 There 이하의 어순이 잘못됐었다. there이하의 주어가 긴 경우 there를 앞으로 이동시키고 길어진 주어는 동사 뒤에 위치시킨다. 이때 동사는 주어의 수에 일치시킨다.

어구 coal 석탄   brownish black 흑 갈색
shiny 빛나는   bury 매장하다
underground 지하(의)

---

mining 채굴   method 방법   surface 표면

정답 (b) There two types of mining methods are → There are two types of mining methods

문법 모의고사

PART I

1 (b)	**2** (a)	**3** (d)	**4** (a)	**5** (c)
6 (a)	**7** (d)	**8** (c)	**9** (c)	**10** (d)
11 (a)	**12** (d)	**13** (c)	**14** (d)	**15** (c)
16 (c)	**17** (b)	**18** (a)	**19** (c)	**20** (d)

PART II

21 (c)	**22** (b)	**23** (a)	**24** (d)	**25** (b)
26 (c)	**27** (a)	**28** (c)	**29** (d)	**30** (a)
31 (d)	**32** (c)	**33** (a)	**34** (b)	**35** (d)
36 (d)	**37** (b)	**38** (d)	**39** (c)	**40** (d)

PART III

41 (d) anywhere → everywhere

42 (d) to business → on business

43 (a) quit → to quit

44 (b) Particular anything → Anything particular

45 (d) in hour → in an hour

PART IV

46 (c) Although → If

47 (a) has been → was

48 (a) smaller as → smaller than

49 (b) were → was

50 (c) millions dollars → millions of dollars

PART I

1

해석 A: 뭐 먹을래, 존?
B: 나도 (너랑) 같은 것으로 먹을게.

해설 첫 번째 화자가 말한 동사 have는 문맥상 '먹다(eat)'의 의미로 쓰였다. '똑같은 것'이란 단어 속에는 이미 서로가 알고 있는 '특정한 것'이라는 의미가 내포되어 있으므로 관사 the를 붙여 the same으로 표현해야 한다.

정답 (b)

2

해석 A: 내가 집까지 태워줄게.
B: 아니야, 그렇게까지 안 해도 돼.

해설 be동사 뒤로 올 수 있는 품사는 명사나 형용사다. 주어는 전체 문장을 받는 it으로 명사 necessity와는 전혀 어울리지 않는다.

정답 (a)

3

해석 A: 너 그 조사 잘했더라.
　　　B: 그렇게 말해주니 고맙다.

해설 to부정사의 의미상 주어를 표현하는 방법을 묻고 있다. 「for + 목적격 + to부정사」의 형태가 일반적이나 사람의 성품을 나타내는 형용사(kind, foolish, careful, good 등)가 오는 경우 for 대신 of를 써야 한다.

어구 do a good job 일을 잘 해내다　　　research 조사

정답 (d)

4

해석 A: 지금 출발해야 할 것 같다.
　　　B: 커피 한 잔 하게 좀 더 있다 가지 그래?

해설 B의 대답에서 A가 '지금 출발 하겠다'의 의미로 말한 것을 알 수 있다. '~해야 한다'라는 뜻을 가지는 조동사가 빈 칸에 필요하다. (a) must가 적절하다.

어구 stay 머물다　　　a cup of coffee 커피 한 잔

정답 (a)

5

해석 A: 클락, 내가 지난번에 본 후로 어떻게 지냈어?
　　　B: 그냥 그렇지 뭐.

해설 문장과 문장을 연결하는 적절한 접속사가 필요하다. 빈 칸을 사이에 두고 한쪽은 단순 과거(saw), 그리고 앞은 현재 완료(have + p.p.)로 쓰였다. 즉 과거의 어느 한 시점부터 현재까지 이르는 시간의 흐름을 지칭하고 있으므로 (c) since가 답이다.

어구 just so-so 그저 그런

정답 (c)

6

해석 A: 마크! 여기서 만나서 반갑다.
　　　B: 안녕, 니콜. 그런데 여긴 웬일이야?

해설 '무슨 일로 이곳에 왔어?'라는 뜻의 영어표현은 동사 bring을 써서 「what brings you here?」로 나타낼 수 있다. 이 같은 어순을 통해 빈 칸에 들어갈 brings you를 답으로 선택할 수 있는데 '무슨 일로'라는 뜻으로 무생물 주어 what이 쓰인 점과 의문사(또는 의문사가 이끄는 문장)는 단수로 받는다는 점도 기억해두자.

어구 fancy 선호함, 좋아함; 좋아하다
　　　What brings you here? 이곳은 무슨 일로 왔어?

정답 (a)

7

해석 A: 이번 주말에 당신과 함께 점심을 함께하고 싶군요.
　　　B: 무슨 일이죠?

해설 I'd like~로 시작하는 '~하고 싶다'라는 표현은 자신의 희망을 상대방에게 다소 높여 말하는 방식이다. 동사 like 뒤에 동사가 오는 경우 동사는 to부정사의 형태가 되고 명사가 오는 경우 to 없이 바로 명사를 취하는 타동사다. have라는 동사가 제시되고 있으므로 to부정사 형태인 (d) to have가 옳다.

어구 What's the occasion? 무슨 일인데?

정답 (d)

8

해석 A: 제가 당신께 샌드위치를 사드리겠습니다.
　　　B: 그러실 필요 없습니다. (직역: 당신을 귀찮게 해드리고 싶지 않은데요.)

해설 동사 buy의 문장 내에서 갖는 구조를 통해 올바른 어순을 선택할 수 있다. buy는 4형식동사로 뒤에 목적어 둘(간접목적어 + 직접목적어)을 취한다. 이를 통해 올바른 어순인 (c) you a sandwich를 답으로 선택할 수 있다.

어구 put A to the bother A를 귀찮게 하다

정답 (c)

9

해석 A: 질이 뉴욕에서 보스턴으로 전근간 지 2년이 됐네.
　　　B: 그래, 정말 그녀가 그리워.

해설 접속사 since를 통해 올바른 동사의 시제를 선택할 수 있다. since는 '~이래로 현재까지'라는 뜻이 있기 때문에 과거의 어느 시점에서 현재까지를 나타내는 현재완료시제와 함께 쓰는 접속사다. 빈 칸 앞의 주절은 현재완료로 표현하지만 since절은 과거의 어느 시점에 해당하는 단순과거형이 되어야 한다. 이를 만족하는 보기는 (c) was다.

어구 transfer 옮기다, 이동하다

정답 (c)

10

해석 A: 너 오늘 정말 예쁘다.
　　　B: 칭찬해줘서 고마워.

해설 동사 look은 '~처럼 보이다'라는 뜻을 가진 2형식 동사로 쓰였다. 주격보어로 형용사를 취해야 하는데 문맥상 놀란 것이 아니라 다른 사람들을 놀라게 하는 능동의 관계에 있으므로 현재분사인 stunning이 정답이다.

어구 stunning 멋진, 매력적인
　　　compliment 칭찬

정답 (d)

11

해석 A: 만나서 반가웠어, 짐.
　　　B: 나야말로.

해설 pleasure와 함께 '~하게 되어 반갑다'는 영어 표현은 it is a pleasure ~ing로 표현할 수 있다. 습관적으로 쓰는 굳어진 표현이므로 문법적 접근보다는 통으로 기억해 두자.

어구 pleasure 기쁨

정답 (a)

12

해석 A: 나 파티에서 빠져도 될까? 감기에 걸렸거든.
　　　B: 물론이지. 몸 조리 잘해.

해설 '실례해도 될까요?'라는 표현은 excuse me 외에도 can I be excused ~라는 수동태 표현으로 나타낼 수도 있다.

어구 can I be excused from A A로부터 실례하다(빠지다)
　　　have a cold 감기 걸리다

정답 (d)

13

해석 A: 제인이 너한테 안부 전해달라고 했어.

B: 고마워. 그녀에게도 안부 전해줘.

해설 '안부를 전하다'는 표현은 동사 give와 함께 give one's regards to someone으로 표현할 수 있다.

어구 tell A hello A에게 안부를 전하다
give one's regards to A A에게 안부를 전하다

정답 (c)

14

해석 A: 오늘 오후에 시간이 있으면 전화 줘.
B: 상황 봐서.

해설 '돌아가는 상황을 일단 봐서'라는 표현은 빈 칸 뒤의 it goes와 함께 how를 써야 한다. 따라서 (d) how가 정답이다.

어구 give A a call A에게 전화하다
see how it goes 상황을 보다

정답 (d)

15

해석 A: 기다리게 해서 미안해. 금방 올게.
B: 괜찮아. 천천히 해.

해설 동사 keep은 여기서 5형식 동사로 쓰였다. 「keep + 목적어 + 목적보어」의 구조에서 기다리는 주체는 you이므로 능동형 분사 waiting으로 표현해야 옳다.

어구 keep A waiting A를 기다리게 하다
in a minute 잠시 후에
take one's time 쉬엄쉬엄 하다

정답 (c)

16

해석 A: 머리를 어떻게 자르실 건가요?
B: 짧게 해주세요.

해설 빈 칸 앞에 조동사 would가 있기 때문에 (a)나 (d)와 같이 원형 동사가 아닌 동사 형태는 올 수 없다. 또한 like 뒤에 동사가 오는 경우에만 to부정사의 형태가 올 수 있으므로 뒤의 명사를 받을 수 있으려면 (c) you like의 형태가 되어야 한다.

정답 (c)

17

해석 A: 마이클, 전화 좀 받아줄래?
B: 안 되겠는데. 내가 지금 다른 일로 꼼짝할 수가 없어서.

해설 어떤 다른 일로 '꼼짝할 수 없거나, 묶여 있다'는 올바른 영어 구어체 표현은 be tied (up)이다. right now라는 단서가 있으므로 현재형 수동태인 (b)가 적절하다.

어구 answer 답하다, 응답하다
be tied (up) 일 등으로 바빠 꼼짝 못하다

정답 (b)

18

해석 A: 당신이 원한다면 제가 도울게요.
B: 도와줘서 진심으로 감사합니다.

해설 '누군가를 돕다'라는 표현으로 help someone out을 쓸 수 있다. 빈 칸 앞에 소유격 your가 쓰였으므로 빈 칸은 명사 상당어구가 되어야 한다. 돕는 대상을 이같이 표현한 (a) helping me out이 적절한 답이다.

어구 appreciate 고마워하다

정답 (a)

19

해석 A: 이것은 내가 낼게. 이번에는 내가 너에게 점심 사고 싶어.
B: 네가 정 그렇다면 그렇게 해.

해설 우리말로 '정 그렇다면'이란 영어식 표현은 if you insist다. 영어에서 습관적으로 쓰다가 굳어진 표현이므로 덩어리째 암기해 두자.

어구 it's on me 내가 지불하겠다
if you insist 정 그렇다면

정답 (c)

20

해석 A: 왜 너는 다이어트하고 있니?
B: 좀 날씬해지려고.

해설 '다이어트하다'의 올바른 형태를 묻고 있다. be on a diet가 올바른 영어식 표현이다. 나머지 보기는 한정사(your, any, the)가 올바르지 못하다.

어구 be on a diet 다이어트하다   slim down 날씬해지다

정답 (d)

PART II

21

해석 한국의 영화가 세계적으로 관심을 끌고 있다고 한다.

해설 동사 say는 수동태가 되면서 뒤에 다른 동사를 달고 나오는 경우 동사는 to부정사의 형태가 되도록 해야 한다. (a)와 (c) 중에서 선택해야 하는데 빈 칸 뒤의 명사 interest(관심)가 있으므로 동사는 타동사의 능동형이 되어야 한다. 따라서 능동형으로 제시한 (c) to be gaining이 정답이다.

어구 film 영화   gain 얻다   interest 관심; 이자

정답 (c)

22

해석 그의 아이디어의 중요성을 깨달은 것은 21세기 초가 되어서였다.

해설 「It's not until A that B」는 「It ~ that」강조구문으로 'B한 것은 (시간상으로) 바로 A가 되어서이다'라는 뜻이다. 형태를 잘 익혀 두도록 하자.

어구 it's not until A that B B한 것은 (시간상으로) A가 되어서다
importance 중요성   realize 깨닫다

정답 (b)

23

해석 고통이 사라지는 데 거의 3일이 소요되었다.

해설 to부정사의 의미상 주어 표현 방법을 묻고 있다. to부정사의 의미상 주어는 「for + 목적격 + to부정사」로 표현할 수 있다. 올바르게 나타낸 보기는 (a) for the pain to go away다.

어구 go away 사라지다

정답 (a)

24

해석 문의 또는 관심 사항이 있으시면 언제든지 저희 웹사이트에 방문하셔서 차에 대해 필요한 모든 원하는 정보를 얻으시오.

해설 콤마(,) 앞뒤로 문맥을 자연스럽게 하는 적절한 답은 '~할 때면 언제든'의 뜻으로 문장을 연결하는 (d) Whenever다. (a) Since

가 부사절을 이끌면 '~때문에'라는 뜻으로 이유의 부사절을 이끌기 때문에 이 경우 문맥이 어색해진다. (b) However는 접속부사가 되는 경우 문장과 문장을 연결할 수 없으며, 복합관계부사가 되면 however 뒤는 형용사나 부사가 와야 한다. (c) What은 명사절을 이끌기 때문에 문장의 구조상 적절치 못하다.

어구 concern 관심; 용무

정답 (d)

25

해석 이 책은 재미있으면서 동시에 교육적이다.

해설 both는 접속사 and와 짝을 이루어 상관접속사가 된다. both A and B를 통해 접속사 and가 필요함을 알 수 있으며 and 앞뒤는 형태와 의미에서 병렬관계를 이루므로 형용사가 필요한데 책의 성질 자체가 '흥미있는' 것이므로 능동의 interesting이 옳다. 따라서 (b) interesting and가 올바른 표현이다.

어구 interest 흥미롭게 하다   instructive 교육적인

정답 (b)

26

해석 죠수아 벨은 세계에서 가장 훌륭한 바이올리니스트 중 한 명이다.

해설 최상급의 올바른 표현을 묻고 있다. 빈 칸 앞에 정관사 the가 있기 때문에 최상급 표현이 되어야 하며 최상급과 더불어 (b)와 (c) 중에서 「one of the 최상급 + 복수명사」 구조에 만족해야 하므로 (c) greatest violinists가 가장 적절한 답이다.

어구 one of the 최상급 + 복수명사 가장 ~한 중에서 하나인

정답 (c)

27

해석 날씨가 좋건 나쁘건, 짐이나 저 모두 모임에는 참석하지 않을 것입니다.

해설 neither A nor B에서 동사의 수는 명사 B에 일치시킨다. B에 해당하는 주어는 I이므로 (a) am이 답이다.

어구 neither A nor B A와 B 모두 아닌
gathering 모임

정답 (a)

28

해석 네가 생각하기에 승리할 것 같은 사람이 아닌 그 일에 가장 적합한 사람에게 투표하라.

해설 문맥을 통해 (c) not을 답으로 선택할 수 있다. 콤마(,)를 사이에 두고 두 내용은 서로 상반된다. 따라서 역접의 부사인 not이 적절한 답이다.

어구 vote 투표하다   whoever 누구나

정답 (c)

29

해석 경기 티켓을 산 맨체스터 유나이티드 팬들의 수는 맨체스터 시티 팬들의 수보다 네 배는 많다.

해설 전체 문장의 주어는 단수 the number다. 따라서 동사는 is가 되어야 하며 빈 칸 뒤의 비교급 표현과 함께 배수를 나타내는 올바른 표현은 (four) times다.

정답 (d)

30

해석 만일 당신이 18세 이하라면, 이 웹사이트 방문 시 반드시 성인과 함께 사이트를 방문해야 합니다.

해설 (c) That은 명사절을 이끄는 접속사이고 (d) However는 접속부사로써, 접속사 역할을 할 수 없다. 문맥상 가정을 나타내는 접속사 (a) If가 가장 자연스럽다.

어구 participation 참석   adult 어른, 성인

정답 (a)

31

해석 우리 집에서 약 두 블록 떨어진 곳에 있다.

해설 'A로부터 약 두 블록 떨어진'이란 올바른 영어표현과 어순은 it's about two blocks from A다.

어구 block 블록(도시의 한 구획)

정답 (d)

32

해석 검사는 3개 부분으로 구성될 것이다.

해설 동사 consist는 자동사기 때문에 수동태로 쓸 수 없지만 '구성되다'로 해석되어 수동태로 착각하기 쉬운 동사다. 자동사가 목적어를 취하기 위해서는 전치사와 결합하는데 consist는 of와 결합하여 consist of의 형태로 쓰인다.

어구 examination 검사   consist of ~로 구성되다
section 부분, 구획

정답 (c)

33

해석 지하철 버스 서비스는 예정대로 오늘 시행된다.

해설 동사 plan과 함께 '예정대로'의 올바른 형태를 묻고 있다. 이는 as와 함께 as planned로 표현 한다. as 뒤에 일반주어와 be동사가 생략되고 굳어진 분사형태로 볼 수 있다. 이때 동사 plan은 '~을 계획하다'라는 뜻의 타동사로 쓰였기 때문에 as planning은 될 수 없다.

어구 operate 작동하다   as planned 예정대로

정답 (a)

34

해석 만약 당신에게 아기가 있다면 천 기저귀를 쓰는 것이 좋다.

해설 빈 칸을 앞뒤로 문장을 연결해야 하므로 접속사가 필요하며 문맥상 '만일 ~한다면'이란 뜻이 되도록 빈 칸은 조건을 나타내는 접속사가 되어야 한다. (c) therefore와 (d) however는 접속부사로 문장과 문장을 연결할 수 없다. 조건의 접속사 if 대신 (b) provided that은 같은 뜻으로 쓸 수 있고 이때 문맥도 자연스럽다.

어구 had better V ~하는 것이 낫다
cloth 천   diaper 기저귀

정답 (b)

35

해석 까마귀들이 일부 농작물에 대대적인 피해를 입혔을 뿐만 아니라, 많은 그 지역 새들에게까지 피해를 입혔다.

해설 'A뿐만 아니라 B도'라는 뜻의 「not only A but also B」 구문으로 문장이 연결되고 있다. not only라는 부정어가 문두에 위치하는 경우 주어와 동사는 도치된다. 보기에서 올바르게 도치된 문장

은 (d) do the crows do다.

어구 not only A but also B A뿐만 아니라 B도
massive 대대적인 　　　 damage 피해
farm crop 농작물 　　　 destroy 파괴하다
local to the area 지역 특산물인(which is/are local to
the area에서 which + be동사가 생략되고 앞의 명사를 후치
수식하는 일종의 형용사 어구로 볼 수 있음)

정답 (d)

36

해석 그녀는 나보다 두 배는 빨리 말한다.

해설 올바른 영어의 배수 표현을 묻고 있다. 「배수사 as 형용사/부
사 as」가 올바른 순서와 표현이며 이를 만족하는 것은 보기 (d)
twice as fast as다.

정답 (d)

37

해석 그는 개 조련사만큼이나 개 치료사이기도 했다.

해설 「as much[many] A as B」 구문을 묻고 있다. '~만큼 이나 ~
한'의 의미를 갖는 이 구문을 통해 (b) as를 답으로 선택할 수 있다.

어구 healer 치료자

정답 (b)

38

해석 가장 가까운 시장은 걸어서 10분 거리에 있다.

해설 '걸어서 10분 거리'라는 올바른 영어표현 방법을 묻고 있다. 이때
시간이나 거리 표시는 단수 취급한다. 따라서 앞에 부정관사 a를
붙인 a ten minute walk이 올바른 표현이다.

어구 nearest 가장 가까운
a ten minute walk 걸어서 10분 거리

정답 (d)

39

해석 그는 직장에서 결코 스트레스를 받은 적이 없다.

해설 빈 칸 앞에 never라는 부정 부사가 문두로 나와 강조하고 있
다. 부정어가 문두에 위치하는 경우 이후의 주어와 동사는 도치
된다. 또한 현재완료(have p.p.) 시제로 제시된 경우 주어는
have/has와 과거분사(p.p.) 사이에 위치하게 된다. (c) has
he been이 이를 만족한다.

어구 stressful 스트레스가 많은 　　　 at work 직장에서

정답 (c)

40

해석 남자는 직사각형의 관에 매장되었는데 그 관 뚜껑의 색깔은 흰색
이었다.

해설 한 문장에 두 개의 주어와 동사(the man was, the lid was)가
있으므로 접속사가 필요하다. 또한 빈 칸은 접속사와 함께 앞의
명사 coffin을 받는 대명사 역할을 해야 한다. 이를 달리 표현하면,
and the lid of it was white가 되고 다시 관계사절로 바꾸면,
the lid of which was white가 된다. 또한 관계대명사 that은
계속적 용법에 쓰이지 않으니 (b) of that은 답이 될 수 없다.

어구 bury 매장하다 　 rectangular 직사각형의
coffin 관 　　　 lid 뚜껑

정답 (d)

41

해석 A: 무슨 일이야, 앤디?
B: 안경을 찾을 수가 없어서.
A: 코트 주머니 뒤져봤어?
B: 물론이지. 안 찾아본 데가 없어.

해설 모든 곳을 찾아봤다는 의미로 연결되어야 정황상 자연스러우
므로 (d)에서 anywhere를 everywhere로 바꿔야 한다.
anywhere는 의문문이나 부정문 또는 양보를 나타내는 평서문
에서 쓸 수 있는 표현이다.

정답 (d) anywhere → everywhere

42

해석 A: 제이, 너는 어디서 왔니?
B: 캐나다에서 왔어.
A: 여기는 휴가차 온 거니?
B: 아니, 사실은 일이 있어서.

해설 '비즈니스 일로'라는 뜻의 영어표현은 on business다. 이때 전
치사는 (d)의 to가 아닌 on이어야 한다.

어구 on vacation 휴가차 　　　 on business 비즈니스 일로

정답 (d) to business → on business

43

해석 A: 신년에는 어떤 결심이라도 했나요?
B: 네. 금연하려고요.
A: 잘됐으면 좋겠네요.
B: 네, 행운을 빌어줘요.

해설 (b)에서 동사 decide는 to부정사를 목적어로 취한다. 동사 quit
을 to quit으로 바꿔야 한다.

어구 make a New Year's resolution 신년 결심(계획)을 짜다
wish me luck 행운을 빌어줘(상대방으로 하여금 자신에게 행
운을 빌어 달라는 표현으로 상대방은 그 화답으로 주로 good
luck이라고 한다.)

정답 (a) quit → to quit

44

해석 A: 넥타이를 찾고 있습니다.
B: 특별히 생각하고 계신 것이라도 있나요?
A: 무늬 없는 붉은 색을 사고 싶습니다.
B: 이것은 어때요?

해설 (b)에서 Particular anything이라는 단어 어순을 Anything
particular로 바꿔야 한다. anything과 같이 -thing으로 끝나
는 대명사는 형용사가 수식하는 경우 후치 수식하기 때문이다.

어구 particular 특별한 　　　 have A in mind A를 염두에 두다
solid 무늬가 없는, 단단한

정답 (b) Particular anything → Anything particular

45

해석 A: 제 컴퓨터를 찾아가도 될까요?
B: 아니요, 여전히 고치고 있는 중입니다.
A: 시간이 얼마나 걸릴까요?
B: 한 시간이면 됩니다.

해설 (d)에서 전치사 in이 시간명사와 결합하면 '~(시간) 후에'라는 의
미가 된다. 이때 뒤의 hour는 가산명사로 관사(an)가 있어야 한

다. 따라서 in hour를 in an hour로 바꿔야 한다.

어구 repair 수리하다   in an hour 한 시간 후에

정답 (d) in hour → in an hour

PART IV

46

해석 (a) 팀 자이언트에서 새로운 직원을 찾고 있습니다. (b) 지원하기 전에 우리의 JOB 페이지를 참고해주세요. (c) 관심이 있으시면, Giant 닷컴으로 이메일을 보내주세요. (d) 귀하에 관한 사항, 즉 이름, 성별, 나이, 기본 정보(출신성분, 경력 등) 등을 알려주시기 바랍니다.

해설 (c)의 접속사가 잘못되었다. 양보의 의미인 Although는 문맥상 어울리지 않는다. 조건을 나타내는 If로 바꿔야 한다.

어구 member 구성원, 직원   have a look at ~을 보다
express 표현하다   interest 관심; 이자
gender 성별
background 배경(출신성분, 경력 등의 기본정보)

정답 (c) Although → If

47

해석 (a) 에볼라 바이러스는 1967년에 처음 알려지게 되었다. (b) 발병은 독일 프랑크푸르트의 실험실에서였고 이를 통해 총 37명이 그 병에 의해 감염되었다. (b) 병을 갖게 된 사람들은 실험실 직원들, 의료진, 환자를 간호하는 가족 구성원들이었다. (c) 감염된 최초의 사람들은 우간다로부터 수입된 아프리카산 녹색 원숭이에 의한 접촉(노출)에 의해서였다.

해설 (a)에서 명백한 과거 시점인 in 1967이 있으므로 동사 has been을 was로 바꿔야 한다.

어구 recognize 인식하다   outbreak 발병
occur 발생하다   laboratory 실험실
sicken 아프게 하다   include 포함하다
medical 의료의   family member 가족 구성원
infect 감염 시키다   expose 노출시키다
import 수입하다

정답 (a) has been → was

48

해석 (a) 나는 잎사귀 크기보다 몇 배나 작은 붉은 개미가 잎사귀 조각을 나른다는 것을 알게 되었다. (b) 개미들은 그들의 가위 같은 턱으로 잎을 자르고 그것들을 자신들의 보금자리로 옮겼다. (c) 잎사귀를 자르는 (일꾼) 개미들은 잎사귀를 먹지 않는다. (d) 오히려, 그들은 잎을 그들의 가장 중요한 식량이 되는 일종의 곰팡이를 기르는 데 사용한다.

해설 (a)에서 비교급 smaller가 있기 때문에 뒤의 as를 than으로 바꿔야 한다. 앞의 (many) times와 함께 올바른 배수 표현을 만들기 위해서라도 smaller than이 되어야 한다.

어구 carry 나르다   reddish 불그스름한
배수사 + 비교급 + than + A A보다 몇 배나 ~한
leaf 잎사귀   scissorlike 가위 같은
jaw 턱   nest 둥지
particular 특별한   fungus 곰팡이

정답 (a) smaller as → smaller than

49

해석 (a) 스페인 점령기 동안 2세기 이상, 필리핀에는 정식 교육 시스템이 없었다. (b) 대부분의 필리핀 사람들이 접근할 수 있는 단 하나의 교육은 주일 학교 문답식 교육이었다. (c) 학교에서 채택된 교과 주제는 미술과 문법에 국한되어 분류되었다. (d) 그리고 (남녀공학이 없어서) 소년 소녀들은 각각의 남학교 또는 여학교를 다녔다.

해설 문장 (b)에서 주어는 the only form이다. 명사의 수가 단수이므로 동사는 were가 아닌 was가 되어야 한다.

어구 century 세기(100년)
formal system of education 정규 교육 시스템
catechism 문답식 교리 교육   separate 분리된

정답 (b) were → was

50

해석 (a) 오늘날 증가하는 기술 산업에서 좋은 품질의 상품을 생산하는 것은 매우 중요하다. (b) 모든 산업과 그것의 제품이 각각 다르더라도 다른 산업체와 경쟁하기 위해 더 좋은 제품을 생산하는 경향이 있다. (c) 매년 기업은 연구와 제품을 만드는 데 수백만 불을 들인다. (d) 기업들은 특허를 통해 그들이 제품을 만드는 데 소비하는 시간과 돈을 지키려는 경향이 있다.

해설 (c) millions와 함께 '수백 만 불'의 올바른 영어표현은 millions of dollars다. of를 넣어야 한다.

어구 growing 증가하는
technology industry 기술 산업
produce 생산하다   high quality 고품질의
product 제품   create 만들다
tend to ~하는 경향이 있다   patent 특허

정답 (c) millions dollars → millions of dollars

Section B 어휘

Chapter 1

UNIT 1 동사+명사 I

EXERCISE

A

1 (d)   2 (a)   3 (e)   4 (b)   5 (c)

B

1 doing   2 taking
3 make   4 made
5 make

PRACTICE

1 (d)   2 (c)   3 (b)   4 (d)   5 (d)
6 (a)   7 (d)   8 (a)

중요 Collocation 정리

1 흥미롭게도, 미쉘은 숙제하는 것을 즐긴다.
2 불평은 절대 하지 말고 최선을 다하기만 해라.
3 나쁜 정책은 나라에 커다란 해를 끼칠 수 있다.
4 담임선생님은 우리들에게 실수를 저지르지 않도록 노력하라고 말씀하셨다.
5 타라는 TEPS 점수를 올리기 위해 힘껏 노력하고 있다.
6 우리는 토론토에서 이틀 밤을 묵기 위해 (방을) 예약했다.
7 윌로우는 그 못생긴 사업가와 결혼하기로 결심했다.
8 학생들이 우리 학교를 아름답게 하자고 제안했다.
9 제시카는 자신의 마을을 떠나겠다는 어려운 선택을 내렸다.
10 크리스는 매일 아침 샤워를 한다.
11 12시간 동안 일하고 나서, 마침내 우리는 휴식을 취했다.
12 매년 수백 만 명의 학생들이 대학 입학시험을 치른다.
13 아침 식사를 하는 것은 건강에 좋다.
14 다음 주에 수지의 생일 파티를 열 계획이다.
15 실은, 그녀의 집을 찾는 데 많은 어려움을 겪었다.

EXERCISE A

1 (d)
정말로 최선을 다한다면 무슨 일이든 해낼 수 있다.

2 (a)
무언가가 어떤 상황에 해를 끼친다면 그 상황을 악화시키는

것이다.

3 (e)
실수를 저지르면 바로잡으려 애써라.

4 (b)
파티를 열면 가능한 한 많은 사람들을 초대하라.

5 (c)
규칙적으로 아침 식사를 하면 건강을 유지할 것이다.

EXERCISE B

1
해석 TV 좀 꺼. 지금 숙제하고 있단 말이야.
해설 '숙제를 하다'라고 할 때 반드시 do를 써야 함에 유의하자. make는 결과에 중점을 두기 때문에, 숙제를 하는 과정에 초점을 맞추는 표현과는 어울리지 않는다.
정답 doing

2
해석 내일 여러 개의 시험을 치른다. 어떤 것을 먼저 해야 할지 모르겠다.
해설 '시험을 치르다'라고 할 때 동사는 take를 써야 한다. make는 결과에 초점을 맞추는 표현이기 때문에, 시험을 치르는 과정에 중점을 두는 어휘와는 어울리지 않는다.
정답 taking

3
해석 두 사람으로 예약하려고 합니다.
해설 '예약'의 결과로서 호텔 객실이나 좌석을 확보할 수 있기 때문에 make를 써야한다.
정답 make

4
해석 오즈는 회의에서 좋은 제안을 했다.
해설 '제안'의 결과로 사람들이 고려하게 됨에 중점을 두기 때문에 make을 써야 한다.
정답 made

5
해석 때때로 어려운 선택을 내려야만 하는 경우도 있다.
해설 '선택'의 결과로 일정한 행동을 해야 함에 중점을 두기 때문에 make을 써야 한다.
정답 make

PRACTICE

1
해석 A: 너 피곤해 보인다.
     B: 응. 좀 쉬어야 할 것 같아.
해설 '휴식을 취하다'라는 뜻의 take a rest를 묻는 문제로 정답은 (d)

다. 동사 take는 본래 '손에 넣다'라는 기본적인 뜻을 갖는다. 이 의미에서 '휴식'을 손에 넣는 것으로 생각하기 때문에 take를 써야 함에 유의하자.

어구 tired 피곤한

정답 (d)

2

해석 A: 내일 시험이 걱정돼.
B: 마음을 편히 먹어. 그냥 최선을 다해.

해설 '최선을 다하다'는 뜻의 do one's best를 묻는 문제로 정답은 (c) 다. 동사 do의 쓰임은 대개 결과보다는 과정이나 행동에 중점을 둔다는 데 유의하자.

정답 (c)

3

해석 A: 내일 파티 하는데. 와 줄래?
B: 아쉽게도 못 가. 다른 일이 있거든.

해설 '파티를 열다'는 뜻의 have a party를 묻는 문제로 정답은 (b) 다. have의 본래 뜻은 '움켜잡다'이다. 이 뜻에서 '가지다'라는 뜻으로 발전했는데, 파티와 같은 행사의 개최를 '움켜잡듯이' 가지는 것으로 생각하기 때문에 have를 써야 함에 유의하자.

정답 (b)

4

해석 A: 어제 늦게까지 안 잤어.
B: 또 그랬니? 그런 습관은 네게 큰 해를 끼칠 수도 있어.

해설 '해를 끼치다'는 뜻의 do harm을 묻는 문제로 정답은 (d)다. do 의 본래 뜻은 '(일정한 곳에) 놓다'이다. 이 뜻으로부터 '일정한 활동을 하다'라는 뜻이 나왔는데, 해(harm)를 일정한 대상에 놓은 것으로 해석하는 원어민의 사고방식을 엿볼 수 있다.

어구 stay up 늦게까지 잠자리에 들지 않다

정답 (d)

5

해석 그것의 소유주를 찾기 위해 모든 노력을 기울였다.

해설 '노력하다'는 뜻의 make an effort를 묻는 문제로 정답은 (d)다. 노력의 결과에 중점을 두기 때문에 make을 써야 함에 유의하자. effort는 '밖으로 (ef←ex) 힘을 내는 것(fort)'으로 분석되어 '노력' 이란 뜻을 나타낸다. 반면, comfort는 '완전히(com) 힘을 내는 것(fort)'으로 분석되어 '위안'을 뜻한다.

어구 affect 정서; 영향을 미치다
comfort 위안   effect 효과   effort 노력

정답 (d)

6

해석 조나단은 발표하면서 끔찍한 실수를 저질렀다.

해설 '실수를 저지르다'는 뜻의 make a mistake를 묻는 문제로 정답은 (a)다. 실수는 '결과'에 중점을 두기 때문에 make를 써야 함에 유의하자.

어구 presentation 발표

정답 (a)

7

해석 버피는 캐나다로 이주하려는 어려운 결정을 내렸다.

해설 '결심하다'는 뜻의 make a decision을 묻는 문제로 정답은 (d) 다. 결심의 '결과'에 중점을 두기 때문에 make를 써야 함에 유의

하자.

어구 move 이주하다, 이사하다

정답 (d)

8

해석 많은 학생들이 영문법을 이해하는 데 큰 어려움을 겪고 있다.

해설 '어려움을 겪다'는 뜻의 have difficulty를 묻는 문제로 정답은 (a) 다. '어려움'을 '움켜잡아 가지다'라고 생각하는 원어민의 발상을 엿볼 수 있다.

정답 (a)

UNIT 2   동사+명사 Ⅱ

EXERCISE

A

1 (e)   2 (a)   3 (d)   4 (b)   5 (c)

B

1 apply   2 dropped
3 repaired   4 shoulder
5 suffered

PRACTICE

1 (d)   2 (b)   3 (a)   4 (b)   5 (a)
6 (d)   7 (c)   8 (c)

중요 Collocation 정리

1 반복은 지식을 흡수하는 데 도움이 된다.

2 그 문제를 해결하기 위해서는 효과적인 방법을 적용해야 한다.

3 로즈메리는 술을 끊겠다는 자신의 맹세를 어겼다.

4 결정을 내리기 전에 늘 사실을 확인하라.

5 머피 박사는 여성문제에 대한 강연을 했다.

6 장관은 살인범을 사형에 처할 것이라는 점을 강력히 시사했다.

7 화가 나서 로라는 도둑을 향해 총을 쏐다.

8 그들은 정당의 실패를 온전히 그녀의 탓으로 돌렸다.

9 놀랍게도, 그녀의 학생 가운데 한 명이 그 장비를 수리했다.

10 이사벨라는 교실 창문 청소를 책임졌다.

11 브리트니 스피어스는 이른 나이에 노래에 대한 재능을 드러냈다.

12 그녀의 고향은 허리케인 카트리나로 인해 피해를 입었다.

13 유감스럽게도, 그 네 명의 형제는 사고에서 살아남지 못했다.

14 청소년들은 많은 변화를 겪기 마련이다.

15 많은 학부모들이 행실이 나쁜 학생들을 퇴학시키는 데 대해

강력한 의견을 표명했다.

EXERCISE A

1 (e)

어떤 것에 대한 지식을 흡수한다면, 그것에 대해 알게 된다.

2 (a)

어떤 일을 하겠다는 맹세를 어기면, 약속을 지키지 않는 것이다.

3 (d)

어떤 것에 대해 강의를 한다면, 그것에 대해 말하는 것이다.

4 (b)

어떤 이를 향해 총을 쏘면, 그 사람은 죽을 수도 있다.

5 (c)

변화를 겪는다면, 사람들이 몰라볼지도 모른다.

EXERCISE B

1

해석 보다 실용적인 방법을 적용할 필요가 있다.

해설 '적용하다'라는 뜻의 apply를 묻는 문제다. reply는 '응답하다'라는 뜻으로 method와 자연스러운 collocation을 만들지 못함에 유의하자.

정답 apply

2

해석 니콜라스는 자신의 계획에 대한 힌트를 주었다.

해설 '힌트를 주다'라고 할 때 drop을 써야 함을 묻는 문제다. fell은 '떨어지다'는 뜻인 fall의 과거형으로 자동사이기 때문에 목적어에 해당하는 a hint가 올 수 없음에 유의하자. 이와 같은 문법적 사항도 정확히 익혀두어야 실제 TEPS 시험에 제대로 대비할 수 있다.

정답 dropped

3

해석 클라라는 장비를 수리했다.

해설 '수리하다'라는 뜻의 repair를 묻는 문제다. 이 문제에서도 appear는 repair와 모양이 비슷하지만 자동사이기 때문에 목적어에 해당하는 the equipment가 이어질 수 없음에 유의해야 한다.

정답 repaired

4

해석 정치가들은 자신들이 하는 일에 대해 책임을 져야 한다.

해설 '(책임을) 지다'라는 뜻의 shoulder를 묻는 문제다. 오답으로 제시된 elbow는 동사로 '팔꿈치로 밀어젖히다'라는 뜻을 나타낸다.

정답 shoulder

5

해석 사라는 그 사고로 인해 피해를 입었다.

해설 '(피해를) 입다'라는 뜻의 suffer를 묻는 문제다. 오답으로 제시된 refer는 대개 to와 함께 쓰여 '~를 지칭하다'라는 뜻을 나타낸다.

정답 suffered

PRACTICE

1

해석 A: 금주하겠다는 맹세를 어기지 마라.
B: 어기지 않을 거야. 결코 실망시키지 않을게.

해설 '맹세를 어기다'라는 뜻의 break a pledge를 묻는 문제다. 이 때 break는 구체적인 물건을 '깨뜨리다'라는 본래의 뜻이 확장되어 추상적인 대상에까지 적용되었다. 마찬가지로, '약속을 어기다' 역시 break a promise로 표현된다.

어구 stop drinking 금주하다   let ~ down ~를 실망시키다
chew 씹다

정답 (d)

2

해석 A: 이 사태에 대해 즉시 부장님께 보고해야 해요.
B: 먼저 사실을 확인해야 할 거 같은데요.

해설 '사실을 확인하다'는 뜻의 check a fact를 묻는 문제다. check는 본래 서양장기에서 '장군을 부르다'라는 뜻을 나타냈는데, 이 뜻으로부터 '저지하다' 그리고 '확인하다'라는 뜻으로 확장되어 쓰인다. '어구' 부분에서 해설한 단어들도 모두 출제 범위에 속하므로 정확히 익혀 두자.

어구 report 보고하다   manager 부장
incident 사태   right away 즉시
peck (새가 부리로) 쪼아대다

정답 (b)

3

해석 A: 그가 사고에서 살아남아서 아주 기뻐요.
B: 저도 그래요. 그렇지만 아슬아슬했어요.

해설 '사고에서 살아남다'라는 뜻의 survive an accident를 묻는 문제다. 이때 survive가 타동사로 쓰이기 때문에 목적어인 an accident가 바로 이어서 와야 함에 주의해야 한다. 그리고 오답으로 제시된 expire, collapse, perish가 대개 자동사로 쓰이기 때문에 바로 다음에 목적어가 올 수 없음에 유의할 필요가 있다.

어구 accident 사고   close call 위기일발
expire 만료되다   collapse 무너지다
perish (사고 등으로) 죽다; 소멸하다

정답 (a)

4

해석 A: 미셸을 거의 못 알아보겠어.
B: 있잖아, 근래에 변화를 겪었거든.

해설 '변화를 겪다'라는 뜻의 undergo a change를 묻는 문제다. undergo는 '일정한 경험 아래를(under) 가다(go)'라는 발상에서 생겨난 단어다. 그리고 영한사전을 통해 제대로 뜻을 알 수 없는 단어 가운데 하나인 underplay가 '평가절하하다'라는 뜻임을 알아두어야 한다. 구동사로는 lay down으로 표현된다.

어구 hardly 거의 ~않다   recognize 알아보다
recently 근래에   prevent 막다
underdo (고기를) 설익히다 underplay 평가절하하다

정답 (b)

5

해석 이해가 지식을 흡수하는 데 있어서 관건이다.

해설 '지식을 흡수하다'라는 뜻의 absorb knowledge를 묻는 문제다. absorb는 '~로부터(ab) 빨아들이다(sorb)'로 분석된다.

absent와 abstain은 각각 '벗어나(abs) 있는(ent)'과 '벗어나(abs) 잡다(tain)'로 분석할 수 있다. abuse는 '벗어나게(ab) 쓰다(use)'로 분석된다.

어구 key 핵심적 측면   absent 결석하다
abuse 남용하다   abstain 삼가다

정답 (a)

6

해석 그 미치광이는 부패한 정치가를 향해 총을 쏘았다.

해설 '총을 쏘다'라는 뜻의 fire a gun을 묻는 문제다. 오답으로 제시된 단어들은 모두 출제 범위이기 때문에 정확히 익혀두어야 한다. 특히 wire의 뜻은 영한사전에 제대로 설명되어 있지 않기 때문에 주의해서 익혀두어야 한다.

어구 madman 미치광이   corrupt 타락한
hire 고용하다   wire 송금하다
tire 지치게 하다

정답 (d)

7

해석 보다 많은 여성들이 사회적 문제에 대해 의견을 표명해야 한다.

해설 '의견을 표명하다'는 뜻의 voice an opinion을 묻는 문제다. 의견표명은 '목소리'를 통해 이루어진다는 데 착안한 표현이다. 오답으로 제시된 단어 가운데 ache은 자동사로 쓰여 '심하지 않은 아픔이 지속되다'라는 뜻을 나타냄에 유의하자.

어구 social 사회적인   issue 쟁점
ache (지속적으로) 아프다   endure 견디다
prohibit 금지하다

정답 (c)

8

해석 정치가는 자신의 견해에 대해 책임을 져야 한다.

해설 '책임을 지다'는 뜻의 shoulder responsibility를 묻는 문제다. 오답으로 제시된 표현들은 모두 신체의 부위를 나타내는데, 해당 신체 부위의 특성과 관련하여 동사로서의 뜻을 나타낼 수 있음에 유의하자. 예컨대 stomach의 경우, 음식물을 '소화하는' 위의 기능을 생각하여, 부당한 대우 등을 '참아낸다'는 뜻을 나타내게 되었다.

어구 view 관점, 견해   stomach 참아내다
arm 무장시키다   head 통솔하다

정답 (c)

UNIT 3   동사＋명사 III

EXERCISE

A

1 (c)	2 (e)	3 (a)	4 (b)	5 (d)

B

1	made	2	took
3	gave	4	cause
5	gave		

PRACTICE

1 (d)	2 (b)	3 (c)	4 (a)	5 (d)
6 (d)	7 (c)	8 (c)		

중요 Collocation 정리

1 경찰은 소녀를 보호하기 위한 조치를 취했다.

2 기자는 자신의 실수에 대해 사죄했다.

3 균형을 유지해라. 그렇지 않으면, 땅으로 떨어질 것이다.

4 몇몇 학부모들이 그 못생긴 교사에 대해 불평을 토로했다.

5 해일은 나라 전체에 막대한 피해를 입혔다.

6 구달 씨는 언제나 명확한 지시를 내린다.

7 변명하지 마라. 그냥 진실을 말해줘!

8 많은 과학자들이 그 액체의 효과를 시험하기 위해 실험을 하고 있다.

9 학교는 5월에 연례 축제를 개최한다.

10 제이슨은 막대한 재산을 벌었지만 도박으로 모두 날렸다.

11 자원봉사자들에게 특별한 선물을 증정했다.

12 사실, 어느 누구도 하룻밤 사이에 버릇을 고칠 수는 없다.

13 그 젊은 근로자는 모든 이들에게 좋은 인상을 주었다.

14 현재의 교육 제도는 학생들의 수요를 충족시키지 못한다.

15 지구 온난화는 환경에 많은 문제를 일으킨다.

EXERCISE A

1 (c)
사과를 한다면, 무언가 잘못을 저지른 것이다.

2 (e)
변명을 한다면, 정직하지 않은 것이다.

3 (a)
축제를 개최한다면, 많은 것을 준비할 필요가 있다.

4 (b)
실험을 한다면, 무엇인가를 알아내려고 하는 것이다.

5 (d)
고객의 수요를 충족시키면 많은 돈을 벌 것이다.

EXERCISE B

1

해석 많은 고객들이 신제품에 대해 불평을 했다.

해설 '불평'의 결과에 중점을 두기 때문에 make를 써야 한다. do는 과정이나 일반적인 행동을 나타낼 때 주로 쓰인다.

정답 made

2

해석 정부는 질병의 확산을 막기 위해 조치를 취했다.

해설 take의 본래 뜻은 '손에 넣다'이다. 이 뜻에서 '확보하다'라는 뜻이 나왔는데, 일정한 조치를 손에 넣듯이 확보하는 것으로 생각하는 원어민의 발상을 엿볼 수 있다.

정답 took

3

해석 실망스럽게도, 경찰관은 우리에게 길을 찾아가는 방법을 알려주지 않았다.

해설 direction에는 '지시'라는 뜻과 함께 '길을 찾아가는 방법'이라는 뜻이 있다. give는 본래 '주다'라는 뜻인데, 이 뜻으로부터 '말해주다'라는 뜻이 생겨났음도 유의하자.

정답 gave

4

해석 부(富)만을 추구하는 것은 당신의 삶에 심각한 문제를 일으킬 수 있다.

해설 cause는 명사로서 '원인'이라는 뜻을, 동사로서 '원인이 되다' 즉 '초래하다'라는 뜻을 나타낸다. 참고로 because는 'be(~에 의해) cause(원인)'로 분석되어 '원인에 의해' 곧 '~하기 때문에'라는 뜻을 나타낸다.

정답 cause

5

해석 그 예의바른 학생은 모든 선생님들에게 좋은 인상을 주었다.

해설 '인상을 주다'는 뜻의 give an impression을 묻는 문제다. give는 본래 '구체적인 대상을 주다'라는 뜻인데, 인상과 같은 추상적인 대상으로 쓰임새가 확장되었다.

정답 gave

PRACTICE

1

해석 A: 늦어서 정말 미안해.
　　　 B: 넌 늘 사과만 하는구나. 지겹지도 않니?

해설 '사과하다'라는 뜻의 make an apology를 묻는 유형으로 정답은 (d)다. '사과'라는 결과에 초점을 맞추기 때문에 make을 써야 함에 유의하자.

어구 tired of ~에 싫증이 난

정답 (d)

2

해석 A: 다음 주에 연례 축제 하는데. 올 수 있니?
　　　 B: 아, 정말? 정말 가고 싶은데, 우선 내 일정을 확인해 봐야 돼.

해설 '축제를 개최하다'라는 뜻의 hold a festival을 묻는 문제로 정답은 (b)다. hold는 본래 '지켜보다'라는 뜻인데, 이로부터 일정한

것을 '보유하다' 또는 '개최하다'라는 뜻이 나왔다.

어구 yearly 연례의(=annual)　　check 확인하다

정답 (b)

3

해석 A: 해롤드가 갑자기 큰돈을 벌었다는 소식 들었니?
　　　 B: 뭐라고? 좀 더 잘 대해줄걸.

해설 '큰돈을 벌다'라는 뜻의 make a fortune을 묻는 문제다. 돈을 번 결과에 중점을 두기 때문에 make를 써야 함에 유의하다. 참고로 '재산을 축적하다'가 accumulate a fortune으로 표현됨도 알아두자.

어구 overnight 하룻밤 사이에
　　　 should have p.p. ~했어야만 했는데

정답 (c)

4

해석 A: 수백만의 아프리카사람들이 굶주리고 있어요.
　　　 B: 음, 즉시 조치를 취해야만 해요.

해설 '조치를 취하다'는 take action으로 표현한다. 그리고 (d)의 lay는 특히 '눕다, 놓여 있다'라는 뜻의 lie와 혼동하지 않도록 주의해야 한다. lay는 '눕히다, 놓아두다'라는 뜻을 나타낸다.

어구 millions of 수백만의　　　 starve 굶주리다
　　　 right away 즉시

정답 (a)

5

해석 성공하기 위해서는 고객들의 수요를 충족시키지 않으면 안 된다.

해설 meet의 본래 뜻은 '~와 마주치다'이다. '수요'와 '마주치는 것'을 '수요를 충족시키는 것'으로 이해하는 원어민의 발상을 엿볼 수 있다.

어구 succeed 성공하다　　　 customer 고객
　　　 part 헤어지다

정답 (d)

6

해석 지시를 할 때는 간단한 단어를 쓰도록 노력하라.

해설 '지시하다'라는 뜻은 give directions로 나타낸다.
이때 directions에는 '길을 찾아가는 방법'이란 뜻도 있음을 기억하자.

정답 (d)

7

해석 나쁜 버릇을 고치는 것은 고되고 오랜 과정이다.

해설 '버릇을 고치다'는 break[shake] a habit으로 표현한다. 다른 동사를 쓰지 않는다는 점에 유의할 필요가 있다. 참고로 '해로운 습관을 버리다'는 뜻은 kick the habit으로 표현된다.

정답 (c)

8

해석 구직 면접에서 좋은 인상을 줄도록 노력하라.

해설 '인상을 주다'는 give an impression으로 표현한다. 동사 give 대신 convey 또는 create를 쓸 수도 있다.

성답 (c)

EXERCISE

A

1 (c)　**2** (a)　**3** (d)　**4** (e)　**5** (b)

B

1 hope　　　**2** on
3 relieve　　**4** enjoyed
5 vacancy

PRACTICE

1 (d)　**2** (b)　**3** (b)　**4** (c)　**5** (a)
6 (c)　**7** (a)　**8** (b)

중요 Collocation 정리

1 그들은 중고 장비에 대한 광고를 게재했다.

2 책을 교정보면서, 에리카는 많은 오타를 찾아냈다.

3 사라는 도전을 감당함으로써 용기를 드러냈다.

4 실제로는, 서로 다른 인종 집단 사이의 차이를 해소하는 것은 불가능하다.

5 때로는 기대를 뛰어넘는 것이 좋은 생각이 아니다.

6 불가능한 목표를 이루려고 하고 있다는 걸 모르겠니?

7 이민자들은 보다 나은 미래에 대한 희망을 품었다.

8 소녀들은 남극으로의 중대한 여행을 시작했다.

9 외로운 어머니는 어린 딸에게 자장가를 흥얼거려 주었다.

10 진통제는 고통을 덜어주어야 하는 법이다.

11 예일대는 미국에서 최고의 명문대학 가운데 하나로 명성을 누려왔다.

12 일부 약품들이 수면을 유발한다는 주장이 제기된다.

13 미국인들은 교역을 증진함으로써 번성을 누렸다.

14 마돈나의 콘서트는 많은 사람들을 끌어들였다.

15 회사는 어리석은 사람을 채용해서 공석을 채웠다.

EXERCISE A

1 (c)
그의 형편없는 책을 교정본다면, 문법적 오류를 많이 발견하게 될 것이다.

2 (a)
누군가가 용기를 드러낸다면, 그 사람은 어려움을 다룰 수 있는 것이다.

3 (d)
두 집단이 차이를 해소한다면, 서로와 사이좋게 지낼 수 있다.

4 (e)
기대를 뛰어넘는다면, 기대한 것보다 더 잘하는 것이다.

5 (b)
목표를 성취한다면, 그 목표를 이루는 것에 성공한 것이다.

EXERCISE B

1

해석 모든 이들은 보다 나은 세상에 대한 희망을 품는다.

해설 '희망을 품다'라는 뜻의 cherish a hope를 묻는 문제다. 오답으로 제시된 slope은 '비탈진 곳'이라는 뜻으로 주어진 맥락에 어울리지 않는다. 이 단어는 동사로 쓰이면 '비탈지다'라는 뜻을 나타낸다.

정답 hope

2

해석 그 나라는 경제 성장으로의 여정을 시작했다.

해설 '여행을 시작하다'라는 뜻의 embark on a journey를 묻는 문제다. 이때 on을 off로 대신할 수 없다. 그리고 이 문장에서 journey는 '발달 과정'이라는 비유적 의미로 활용되었음도 기억하자.

정답 on

3

해석 아스피린을 좀 복용해 봐. 고통을 덜어내는 데 도움이 될 거야.

해설 '고통을 덜어내다'라는 뜻의 relieve pain을 묻는 문제다. 오답으로 제시된 cause는 '초래하다'라는 뜻을 나타내기 때문에 주어진 맥락에 맞지 않는다. 이 단어와 관련된 말인 because는 '원인(cause)에 의해(be)'로 분석된다.

정답 relieve

4

해석 그 회사는 이상적인 직장으로서의 명성을 누려왔다.

해설 '명성을 누리다'라는 뜻의 enjoy a reputation을 묻는 문제다. 오답으로 제시된 join은 '가입하다(또는 합류하다)'라는 뜻으로 주어진 맥락에 맞지 않는다. 참고로 reputation은 '다시(re) 생각나게(put) 하는(at) 것(ion)'으로 분석된다.

정답 enjoyed

5

해석 아무도 그 직책에 지원하지 않아서 그들은 공석을 채울 수 없었다.

해설 '공석을 채우다'라는 뜻의 fill a vacancy를 묻는 문제다. 오답으로 제시된 vacation은 '휴가(또는 방학)'라는 뜻으로 주어진 맥락에 어울리지 않는다.

정답 vacancy

PRACTICE

1

해석 A: 내 중고 컴퓨터를 어떻게 팔 수 있는지 알려줄래?
B: 지역 신문에 광고를 게재하는 게 어때?

해설 '광고를 게재하다'라는 뜻의 place an advertisement를 묻는 문제다. 본래 place는 '개방된 공간'이라는 뜻을 나타내는데, 광고를 일정한 '공간'에 모아두는 데 착안하여 place an advertisement라는 표현이 생겨났다. 그리고 선택지 가운데 please가 '기쁘다'라는 뜻이 아니라는 점을 꼭 기억해야 한다.

어구 used 중고의   local 지역의
jog 조깅하다   please 즐겁게 하다

정답 (d)

2

해석 A: 그녀의 용기에 아주 감명을 받았어.
B: 나도 그래. 아무도 그녀가 그런 용기를 드러내리라고 예상하지 못했어.

해설 '용기를 드러내다'라는 뜻의 display courage를 묻는 문제다. 선택지 가운데 disappear는 자동사로만 쓰이기 때문에 courage와 같은 목적어가 바로 다음에 올 수 없다. 그리고 disprove와 discuss는 주어진 맥락에 적합하지 않다.

어구 impress 감명을 주다   disappear 사라지다
disprove 반증하다

정답 (b)

3

해석 A: 에리카가 시험을 얼마나 잘 치렀어요?
B: 놀랍게도, 기대를 뛰어넘었어요.

해설 '기대를 뛰어넘다'라는 뜻의 exceed expectations를 묻는 문제다. exceed는 '밖으로(ex) 가다(ceed)'로 분석되는데, 일정한 한계 밖으로 가는 것으로 생각하기 때문에 '뛰어넘다'라는 뜻을 갖게 되었다. 참고로 express는 '밖으로(ex) 누르다(press)'로 분석된다.

어구 experience 경험하다   express 표현하다
exchange 교환하다

정답 (b)

4

해석 A: 회의가 어떻게 됐어요?
B: 실망스럽게도, 참석자들을 조금밖에 끌어들이지 못했어요.

해설 '(참석하는) 사람들을 끌어들이다'라는 뜻의 attract a turnout을 묻는 문제다. attract는 '향해서(at←ad) 끌다(tract)'로 분석된다. 선택지 가운데 apply는 바로 다음에 for나 to가 오면 '신청하다'라는 뜻을, 목적어가 와서 타동사로 쓰이면 '적용하다; (화장품 등을) 바르다'라는 뜻을 나타낸다.

어구 conference 회의   disappointment 실망
apply 적용하다   agree 동의하다
astonish 깜짝 놀라게 하다

정답 (c)

5

해석 편집자는 질(質)을 높이기 위해 그 책을 여러 번 교정했다.

해설 '책을 교정보다'라는 뜻의 proofread a book을 묻는 문제다. 선택지 가운데 promote는 '앞으로(pro) 움직이다(mot[e])'로 분석된다. 이와 관련된 단어인 emotion은 '밖으로(e) 움직이는 (mot) 것(ion)'으로 분석되는데, 일정한 정서는 밖으로 드러내려고 하는 경향이 있기 때문에 '정서'라는 뜻을 갖는다.

어구 editor 편집자   improve 향상시키다
quality 품질   promote 승진시키다
propose 제안하다   prosper 번창하다

정답 (a)

6

해석 힐러리는 목표를 성취하기 위해 할 수 있는 모든 일을 다 했다.

해설 '목표를 성취하다'라는 뜻의 attain a goal을 묻는 문제다. attain은 '향해서(at←ad) 건드리다(tain)'로 분석된다. 선택지 가운데 attack이 '공격하다'라는 뜻에서 발전하여 '(심하게) 비판하다'라는 뜻과 '(문제를) 다루다'라는 뜻도 나타낸다는 점을 익혀두자.

어구 attend 참석하다   attach 첨부하다   attack 공격하다

정답 (c)

7

해석 두 집단 사이의 차이를 창의적인 방식으로 해소하도록 노력하라.

해설 '차이를 해소하다'라는 뜻의 resolve differences를 묻는 문제다. resolve는 '완전히(←다시: re) 풀다(solve)'로 분석된다. 이 단어에서 접두사 re-가 '완전히'라는 뜻을 나타내는 것은 어떤 일을 '다시' 하는 것을 반복하면 '완전하게' 해낼 수 있다는 생각 때문임도 참고하자.

어구 creative 창의적인   rely 의존하다   respond 반응하다
regret 후회하다

정답 (a)

8

해석 삶을 풍요롭게 하기 위한 여정을 시작하라!

해설 '여행을 시작하다'라는 뜻의 embark on a journey를 묻는 문제다. 선택지 가운데 employ와 embarrass는 둘 다 타동사이기 때문에 on과 같은 전치사가 바로 이어질 수 없다. 반면 자동사인 emerge는 바로 다음에 전치사로 from이 오는 것이 보통이다.

어구 enrich 풍요롭게 하다   employ 고용하다
embarrass 창피하게 하다   emerge 나타나다

정답 (b)

UNIT 5 명사+동사

EXERCISE

A

1 (b)   **2** (d)   **3** (e)   **4** (a)   **5** (c)

B

1 circulate   **2** reigned
3 function   **4** expires
5 broke

PRACTICE

1 (a)   **2** (d)   **3** (c)   **4** (c)   **5** (d)
6 (b)   **7** (a)   **8** (b)

중요 Collocation 정리

1 비행기는 몇 분 동안 지상에서 활주하고 나서 이륙했다.

2 혈액은 몸 전체에 걸쳐 순환한다.

3 그 정치인이 물러나고 나서 위기는 완화되었다.

4 그때 이래로 일본의 밀 수요는 증가해왔다.

5 놀랍게도 기관은 완벽하게 기능을 발휘했다.

6 독립을 위한 그들의 투쟁은 수십 년 동안 맹위를 떨쳤다.

7 그들의 대단한 노력으로 인해, 빈부 격차는 줄어들었다.

8 그를 처음 보았을 때, 가슴이 심하게 두근거렸다.

9 유감스럽게도, 감염은 급속히 확산되었다.

10 현명한 왕은 반세기 동안 집권했다.

11 유가가 급격히 상승하자 시장은 침체에 빠졌다.

12 그들 사이의 심한 차이 때문에 협상은 결렬되었다.

13 그녀의 여권은 2002년 6월 29일에 만료되었다.

14 3월에 호텔 요금이 30퍼센트만큼 내렸다.

15 스캔들이 터지고 나자 회장은 회사를 떠나야만 했다.

EXERCISE A

1 (b)

비행기가 지상에서 활주하면, 공중을 날고 있는 것이 아니다.

2 (d)

위기가 완화되면, 그 위기에 대해 걱정할 필요가 없다.

3 (e)

수요가 증가하면, 보다 많은 제품을 팔 수 있다.

4 (a)

심장이 두근거리면, 어떤 것에 대해 격한 감정을 갖는 것이다.

5 (c)

시장이 침체에 빠지면, 많은 사람들이 불행을 느낀다.

EXERCISE B

1

해석 혈액이 어떻게 인체 내에서 순환하는 것일까?

해설 '혈액이 순환하다'라는 뜻의 blood circulates를 묻는 문제다. 오답으로 제시된 surround는 '둘러싸다'라는 뜻의 타동사이기 때문에, 목적어가 제시되어 있지 않은 주어진 문장에 어울리지 않는다.

정답 circulate

2

해석 여왕은 1789년부터 1876년까지 집권했다.

해설 '집권하다'라는 뜻의 reign을 묻는 문제다. 오답으로 제시된 rein은 '억제하다'라는 뜻의 타동사로 쓰이기 때문에 주어진 맥락에 맞지 않는다. 이 단어는 대개 reins라는 형태로 '고삐'라는 뜻으로도 쓰인다.

정답 reigned

3

해석 심하게 손상되었기 때문에, 기관은 작동하지 않았다.

해설 '작동하다'라는 뜻의 function을 묻는 문제다. 오답으로 제시된

mention은 '언급하다'라는 뜻의 타동사로 쓰이기 때문에 주어진 맥락에 어울리지 않는다. 특히 mention 바로 다음에 about을 쓸 수 없음에 유의하자.

정답 function

4

해석 여권이 만료되면, 사용할 수가 없다.

해설 '만료되다'라는 뜻의 expire를 묻는 문제다. 오답으로 제시된 express는 '표현하다'라는 뜻의 타동사로 쓰이기 때문에 주어진 맥락에 어울리지 않는다. 반면 expire는 자동사로만 쓰인다는 점도 기억해두자.

정답 expires

5

해석 스캔들이 터졌을 때, 모든 이들이 충격을 받았다.

해설 '스캔들이 터지다'라는 뜻의 a scandal breaks를 묻는 문제다. 오답으로 제시된 freeze는 '얼다; 얼게 하다'라는 뜻을 주로 나타내기 때문에 주어진 맥락에 어울리지 않는다.

정답 broke

PRACTICE

1

해석 A: 충돌 사고가 어떻게 일어났죠?
B: 비행기가 지상을 활주할 때, 트럭이 비행기에 충돌했어요.

해설 '비행기가 지상에서 활주하다'라는 뜻의 an airplane taxis를 묻는 문제다. taxi는 물론 명사로서 '택시'라는 뜻도 나타낸다. 그리고 선택지 가운데 trying은 형용사로서 '시련을 안겨주는'이란 뜻을 나타냄도 알아두자.

어구 collision 충돌 사고   crash 충돌하다
tire 피로하게 하다   tax 과세하다

정답 (a)

2

해석 A: 토고 여행을 예약하고 싶습니다.
B: 죄송합니다만, 손님, 여권이 만료되셨는데요.

해설 '만료되다'라는 뜻의 expire를 묻는 문제다. 선택지 가운데 explain은 '설명하다'라는 뜻으로 explain something to someone과 같은 형태로 쓰이기 때문에 정답이 될 수 없다. explain은 특히 explain someone something과 같은 형태로 절대로 쓸 수 없음에 유의해야 한다.

어구 reservation 예약   explain 설명하다
exist 존재하다   explode 폭발하다

정답 (d)

3

해석 A: 브루스 파커가 회장 자리에서 언제 물러났죠?
B: 스캔들이 터진 2007년에요.

해설 '스캔들이 터지다'라는 뜻의 a scandal breaks를 묻는 문제다. 선택지 가운데 destroy는 타동사로만 쓰이고, interrupt는 주로 타동사로 쓰이기 때문에 정답이 될 수 없다. 그리고 smash는 '부수어지다'라는 자동사로도 쓰일 수 있지만, 물체에 대해 쓰는 말이기 때문에 정답이 될 수 없다.

어구 step down 물러나다   president 회장; 대통령
destroy 파괴하다   interrupt 방해하다

smash 때려 부수다

정답 (c)

4

해석 A: 그 나라에서 감염이 급속히 확산되고 있어요.
B: 즉각적인 조치를 취해야 합니다.

해설 '감염이 확산되다'라는 뜻의 an infection spreads를 묻는 문제다. 선택지 가운데 repair, remove, support는 모두 타동사이기 때문에 정답이 될 수 없다. 반면 spread는 자동사로도 쓰이고 타동사로도 쓰인다.

어구 rapidly 급속히   take action 조치를 취하다
immediate 즉각적인   repair 수리하다
remove 제거하다   support 뒷받침하다

정답 (c)

5

해석 수요는 15%만큼 증가할 것으로 예상된다.

해설 '수요가 증가하다'라는 뜻의 a demand rises를 묻는 문제다. 선택지 가운데 raise는 특히 rise와 혼동하지 않도록 주의해야 한다. 그리고 rise와 형태가 비슷하지만 arise에는 '오르다'라는 뜻이 없음도 꼭 기억하자.

어구 raise 올리다   arise (문제 등이) 발생하다   rip 찢다

정답 (d)

6

해석 여자친구를 보았을 때, 병사의 가슴은 두근거리기 시작했다.

해설 '심장이 두근거리다'라는 뜻의 a heart pounds를 묻는 문제다. 선택지 가운데 found는 타동사로만 쓰이기 때문에 주어진 맥락에 어울리지 않음에 유의해야 한다. 이 단어는 '찾다'라는 뜻의 find의 과거형이나 과거분사와 모양이 같지만, 서로 관련이 없음에 유의하자. found는 라틴어 계열의 단어이고, find는 순수영어 계열의 단어이기 때문이다.

어구 soldier 병사   found 설립하다
pour 쏟아 붓다   foul 반칙을 저지르다

정답 (b)

7

해석 협상이 결렬되자, 양 당사자는 전쟁을 치를 각오를 했다.

해설 '협상이 결렬되다'는 뜻의 negotiations collapse를 묻는 문제다. 주어진 맥락을 감안할 때, '성공하다'라는 뜻의 succeed가 정답이 될 수는 없다. 그리고 substitute는 자동사로 쓰일 때 '대신 일해주다'라는 뜻이기 때문에 주어진 문장에 어울리지 않는다.

어구 party 당사자   ready to ～할 각오가 되어 있는
collaborate 협력하다   substitute 대체하다

정답 (a)

8

해석 빈부 격차가 금방이라도 줄어들 가능성은 높지 않다.

해설 '격차가 줄어들다'는 뜻의 a gap narrows를 묻는 문제다. 선택지 가운데 narrate와 name은 타동사로만 쓰이고, borrow는 주로 타동사로 쓰이기 때문에, 주어진 맥락에 어울리지 않음에 유의해야 한다.

어구 unlikely to ～할 가능성이 낮은   narrate 내레이션을 하다
borrow 빌리다   name 이름을 짓다

정답 (b)

UNIT 6   형용사+명사 I

EXERCISE

A

1 (d)	2 (a)	3 (c)	4 (e)	5 (b)

B

1	factor	2	intense
3	job	4	superficial
5	heroic		

PRACTICE

1 (b)	2 (d)	3 (c)	4 (c)	5 (a)
6 (a)	7 (b)	8 (c)		

중요 Collocation 정리

1 사라 브라잇만은 가수로서의 능력이 뛰어나다.

2 그 어린 아이들이 그 문제를 철저하게 분석했다.

3 자유와 책임 사이에서 섬세한 균형을 유지해야만 한다.

4 라듐의 발견은 물리학의 주요한 발전이었다.

5 안젤리나 졸리가 회장 직책의 유력한 후보였다.

6 결국엔 건설적인 비판이 작가로서 성공하는 데 도움을 준다.

7 남편과 이혼하는 것은 그녀의 삶에서 중대한 결정이었다.

8 그의 굉장한 노력은 페니실린의 발견으로 귀결되었다.

9 자신감은 성공하는 데 있어 주된 요인이다.

10 급진적인 여성운동가들은 결혼이 금지되어야 한다고 주장한다.

11 팀은 프로젝트에 대해 뛰어난 점수를 받았다.

12 그녀는 인류를 심하게 증오해서 여러 건의 살인을 저질렀다.

13 책을 쓰는 것은 시간이 많이 소요되는 일이다.

14 피상적인 지식은 어떤 통찰도 제공할 수 없다.

15 사실, 마릴린 먼로는 비참하게 살았다.

EXERCISE A

1 (d)
뛰어난 능력이 있다면, 어떤 일을 아주 잘 하는 것이다.

2 (a)
어떤 것을 철저하게 분석한다면, 그것을 매우 주의 깊게 검토하는 것이다.

3 (c)
어떤 직책에 대한 유력한 후보자라면, 채용될 가능성이 높다.

4 (e)
중대한 결정을 내린다면, 삶이 극적으로 바뀔 것이다.

5 (b)
급진적인 여성 운동가라면, 남성들을 증오할 가능성이 높다.

EXERCISE B

1
해석 그가 그 대학에 지원하기로 결정한 데 있어 명성이 주된 요인이었다.
해설 '주된 요인'이라는 뜻의 a key factor를 묻는 문제다. 오답으로 제시된 fact는 '사실'이라는 뜻으로 주어진 맥락에 어울리지 않는다. 또한 이 표현에서 key가 '결정적인'이라는 뜻의 형용사로 쓰인다는 점도 알아두자.
정답 factor

2
해석 심한 증오는 사랑의 표현일 수 있다.
해설 '심한 증오'라는 뜻의 intense hatred를 묻는 문제다. 오답으로 제시된 intensive는 '집중적인; 집약적인'이라는 뜻으로 주어진 맥락에 어울리지 않음에 유의해야 한다. 감정이 아니라, 활동을 표현하는 데 쓰이기 때문이다.
정답 Intense

3
해석 꽃을 기르는 것은 시간이 많이 소요되는 일이다.
해설 '시간이 많이 소요되는 일'이란 뜻의 a time-consuming job을 묻는 문제다. 오답으로 제시된 work도 '일'이란 뜻을 나타내지만, 셀 수 없는 명사로 쓰이기 때문에 a와 결합할 수 없음에 유의해야 한다. 반면 work이 '작품'이라는 뜻으로 쓰일 때는 셀 수 있는 명사로 활용된다.
정답 job

4
해석 많은 사람들이 자신들의 피상적인 지식을 자랑한다.
해설 '피상적인'이란 뜻의 superficial을 묻는 문제다. 오답으로 제시된 official은 '공식적인'이란 뜻으로 주어진 맥락에 어울리지 않는다. 참고로 boast는 타동사로서 '(바람직한 것을) 보유하다'라는 뜻으로도 쓰인다.
정답 superficial

5
해석 그들은 굉장한 노력으로 자신들의 나라를 용감하게 지켰다.
해설 '굉장한 노력'이라는 뜻의 heroic efforts를 묻는 문제다. 오답으로 제시된 hesitant는 '망설이는'이란 뜻으로 주어진 맥락에 적합하지 않다. '용감하게(bravely)'와 '망설이는' 것이 서로 어울릴 수는 없기 때문이다.
정답 heroic

PRACTICE

1
해석 A: 마이클 위에 대해 어떻게 생각하세요?
B: 음, 골프선수로서는 능력이 뛰어나지만 뭔가가 결여된 거 같아요.

해설 '뛰어난 능력'이란 뜻의 exceptional ability를 묻는 문제다. B의 응답의 후반부에서 부정적인 면을 말했기 때문에 but 이전의 전반부에서는 긍정적인 측면이 언급되어야 함에 유의하자. 그리고 odd는 odd jobs(허드렛일)라는 표현에도 활용됨을 기억하자.
어구 lack ~가 결여되다   irregular 불규칙적인   odd 기이한
정답 (b)

2
해석 A: 브루스한테 왜 그렇게 화가 났어?
B: 그의 말은 건설적인 비판이 아니었거든.
해설 '건설적인 비판'이란 뜻의 constructive criticism을 묻는 문제. '건설적인'을 뜻하는 constructive는 '함께(con) 짓는(struct) 경향이 있는(ive)'으로 분석된다. 반면 '파괴적인'을 뜻하는 destructive는 '짓지(struct) 않는(de) 경향이 있는(ive)'으로 분석된다.
어구 mad 화가 난   comment 논평
destructive 파괴적인   negative 부정적인
정답 (d)

3
해석 A: 축하해! 뛰어난 점수를 받았다고 들었어!
B: 고마워. 그냥 최선을 다했을 뿐이야.
해설 '뛰어난 점수'를 뜻하는 an excellent grade를 묻는 문제다. A가 축하를 하고 있고, B가 '최선을 다했다'라고 했으므로 빈 칸에는 긍정적인 의미를 나타내는 말이 오는 것이 자연스럽다. 이처럼 주어진 맥락을 정확히 파악하는 습관을 들이자.
어구 Congratulations 축하해   do one's best 최선을 다하다
failing grade 낙제점   poor 형편없는; 가난한
정답 (c)

4
해석 A: 앨버트 아인슈타인이 왜 그렇게 유명한지 아니?
B: 물리학에서 주요한 발전을 이루어냈거든.
해설 '주요한 발전'을 뜻하는 a major breakthrough를 묻는 문제다. A가 아인슈타인이 왜 '유명한지'를 질문했고, B가 그에 대해 응답하고 있기 때문에 유명한 것을 뒷받침할 만한 내용이 나와야 함에 유의해야 한다.
어구 famous 유명한   physics 물리학
inferior 열등한   unimportant 하찮은
lower 열등의
정답 (c)

5
해석 이라크에 전쟁을 선포한 것은 그 나라의 역사에서 중대한 결정이었다.
해설 '중대한 결정'을 뜻하는 a crucial decision을 묻는 문제다. '전쟁'의 중요성을 감안할 때 다른 선택지들은 정답이 될 수 없음에 유의해야 한다. crucial에는 '중대한'이란 뜻과 함께 '결정적인'이란 뜻도 있다.
어구 declare 선언하다   modest 겸손한
humble 겸손한   shy 수줍음을 타는
정답 (a)

6
해석 그럼에도 불구하고, 힐러리 클린턴이 유력한 미국 대통령 후보이다.

해설 '유력한 후보'를 뜻하는 a leading candidate를 묻는 문제다. 선택지 가운데 listening이나 learning이 candidate와 어울리는 것이 완전히 불가능하지는 않지만, 이와 같은 어휘 영역에서는 상식에 보다 부합하는 정답을 택해야 함을 명심해야 한다.

어구 still 여전히; 그럼에도 불구하고　　**position** 직책
lazy 게으른

정답 (a)

7

해석 명상은 심한 증오를 자비심으로 바꾸는 데 도움이 될 수 있다.

해설 '심한 증오'라는 뜻의 intense hatred를 묻는 문제다. '증오'와 '자비심'이 대조를 이루기 때문에, 다른 선택지가 정답이 될 수 없음에 유의해야 한다. intense는 '안으로(in) 뻗은(tense)'로 분석되는데, '의도하다'는 뜻의 intend와 관련이 있는 단어이다.

어구 meditation 명사　　　　compassion 동정심
intelligent 지적인　　　　intelligible 쉽게 이해되는
interim 과도적인

정답 (b)

8

해석 제 견해로는, 쟁점에 대한 보다 철저한 분석이 필요합니다.

해설 '철저한 분석'이라는 뜻의 a thorough analysis를 묻는 문제다. 문장에서 '보다 ~한 분석이 필요하다'라고 말하므로, '철저한'과 같은 말이 오는 것이 자연스럽다. incomplete이나 inaccurate은 thorough와 달리 특별한 노력을 요하지 않기 때문이다.

어구 in someone's opinion ~의 견해로는
issue 문제, 쟁점　　　　incomplete 불완전한
inaccurate 부정확한　　miserable 비참한

정답 (c)

UNIT 7 형용사+명사 Ⅱ

EXERCISE

A

1 (e)　　2 (c)　　3 (d)　　4 (a)　　5 (b)

B

1　mail　　　　2　urgent
3　Sensational　4　primary
5　grave

PRACTICE

1 (a)　　2 (d)　　3 (c)　　4 (c)　　5 (d)
6 (b)　　7 (b)　　8 (a)

중요 Collocation 정리

1 국내 우편으로 배송하는 경우 대략 이틀에서 사흘이 소요된다.

2 그 어리석은 사람을 채용한 것은 중대한 실수였다.

3 보다 질적으로 우수한 책들에 대한 급박한 필요가 있다.

4 그 신문은 선정적인 뉴스로 악명이 높다.

5 우리의 일차적인 목적은 건강한 사회를 만드는 것이다.

6 새로운 정책에 대한 반대 의견이 많이 제시되었다.

7 어떤 이들은 공산주의가 사회에 대한 왜곡된 관점이라고 생각한다.

8 실제로, TV에 나타나는 폭력은 심각한 문제다.

9 안젤리나 졸리는 그들의 삶의 가혹한 현실에 충격을 받았다.

10 우리의 풍부한 자원을 현명하게 쓸 필요가 있다.

11 브룩 쉴즈는 패션모델로서 급여를 넉넉하게 받았다.

12 믿을 만한 출처로부터 그들이 우리 시(市)를 공격할 계획이라고 들었다.

13 위원회는 위험을 피하기 위해 신중한 조치를 취했다.

14 이른바 '진솔한' 회담은 아무런 결실도 맺지 못했다.

15 돼지를 잔혹하게 다루는 것을 당장 멈추어야 한다.

EXERCISE A

1 (e)
중대한 실수를 저지른다면, 어려움에 처할 것이다.

2 (c)
관점이 왜곡되어 있다면, 현상을 있는 그래도 볼 수 없다.

3 (d)
어떤 나라가 자원이 풍부하다면, 그 나라는 부유해질 가능성이 높다.

4 (a)
넉넉하게 급여를 받는다면, 일이 보람 있을 가능성이 높다.

5 (b)
믿을 만한 출처로부터 어떤 것을 들었다면, 그것은 사실일 가능성이 높다.

EXERCISE B

1

해석 국내 우편은 많은 방식으로 분류될 수 있다.

해설 '국내 우편'을 뜻하는 domestic mail을 묻는 문제다. 발음이 똑같지만 male은 '남성'이라는 뜻의 명사로 쓰일 때 셀 수 있는 명사이기 때문에 단수로 쓰이면 a와 같은 말이 와야 한다. 따라서 정답이 될 수 없다.

정답 mail

2

해석 보다 자격을 갖춘 교사들에 대한 급박한 필요가 있다.

해설 '급박한 필요'라는 뜻의 an urgent need를 묻는 문제다. 오답으로 제시된 urban은 '도시의'라는 뜻으로 주어진 맥락에 맞지 않는다. 자격을 갖춘 교사에 대한 수요가 도시에 한정된다고 보기 힘들기 때문이다.

정답 urgent

3

해석 선정적인 뉴스는 읽을 만한 가치가 없다.

해설 '극히 자극적인 뉴스'라는 뜻의 sensational news를 묻는 문제다. 오답으로 제시된 proportional은 '비례의'라는 뜻으로 news와 어울리기에 부적합한 말이다. 그리고 news는 어떤 경우에도 셀 수 없음에 유의하자.

정답 Sensational

4

해석 그들의 일차적 목적은 많은 돈을 버는 것이다.

해설 '일차적 목적'이라는 뜻의 a primary objective를 묻는 문제다. 오답으로 제시된 emotional은 '감정적인, 정서적인'이란 뜻으로 주어진 맥락에 어울리지 않는다. 돈을 버는 것이 '정서적인 목적'이라고 할 수는 없기 때문이다.

정답 primary

5

해석 지구 온난화는 심각한 문제다.

해설 '심각한 문제'라는 뜻의 a grave problem을 묻는 문제다. 오답으로 제시된 respectable은 '훌륭한'이란 뜻으로 주어진 맥락에 어울리지 않는다. 참고로 명사로서 grave는 '무덤'이란 뜻을 나타낸다.

정답 grave

PRACTICE

1

해석 A: 캐시가 왜 빌과 결혼했는지 아니?
B: 빌이 급여를 넉넉하게 받고 있으니까.

해설 '넉넉한 급여'라는 뜻의 a handsome salary를 묻는 문제다. handsome의 뜻을 '잘생긴'으로만 알고 있기 쉬운데, 이처럼 '넉넉한'이란 뜻이 있음도 알아두어야 한다. 반면, '잘생긴'과 비슷한 뜻을 나타내는 beautiful이나 pretty에는 '넉넉한'이란 뜻이 없음에 주의하자.

어구 earn (돈을) 벌다   ugly 추한

정답 (a)

2

해석 A: 믿을 만한 출처로부터 우리 회사가 수천 명을 해고할 거라는 말을 들었어.
B: 뭐라고? 회사가 잘 돌아가는 줄 알았는데.

해설 '믿을 만한 출처'라는 뜻의 a reliable source를 묻는 문제다. 나머지 선택지들은 주어진 맥락에 어울리지 않는다. reliable은 '완전히(←다시: re) 묶을(li) 수 있는(able)'으로 분석된다. 동사형인 rely는 on과 함께 '~에 의존하다'라는 뜻을 나타낸다는 점도 알아두어야 한다.

어구 lay off (일시적으로) 해고하다   religious 종교적인
relieved 안도하는   relive (기억을) 되살리다

정답 (d)

3

해석 A: 전문가로서 법원의 결정에 대해 어떻게 생각하십니까?
B: 중대한 실수라고 봐요. 아무도 받아들이려고 하지 않을 거예요.

해설 '중대한 실수'라는 뜻의 a serious mistake을 묻는 문제다. B의 말에서 '아무도 받아들이지 않을 것'이라는 언급이 있기 때문에, 빈 칸에 긍정적인 내용이 올 수 없다. 그리고 cheerful, delightful에서 접미사 −ful은 '~으로 가득한'이란 뜻을 나타냄도 알아두자.

어구 expert 전문가   accept 받아들이다, 수용하다
cheerful 유쾌한   pleasant 즐거운
delightful 몹시 즐거운

정답 (c)

4

해석 A: 보다 헌신적인 자원봉사자들에 대한 필요가 급박해.
B: 정말 맞는 말이야!

해설 '급박한 필요'라는 뜻의 an urgent need를 묻는 문제다. urgent는 '재촉하고(urg[e]) 있는(ent)'으로 분석된다. useless는 '쓸모가(use) 없는(less)'으로 분석되는데, 접미사 −less는 많이 쓰이므로 뜻을 정확히 알아두자.

어구 dedicated 헌신적인   volunteer 자원봉사자
usable 쓸 만한   useless 쓸모없는
urban 도시의

정답 (c)

5

해석 물론, 소음 공해는 심각한 문제다.

해설 '심각한 문제'라는 뜻의 a grave problem을 묻는 문제다. 주어진 문장이 '물론'으로 시작하고 있기 때문에 상식적으로 적합한 단어를 선택해야 함에 유의하자. junior는 '~보다 등급이 하위인'이라는 뜻을 나타낼 때 전치사로 반드시 to가 와야 함도 기억하자.

어구 pollution 오염, 공해   junior (등급이) 하위인
favorable 호의적인   minor 경미한

정답 (d)

6

해석 교육의 일차적 목적은 마음을 자유롭게 하는 것이다.

해설 '일차적 목적'이란 뜻의 a primary objective를 묻는 문제다. 나머지 선택지들은 주어진 맥락에 전혀 어울리지 않는다. depressed는 '아래로(de) 누름을(press) 당한(ed)'으로 분석된다. 그리고 resentful은 '다시(re) 느끼는(sent) 것으로 가득한(ful)'으로 분석된다.

어구 education 교육   free 자유롭게 하다
depressed 우울한   prosperous 번창하는
resentful 분개한

정답 (b)

7

해석 민주 시민으로서, 반대 의견을 존중해야 한다.

해설 '반대 의견'이란 뜻의 an opposing opinion을 묻는 문제다. 다른 선택지들은 주어진 맥락에 어울리지 않는다. opposing은 '대립하여(op) 놓여져(pos[e]) 있는(ing)'으로 분석된다. 이 단어는 '함께(com) 놓다(pose)'로 분석되어 '구성하다'를 뜻하는 compose와 어근 pose를 공유한다.

어구 democratic 민주적인   respect 존중하다
ineffective 비효과적인   feeble 연약한
sadden 슬프게 하다

정답 (b)

8

해석 풍부한 자원이 항상 경제 성장으로 귀결되지는 않는다.

해설 '풍부한 자원'이라는 뜻의 abundant resources를 묻는 문제다. 역시 나머지 선택지들은 주어진 맥락에 맞지 않는다. abundant 는 '벗어나서(ab) 물결치고(und) 있는(ant)'으로 분석된다. '벗어나서 물결치다'는 '넘쳐흐르다'는 의미로 발전했다. 따라서 현재의 '풍부한'이란 뜻을 나타내게 되었다.

어구 lead to ~로 귀결되다　　economic 경제의
　　 absurd 터무니없는　　abuse 학대하다; 남용하다
　　 abstract 추상적인

정답 (a)

UNIT 8　동사+부사 Ⅰ

EXERCISE

A

1 (c)　　2 (e)　　3 (a)　　4 (d)　　5 (b)

B

1	warmly	2	wildly
3	greatly	4	carefully
5	strongly		

PRACTICE

1 (d)　　2 (b)　　3 (c)　　4 (a)　　5 (c)
6 (b)　　7 (c)　　8 (d)

중요 Collocation 정리

1　액자를 조심스럽게 다루어라. 그렇지 않으면, 산산조각이 날 것이다.

2　학생들은 반장을 신중하게 선택했다.

3　그 이상한 선생님은 감히 수업 시간에 평상복을 입으려고 했다.

4　유감스럽게도, 그 탁월한 영화는 완전히 망했다.

5　대다수 학생들은 교장 선생님을 몹시 미워했다.

6　보급품은 병사들 사이에서 균등하게 배분되었다.

7　모든 이들이 빨간 넥타이를 매는 것에 완전히 동의했다.

8　졸업반 학생들은 그 댄스파티를 한껏 즐겼다.

9　그의 마을은 해일로 심하게 타격을 입었다.

10　그 근로자는 그의 나태함으로 인해 심하게 비난을 받았다.

11　여름철에는 비가 심하게 내린다.

12　많은 승객들이 충돌 사고에서 심하게 부상을 입었다.

13　우리는 모든 이들이 소중한 사람이라고 굳게 믿고 있다.

14　호스트 패밀리가 우리 학생들을 따뜻하게 맞이해 주었다.

15　많은 교사들은 윌로우가 그 서류를 훔쳤다고 억측을 했다.

EXERCISE A

1　(c)
어떤 것을 조심스럽게 다루면 그것이 손상될 가능성은 높지 않다.

2　(e)
평상복을 입으면 격식을 갖춘 파티에는 갈 수 없다.

3　(a)
여러분이 누군가를 몹시 미워하면 그 사람도 여러분을 좋아하지 않을 것이다.

4　(d)
모든 이들이 어떤 일을 하기로 완전히 동의하면 아무도 그 계획에 반대하지 않는다.

5　(b)
비가 심하게 내리면 바깥에 나가서 놀 수 없다.

EXERCISE B

1

해석 친절한 집주인이 그들을 따뜻하게 맞이해 주었다.

해설 '따뜻하게 맞이하다'라는 뜻의 greet warmly를 묻고 있다. weakly는 '약하게'라는 뜻이기 때문에 greet과는 자연스럽게 어울리지 않음에 유의하자.

정답 warmly

2

해석 크리스티는 오빠가 도망갔다고 억측했다.

해설 '억측하다'는 guess wildly로 표현한다. politely는 '정중하게'라는 뜻으로 guess와는 어울리지 않는 부사다.

정답 wildly

3

해석 학생들 모두 축제를 한껏 즐겼다.

해설 '한껏 즐기다'는 enjoy greatly로 표현한다. 부사로 쓰이는 hard는 '열심히' 또는 '심하게'라는 뜻을 나타내기 때문에 enjoy 와는 어울리지 않는다.

정답 greatly

4

해석 회원들이 후보자들을 신중하게 선택했다.

해설 '신중하게 고르다'라는 choose carefully로 표현한다. uselessly는 '헛되이'라는 뜻으로 choose와 자연스럽게 연결되지 않음에 유의하자.

정답 carefully

5

해석 우리는 우리나라가 우리 모두에게 소중하다고 굳게 믿는다.

해설 '굳게 믿다'는 believe strongly로 표현한다. unkindly는 '불친절하게'라는 뜻으로 believe와 어울리지 않는다.

정답 strongly

PRACTICE

1

해석 A: 매리를 어떻게 생각하니?
B: 솔직히 말해서 몹시 미워해.

해설 '몹시 미워하다'는 hate deeply로 나타낸다. deeply는 감정이나 믿음의 정도가 아주 강함을 나타내는 부사다. 다른 부사들은 hate와 어울리기에는 쓰임새가 맞지 않는다.

어구 thinly 듬성하게   thickly 조밀하게
closely 면밀하게

정답 (d)

2

해석 A: 논의는 어떻게 되었니?
B: 유감스럽게도 완전히 실패했어.

해설 '완전히 실패하다'는 fail completely로 나타낸다. completely는 정도가 완전함을 나타내는 부사다. 참고로 hopefully는 문장 부사로서 '희망하건대'라는 뜻으로도 쓰이는데, 이 표현의 허용 여부에 대해서는 논란이 있지만 일상적으로 널리 쓰이기 때문에 함께 알아두자.

어구 delightfully 기쁘게   happily 행복하게
hopefully 희망에 겨워

정답 (b)

3

해석 A: 이 꽃병을 어디에다 두어야 해요?
B: 이봐요. 조심스럽게 다루어요! 쉽게 깨지니까요.

해설 '조심스럽게 다루다'는 handle carefully로 표현한다. carelessly는 carefully의 반의어인데, 주어진 맥락에 어울리지 않는다. 참고로 coldly는 일정한 행동을 '따뜻한 감정 없이' 하는 것을 나타내는 부사로 주로 쓰인다.

어구 carelessly 경솔하게   coldly 냉담하게
warmly 따뜻하게

정답 (c)

4

해석 A: 샌디에이고의 날씨는 어때요?
B: 비가 심하게 내리고 있어요. 외출을 할 수가 없어요.

해설 '비가 심하게 내리다'는 rain heavily로 나타낸다. heavily는 정도나 양이 심함을 나타내는 뜻으로 주로 쓰이는 부사다. 참고로 darkly는 대개 '슬프게' 또는 '험악하게'라는 뜻을 나타내는 부사다.

어구 darkly 음울하게   softly 부드럽게
brightly 환하게

정답 (a)

5

해석 유감스럽게도 제시카는 사고에서 심하게 부상을 입었다.

해설 '심하게 부상을 입다'는 injure severely로 표현한다. severely는 '정도가 심하게' 또는 '엄하게'라는 뜻을 나타내는 부사로 주로 쓰인다.

어구 pleasantly 즐겁게   humorously 익살맞게
incorrectly 부정확하게

정답 (c)

6

해석 그 교사는 학생들을 이해하지 못하는 데 대해 심하게 비난을 받았다.

해설 '심하게 비난하다'는 criticize harshly로 표현한다. harshly는 비판이나 처벌 등이 가혹함을 나타내는 부사로 주로 쓰인다. dully가 '지루하게', '어리석게', '활기 없이'라는 다양한 뜻을 나타냄도 기억해 두자.

어구 lovingly 정답게   sweetly 달콤하게
dully 활기 없이

정답 (b)

7

해석 마침내 그들은 함께 보다 나은 공동체를 만들자는 데 완전히 동의했다.

해설 '완전히 동의하다'는 agree fully로 나타낸다. fully는 정도가 완전함을 나타내는 부사다. 참고로 sharply가 '급격하게', '냉담하게', '심하게', '날카롭게' 등의 다양한 의미로 쓰이는 부사라는 점도 기억하자.

어구 unluckily 불행하게도   sharply 날카롭게
rudely 무례하게

정답 (c)

8

해석 이익금은 근로자들 사이에서 균등하게 나누기로 되어 있었다.

해설 '균등하게 나누다'는 divide equally로 나타낸다. equally는 '똑같은 정도로', '똑같은 양으로'라는 뜻을 나타내는 부사다. 참고로 lightly가 '가볍게', '적은 양으로', '함부로' 등을 나타내는 부사임도 익혀두자.

어구 toughly 혹독하게   strongly 굳게
lightly 가볍게

정답 (d)

UNIT 9   동사+부사 II

EXERCISE

A

| 1 (c) | 2 (e) | 3 (a) | 4 (b) | 5 (d) |

B

1 calmly	2 flatly
3 impartially	4 dimly
5 utterly	

PRACTICE

| 1 (d) | 2 (b) | 3 (a) | 4 (c) | 5 (c) |
| 6 (b) | 7 (d) | 8 (a) | | |

중요 Collocation 정리

1 소녀들은 개집을 지으려는 계획에 맹렬히 반대했다.

2 놀랍게도, 미셸 파이퍼는 차분히 반응해냈다.

3 전구는 작은 방에서 희미하게 빛났다.

4 선생님들은 대부분 그녀의 성취에 아주 기뻐했다.

5 에리카 김은 그 계약에 대해 새빨간 거짓말을 했다.

6 황망하게도, 기자는 그 끔찍한 사건을 생생하게 묘사했다.

7 패리스 힐튼은 처음 만난 이래로 현격하게 변했다.

8 모든 이들은 능력에 따라 공정하게 평가받아야 한다.

9 이번 선거는 우리나라의 장래에 심하게 영향을 미칠 것이다.

10 진심으로 여러분 모두가 행복하기를 바랍니다.

11 일부 미국인들은 이라크와 전쟁을 해야 한다고 완고하게 주장했다.

12 경찰은 안젤리나의 집을 철저히 수색했다.

13 대중은 그들의 끔찍한 상황을 완전히 무시했다.

14 유감스럽게도, 나는 문을 잠가야 하는 것을 완전히 잊어버렸다 .

15 그들은 그 순진무구한 아이를 보호하는 일을 의도적으로 소홀히 했다.

EXERCISE A

1 (c)
계획을 맹렬히 반대한다면, 단연코 반대하는 것이다.

2 (e)
어떤 이를 아주 기쁘게 만들면, 그 사람은 매우 행복하다.

3 (a)
어떤 것을 생생하게 묘사하면, 사람들은 그것이 어떻게 생겼는지 안다.

4 (b)
어떤 일이 일어나기를 진정으로 바란다면, 그 일이 생기기를 정말로 원하는 것이다.

5 (d)
어떤 것을 완전히 무시한다면, 그것에 대해 전혀 주의를 기울이지 않는 것이다.

EXERCISE B

1

해석 화가 났지만, 메리는 차분하게 반응했다.

해설 '차분히 반응하다'라는 뜻의 react calmly를 묻는 문제다. 오답으로 제시된 strongly는 '강렬히' 또는 '강력하게'라는 뜻으로, 문장이 although로 시작하기 때문에 주어진 맥락에 어울리지 않음에 유의해야 한다.

정답 calmly

2

해석 사고에 대해 어떻게 새빨간 거짓말을 할 수 있니?

해설 '새빨간 거짓말을 하다'라는 뜻의 lie flatly를 묻는 문제다. fairly는 '공정하게'라는 뜻이기 때문에 '거짓말하다'라는 뜻의 lie와 자

연스럽게 연결될 수 없음에 유의하자.

정답 flatly

3

해석 각 후보자를 공정하게 판단하기로 되어 있었다.

해설 '공정하게 판단하다'라는 뜻의 judge impartially를 묻는 문제다. 오답으로 제시된 impatiently는 '조바심을 내면서'라는 뜻으로 '~해야 하는 법이다'라는 뜻의 be supposed to ~가 쓰인 문장에 어울리지 않는다.

정답 impartially

4

해석 탁자 위에서, 촛불은 희미하게 빛났다.

해설 '희미하게 빛나다'라는 뜻의 glow dimly를 묻는 문제다. 오답으로 제시된 randomly는 '무작위로'라는 뜻으로 '빛나다'라는 뜻의 glow와 자연스럽게 어울리지 않음에 유의하자.

정답 dimly

5

해석 나는 그 일에 대해 완전히 잊어버렸다.

해설 '완전히 잊어버리다'라는 뜻의 forget utterly를 묻는 문제다. 오답으로 제시된 urgently는 '급박하게'라는 뜻으로 '잊다'라는 뜻의 forget과는 어울리지 않는다.

정답 utterly

PRACTICE

1

해석 A: 제 생각에는, 그들이 계획을 맹렬히 반대할 거예요.
　　 B: 왜 그렇게 생각하죠?

해설 '맹렬히 반대하다'는 뜻의 oppose bitterly를 묻는 문제다. 오답으로 제시된 표현들은 모두 일정한 맛을 나타내는 형용사에서 유래한 부사들인데, 각각의 뜻을 참고적으로 알아두자. 그리고 '기쁨과 슬픔이 교차하는' 감정을 뜻하는 bittersweet(씁쓸하면서 달콤한)이란 표현도 기억하자.

어구 in one's opinion ~의 생각에는　　sweetly 유쾌하게
saltily 저급하게　　spicily 저속하게

정답 (d)

2

해석 A: 폴이 매우 차분한 반응을 보여 놀랐어.
　　 B: 나도 그래. 그의 자제력이 인상 깊었어.

해설 '차분히 반응하다'라는 뜻의 react calmly를 묻는 문제다. B의 말 가운데 self-control(자제)이라는 말이 있기 때문에, 다른 말들이 정답이 될 수 없음에 유의해야 한다. 이처럼 실제 TEPS 어휘 영역에서는 전후 맥락으로 보아 자연스러운 표현을 선택할 것을 요구한다는 점을 명심하자.

어구 self-control 자제심　　impressive 인상적인
violently 격렬하게　　rudely 무례하게
aggressively 직극직으로

정답 (b)

3

해석 A:당신과 함께 일한 것이 큰 기쁨이었습니다.
　　 B: 새로운 분야에서 성공적으로 경력을 개척하기를 진심으로 바랍니다.

해설 '진심으로 바라다'라는 뜻의 sincerely hope을 묻는 문제다. 오답으로 제시된 부사들 가운데 insignificantly는 형용사 insignificant에서 유래했는데, 이 형용사가 크게 '전혀 중요하지 않은'과 '무의미한'이라는 두 가지 의미를 나타낸다는 점을 기억해 두자.

어구 successful 성공적인 　　career 경력
　　field 분야 　　dishonestly 기만적으로
　　insignificantly 미미하게 　　deceitfully 기만적으로

정답 (a)

4

해석 A: 케이트가 나를 완전히 무시했어! 어떻게 그럴 수가 있지?
　　B: 아, 걔가 아주 형편없는 애란 거 몰랐니?

해설 '완전히 무시하다'라는 뜻의 ignore totally를 묻는 문제다. '형편없는 사람'으로 옮긴 jerk는 '상황에 맞지 않는 행동으로 다른 사람의 감정을 해치는 이'라는 뜻임에 유의하자. 그리고 '따뜻한'이란 뜻의 형용사 warm에서 나온 부사 warmly는 사람을 '따뜻하게' 대하는 상황을 나타낼 수 있다.

어구 jerk 형편없는 사람 　　fairly 공정하게
　　welcomingly 환영하여 　　warmly 따스하게

정답 (c)

5

해석 청중들은 그녀의 아름다운 음악에 아주 기뻐했다.

해설 '아주 기뻐하는'이란 뜻의 highly pleased를 묻는 문제다. high와 highly를 혼동하기 쉬운데, 우선 high가 '(위쪽으로) 높게'라는 뜻을 나타냄을 기억할 필요가 있다. 반면 highly는 '정도가 높게'라는 뜻이기 때문에 '아주(very)'로 옮길 수 있다.

어구 high 높게 　　cheaply 값싸게
　　poorly 형편없게

정답 (c)

6

해석 아넷이 현격하게 변해서 아무도 그녀를 못 알아봤다.

해설 '현격하게 변하다'라는 뜻의 change radically를 묻는 문제다. radically는 형용사 radical에서 나왔는데, radical의 본래 의미는 '뿌리의'이다. 이 뜻으로부터 '뿌리까지 바뀌는'으로 발상이 확장되어 '근본적인, 현격한'이란 뜻으로 발전했음에 유의하자.

어구 furiously 격분해서 　　lazily 게으르게
　　thankfully 다행스럽게도

정답 (b)

7

해석 인종차별주의자들이 흑인을 공정하게 판단하는 것은 불가능하다.

해설 '공정하게 판단하다'라는 뜻의 judge impartially를 묻는 문제다. 인종차별주의자(racist)에 대해 말하는 것이기 때문에 맥락으로 보아, 빈 칸에는 긍정적인 특성이 나와야 한다. 답지 가운데 긍정적인 특성을 나타내는 부사는 impartially밖에 없다.

어구 racist 인종차별주의자 　　African Americans 흑인
　　impatiently 조바심을 내며 　　improperly 부적절하게
　　impolitely 무례하게

정답 (d)

8

해석 음악은 인간의 정서에 심하게 영향을 끼칠 수 있다.

해설 '심하게 영향을 미치다'라는 뜻의 affect profoundly를 묻는 문

제다. profoundly는 '바닥(found) 아래의(pro)'로 분석되는 형용사 profound에서 나왔다. 그리고 TEPS 어휘 영역의 문제를 풀 때는 가능한 한 상식적으로 올바른 판단을 해야 함에 유의하자. 음악과 인간 정서 사이의 관계를 생각할 때, (b), (c), (d)는 일반적으로 부적절하다.

어구 affect ~에 영향을 미치다 　　emotion 정서
　　irritably 짜증스럽게 　　indifferently 무관심하게
　　incorrectly 부정확하게

정답 (a)

UNIT 10　부사+형용사

EXERCISE

A

1 (d)　　2 (b)　　3 (a)　　4 (c)　　5 (e)

B

1 mutually　　2 actively
3 happily　　4 absolutely
5 ideally

PRACTICE

1 (d)　　2 (d)　　3 (c)　　4 (a)　　5 (b)
6 (b)　　7 (a)　　8 (c)

중요 Collocation 정리

1 그들은 연못의 소유에 대한 상호 수용 가능한 합의에 이르렀다.

2 법적 구속력이 있는 계약은 책임감 있는 성인이 되도록 해준다.

3 마을 사람들은 전통 의상을 완전히 차려 입었다.

4 그 지역에서 비즈니스를 하는 것은 지극히 위험하다.

5 두 집단은 서로 전혀 다르다.

6 말콤은 흑인들을 위한 사회적 운동에 적극적으로 관여했다.

7 신체적으로 건강한 사람들에게만 밀림으로의 위험한 여행이 허용된다.

8 시상식에 초대를 받아서 대단히 영광스러웠다.

9 그 산을 정복하는 것은 거의 불가능하다.

10 메리안느는 7명의 자녀를 두면서 행복한 결혼 생활을 누렸다.

11 호신술을 익히는 것이 절대적으로 필요하다.

12 전문가들은 평화회담의 결과에 대해 신중하게 낙관론을 펴고 있다.

13 그녀의 새로운 노래들은 아일랜드 전통 음악에 깊이 뿌리를 내리고 있다.

14 이것이 초래할지도 모르는 어떤 불편에 대해서는 심심한 유감의 뜻을 전합니다.

15 그 회사는 수제 가구를 생산하기에 완벽하게 적합하다.

EXERCISE A

1 (d)

합의가 법적 구속력이 있다면, 그 합의를 이행해야만 한다.

2 (b)

어떤 것이 지극히 위험하다면, 그것을 하지 않는 편이 낫다.

3 (a)

두 가지가 서로와 전혀 다르다면, 그 두 가지는 똑같지 않다.

4 (c)

신체적으로 건강하다면, 강하고 건강한 것이다.

5 (e)

어떤 것이 거의 불가능하다면, 그것을 해내는 것은 가능하지 않다.

EXERCISE B

1

해석 그들은 서로 받아들일 수 있는 조건으로 합의했다.

해설 '서로 받아들일 수 있는'이란 뜻의 mutually acceptable을 묻는 문제다. 오답으로 제시된 regrettably는 '애석하게도'라는 뜻으로 문장부사로 주로 쓰이기 때문에 정답이 될 수 없다. 참고로 regretfully도 regrettably와 같은 뜻을 나타낸다.

정답 mutually

2

해석 그들은 적극적으로 인도주의적인 노력을 펼쳤다.

해설 '적극적으로 관여하는'이란 뜻의 actively engaged를 묻는 문제다. angrily는 '화가 나서'라는 뜻으로 '인도주의적인 노력'과 자연스럽게 어울리지 않는다. 그리고 engaged와 같이 ─ed형을 써야 함에 유의하자.

정답 actively

3

해석 팀은 행복한 결혼 생활을 누리며 아내를 아주 사랑했다.

해설 '결혼 생활이 행복한'이란 뜻의 happily married를 묻는 문제다. 오답으로 제시된 mournfully는 '애도하여'라는 뜻으로 주어진 맥락에 어울리지 않는다. 참고로 mournful은 '구슬픈'이란 뜻을 나타낸다.

정답 happily

4

해석 우리의 환경을 보호하는 일이 절대적으로 필요하다.

해설 '절대적으로 필요한'이란 뜻의 absolutely necessary를 묻는 문제다. 오답으로 제시된 unattractively는 '매력 없게'라는 뜻으로 주어진 맥락에 어울리지 않는다. 반의어는 물론 attractively 이다.

정답 absolutely

5

해석 위치 때문에, 그 마을은 관광하기에 완벽하게 적합하다.

해설 '이상적으로 적합한'이란 뜻의 ideally suited를 묻는 문제나. 오답으로 제시된 idly는 '게을리'라는 뜻으로 ideally와 형태가 다소 비슷하지만 주어진 맥락에 전혀 어울리지 않는다. 형용사 idle의 부사 형태이다.

정답 ideally

PRACTICE

1

해석 A: 나는 우주를 탐험하고 싶은 열망이 아주 강해.
B: 음, 있잖아, 지극히 위험할 수도 있어.

해설 '지극히 위험한'이란 뜻의 extremely dangerous를 묻는 문제다. 나머지 선택지들은 주어진 맥락에 적합하지 않음에 유의해야 한다. 이 가운데 expertly는 형용사로서의 expert의 부사 형태이다. 형용사일 때 expert는 '능숙한; 전문적인'이란 뜻을 나타낸다.

어구 eager to ~하기를 열망하는   explore 탐험하다
expressionlessly 무표정하게   expertly 전문적으로 expensively 값비싸게

정답 (d)

2

해석 A: 클라라는 어떻게 됐니?
B: 아, 결혼 생활을 행복하게 하며 보스턴에 살고 있어.

해설 '결혼 생활이 행복한'이란 뜻의 happily married를 묻는 문제다. 다른 선택지들은 '결혼한'이란 말을 꾸미기에 적합한 단어들이 아님에 유의하자. 그 가운데 enormously는 '기준(norm)의 밖에 있는(e) 것으로 가득한(ous) 방식으로(ly)'라고 분석되어 '막대하게'라는 뜻을 나타낸다.

어구 enormously 막대하게   irregularly 불규칙적으로
slightly 약간

정답 (d)

3

해석 A: 그의 선거 운동에 대해 어떻게 생각하세요?
B: 결과에 대해 신중하게 낙관하는 편이랍니다.

해설 '신중하게 낙관적인'이란 뜻의 cautiously optimistic을 묻는 문제다. 나머지 선택지들은 optimistic을 꾸미기에 부적합하다. cautiously는 '주의하는(caut[i]) 것으로 가득한(ous) 방식으로(ly)'라고 분석된다.

어구 election campaign 선거 운동   result 결과
gloomily 우울하게   ridiculously 어처구니없게
elegantly 우아하게

정답 (c)

4

해석 A: 실수에 대해 정말 죄송합니다.
B: 괜찮아요. 완벽한 사람은 아무도 없잖아요.

해설 '대단히 미안한'이란 뜻의 terribly sorry를 묻는 문제다. 나머지 선택지들은 '미안한'을 뜻하는 sorry와 자연스럽게 어울리지 않는다. 부사 terribly는 이처럼 '대단히'라는 뜻과 함께 '몹시 심하게'라는 뜻도 나타낸다.

어구 perfect 완벽한   brightly 환하게
gratefully 감사하게   mistakenly 그릇되게

정답 (a)

5

해석 마음을 다스리는 법을 배우는 것이 절대적으로 필요하다.

해설 '절대적으로 필요한'이란 뜻의 absolutely necessary를 묻는 문제다. 나머지 선택지들은 necessary와 자연스럽게 연결되지 않는다. absolutely는 '벗어나게(ab) 풀어줌(sol)을 당한(ute) 방식으로(ly)'라고 분석되는데, '결함으로부터 벗어나게 한다'는 발상에서 '완전하게'라는 뜻이 본래 의미였다.

어구 control 통제하다   absently 멍하니
absurdly 터무니없게   abusively 거칠게

정답 (b)

6

해석 계약이 법적 구속력이 없어서 귀하는 아무런 책임도 없습니다.

해설 '법적 구속력이 있는'이란 뜻의 legally binding을 묻는 문제다. 나머지 선택지들은 계약 관계에서 쓰이기에 적합하지 않다. legally는 '법률(leg)에 따른(al) 방식으로(ly)'라고 분석되는데, 반의어는 illegally(불법적으로)이다.

어구 contract 계약   responsibility 책임
emotionally 감정적으로   instinctively 본능적으로
unconsciously 무의식적으로

정답 (b)

7

해석 영예로운 상을 수상하게 되어 대단히 영광스러웠다.

해설 '대단히 영광스러운'이란 뜻의 greatly honored를 묻는 문제다. 주어진 문장에 prestigious award라는 말이 있기 때문에 나머지 선택지들은 적합하지 않다. highly honored도 '대단히 영광스러운'이란 뜻을 나타낸다.

어구 prestigious 영예로운   award 상
shallowly 얕게   poorly 형편없게
uncertainly 불확실하게

정답 (a)

8

해석 사고력이 있는 컴퓨터를 개발하는 일은 거의 불가능하다.

해설 '거의 불가능한'이란 뜻의 practically impossible을 묻는 문제다. practically에는 '실제적으로'라는 뜻도 있음을 익혀두자. 참고로 innocently는 '해를 끼치지(noc) 않고(in) 있는(ent) 방식으로(ly)'라고 분석된다.

어구 develop 개발하다   innocently 순박하게
ignorantly 무지(無知)하게   hastily 성급하게

정답 (c)

Chapter 2

UNIT 1 동사(필수어휘) Ⅰ

EXERCISE

A
1 (c)   2 (a)   3 (e)   4 (b)   5 (d)

B
1   avoid   2   cancel
3   join   4   Earning
5   hired

PRACTICE

1 (d)   2 (b)   3 (b)   4 (d)   5 (c)
6 (d)   7 (b)   8 (b)

중요 Collocation 정리

1 어떤 까닭인지 레이첼은 나를 피한다.

2 에단은 나이치고는 처신을 잘한다.

3 놀랍게도, 그들의 결혼은 취소되었다.

4 많은 새들로 인해 항공편이 지연되었다.

5 타이거 우즈는 2006년에 대략 1억 달러를 벌어들였다.

6 그 꽃병을 깨뜨린다면 심각한 문제에 직면하게 될 것이다.

7 대니얼은 차를 충분히 팔지 못해서 해고당했다.

8 다이애나는 그의 유익한 충고로부터 많은 이득을 얻었다.

9 끔직한 일이 누구에게나 일어날 수 있다.

10 그레고리는 슈퍼마켓에 고용되었다.

11 많은 학생들이 그 이상한 교사를 흉내 내는 것을 즐겼다.

12 이 책은 많은 악어 사진들을 포함하고 있다.

13 그 유명한 투수가 팀에 합류하자, 많은 것들이 변했다.

14 격언에 이르기를, '외모로 판단해서는 안 된다.'

15 그들의 우정은 그 가수가 사망한 1999년까지 지속되었다.

EXERCISE A

1 (c)
처신을 잘한다면 사람들이 당신을 좋아할 것이다.

2 (a)
해고당하면 돈을 버는 데 어려움을 겪을 것이다.

3 (e)
나쁜 일이 선량한 사람들에게 일어나면 그들은 그런 어려움을 극복해 낼 것이다.

4 (b)
문제에 직면하면 해결하기 위해 최선을 다하라.

5 (d)

누군가를 흉내 내면 그 사람은 당신을 좋아하지 않을 것이다.

EXERCISE B

1

해석 낯선 사람과 대화하는 것을 피하도록 늘 노력하라.

해설 '～하는 것을 피하다'는 avoid로 표현해야 한다. 이에 반해 prevent는 '사람이나 사물이 어떤 것을 하지 못하도록 막다'라는 뜻을 나타낸다. 따라서 주어진 맥락에 자연스럽게 어울리는 것은 avoid다.

정답 avoid

2

해석 유감스럽게도, 콘서트를 취소하는 수밖에 없다.

해설 '취소하다'는 뜻은 cancel로 표현한다. catch는 '붙잡다'라는 뜻이기 때문에 concert라는 말과는 어울릴 수 없다.

정답 cancel

3

해석 아주 많은 학생들이 그 축구팀에 합류하고 싶어 한다.

해설 '합류하다'는 join으로 나타낸다. joke는 '농담하다'라는 뜻의 자동사이기 때문에 the soccer team과 같은 목적어가 바로 이어질 수 없음에 유의하자.

정답 join

4

해석 돈을 버는 것이 삶의 전부는 아니다.

해설 '돈을 벌다'는 earn money 또는 make money로 표현한다. 동사 work는 '작동시키다' 또는 '효과가 있다'라는 뜻이기 때문에 문맥상 어울리지 않는다.

정답 Earning

5

해석 솔직히 말하자면, 우리는 형편없는 사람을 고용했다.

해설 '고용하다'는 hire로 나타낸다. rent는 '돈을 주고 집이나 방, 또는 물건을 임대하다'라는 뜻으로 쓰이기 때문에 정답이 될 수 없다.

정답 hired

PRACTICE

1

해석 A: 중요한 사람을 만날 거야. 처신을 잘 해!
　　B: 걱정 마세요, 엄마. 말썽 피우지 않을게요.

해설 내용으로 보아 '처신을 바로 하라'는 말이 와야 한다. 이때 쓰는 표현이 Behave yourself!이다. 참고로 Act your age!라고 하면 '나이에 맞게 행동하라'는 뜻이 된다.

어구 misbehave 못되게 굴다　　act 행동하다
　　mind 신경 쓰나

정답 (d)

2

해석 A: 내일 행사 때문에 몹시 흥분이 돼.
　　B: 나도 그래. 행사에 흥미로운 활동들이 많이 있어.

해설 '포함하다'라는 뜻은 include로 표현한다. 이 단어는 '안으로(in) 닫다(clude)'로 분석된다. 반면 exclude는 '밖으로(ex) 닫다(clude)'로, conclude는 '완전히(con) 닫다(clude)'로 분석되면서 각각의 뜻을 나타낸다.

어구 event 행사　　　　　　　　activity 활동
　　conclude 결론짓다　　　　　exclude 배제하다

정답 (b)

3

해석 A: 안젤라는 근사한 여자임에 틀림없어. 그녀는 정말 예쁘거든.
　　B: 사람을 결코 외모로 판단하지 마.

해설 '판단하다'는 judge로 나타낸다. 명사로서 '판사'를 뜻하기도 하는 이 단어에는 '판결을 내리다'라는 뜻도 있음을 기억해두자.

어구 appearance 외모　　misunderstand 오해하다

정답 (b)

4

해석 A: 축하드려요! 채용되셨습니다.
　　B: 정말요? 이 회사에서 일하게 되어 정말 기뻐요.

해설 주어진 맥락으로 보아 '고용된' 상황임을 알 수 있다. '고용하다'는 hire로 나타낸다. 참고로 '해고하다'는 fire, dismiss, lay off (일시적 해고) 등으로 나타낸다.

어구 Congratulations! 축하드려요!　　fire 해고하다
　　shoot 사살하다

정답 (d)

5

해석 허리케인 때문에 내가 이용할 항공편이 지연되었다.

해설 맥락으로 보아 항공편이 지연되었음을 알 수 있다. delay로 표현해야 함에 유의하자. 그리고 book이 동사로 쓰일 때 '예약하다'라는 뜻이 있음도 함께 기억해두자.

어구 praise 칭찬하다
　　book 예약하다(=reserve, make a reservation)

정답 (c)

6

해석 때로는 좋은 일이 나쁜 사람들에게 일어나기도 한다.

해설 '(어떤 일이) 일어나다'는 뜻은 happen으로 표현한다. 간단한 단어지만 출제 빈도가 높으므로 정확히 알아두자.

어구 appear 나타나다　　hurt 다치게 하다

정답 (d)

7

해석 다른 사람의 말을 흉내 내는 것은 그리 좋은 생각이 아니다.

해설 '흉내 내다'는 뜻은 imitate로 나타낸다. resemble과 혼동할 수 있는데, 이 단어는 모습이나 태도가 닮았다는 뜻이기 때문에 모방과는 다르다.

어구 speech 말; 연설　　resemble 닮다　　disappear 사라지다

정답 (b)

8

해석 어려움에 직면하면 침착함을 유지하려고 노력하라.

해설 'face～' 또는 'be faced with～'는 '～에 직면하다'라는 뜻을 나타낸다.

어구 remain calm 침착함을 유지하다　　locate (위치를) 찾다

avoid 피하다

정답 (b)

UNIT 2 동사(필수어휘) Ⅱ

EXERCISE

A
1 (c)   2 (a)   3 (e)   4 (b)   5 (d)

B
1 patrolled   2 quitting
3 recommended   4 ship
5 stores

PRACTICE

1 (a)   2 (d)   3 (c)   4 (c)   5 (d)
6 (b)   7 (b)   8 (c)

중요 Collocation 정리

1 그 어린 여자 아이는 중요한 정보를 친구들한테 누설했다.
2 우리는 모든 이들이 춤을 출 수 있어야 한다고 주장한다.
3 제시카는 CIA의 수장(首長)으로 지명되었다.
4 놀랍게도, 매리는 국가시험에 합격했다는 통보를 받았다.
5 남자가 여자보다 더 낫다는 아이디어에 강력히 반대한다.
6 아버지는 그 사람의 인종차별적인 말에 감정이 심하게 상하셨다.
7 다섯 마리의 뱀이 브리트니의 집을 순찰했다.
8 잘 해내기 위해, 가능한 한 자주 연습해야 한다.
9 복권에 당첨되고 나서, 브루스는 일을 그만두었다.
10 그녀의 전문성은 언어학에서 천문학에까지 이른다.
11 윌리엄 진저를 아무런 망설임도 없이 추천한다.
12 그 도시에는 아일랜드계 이민자들이 정착했다.
13 아마존닷컴은 도서를 국제적으로 배송해준다.
14 인간의 두뇌에는 많은 정보가 저장되어 있다.
15 마을사람들은 실종된 여자 아이를 애써서 추적하고 있었다.

EXERCISE A

1 (c)
누군가에게 비밀을 누설하면, 그 사람은 필경 다른 이들에게 그것에 대해 말할 것이다.

2 (a)
어떤 일을 수행해야 한다고 주장한다면, 그 일을 하는 것이

중요하다고 말하는 것이다.

3 (e)
누군가가 어떤 것을 통보한다면, 그 사람은 중요한 일을 말하는 것이다.

4 (b)
당신이 어떤 것에 반대한다면, 그것에 대해 강한 이의(異議)를 갖는 것이다.

5 (d)
어떤 것이 당신의 감정을 상하게 한다면, 그것 때문에 감정이 나빠지는 것이다.

EXERCISE B

1
해석 경찰은 며칠 밤 동안이나 그녀의 집을 순찰했다.
해설 '순찰하다'라는 뜻의 patrol을 묻는 문제다. 오답으로 제시된 patronize는 '(상대를) 낮추어보고 대하다'라는 뜻으로 주로 쓰인다. 이 단어에는 '단골 고객이 되다'라는 뜻도 있다.
정답 patrolled

2
해석 직장을 그만두기 전에, 많은 것에 대해 생각해 보아야 한다.
해설 '그만두다'라는 뜻의 quit을 묻는 문제다. 오답으로 제시된 anger는 '화나게 하다'라는 뜻으로 주어진 맥락에 어울리지 않는다. 이 단어는 '분노'라는 뜻의 명사로도 쓰인다.
정답 quitting

3
해석 그녀의 책은 전문 작가들로부터 적극적인 추천을 받았다.
해설 '추천하다'라는 뜻의 recommend를 묻는 문제다. 오답으로 제시된 respond는 '반응하다; 응답하다'라는 뜻인데, 특히 '반응하다'라는 뜻일 때는 자동사이기 때문에 수동태로 쓸 수 없음에 유의하자.
정답 recommended

4
해석 아프리카에서 미국으로 뱀을 운송하는 데 얼마나 비용이 들까?
해설 '운송하다'라는 뜻의 ship을 묻는 문제다. 오답으로 제시된 chip은 '(일부가) 깨지다; 깎아내다'라는 뜻으로 주어진 맥락에 어울리지 않는다.
정답 ship

5
해석 그 가게는 많은 제품들을 저장하고 있다.
해설 '저장하다'라는 뜻의 store를 묻는 문제다. 오답으로 제시된 score는 '득점하다'라는 뜻으로 주어진 맥락에 적합하지 않다.
정답 stores

PRACTICE

1
해석 A: 많은 사람들이 그 계획 때문에 들떠 있어.
B: 그렇지만 나는 그 계획에 강력히 반대해.

해설 '반대하다'라는 뜻의 object를 묻는 문제다. 다른 선택지들은 주로 타동사로 쓰이기 때문에 전치사 to가 바로 이어질 수 없다. 참고로 oppose는 be opposed to ~라는 형태로 '~에 반대하다'라는 뜻을 나타낼 수 있다. 참고로 object는 '반대하여(ob) 던지다'로, subject는 '아래로(sub) 던지다(ject)'로 각각 분석된다.

어구 excited 흥분한 strongly 강력하게
oppose 반대하다 subject 종속시키다
project 추정하다

정답 (a)

2
해석 A: 그녀에게 사과하는 편이 나을 거 같은데.
B: 음, 어쩌면. 그렇지만 그녀의 감정을 상하게 할 의도는 아니었는데.

해설 '감정을 상하게 하다'라는 뜻의 offend를 묻는 문제다. 이 단어는 '향해서(of←ob) 치다(fend)'로 분석된다. 이 단어와 어근 fend를 공유하는 defend는 '치는 것을(fend) 막다(de)'로 분석된다. 그리고 선택지 가운데 effect가 '영향, 효과'라는 명사로서 쓰인다는 점도 익혀두자.

어구 apologize 사과하다 mean to ~할 의도이다
offer 제의하다 attend 참석하다
effect 초래하다

정답 (d)

3
해석 A: 엔야가 어젯밤 콘서트에서 공연을 잘한 거 같아.
B: 나도 그렇게 생각해. 그녀는 정말로 뛰어난 가수인 거 같아.

해설 '수행하다'라는 뜻의 perform을 묻는 문제다. perform에는 주어진 예문에서와 같이 '공연하다'라는 뜻도 있음을 익혀두자. 다른 선택지들은 모두 타동사로 쓰이기 때문에 빈 칸에 들어갈 수 없다. perform이 '완전히(per) 이루어내다(form)'로 분석되는 데 반해, reform은 '다시(re) 모양을 만들다(form)'로 inform은 '향해서(in) 모양을 만들다(form)'로 분석된다.

어구 excellent 탁월한 perfect 완성하다 inform 알리다
reform 개혁하다

정답 (c)

4
해석 A: 훌륭한 변호사를 추천해 주시겠어요?
B: 아바 카펜터에게 연락해 보시는 게 어때요? 그녀는 일을 잘 알아요.

해설 '추천하다'라는 뜻의 recommend를 묻는 문제다. 선택지 가운데 command와 commend는 혼동하기 쉬우므로 뜻을 정확하게 알아둘 필요가 있다. recommend는 '다시(re) 칭찬하다(commend)'로 분석할 수 있다. 그리고 '연락하다'라는 뜻의 contact가 타동사라는 점도 기억해 두어야 한다.

어구 contact 연락하다 command 명령하다
recollect 기억해내다 commend 칭찬하다

정답 (c)

5
해석 그들은 시(市)가 교육에 보다 많은 돈을 투자해야 한다고 주장한다.

해설 '주장하다'라는 뜻의 maintain을 묻는 문제다. 이 단어는 '손에(main) 잡다(tain)'로 분석된다. 반면 contain은 '함께(con) 잡다(tain)'로, retain은 '완전히(←다시: re) 잡다(tain)'로, obtain은 '향해서(ob) 잡다(tain)'로 각각 분석된다.

어구 invest 투자하다 contain 포함하다
retain 보유하다 obtain 획득하다

정답 (d)

6
해석 낮은 급여에 화가 나서, 데이비드는 직장을 그만두었다.

해설 '그만두다'라는 뜻의 quit을 묻는 문제다. 이 뜻의 quit은 자동사로도 쓰인다. 그리고 선택지 가운데 recall에 '(결함이 있는 제품을) 회수하다'라는 뜻과 '(중요 인물 등을) 소환하다'라는 뜻도 있음을 익혀두자.

어구 anger 화나게 하다 suit ~에 어울리다
destroy 파괴하다 recall 기억해내다

정답 (b)

7
해석 놀랍게도, 그들은 디트로이트로 자동차를 배송할 수 있었다.

해설 '운송하다'라는 뜻의 ship을 묻는 문제다. 본래 이 단어는 선박을 이용하여 물품을 운송한다는 뜻을 나타냈는데, 의미가 확장되어 비행기나 트럭 등과 같은 항공편이나 육상 교통수단으로 운송한다는 뜻도 갖게 되었다.

어구 shop (상품을 사러) 가게에 들르다 shoot (총 등을) 쏘다
shock 충격을 주다

정답 (b)

8
해석 가격은 77달러에서 122달러에 이른다.

해설 '(일정한) 범위에 이르다'라는 뜻의 range를 묻는 문제다. '범위'라는 뜻의 명사로도 쓰이는 range가 over와 함께 '(대화 등에서) 다양한 주제를 다루다'라는 뜻을 나타내기도 한다는 점을 알아두자.

어구 exchange 교환하다 charge (요금을) 부과하다
arrange 마련하다

정답 (c)

UNIT 3 명사(필수어휘)

EXERCISE

A

1 (c)　　**2** (e)　　**3** (d)　　**4** (b)　　**5** (a)

B

1 anniversary　　**2** field
3 housing　　　　**4** lot
5 manuscript

PRACTICE

1 (a)　**2** (d)　**3** (c)　**4** (b)　**5** (b)
6 (d)　**7** (a)　**8** (c)

중요 Collocation 정리

1 많은 부부들은 선물을 주고받음으로써 결혼기념일을 경축한다.

2 새로운 정책은 패션업계의 갑작스런 호황으로 이어졌다.

3 유명 인사들은 행복한 삶을 영위하는가?

4 우리는 교통 체증을 피하기 위해 우회했다.

5 유명한 사설에서 교수는 정부를 혹독하게 비판했다.

6 분자 생물학이라는 분야는 지성뿐만 아니라 창의성을 요구한다.

7 그가 한 말의 핵심은 행복이 외부가 아니라 내부로부터 비롯된다는 것이었다.

8 값싼 주택을 공급하는 것이 선거의 주요 쟁점이었다.

9 그런 말은 모욕으로 간주될 수 있다.

10 여성 운동은 나라의 사회적 상황에 영향을 미쳤다.

11 긍정적으로 생각함으로써 운명이 좋아지도록 애쓰라.

12 엄격한 편집자는 많은 원고들을 거부했다.

13 진화라는 개념은 상당히 오도하는 개념이다.

14 그녀를 떠나보낼 수밖에 없었다.

15 많은 학생들에게, 쉬는 시간은 재미있게 노는 시간이다.

EXERCISE A

1 (c)
의류업계가 호황이라면, 사람들이 옷을 많이 사는 것이다.

2 (e)
여러분이 유명 인사라면, 많은 사람들이 여러분을 좋아할 것이다.

3 (d)
잡지에서 재미있는 사설을 읽는다면, 그 잡지를 구독하고 싶어 할지도 모른다.

4 (b)
누군가가 하는 말의 핵심을 안다면, 그 사람이 하고 싶어 하는 말을 이해하는 것이다.

5 (a)
누군가를 모욕한다면, 그 사람이 화를 낼 것이다.

EXERCISE B

1

해석 다음 주 월요일이 우리의 20번째 결혼기념일이다.

해설 '기념일'이라는 뜻의 anniversary를 묻는 문제다. 오답으로 제시된 adversity는 '역경, 고난'이라는 뜻으로 특히 발음이 비슷해서 anniversary와 혼동할 수 있으므로 주의해야 한다.

정답 anniversary

2

해석 에릭은 인지 언어학이라는 분야에 관심이 있다.

해설 '분야'라는 뜻의 field를 묻는 문제다. 오답으로 제시된 shield는 '방패'라는 뜻으로 field와는 관계가 없다. shield에는 '경찰관이 착용하는 배지'라는 뜻도 있다.

정답 field

3

해석 저렴한 주택은 모든 이들에게 중요하다.

해설 '주택'이라는 뜻의 housing을 묻는 문제다. 이때 housing을 셀 수 없는 명사로 쓰인다. 반면 '집'을 뜻하는 house는 셀 수 있는 명사이기 때문에 단수형일 때는 a와 같은 말이 반드시 앞에 와야 한다.

정답 housing

4

해석 어떻게 하면 내 운명이 더 나아지게 할 수 있을까?

해설 '운명'이란 뜻의 lot을 묻는 문제다. 오답으로 제시된 rot은 lot과 발음을 혼동할 수 있지만, '부패 (과정)'라는 뜻으로 주어진 맥락에 전혀 어울리지 않는다. lot의 뜻이 생소할 수 있으므로 정확히 익혀두자.

정답 lot

5

해석 출판사로서, 저희는 귀하의 뛰어난 원고에 감명을 받았습니다.

해설 '원고'라는 뜻의 manuscript를 묻는 문제다. 오답으로 제시된 manicure는 '매니큐어'라는 뜻으로 주어진 맥락에 전혀 어울리지 않는다. 참고로, 두 단어는 '손'을 뜻하는 man(u)이라는 어근을 공유한다.

정답 manuscript

PRACTICE

1

해석 A: 결혼 10주년을 어떻게 기념할 생각이니?
　　　B: 곰으로 여행을 떠날까 싶어.

해설 '기념일'을 뜻하는 anniversary를 묻는 문제다. 이 단어는 '해마다(ann[i]) 방향을 돌리는(vers[e]) 것(ary)'으로 분석된다. '향해서(ad) 방향을 돌리는(verse)'으로 분석되는 adverse(불리한)

와 어근 vers를 공유한다.

어구 celebrate 경축하다　　　　glossary 용어 해설집
　　　necessity 필요성　　　　density 밀도

정답 (a)

2

해석 A: 그의 강연의 요점이 뭐니?
　　　B: 근본적으로, 그는 이라크에 군대를 보내는 것에 반대해.

해설 '요점'이라는 뜻의 gist를 묻는 문제다. 이 단어는 본래 '소송의 근거'라는 뜻을 나타내는데, 이 뜻으로부터 '요점'이라는 뜻으로 의미가 확장되었다. 그리고 영한사전의 불충분한 설명과 달리, guilt에는 '죄책감'이라는 뜻이 있음도 익혀두자.

어구 lecture 강연, 강의　　　　basically 근본적으로
　　　opposed to ~에 반대하는　troop 군대
　　　germ 세균　　　　　　　　gum 잇몸; 껌
　　　guilt 죄책감

정답 (d)

3

해석 A: 어떻게 자기 아들한테 모욕을 줄 수 있어요?
　　　B: 정말 미안해. 그렇지만, 그럴 생각은 아니었어.

해설 '모욕'이란 뜻의 insult를 묻는 문제다. 이 단어는 '위로(in) 뛰다(sult)'로, result는 '되돌아서(re) 뛰다(sult)'로 분석된다. 반면 consult는 '함께(con) 구하다(sult)'로 분석되기 때문에 다른 단어들과 다르다.

어구 dreadfully 아주　　　　mean to ~할 작정이다
　　　consult 상의　　　　　result 결과

정답 (c)

4

해석 A: 어떻게 할 작정이니?
　　　B: 집을 파는 수밖에 없을 거 같아.

해설 '선택'이란 뜻의 option을 묻는 문제다. 이 단어는 '고르는(opt) 것(ion)'으로 분석된다. 그리고 adoption은 '향해서(ad) 고르는 (opt) 것(ion)'으로 분석되어, 본래 '계획이나 방법을 채택하는 것' 이란 뜻을 나타냈다. 이 의미로부터 '입양'이란 뜻으로 확장되었다.

어구 consumption 소비　　adoption 입양　　assumption 가정

정답 (b)

5

해석 1990년대에는 건설업계가 호황이었다.

해설 '호황'이라는 뜻의 boom을 묻는 문제다. 이 뜻으로 쓰일 때 boom은 대개 단수형을 취한다. 선택지 가운데 room에는 '여유 공간'이라는 뜻이 있는데, 이 뜻에서는 셀 수 없는 명사임에 특히 유의해야 한다.

어구 construction 건설　　　　room 방; 여유 공간
　　　groom 신랑　　　　　　　mushroom 버섯

정답 (b)

6

해석 안셀리나 솔리와 같은 유명 인사는 훌륭한 역할 모델이다.

해설 '유명 인사'라는 뜻의 celebrity를 묻는 문제다. 선택지 가운데 security는 복수형으로 쓰이면 '주식이나 채권과 같은 유기 증권' 을 뜻한다. 이 뜻을 제외한 나머지 뜻에서는, 예컨대 '안보,' '보안,' '경비'와 같은 뜻일 때는 모두 셀 수 없는 명사라는 점을 익혀두어야 한다.

어구 role model 역할 모델　　celebration 축하 (행사)
　　　miscellany 잡동사니　　　securities 유가 증권

정답 (d)

7

해석 우월성이라는 개념은 다양한 방식으로 이해될 수 있다.

해설 '개념'을 뜻하는 notion을 묻는 문제다. 똑같은 뜻을 나타내는, 다소 어려운 단어로 construct를 들 수 있다. 이 단어는 흔히 '건 설하다'라는 뜻의 동사로만 아는 경향이 있는데, 명사로서 '개념' 을 뜻함도 익혀두자.

어구 superiority 우월성　　　　lotion 로션
　　　promotion 승진; 판촉
　　　portion (나머지와 구별되는) 부분

정답 (a)

8

해석 많은 이들은 언어학이라는 분야에 매력을 느낀다.

해설 '분야'라는 뜻의 field를 묻는 문제다. 선택지 가운데 yield는 '양 보하다'라는 뜻의 동사로만 알기 쉬운데, '산출량'이라는 뜻의 셀 수 있는 명사로도 쓰임에 유의해야 한다. 이 단어의 본래 뜻은 '대 가를 치르다'이다.

어구 fascinate 매혹시키다　　　linguistics 언어학
　　　yield 산출량　　　　　　　pasture 목초지
　　　meadow 초원

정답 (c)

UNIT 4　형용사(필수어휘)

EXERCISE

A

1 (c)　　2 (e)　　3 (a)　　4 (b)　　5 (d)

B

1　Emotional　　2　ideal
3　normal　　　 4　fashionable
5　Sensitive

PRACTICE

1 (c)　　2 (c)　　3 (a)　　4 (b)　　5 (d)
6 (b)　　7 (a)　　8 (b)

중요 Collocation 정리

1　오즈에게는 한밤중에 코를 고는 짜증스런 버릇이 있다.

2　회의를 가능한 한 짧게 진행하도록 하라.

3　헌신적인 자원봉사자들이 수천 명의 생명을 구해냈다.

4　감정적인 문제가 교사로서의 역할 수행에 영향을 미칠 수 있다.

5　미니스커트는 1960년대에 유행했다.

6　이 팔찌는 진짜 은으로 만든 것이다.

7　우리가 이상적인 세상에 살고 있는 게 아니란 것을 알지 못하니?

8 모든 소녀들이 그녀의 지성을 시샘했다.

9 P2P 네트워크를 차단하는 것이 적법한가?

10 현미경이 당신에게 사물의 세세한 사항을 보여줄 수 있다.

11 미친 사람들조차도 때로는 정상적인 행동을 나타낼 수 있다.

12 많은 한국인들은 나라를 통일할 수 있을 것이라고 낙관한다.

13 자신에 대해 인내심을 가지면 멋진 일들이 일어날 것이다.

14 그들이 제시하는 가격이 적당한 거 같은데.

15 사라는 다른 이들의 마음을 읽을 수 있는, 감수성이 예민한 소녀였다.

EXERCISE A

1 (c)
어떤 것이 짜증나게 한다면, 그것은 약간 화가 나게 하는 것이다.

2 (e)
어떤 일을 하는 데 헌신한다면, 그것을 하기 위해 아주 열심히 노력하는 것이다.

3 (a)
누군가와 진정한 우정을 맺는다면, 그 우정은 진실한 것이다.

4 (b)
어떤 것이 합법적이라면, 법적으로 그것을 할 수 있다.

5 (d)
어떤 것에 대해 낙관적이라면, 그것이 성공할 것이라고 믿는 것이다.

EXERCISE B

1
해석 정서적으로 건강한 상태는 일상생활에서 매우 중요하다.

해설 '감정적인' 또는 '정서적인'이란 뜻을 나타내는 emotional을 묻는 문제다. 오답으로 제시된 motionless는 '정지된'이란 뜻으로 health와 자연스럽게 연결되지 않는다. motionless에서 less라는 접미사는 '~이 없는'이란 뜻을 나타냄도 알아두자.

정답 Emotional

2
해석 가까운 장래에 이상적인 세계가 도래할까?

해설 '이상적인'이란 뜻의 ideal을 묻는 문제다. 오답으로 제시된 idle은 '게으른'이란 뜻으로 본래 의미는 '가치 없는'이며 순수 영어에 속한다. 반면 ideal은 본래 '아이디어(idea)와 관련된(al)'으로 분석되는, 라틴어 계열 어휘에 속한다.

정답 ideal

3
해석 때때로 스트레스를 느끼는 것은 정상적이다.

해설 '정상적인'을 뜻하는 normal을 묻는 문제다. normal은 '기준(norm)과 관련된(al)'으로 분석되는 단어이다. 반면 오답으로 제시된 minimal은 '최소한의'라는 뜻으로 '최소(minim)와 관련된(al)'으로 분석된다.

정답 normal

4
해석 모든 일에 대해 정부를 탓하는 것이 유행이 되어 버렸다.

해설 '유행하는'이란 뜻의 fashionable을 묻는 문제다. 오답으로 제시된 fascinated는 '매혹된'이란 뜻으로 대개 사람이 다른 사람이나 대상에 대해 강한 매력을 느끼는 것을 나타내기 때문에 정답이 될 수 없다.

정답 fashionable

5
해석 감수성이 예민한 사람들은 현명하면서 친절하다.

해설 '감수성이 예민한'이란 뜻의 sensitive를 묻는 문제다. 이 단어에 '민감한'이란 뜻이 있음도 기억해두어야 한다. 오답으로 제시된 senseless는 '무의미한' 또는 '무감각의'라는 뜻을 나타낸다.

정답 Sensitive

PRACTICE

1
해석 A: 론을 더 이상 못 봐주겠어.
　　 B: 이해해. 걘 아주 짜증나는 애야.

해설 '짜증나게 하는'이란 뜻의 annoying을 묻는 문제다. annoyed가 '짜증나는'이란 뜻으로 '일정한 감정을 가진' 상태를 뜻하는 데 반해, annoying은 사람으로 하여금 '일정한 감정을 가지도록 만드는' 것을 나타낸다는 점에 특히 유의해야 한다. 이 점은 pleasing과 pleased에 대해서도 마찬가지로 적용된다는 점도 기억하자. 그리고 선택지에서 제시된 understanding의 뜻도 정확히 알아두어야 한다.

어구 stand 참다　　　　　　　guy 녀석, 사람
　　 charming 매력적인　　　understanding 이해심 있는
　　 pleasing 만족스러운

정답 (c)

2
해석 A: 언니를 왜 그렇게 시샘하니?
　　 B: 언니는 모든 걸 가졌지만, 난 아무것도 없잖아.

해설 '시샘하는'이란 뜻의 jealous를 묻는 문제다. B의 말을 통해 자신이 가지지 못한 것을 가진 이에 대한 '시샘'의 마음을 짐작할 수 있다. 그리고 proud는 대개 '자랑스러워하는'이란 뜻이지만, '어구'에서 밝힌 바와 같이 '거만한'이란 뜻도 있음을 기억해야 한다. '자랑스러워하는' 마음이 지나친 경우 '거만한' 마음이 되기 때문이다.

어구 modest 겸손한　　　　　proud 거만한
　　 shy 수줍음을 타는

정답 (c)

3
해석 A: 그의 경기에 대해 어떻게 그렇게 낙관할 수 있니?
　　 B: 난 그가 이길 것을 아니까.

해설 '낙관적인'이라는 뜻의 optimistic을 묻는 문제다. optimistic은 '가장 좋을(optim) 것이라 믿는 사람(ist)과 관련된(ic)'으로 분석된다. 반면 이와 반대되는 pessimistic은 '가장 나쁠(pessim) 것이라 믿는 사람(ist)과 관련된(ic)'으로 분석된다. 그리고 선택지의 concerned 다음에 about이 오면 '~에 대해 우려하는'이란 뜻을, 반면 with가 오면 '~에 관여하는'이란 뜻을 나타냄에 유의해야 한다.

어구 concerned 우려하는   humble 겸손한
　　pessimistic 비관적인

정답 (a)

4

해석 A: 가격이 적당한 거 같아.
　　B: 농담하니? 너무 높은 가격이야.

해설 '(가격 등이) 적당한'이란 뜻의 reasonable을 묻는 문제다. B
가 너무 높은 가격이라고 하며 반박했기 때문에 A는 적당한 가
격이라고 말해야 한다. 그리고 일반적으로 price(가격)에 대해
서는 cheap(값싼)이나 expensive를 쓰지 않고 low(낮은)나
high(높은)를 써야 함에 유의하자.

어구 expensive 값비싼   unattractive 매력이 없는
　　unreliable 신뢰할 수 없는

정답 (b)

5

해석 그녀와의 잠깐의 조우에서, 인생에 대해 많은 것을 배웠다.

해설 '잠깐의'라는 뜻의 brief를 묻는 문제다. brief에 '간략한'이란 뜻
이 있음도 함께 알아두어야 한다. 선택지에서 arrogant는 '많은
것을 배웠다'라는 내용과 어울리지 않는다. 그리고 innovative
는 아이디어나 어떤 일을 수행하는 방식에 대해 주로 쓰는 말이기
때문에 정답이 될 수 없음에 유의하자.

어구 encounter 조우(遭遇)   arrogant 오만한
　　innovative 혁신적인   incorrect 부정확한

정답 (d)

6

해석 오프라 윈프리는 여성들에게 자신감을 불어넣는 데 헌신하고 있다.

해설 '헌신하는'이란 뜻의 dedicated를 묻는 문제다. 참고로
empower에는 '어구'에서 해설한 '자신감을 불어넣다'라는 뜻과
'해석'에서 제시한 '권한을 주다'라는 뜻이 모두 있음에 유의하자.
그리고 uncomfortable 다음에는 전치사로 about이나 with가,
uninterested 다음에는 전치사로 in이 와야 함에 주의해야 한다.

어구 empower 권한을 주다   dishonest 부정직한
　　uncomfortable 불편한   uninterested 관심이 없는

정답 (b)

7

해석 남자들이 귀걸이를 하는 것이 유행하게 되었다.

해설 '유행하는'이란 뜻의 fashionable을 묻는 문제다. committed
다음에는 전치사로 to가 와야 한다. 반면 capable은 바로 다음
에는 of -ing가 와서 '(최대로 하여) ~할 수 있는'이란 뜻을 나타
낸다. 이와 같은 단어의 쓰임새를 정확히 알아두어야만 어휘 영역
에서 고득점을 얻을 수 있음을 명심하자.

어구 earring 귀걸이   committed 헌신적인
　　unclear 불명료한   capable 능력이 있는

정답 (a)

8

해석 진정한 우정은 사람을 강하게 만들 수 있다.

해설 '진정한'이란 뜻의 genuine을 묻는 문제다. 전후 맥락으로 보아,
genuine friendship이 자연스럽다. 왜냐하면 '진정한 우정'이
되어야 사람을 강하게 해 줄 수 있기 때문이다. 이처럼 상식에 맞
으면서 주어진 맥락에 가장 잘 어울리는 선택지가 정답이 된다는
점을 명심하자.

어구 feeble 연약한   cowardly 비겁한
　　untrustworthy 신뢰할 수 없는

정답 (b)

UNIT 5 의미(혼동어휘) I

EXERCISE

A
1 (d)　　2 (a)　　3 (e)　　4 (c)　　5 (b)

B
1　effect　　2　clothes
3　cook　　4　stealing
5　accept

PRACTICE

1 (d)　　2 (b)　　3 (c)　　4 (a)　　5 (a)
6 (c)　　7 (d)　　8 (a)

중요 Collocation 정리

1　마지막 부분을 제외하고 제안을 받아들이기로 결정했다.

2　흡연의 효과는 건강에 부정적인 영향을 끼친다.

3　린지로부터 빌린 책을 빌려주었다.

4　일부 작가들이 어린애처럼 순수한 데 반해, 다른 작가들은 유
　치하다.

5　이 옷은 명주로 만들어졌다.

6　요리사는 다양한 주방 도구를 사용하는 데 매우 능숙하다.

7　우스운 영화를 보는 것은 아주 재미있었다.

8　두 여자는 가게를 털어서 많은 돈을 훔쳤다.

EXERCISE A

1　(d)
　파티에 대한 초대를 받아들이면 참석할 것이 거의 확실하다.

2　(a)
　어떤 것이 상황에 영향을 미치면 그 상황은 그것에 의해 변화
　될 것이다.

3　(e)
　어린애처럼 순수하다면 많은 이들이 그런 순진무구함을 좋아
　할 것이다.

4　(c)
　누군가로부터 어떤 것을 빌리면 되돌려주어야 한다.

5　(b)
　은행을 털면 감옥에 가게 될 것이 거의 확실하다.

EXERCISE B

1

해석 지구 온난화의 영향이 그렇게 크지 않을지도 모른다.

해설 '영향'이나 '효과'라는 뜻의 명사는 effect다.

정답 effect

2

해석 그 옷은 정말 이상하다.

해설 cloth는 '천'을, clothes는 '옷'을 나타낸다.

정답 clothes

3

해석 그 요리사는 가능한 모든 요리법을 알고 있다.

해설 cook은 '요리사'를, cooker는 '주방 도구'를 뜻한다.

정답 cook

4

해석 보석을 훔치고 나서, 줄리엣은 아주 행복해 했다.

해설 rob의 목적어는 사람이나 장소이며, steal의 목적어는 훔치는 물건이다.

정답 stealing

5

해석 조건이 터무니없다. 받아들일 수 없다.

해설 '받아들이다'는 accept로 표현해야 한다.

정답 accept

PRACTICE

1

해석 A: 언짢아 보이네, 무슨 일이니?
B: 핸드백을 도난당한 거 같아.

해설 어떤 물품을 훔치는 것은 steal로 나타낸다. rob 바로 다음에는 사람 또는 장소가 와야 한다. 참고로 purse가 영국식 영어에서는 '지갑'이라는 뜻을 나타낸다. 미국식 영어에서는 '지갑'을 wallet으로 나타내는 것이 보통이다.

어구 upset 언짢은 　purse 핸드백, 지갑 (영국식)
lend 빌려주다

정답 (d)

2

해석 A: 쥬디, 제의 받은 일자리를 수락할 거니?
B: 실은 잘 모르겠어. 복리 혜택이 그리 좋지 않거든.

해설 '받아들이다'는 accept로 표현한다. (a) acquire로 정답을 착각하지 않도록 유의해야 한다. '일자리 제의'를 이미 받은 상태에서 이를 수락할 것인가 말 것인가를 결정하는 상황이기 때문이다.

어구 job offer 일자리 제의 　benefits package 복리 혜택
acquire 획득하다 　exchange 교환하다
acclaim 격찬하다

정답 (b)

3

해석 A: 로라, 새 요리사에 대해 어떻게 생각하니?
B: 음, 적어도 요리는 잘하잖아. 그게 그 사람 일이잖아.

해설 '요리사'는 cook으로 나타내야 한다. cooker(주방 도구)가 아님에 주의하자.

어구 at least 적어도 　cashier 계산원
bank teller 은행 창구 직원

정답 (c)

4

해석 A: 와, 이 천은 촉감이 아주 부드러워!
B: 응. 비단이나 그런 종류 같아.

해설 A의 대사에서 동사가 feels로 단수형이기 때문에 빈 칸은 단수형이 와야 한다. 따라서 정답은 (a)다. 참고로 (d)의 clothing은 셀 수 없는 명사이기 때문에 복수형은 잘못되었다. 이와 같은 문법적 제약을 TEPS에서는 단어의 쓰임새로 파악하기 때문에 어휘를 학습할 때도 정확히 익혀두어야 한다.

어구 silk 비단, 명주 　dress 드레스 　clothing (불가산명사) 의복

정답 (a)

5

해석 제임스를 빼고 남자애는 모두 왕자처럼 소중한 존재이다.

해설 맥락으로 보아 '~를 제외하고'가 가장 자연스럽다. Frances Hodgson Burnett 원작의 영화 a Little Princess의 한 구절인 Every girl is a princess의 변형인데, except의 쓰임새를 정확히 익힐 수 있는 문장이다.

어구 excel 능가하다 　exceed 초과하다
exercise 운동하다; 행사하다

정답 (a)

6

해석 어린애 같은 그녀의 순진무구함 때문에 모든 이들이 메리 제인 왓슨을 좋아한다.

해설 '어린애 같이 순진무구한'이란 뜻은 childlike로 나타낸다. (a)에서 접미사 less가 '~이 없는'이란 뜻을 나타낸다는 점도 알아두자. 반대의 뜻을 나타내는 접미사는 ful로 '~로 가득한'이란 뜻이다.

어구 innocence 순진무구함 　childless 자녀가 없는
childproof 아동에게 안전한

정답 (c)

7

해석 그녀의 우스운 농담은 늘 우리로 하여금 한껏 웃게 한다.

해설 '우스운'이란 뜻은 funny로 나타내야 함에 유의하자.

어구 hard 심하게 　　　　fund 자금을 제공하다
diligent 부지런한 　　lazy 게으른

정답 (d)

8

해석 여러분의 행복은 여러분 파트너의 행복에 크게 영향을 미칠 수 있습니다.

해설 '영향을 미치다'는 affect로 나타내야 한다. 나머지 표현도 중요하므로 기억해두자.

어구 approach 접근하다 　attack 공격하다 　assign 배당하다

정답 (a)

EXERCISE

A

1 (d) 2 (a) 3 (e) 4 (b) 5 (c)

B

1 delightful 2 efficient
3 imaginary 4 literary
5 principal

PRACTICE

1 (a) 2 (d) 3 (c) 4 (b) 5 (c)
6 (d) 7 (a) 8 (b)

중요 Collocation 정리

1 그들이 업무에서 서로를 보완해 주었을 때, 모든 이들이 그들을 칭찬했다.

2 기쁜 일들이 일어나면 즐거워하게 된다.

3 능숙한 근로자들은 언제나 효과적인 방식으로 일한다.

4 상상력이 풍부한 작가들은 상상의 동물들을 잘 만들어 낸다.

5 글을 아는 이들만이 문학 작품을 즐겨 읽을 수 있다.

6 강연의 주제는 '객체의 본질에 관해서'이다.

7 우리 교장 선생님은 민주주의의 기본 원칙을 존중하신다.

8 은퇴한 디자이너는 보다 일찍 사임했어야만 했는데 그러지 못했다고 생각했다.

EXERCISE A

1 **(d)**
어떤 것을 칭찬한다면, 그것에 대해 좋게 말하는 것이다.

2 **(a)**
어떤 것이 매우 기쁘게 한다면, 그것은 여러분을 매우 행복하게 만든다.

3 **(e)**
어떤 사람이 일에 능숙하다면, 그 사람은 일을 매우 잘하는 것이다.

4 **(b)**
어떤 사람이 식자(識字)가 들었다면, 그 사람은 읽거나 쓸 줄 안다.

5 **(c)**
회사에서 사임한다면, 더는 그 회사에서 근무하지 않는 것이다.

EXERCISE B

1

해석 아이러니하게도, 매우 기쁜 일이 나쁜 사람들에게 일어날 수 있다.

해설 '매우 기쁘게 하는'이란 뜻의 delightful을 묻는 문제다. 오답으로 제시된 delighted는 '매우 기뻐하는'이란 뜻으로 사람이 그런 감정을 갖는다는 뜻이기 때문에 정답이 될 수 없다.

정답 delightful

2

해석 능숙하게 일하는 사람은 시간을 허비하지 않는다.

해설 '능숙한'이란 뜻의 efficient를 묻는 문제다. 오답으로 제시된 effective는 '효과적인'이란 뜻으로 본래 용도에 맞게 기능을 발휘함을 나타내는 말이기 때문에 주어진 맥락에 맞지 않는다. 참고로 efficient에는 '허비하지 않는'이란 뜻이 들어 있음에도 유의하자.

정답 efficient

3

해석 용은 상상의 동물이다.

해설 '상상의'라는 뜻의 imaginary를 묻는 문제다. 오답으로 제시된 imaginative는 '상상력이 풍부한'이란 뜻과 함께, '창의적인'이라는 뜻이 있음도 알아두어야 한다. 어떤 의미로든 용이 그런 동물이라고 할 수 없으므로 정답은 imaginary이다.

정답 imaginary

4

해석 다양한 문학 장르가 있다.

해설 '문학의'라는 뜻의 literary를 묻는 문제다. 오답으로 제시된 literate는 '읽고 쓸 줄 아는'이란 뜻이기 때문에 주어진 맥락에 어울리지 않음에 유의하자.

정답 literary

5

해석 이 프로그램의 주된 목적은 인격을 배양하는 것이다.

해설 '주요한, 주된'이라는 뜻의 principal을 묻는 문제다. 오답으로 제시된 principle은 '원리, 원칙'이라는 뜻의 명사로 쓰임에 유의해야 한다. 반면 principal은 형용사와 명사로 쓰일 수 있다.

정답 principal

PRACTICE

1

해석 A: 메리와 산드라는 서로 사이가 좋은 거 같아.
B: 응. 정말 서로 잘 어울려.

해설 '보완하다'라는 뜻의 complement를 묻는 문제다. 선택지 가운데 compare에는 '비유하다'라는 뜻도 있음을 기억하자. 그리고 compete은 자동사로만, complain은 주로 자동사로 쓰이기 때문에 주어진 문장에 쓰일 수 없음에 유의해야 한다.

어구 get along 사이좋게 지내다 compare 비교하다
compete 겨루다   complain 불평하다

정답 (a)

2

해석 A: 왜 그렇게 기뻐하니?
B: 아빠가 될 거라서.

해설 '매우 기뻐하는'이란 뜻의 delighted를 묻는 문제다. 오답으로 제시된 단어 가운데 dismissed는 동사 dismiss의 과거분사 형태이다. dismiss에는 '해고하다'라는 뜻과 함께 '도외시하다', 그리고 '해산시키다'라는 뜻이 있음도 알아두어야 한다.

어구 delicious 맛있는　dismissed 해고된
disobedient 반항적인

정답 (d)

3

해석 A: 모든 사람들이 마리엔이 일 잘하는 비서라고들 해.
B: 응. 그녀는 일을 어떻게 해야 하는지 잘 알아.

해설 '일에 능숙한'이란 뜻의 efficient를 묻는 문제다. 참고로 B의 말에서 knows what she is doing은 '자신의 일에 대한 지식이나 기술을 갖추고 있다'라는 뜻이다. 따라서 (a), (b), (d)의 선택지는 모두 정답이 될 수 없다.

어구 secretary 비서　inattentive 부주의한
arrogant 오만한　furious 격분한

정답 (c)

4

해석 A: 회사에서 물러날까 싶습니다.
B: 뭐라고요? 있잖아요, 당신은 우리 회사에 좋은 자산이었어요.

해설 '사임하다'라는 뜻의 resign을 묻는 문제다. A의 말에서와 같이 resign 바로 다음에는 전치사로 from이 오는 경우가 많다. 반면 (a)의 dismiss는 타동사이기 때문에 바로 다음에 전치사가 오지 않는다. 그리고 apply 다음에는 전치사로 for나 to가, reside 다음에는 전치사로 in이 오는 것이 보통이다.

어구 asset 자산　dismiss 해고하다
apply 지원하다　reside 거주하다

정답 (b)

5

해석 낙태는 여전히 논란이 되는 주제이다.

해설 '주제'라는 뜻의 subject를 묻는 문제다. 선택지로 제시된 단어들은 모두 ject라는 어근을 공유하는데, '던지다'라는 뜻을 나타낸다. 참고로 object는 '향해서(ob) 던지다(ject)'로, project는 '앞으로(pro) 던지다(ject)'로, subject는 '아래로(sub) 던지다(ject)'로, injection은 '안으로(in) 던지는(ject) 것(ion)'으로 각각 분석된다.

어구 abortion 낙태　debate 논쟁하다
object 물체, 대상　project 계획, 기획
injection 주사, 주입

정답 (c)

6

해석 상상력이 풍부한 사람들은 창의적인 해결책을 잘 내놓는다.

해설 '상상력이 풍부한'이란 뜻의 imaginative를 묻는 문제다. 주어진 문장의 creative(창의적인)와 자연스럽게 이어져야 하기 때문에 다른 선택지가 정답이 될 수 없음에 유의해야 한다. 참고로 imaginable은 '생각해낼 수 있는 것 가운데 최고이거나 최악인' 대상임을 나타낼 때 주로 쓰인다.

어구 come up with 생각해내다　creative 창의적인
solution 해결책　imaginary 상상의
imagined 상상된　imaginable 상상할 수 있는

정답 (d)

7

해석 다른 사람들에 대한 존중은 민주주의의 기본 원칙이다.

해설 '원리, 원칙'이란 뜻의 principle을 묻는 문제다. 선택지 가운데 principal은 명사로 쓰일 때는 '교장'이라는 뜻을 나타낸다. 그리고 probability는 the probability of -ing 또는 a probability that ～라는 형태로 주로 쓰임도 기억해두자.

어구 basic 기본적인　democracy 민주주의
principal 교장　probability 가능성
prohibition 금지

정답 (a)

8

해석 읽고 쓸 줄 아는 사람들은 글을 읽지 못하는 사람들보다 훨씬 더 많은 것을 성취할 수 있다.

해설 '읽고 쓸 줄 아는'이란 뜻의 literate를 묻는 문제다. 주어진 문장에서 those who can't read와 대조를 이루어야 하기 때문에 literal과 같은 말이 정답이 될 수 없음에 유의해야 한다. 그리고 ironic에 '(본래 의도와) 상반되는 것 같은'이란 뜻이 있음도 알아두자.

어구 achieve 성취하다　literal 글자 그대로의
irrational 비합리적인　ironic 반어적인

정답 (b)

UNIT 7　형태(혼동 어휘)

EXERCISE

A

1 (d)　2 (b)　3 (e)　4 (c)　5 (a)

B

1　commanded　2　Conscientious
3　products　4　Economic
5　Awards

PRACTICE

1 (d)　2 (d)　3 (a)　4 (b)　5 (b)
6 (c)　7 (c)　8 (a)

중요 Collocation 정리

1　빌이 팀을 아주 잘 지휘했을 때, 모든 이들이 그를 칭찬했다.

2　양심적인 사람들은 도덕적 가치를 의식한다.

3　경제적 사고는 낭비 없는 생활 방식으로 귀결될 수 있다.

4　직원들은 모두 개인적인 문제로 인해 영향을 받을 수 있다.

5　물리학자는 그 의사의 잘못된 의료 행위를 비판했다.

6　농산물은 다양한 종류의 농업 제품을 포함한다.

7　상은 일종의 보상으로 간주될 수 있다.

8　어떤 것을 올리면 올라가게 된다.

EXERCISE A

1 (d)

어떤 사람을 칭찬하면, 그 사람은 행복해질 것이다.

2 (b)

어떤 것을 의식한다면, 그것이 존재한다는 것을 아는 것이다.

3 (e)

개인적인 문제가 있다면, 그 문제는 자신에게만 영향을 미친다.

4 (c)

의사라면, 환자를 치료한다.

5 (a)

어떤 것이 오르면, 그것은 떨어지는 것이 아니다.

EXERCISE B

1

해석 레이첼은 학생들에게 교실을 청소하라고 명령했다.

해설 '명령하다'라는 뜻의 command를 묻는 문제다. '추천하다'라는 뜻의 recommend 다음에는 -ing형이나 that절이 오는 것이 일반적이기 때문에 정답이 될 수 없음에 유의하자.

정답 commanded

2

해석 양심적인 사람들은 거짓말을 하지 않는다.

해설 '양심적인'이란 뜻의 conscientious를 묻는 문제다. 오답으로 제시된 scientific은 '과학적인'이란 뜻으로 주어진 맥락에 어울리지 않는다. 참고로 이 단어는 '알고(sci) 있도록(ent) 만드는([i]fic)'으로 분석된다.

정답 Conscientious

3

해석 많은 제품들이 형편없게 만들어진다.

해설 '제품'이란 뜻의 product를 묻는 문제다. '농산물'을 뜻하는 produce는 셀 수 없는 명사이기 때문에 복수형으로 쓰일 수 없다. 반면 대개 셀 수 있는 명사로 쓰이는 product는 복수형으로 쓰일 수 있다.

정답 products

4

해석 경제 성장은 모든 나라에 중요하다.

해설 '경제와 관련된'이란 뜻의 economic을 묻는 문제다. economical은 '허비하지 않는'이란 뜻으로 주어진 맥락에 자연스럽지는 않다. 이와 같은 경우에도 '경제 성장'이 일반적인 표현이라는 상식을 활용해야 함에 유의하자.

정답 Economic

5

해석 그들은 아카데미상 수상식에 참석했다.

해설 '상'을 뜻하는 award를 묻는 문제다. 오답으로 제시된 reward는 '보상'이라는 뜻으로 주어진 맥락에 어울리지 않는다. 이처럼 '~상'을 나타낼 때 쓰이는 말이 대개 award라는 점도 기억해두자.

정답 Awards

PRACTICE

1

해석 A: 그의 발표는 형편없었어요!
B: 음, 저는 그가 중요한 문제를 제기했다고 생각했는데요.

해설 '올리다'라는 뜻의 raise를 묻는 문제다. B에서 raise는 이 뜻에서 확장된 '(문제를) 제기하다'라는 뜻으로 쓰였다. 그리고 타동사 fell은 규칙변화를 하기 때문에 fell — felled — felled로 활용됨에 유의하자. 반면 자동사인 fall은 fall — fell — fallen으로 활용된다.

어구 presentation 발표　　fall 떨어지다
fell (나무를) 베어내다

정답 (d)

2

해석 A: 축하해! 최고의 연설상을 수상했다면서.
B: 고마워. 그냥 최선을 다했어.

해설 '상'을 뜻하는 award를 묻는 문제다. 선택지 가운데 reward는 '보상'이라는 뜻으로 주어진 맥락에 적합하지 않다. 그리고 regard에 '호감 어린 존경'이란 뜻도 있음을 익혀두자.

어구 Congratulations! 축하해요!　　speech 연설; 말
regard 고려　　guard 경비

정답 (d)

3

해석 A: 어머니의 직업이 뭐니?
B: 의사신데, 보스턴 병원에서 근무하셔.

해설 '의사'를 뜻하는 physician을 묻는 문제다. 이와 같은 문제에서도 역시 상식적인 판단에 따라 정답을 택해야 한다. 마술사(magician)가 병원에서 근무하는 것이 전혀 불가능하지는 않지만 일반적이지 않기 때문에 정답이 될 수 없다. 이처럼 어휘 영역에서 상식적인 판단을 따라야 하는 경우가 종종 있다는 점을 명심하자.

어구 musician 음악가　　magician 마술사

정답 (a)

4

해석 A: 개인적인 질문을 드려도 될까요?
B: 물론이죠! 어떤 점을 알고 싶으신가요?

해설 '개인적인'을 뜻하는 personal을 묻는 문제다. B가 자신에 대해 무엇을 알고 싶은가 라고 했기 때문에 '개인적인'이라는 말이 가장 적절하다. 참고로 접미사 -al은 '~의', '~와 관련된'이란 뜻을 나타낸다.

어구 seasonal 계절적인　　national 전국적인; 국가적인; 국립의

정답 (b)

5

해석 경제 발전은 정치적 불확실성 때문에 저해될 수 있다.

해설 '경제와 관련된'을 뜻하는 economic을 묻는 문제다. 정치적 불확실성과의 관련을 말하고 있기 때문에, economic이 자연스럽다. 참고로 접미사 -ic의 기본적인 의미는 '~의 특성을 갖는'이다.

어구 development 발전　　discourage 저해하다
uncertainty 불확실성　　atomic 원자의; 원자력의
comic 희극적인　　automatic 자동적인

정답 (b)

6

해석 양심적인 사람들은 어떤 것도 훔치지 않을 것이다.

해설 '양심적인'이란 뜻의 conscientious를 묻는 문제다. 이 단어는 '완전히(con) 알고(sci) 있는(ent) 것으로 가득한([i]ous)'으로 분석된다. 이 단어의 명사 형태인 conscience(양심)는 '완전히 (con) 알고(sci) 있는 것(ence)'로 분석된다. 이 단어들에서 앞은 도덕에 관한 것으로 생각된다.

어구 steal 훔치다   consequent 결과적인
economical 허비하지 않는

정답 (c)

7

해석 그것은 정말 좋은 책이다. 아주 훌륭하다.

해설 '칭찬하다'라는 뜻의 commend를 묻는 문제다. 주어진 문장에서 have a lot to commend it은 '칭찬할 만한 요소가 많다'라는 뜻으로, 곧 '아주 훌륭하다'는 뜻을 나타낸다. commend를 command와 혼동하지 않도록 다시 한 번 주의하자.

어구 commit (범죄 등을) 저지르다   comment 논평하다

정답 (c)

8

해석 그 회사는 양질의 제품으로 유명하다.

해설 '제품'을 뜻하는 product를 묻는 문제다. '농산물'을 뜻하는 produce, 그리고 명사로서의 conduct와 refuse는 모두 셀 수 없는 명사이기 때문에, 선택지에서와 같이 복수형으로 쓸 수 없음에 유의해야 한다. 명사가 셀 수 있는가 그렇지 않은가는 Longman Dictionary of Contemporary English처럼 신뢰할 수 있는 영영사전을 기준으로 해야 함을 명심하자.

어구 quality 양질의   conduct 행실
refuse 쓰레기

정답 (a)

Chapter 3

UNIT 1 동사와 particle의 결합(구동사) Ⅰ

EXERCISE

A

| 1 (d) | 2 (e) | 3 (a) | 4 (c) | 5 (b) |

B

1 on   2 out
3 up   4 down
5 without

PRACTICE

| 1 (c) | 2 (a) | 3 (c) | 4 (d) | 5 (b) |
| 6 (d) | 7 (c) | 8 (c) | | |

중요 Collocation 정리

1 그의 정신 나간 행동은 어떠한 것으로도 설명이 되지 않는다.

2 PSP가 고장 나서 영화를 전혀 볼 수 없었다.

3 7년 동안이나 다투고 나서, 부부는 결국 헤어졌다.

4 사실 브리트니 스피어스는 전통적인 방식으로 양육되었다.

5 이코노미스트지(誌)에서 한국에 관한 불쾌한 기사를 접했다.

6 우리는 십대의 흡연 문제를 다루어야 한다.

7 사실, 성공은 창의력에 의존한다.

8 공기 없이 4분 이상 생존할 수 없다.

9 올해는 크리스마스가 화요일이다.

10 따분한 그 교사가 내게 한 말이 아직도 이해가 되지 않는다.

11 아니 이런! 이 바보 같은 알람시계가 여섯 시에 울렸어야 되는데.

12 과제를 제때 제출하지 않으면 그 교수가 엄청 화를 낼 거야.

13 버피는 작별 인사도 없이 무례하게 전화를 끊었다.

14 귀하를 직접 뵙게 되기를 고대합니다.

15 공기는 몇 가지 기체로 구성되어 있다.

EXERCISE A

1 (d)
어떤 것이 어떤 이의 행동을 설명한다면 그것은 그 사람이 일정하게 행동하는 이유다.

2 (e)
어떤 사람과 갈라서면 그 사람과의 관계가 끝난 것이다.

3 (a)
어떤 이와 우연히 마주치는 것은 우연으로 그 사람을 만나는 것이다.

4 (c)

성공이 어떤 것에 달려 있다면 그것 없이는 성공할 수 없다.

5 (b)

어떤 이를 만날 것을 고대한다면 그 사람과의 만남 때문에 흥분한 것이다.

EXERCISE B

1

해석 올해는 그녀의 생일이 일요일이다.

해설 '(날짜 등이) ~에 해당하다'라는 뜻은 '접촉'을 나타내는 전치사 on을 써서 표현한다.

정답 on

2

해석 훌륭한 교사는 학생들의 행동을 이해하려고 노력한다.

해설 '밖으로 드러내어'를 뜻하는 out을 써야 함에 주의하자.

정답 out

3

해석 물질은 원자로 구성되어 있다.

해설 '완전히'를 뜻하는 up을 써야 함에 유의하자.

정답 up

4

해석 유감스럽게도, 그녀의 차는 도로 한가운데서 고장 났다.

해설 '부정적인 상태로'라는 뜻을 나타내는 down을 써야 함에 주의하자.

정답 down

5

해석 물 없이 며칠은 살 수 있다.

해설 문맥상 '~없이'를 나타내는 without을 써야 자연스럽다.

정답 without

PRACTICE

1

해석 A: 앨리스가 아주 슬퍼 보이던데.
B: 아, 남자친구랑 갈라선 거 몰랐어?

해설 맥락으로 보아 '~와 갈라서다'라는 뜻의 break up with가 필요함을 알 수 있다. up은 본래 '위로'라는 뜻인데, '위'에 해당하는 하늘이 '완전함'을 상징하기 때문에 '완전히'라는 뜻을 나타내게 되었음을 알아두자.

어구 make up (with~) ~와 화해하다
grow up (어른으로) 성장하다   call up 전화를 걸다

정답 (c)

2

해석 A: 이런 어리석은 실수를 어떻게 실명할 거니?
B: 어, 나도 사람이잖아.

해설 맥락으로 보아 '설명하다'라는 뜻이 account for가 필요하다. 이때 for는 '이유를 밝혀'라는 뜻을 나타낸다.

어구 allow for (어려움 등을) 감안하다

fall for (계략에) 속아 넘어가다
make for ~를 향해 가다

정답 (a)

3

해석 A: 다음 주에 토고를 방문할 것을 고대하고 있어.
B: 음, 그 나라가 방문하기에 좋은 곳은 아닌 것 같은데.

해설 '고대하다'라는 뜻의 look forward to를 써야하므로 정답은 (c)다. 이때 forward는 '시간적으로 앞서서'라는 뜻을 나타낸다.

어구 backward 뒤쪽으로   downward 아래쪽으로
toward 향해서

정답 (c)

4

해석 A: 제시카랑 언제 화해할 작정이니?
B: 그 이야긴 그만 해. 그 얘긴 더이상 하고 싶지 않아.

해설 '화해하다'라는 뜻의 make up with를 묻는 문제다.

어구 drop (논의 등을) 중지하다   bring up (이야기 등을) 꺼내다
hang up 전화를 끊다
come up with (해결책 등을) 생각해내다

정답 (d)

5

해석 그는 100달러짜리 지폐를 우연히 발견하고는 경찰서로 갔다.

해설 '마주치다'라는 뜻의 come across를 묻는 문제다.

어구 get across (생각 등을 제대로) 전달하다
put across (생각 등을) 이해시키다

정답 (b)

6

해석 우리나라의 미래는 아이들에게 달려 있다.

해설 '~에 의존하다' 또는 '~에 달려 있다'는 뜻의 depend on을 묻는 문제다.

어구 feed on (동물이) ~를 주로 먹고 살다
go on 계속하다; 일어나다   carry on 계속하다

정답 (d)

7

해석 우리는 즉시 그 문제를 다루어야 합니다.

해설 '다루다'라는 뜻의 deal with를 묻는 문제다.

어구 live with 동거하다; 인내하다   go with ~와 어울리다

정답 (c)

8

해석 유감스럽게도, 많은 성인들이 형편없는 방식으로 양육되었다.

해설 '양육하다'는 뜻의 bring up을 묻는 문제다.

어구 add up (말이) 되다   show up 나타나다; 창피를 주다
dig up (정보 등을) 파헤치다

성답 (c)

UNIT 2 동사와 particle의 결합(구동사) Ⅱ

EXERCISE

A

1 (c)　　2 (a)　　3 (e)　　4 (b)　　5 (d)

B

1 mess　　　　2 running
3 saw　　　　4 show
5 turn

PRACTICE

1 (b)　2 (a)　3 (c)　4 (d)　5 (d)
6 (b)　7 (a)　8 (c)

중요 Collocation 정리

1 가격은 (이미) 여러 번 할인된 거예요!
2 과음을 함으로써 인생을 망칠 수도 있다.
3 아버지가 사망했을 때, 에릭은 슬픔으로 제정신이 아니었다.
4 그 요리법은 여러 세대에 걸쳐 전수되었다.
5 노력이 결실을 맺어 그녀는 많은 돈을 벌었다.
6 영어의 리듬을 익히기 위해 노력하라.
7 산드라가 갑자기 차를 세웠을 때 아주 놀랐다.
8 많은 아시아인들은 위안을 얻기 위해 명상에 의지한다.
9 유감스럽게도, 신디는 힘이 소진되어 갔다.
10 에이미는 남자친구를 배웅하러 기차역에 갔다.
11 내 꿈은 가난한 이들을 돕는 단체를 설립하는 것이다.
12 너무도 많은 배우들이 값비싼 옷을 자랑해댄다.
13 다양한 출처로부터 지식을 흡수하기 위해 노력하라.
14 드류는 어젯밤 밤새도록 토했다.
15 그것은 거절하기에는 너무 좋은 제의였다.

EXERCISE A

1 (c)
어떤 것의 가격이 할인되면, 값이 더 저렴해진 것이다.

2 (a)
친구 가운데 한 명이 사망한다면, 슬퍼하게 될 것이다.

3 (e)
열심히 일한 것이 득이 된다면, 성공하게 될 것이다.

4 (b)
차를 도로변에 세우면, 차를 멈추는 것이다.

5 (d)
누군가에게 의지한다면, 그 사람을 신뢰하는 것이다.

EXERCISE B

1
해석 나쁜 사람들과 사귐으로써 인생을 망칠 수도 있다.
해설 '망치다'라는 뜻의 mess up을 묻는 문제다. show up은 '나타나다'라는 뜻을 나타내는데, 두 구동사에서 up은 모두 '완전히(completely)'라는 뜻을 나타냄을 기억하자.
정답 mess

2
해석 실은 그들의 인내심도 소진되어 갔다.
해설 '~이 다 떨어지다'라는 뜻의 run out of를 묻는 문제다. grow out of는 '옷이 맞지 않을 정도로 커지다'라는 뜻을 나타내는데, 이때 out of는 '벗어나서'라는 뜻으로 쓰였다.
정답 running

3
해석 우리는 손님들을 공항에서 배웅했다.
해설 '배웅하다'라는 뜻의 see off를 묻는 문제다. call off는 '취소하다'라는 뜻을 나타낸다. 이때 off는 '중지하여'라는 뜻으로 쓰였다.
정답 saw

4
해석 능력을 과시하지 않도록 노력하라.
해설 '과시하다'라는 뜻의 show off를 묻는 문제다. turn off는 '전기 기구 등을 끄다'라는 뜻을 나타낸다. 이때 off는 '중지하여'라는 뜻으로 쓰였다.
정답 show

5
해석 그 제의를 거절한 것은 어리석었다.
해설 '거절하다'라는 뜻의 turn down을 묻는 문제다. settle down은 '정착하다'라는 뜻을 나타낸다. 이때 down은 '완전히'라는 뜻으로 쓰였다.
정답 turn

PRACTICE

1
해석 A: 제시카가 오늘 왜 결근했는지 아니?
B: 할아버지가 어젯밤에 돌아가셨거든.
해설 '사망하다'라는 뜻의 pass away를 묻는 문제다. explain away와 throw away에서 away는 '없애서'라는 뜻을 나타낸다. 반면, give away에서 away는 '다른 곳으로 옮겨서'라는 뜻을 나타낸다. 이 뜻은 '없애서' 또는 '사라져서'라는 뜻에서 확장된 것임을 기억하자.
어구 absent 결근한　　　explain away 해명하다
give away (공짜로) 주다
throw away (불필요한 것을) 버리다
정답 (b)

2
해석 A: 서둘러! 시간이 없단 말이야.
B: 너무 재촉하지 마. 시간이 있긴 있잖아.
해설 '~이 다 떨어지다'라는 뜻의 run out of를 묻는 문제다. 선택지

가운데 figure는 out과 어울려 '알아내다; 이해하다'라는 뜻으로 쓰인다. 그리고 break은 out of와 어울려 '(구태 등으로부터) 벗어나다'라는 뜻을 나타낸다. 반면 work은 out과 어울려 '해결책을 알아내다; 운동하다'라는 뜻으로 쓰인다. 이처럼 구동사로서 figure와 work은 out of와 어울리지 않에 주의하자.

어구 hurry up 서두르다 pushy 강압적인

정답 (a)

3

해석 A: 그 조리법 어디에서 배웠어요?
　　　B: 아, 할머니로부터 전수된 거예요.

해설 '물려주다'라는 뜻의 pass down을 묻는 문제다. break은 down과 어울리면 '고장 나다'라는 뜻을 나타낸다. cut은 down과 어울려 '감소시키다'라는 뜻으로 쓰인다. fall은 down과 어울리면 '(건물 등이) 붕괴되다'라는 뜻을 나타낸다. 이 가운데 break down과 fall down에서 down은 '파괴되어'라는 뜻을, cut down에서 down은 '아래로'라는 뜻을 각각 나타낸다.

어구 recipe 요리법

정답 (c)

4

해석 A: 몬트리올 여행은 어땠어요?
　　　B: 환상적이었죠. 프랑스어도 좀 익혔고요.

해설 '익히다'라는 뜻의 pick up을 묻는 문제다. break up은 '(이성과) 갈라서다'라는 뜻을, make up은 '구성하다; 화해하다'라는 뜻을, let up은 '(날씨 등이) 누그러지다'라는 뜻을 나타낸다. break up과 make up에서 up은 '완전히'라는 뜻으로, let up에서 up은 '제한되어'라는 뜻으로 쓰였다.

어구 fantastic 환상적인

정답 (d)

5

해석 너무도 많은 사람들이 돈을 추구하다가 인생을 망친다.

해설 '망치다'라는 뜻의 mess up을 묻는 문제다. show up은 '나타나다'라는 뜻을, look up은 '(정보 등을) 찾아보다'라는 뜻을, bring up은 '양육하다; (문제 등을) 꺼내다'라는 뜻을 나타낸다. show up과 look up에서 up은 '완전히'라는 뜻으로, bring up에서 up은 '향상시켜'라는 뜻으로 쓰였다.

어구 pursue 추구하다

정답 (d)

6

해석 브라이언의 노고가 결실을 맺어 부사장으로 승진되었다.

해설 '(결국엔) 득이 되다'라는 뜻의 pay off를 묻는 문제다. go off는 '폭발하다'라는 뜻을, let off는 '(책임을 묻지 않고) 봐주다'라는 뜻을, lay off는 '해고하다'라는 뜻을 나타낸다. 이러한 뜻은 모두 off의 기본적인 의미인 '떼어내어'라는 뜻에서 발전했는데, 이 가운데 let off에서 off는 '줄여주어서'라는 뜻으로 쓰였다.

어구 promote 승진시키다 vice president 부회장, 부사장

정답 (b)

7

해석 많은 언어 전문가들은 참조를 위해 옥스퍼드 영어사전에 의지하다

해설 '의지하다'라는 뜻의 rely on을 묻는 문제다. put on은 '(옷 등을) 착용하다'라는 뜻을, go on은 '지속되다'라는 뜻을, live on은 '~를 주식으로 하다'라는 뜻을 나타낸다. put on에서 on은 '접촉

하여'라는 뜻으로, go on에서 on은 '지속하여'라는 뜻으로, live on에서 on은 '소비하여'라는 뜻으로 쓰였다.

어구 expert 전문가 reference 참조

정답 (a)

8

해석 레베카는 그 클럽에 가입하고 싶은 유혹을 거부했다.

해설 '거절하다, 거부하다'라는 뜻의 turn down을 묻는 문제다. let down은 '실망시키다'라는 뜻을, mark down은 '할인하다'라는 뜻을, write down은 '써 두다'라는 뜻을 나타낸다. let down에서 down은 '좋지 않은 상태로'라는 뜻으로, mark down에서 down은 '아래로'라는 뜻으로, write down에서 down은 '기록하여'라는 뜻으로 쓰였다.

어구 temptation 유혹 join 가입하다

정답 (c)

UNIT 3 숙어 I

EXERCISE

A

| 1 (b) | 2 (e) | 3 (a) | 4 (c) | 5 (d) |

B

1	Greek	2	blue
3	die	4	ear
5	fiddle

PRACTICE

| 1 (a) | 2 (c) | 3 (d) | 4 (b) | 5 (b) |
| 6 (a) | 7 (d) | 8 (d) |

중요 Collocation 정리

1 그냥 즐겁게 이곳에 머무르세요. 숨겨진 의도 같은 것은 없습니다.

2 어떻게 절친한 친구를 저버릴 수가 있었죠?

3 아주 놀랍게도, 노란 버스가 돌연히 나타났다.

4 말을 둘러대지 마! 그냥 진실을 말해줘!

5 사실, 마돈나는 수십 억 달러를 벌어들이는, 수익의 원천이었다.

6 일부 정치인들은 끔찍한 사태에 대해 동정하는 체했다.

7 결정은 이미 내려졌고, 우리는 끝까지 싸울 각오가 되어 있다.

8 인기 말이어서, 대통령은 나라에 대한 영향력이 없었나.

9 아주 총명했기 때문에, 카산드라는 상황에 맞게 행동하는 데 능했다.

10 사실, 그들은 생계를 유지하는 데 어려움을 겪었다.

11 그는 자녀들 앞에서 체면을 잃고 싶지 않았다.

12 많은 이들은 자신들이 아주 건강하다고 잘못 생각한다.

13 로건은 백만장자들을 위해 일하면서 거액을 챙겼다.

14 유감스럽게도, 고위직 진입 장벽이 여전히 미국에 존재한다.

15 분자생물학이라고? 전혀 이해가 안 되는걸.

EXERCISE A

1 (b)
숨은 의도가 있다면, 어떤 일을 하는 데 대해 비밀스런 목적을 가지는 것이다.

2 (e)
누군가를 저버린다면, 더 이상 그 사람을 돕지 않는 것이다.

3 (a)
말을 둘러댄다면, 진실을 말하는 것이 아니다.

4 (c)
동정하는 체한다면, 진심이 아닌 것이다.

5 (d)
체면을 잃는다면, 사람들이 존중하지 않을 것이다.

EXERCISE B

1

해석 인지 언어학이라고? 전혀 이해가 안 되는걸.

해설 '전혀 알아듣지 못하다'라는 뜻의 'be Greek'을 묻는 문제다. 이때 Greek을 Latin과 같은 말로 대체할 수 없다. 그리스어가 특히 영어와 전혀 다른 철자를 쓰기 때문에 배우기에 어려운 언어로 생각되기 때문이다.

정답 Greek

2

해석 큰 곰이 돌연히 나타났다.

해설 '돌연히'라는 뜻의 out of the blue를 묻는 문제다. 이때 blue를 red와 같은 다른 색깔로 대신할 수 없음에 유의해야 한다. 본래 '푸른 하늘에서'라는 발상에서 비롯된 숙어이기 때문이다.

정답 blue

3

해석 결정이 이미 내려져서 되돌릴 수 없다.

해설 '결정이 이미 내려지다'라는 뜻의 The die is cast를 묻는 문제다. 오답으로 제시된 dye는 '염색약'이란 뜻으로 die와 발음이 같지만 관련성이 없음에 유의해야 한다.

정답 die

4

해석 상황에 따라 처리하는 수밖에 없다.

해설 '상황에 따라 처리하다'는 뜻의 play it by ear를 묻는 문제다. 본래 이 표현에는 악보 없이 연주한다는 발상이 들어 있기 때문에 ear를 eye로 대체할 수 없다. 이처럼 숙어가 고정된 표현이라는 점을 기억해 두어야 한다.

정답 ear

5

해석 비록 여든 살이지만, 그녀는 매우 건강하다.

해설 '매우 건강한'이란 뜻의 as fit as a fiddle을 묻는 문제다. 역시 숙어로서 고정된 표현이기 때문에 fiddle을 violin으로 대신할 수 없다.

정답 fiddle

PRACTICE

1

해석 A: 숨은 의도가 있는 것 같은데요.
B: 무슨 말씀이세요? 저는 그냥 도와드리려고 하는 거예요.

해설 '숨은 의도'를 뜻하는 a hidden agenda를 묻는 문제다. 선택지의 다른 숙어들도 그 뜻을 정확히 익혀두어야 한다. 대화로부터 알 수 있듯이, 다른 선택지들은 주어진 맥락에 어울리지 않는다.

어구 a bad/rotten apple 악영향을 미치는 사람
the last straw 인내의 한도를 넘게 만드는 일
a stitch in time 제때의 적절한 조치

정답 (a)

2

해석 A: 네가 말을 둘러대는 데 질렸어.
B: 음, 적어도, 네 감정을 해치진 않았어.

해설 '말을 둘러대다'는 뜻의 beat around the bush를 묻는 문제다. 그리고 선택지 가운데 숙어 tighten your belt의 의미를 풀어 설명하면, '예전보다 덜 소비하려고 애쓰다'이다.

어구 sick and tired of ~에 질린
pack your bags 살던 곳을 떠나다
tighten your belt 허리띠를 졸라매다
fit/fill the bill (필요에) 딱 맞다

정답 (c)

3

해석 A: 저 어리석은 정치인이 또 다시 동정하는 체했어.
B: 어쩌면 진심을 표현했을 수도 있지.

해설 '동정하는 체하다'는 뜻의 shed crocodile tears를 묻는 문제다. 선택지의 숙어 가운데 kick the bucket은 다소 고풍스러운 표현인데, 유머로 하는 말에서 '죽다'라는 뜻을 나타낸다.

어구 politician 정치인   kick the bucket (유머조로) 죽다
get even with ~에게 복수하다
get the picture (상황을) 헤아리다

정답 (d)

4

해석 A: 새 프로그램 사용할 줄 아니?
B: 설명서를 읽어보았는데, 전혀 이해가 안 되는데.

해설 '전혀 이해가 되지 않는다'라는 뜻의 'be all Greek'을 묻는 문제다. 앞에서 살펴보았듯이, 숙어가 고정된 표현이기 때문에 이 표현의 Greek을 다른 외국어를 나타내는 말로 대신할 수 없다.

어구 software 소프트웨어   manual 사용 설명서

정답 (b)

5

해석 그 사고는 돌연히 일어났다.

해설 '돌연히'라는 뜻의 out of the blue를 묻는 문제다. 선택지의 숙어 가운데 in the red는 장부의 차변(借邊)을 빨간 색으로 작성하던 관행에서 비롯된 표현이다.

어구 on the tip of one's tongue (이름 등이) 막 떠오르는
off the record 비공개를 전제로
in the red 적자 상태인

정답 (b)

6

해석 그러니까, 따라야 할 대본이 없다고요? 좋아요, 즉흥적으로 연기할게요.

해설 '상황에 따라 처리하다'라는 뜻의 play it by ear를 묻는 문제다. 선택지의 숙어 가운데 make the grade에서, grade는 '등급'을 뜻한다고 보는 것이 일반적이다.

어구 script 대본   bear fruit 결실을 맺다
go Dutch 각자 부담하다   make the grade
(요구되는) 수준을 충족시키다

정답 (a)

7

해석 스캔들이 터졌을 때, 노이는 체면을 잃었다.

해설 '체면을 잃다'라는 뜻의 lose face를 묻는 문제다. 선택지의 숙어 가운데 burn the midnight oil과 같은 뜻의 표현으로 burn the candle at both ends를 들 수 있다. 함께 익혀 두어야 한다.

어구 burn the midnight oil 밤늦게까지 일하다
hit the nail on the head 정곡을 찌르다
sell like hot cakes 날개 돋친 듯 팔리다

정답 (d)

8

해석 저 고급 자동차를 사려면 거액이 들 것이다.

해설 '거액'을 뜻하는 a small fortune을 묻는 문제다. 선택지의 숙어 가운데, a gray area는 '회색 지대'라고 옮길 수도 있는데, 그 뜻을 풀어 설명한 것이 어구의 해설이다. 모두 익혀 두자.

어구 fancy 고급의
a gray area 어느 쪽인지 분명하지 않은 대상
a close call 가까스로 사고나 재난을 피함
a white lie 선의의 거짓말

정답 (d)

UNIT 4   숙어 Ⅱ

EXERCISE

A
1 (b)   2 (d)   3 (a)   4 (e)   5 (c)

B
1   seventh   2   letter
3   red   4   long
5   tab

PRACTICE

1 (c)   2 (d)   3 (a)   4 (a)   5 (d)
6 (c)   7 (b)   8 (a)

중요 Collocation 정리

1 우승했을 때, 에이미는 더할 나위 없이 행복했다.
2 그렉은 우스운 농담으로 어색한 분위기를 깨뜨리려고 했다.
3 줄리엣은 로미오와 작년에 결혼했다.
4 그녀의 충고를 엄밀히 따르는 것이 더 나을 텐데.
5 그들은 새로운 다리를 지어도 좋다는 허가를 받았다.
6 수잔 스미스는 그냥 평범한 인물이다.
7 놀랍게도, 두 후보자는 막상막하였다.
8 나쁜 사람들이 취한 화해 제스처를 받아들여서는 안 된다.
9 명확성은 좋은 글의 핵심적인 요소다.
10 슈퍼모델이었지만, 크리스티는 대중의 시선을 끌지 않으려고 애썼다.
11 그의 무례한 말은 많은 이들을 격분하게 만들었다.
12 경험칙으로 볼 때, 10살 난 아이가 설명을 이해할 것인지를 자문해 보라.
13 사람들을 화성에 보낸다고? 너무 가능성이 희박한 일이야.
14 그가 점심값을 치러야 할 차례였다.
15 그 일은 직원들에게 주의를 촉발한 일이었다.

EXERCISE A

1   (b)
어색한 분위기를 깨뜨린다면, 사람들이 보다 편안하게 느낄 것이다.

2   (d)
어떤 사람과 '매듭을 짓는다'면, 그 사람과 결혼하는 것이다.

3   (a)
여러분이 평범한 근로자라면, 뛰어나게 일을 해내는 것은 아니다.

4 (e)

대중의 시선을 끌지 않는다면, 사람들이 알아차리지 못할 것이다.

5 (c)

어떤 것이 성공의 핵심적인 요소라면, 그것은 성공하는 데 꼭 필요하다.

EXERCISE B

1

해석 그 소식을 들었을 때, 더할 나위 없이 행복했다.

해설 '더할 나위 없이 행복한'이란 뜻의 in seventh heaven을 묻는 문제다. 이 표현은 숙어로 고정된 표현이기 때문에, seventh를 다른 숫자로 대신할 수 없음에 유의해야 한다.

정답 seventh

2

해석 명령을 엄밀히 따르는 편이 현명할 것이다.

해설 '지극히 정확하게'라는 뜻의 to the letter를 묻는 문제다. 이때 letter는 '글자'라는 뜻을 나타내기 때문에 관련이 있다고 해서 sound(소리)라는 단어로 대신할 수 없음에 유의해야 한다.

정답 letter

3

해석 그녀의 무례한 행동에 그는 격분했다.

해설 '격분하다'라는 뜻의 see red를 묻는 문제다. 이때 red는 분노를 상징하는 단어이기 때문에, 색깔을 나타내는 다른 단어로 아무렇게나 대체할 수 없음에 유의해야 한다.

정답 red

4

해석 그 질병을 치유하는 일은 가능성이 희박하다. 거의 불가능하다.

해설 '가능성이 희박한 일'을 뜻하는 a long shot을 묻는 문제다. 먼 거리를 사격한다는 발상이 들어 있기 때문에, long을 short을 대신할 수 없음에 유의해야 한다. 이처럼 숙어는 대개 고정된 표현이다.

정답 long

5

해석 제가 한 턱 낼게요. 제가 비용을 치르겠습니다.

해설 '비용을 치르다'라는 뜻의 pick up the tab을 묻는 문제다. 발음이 다소 비슷하지만 cab은 '택시'라는 뜻으로 tab을 대신할 수 없다.

정답 tab

PRACTICE

1

해석 A: 어떻게 어색한 분위기를 깼니?
B: 아, 그냥 우스운 농담을 해서 마음껏 웃었어.

해설 '어색한 분위기를 깨뜨리다'라는 뜻의 break the ice를 묻는 문제다. 나머지 선택지들은 모두 주어진 맥락에 맞지 않는데, (d)의 경우에도 A가 B의 일에 대해 모르는 상태에서 질문하는 것이기 때문에 어울리지 않는다.

어구 crack a joke 농담하다　　lose heart 낙심하다
live from hand to mouth 겨우겨우 연명하다
stick to your guns (자신이 정한) 입장을 고수하다

정답 (c)

2

해석 A: 올해에 백만 달러를 벌 계획이야.
B: 가능성이 희박한 일이겠다.

해설 '가능성이 희박한 일'을 뜻하는 a long shot을 묻는 문제다. 선택지의 숙어 가운데 red tape은 셀 수 없는 명사로 쓰이기 때문에 빈 칸에 적합하지 않다. 참고로 이 숙어는 공문서를 빨간색 끈으로 묶는 관습에서 유래했다.

어구 a big fish 유력 인사
have a green thumb 원예에 소질이 있다
red tape (성가신) 형식적 절차

정답 (d)

3

해석 A: 축하해! 결혼한다면서.
B: 고마워. 더할 나위 없이 행복해.

해설 '더할 나위 없이 행복한'이란 뜻의 in seventh heaven을 묻는 문제다. 선택지의 숙어 가운데 a full-time job은 본래 '정식 직원으로서의 일'을 뜻하는데, 이 의미와 함께 어구에서 설명한 뜻을 가짐을 익혀 두자.

어구 just around the corner 임박한
be all ears 귀를 바짝 기울이다
a full-time job 고된 노력과 많은 시간이 소요되는 일

정답 (a)

4

해석 A: 오늘 저녁 식사는 내가 계산할게.
B: 웬일이니?

해설 '비용을 치르다'라는 뜻의 pick up the tab을 묻는 문제다. 선택지의 숙어 가운데 blow the lid off에서 blow는 take이나 life로 대신할 수 있다. keep up with the Joneses에서 Joneses에 대해서는 Arthur Momand의 만화 제목에서 유래했다는 입장과 '옆집 이웃'을 뜻한다는 입장으로 나뉜다.

어구 keep up with the Joneses (남들과 같아 보이려고) 허세를 부리다　　blow the lid off ～의 진상을 알리다
call someone names ～를 욕하다

정답 (a)

5

해석 어려움은 삶의 핵심적인 요소이다.

해설 '핵심적인 요소'라는 뜻의 part and parcel을 묻는 문제다. 선택지의 숙어 가운데 the real McCoy의 유래에 대해서는 여러 입장이 있는데, 누가 McCoy였는지에 대해 위스키 제조업자라는 설과 밀수꾼이라는 설 등이 다양하게 제시되었다.

어구 the dos and don'ts (특정한 상황에서) 지켜야 할 사항들
melting pot 다양한 집단들이 융화되는 곳
the real McCoy (값진) 진품

정답 (d)

6

해석 그를 깊이 존경했기 때문에, 그의 명령을 엄밀하게 따랐다.

해설 '지극히 정확하게'라는 뜻의 to the letter를 묻는 문제다. 선택

지의 숙어 가운데 on cloud nine의 유래에 대해서는 '가장 높은 구름이 있는 곳에서'라는 데서 유래했다고 보는 견해가 유력하다.

어구 on cloud nine 매우 흡족한
under the weather 몸이 (약간) 아픈
at a snail's pace 너무 느리게

정답 (c)

7

해석 그의 버릇없는 행동에 우리는 격분했다.

해설 '격분하다'라는 뜻의 see red를 묻는 문제다. 선택지의 숙어 가운데 bury the hatchet은 평화 협정을 맺을 때 족장들의 도끼를 묻는, 미국 인디언들의 전통에서 비롯되었다고 보는 것이 일반적이다.

어구 follow suit (다른 사람을) 따라하다
lend someone a hand 도와주다
bury the hatchet 화해하다

정답 (b)

8

해석 한 달 동안 데이트를 하고 나서, 그들은 결혼하기로 결정했다.

해설 '결혼하다'라는 뜻의 tie the knot을 묻는 문제다. 나머지 표현들도 뜻을 정확히 익혀 두자.

어구 get the hang of ~를 다루는 요령을 터득하다
let off steam (활동을 통해) 분노나 흥분을 해소하다
add insult to injury (이미 나쁘게 대한 사람을) 더 곤경에 처하게 하다

정답 (a)

▌Chapter 4

UNIT 1 고급 어휘 I

EXERCISE

A
1 (c) 2 (e) 3 (a) 4 (b) 5 (d)

B
1 abuse 2 aspect
3 circumstances 4 commanded
5 decreased

PRACTICE
1 (b) 2 (c) 3 (d) 4 (b) 5 (c)
6 (a) 7 (b) 8 (c)

중요 Collocation 정리

1 매우 놀랍게도, 그들의 자녀들은 약물 남용으로 체포당했다.

2 훌륭한 교사는 학생들에게 정확한 지식을 제공한다.

3 그들은 도시 생활에 적응하는 데 많은 어려움을 겪었다.

4 프레드는 자신의 개구리에 대해 깊은 애정을 갖고 있었다.

5 그 소설은 그녀의 삶의 모든 측면을 탐구한다.

6 그 능숙한 비서는 회사에 커다란 자산이었다.

7 부유한 사람조차도 파산할 수 있다.

8 최대 다수에게 최대 이익을 제공해야 한다.

9 여행은 생각의 지평을 넓혀줄 수 있다.

10 친구를 선택하는 데 특히 주의를 기울여라.

11 그 상황에서는 그것이 최선의 방법이었다.

12 신부(神父)는 악령에게 희생자의 몸에서 나오라고 명령했다.

13 MP3 플레이어의 인기는 감소했다.

14 다이아몬드가 아주 견고하다는 것은 잘 알려진 사실이다.

15 자신의 나라에 대한 감정을 묘사하라.

EXERCISE A

1 (c)
어떤 것이 정확하다면 올바른 것이다.

2 (e)
새로운 환경에 적응한다면 그 환경에서 행복하게 살 수 있다.

3 (a)
파산한다면 돈이 한 푼도 없는 것이다.

4 (b)
조심하는 것은 위험을 피하려고 애쓰는 것이다.

5 (d)
어떤 것이 견고하다면 오래 지속될 수 있는 것이다.

EXERCISE B

1
해석 사실 약물 남용은 심각한 범죄다.
해설 abuse는 '남용'을, reuse는 '재사용'을 뜻한다.
정답 abuse

2
해석 그녀의 어떤 면이 가장 마음에 들어요?
해설 aspect는 '측면'을, respect는 '존중'을 뜻한다.
정답 aspect

3
해석 그런 상황이라면 어떻게 하시겠어요?
해설 circumstances는 '상황'을, instance는 '경우'를 뜻한다.
정답 circumstances

4
해석 부모는 자녀들에게 조용히 하라고 명했다.
해설 command는 '명령하다'를, commend는 '칭찬하다'를 뜻한다.
정답 commanded

5

해석 유가가 작년에 7.7% 하락했다.

해설 decrease는 '감소하다'를, include는 '포함하다'를 뜻한다.

정답 decreased

PRACTICE

1

해석 A: 제나는 어째서 자기 딸에게 그렇게 못되게 굴어요?
　　 B: 딸에게 애정이 전혀 없거든요.

해설 맥락으로 보아 '애정'이라는 뜻의 affection이 필요하다. 참고로 attention은 '향해서(at) 뻗는(tent) 것(ion)'으로, distrust는 '믿지(trust) 않음(dis)'으로 분석되어 각각의 뜻을 나타낸다.

어구 attention 주의, 관심　hatred 증오　distrust 불신

정답 (b)

2

해석 A: 대니얼이 왜 체포되었나요?
　　 B: 아동 학대 혐의를 받고 있었어요.

해설 '학대'를 뜻하는 abuse를 묻는 문제다. 참고로 suspect는 '부정적으로(sus) 바라보다(spect)'로 분석되어 '혐의를 두다'라는 뜻을 나타낸다.

어구 arrest 체포하다　　　suspect 혐의를 두다
　　 clause (법률의) 조항　cause 원인; (대의)명분
　　 louse (곤충) 이

정답 (c)

3

해석 A: 내일 있을 야영 때문에 몹시 흥분이 돼요.
　　 B: 극히 조심하세요! 날씨가 위험하게 변할 수도 있어요.

해설 '조심하는'이란 뜻의 cautious를 묻는 문제다.

어구 extremely 지극히　　 turn 바뀌다
　　 delicious 맛있는　　　ambitious 야망이 있는

정답 (d)

4

해석 A: 돈 좀 빌려 줄래?
　　 B: 아, 내가 빈털터리라고 말 안 했었나?

해설 '파산한' 또는 '빈털터리의'라는 뜻의 bankrupt를 묻는 문제다. 참고로 corrupt는 '완전히(cor) 부서진, 찢긴(rupt)'이라는 뜻에서 '타락한'이란 뜻으로 발전했다.

어구 corrupt 타락한　healthy 건강한, 건강에 좋은
　　 exhausted 기진맥진한

정답 (b)

5

해석 일을 아주 잘하기 때문에 마리아는 우리 회사의 큰 자산이다.

해설 '자산'을 뜻하는 asset을 묻는 문제다. 참고로 repression은 '완전히(re) 누르는(press) 것(ion)'으로, aggression은 '향해서(ag) 가는(gress) 것(ion)'으로, regression은 '뒤로(re) 가는(gress) 것(ion)'으로 분석된다.

어구 efficient 일을 잘하는, 효율적인　　 repression 억압
　　 aggression 공격　　　　　　　　 regression 퇴화

정답 (c)

6

해석 튼튼한 집을 짓기 위해서는 견고한 재료가 필요하다.

해설 '견고한'이란 뜻의 durable을 묻는 문제다.

어구 independent 독립적인　faulty 결함이 있는

정답 (a)

7

해석 정보화 시대에 살아남기 위해서는 정확한 정보가 필요하다.

해설 '정확한'이란 뜻의 accurate를 묻는 문제다.

어구 survive 살아남다　　　　　impolite 무례한
　　 diligent 부지런한　　　　　 tough 질긴

정답 (b)

8

해석 많은 남성들은 자신들의 감정을 설명하는 데 어려움을 겪는다.

해설 '기술(記述)하다'라는 뜻의 describe를 묻는 문제다. 참고로 subscribe는 '아래에(sub) 쓰다(scribe)'로, prescribe는 '미리(pre) 쓰다(scribe)'로, transcribe는 '건너서(trans) 쓰다(scribe)'로 분석된다.

어구 subscribe 구독하다　prescribe 처방하다
　　 transcribe 전사(轉寫)하다

정답 (c)

UNIT 2　고급 어휘 Ⅱ

EXERCISE

A

| 1 (c) | 2 (e) | 3 (a) | 4 (b) | 5 (d) |

B

1	facilitate	2	frequented
3	generous	4	habitat
5	hostile		

PRACTICE

| 1 (b) | 2 (d) | 3 (c) | 4 (c) | 5 (a) |
| 6 (a) | 7 (d) | 8 (b) | | |

중요 Collocation 정리

1 메리는 가난한 아이들을 교육하는 데 헌신했다.

2 아이러니하게도, 정교한 계획은 종종 단순한 이유로 실패한다.

3 소년들은 너무도 배가 고파서 엄청나게 큰 피자를 먹었다.

4 고아원은 1777년에 설립되었다.

5 간호사의 역할은 치유를 촉진하는 것이다.

6 신앙요법이란 주제에 익숙한 사람들은 그리 많지 않다.

7 해리 포터는 가공의 인물이다.

8 짐은 이혼 절차를 마무리하고 다른 여자와 결혼했다.

9 그 묘지에는 흡혈귀들이 자주 들렀다.

10 수지는 어려움에 처한 이들은 누구든 도우려고 하는, 잘 베푸는 여성이다.

11 외국어를 배우는 과정은 점진적인 과정이다.

12 이 책은 TEPS 시험에서 보다 높은 점수를 보증할 수 있다.

13 연못이 그것의 자연적인 서식지이다.

14 이처럼 적대적인 세상에서 어떻게 살아남을 수 있을까?

15 한국 교사들은 학생들을 보다 자비롭게 대해야 한다.

EXERCISE A

1 (c)
여러분이 어떤 사람을 교육하면, 그 사람은 여러분으로부터 가르침을 받는다.

2 (e)
어떤 것이 막대하면, 그것은 지극히 큰 것이다.

3 (a)
어떤 조직을 설립하면, 그 조직이 형성되는 것이다.

4 (b)
어떤 것에 익숙하면, 그것을 아주 잘 아는 것이다.

5 (d)
어떤 것을 마무리하면, 그것을 완성하는 것이다.

EXERCISE B

1
해석 언어교사는 언어를 학습하는 과정을 촉진해야 한다.
해설 '촉진하다'라는 뜻의 facilitate를 묻는 문제다. 오답으로 제시된 block은 '가로막다'라는 뜻으로 facilitate의 반의어이다. '∼해야 한다'는 당위를 나타내는 should가 쓰였기 때문에 facilitate가 자연스러움에 유의하자.
정답 facilitate

2
해석 그 교회에는 신앙심이 깊은 사람들이 자주 들렀다.
해설 '자주 들르다'라는 뜻의 frequent를 묻는 문제다. 오답으로 제시된 frozen은 '얼리다'는 뜻의 freeze의 과거분사이다. 이 뜻일 때는 대개 액체를 나타내는 말과 어울리므로 정답이 아님을 알 수 있다.
정답 frequented

3
해석 잘 베푸는 교사는 학생들을 기꺼이 도우려고 한다.
해설 '후하게 베푸는'이란 뜻의 generous를 묻는 문제다. 오답을 제시된 genetic은 '유전의'라는 뜻으로 '태생의'라는 뜻의 gene-라는 어근을 generous와 공유하지만 뜻이 다르게 발전한 경우이다.
정답 generous

4
해석 우리는 그것의 서식지를 보호하기 위해서 할 수 있는 모든 일을 하고 있다.
해설 '서식지'라는 뜻의 habitat을 묻는 문제다. 오답으로 제시된 habit은 '습관'이란 뜻으로, '가지다'라는 뜻의 hab-라는 어근을 공유하지만 뜻이 다르게 발전한 경우이다.
정답 habitat

5
해석 미국은 이민자들에 대해 적대적이다.
해설 '적대적인'이란 뜻의 hostile을 묻는 문제다. 오답으로 제시된 horrific은 '끔찍한'이란 뜻으로 '떨리도록(horr) 만드는(ific)'으로 분석된다.
정답 hostile

PRACTICE

1
해석 A: 낯익은 분 같네요.
　　 B: 회의에서 만났던 거 기억 안 나세요?
해설 '익숙한'이란 뜻의 familiar를 묻는 문제다. 선택지 가운데 fancy는 동사로 '상상하다'라는 뜻을, 형용사로 '화려한'이란 뜻을, 명사로 '(변덕스런) 호감'이란 뜻을 나타낸다. 이 단어는 '환상'을 뜻하는 fantasy를 줄인 형태다. 그리고 fanatic은 '신전(fan)에 의해 영향을 받게 된(atic)'으로 분석된다.
어구 conference 회의　　false 틀린; 가짜의
　　 fancy 고급의　　fanatic 극히 열광적인
정답 (b)

2
해석 A: 저 가게에는 부유한 부인들이 자주 출입해.
　　 B: 주인은 손쉽게 떼돈을 벌겠네.
해설 '자주 들르다'는 뜻의 frequent를 묻는 문제다. 이 단어는 '빈번한'이란 뜻의 형용사로도 쓰인다. freshen과 frighten에는 접미사 -en이 들어 있는데, '만들다'라는 기본적인 뜻을 나타냄을 기억하자. 접미사 -en은 순수영어 계열의 어근과 결합하는 것이 원칙이다.
어구 lady 귀부인　　owner 주인
　　 be laughing all the way to the bank 손쉽게 많은 돈을 벌어들이다　　freshen 잔을 다시 채워주다
　　 free 풀어주다　　frighten 겁에 질리게 하다
정답 (d)

3
해석 A: 언제 그 계획을 끝낼 거니?
　　 B: 이번 달 말까지는 마무리할 생각이야.
해설 '마무리하다'라는 뜻의 finalize를 묻는 문제다. commence는 '완전히(com) 시작하다([m]ence)'로 분석된다. 다음으로 cease는 명사로서 without cease(멈추지 않고)라는 표현에 활용된다. 그리고 launch는 '발시하다; 진수시키다'라는 뜻노 나타냄을 기억해야 한다.
어구 complete 끝내다　　commence 개시하다
　　 cease 중지하다　　launch 착수하다
정답 (c)

4

해석 A: 박물관의 역사에 대해 말씀해 주시겠어요?
B: 1789년에 설립되었고 2002년에 개축되었습니다.

해설 '설립하다'라는 뜻의 establish를 묻는 문제다. estimate는 명사로서 '견적'이란 뜻도 나타낸다. escape은 바로 다음에 unharmed와 같은 말이 와서 '다치지 않고 피하다'라는 표현으로 쓰이기도 한다. 그리고 '바래다주다'로 옮길 수 있는 escort가 타동사라는 점도 알아두어야 한다.

어구 renovate (건물을) 개축하다   estimate 추산하다
escape 달아나다   escort 호송하다

정답 (c)

5

해석 남성들에게 여권에 대해 교육해야만 한다.

해설 '교육하다'라는 뜻의 educate을 묻는 문제다. endure는 '지속되게(dur[e]) 만들다(en)'로 분석되는데, 이 단어와 어근 dur를 공유하는 단어로 durable(견고한)을 들 수 있다. enjoy는 '기쁨을(joy) 만들다(en)'로 분석된다.

어구 women's rights 여권   edit 편집하다
endure 견디다   enjoy 즐기다

정답 (a)

6

해석 새로운 단어를 배우는 과정을 촉진하는 방법이 많이 있다.

해설 '촉진하다'라는 뜻의 facilitate을 묻는 문제다. 이 단어의 어근인 facil은 '쉬운'이라는 뜻인데, facile이라는 형태로 '손쉬운'이란 뜻의 단어로 쓰인다는 점도 기억해두자. 이처럼 단어 끝에 오는 -e는 뜻을 나타내지 못한다. faint는 형용사로서 '희미한; 거의 가망이 없는'이란 뜻을 나타내기도 한다.

어구 process 과정   faint 기절하다
fade (빛깔이) 바래다   fake 위조하다

정답 (a)

7

해석 톰이 어려움을 극복하도록 수잔이 도와준 것은 자상한 일이었다.

해설 '후하게 베푸는'이란 뜻의 generous를 묻는 문제다. 선택지 가운데 mean이 어구에서 설명한 것처럼 형용사로도 쓰임을 알아두어야 한다. 참고로 no mean feat(대단한 일)이라는 표현도 함께 기억하자. 그리고 famous는 '명성(fam[e])으로 가득한(ous)'으로 분석된다.

어구 overcome 극복하다   mean 짓궂은
furious 격분한

정답 (d)

8

해석 동물 권리를 주장하는 많은 단체들은 소를 보다 자비롭게 대할 것을 요구하고 있다.

해설 '자비로운'이란 뜻의 humane을 묻는 문제다. hostile은 '적(host)에 어울리는(ile)'으로 분석된다. 그리고 violent는 '다치게(viol) 하고 있는(ent)'으로 분석된다. 접미사 −ile과 −ent는 자주 접하게 되므로 그 뜻을 정확히 알아두자.

어구 treatment 대우   cruel 잔인한
hostile 적대적인   violent 난폭한

정답 (b)

UNIT 3 고급 어휘 Ⅲ

EXERCISE

A

1 (c)	2 (d)	3 (a)	4 (e)	5 (b)

B

1 ignorance   2 laudable
3 isolation   4 legitimate
5 linguistic

PRACTICE

1 (c)	2 (a)	3 (d)	4 (c)	5 (d)

6 (a)   7 (b)   8 (b)

중요 Collocation 정리

1 건강한 정체성을 형성하는 것은 어렵다.

2 나는 그들이 자신들의 전통을 모르는 데 대해 실망했다.

3 돈으로 어떤 것이든 살 수 있다는 것은 환상이다.

4 자신의 일에 완전히 몰입하면 성공할 수 있다.

5 우리나라가 그처럼 모욕을 당해서 우리는 격분했다.

6 어학원은 타갈로그어에 대한 기초 강습을 제공한다.

7 에단은 신뢰할 수 있다. 그는 정직한 인물이니까.

8 천성적으로 수줍음이 많아서, 조셉은 고립되어 살아가는 것을 더 좋아했다.

9 그의 형편없는 결정 때문에 우리의 삶은 위험에 빠졌다.

10 같은 마을에서 자라나서, 니콜은 나오미에 대해 친밀감을 느꼈다.

11 그녀가 어린 여동생들을 돌본 것은 갸륵한 일이었다.

12 결혼한 여성과 관계를 맺는 것은 합법적이지 않다.

13 과학자들은 인간의 언어 능력을 온전히 설명하지 못한다.

14 사실, 명상은 수동적인 과정이 아니다.

15 도덕적 가치에 바탕을 두어 결정을 내려야만 한다.

EXERCISE A

1   (c)
정체성을 형성한다면, 자신이 누구인지 알게 된다.

2   (d)
어떤 것이 환상이라면, 그것은 거짓된 것이다.

3   (a)
인격적 완결성을 갖춘 인물이라면, 정직하다.

4   (e)
어떤 것을 위험에 빠뜨린다면, 그것은 안전하지 않다.

5 (b)

어떤 것이 격분시킨다면, 매우 화가 나게 하는 것이다.

EXERCISE B

1

해석 교사는 과학의 기초에 대한 무지(無知)를 드러냈다.

해설 '무지'를 뜻하는 ignorance를 묻는 문제다. appearance는 '외모; 출현'이라는 뜻으로 주어진 맥락에 어울리지 않는다. 이 단어는 '향해서(ap←ad) 나타나고(pear) 있는 것(ance)'으로 분석된다.

정답 ignorance

2

해석 그녀가 그토록 친절한 말을 한 것은 가륵한 일이었다.

해설 '칭찬할 만한'이란 뜻의 laudable을 묻는 문제다. 오답인 audible은 '들을(aud) 수 있는(ible)'으로 분석되는데, 이 뜻 그대로 쓰이는 단어이다.

정답 laudable

3

해석 고립되어 살아가는 것은 불쾌할 수도 있다.

해설 '고립'이라는 뜻의 isolation을 묻는 문제다. 오답인 location은 '위치'라는 뜻인데, '놓아두도록(loc) 만드는(at[e]) 것(ion)'으로 분석된다. 이 단어에는 영화의 '야외 촬영지'라는 뜻도 있다.

정답 isolation

4

해석 약한 동물들을 사냥하는 것이 적법한 일인가?

해설 '적법한'이란 뜻의 legitimate을 묻는 문제다. 오답인 intimate는 '친밀한'이란 뜻으로 '가장 깊어지게(intim) 된(ate)'으로 분석된다.

정답 legitimate

5

해석 기능 문법과 같은 많은 언어학 이론이 있다.

해설 '언어의'를 뜻하는 linguistic을 묻는 문제다. 오답인 optimistic은 '낙관적인'이란 뜻으로, '가장 좋은(optim) 것이라 믿는 사람(ist)과 관련된(ic)'으로 분석된다.

정답 linguistic

PRACTICE

1

해석 A: 배락 오바마를 어떻게 생각하세요?
B: 무엇보다도, 그는 정직해요. 인격적 완결성을 갖춘 인물입니다.

해설 '인격적 완결성'을 뜻하는 integrity를 묻는 문제다. 선택지 가운데 corruption은 '완전히(cor←com) 찢어진(rupt) 것(ion)'으로 분석되는데, 이 뜻으로부터 '부패, 타락'이라는 뜻이 생겨났다. 이 단어에서와 같이 접두사 com-은 '함께'라는 뜻에서 확장되어 '완전히'라는 뜻을 나타낼 수도 있다.

어구 intelligence 지성　　　corruption 타락
minority 소수 집단

정답 (c)

2

해석 A: 돈을 모두 주식에 투자하기로 결심했어.
B: 그런 결정이 네 돈을 위험에 빠뜨릴 텐데.

해설 '위험'을 뜻하는 jeopardy를 묻는 문제다. 선택지 가운데 jealousy는 '시샘(jeal)으로 가득한(ous) 상태(y)'로 분석된다. 참고로, 접미사 −y는 '상태'나 '조건' 또는 '특성'이란 뜻을 나타낸다.

어구 invest 투자하다　　　stock 주식
jealousy 시샘　　　jewelry 장신구

정답 (a)

3

해석 A: 안젤리나 졸리가 아이를 한 명 더 입양했어요.
B: 그녀가 그렇게 한 것은 칭찬할 만한 일입니다.

해설 '칭찬할 만한'이란 뜻의 laudable을 묻는 문제다. 선택지 가운데 avoidable은 '바깥으로(a) 비워낼(void) 수 있는(able)'으로 분석된다. 물론, readable는 '읽을(read) 수 있는(able)'으로 분석된다.

어구 adopt 입양하다; 채택하다　　readable 읽을 만한
avoidable 피할 수 있는　　audible 들을 수 있는

정답 (d)

4

해석 A: 명상이 정신 건강을 향상시킬 수 있나요?
B: 단연코 그렇습니다. 명상은 마음을 완전히 이완시키는 데 도움이 됩니다.

해설 '명상'을 뜻하는 meditation을 묻는 문제다. 선택지 가운데 irritation은 '안으로(ir) 올라오게(rit) 만드는(at[e]) 것(ion)'으로 분석된다. 이 단어는 짜증이라는 뜻일 때는 셀 수 없는 명사로, '짜증거리'라는 뜻일 때는 셀 수 있는 명사로 쓰인다.

어구 mental 정신적인　　　definitely 확실히
completely 완전히　　　station (사회적) 지위
irritation 짜증　　　invitation 초대

정답 (c)

5

해석 많은 이들에게, 정체성을 형성하는 것은 복잡한 과정이다.

해설 '정체성'을 뜻하는 identity를 묻는 문제다. 선택지에서 quantity는 '얼마나 많은가 하는(quant) 특성(ity)'으로, entity는 '존재하는(ent) 특성(ity)'으로, property는 '특유한(proper) 상태(ty)'로 분석된다.

어구 complex 복잡한　　　quantity 양
entity 실체　　　property 속성; 소유물

정답 (d)

6

해석 모르는 게 약이라는 말이 사실인가?

해설 '무지(無知)'를 뜻하는 ignorance를 묻는 문제다. 선택지 가운데 arrogance는 '향해서(ar←ad) 요구하고(rog) 있는 것(ance)'으로, insurance는 '확실하게(sur[e]) 만들고(in) 있는 것(ance)'으로 각각 분석된다.

어구 bliss 지극한 행복　　　arrogance 오만
appearance 출현　　　insurance 보험

정답 (a)

7

해석 순진무구한 아이들이 아주 많이 죽임을 당해서 우리는 격분했다.

해설 '격분시키다'라는 뜻의 infuriate을 묻는 문제다. 선택지 가운데 calm은 '차분한'이란 뜻의 형용사로만 알기 쉬운데, '진정하다; 진정시키다'라는 뜻의 동사로 활용될 수 있음도 익혀 두어야 한다. 그리고 satisfy는 '충분하게(satis)+만들다(fy)'로 분석된다.

어구 innocent 순진무구한　　calm 진정시키다
　　satisfy 만족시키다　　desire 갈망하다

정답 (b)

8

해석 우리가 영원히 살 수 있다는 것은 환상이다.

해설 '환상'을 뜻하는 illusion을 묻는 문제. inclusion은 '안으로(in) 닫는(clus) 것(ion)'으로, exclusion은 '밖으로(ex) 닫는(clus) 것(ion)'으로, inclination은 '향해서(in) 굽도록(clin) 만드는 (at[e]) 것(ion)'으로 분석된다.

어구 forever 영원히　　inclusion 포함
　　exclusion 제외　　inclination 성향

정답 (b)

UNIT 4　고급 어휘 Ⅳ

EXERCISE

A

1 (e)　　**2** (c)　　**3** (a)　　**4** (b)　　**5** (d)

B

1 native　　**2** pacific
3 patriot　　**4** perturbed
5 prejudice

PRACTICE

1 (d)　　**2** (d)　　**3** (c)　　**4** (a)　　**5** (b)
6 (b)　　**7** (d)　　**8** (b)

중요 Collocation 정리

1 감자는 아일랜드 원산이 아니다.

2 로버트는 아버지로서의 의무를 게을리했다.

3 그 교사는 욕설을 하는 것으로 악명이 높다.

4 우리에게는 우리나라를 지켜야 할 의무가 있다.

5 자손을 생산하는 것은 종(種)의 생존에 필수적이다.

6 아동을 학대하는 것은 극히 부당한 일이다.

7 영국은 일본에 화해 제스처를 취했다.

8 놀랍게도, 대부분의 바이킹들은 평화적인 사람들이었다.

9 애국자였기에, 잔 다르크는 자신의 나라를 지키는 데 헌신했다.

10 빌 스미스는 그 술집의 단골손님이다.

11 많은 이들은 대통령이 약속을 어겨서 동요되었다.

12 때로는 전례를 깨뜨릴 필요가 있다.

13 그 기구는 여성에 대한 편견을 없애기 위해 노력하고 있다.

14 그 원소에는 재미있는 속성들이 있다.

15 행복을 추구하는 것은 쉬운 과정이 아니다.

EXERCISE A

1 (e)
　의무를 소홀히 한다면, 해야 하는 일을 하지 않는 것이다.

2 (c)
　나쁜 것으로 악명이 높다면, 그것을 하는 것으로 유명한 것이다.

3 (a)
　어떤 것을 해야 할 의무가 있다면, 그것을 해야만 한다.

4 (b)
　자손을 생산한다면, 자녀를 갖는 것이다.

5 (d)
　어떤 것이 극히 부당하다면, 사람들이 그것에 대해 안 좋게 생각하는 것이다.

EXERCISE B

1

해석 영어 원어민 화자조차도 그런 실수를 저지른다.

해설 '토착의'라는 뜻의 native를 묻는 문제다. 오답인 negative는 '부정하도록(neg) 만드는(at[e]) 경향이 있는(ive)'으로 분석되는데, '부정적인'으로 옮길 수 있다.

정답 native

2

해석 우리 한국인들은 평화적인 민족이다. 우리는 평화를 사랑한다.

해설 '평화적인'을 뜻하는 pacific을 묻는 문제다. 오답인 warlike은 '호전적인'이란 뜻으로, '전쟁(war) 같은(like)'으로 분석되며 본래 '전쟁할 준비가 되어 있는'이란 뜻이었다. 지금은 이 뜻이 사라지고 '호전적인'이란 뜻으로 주로 쓰인다.

정답 pacific

3

해석 네이단 헤일은 애국자였다. 그는 나라를 사랑했다.

해설 '애국자'를 뜻하는 patriot을 묻는 문제다. 오답으로 제시된 traitor는 '반역자'라는 뜻인데, '넘겨(tra) 주는(it) 사람(or)'으로 분석된다.

정답 patriot

4

해석 수지는 가장 친한 친구가 배신을 해서 언짢았다.

해설 '언짢은'을 뜻하는 perturbed를 묻는 문제다. 오답으로 제시된 pleased는 '즐거워하는'을 뜻하는데, 이처럼 감정을 나타내는 말이 -ed로 끝나면 일정한 감정을 갖게 된다는 것을 뜻함에 유의해야 한다.

정답 perturbed

5

해석 노인들에 대한 편견을 없애기가 매우 어렵다.

해설 '선입견'을 뜻하는 prejudice를 묻는 문제다. 오답으로 제시된 prelude는 '전주곡; 서막'이란 뜻으로 '미리(pre) 노는 것(lude)'로 분석된다.

정답 prejudice

PRACTICE

1

해석 A: 그들이 왜 이혼했죠?
B: 톰이 남편으로서의 의무를 소홀히 했거든요.

해설 '소홀히 하다'라는 뜻의 neglect를 묻는 문제다. collect는 '함께(col) 모으다(lect)'로, recollect는 '다시(re) 함께(col) 모으다(lect)'로, elect는 '밖으로(e) 골라내다(lect)'로 분석된다. 이처럼 어근 lect에는 '모으다'라는 뜻과 '골라내다'라는 뜻이 있다.

어구 divorce 이혼하다   collect 수집하다
recollect 기억해내다   elect 선출하다

정답 (d)

2

해석 A: 그들의 화해 제스처를 받아들여야 하나요?
B: 그렇게 하지 않는 편이 나아요. 그들에게는 숨은 의도가 있어요.

해설 '화해 제스처'를 뜻하는 overtures를 묻는 문제다. 선택지 가운데 structure는 '지은(struct) 것(ure)'으로 분석되는데, 이 단어와 어근 struct를 공유하는 단어로 construct를 들 수 있다. construct는 '함께(con) 짓다(struct)'로 분석되어 '건설하다'라는 뜻을 나타낸다.

어구 hidden agenda 숨겨진 의도   feature 특징
structure 구조   culture 문화

정답 (d)

3

해석 A: 그의 말에 대해 어떻게 느꼈니?
B: 아, 그가 아주 심한 인종차별주의자여서 언짢았어.

해설 '언짢은'을 뜻하는 perturbed를 묻는 문제다. 선택지 가운데 grateful은 '고마움(grate)으로 가득한(ful)'으로 분석되는데, 순수영어 계열의 단어다. '~으로 가득한'을 뜻하는 접미사 –ous가 주로 라틴어 계열의 단어와 결합하는 데 반해, 같은 뜻의 –ful은 순수영어 계열의 단어와 결합한다.

어구 remark 말, 언급   racist 인종차별주의자
proud 자랑스러운   naive 순진한
grateful 고마워하는

정답 (c)

4

해석 A: 남자가 여자보다 과학을 더 잘한다고 생각해.
B: 그것은 여성에 대한 흔한 편견이야.

해설 '선입견'을 뜻하는 prejudice를 묻는 문제다. 선택지 가운데 pregnancy는 '태어나기(gn) 이전(pre) 상태(ancy)'로, preface는 '앞서(pre) 말하는 것(face)'으로 각각 분석된다.

어구 common 흔한, 공동의   cowardice 비겁함
pregnancy 임신   preface 서문

정답 (a)

5

해석 그 정권은 국민들을 아사시키는 것으로 악명이 높다.

해설 '악명이 높은'을 뜻하는 notorious를 묻는 문제다. furious는 '격분(furi)으로 가득한(ous)'으로, various는 '다양한(vari) 것으로 가득한(ous)'으로, glorious는 '영광(glori)으로 가득한(ous)'으로 분석되는데, 모두 라틴어 계열의 단어들이다.

어구 regime 정권   starve 굶겨 죽이다
furious 격분한   various 다양한
glorious 영예로운

정답 (b)

6

해석 가난한 사람들을 나쁘게 대하는 것은 극히 부당하다.

해설 '극히 부당한'을 뜻하는 outrageous를 묻는 문제다. gorgeous는 '수녀의 베일(gorge)로 가득한(ous)'로 분석되는데, 이 의미에서 '우아한'이란 뜻으로 의미가 확장되었다. simultaneous는 '동시의(simul) 순간(tane)으로 가득한(ous)'으로 분석된다. 역시 라틴어 계열의 단어다.

어구 badly 사악하게   gorgeous 외모가 수려한
simultaneous 동시의   generous 후하게 베푸는

정답 (b)

7

해석 캐슈는 브라질이 원산이다.

해설 '토착의'를 뜻하는 native를 묻는 문제다. active는 '행동하는(act) 경향이 있는(ive)'으로, passive는 '아파하는(pass) 경향이 있는(ive)'으로, conservative는 '보존하도록(conserv) 만드는(at[e]) 경향이 있는(ive)'으로 각각 분석된다.

어구 cashew 캐슈(옻나무과의 수목)   active 활발한
passive 수동적인   conservative 보수적인

정답 (d)

8

해석 진정한 애국자라는 것은 자신의 나라를 무조건적으로 사랑하는 것을 뜻한다.

해설 '애국자'를 뜻하는 patriot을 묻는 문제다. 선택지 가운데 tailor가 동사로도 쓰여 '특정한 수요에 정확히 맞추다'라는 뜻을 나타낸다는 점도 익혀두자. 그리고 주어진 맥락을 고려할 때, '학자'를 정답으로 하기는 부적절하다는 것도 기억하자. 상식적인 판단이 요구되기 때문이다.

어구 unconditionally 무조건적으로   traitor 반역자
tailor 재단사   scholar 학자

정답 (b)

EXERCISE

A

1 (b) **2** (d) **3** (e) **4** (a) **5** (c)

B

1 quota **2** relevant
3 tendency **4** tolerant
5 security

PRACTICE

1 (c) **2** (a) **3** (b) **4** (c) **5** (d)
6 (d) **7** (a) **8** (b)

중요 Collocation 정리

1 윌로우는 자신의 할당량을 채우기 위해 아주 열심히 노력하고 있다.

2 그녀의 미소는 언제나 따스함과 동정심을 발산한다.

3 합리적으로 선택하기 위해서는 많은 요소들을 고려해야 한다.

4 그의 주장은 우리의 논의와는 연관성이 없다.

5 민주주의를 수호하기 위해서는 표현의 자유를 허용해야 한다.

6 다행스럽게도, 우리는 외딴 곳에 있는 해변을 찾아내어 재미있게 놀았다.

7 부(富)는 거짓된 안정감을 줄 수 있다.

8 그들의 관계는 안정적이지 못했다.

9 법규는 항상 헬멧을 착용하도록 규정한다.

10 불확실한 시대에는 사람들이 미신을 믿게 된다.

11 천성적으로 사려가 깊어, 수지는 그 상황에서 어떻게 말해야 할지를 정확히 알았다.

12 사장은 직원들을 학대하는 성향이 있다.

13 올리비아는 놀랄 정도로 비판에 대해 관용한다.

14 그의 발언은 전혀 터무니없는 말이다. 전혀 말이 되지 않는다.

15 허영심 때문에, 그녀는 비싼 집을 사기로 결심했다.

EXERCISE A

1 (b)
따스함을 발산한다면, 필경 사람들이 좋아할 것이다.

2 (d)
합리적인 결정을 내린다면, 그 결정은 훌륭한 결정이다.

3 (e)
외딴 마을을 방문한다면, 외로움을 느낄지도 모른다.

4 (a)
미신을 믿는다면, 과학적으로 사고하지 않는 것이다.

5 (c)
사려가 깊다면, 다른 사람들의 감정을 해치지 않는다.

EXERCISE B

1

해석 할당량을 채우지 못했을 때, 에이미는 좌절감을 느꼈다.

해설 '할당량'을 뜻하는 quota를 묻는 문제다. 오답인 quiver는 '약간의 떨림'을 뜻하는 말이기 때문에, 주어진 맥락에 어울리지 않는다. 이 단어는 동사로 쓰이면 '추위나 두려움 등으로 떨다'라는 뜻을 나타낸다.

정답 quota

2

해석 직책에 지원하려면, 모든 관련 서류를 앤에게 보내시오.

해설 '연관성이 있는'을 뜻하는 relevant를 묻는 문제다. 오답인 relative는 '상대적인'이란 뜻으로 주어진 맥락에 맞지 않는다. 이 단어는 '다시(re) 옮기는(lat) 경향이 있는(iv)'으로 분석된다.

정답 relevant

3

해석 남자들은 스포츠를 즐기는 경향이 있다.

해설 '경향'을 뜻하는 tendency를 묻는 문제다. dependence는 '의존'이란 뜻으로 셀 수 없는 명사이다. 이 단어는 '아래에(de) 달려(pend) 있는 것(ence)'으로 분석된다.

정답 tendency

4

해석 관용하는 사회는 성숙한 사회이다.

해설 '관용하는'을 뜻하는 tolerant를 묻는 문제다. 오답인 ignorant는 '무지한, 무식한'이란 뜻으로, '알지(gnor) 못하고(i) 있는(ant)'으로 분석된다.

정답 tolerant

5

해석 안전을 확보하기 위해, 많은 장치들이 설치되었다.

해설 '안정감'을 뜻하는 security를 묻는 문제다. 이 문제에서는 security가 '안전'이란 뜻으로 쓰였다. 오답인 impurity는 '불순함; 불순물'이란 뜻으로, '순수하지(pur[e]) 못한(im) 상태(ity)'로 분석된다.

정답 security

PRACTICE

1

해석 A: 사만다가 이 달의 최우수 직원상을 받았어요.
　　B: 그녀는 판매 할당량을 초과 달성했으니까요.

해설 '할당량'을 뜻하는 quota를 묻는 문제다. '할당량을 채우다'라는 뜻은 meet[fill] a quota로 표현된다. 그리고 quotation과 date에 각각 '시세'와 '대추야자'라는 뜻이 있음도 익혀두자.

어구 employee 직원 　　award 상
　　 exceed 뛰어넘다 　　data 자료
　　 quotation 인용구; 시세 　　date 날짜; 대추야자

정답 (c)

2

해석 A: 수지를 어떻게 설명하실 수 있나요?
　　B: 음, 그녀는 친절과 동정심을 발산해요.

해설 '발산하다'라는 뜻의 radiate을 묻는 문제다. negotiate은 '쉽지 (ot[i]) 않도록(neg) 만들다(ate)'로, initiate은 '안으로(in) 가도록(it[i]) 만들다(ate)'로, fascinate은 '주문(呪文)을(fascin) 만들다(ate)'로 각각 분석된다.

어구 describe 기술하다, 설명하다
　　compassion 동정심　　　negotiate 협상하다
　　initiate 시작하다　　　　fascinate 매혹시키다

정답 (a)

3

해석 A: 그의 연령을 고려해야 하나요?
　　B: 절대로 아니죠. 연령은 연관된 요소가 아니에요.

해설 '연관성이 있는'을 뜻하는 relevant를 묻는 문제. 선택지 가운데 separate은 '따로(se) 마련하도록(par) 만들다(ate)'로 분석되는데, 동사로 쓰일 때 '별거하다'라는 뜻이 있음도 알아두어야 한다.

어구 take into account 고려하다
　　factor 요인, 요소　　　relative 상대적인
　　separate 별개의　　　　similar 유사한

정답 (b)

4

해석 A: 나는 13이 불길한 숫자라고 믿어.
　　B: 뭐라고? 너가 그렇게 미신을 믿는 줄 몰랐는데.

해설 '미신을 믿는'이란 뜻의 superstitious를 묻는 문제. 선택지 가운데 sensible은 '느낄(sens) 수 있는(ible)'으로, sensual은 '감각(sens[u])과 관련된(al)'으로 각각 분석된다. 어구에서 해설한 뜻을 정확히 익혀두자.

어구 scientific 과학적인　　sensible 양식이 있는
　　sensual 관능적인

정답 (c)

5

해석 합리적인 사람이라면 그토록 어리석은 일은 하지 않을 텐데.

해설 '합리적인'을 뜻하는 rational을 묻는 문제. rational은 '비율 (ration)에 따른(al)'으로 분석할 수도 있는데, 손익의 비율을 따지는 것이 '합리적인' 것이라는 발상에서 현재의 뜻을 갖게 되었다.

어구 stupid 어리석은　　　　absurd 터무니없는
　　illogical 비논리적인　　　awkward 어색한; 서투른

정답 (d)

6

해석 패트릭은 외딴 섬으로 가서 고립되어 살았다.

해설 '외딴'이란 뜻의 secluded를 묻는 문제. 선택지 가운데 festive는 '축제(fest)를 하는 경향이 있는(ive)'으로 분석되는데, 본래 '축제의, 축제에 어울리는'이란 뜻을 나타내었다. 이 뜻에서 '들뜬'이란 의미가 나왔는데, 두 의미를 모두 익혀두어야 한다.

어구 isolation 고립　　　　crowded (사람들로) 혼잡한
　　noisy 시끄러운　　　　festive 들뜬

정답 (d)

7

해석 사려 깊음은 동정심을 요구한다.

해설 '감정을 해치지 않는'이란 뜻의 tactful을 묻는 문제. 이 단어의 뜻에 대한 영한사전의 일반적인 풀이는 '재치있는, 약삭빠른'인데, 이 정의는 영어 원래의 어감과 차이가 너무 심하다는 단점이 있다. '다른 사람의 감정을 상하게 하는 말이나 행동을 하지 않는'이란 정확한 뜻을 익혀두어야 한다.

어구 require 요하다　　　　sympathy 동정심
　　mischievous 장난기가 있는
　　indifferent 무관심한　　fearful 두려워하는

정답 (a)

8

해석 한국인들이 그런 문법적 실수를 저지르는 경향이 있다.

해설 '경향'을 뜻하는 tendency를 묻는 문제. 선택지 가운데 confidence는 '완전히(con) 믿고(fid) 있는 것(ence)'으로, currency는 '달리고(curr) 있는 것(ency)'로 분석된다. currency에 어구에서 밝힌 바와 같이 '통용'이라는 뜻도 있다는 점을 익혀 두어야 한다.

어구 grammatical 문법적인　　dependence 의존
　　confidence 자신감, 신뢰　currency 통화(通貨); 통용

정답 (b)

▍Chapter 5

UNIT 1　일상 구어체 표현 I

EXERCISE

A

| 1 (d) | 2 (b) | 3 (e) | 4 (a) | 5 (c) |

B

1　Come　　　2　Get
3　give　　　　4　chin
5　Beats

PRACTICE

| 1 (d) | 2 (d) | 3 (b) | 4 (a) | 5 (c) |
| 6 (c) | 7 (a) | 8 (b) | | |

중요 Collocation 정리

1　네가 결정을 내려야 한다. 공이 네게로 넘어왔으니까.

2　그가 우리한테 왜 그렇게 화가 났지? — 모르겠는걸.

3　같이 힐래? — 아니, 이미 해봐서 관심 없어.

4　생각해 보니까 궁금한데, 어떻게 내 아파트를 찾아냈지?

5　그 정도면 됐어! 그만해!

6　어쩌면 그들이 도와줄 거야. — 가능성이 없어!

7　여성들이여, 정신을 차려라! 이상형의 남자란 존재하지 않는다.

8 리차드, 제발 그만해! 더이상 불평을 들어줄 순 없어.

9 브루스를 다시는 안 볼 거야. 걘 끝났어.

10 남자친구가 없어. — 나도 같은 처지야.

11 디지털 카메라를 빌려도 될까요? —그렇게 하세요!

12 기운 내! 다음번에는 더 잘 할 수 있어.

13 제이 케이 롤링? 그 이름은 잘 기억이 나지 않는다.

14 제발 속도를 줄여! 나중에 후회하느니 미리 조심하는 게 낫잖아.

15 해고당했어! — 같은 처지야.

EXERCISE A

1 (d)

결정을 내릴 차례라면 조치를 취해야 한다.

2 (b)

'모르겠는데.'라고 말한다면, 어떤 것을 이해하지 못한다는 뜻이다.

3 (e)

'해봐서 더이상 관심이 없어.'라고 말한다면, 어떤 것에 관심이 없다는 뜻이다.

4 (a)

'그만해.'라고 말한다면, 누군가가 어떤 일을 그만두기를 바라는 것이다.

5 (c)

어떤 것이 어렴풋이 기억나면, 그것을 기억할 수 있다고 믿는 것이다.

EXERCISE B

1

해석 생각해 보니까 궁금한데, 어떻게 그녀의 주소를 알았지?

해설 '생각해 보니까'라는 뜻의 come to think of it을 묻는 문제다. 이 표현은 고정된 관용표현이기 때문에 come을 의미가 연결되는 go로 바꾸어 쓸 수 없음에 유의해야 한다. 따라서 표현 전체를 하나로 묶어서 기억하자.

정답 Come

2

해석 소년이여, 정신을 차리라! 세상은 위험한 곳이다.

해설 '정신 차려!'라는 뜻의 Get real!을 묻는 문제다. turn도 get과 마찬가지로 변화를 나타낼 수 있긴 하지만, 이 표현에서 get을 대신할 수 없다. 참고로, turn traitor to는 '배신하다'라는 뜻을 나타낸다.

정답 Get

3

해석 톰, 그만해! 그건 터무니없어.

해설 '그만해'라는 뜻의 give me a break을 묻는 문제다. '도와주다'라는 뜻일 때는 give/lend a hand라고 해서 lend가 give를

대신할 수 있지만, 이 표현에서는 대신할 수 없음에 유의하자.

정답 give

4

해석 기운 내! 기회가 또 있으니까.

해설 '기운 내!'라는 뜻의 Keep your chin up!을 묻는 문제다. 이 표현은 Chin up!으로 쓸 수도 있다. 그렇지만 이 때의 chin을 nose로 대신할 수는 없다. 역시 고정된 표현이기 때문이다.

정답 chin

5

해석 케이트가 왜 그만두었니? — 모르겠는걸.

해설 '모른다'라는 뜻의 Beats me를 묻는 문제다. 이때 beat은 '놀라게 하다' 곧 '제대로 이해하지 못하는 상태에 빠뜨리다'라는 뜻으로 쓰였다. 따라서 단순히 '때리다'라는 뜻의 hit으로 대신할 수 없음에 유의하자.

정답 Beats

PRACTICE

1

해석 A: 그들이 왜 이탈리아로 이주하기로 결심했니?
B: 모르겠는걸.

해설 '모르겠는걸.'이란 뜻의 Beats me를 묻는 문제다. 관용표현이기 때문에 단순히 '때리다'라는 뜻을 나타내는 다른 단어로 대체할 수 없다. 참고로 strike a balance between은 '~사이에 균형을 맞추다'라는 뜻이다.

어구 move 이사하다 strike 치다
knock 두드리다 punch 주먹으로 때리다

정답 (d)

2

해석 A: 크게 파티 하는데, 같이 갈래?
B: 아니, 이미 해봐서 관심이 없어.

해설 '더이상 관심이 없다'라는 뜻의 been there, done that을 묻는 문제다. 역시 관용표현이기 때문에 been이나 done을 다른 단어로 대신할 수 없다. 참고로 join은 '합류하다, 가입하다, 같이 가다'라는 뜻일 때 모두 타동사이기 때문에 전치사 with과 함께 쓸 수 없음에 유의해야 한다.

어구 join 합류하다; 가입하다; 같이 가다

정답 (d)

3

해석 A: TEPS 시험에서 떨어졌어!
B: 나도 같은 처지야! 너무 어려웠어.

해설 '같은 처지이다'라는 뜻의 Join the club을 묻는 문제다. 역시 고정된 표현이기 때문에 join을 다른 단어로 대신할 수 없다. 그리고 앞에서 살펴보았듯이, join이 타동사이기 때문에 join in the club과 같이 쓸 수 없음에 유의해야 한다.

어구 fail (시험에) 낙제하다 enjoy 즐기다

정답 (b)

4

해석 A: 브리트니 스피어스가 누구인지 아니?
B: 그 이름은 잘 기억이 나지 않는 걸.

해설 '(어렴풋이) 기억나다'라는 뜻의 ring a bell을 묻는 문제다. 이때 ring은 '(종을) 울리다'라는 본래의 뜻으로 쓰였는데, '종'이 '어떤 것을 기억하도록 하는 장치'라는 의미를 갖기 때문에 '기억나다'라는 뜻으로 발전했다.

정답 (a)

5

해석 우리가 기다릴 필요가 있어. 그녀가 결정을 내릴 차례거든.

해설 '누가 결정을 내릴 차례이다'라는 뜻의 The ball is in someone's court를 묻는 문제다. 이 때 court는 '테니스 코트'라는 뜻으로 쓰였다. 본래 이 표현은 테니스 경기에서 '공이 상대편에 있다'는 뜻으로, 이 의미에서 현재의 비유적 의미로 발전했다.

어구 ring (권투 등의) 링; 고리   field 들판; 분야

정답 (c)

6

해석 패리스 힐튼은 더 이상 중요하지 않아. 더 이상 그녀한테 관심이 없어.

해설 '더 이상 중요하지 않다'라는 뜻의 someone is history를 묻는 문제다. history(역사)는 과거의 일을 주로 다루기 때문에, 그러한 의미에서 '이미 지난 일이어서 더 이상 중요하지 않은 것'이라는 뜻으로 발전했다.

어구 politics 정치   economy 경제   society 사회

정답 (c)

7

해석 제발 그만해! 내가 그렇게 순진하지는 않아.

해설 '그만해!'라는 뜻의 Give me a break!을 묻는 문제다. 이 표현은 대개 상대방이 속이려고 하거나 짜증나게 하는 것을 그만두라고 말할 때 쓰인다. 이때 break은 '휴식'이라는 의미로 파악할 수 있는데, 고정된 표현이기 때문에 비슷한 뜻의 단어로 대신할 수 없음에 유의하자.

어구 naive 순진한   leave 휴가   holiday 휴일

정답 (a)

8

해석 정신 차려! 안정성 같은 것이란 존재하지 않아.

해설 '정신 차려!'라는 뜻의 Get real!을 묻는 문제다. 선택지 가운데 go나 turn은 get과 같이 변화를 나타낼 수 있지만, 관용표현이기 때문에 get을 대신할 수 없다. 그리고 go 다음에는 좋지 않은 상태를 나타내는 말이 오는 것이 보통이라는 점도 기억하자.

어구 security 보안; 안정성

정답 (b)

UNIT 2 일상 구어체 표현 Ⅱ

EXERCISE

A

1 (d)	2 (a)	3 (c)	4 (e)	5 (b)

B

1	nuts	2	nutshell
3	thought	4	leg
5	neck		

PRACTICE

1 (a)	2 (c)	3 (b)	4 (d)	5 (c)
6 (a)	7 (a)	8 (d)		

중요 Collocation 정리

1 톰 크루즈가 네 파티에 왔다고? 농담이겠지.

2 첫 공연 때문에 너무 떨려. — 괜찮을 거야. 행운을 빌게!

3 학생은 정신병이 있는 척해서 그녀를 놀렸다.

4 이 이야기에 대해 아무한테도 말하지 않아야 돼. — 비밀을 지킬게.

5 네 노트북 컴퓨터 써도 되니? — 물론이지.

6 재미있네. 똑같은 걸 생각하고 있었거든. — 정신이 위대한 사람들은 생각도 비슷해.

7 사진기 갖고 왔니? — 아, 깜빡했다.

8 데이비드가 짜증나게 하기 시작했어. 그러니까, 걔 때문에 미치겠어.

9 라이언은 아내가 바람을 피웠다는 사실을 알고서는 몹시 화를 냈다.

10 요컨대 자신을 믿어야 한다.

11 그가 사라져서 천만다행이다. 그는 정말 골칫거리였다.

12 원하는 것은 어떤 것이든 가질 수 있어. 그냥 좋은 것으로 골라.

13 여행을 시작해서 라스베이거스로 향해야 할 때이다.

14 노곤해서 평소보다 일찍 잠자리에 들었다.

15 아, 잠깐만요. 다시 생각해 보니까, 커피가 좋겠네요.

EXERCISE A

1 (d)
'실마?'라고 말한다면, 어떤 사람이 한 말을 믿지 않는 것이다.

2 (a)
'행운을 빌게.'라고 말한다면, 누군가에게 행운을 빌어주는 것이다.

3 (c)

'비밀을 지킬게'라고 말한다면, 누구에게도 비밀을 말하지 않겠다는 뜻이다.

4 (e)

'도로를 친다'라고 하면, 여행을 시작하는 것이다.

5 (b)

'자루를 친다'라고 하면, 잠자리에 드는 것이다.

EXERCISE B

1

해석 힐러리는 자신이 속았다는 사실을 알았을 때 몹시 화를 냈다.

해설 '몹시 화를 내다'라는 뜻의 go nuts를 묻는 문제다. 이때 nuts는 '정신 이상의'라는 뜻을 나타내기 때문에, 단순히 '완두'를 뜻하는 peas로 대체할 수 없다. 일종의 숙어에 해당한다고 분석할 수도 있다.

정답 nuts

2

해석 요컨대 교육 수준을 향상시켜야 한다.

해설 '요컨대'를 뜻하는 in a nutshell을 묻는 문제다. '조가비'를 뜻하는 seashell이 모양이 비슷하다고 해서 nutshell 대신 쓸 수 없다. 역시 숙어라고 해석할 수 있기 때문이다.

정답 nutshell

3

해석 아, 다시 생각해 보니까, 내일 떠나겠습니다.

해설 '다시 생각해 보니까'를 뜻하는 on second thought를 묻는 문제다. 발음이 혼동될 수 있는 sought는 seek(구하다)의 과거형/과거분사로서 thought와 달리 명사로 쓰일 수 없다.

정답 thought

4

해석 앤소니는 경찰관인 척해서 그녀를 놀렸다.

해설 '장난삼아 놀리다'라는 뜻의 pull someone's leg를 묻는 문제다. 본래 발상이 '다리를 걸어 넘어뜨리는 것'이기 때문에 leg을 '팔'을 뜻하는 arm으로 대체할 수 없음에 유의해야 한다.

정답 leg

5

해석 설거지는 골칫거리이다.

해설 '골칫거리'라는 뜻의 a pain in the neck을 묻는 문제다. 이 표현도 역시 숙어로 파악되기 때문에 neck을 '무릎'을 뜻하는 lap으로 대신할 수 없음에 주의해야 한다.

정답 neck

PRACTICE

1

해석 A: 제시카 알바랑 결혼해!
B: 설마?

해설 '설마?'라는 뜻의 Are you kidding me?를 묻는 문제다. 선택지 가운데, nag이 '들볶다'라는 의미와 함께 '바가지를 긁다'라는

뜻과 '지속적으로 고통을 안겨주다'라는 뜻을 나타낸다는 점을 익혀두어야 한다. 본래 의미는 '긁다'이다. 이 뜻으로부터 현재의 여러 의미가 파생되었다.

어구 pig oneself 게걸스럽게 먹다   dig 파다   nag 들볶다

정답 (a)

2

해석 A: 드루실라의 영어는 아주 완벽해요.
B: 어쩌면, 외국인인 척하면서 놀리는 줄도 몰라요.

해설 '장난삼아 놀리다'라는 뜻의 pull someone's leg을 묻는 문제다. 선택지의 다른 표현들도 의미를 정확히 익혀두어야 한다. 물론, 주어진 맥락을 고려할 때 (c) 이외의 다른 선택지는 정답이 될 수 없다.

어구 pretend ~인 체하다
reap the harvest of ~의 (좋거나 나쁜) 결과를 얻다
give somebody the cold shoulder 냉대하다
leave no stone unturned 모든 노력을 다 해보다

정답 (c)

3

해석 A: 문을 모두 확인했니?
B: 아 이런! 완전히 깜빡해버렸네.

해설 '깜빡하다'라는 뜻의 It slipped someone's mind를 묻는 문제다. 이때 slip은 '빠져나가다'라는 의미를 나타내는데, 뜻이 관련이 있다고 해서 다른 선택지로 대신할 수 없음에 유의해야 한다. 표현을 정확히 익혀 두자.

어구 miss 놓치다; 그리워하다

정답 (b)

4

해석 A: 그녀의 디지털카메라를 망가뜨렸어.
B: 그녀가 그 사실을 알면 몹시 화를 낼 거야.

해설 '몹시 화를 내다'는 뜻의 go nuts를 묻는 문제다. 선택지 가운데 ring true는 부정문에서 쓰이는 경우가 많다. 그리고 eat one's words는 바로 앞에 have[has, had] to가 오는 경우가 흔하다.

어구 ring true 사실인 것 같다
eat one's words 자신의 말이 틀렸음을 인정하다
cut one's teeth on ~에서 초임 시절을 보내다

정답 (d)

5

해석 나한테 어떤 것이든 말해도 돼. 비밀을 지킬 거니까.

해설 '비밀을 지키다'라는 뜻의 one's lips are sealed를 묻는 문제다. 말하기와 관련된 것이 '입술(lip)'이기 때문에, 다른 표현으로 대체할 수 없다. 물론, 숙어로 파악해도 된다.

정답 (c)

6

해석 요컨대 스스로가 (진리를) 찾아내야만 한다.

해설 '요컨대'라는 뜻의 in a nutshell을 묻는 문제다. 다른 선택지들은 어구에서 밝힌 바와 같이, 전치사 at이나 on 등과 어울려 설명한 것과 같은 의미를 나타낸다. 각각의 뜻을 정확히 익혀두자.

어구 on a roll 행운이나 성공을 맞이한
at a loss 어찌할 바를 모르는
at home 마음이 편한

정답 (a)

7

해석 아, 떠나야 할 때이구나. 안녕!

해설 '(여행 등을) 떠나다'라는 뜻의 hit the road를 묻는 문제다. 나머지 표현들도 뜻을 정확히 알아두자.

어구 hit home (비판 등이) 정곡을 찌르다; 부정적인 영향을 미치다
keep one's fingers crossed 행운을 빌다
get cold feet (소심하여) 주저하다

정답 (a)

8

해석 아, 다시 생각해 보니까, 창문측 좌석이 좋겠네요.

해설 '다시 생각해 보니까'를 뜻하는 on second thought를 묻는 문제. 선택지 가운데 (a)는 down-to-earth라는 형태로 '현실적인'이란 뜻을 나타내기도 한다. 각 표현의 뜻을 정확히 익혀 두자. 무엇보다도 자연스러운 맥락에서 표현을 익히는 것이 바람직하다는 점을 명심하자.

어구 come (back) down to earth (따분한) 일상으로 돌아오다
on edge 초조한
let somebody off the hook 책임을 모면하게 하다

정답 (d)

어휘 모의고사

PART I

1 (b)	2 (c)	3 (b)	4 (b)	5 (b)
6 (b)	7 (a)	8 (a)	9 (a)	10 (d)
11 (d)	12 (b)	13 (d)	14 (b)	15 (c)
16 (a)	17 (c)	18 (b)	19 (b)	20 (c)
21 (d)	22 (a)	23 (a)	24 (b)	25 (d)

PART II

26 (d)	27 (d)	28 (d)	29 (a)	30 (a)
31 (c)	32 (b)	33 (c)	34 (a)	35 (d)
36 (c)	37 (a)	38 (d)	39 (d)	40 (d)
41 (d)	42 (c)	43 (a)	44 (d)	45 (c)
46 (d)	47 (a)	48 (c)	49 (b)	50 (c)

PART I

1

해석 A: 어떻게 된 거니?
B: 아무도 몰라. 근데 많은 사람들이 입원했어.

해설 '(일이) 일어나다'라는 뜻의 필수 동사 happen을 묻는 문제. 선택지 가운데 place는 타동사로 쓰이기 때문에 정답이 될 수 없음에 유의해야 한다. 또한 이와 같은 일상적 표현에서는 순수영어 계열에 속하는 happen이 라틴어 계열에 속하면서 '발생하다'라는 뜻을 나타내는 occur에 비해 자연스럽다는 점도 익혀두어야 한다.

어구 be hospitalized 입원하다   ease 완화되다
lie (-lay -lain) 눕다

정답 (b)

2

해석 A: 글로리아는 정말 나쁜 사람이야.
B: 그런 말을 하기 전에 사실을 확인하는 편이 나을 거야.

해설 '사실을 확인하다'라는 뜻의 collocation인 check a fact를 묻는 문제. 선택지 가운데 fail은 '실패하다'라는 뜻일 때는 자동사로만 쓰이기 때문에 주어진 맥락에 어울리지 않는다. 이처럼 특히 동사의 경우에 자동사인가 타동사인가를 반드시 확인하는 습관을 들여야 한다.

어구 comment 말, 논평   beat 때리다   fail 실패하다

정답 (c)

3

해석 A: 로라 선생님과의 내일 진료 예약을 취소하고 싶습니다.
B: 알겠어요, 고객님. 취소 양식을 작성해 주시겠어요?

해설 '취소하다'라는 뜻의 필수 동사 cancel을 묻는 문제. 선택지 가운데 agree는 that절이나 to부정사가 바로 다음에 오지 않으면 자동사로 쓰이기 때문에 정답이 될 수 없다. 반면 divide와 greet은 주어진 맥락에 전혀 어울리지 않는다. 그렇지만 TEPS 어휘 영역의 출제 범위에 속하므로 뜻을 정확히 익혀두어야 한다.

어구 appointment (만날) 약속   fill out (양식을) 작성하다
cancellation 취소   agree 동의하다
divide 나누다   greet 맞이하다

정답 (b)

4

해석 A: 데이비드가 왜 체포되었나요?
B: 경찰 말로는 회사에서 많은 돈을 훔쳤대요.

해설 '훔치다'를 뜻하는 steal을 묻는 문제. steal은 특히 rob과 혼동하기 쉬운데, rob의 목적어로 사람이나 장소가 와야 하는 데 반해 steal의 목적어로 훔치는 물건이 온다는 점을 익혀 두면 혼동을 피할 수 있다. 선택지 가운데 guess는 바로 다음에 의문사가 오지 않으면 자동사로 쓰이기 때문에 정답이 될 수 없음에 유의해야 한다.

어구 arrest 체포하다   cause 일으키다
guess 추측하다   injure 부상을 입히다

정답 (b)

5

해석 A: 오늘 저녁 예약하고 싶습니다.
B: 알겠습니다, 손님. 몇 분이시죠?

해설 '예약하다'라는 뜻의 collocation인 make a reservation을 묻는 문제. 선택지 가운데 effort와 apology가 make와 어울릴 수 있는 데 반해, impression은 주로 give와 어울린다. 이처럼 각각의 명사가 자연스럽게 어울리는 동사를 확인하는 습관을 들여야 한다.

어구 effort 노력   apology 사과, 사죄   impression 인상

정답 (b)

6

해석 A: 연례 축제가 이번 주말에 개최될 거야!
B: 아, 정말? 빨리 그 날이 왔으면!

해설 '축제를 개최하다'라는 뜻의 collocation인 hold a festival을 묻는 문제. 이때 hold를 대신하여 선택지의 다른 동사들을 쓸 수 없음에 유의해야 한다. 이처럼 collocation의 경우에는 조합

이 자유롭지 않은 것이 보통이기 때문에 자연스러운 collocation
이 어떤 것인지를 꼭 확인해 두어야 한다.

어구 annual 연례의

정답 (b)

7

해석 A: 수백만 명의 아프리카 아동들이 굶주리고 있어.
B: 즉각적인 조치를 취해야만 할 거 같은데.

해설 '조치를 취하다'라는 뜻의 collocation인 take action을 묻는
문제. 역시 자연스러운 collocation이어야 하기 때문에 선택
지의 다른 동사들로 take를 대체할 수 없음에 유의해야 한다.

어구 starve 굶주리다   immediate 즉각적인

정답 (a)

8

해석 A: 우리 회사가 수천 명의 직원을 새로 뽑을 계획이야.
B: 와! 회사가 정말 잘 되나 보다.

해설 '고용하다'라는 뜻의 필수 동사인 hire를 묻는 문제. B의 말을
감안하면 '해고하다'라는 뜻의 fire는 주어진 맥락에 자연스럽게
어울리지 않는다. 다른 선택지들도 역시 어색함에 유의해야 한다.

어구 fire 해고하다   avoid 피하다   delay 지연시키다

정답 (a)

9

해석 A: 가격이 적정한 거 같지 않니?
B: 사실은 약간 너무 높아.

해설 '(가격이) 적정한'이란 뜻의 필수 형용사인 reasonable을 묻는
문제. 나머지 형용사들도 모두 출제 범위에 속하기 때문에 뜻을
정확히 익혀두어야 한다. 모두 주어진 맥락에는 어울리지 않는다.

어구 actually 실은   patient 인내심이 강한
optimistic 낙관적인   genuine 진정한

정답 (a)

10

해석 A: 회의에서 낙태 문제를 다루어야 한다고 생각합니다.
B: 너무 예민한 주제라고 생각하지 않으세요?

해설 '다루다'라는 뜻의 구동사 deal with를 묻는 문제. 선택지의 다
른 구동사들도 정답과 마찬가지로 출제 빈도가 높은 구동사들이기
때문에 뜻을 정확히 익혀두어야 한다.

어구 abortion 낙태   delicate 조심스럽게 다루어야 하는
account for 설명하다   break up (이성끼리) 갈라서다
come across (우연히) 마주치다

정답 (d)

11

해석 A: 공석을 채워줄 사람이 몹시 필요해.
B: 그렇다면, 어떤 사람을 추천해도 될까요?

해설 '공석을 채우다'라는 뜻의 collocation인 fill a vacancy를 묻는
문제. 선택지에서 attract는 a turnout과 함께 쓰여 '(참석하
는) 사람들을 끌어들이다'는 뜻을, attain은 a goal과 함께 '목표
를 성취하다'라는 뜻을, embark는 embark on a journey라
는 형태로 '여행을 시작하다'라는 뜻을 각각 나타낸다.

어구 badly 몹시   recommend 추천하다
attract 끌어들이다   attain 성취하다

embark on ~를 시작하다

정답 (d)

12

해석 A: 누가 장비를 수리할 수 있다고 생각하니?
B: 샐리한테 연락하는 게 어때? 기계를 정말 잘 고치거든.

해설 '장비를 수리하다'라는 뜻의 collocation인 repair equipment
를 묻는 문제. 선택지 가운데 slump와 function은 모두 자동
사로만 쓰이기 때문에 정답이 될 수 없다. 반면 quit은 B의 말을
감안할 때 주어진 맥락에 어울리지 않는다.

어구 contact 연락하다   fix 수리하다
quit 그만두다   slump 침체에 빠지다
function 작동하다

정답 (b)

13

해석 A: 안젤리나가 너무 많은 책임을 져왔다고 생각합니다.
B: 무슨 뜻인지는 알겠지만, 그녀한테 의존하는 수밖에 없었어요.

해설 '책임을 지다'라는 뜻의 collocation인 shoulder responsibility를 묻는 문제. 선택지 가운데 deliver는 a lecture와
어울려 '강연하다'라는 뜻을, absorb는 knowledge와 어울려
'지식을 흡수하다'라는 뜻을 각각 나타낸다.

어구 have no choice but to ~할 수밖에 없다
compliment 칭찬하다   deliver 배달하다
absorb 흡수하다

정답 (d)

14

해석 A: 아들이 사고에서 살아남아서 천만다행이에요.
B: 네, 그렇지만 아드님이 보다 조심을 했어야만 했는데요.

해설 '사고에서 살아남다'라는 뜻의 collocation인 survive an
accident를 묻는 문제. 이때 survive가 타동사로 쓰이기 때
문에 바로 다음에 the accident와 같은 목적어가 온다는 점에
특히 유의해야 한다. 우리말의 사고 방식을 따르지 않도록 주의하
자.

어구 finalize 마무리하다   educate 교육하다
resign 사임하다

정답 (b)

15

해석 A: 이 프로그램을 쓰는 방법을 모르겠어.
B: 사용 설명서를 다시 한 번 읽어보는 게 어때?

해설 '이해하다'라는 뜻의 구동사인 figure out을 묻는 문제. 나머지
구동사들도 역시 출제 빈도가 높으므로 뜻을 정확히 알아두자.

어구 manual 사용 설명서   hand in (과제 등을) 제출하다
hang up (전화를) 끊다   make up 구성하다; 화해하다

정답 (c)

16

해석 A: 캐시가 시험에 합격해서 아주 기뻐요.
B: 저도 그래요. 그녀의 노고가 결국에 결실을 맺은 것이죠.

해설 '(결국엔) 득이 되다'라는 뜻의 구동사 pay off를 묻는 문제. 역
시 나머지 구동사들도 출제 빈도가 높으므로 정확히 익혀두자.

어구 mark down 할인하다   pull over (도로변에) 차를 세우다

turn down (제의 등을) 거절하다

정답 (a)

17

해석 A: 엘리사에 대해 어떻게 생각하세요?
B: 아, 일을 잘하는 비서입니다. 자기 일을 잘 알아요.

해설 '효과적인'을 뜻하는 effective와 혼동될 수 있는 efficient를 묻는 문제다. efficient는 '효율적인; 일에 능숙한'이란 뜻을 나타낸다. 다른 선택지들도 역시 출제 범위에 속하므로 뜻을 정확히 익혀 두자.

어구 secretary 비서　　　fictional 가공의
familiar 익숙한　　　generous 후하게 베푸는

정답 (c)

18

해석 A: 입사를 환영해요. 모두들 당신이 우리 회사에 커다란 자산이 될 거라고 그러더군요.
B: 아, 과찬이에요. 어떻든, 함께 일하게 되어 기쁩니다.

해설 '자산'을 뜻하는 고급 단어인 asset을 묻는 문제다. 앞서 공부한 것처럼 이 단어는 '충분한 것을(set) 향한(as←ad)'으로 분석된다. 이 뜻으로부터 '자산'이란 뜻으로 확장되었는데, A의 말과 같은 맥락에도 활용됨을 익혀 두어야 한다. 나머지 단어들도 출제 범위에 속하므로 정확히 익혀 두자.

어구 flatter 아첨하다　　　abuse 남용; 학대　　　aspect 측면
circumstance 주위 상황

정답 (b)

19

해석 A: 회의에서 왜 기업의 책임이라는 문제를 제기했죠?
B: 토의와 연관성이 있다고 생각했어요.

해설 '의문을 제기하다'라는 뜻의 collocation인 raise the question을 묻는 문제다. raise의 뜻을 단순히 '올리다'로 알기 쉬운데, 이처럼 중요한 쓰임새가 있다는 점도 익혀두어야 한다. 출제 빈도가 매우 높으므로 정확히 알아두자. 다른 동사들도 뜻에 유의해서 익혀두어야 한다.

어구 corporate 기업의　　　relevant 연관성이 있는
establish 설립하다　　　offend 감정을 상하게 하다
leak (비밀을) 누설하다

정답 (b)

20

해석 A: 이 차는 견고합니까?
B: 네, 그렇습니다. 사실, 거의 20년 정도 지속될 수 있어요.

해설 '견고한'이란 뜻의 고급 단어인 durable을 묻는 문제다. 이 단어는 앞서 살펴본 바와 같이, '지속될(dur) 수 있는(able)'으로 분석된다. 나머지 고급 단어들도 자연스러운 맥락에서 뜻을 정확히 익혀두어야 한다.

어구 last 지속되다　　　hostile 적대적인
humane 자비로운　　　gradual 점진적인

정답 (c)

21

해석 A: 시카고로 이사 가게 되어 정말 흥분돼!
B: 특히 조심해라! 시카고는 아주 위험한 도시니까.

해설 '조심하는'이란 뜻의 고급 단어인 cautious를 묻는 문제다. 앞서

살펴본 바와 같이, 이 단어는 '주의하는 것(caut[i])으로 가득한(ous)'으로 분석된다. 다른 단어들도 뜻과 쓰임새를 정확히 익혀 두자.

어구 move 이사하다　　　extremely 극히
accurate 정확한　　bankrupt 파산한　　effective 효과적인

정답 (d)

22

해석 A: 어쩌면 그들이 우리가 숙제하는 걸 도와줄지도 몰라.
B: 가능성이 없어. 그들은 우리한테 신경을 쓰지 않거든.

해설 '희박한 가능성'을 뜻하는 일상 구어체 표현인 fat chance를 묻는 문제다. 앞서 살펴본 바와 같이, 이 표현에서는 fat의 '풍부한'이란 뜻이 반어적으로 활용된다. 나머지 표현들도 출제 빈도가 높은 편이므로 정확히 익혀두자.

어구 join the club 같은 (어려운) 처지인걸
Be my guest! 그렇게 하세요!
ring a bell (어렴풋이) 기억나다

정답 (a)

23

해석 A: 그들을 신뢰할 수 있을까요?
B: 아니, 그럴 수 없습니다. 그들에게는 숨은 의도가 있어요.

해설 '숨은 의도'를 뜻하는 a hidden agenda를 묻는 문제다. agenda에 '의제'라는 뜻이 있음도 알아두어야 한다. 나머지 표현들도 모두 자주 출제되므로 뜻과 쓰임새를 정확히 익혀두자.

어구 trust 신뢰하다　　　　　a pain in the neck 골칫거리
a long shot 가능성이 희박한 일
a rule of thumb 경험칙, 대략적인 방법

정답 (a)

24

해석 A: 어색한 분위기를 깨뜨리는 가장 좋은 방법이 무엇인가요?
B: 농담을 해서 사람을 웃기시면 돼요. 그러면 사람들이 보다 편하게 느낄 거예요.

해설 '어색한 분위기를 깨뜨리다'라는 뜻의 숙어인 break the ice를 묻는 문제다. 다른 숙어들도 모두 출제 빈도가 높으므로 정확히 익혀두어야 한다.

어구 crack a joke 농담하다
play it by ear (계획 없이) 상황에 따라 처리하다
pick up the tab 비용을 치르다
make ends meet 겨우 살아갈 정도의 수입만 있다

정답 (b)

25

해석 A: 말을 둘러대지 마라. 그냥 정말로 생각하는 바를 말해줘.
B: 그렇지만 일이 그렇게 단순한 게 아니잖아.

해설 '말을 둘러대다'라는 뜻의 숙어인 beat around the bush를 묻는 문제다. 그리고 일상 구어체 표현에 속하는 다른 표현들도 실제로는 숙어로 분류할 수 있다. 특성이 숙어와 비슷한 짐이 많기 때문이다. 모두 출제 빈도가 높은 표현들이느로 활용되는 자연스러운 맥락을 정확히 익혀두자. 그것이 숙어를 학습하는 가장 효과적이고 효율적인 방법이기 때문이다.

어구 pull someone's leg 장난삼아 놀리다
it slipped one's mind 깜빡하다
go nuts 몹시 화를 내다, 흥분하다

PART II

26

해석 그 집을 사기 위해서 미셸은 은행으로부터 많은 돈을 빌려야 했다.

해설 '빌리다'라는 뜻의 borrow를 묻는 문제다. 이 단어는 특히 lend 와 혼동하지 않도록 유의해야 한다. 예문에서와 같이 borrow는 from과 함께 쓰이는 경우가 많은데, 두 단어에 모두 ro가 들어 있다는 점을 기억하면 혼동을 피할 수 있다. 그리고 rob의 목적어 로 반드시 사람이나 장소가 와야 한다는 점을 다시 한 번 기억하자.

어구 lend 빌려주다   rob 빼앗다   lie 눕다; 거짓말하다

정답 (d)

27

해석 흡연은 건강에 해를 끼친다.

해설 '해를 끼치다'라는 뜻의 collocation인 do harm을 묻는 문제다. 이 표현에서 do를 cause로 대신할 수는 있지만, 선택지의 다른 동사로 대신할 수는 없다. 이처럼 collocation은 결합할 수 있는 표현을 제약하기 때문에 자연스러운 collocation을 익히는 것이 매우 긴요하다는 점을 명심하자.

어구 smoking 흡연

정답 (d)

28

해석 성인으로서, 성숙한 선택을 내려야 한다.

해설 '선택하다'라는 뜻의 collocation인 make a choice를 묻는 문 제다. 이때 make를 exercise로 대신할 수 있지만, 선택지의 다른 동사로 대신할 수는 없음에 유의해야 한다. 또한 우리말에 이끌려 선택지 (a) do를 정답으로 선택하지 않도록 주의하자.

어구 adult 성인   mature 성숙한

정답 (d)

29

해석 모든 고객의 수요를 충족시키는 일은 거의 불가능하다.

해설 '수요를 충족시키다'라는 뜻의 collocation인 meet the need 를 묻는 문제다. 이때 meet을 fill이나 satisfy로 대신할 수는 있 지만, 선택지의 다른 동사들로 대신할 수는 없다. 그리고 part가 동사로도 쓰일 수 있음도 알아두자.

어구 practically 거의   customer 고객
part 동) 헤어지다

정답 (a)

30

해석 한국의 전력 수요는 상당히 증가할 것으로 예상된다.

해설 '수요가 증가하다'라는 뜻의 collocation인 a demand rises 를 묻는 문제다. 선택지 가운데 raise는 타동사로만, 그리고 handle은 주로 타동사로 쓰이는 말이기 때문에 주어진 맥락 에 어울리지 않는다. 동사의 자동사/타동사 여부도 Longman Dictionary of Contemporary English(http://www. ldoceonline.com)를 통해 정확히 확인할 수 있다.

어구 electricity 전력   demand 수요
significantly 상당히   pound (심장이) 두근거리다
handle 다루다

정답 (a)

31

해석 우리 사회는 불법 이민이라는 문제에 직면해 있다.

해설 '(문제 등에) 직면하다'라는 뜻의 필수 동사인 face를 묻는 문제다. 선택지 가운데 behave는 자동사이기 때문에 주어진 맥락에 어 울리지 않는다. 그리고 다른 선택지들은 내용에 맞지 않기 때문에 정답이 될 수 없다.

어구 society 사회   illegal 불법적인
immigration 이민   behave 처신하다
gain (이익 등을) 얻다   imitate 흉내 내다

정답 (c)

32

해석 실용적인 방법을 적용하는 것은 언제나 괜찮은 아이디어이다.

해설 '방법을 적용하다'라는 뜻의 collocation인 apply a method 를 묻는 문제다. 이때 apply를 employ로 대신할 수는 있지만, 선택지의 다른 동사로 대신 할 수는 없다. 그리고 선택지 가운데 glow는 자동사이기 때문에, 빈 칸에 들어갈 수 없음에 유의해야 한다.

어구 practical 실용적인   break 어기다
suffer (피해 등을) 겪다   glow 빛나다

정답 (b)

33

해석 우리 사회는 많은 변화를 겪고 있다.

해설 '변화를 겪다'라는 뜻의 collocation인 undergo a change를 묻는 문제다. 다른 선택지들은 voice an opinion(의견을 표명 하다), fire a gun(총을 쏘다), drop a hint(힌트를 주다)와 같 이 활용된다. 각각의 collocation을 정확히 익혀두자.

어구 voice (의견 등을) 표명하다   fire (총 등을) 쏘다
drop (힌트를) 주다

정답 (c)

34

해석 그 상은 영어로 글을 잘 쓰는 학생에게 주어진다.

해설 '상'을 뜻하는 award를 묻는 문제다. 이 단어는 '보상'을 뜻하 는 reward와 혼동하지 않도록 주의해야 한다. 선택지 가운데 personnel을 '개인적인'이란 뜻을 나타내는 personal과 혼동 하지 않도록 유의하자.

어구 present 증정하다   personnel 직원 전체
ignorance 무지(無知)   integrity 인격적 완결성

정답 (a)

35

해석 그녀의 여권은 두 달 전에 만료되어, 그녀가 더이상 쓸 수 없었다.

해설 '여권이 만료되다'라는 뜻의 collocation인 a passport expires를 묻는 문제다. 다른 동사들도 어구에서 해설한 것과 같 은 의미로 명사와 어울려서 쓰임에 유의하자. 특히 형태가 특이한 taxi의 뜻은 정확히 알아두자.

어구 taxi (비행기가) 지상에서 활주하다
rage (싸움 등이) 격하게 계속되다
reign (왕 등이) 집권하다

정답 (d)

36

해석 건설적인 비판을 받아들이기 위해서는, 자신에게 솔직해질 필요가 있다.

해설 '건설적인 비판'이란 뜻의 collocation인 constructive criticism을 묻는 문제다. 다른 선택지들은 각각 a miserable life(비참한 삶), superficial knowledge(피상적인 지식), domestic mail(국내 우편)과 같이 활용된다. 주어진 맥락을 고려할 때, constructive가 가장 자연스러움에 유의하자.

어구 accept 받아들이다   honest 정직한
miserable 비참한   superficial 피상적인
domestic 국내의

정답 (c)

37

해석 놀랍게도, 수면은 학습 능력에 영향을 미칠 수 있다.

해설 '영향을 미치다'라는 뜻의 affect를 묻는 문제다. 이 단어는 특히 동사로서 '초래하다'라는 뜻을 나타내는 effect와 혼동하지 않도록 유의해야 한다. affect에서 af가 '향해서'를 뜻하는 ad의 변형임을 기억하면 혼동을 피할 수 있다. 일정한 대상을 '향해서' 영향을 미치게 되기 때문이다.

어구 surprisingly 놀랍게도   learning 학습
effect 초래하다   insist 주장하다
ignore 무시하다

정답 (a)

38

해석 이 책을 공부하면 높은 점수가 보장된다.

해설 '보증하다'라는 뜻의 고급 단어인 guarantee를 묻는 문제다. 주어진 문장의 맥락을 감안할 때, 다른 선택지들이 정답이 될 수 없음에 유의해야 한다. 실제 시험에서는 짧은 시간에 문제를 풀어나가야 하기 때문에, 평소에 전후 맥락을 파악하는 습관이 완전히 몸에 배어 있어야 함을 명심하자.

어구 oppose 반대하다   judge 판단하다
neglect 소홀히 하다

정답 (d)

39

해석 어떤 이들은 인터넷이 민주주의의 확산을 촉진하는 데 기여한다고 생각한다.

해설 '촉진하다'라는 뜻의 고급 단어인 facilitate를 묻는 문제다. 이 단어는 '쉽게(facil) 되도록(it) 만들다(ate)'로 분석된다. 선택지 가운데 frequent가 '빈번한'이란 형용사로도 쓰인다는 점도 함께 익혀두자.

어구 spread 확산   frequent 자주 들르다
react 반응하다   search 수색하다

정답 (d)

40

해석 그들의 자연 서식지는 인간의 활동에 의해 위협을 받고 있다.

해설 '서식지'를 뜻하는 고급 단어인 habitat를 묻는 문제다. 이 단어는 '가지게(hab) 된(it) 것(at)'으로 분석된다. 다른 단어들도 어휘 영역의 출제 범위에 속하므로 뜻과 쓰임새를 성확히 익혀두자.

어구 natural 자연적인   threaten 위협하다
activity 활동   principal 교장 선생님

housing 주택   insult 모욕

정답 (d)

41

해석 부부는 일본으로 여행을 떠남으로써 결혼기념일을 경축했다.

해설 '기념일'을 뜻하는 필수 명사인 anniversary를 묻는 문제다. 앞에서 살펴본 바와 같이, 이 단어는 '해마다(ann[i]) 방향을 돌리는(vers[e]) 것(ary)'으로 분석된다. 다른 단어들도 뜻과 쓰임새를 정확히 알아두자.

어구 celebrate 경축하다   recess (학교의) 쉬는 시간
landscape 전반적 상황   adversity 역경, 고난

정답 (d)

42

해석 우리는 우회했지만 예상보다 일찍 그곳에 도착했다.

해설 '우회'를 뜻하는 필수 명사인 detour를 묻는 문제다. 참고로 '우회하다'라는 뜻은 take[make] a detour로 표현된다. 우리말에 이끌려 do a detour로 표현하지 않도록 특히 주의해야 한다. 이처럼 영어와 우리말은 발상의 차이가 크기 때문에 영어 본래의 어감을 정확히 익혀야 함을 명심하자.

어구 boom 호황   gist 요점, 핵심   notion 개념

정답 (c)

43

해석 우리 회사는 '한국의 최고 직장'으로 지명되었다.

해설 '지명하다'라는 뜻의 필수 동사인 nominate을 묻는 문제다. 라틴어 계열에 속하는 이 단어는 '이름을(nomin) 만들다(ate)'로 분석된다. 다른 단어들도 모두 출제 범위에 속하므로 뜻과 쓰임새를 정확히 익혀두자.

어구 workplace 직장   leak (비밀을) 누설하다
patrol 순찰하다   trace 추적하다

정답 (a)

44

해석 시간이 많지 않습니다. 따라서 관련이 있는 질문만 해주십시오.

해설 '연관성이 있는'이란 뜻의 고급 단어인 relevant를 묻는 문제다. 앞에서 살펴본 바와 같이, relevant는 '소유하고(relev) 있는(ant)'으로 분석된다. 그리고 앞에서 언급했듯이 tactful의 정확한 의미를 익혀두어야 한다.

어구 secluded 외딴   tactful 감정을 해치지 않는
outrageous 극히 부당한

정답 (d)

45

해석 그의 전문성은 물리학에서 나노테크놀로지에까지 이른다.

해설 '(일정한) 범위에 이르다'라는 뜻의 필수 동사인 range를 묻는 문제다. 이 단어는 명사로서 '범위; 산맥'이란 뜻을 나타내기도 한다. 선택지로 제시된 다른 동사의 뜻과 쓰임새도 정확히 익혀두어야 한다.

어구 expertise 전문성   physics 물리학
notify 통보하다   store 저장하다
perform 수행하다

정답 (c)

46

해석 그 품목을 멕시코로 운송하는 데는 시간이 많이 걸릴 것이다.

해설 '운송하다'라는 뜻의 필수 동사인 ship을 묻는 문제다. 선택지 가운데 maintain은 '손에(main) 잡다(tain)'로 분석되는데, 이때 어근 main을 '주된'의 의미인 형용사 main과 혼동해서는 안 된다. 형용사 main이 순수영어 계열인 데 반해, 동사 maintain은 라틴어 계열이기 때문이다. 따라서 우연히 형태가 같을 뿐, 의미가 서로 연결되지 않음에 유의하자.

어구 item 품목　　　　　　settle 정착하다
　　　maintain 주장하다　　object 반대하다

정답 (d)

47

해석 폭력은 문제를 해결하는 적당한 방법이 아니다.

해설 '적법의'를 뜻하는 고급 단어인 legitimate을 묻는 문제다. 앞에서 살펴본 바와 같이 이 단어는 '합법적이(legitim) 되도록 만들다(ate)'로 분석된다. 참고로 이처럼 '~하게 만들다'를 뜻하는 접미사로는 -ate, -ify, -ize, en-이 있는데, 이 가운데 en-만이 순수영어 계열에 속한다.

어구 violence 폭력　　　　　notorious 악명이 높은
　　　perturbed 언짢은　　　stable 안정적인

정답 (a)

48

해석 E2 비자에 대해 할당량을 엄하게 책정해야 한다.

해설 '할당량'을 뜻하는 고급 단어인 quota를 묻는 문제다. 선택지 가운데 jeopardy는 대개 place[put] something in jeopardy라는 형태로 쓰여 '어떤 것을 위험에 빠뜨리다'라는 뜻을 나타낸다.

어구 strict 엄한　　　　　　prejudice 선입견
　　　obligation 의무, 책임　jeopardy 위험

정답 (c)

49

해석 미국인들은 위기가 있을 때 단결하는 경향이 있다.

해설 '경향, 성향'을 뜻하는 고급 단어인 tendency를 묻는 문제다. 뜻이 나타내는 추상성 때문에 셀 수 없는 명사로 생각하기 쉬운데, 셀 수 있는 명사로만 쓰인다. 일정하게 한정된 경향을 나타낸다고 생각하기 때문이다. 특히, 명사의 학습에서는 셀 수 있는가 없는가를 확인하는 것이 긴요하다는 점을 명심하자.

어구 unite 단결하다　　　　crisis 위기
　　　immersion 몰입　　　identity 정체성; 동일성
　　　pursuit 추구

정답 (b)

50

해석 협약은 직원들이 유니폼을 입어야만 한다고 규정한다.

해설 '규정하다'라는 뜻의 고급 단어인 stipulate를 묻는 문제다. TEPS의 어휘 영역은 점차 난이도가 높아지는 경향이 있기 때문에 특히 이와 같은 고급 어휘의 학습이 매우 중요하다. 어원 분석을 활용하되, 자연스러운 맥락에서 활용되는 것을 주의 깊게 익히는 것이 고급 어휘 학습의 가장 효과적인 방법임을 명심하자. 물론, 맥락의 활용은 다른 어휘 범주의 학습에 대해서도 가장 효과적인 방법이다.

어구 agreement 협정　　　　safeguard 보호하다
　　　radiate (감정을) 발산하다　infuriate 격분시키다

정답 (c)

Chapter 1

UNIT 1   주제 찾기

EXERCISE

1-1 (c)   1-2 (a)   2-1 (a)   2-2 (a)

PRACTICE

1 (d)   2 (b)

유형 정리

1   주제가 앞부분에 있는 경우

해석 영어를 배우는 것은 이상한 습관을 가진 사람과 연애하는 것과 같다. "성공하기" 위해서는 그런 습관에 익숙해져야 한다. 마찬가지로, 영어에는 많은 학습자들이 이해하는 데 어려움을 겪는 이상한 "습관"들이 많이 있다. 그런 습관들은 대개 일반적인 규칙의 예외들이다. 그렇지만 일단 그런 예외들에 익숙해지면 영어 실력이 상당히 향상될 것이다.

어구 date ~와 여데이트하다;대추야자
get used to ~에 익숙해지다
likewise 마찬가지로(=similarly)
improve 향상되다;향상시키다

2   주제가 뒷부분에 있는 경우

해석 복구된 기억이란 어떤 사건을 기억해내는 데 성공했다고 잘못 믿는 것을 말한다. 그런 일은 대개 아동기의 학대에 관한 것이다. 문제는 물론 복구된 기억이 틀린 것이라는 데 있다. 단지 어떤 일을 경험했다고 상상하는 것일 뿐이다. 그러나 그 일은 일어난 적이 없다. 따라서 복구된 기억을 조장해서는 안 된다.

어구 recover 회복하다, 복구하다   event (발생한) 일, 사건
abuse 학대; 남용   memory 기억; 기억력
encourage 격려하다; 조장하다

3   주제가 암시되어 있는 경우

해석 불필요한 파일을 정말로 삭제하고 싶은가? 비밀을 안전하게 유지하기를 정말로 바라는가? 그렇다면 BC Wipe이라는 프로그램을 써 보라. 이 '(정보) 삭제' 프로그램은 불필요한 파일을 완전히 제거하여 누구도 제거된 파일을 찾거나 복구할 수가 없다. 따라서 이 간단한 프로그램을 사용하여 파일을 제거하면 복구할 수 있는 방법은 전혀 없다. 매우 편리하다고 생각되지 않는가?

어구 delete 삭제하다   unnecessary 불필요한(=unneeded)
once and for all 완전히, 최종적으로
restore 복구하다   convenient 편리한

EXERCISE

1-1

해석 (a) 우리는 아주 오랫동안 서로를 알고 지냈죠. (b) 그래서 저를 당연한 존재로 여길지도 모르겠네요. (c) 그러나 그대는 제게 특별한 숙녀랍니다.

해설 일종의 연애편지인데, 말하고자 하는 바의 요지는 마지막 문장이다. 따라서 정답은 (c)다. (a)와 (b)는 (c)를 말하기 위한 배경을 제공하는 역할을 맡고 있다.

어구 take A for granted A를 당연한 것으로 여기다

정답 (c)

1-2

해석

Q. 이 글은 주로 무엇을 말하고 있나?
(a) 어느 숙녀에 대한 사랑
(b) 우정의 중요성

해설 주어진 글에서 (c)가 글의 주제이기 때문에 정답은 (a)다. 주어진 글의 (a)와 (b)부분에서는 서로 오래 알고 지내는 사이라는 것을 확인할 수 있는데 (c)에서 보다 더 깊은 관계를 말하고 있으므로 '(b) 우정의 중요함'은 답이 될 수 없다.

정답 (a)

2-1

해석 (a) 소음 공해는 심각한 문제다. (b) 소음 공해 때문에 청각을 영구적으로 잃을 수도 있다. (c) 또한 소음 공해는 여러 가지 점에서 건강에 해를 끼친다.

해설 소음 공해의 심각성을 말하고 있으므로 정답은 (a)다. (b)와 (c)는 소음 공해가 왜 심각한 문제인지를 예를 들어 설명하고 있기 때문에 주제를 보충 설명하는 문장들에 해당된다.

어구 serious 심각한; 진지한   hearing 청각
permanently 영원히

정답 (a)

2-2

해석

Q. 이 글의 가장 적절한 제목은 무엇인가?
(a) 소음 공해 문제
(b) 건강의 중요성

해설 2-1번 문제에서 확인했듯이, 주어진 글의 중심 내용은 '소음 공해의 심각성'이다. 이와 연결되는 것은 (a)다.

어구 noise pollution 소음 공해

정답 (a)

PRACTICE

1

해석 독일의 통일 과정은 험난했다. 짐작할지 모르지만, 동독정권은 동독인들이 민주적인 개혁을 요구하는 것을 막으려고 했다. 동독 정부는 국민들이 동독 정권에 위협이 되는 것으로 간주되는, 구소련의 간행물을 읽는 것을 허용하지 않았다. 또한 동독인들이 서독으로 탈출하는 것을 막으려는 시도들도 있었다. 이런 장애에도 불구하고 독일인들은 성공적으로 나라를 통일시켰다.

Q. 글의 제목으로 가장 알맞은 것은?

(a) 민주적인 개혁의 중요성
(b) 동독과 서독 사이의 우호적인 관계
(c) 서독으로의 탈출
(d) 동독과 서독의 통일

해설 주제가 앞부분에 있는 경우로 정답은 (d)다. 전체적으로 독일 통일의 험난한 과정을 서술했다. 보기 가운데 (a)는 지나치게 일반적인 설명으로 글 전체의 내용과 맞지 않다. (b)는 글의 내용과 어긋난다. (c)는 글의 세부적인 내용이기 때문에 전체에 대한 제목으로는 적절하지 않다. 이와 같이 주제나 제목을 묻는 문제에서는 보기의 구성이 대체로 이 문제와 비슷하다는 점을 기억해두자.

어구 reunification (재)통일   regime 정권
stop A from~ A가 ~하는 것을 막다
call for 요구하다   reform 개혁
publication 출판; 간행물   attempt 시도
escape 탈출하다   obstacle 장애(물)
reunify (재)통일하다

정답 (d)

2

해석 한때 어떤 이들은 악어가 공룡의 선조라고 생각했다. 사실 공룡과 악어는 공통점이 많다. 이빨, 두개골, 턱의 구조가 매우 비슷하다. 그러나 공룡은 악어로부터 발달되지 않았다. 주된 이유는 이 두 파충류가 거의 동시에 지구상에 나타났기 때문이다. 그러면 공룡은 어떤 동물로부터 진화한 것일까?

Q. 글의 주된 내용은 무엇인가?

(a) 공룡의 이빨
(b) 공룡의 선조
(c) 악어와 공룡의 관계
(d) 악어의 출현

해설 글의 주된 내용이 '공룡의 선조'에 관한 내용이기 때문에 정답은 (b)다. (a)와 (d)는 세부적인 내용으로 전체 내용을 포괄하지 못한다. (c)를 정답으로 착각할 수도 있지만 첫 번째 문장과 마지막 문장을 통해 '공룡의 선조'라는 문제를 제기했기 때문에 정답이 될 수 없음에 유의하자. 항상 첫 문장과 마지막 문장이 중요함을 기억해두자.

어구 once 한 번; 한때   ancestor 선조, 조상
have in common 공통점을 갖다   skull 두개골
similar 유사한   reptile 파충류   evolve 진화하다

정답 (b)

EXERCISE

1 (c)   2 (b)

PRACTICE

1 (d)   2 (b)

유형 정리

1   특성

해석 오늘날 교사를 존경하는 사람들은 많지 않다. 이 현상의 원인은 다양한데, 그 가운데 하나는 교사들이 해야 하는 바를 효과적으로 하지 못한다는 데 있다. 근본적으로, 자신의 과목을 효율적으로 가르칠 수 있는 교사들이 충분하지 않다. 이 문제를 다루기 위해서는, 교사를 평가하고 보상하는 데 있어 구조적인 개혁을 실행해야 한다.

어구 a variety of 다양한   effectively 효과적으로
be supposed to ~하기로 되어 있다
basically 근본적으로   efficient 효율적인
address (문제를) 다루다   structural 구조적인
reform 개혁   evaluate 평가하다
reward 보상하다

2   조건

해석 두뇌에서 세로토닌의 양이 감소하는 것은 우울증의 발병과 밀접하게 관련되어 있다. 이것은 주로 세로토닌이 감정적 스트레스를 얼마나 효과적으로 다루는가에 영향을 미치기 때문이다. 신경 전달 물질인 세로토닌의 기능은 두뇌의 정서적 방어 체계를 조직하는 것이다. 따라서 두뇌에 세로토닌이 충분하지 않으면, 두뇌는 감정적 스트레스에 성공적으로 대처할 수 없다.

어구 decrease 감소   quantity 양
serotonin 세로토닌(혈액이나 뇌 속의 혈관수축물질)
closely 긴밀하게   related to ~와 관련된
onset 발병; 시작   depression 우울증
deal with 다루다   emotional 정서적인
function 기능
neurotransmitter 신경 전달 물질
organize 조직하다   defense 방어
cope with 대처하다   successfully 성공적으로

3   제외 항목

해석 2007년 11월 26일, 여수는 2012년 세계박람회를 개최하는 곳으로 선정되었다. 한국의 이 항구 도시는 77표 대 63표로 모로코의 탕헤르를 따돌렸다. 전문가들은 한국 도시인 여수의 '살아 있는 바다 숨 쉬는 연안'이라는 주제가 모로코의 항구 도시를 이기는 데 기여했다고 말했다. 세계박람회 행사는 많은 사람들을 끌어들여 한국에 막대한 이익을 창출한 것으로 예상된다.

어구 hold (행사를) 개최하다   port 항구
defeat 패배시키다   vote 투표; 득표
analyst 전문가; 분석가   theme 주제
contribute to ~에 기여하다   draw 끌어들이다
create 창조하다   huge 막대한

profit 이익, 이득

EXERCISE

1

해석 수잔나 타마로의 '마음을 따르라'는 아주 놀라운 소설이다. 이 감동적인 이야기에서, 할머니는 손녀에게 편지를 쓴다. 매우 인상적인 편지들에서, 할머니는 사람이라는 것의 의미에 대해 말한다. 실은, 이 현명한 여인은 우리들 각자에게 우리 자신의 마음에 바탕을 두어 선택을 내려야 한다고 조언한다. 오늘날 우리가 직면하고 있는 많은 도전을 감안할 때, 그녀의 충고는 언제나 그렇듯이 시의적절하다.
(a) 시대에 뒤진 소설이다.
(b) 주로 젊은 여성을 겨냥했다.
(c) 편지 형식으로 쓰였다.

해설 세부사항 가운데 특성을 묻는 문제다. (a)는 글의 마지막 문장에서 말한 바와 정반대되는 내용이기 때문에 정답이 될 수 없다. (b)는 본문에서 '우리들 각자에게'라는 말이 있기 때문에 역시 정답이 아니다. 따라서 정답은 본문의 내용과 일치하는 (c)다.

어구 amazing 아주 놀라운 　　touching 감동적인
elderly 늙은 　　dazzling 매혹적인
challenge 도전 　　confront 직면하다
timely 시의적절한
as ~ as ever 변함없이, 여전히 ~한(하게)

정답 (c)

2

해석 많은 사람들은 인터넷이 우리의 삶을 향상시켰다고 생각한다. 예컨대, 우리는 외출하지 않고서 많은 일을 할 수 있다. 그렇지만 유감스럽게도, 우리는 많은 소중한 것들을 잃었다. 무엇보다도, 아주 많은 사람들이 대면 접촉의 중요성을 망각하게 되었다. 대면 접촉을 통해서만 진정한 관계를 형성할 수 있다. 따라서 인터넷은 우리의 삶을 중요하게 '향상시킨' 것이 아니다.
(a) 우리가 신체를 움직이지 않고서도 많은 일을 할 수 있게 한다.
(b) 다른 사람들과의 진정한 우정을 형성하는 데 도움이 되지 않는다.
(c) 일상적인 것들의 소중함을 깨닫는 데 도움이 된다.

해설 일종의 조건으로 분석할 수도 있는 이유를 묻는 문제다. (a)는 삶을 향상시킨 이유로 생각될 수 있기 때문에 정답이 될 수 없다. (c)는 글에서 다루고 있지 않기 때문에 역시 정답이 아니다. 따라서 정답은 글의 내용과 연결되는 (b)다.

어구 improve 향상시키다 　　for instance 예를 들어
go out 외출하다 　　precious 소중한
more than anything else 무엇보다도
unaware 의식하지 못하는 　　face-to-face 대면의
communication 의사소통 　　interaction 상호작용

정답 (b)

PRACTICE

1

해석 루드윅 위겐스타인은 천재 논리학자였다. 버트렌 러셀의 '수학 원론'을 읽고 나서, 그는 논리에 대해 배우는 데 꽤 관심을 갖게 되었다. 그래서 러셀에게서 배우기 위해 케임브리지 대학에 다녔다. 일 년이 지나기도 전에, 러셀은 위겐스타인에게 가르칠 게 남아 있지 않다고 느꼈다. 그처럼 뛰어난 천재였기에, 위겐스타인은 스스로 논리를 탐구하기로 마음먹었다.

Q. 다음 중 어떤 것이 루드윅 위겐스타인에 대한 가장 적절한 설명인가?
(a) 옥스퍼드 대학을 다녔다.
(b) 버트렌 러셀에게 논리를 가르쳤다.
(c) 논리에 대해 배우는 데 어려움이 컸다.
(d) 논리에 능했다.

해설 세부사항 가운데 특성을 묻는 유형이다. (a)는 위겐스타인이 케임브리지대학을 다녔다고만 되어 있기 때문에 정답이 될 수 없다. (b)와 (c)는 글의 내용과 정반대로 서술되어 있다. 따라서 정답은 글의 내용과 완전히 일치하는 (d)다.

어구 genius 천재 　　logician 논리학자
principle 원리, 원칙 　　pass (시간이) 지나다
explore 탐구하다, 탐험하다

정답 (d)

2

해석 과학이 사랑을 설명할 수 있을까? 어떤 사람들은 이 질문에 긍정적으로 답하고 여성들이 특정한 유형의 남성들에게 매력을 느끼는 데 대한 '과학적인' 설명을 제공하려고 한다. 예컨대, 일부 과학자들은 젊은 여성들이 늙은 남성을 사랑하도록 유전적으로 프로그램화되어 있다고 주장한다. 그러나 '늙은'이란 나이가 얼마인 것을 말하는가? 80세나 90세를 말하는가? 그리고 '젊은'이란 나이가 얼마인 것을 말하는가? 10세나 12세인가? 또한 왜 젊은 여성은 한 남성만을 사랑하는가? 필경, 과학은 사랑에 대한, 우리의 이해에 기여할 것이 아무것도 없다고 해야 할 것이다.

Q. 글에 따르면, 다음 중 어떤 것이 올바른 설명인가?
(a) 늙은 여성은 젊은 남성을 사랑하도록 유전적으로 프로그램화되어 있다.
(b) 과학은 사랑을 만족스럽게 설명하지 못한다.
(c) 여성은 동시에 많은 남성들을 사랑하는 경향이 있다.
(d) 과학이 우리가 사랑을 이해하는 것을 도울 가능성이 높다.

해설 역시 세부사항 가운데 특성을 묻는 문제다. (a)는 글에 나타나 있지 않기 때문에 정답이 될 수 없다. (c)와 (d)는 본문의 내용에 어긋난다. 따라서 정답은 글의 내용과 일치하는 (b)다.

어구 scientific 과학적인 　　explanation 설명
attracted to ~에 매력을 느끼는
particular 특정한 　　genetically 유전적으로
program 자동적으로 행동하도록 만들다
probably 필경
contribute to ~에 기여하다, 공헌하다

정답 (b)

EXERCISE
1 (b)   2 (b)
PRACTICE
1 (c)   2 (d)

유형 정리

1 특성

해석 서태지의 컴백은 환영받는 컴백인가? 그의 열렬한 일부 팬들은 이에 대해 긍정하면서 서태지의 8집 앨범을 구입하기를 고대한다. 이들에 따르면, 이 논란을 불러일으키는 가수가 우리 사회에 '가르칠' 것이 많다고 한다. 다른 이들은 의견이 다르다. 이들은 논란의 여지가 있었던 그의 4집 앨범처럼, 8집 앨범이 예술적 탁월성이 결여될 수도 있다고 우려한다.

어구 comeback (지위나 활동 등으로의) 복귀
welcome 환영받는   ardent 열렬한
controversial 논란이 많은   disagree 동의하지 않다
concerned 우려하는   problematic 문제가 많은
lacking in ~이 결여된   artistic 예술적
excellence 탁월성

2 결과

해석 요즘 너무도 많은 사람들이 세계의 다양한 분쟁을 이해하는 데 있어 역사의 중요성을 인식하지 못한다. 예컨대 많은 미국인들은 미국과 이라크 사이의 전쟁에 대해 모든 것을 아는 체 하면서도 이라크의 역사에 대해 배우려고도 하지 않는다. 이런 종류의 무지(無知)는 잘못된 여론과 부적절한 정책으로 귀결될 것이다.

어구 unaware 의식하지 못하는   various 다양한
conflict 분쟁, 갈등   pretend to ~인 체 하다
ignorance 무지(無知)   public opinion 여론
inappropriate 부적절한
policy 정책; 보험증서(insurance~)

3 추리

해석 2008년 2월 10일, 화재가 발생하여 한국의 국보 제1호인 남대문을 불태워버렸다. 다음 날, 경찰은 용의자를 체포하여 밤새 심문했다. 방화범은 한국에서 가장 귀중하게 여겨지는 성문(城門)에 불을 질렀음을 시인했다. 경찰에 따르면, 그 남자는 토지 분쟁에 분노하여 일반 대중을 겨냥한 범죄를 저지름으로써 격한 감정을 해소하기로 결심했다고 한다.

어구 break out (나쁜 일이) 발발하다 burn down 전소시키다
treasure 보물   arrest 체포하다
suspect 용의자   question 심문하다
overnight 밤새도록   arsonist 방화범
set fire to ~에 불을 지르다   treasured 소중하게 여겨지는
gate 문, 성문   anger 분노시키다
dispute 분쟁
blow off steam 좋지 않은 감정을 해소하다
commit a crime 범죄를 저지르다

1

해석 우주 관광은 괜찮은 아이디어일까? 리차드 브랜슨과 같은 사람들은 그렇게 생각하여 일반 대중이 우주 관광을 할 수 있도록 만들 계획인 것 같다. 사실, 브랜슨은 대략 200건의 우주여행 예약이 이루어졌다고 주장한다. 물론, 수십만 달러가 소요될 것이다. 그러나 우주여행이 그만한 돈을 들일 만큼 가치가 있을까? 그냥 '재미'있게 놀기 위해 정말로 우주여행을 해야 하는 것일까? 그런 돈을 보다 의미 있는 활동에 소비하는 게 낫지 않을까?
(a) 리차드 브랜슨은 억만장자이다.
(b) 우주여행은 값비쌀 것이다.
(c) 우주여행은 따뜻할 것이다.

해설 추론 유형 가운데 '특성'에 해당하는 문제다. 일단 글에서 리차드 브랜슨이 억만장자라는 말이 전혀 언급되지 않았기 때문에 (a)는 정답이 될 수 없다. 그리고 (c)는 글에서 우주여행이 재미있을 것이라고 암시하기 때문에 정답이 될 수 없다. 따라서 정답은 (b)다.

어구 tourism 관광   available 이용할 수 있는
approximately 대략   reservation 예약
space travel 우주여행   worth 가치가 있는
meaningful 유의미한

정답 (b)

2

해석 스웨덴 신문과의 인터뷰에서, 도리스 레싱은 만약 배럭 오바마가 미국의 다음 대통령으로 선출된다면 틀림없이 암살당할 것이라고 말했다. 레싱은 KKK와 같은 인종차별주의 집단이 흑인 오바마를 '살해'할지도 모른다고 우려했다. 그녀에 따르면, 힐러리 클린턴이 미국 최초의 여성 대통령이 된다면 상황이 보다 차분할지도 모른다고 한다.
(a) 버락 오바마는 미국의 44대 대통령이다.
(b) 레싱은 오바마의 안전에 대해 걱정한다.
(c) 힐러리 클린턴은 미국 최초의 여성 대통령이다.

해설 추론 유형 가운데 '추리'에 해당하는 문제다. 글의 내용에서 가정법을 썼기 때문에 아직 일어나지 않은 일이라는 점을 추리할 수 있다. 따라서 (a)와 (c)는 정답이 될 수 없다. 반면 (b)는 글의 내용에서 자연스럽게 추리되므로 바로 정답이다.

어구 elect 선출하다   surely 확실히
assassinate 암살하다   racist 인종 차별주의자(의)
murder 살해하다   calm 차분한

정답 (b)

PRACTICE

1

해석 2008년 2월 11일, 블랙베리의 이메일 서비스에 이상이 생겨서 수많은 사용자들이 메시지를 보내거나 받을 수 없었다. 그렇지만 음성 서비스와 SMS 서비스는 중단되지 않았다. 몇 시간 동안 중단되고 나서, 서비스는 복구되었다. 이 서비스 중단은 블랙베리 스마트폰의 개선을 목적으로 한 업그레이드에서 비롯되었다. 유사한 서비스 단절 사태가 지난해에도 발생했다.

Q. 글로부터 추론할 수 있는 것은 무엇인가?
(a) 블랙베리 스마트폰은 견고하다.
(b) 서비스가 중단되는 동안에, 사용자들은 SMS 서비스를 이용할 수 없었다.
(c) 서비스 중단 사태는 몇 시간 동안 지속되었다.
(d) 서비스 중단 사태는 컴퓨터 바이러스 때문에 발생했다.

해설 추론 유형 가운데 '특성'에 해당하는 문제다. (a)는 글을 통해 알 수 없고, (b)는 내용과 반대이기 때문에 정답이 될 수 없다. 그리고 (d)는 업그레이드가 원인이라고 했기 때문에 정답이 될 수 없다. 따라서 정답은 (c)다.

어구 break down 고장 나다
prevent A from −ing A가 ~하는 것을 막다
interrupt 방해하다   outage 정전; 기능 정지
restore 복구하다
result from ~으로부터 비롯되다
aim at ~을 목표삼다   similar 유사한
disruption 중단, 단절

정답 (c)

2

해석 단지 15세였을 때, 조앤 바에즈는 마틴 루터 킹 주니어 목사가 비폭력과 민권에 대해 논의하는 것을 들었다. 바에즈는 목사의 연설에 깊이 감동을 받아 그 두 가지 대의명분을 증진시키는 데 삶을 헌신하기로 결심했다. 베트남 전쟁이 발발하고 나서, 그녀는 종종 반전 항의 시위에 참가했었다. 자신의 콘서트에서, 바에즈는 청중들에게 군에 입대하지 말라고 말했다. 이후에, 그녀는 인권 운동을 지원하는 것이 목적인 국제인권보호회 인권 위원회를 설립했다.

Q. 글로부터 추론할 수 있는 것은 무엇인가?
(a) 바에즈는 베트남 전쟁이 싸울 만한 가치가 있다고 믿었다.
(b) 바에즈는 루터 킹 주니어 목사와 친교 관계를 맺었다.
(c) 바에즈는 미국의 이익을 추구하는 데 관심이 있었다.
(d) 바에즈는 정치운동가였다.

해설 바에즈가 반전 시위에 참가한 것을 생각하면 (a)는 정답이 될 수 없다. (b)는 사실 관계가 올바르긴 하지만, 주어진 글에 나타나 있지 않기 때문에 정답이 아니다. (c)는 바에즈가 '비폭력'과 '민권'이라는 두 가지 대의명분의 증진에 헌신했다는 점에서 정답이 될 수 없다. 따라서 정답은 (d)다.

어구 nonviolence 비폭력   civil rights 민권
move 감동시키다
dedicate 헌신하다; 한정하다
promote 증진하다; 승진시키다   cause 대의명분; 원인
break out (전쟁 등이) 발생하다 protest 항의
military forces 군대   establish 설립하다
human rights 인권

정답 (d)

UNIT 4 일관성에서 벗어난 것

EXERCISE
1 (d)   2 (c)
PRACTICE
1 (b)   2 (d)

유형 정리

1 전혀 관련 없는 문장

해석 기업이 비윤리적 활동에 관여한다면 살아남지 못할 것이라고 생각합니다. (a) 또한 저는 제 고객에 대한 깊은 책임감을 갖고 있습니다. (b) 어떤 식으로든 고객을 해치는 것이 막대한 이득을 가져올 것이라고는 전혀 믿지 않습니다. (c) 제 고객들과 친근한 관계를 유지하고 있다는 점을 언급해야만 합니다. (d) 더욱이, 회사가 도덕적으로 적법한 방식으로 모든 일과 고객을 다루어야 한다는 것을 분명하게 의식하고 있습니다.

어구 survive 생존하다   engage in ~에 관여하다
unethical 비윤리적인   keen 예리한
responsibility 책임   client 고객
substantial 상당한   sharply 예리하게
aware 의식하는   morally 도덕적으로
legitimate 적법한

2 입장이 다른, 관련된 문장

해석 1911년 8월 21일, 모나리자 그림이 루브르에서 도난당했다. (a) 처음에 사람들은 길리움 아폴리네어가 도둑이라고 생각했다. (b) 그렇지만 어떤 이들은 빈센조 페루지아가 그 그림을 훔쳤다고 생각했다. (c) 이것은 아폴리네어가 그 박물관을 탐탁지 않게 여겼기 때문이었다. (d) 그렇지만 아폴리네어는 파블로 피카소가 그 대작을 훔쳤다고 의심했다.

어구 steal 훔치다   thief 도둑
approve of ~를 긍정적으로 여기다 cf. approve 승인하다
suspect 의심하다   masterpiece 대작

3 초점이 다른, 관련된 문장

해석 버나드 케틀웰은 나방 실험으로 유명했다. (a) 그에 따르면, 산업화된 지역에서는 어두운 색깔의 나방이 밝은 색깔의 나방에 비해 더 잘 생존한다고 한다. (b) 이것은 밝은 색깔의 나방이 오염되어서 어두운 색깔을 띠게 된 나무 곁에서 보다 쉽게 눈에 띄기 때문이었다. (c) 유감스럽게도, 그의 방법은 전혀 과학적이지 않았다. (d) 케틀웰은 헌신적인 교사였다.

어구 moth 나방   dark−colored 짙은 색의
light−colored 옅은 색의   industrial 산업의
pollute 오염시키다   darken 어둡게 하다
dedicated 헌신적인

EXERCISE

1

해석 2008년 2월 24일, 랄프 네이더는 대통령 선거에 출마하겠다고 발표했다. (a) NBC에 따르면, 네이더는 '제퍼슨적인 혁명'에 대한 급박한 필요가 있다고 믿는다고 한다. (b) 버락 오바마와 힐러리 클린턴은 모두 그의 결정을 비판했다. (c) 그들은 네이더의 결심이 공화당을 돕게 될 것이라고 우려했다. (d) 어떻든, 오바마와 힐러리는 서로를 증오했다.

해설 네이더의 대통령 선거 출마 선언을 오바마와 힐러리가 비판한다는 것이 주된 내용이다. (d)는 이런 내용의 흐름과 전혀 관계가 없기 때문에 정답이다.

어구 announce 발표하다   run for 출마하다
urgent 급박한   Jeffersonian 제퍼슨적인
revolution 혁명   criticize 비판하다
concerned 우려하는
the Republican Party 공화당

정답 (d)

2

해석 학생들이 흥미를 느끼도록 만드는 것이 어려울지도 모르지만, 교사는 수업 시간에 논의되는 주제에 대해 학생들이 공감하도록 만들기 위해 노력해야 한다. (a) 교사가 일정한 주제가 학생들에게 호소력이 없다고 생각하면 다른 흥미로운 주제를 선택할 수 있다. (b) 이것은 학생들이 주제를 흥미 있게 생각하지 않으면 그 주제에 대해 말을 할 가능성이 낮기 때문이다. (c) 어쨌든, 우리 학생들은 전반적으로 게으르다. (d) 따라서 토론 주제를 선택할 때는, 학생의 정서적 필요를 감안해야만 한다.

해설 토론 수업에서 학생의 정서적 요구에 부합하는 흥미로운 주제를 선택해야 함을 다룬 글이다. (c)는 이런 내용과 전혀 관계없는 내용이므로 정답이다.

어구 engage 흥미 있게 만들다
relate to ~에 공감하다; ~에 관계가 있다
certain 일정한, 확실한　　appealing 호소력이 있는
engaging 흥미로운　　generally 전반적으로
take A into account A를 고려하다, 참작하다

정답 (c)

PRACTICE

1

해석 샌디에이고에 기반을 둔 웰빙회사인 RealAge는 생물학적인 나이를 알아내는 독특한 도구를 제공한다. (a) http://www.realage.com/을 방문하여 무료 RealAge 검사를 받아 보라. (b) 다른 웹사이트들도 유사한 검사도구를 제공한다. (c) 검사 결과는 여러분의 RealAge가 생년월일에 따른 나이와 아주 다를 수 있어서 충격적일 수도 있다. (d) 예컨대 생년월일에 따른 나이가 36세라 하더라도 RealAge가 25세일 수도 있다.

해설 첫 번째 문장에서 '독특한 도구'라고 했으므로 다른 웹사이트들이 유사한 도구를 제공한다는 것은 주어진 글의 입장과 다르다. 따라서 정답은 (b)다. 참고로 실제로 지문에서 언급한 웹사이트에서 설명한 서비스를 제공하니 이용해 보기 바란다.

어구 based ~에 기반을 둔　　wellness 건강, 웰빙
unique 독특한　　biological 생물학적인
free 무료의　　similar 유사한

정답 (b)

2

해석 한번은 현대 사회가 직면한 주요 문제에 대해 논의했는데, 그녀는 '인간적인' 의사소통 문제를 주저하지 않고 언급했습니다. (a) 그녀가 분명하게 지적했듯이, 예술도 의사소통을 위한 매체입니다. (b) 그녀는 예술이 감수성이 예민한 사람들이 있는 세상을 만들 수 있다고 생각합니다. (c) 그런 세상이 나타난다면, 사람들은 진정으로 인간적인 의사소통을 하게 될 것입니다. (d) 제3차 세계대전이 일어날 것입니다.

해설 '인간적인' 의사소통을 위한 예술의 역할을 다룬 글이다. 전체 글의 흐름으로 보아 제3차 세계대전의 발발은 내용과 아무런 관련이 없다. 따라서 정답은 (d)다.

어구 major 주요한　　confront 직면하다
hesitant 주저하는　　mention 언급하다
humane 자애로운; 인도적인　　medium 매체; 영매
sensitive 감수성이 예민한　　engaged in ~에 관여하는
break out (전쟁 등이) 발발하다

정답 (d)

Chapter 2

UNIT 1　빈 칸이 처음에 있는 경우

EXERCISE
1 (c)　　2 (b)

PRACTICE
1 (d)　　2 (b)

유형 정리

1　전체 내용의 요약

해석 고대 그리스에서는 사람들이 신에 대해 자유롭게 말할 수가 없었다. 만약 도시의 신을 험담한다면 곤경에 처할 수도 있었다. 이것은 신을 중시하는 것이 사회생활의 중요한 일부였기 때문이다. 많은 이들은 신만이 사람들이 서로서로 잘 어울려 살아갈 수 있게 한다고 생각했다. 그래서 일부 사람들은 신에 대한 '존경'을 나타내기 위해 역사상 가장 현명한 사람을 죽이기까지 했다.

어구 free to V 자유롭게 ~할 수 있는
speak ill of ~를 나쁘게 말하다
get into trouble 곤란에 처하다
get along with ~와 사이좋게 지내다

2　배경 지식 제공

해석 번역이란 늘 고된 일이다. 놀랍게도 번역은 때때로 과학 지식에 영향을 끼치기도 한다. 예컨대, 이탈리아의 과학자 지오바니 비르지노 스치아파렐리는 화성 표면에서 본 것을 설명하기 위해 canali라는 단어를 사용했다. 일부 사람들은 이 단어를 운하(canal)로 번역했다. 이러한 번역은 화성에 운하를 지을 수 있는 지적인 생명체가 있을 수도 있다는 것을 암시하는 것이다. 올바른 번역은 수로(channel)인데, 운하와 달리 수로는 지적인 존재에 의해 만들어지는 것이 아니다.

어구 translation 번역　　affect ~에 영향을 미치다
describe 묘사하다, 기술(記述)하다
surface 표면　　suggest 제안하다; 시사하다
intelligent 지적인　　canal 운하
channel 수로

3　반박하려는 내용

해석 많은 이들이 '디 워'보다 더 형편없는 영화는 있을 수 없다고 말한다. 그러나 이 영화가 정말 그렇게 형편없을까? 이 영화를 정말로 주의 깊게 본다면, 이 놀라운 영화의 줄거리가 탄탄하다는 것을 알게 될 것이다. (영화 속의) 남자는 세상에 평화를 가져오기 위해 쓰여야 할 여자를 보호해야 할 운명이었다. 그러나 그는 그녀와 사랑에 빠져 세상으로부터 도망가려고 했다. 그렇지만 결국엔 그들의 사랑은 오래 갈 수 없었다. 꽤 슬프지 않은가? 이 영화는 또한 우리에게 '세상을 구해야 하는가 아니면 우리의 마음을 따라야 하는가?'라는 심오한 의문을 제기한다.

어구 terrible 끔찍한; 형편없는　　solid 고체의; 탄탄한
plot 줄거리; 계략
run away from ~로부터 도망가다
last 마지막의; 지속되다

EXERCISE

1

해석 소개팅은 <u>따분할 수도 있다</u>. 세상에는 어리석은 남자들이 많이 있어서 소개팅에서 만나는 사람이 그런 남자 가운데 하나일 수도 있다. 외모에만 관심이 있는 남자와 대화를 나눈다고 상상을 해 보라. 그 사람은 여러분의 마음을 헤아리지 못한다. 예술도 이해하지 못한다. 우둔한 사람이다. 계속 시계를 쳐다보게 될지도 모른다. 시간이 빨리 갔으면 하고 바란다. 재미있는 이야깃거리를 찾을 수가 없다. 그냥 그 남자를 떠나버렸으면 하고 바란다.

(a) 삶을 흥미진진하게 할
(b) 삶의 진정한 의미를 깨우치게 할
(c) 따분할

해설 글 전체에 걸쳐서 미팅이나 소개팅이 따분할 수도 있음을 말하고 있다. '시계를 쳐다본다'거나 '시간이 빨리 갔으면 하고 바란다' 등의 내용은 모두 지루한 상황을 말하고 있으므로 정답은 (c)다. (a)는 이런 내용과 정반대되는 내용이고 (b)는 글의 내용과 거리가 멀다.

어구 blind date 미팅, 소개팅   boring 지루한, 따분한
date 데이트 상대   looks 외모
appreciate 이해하다; 감사하다
dull 우둔한; 무딘

정답 (c)

2

해석 어떤 이들은 명상을 하기 위해서는 <u>스승의 도움이 필요하다고</u> 말한다. 그러나 그렇지가 않다. 명상이란 자신의 내면을 바라보려고 노력하는 것이다. 자신의 내면에는 좋은 것도 있고 나쁜 것도 있다. 명상을 하기 위해서는 그것들을 있는 그대로 보아야 한다. 어떤 스승도 그 일을 대신해줄 수는 없다. 자신만이 자신의 내면을 볼 수 있다. 요컨대, 명상이란 외부의 도움을 필요로 하지 않는다.

(a) 많은 돈을 써야 한다고
(b) 스승의 도움이 필요하다고
(c) 자신을 편안한 상태로 하는 편이 낫다고

해설 글 전체에 걸쳐서 명상을 하는 데 외부의 도움이 필요하지 않다는 점을 누차 언급하고 있으므로 정답은 (b)다. (a)는 글에서 전혀 언급되어 있지 않고, (c)는 명상의 전제 조건일 수는 있겠지만 글에서 말하고자 하는 바와는 거리가 멀다.

어구 meditate 명상하다; 꾀하다   meditation 명상
in short 요컨대   require 요하다

정답 (b)

PRACTICE

1

해석 제라드 램버트는 1886년에 미국에서 태어났다. 어떤 의미에서, 그는 <u>건축가가 되기로 되어</u> 있었다. 왜냐하면 콜롬비아 대학에서 건축학을 전공했기 때문이다. 그렇지만, 놀랍게도 그는 성공적인 광고인이 되었다. 일례로, 아버지의 발명품인 Listerine을 광고하기 위해 그는 뛰어난 아이디어를 생각해냈다. 그는 사람들에게 그 새로운 구강청정제를 사용함으로써 사교적 상황에서 체면을 살릴 수 있다고 말했다.

Q. 빈 칸에 들어갈 가장 적절한 보기를 선택하시오.
(a) 용감한 병사가 되기로 되어
(b) 훌륭한 광고인이 되기로 되어
(c) 발명가가 되기로 되어
(d) 건축가가 되기로 되어

해설 주의해야 하는 문제 유형이다. 정답은 (d)인데, 밑줄 친 부분이 들어 있는 문장에 대한 설명이 바로 다음 문장이기 때문이다. 대학에서 건축학을 전공했으므로 건축가가 되는 것이 자연스럽다. 나머지 내용은 모두 이에 어긋난다. 이처럼 빈 칸 채우기 유형에서는 전후 흐름을 판단해야 함을 기억하자.

어구 be supposed to ~하기로 되어 있다
architect 건축가   major in ~를 전공하다
architecture 건축학; 건축 양식
advertiser 광고인, 광고주
come up with ~를 생각해내다
mouthwash 구강세척제   save face 체면을 살리다

정답 (d)

2

해석 TV 프로그램인 버피 더 뱀파이어 슬레이어는 여러 해 동안 아주 많은 미국인들로부터 사랑을 받았다. 2003년에 이 TV 시리즈가 종영되었을 때, 수백만의 미국인들은 버피와 그의 친구들을 떠나보내고 싶지 않아 하면서 울었다. 이것은 이 프로가 아주 놀라워서가 아니라 이 프로가 있다는 것이 많은 미국인들로 하여금 사랑과 배려를 받고 있다고 느끼게 했기 때문이었다. 이렇게 이 프로는 미국인들에게 위안을 주었다.

Q. 빈 칸에 들어갈 가장 적절한 보기를 선택하시오.
(a) 로부터 미움을 받았다
(b) 로부터 사랑을 받았다
(c) 에게 아무런 의미도 갖지 못했다
(d) 에게 나쁜 영향을 미쳤다

해설 전반적인 글의 흐름을 통해 (b)를 답으로 선택할 수 있다. 내용 가운데 이 프로가 미국인들에게 '사랑과 배려'를 베풀었고 '위안을 주었다'는 말이 나오기 때문에, 이에 대한 미국인들의 자연스러운 반응은 이 프로에 대해 애정을 갖는 것으로 해석할 수 있다. 이는 이 프로의 종영에 대한 미국인들의 반응으로도 이해할 수 있다. 글의 전반적인 흐름을 파악해야 하는 문제인데, 이것이 빈 칸 채우기의 전형적인 유형임을 명심하자.

어구 slayer 살인자   unwilling to ~하기를 꺼려하는
presence 존재   comfort 위로하다

정답 (b)

UNIT 2 빈 칸이 중간에 있는 경우

EXERCISE
1 (b)   2 (b)

PRACTICE
1 (c)   2 (b)

유형 정리

1 주제 관련 내용

해석 많은 발명들은 호기심이 많은 과학자들에 의해 이루어진다. 펄시 스펜서의 예를 들어보자. 그는 레이딘사(社)에 근무하는 과학자였다. 한 번은 그가 자전관(磁電管)을 마주보게 되었는데, 주머니에 들어 있던 막대사탕이 녹았다는 사실을 알아차렸다. 이후에 그는

자전관 앞에 팝콘을 놓아두었는데, 팝콘이 뻥 하고 터지는 것을 바라보았다. 이런 관찰에 바탕을 두어, 그는 전자렌지를 발명했다.

어구 invention 발명, 발명품   curious 호기심이 많은
happen to 우연히 ~하다   face ~로 향하다
magnetron 자전관(磁電管)   notice 알아차리다
candy bar 막대사탕   thaw 녹다
pop 뻥하고 터지다   based on ~에 바탕을 둔
observation 관찰 *cf.* observance 준수
microwave oven 전자렌지

2 연결 내용

해석 한때 소크라테스는 '성찰하지 않은 삶은 살 가치가 없다'고 말했다. 그가 의미했던 바는 어떤 방식으로 살아가고 있는지를 검토해야 한다는 것이다. 우리 자신의 만족만을 위해 살아가는가? 가치 있는 명분을 위해 살아가는가? 우리는 정말 우리 자신을 아는 것일까? 소크라테스에 따르면, 너무도 많은 사람들이 삶의 진정한 의미를 모른다고 한다. 자기 성찰을 통해서만 존재의 의미를 찾을 수 있다.

어구 unexamined 검토되지 않은   worth –ing ~할 가치가 있는
examine 검토하다   satisfaction 만족
worthy 가치 있는   cause 대의명분; 원인
self–examination 자기 성찰   existence 존재

3 반전

해석 요즘, 많은 한국 여성들은 남자친구들에게 초콜릿을 사서 주는 것으로 발렌타인데이를 경축한다. 그들은 그렇게 하는 것이 사랑을 표현하는 유일한 방법이라고 생각하는 것 같다. 그러나 그렇지가 않다. 전통적으로, 사람들은 사랑의 쪽지를 교환함으로써 발렌타인데이를 경축했다. 실은, 이런 전통적 방식이 그런 하찮은 과자류를 사는 것보다 훨씬 더 낭만적이다.

어구 celebrate 경축하다   express 표현하다
traditionally 전통적으로   exchange 교환하다
note 쪽지   romantic 낭만적인
silly 하찮은; 어리석은

EXERCISE

1

해석 사이버스토킹은 다른 사람을 스토킹하기 위해 인터넷을 사용하는 것을 말한다. 사이버스토커들은 목표로 하는 인물을 찾기 위해 다양한 방법을 사용한다. 예컨대 그들은 야후, 구글, 그리고 MSN과 같은 검색 엔진을 이용한다. 온라인 포럼과 채팅룸도 그런 나쁜 사람들에 의해 자주 이용된다. 세컨드라이프와 같은 온라인 공동체도 사이버스토커의 희생자를 찾는 '유용한' 방법이 될 수 있다.
(a) 경찰을 피하기 위해
(b) 목표로 하는 인물을 찾기 위해
(c) 범죄 피해자를 돕기 위해

해설 주제 관련 내용을 묻는 문제다. 다양한 예가 제시되어 있는데, 그 예들은 모두 마지막 문장에서 설명하듯이, '희생자를 찾기 위한' 방법들에 해당된다. 따라서 정답은 이와 연결되는 (b)다.

어구 cyberstalking 사이버스토킹   stalk 몰래 접근하다
a variety of 다양한   target 표적
search engine 검색 엔진   community 공동체
victim 희생자

정답 (b)

2

해석 리즈 위더스푼은 탁월한 배우일 뿐만 아니라 인정이 많은 인물이다. 다른 여성들을 아끼기 때문에, 위더스푼은 아본 재단의 명예 의장직을 수행하기로 결심했다. 재단의 사명은 '전 세계적으로 여성의 삶을 향상시키는' 것이다. 재단과 함께, 위더스푼은 사람들이 유방암과 가정폭력을 예방하는 일의 중요성을 인식하도록 하기 위해 열심히 노력하고 있다.
(a) 전세계를 여행하고 싶기
(b) 다른 여성들을 아끼기
(c) 아동들을 아끼기

해설 연결 내용을 묻는 문제다. 바로 앞에서 '인정이 많은 인물'이라고 말했고, 그 다음에 이어지는 내용들이 모두 Witherspoon이 다른 여성들을 위해 일하는 내용이므로 정답은 (b)다.

어구 excellent 뛰어난   actor 배우
caring 인정이 많은
serve as ~의 역할을 하다   honorary 명예직의
chairperson 의장   foundation 재단
mission 사명   globally 전 세계적으로
aware of ~를 의식하는   domestic violence 가정폭력

정답 (b)

PRACTICE

1

해석 생강이 위약(僞藥)보다 정말로 멀미가 가시는 데 도움이 될까? 어떤 연구는 이런 주장을 뒷받침한다. 다른 연구들은 그렇지 않다. 예컨대 미시간대학 의료센터에 의한 연구는 생강이 위약보다 멀미를 예방하는 데 훨씬 더 효과적이라는 점을 입증했다. 반면, 아르핀과 그의 동료들에 의한 연구는 생강과 위약 사이에 효능에서 큰 차이가 없다는 점을 밝혀냈다.

Q. 문장을 가장 알맞게 완성하는 선택지를 고르시오.
(a) 과학자들이 그 사실을 알고 있었기 때문이다.
(b) 많은 실험이 있었기 때문이다.
(c) 다른 연구들은 그렇지 않다.
(d) 다른 연구들이 그것을 증명하는 데 도움이 된다.

해설 주제 관련 내용을 묻는 문제다. 전체 내용에서 생강과 위약 사이의 효능에 대한 차이가 있다는 연구 결과와 그렇지 않다는 연구 결과가 제시되므로, 정답은 (c)다. 다른 선택지들은 전체 글의 흐름에 어울리지 않는다.

어구 ginger 생강   relieve (고통을) 경감하다
motion sickness 멀미   placebo 위약(僞藥)
support 뒷받침하다   effective 효과적인
prevent 예방하다   on the other hand 반면
colleague 동료   significant 차이가 큰
efficacy 효능

정답 (c)

2

해석 경영은 사업에 관한 것이 아니라 사람에 관한 것이며, 글로벌경영도 예외가 아니다. 훌륭한 경영은 인간의 본성에 대한 보다 깊이 있는 이해에서만 비롯된다. 글로벌 경영의 경우에는, 또한 문화적 차이를 고려해야 한다. 그렇지만 이것은 인간의 본성이 문화마다 다르다는 것을 뜻하지는 않는다. 이것은 인간의 본성이 문화에 따라 서로 다른 방식으로 표현될 수 있다는 것을 뜻한다.

Q. 문장을 가장 알맞게 완성하는 선택지를 고르시오.

(a) 정치적 요인을 살펴봐야
(b) 문화적 차이를 고려해야
(c) 글로벌 비즈니스의 진정한 목적을 생각해야
(d) 사회와 개인 사이의 관계를 검토해야

해설 연결 내용을 묻는 문제다. 바로 다음에서 문화적 차이가 언급되기 때문에 (b)가 가장 자연스럽다. 또한 바로 앞에 '글로벌 경영의 경우'라는 말이 있기 때문에 세계 여러 지역을 대상으로 한다는 점을 짐작할 수 있다.

어구 management 경영
be concerned with ~와 관계되다
global 세계적인   exception 예외
understanding 이해
human nature 인간의 본성   vary 다르다
express 표현하다   according to ~에 따라

정답 (b)

UNIT 3   빈 칸이 마지막에 있는 경우

EXERCISE

1 (c)   2 (b)

PRACTICE

1 (d)   2 (b)

유형 정리

1   중심 내용

해석 근본적으로, 새로운 언어를 배우는 것은 그 언어로 의미를 구성하는 방법을 배우는 과정이다. 짐작할 수 있듯이, 새로운 언어에는 의미 있는 문장을 구성하기 위한 다른 규칙이 있을 수도 있다. 보다 중요한 사항으로, 새로운 언어에는 우리가 살아가는 세상을 해석하는 다른 방식이 있을지도 모른다. 이런 의미에서, 다른 언어를 배우는 것은 그 언어로 생각하는 방법을 배우는 과정이다.

어구 basically 근본적으로   process 과정
construct 구성하다; 개념   meaningful 의미 있는
interpret 해석하다; 통역하다

2   결론

해석 너무도 많은 사람들이 수단이 항상 목적에 의해 정당화된다고 믿는다. 이것은 그들이 어떤 대가를 치르더라도 좋은 결과를 보고 싶어하기 때문일 수도 있다. 그렇지만 그런 사람들은 모든 행동에는 긍정적이든 부정적이든 몇몇 종류의 결과가 발생한다는 것을 의식할 필요가 있다. 많은 경우에, '잘못된' 수단의 결과는 다른 사람들을 다치게 할 수 있다. 이것은 '올바른' 목적을 성취하기 위해 어떤 수단이든 정당화하려고 하는 그런 종류의 사고로부터 비롯된 것이다. 따라서 수단은 윤리적 성찰에 의해 통제를 받아야 한다.

어구 means 수단, 방법   justify 정당화하다
end 목적   cost 대가
effect 효과, 결과   positive 긍정적인
negative 부정적인
result from ~으로부터 비롯되다

---

achieve 성취하다   thus 따라서
ethical 윤리적인   consideration 성찰, 고려

3   내용 요약

해석 디자인이 생활의 모든 측면에 영향을 미치는 시대에, 훌륭한 디자이너는 다양한 특성을 개발해야만 한다. 물론, 아름다움에 대한 예리한 감각을 가져야 한다. 또한 인간의 기능에 대한 깊은 이해를 성취해야만 한다. 마지막으로 창의력을 길러야만 한다. 요컨대 이 시대의 훌륭한 디자이너는 미(美)를 감상할 수 있어야 하고, 인간이 어떻게 기능하는지를 이해해야 하며, 창의적이어야 한다.

어구 age 시대   affect 영향을 미치다
aspect 측면   various 다양한
quality 특성, 품질   keen 예리한
in addition 더욱이   functioning 기능성
creativity 창의성   in short 요컨대
appreciate 이해하다; 감사하다
creative 창의적인

EXERCISE

1

해석 심지어 오늘날에도, 많은 사람들은 우리가 두뇌의 10%만을 활용한다고 생각한다. 그렇지만 에릭 추들러 박사에 따르면, 그런 주장을 뒷받침하는 '어떤 과학적 증거도 없다'고 한다. 박사는 모든 신경세포들이 항상 기능한다고 지적한다. 또한 보다 큰 두뇌가 우리에게 이점을 주지 않는다면 왜 발달되었겠는가라고 질문한다. 요컨대 우리가 두뇌의 10%만을 활용한다는 주장은 <u>잘못된 믿음이다.</u>
(a) 많은 점에서 우리에게 도움이 된다
(b) 연구를 더 요한다
(c) 잘못된 믿음이다

해설 중심 내용을 묻는 문제다. 두 번째 문장에서 '우리가 두뇌의 10%만을 활용한다'는 주장을 뒷받침하는 과학적 증거가 없다고 했으므로, 이 주장은 잘못된 믿음이라는 것을 알 수 있다. 따라서 정답은 (c)다.

어구 brain 두뇌   evidence 증거
support 뒷받침하다   point out 지적하다
nerve cell 신경 세포   work 작동하다
develop 발달시키다   advantage 이점
myth 잘못된 믿음; 신화

정답 (c)

2

해석 행동과 가치관의 변화가 인종 갈등과 관련된 문제를 해결할 수 있는가? 물론 그렇지는 않다. 이것은 인종 갈등이 일정한 행동 유형이나 가치관으로부터가 아니라, 서로 다른 집단들 사이의 권력 투쟁으로부터 비롯되기 때문이다. 결과적으로, 인종 차별은 사회의 정치·경제적 구조에 반영되어 있고 또한 그에 의해 강화된다. 따라서 미국에서의 인종 갈등을 해소하기 위해서는, <u>미국 사회의 정치·경제적 구조를 바꾸어야만 한다.</u>
(a) 미국 사회의 행동 유형과 가치관을 바꾸다
(b) 미국 사회의 정치·경제적 구조를 바꾸다
(c) 미국 사회의 인종 차별을 무시하다

해설 결론을 묻는 문제다. 인종 갈등이나 차별이 사회의 정치·경제적 구조와 밀접하게 관련을 맺는다는 입장이므로 이에 따른 결론은 (b)다. (a)는 글에서 부정하는 입장이기 때문에 정답이 될 수 없다.

또한 (c)는 문제를 해결하는 태도가 아니므로 정답이 될 수 없다.

어구 behavior 행동 　　　　values 가치관
related to ~와 관련된 　　racial 인종의
conflict 갈등
result from ~으로부터 비롯되다
struggle 투쟁 　　　　　power 권력
certain 일정한; 확실한 　onsequently 결과적으로
discrimination 차별 　　reflect 반영하다
reinforce 강화하다 　　structure 구조
resolve 해소하다

정답 (b)

PRACTICE

1

해석 안개와 박무(薄霧) 사이에는 몇 가지 차이가 있다. 첫째, 안개가 박무보다 더 두껍다. 둘째, 안개가 낄 때 바라보는 데 더 큰 어려움이 생긴다. 가시거리가 1킬로미터 미만이면, 안개가 있다는 것을 안다. 가시거리가 1킬로미터에서 2킬로미터 사이이면, 박무가 있는 것이다. 그렇지만, 이런 차이에도 불구하고, 안개와 박무는 모두 지표에 접촉하는 구름이다.

Q. 문장을 가장 알맞게 완성하는 선택지를 고르시오.
(a) 하늘 높이 오르다
(b) 많은 도시에서 대기 오염을 일으킨다
(c) 건강의 소중함을 일깨워주다
(d) 지표에 접촉하다

해설 '차이에도 불구하고'라는 말이 있기 때문에, 안개와 박무 사이의 공통점이 제시되어야 한다. 선택지 가운데 (a)와 (b)는 상식적으로 올바른 내용이 아니다. 반면 (c)는 전혀 관계없는 내용이다. 따라서 정답은 (d)다.

어구 fog 안개 　　　　　mist 박무(薄霧)
visibility 가시거리 　　exist 존재하다
present 존재하는 　　　contact 접촉하다
surface 표면

정답 (d)

2

해석 영화 스파이더맨2는 이 잔혹한 세상에서 진정한 영웅으로 살아가는 것이 무엇인가를 끊임없이 상기시키는 영화이다. 영화에서, 피터 파커는 초영웅으로서 그리고 대학생으로서의, 자신의 이중 정체성 때문에 많이 괴로워한다. 너무도 괴로워해서 그냥 평범한 삶을 영위하기를 원하는데, 그래서 영웅으로서 행동하는 것을 그만두기로 결심한다. 그러나 강한 의무감 때문에 그는 초영웅으로서의 역할로 되돌아와서 도시를 파괴로부터 구해낸다. 이런 의미에서, 파커는 좋은 사람일 뿐만 아니라 또한 진정한 영웅이다.

Q. 문장을 가장 알맞게 완성하는 선택지를 고르시오.
(a) 뛰어난 대학생
(b) 진정한 영웅
(c) 유명한 배우
(d) 정신병자

해설 중심 내용을 묻는 문제다. 첫 번째 문장에서 '진정한 영웅'을 말했고, 이에 따라 글 전체는 진정한 영웅이라는 것이 무엇을 뜻하는가를 밝히는 내용으로 구성되어 있다. 따라서 정답은 (b)다.

어구 constant 끊임없는 　　reminder 상기시키는 것
hero 영웅 　　　　　　cruel 잔혹한
suffer 괴로워하다 　　dual 이중의

identity 정체성 　　　　superhero 초영웅
severely 혹독하게 　　ordinary 평범한
sense of duty 의무감 　destruction 파괴

정답 (b)

UNIT 4 연결어 선택

EXERCISE
1 (c) 　　　**2** (b)

PRACTICE
1 (d) 　　　**2** (b)

유형 정리

1 역접

해석 어린 아이였을 때, 발레 동작을 배웠다. 발레의 섬세한 아름다움 때문에 발레리나가 되겠다고 결심할 뻔 했다. 그렇지만 아름다움을 영구적인 방식으로 포착하는 데 훨씬 더 관심이 있었기 때문에 생각을 바꾸었다. 그럼에도 불구하고, 발레 수업은 인간의 형체의 아름다움에 대해 많은 것을 가르쳐주었다. 인체의 모든 부분이 완벽하게 균형을 이룰 때, 인체는 진정한 아름다움이 무엇인지를 보여줄 수 있다.

어구 ballet 발레 　　　　　movement 동작
subtle 미묘한 　　　　ballerina 발레리나
capture 포착하다 　　permanent 영구적인
nevertheless 그럼에도 불구하고
form 모양 　　　　　balance 균형

2 결과

해석 미국인 선생님으로부터 처음으로 꾸지람을 들었을 때, 나는 한국과 미국의 문화 차이 때문에 곤혹스러웠다. 한국에서는 연장자가 꾸짖으면, 연장자와의 시선 접촉을 피하고 그냥 아래를 내려다보아야 한다. 당연히, 그 미국인 선생님이 꾸짖을 때, 시선 접촉을 피하려고 했는데, 이 때문에 그 선생님은 화가 나셨다. 뭔가 잘못되었음에 틀림없다고 느꼈다. 그래서 '미국인들은 연장자에 대한 존경심을 어떻게 표현할까?'라고 궁금하게 되었다.

어구 admonish 꾸짖다 　　puzzled 곤혹스러운
cultural 문화적인 　　elder 연장자
scold 꾸짖다 　　　　avoid 피하다
eye contact 시선 접촉 　naturally 당연히
tell off 꾸짖다 　　　respect 존경, 존중

3 보완

해석 제니퍼 스미스는 수학 분야에서 아주 많은 상을 수상했습니다. 물론, 그 상들은 스미스 양에 대해 많은 것을 말해줄 수 있습니다. 그렇지만, 보다 중요한 사항으로, 스미스 양은 수학의 진정한 목적이 궁극적인 진리에 도달하는 것이라는 점을 알고 있습니다. 동시에, 스미스 양은 사람들의 행동 방식을 결정하는 것이 무엇인지에 대해 아주 호기심이 많은, 순진무구한 소녀입니다. 스미스 양은 자신을 둘러싼 모든 가능성을 기꺼이 탐구하려고 하는, 순진무

구한 소녀입니다.

어구 award 상   field 분야
mathematics 수학
be aware that ~라는 것을 의식하다
ultimate 궁극적인   innocent 순진무구한
what makes ~ tick ~의 행동 방식을 결정하다
explore 탐구하다; 탐험하다

EXERCISE

1

해석 2007년 2월 2일, 치자색 눈이 서부 시베리아에 내렸다. 어떤 이들은 그 눈이 대기 오염 때문에 생겼을 수도 있다고 염려했다. 관계 당국은 이 이상한 현상을 설명할 수 없었다. 후에 그 눈이 유독하지 않다는 사실이 밝혀졌다. <u>그럼에도 불구하고</u>, 주민들은 그 눈을 사용하지 말라는 명령을 받았다. 이것은 주로 그 눈에 들어 있는 철의 함량이 평상시보다 더 높았기 때문이다.
(a) 예컨대
(b) 따라서
(c) 그럼에도 불구하고

해설 역접의 연결어를 묻는 문제다. 눈이 유독하지 않다는 내용과 사용해서는 안 된다는 내용은 대립 관계에 있기 때문에 역접의 연결어가 자연스럽다. (a)의 예시나 (b)의 결과를 나타내는 연결어가 올 수 없다. 따라서 정답은 (c)다.

어구 orange-yellow 치자색   western 서부의
air pollution 대기 오염
authorities concerned 관계 당국
phenomenon 현상   toxic 유독한
resident 주민   content 함유량

정답 (c)

2

해석 '널 증오해, 너도 날 증오해, 우리는 문제 가정이야'라고 안티 바니 노래 가운데 한 곡은 시작한다. 어떤 이들은 그런 노래들이 그 어리석은 등장인물을 놀리는 우스운 방법일 뿐이라고 생각할지도 모른다. 그렇지만 문제는 그런 노래들에 깊은 증오가 분명하게 반영되어 있다는 것이다. 널리 알려져 있듯이, 증오는 해소하기가 쉽지 않다. <u>따라서</u> 그런 노래들을 보다 심각하게 받아들일 필요가 있다.
(a) 그렇지만
(b) 따라서
(c) 이와는 대조적으로

해설 결과의 연결어를 묻는 문제다. 증오가 해소하기 쉽지 않다는 점에서 증오가 배어 있는 노래들을 보다 심각하게 받아들여야 한다고 결론을 내릴 수 있으므로 정답은 (b)다. 역접을 나타내는 (a)나 (c)가 정답이 될 수 없다.

어구 hate 증오하다
dysfunctional family 문제 가정
funny 우스운   make fun of ~를 놀리다
character 등장인물   clearly 분명하게
reflect 반영하다   hatred 증오
resolve 해소하다
take A seriously A를 심각하게 받아들이다

정답 (b)

PRACTICE

1

해석 매트펀 읍은 내게는 내 자신의 고향인 것처럼 들린다. 실은, 나는 도시가 아니라 시골에서 자라났다. 그리고 내 생각에는 시골 생활이 정서적 성장에 좋은 영향을 미치는 것 같다. 반면, 대도시에서의 생활은 종종 우리 감정에 부정적으로 영향을 미친다. 이것은 주로 사람들이 대도시에서는 다른 사람들을 진정으로 알게 되는 기회를 많이 갖지 못하기 때문이다.

Q. 문장을 가장 알맞게 완성하는 선택지를 고르시오.
(a) 그래서
(b) 어떻든
(c) 예컨대
(d) 반면

해설 역접의 연결어를 묻는 문제다. 시골 생활과 대도시에서의 생활이 대립 관계에 있으므로 정답은 (d)다. (a)의 결과나 (c)의 예시를 나타내는 선택지가 정답이 될 수 없음에 유의해야 한다.

어구 town 읍
sound as if ~인 것처럼 들리다
hometown 고향   in the country 시골에서
impact 영향   emotional 정서적인
growth 성장   affect 영향을 미치다
negative 부정적인   opportunity 기회

정답 (d)

2

해석 단지 보다 자주 글을 쓴다고 해서 글 쓰는 능력이 향상될까? 대개는 그렇지 않다. 부분적인 이유는 글쓰기가 자기 자신의 아이디어를 검토할 것을 요구하기 때문이다. 자신의 생각을 살펴보면, 생각 가운데 대부분이 충분히 명확하지 않다는 것을 알게 되어 놀랄 것이다. 덧붙여, 그런 생각들을 강력하게 표현할 것이 기대된다. 물론, 이것은 노고와 창의성을 함의한다. <u>따라서</u> 글을 잘 쓰기 위해서는, 명확하게 그리고 창의적으로 생각하는 법을 배워야 한다.

Q. 문장을 가장 알맞게 완성하는 선택지를 고르시오.
(a) 그럼에도 불구하고
(b) 따라서
(c) 대신에
(d) 다행스럽게도

해설 결과의 연결어를 묻는 문제다. 글 쓰는 능력을 향상시키기 위해서는 명확하게 생각하고 강력하게 표현할 수 있어야 한다고 했으므로, 이에 대한 결론에 해당하는 문장 앞에는 (b)와 같은 연결어가 오는 것이 자연스럽다.

어구 skill 능력   improve 향상되다
require 요구하다   examine 검토하다
clear 명확한   in addition 더욱이
powerfully 강력하게   imply 함의하다
creativity 창의성   clearly 명확하게
creatively 창의적으로

정답 (b)

Chapter 3

UNIT 1 전반적 정보 Ⅰ

EXERCISE
1 (c)   2 (b)

PRACTICE
1 (c)   2 (b)

유형 정리

1 주제 찾기

해석 사실, 조안 캐틀린 롤링은 천재 작가이다. 겨우 여섯 살 때, 그녀는 최초의 판타지 이야기를 썼다. 이 이야기는 병든 토끼와, 엄청나게 큰 꿀벌을 포함한 그 병든 토끼의 친구들에 관한 것이었다. 학교에 다니면서, 그녀는 자신의 책에 등장하는 인물들에 대한 아이디어를 얻었다. 기차를 타고 런던으로 여행하면서, 판타지소설들에 대한 아이디어를 떠올렸는데, 이 판타지 소설은 이후에 해리 포터 시리즈로 알려지게 되었다.

어구 genius 천재   fantasy 공상; 판타지
huge 거대한   character 등장인물; 성격

2 제목 정하기

해석 나노테크놀러지는 원자만큼 아주 작은 장치를 개발하는 것과 관련된다. 어떤 이들은 그렇게 작은 장치를 일상생활에서는 쓸 수 없다고 생각한다. 글쎄, 어쩌면 그것이 가능할지도 모른다. 그렇지만 현재 그 기술은 얼룩에 저항할 수 있는 옷, 그리고 해로운 세균을 죽일 수 있는 붕대를 만드는 데 쓰인다. 많은 과학자들은 나노테크놀러지가 훨씬 더 많은 면에서 일상생활을 향상시키는 데 사용될 것이라고 예측한다.

어구 be concerned with ~에 관계되다   tiny 극미한
stain 얼룩; 오점   germ 세균

3 글의 목적 파악

해석 혈액형과 성격 사이에 관계가 있을까? 1927년에 다케지 후루카와는 자신이 출간한 한 논문에서 혈액형을 검토함으로써 성격에 대해 보다 많은 것을 알아낼 수 있다고 주장했다. 그의 주장은 과학적 근거가 전혀 없었지만, 마사히코 노미와 같은 일부 사람들은 후루카와가 옳다고 생각했다. 노미는 그런 잘못된 믿음에 바탕을 두어 책을 쓰기까지 했다.

어구 relationship 관계, 관련   blood type 혈액형
personality 성격   publish 출간하다
examine 검토하다; 진찰하다   basis 기초, 토대
mistaken 그릇된

EXERCISE

1

해석 경제가 성장하면, 농장에서 일하는 사람들의 숫자가 줄어든다. 대신, 보다 많은 사람들이 공장과 서비스업계에서 일한다. 따라서 보다 많은 사람들이 시골 지역보다 도시에서 살게 된다. 경제 성장의 초기 단계에서는 도시가 공장을 짓는 데보다 공공 설비에 보다 많은 돈을 소비한다. 후기 단계에서는 공장을 짓는 데 보다 많은 돈이 소비된다.

(a) 현명하게 돈을 소비하는 방법
(b) 시골 지역에 공장 짓기
(c) 경제 성장의 단계

해설 전반적으로 경제 성장의 단계를 설명하고 있으므로 정답은 (c)다. (a), (b) 모두 글의 내용과 거리가 멀거나 내용과 일치하지 않는다. 오답의 유형도 더불어 파악해두자.

어구 economy 경제(체제)   industry 산업; 근면
rural 시골의   stage 무대; 단계
public 대중; 공공의   facility 설비; 재능
construct 개념; 건설하다

정답 (c)

2

해석 현재 과학자들은 외계인이 존재하는지 또는 그렇지 않는지를 모른다. 그렇지만 많은 과학자들은 일정한 조건만 충족된다면 다른 행성에 외계인이 살 수 있다고 믿는다. 과학자들 대부분은 그런 조건이 지구의 조건과 비슷해야 한다고 생각한다. 일부 과학자들은 그런 조건 없이도 살 수 있는 다른 형태의 생명체가 있을 수도 있다고 믿는다. 어느 쪽이 옳은지는 시간이 흘러야만 알 수 있을 것이다.

(a) 중요한 문제에 답하지 못하는 과학자들을 비판하기 위해서
(b) 외계인에 대한 서로 다른 입장을 설명하기 위해서
(c) 외계인이 존재하지 않는다는 것을 증명하기 위해서

해설 전체적으로 외계인의 존재에 대한 서로 다른 입장을 설명하고 있으므로 정답은 (b)다. (a)는 지나치게 일반적인 내용으로 글의 내용과 어울리지 않는다. 반면 (c)는 글에서 취한 입장과 다르기 때문에 정답이 될 수 없다.

어구 alien 외국인; 외계인   certain 일정한; 확실한
condition 조건; 상태

정답 (b)

PRACTICE

1

해석 요즘 많은 언어순수주의자들은 문자 메시지를 보내는 것에 대해 분노한다. 그들 생각에는 문자 메시지를 보낼 때 쓰는 짧은 '말'들이 훌륭한 영어가 아니다. 그들은 BTW(by the way, 그건 그렇고)와 IMO(in my opinion, 내 생각으로는)와 같은 표현에 눈살을 찌푸린다. 짐작할 수 있듯이, 그들은 이모티콘을 결코 좋아하지 않는다. 그들의 입장도 일리가 있을 수 있지만, 많은 이들은 일상생활에서 의사소통하는 쓸모 있는 방식에 대해 언어순수주의자들이 과민 반응한다고 느낀다.

Q. 글의 제목으로 가장 알맞은 것은?
(a) 일상생활에서 문자 메시지를 보내는 것의 중요성
(b) 이모티콘을 정확하게 쓰는 방법
(c) 간단한 표현에 대해 분노하는 언어순수주의자들
(d) 훌륭한 영어를 쓰는 것의 중요성

해설 전반적으로 문자 메시지에서 쓰이는 축약된 표현에 대해 언어순수주의자들이 분노하고 있다는 내용을 다루기 때문에 정답은 (c)다. 정답을 (d)로 착각할 수도 있지만, 이 글이 문자 메시지에서 쓰이는 간단한 표현에 대한 언어순수주의자들의 반응에 초점을 맞추고 있기 때문에 정답은 될 수 없다. 전반적인 흐름과 함께 어디에 초점을 맞추는지를 파악하는 연습이 필요하다.

focus on ~에 초점을 맞추다
meet the need 수요를 충족시키다

attend 참석하다   meeting 회의
common 공동의   interests 이익

develop 개발하다   materials 자료, 재료

2

해석 안젤리나 졸리가 베버리힐즈 고등학교를 다닐 때 그녀는 범상치 않았다. 이것은 특히 그녀가 가난한 집안 출신이기 때문이었다. 급우들 대부분은 부유한 가족 출신이어서 그녀를 깔보았다. 그 당시 그녀는 빼빼 말랐는데, 이 때문에도 그녀는 다른 학생들 사이에서 인기가 없었다. 그래서 안젤리나는 자신에 대한 믿음을 잃고 자해하기 시작했다.

Q. 글의 목적은 무엇인가?
(a) 졸리의 나쁜 습관을 비판하기 위해서
(b) 졸리의 고등학교 시절을 설명하기 위해서
(c) 졸리의 자만심에 대한 불만을 나타내기 위해서
(d) 졸리의 정서적인 문제에 대해 문의하기 위해서

해설 전반적으로 안젤리나 졸리의 고등학교 시절을 기술하고 있기 때문에 정답은 (b)다. 정답을 (d)로 착각하지 않도록 주의해야 하는데, 졸리의 정서적인 문제가 드러나긴 했지만, 이에 대해 의문을 제기하는 것이 아니고, 전반적으로 고등학교 생활에 대해 묘사하고 있으므로 정답이 될 수 없다. 이처럼 '매력적인 오답'을 정답으로 택하지 않기 위해서는 글의 전체 흐름을 정확히 읽어내야 한다.

어구 attend 참석하다, 다니다
odd one out 유별란 사람[사물]
mainly 주로   look down on ~를 멸시하다
skinny 빼빼 마른   unpopular 인기 없는
faith 굳은 믿음

정답 (b)

UNIT 2 전반적 정보 Ⅱ

EXERCISE
1 (b)   2 (c)

PRACTICE
1 (d)   2 (b)

유형 정리

1 대상 독자

해석 저는 Hope Publishers의 편집장인 에릭 존스입니다. 저희는 양질의 ELT 서적을 만들어내는 출판사입니다. 1999년 이래로, 영어를 학습하는 일본인의 수요를 충족시키는 데 중점을 두면서 천 권이 넘는 책을 출간했습니다. 귀사와 마찬가지로, 저희는 미국의 애틀랜타에서 개최되는 제53회 IRA 컨벤션에 참석할 예정입니다. 새로운 녹해 교재를 개발하는 데 있어 상농의 이익을 논의하기 위해 그 곳에서 모임을 가질 수 있는지 궁금합니다.

어구 editor-in-chief 편집장
publishing company 출판사
produce 생산하다   quality 품질; 특성
title 서적   publish 출판하다

2 저자의 직종

해석 예멘을 처음으로 방문했을 때, 납치가 아주 빈번하다는 사실을 알고서 충격을 받았다. 물론, 위험한 나라들을 많이 여행했었다. 그렇지만 나는 가이드에게 '예전에 이처럼 위협을 느꼈던 적이 없다'라고 말했다. 가이드는 그 악명 높은 나라에서는 납치가 '전통'이라고 설명했다. 그에 따르면, 예멘의 다양한 부족들은 외국인을 협상 카드로 사용하는 것을 아무렇지도 않게 생각한다고 한다.

어구 shocked 충격을 받은   kidnap 납치하다
common 흔한; 공통의   guide 안내자
threaten 위협하다   tradition 전통
notorious 악명 높은   various 다양한
tribe 부족, 종족
think nothing of ~를 아무렇지도 않게 여기다
bargaining chip 협상 카드

3 저자의 태도

해석 문제는 헤어스타일에 대한 귀하의 선호도에 관한 것입니다. 오필리아가 저희에게 귀하의 머리가 길다고 알려왔습니다. 저는 모든 이들이 자신의 헤어스타일을 선택할 귀중한 권리가 있으며 누구도 다른 사람의 문제에 간섭할 권리가 없다고 굳게 믿습니다. 그렇지만 우리나라의 보수적인 분위기를 감안할 때, 헤어스타일에 대한 귀하의 선호도가 바뀔 수 있는 가능성에 대해 탐구할 필요가 있습니다.

어구 matter 문제
concerned with ~와 관계되는 *cf.* concerned about ~에
대해 우려하는   preference 선호도
inform 알리다   firmly 확고하게
precious 소중한
decide on (숙고하고 나서) 선택하다
interfere with 간섭하다   conservative 보수적인
atmosphere 분위기   possibility 가능성

EXERCISE

1

해석 합리적인 정책을 채택하여 추구하는 것이 절대적으로 필요하다는 점을 명심해야만 합니다. 그렇지 않으면, 소중한 우리나라는 많은 손실을 입게 될 것입니다. 그런 정책을 형성하기 위해서는, 성취 가능한 목표를 설정하고 우리나라의 이익을 추구해야 합니다. 이것이 너무도 쉬운 것처럼 들릴지도 모르지만, 실제 세계에서 합리적 정책을 추구하는 것이 얼마나 어려운지를 알게 될 것입니다.
(a) 교수들
(b) 정책 입안자들
(c) 무용수들

해설 주어진 글에서 합리적인 정책 추구의 중요성을 강조했기 때문에 실제로 정책을 입안하는 이들을 대상으로 한 글임을 알 수 있다. 따라서 정답은 (b)다. (a)의 교수들이 정책 입안에 관여할 수도 있지만 반드시 그런 것이 아니기 때문에 정답이 될 수 없음에 유의해야 한다.

어구 keep in mind 명심하다   absolutely 절대적으로

adopt 채택하다; 입양하다
rational 합리적인
otherwise 그렇지 않다면
shape 형성하다
seek 추구하다; 찾다

pursue 추구하다
policy 정책; 보험증서
suffer (나쁜 일) 겪다
attainable 실현가능한
interests 이익

정답 (b)

2

해석 이 주장은 자유민주주의의 본성에 대한 오해에 바탕을 두고 있다. 자유민주주의의 기본 원칙을 부인한다고 하더라도, 그것이 자유민주주의가 틀렸다는 것을 뜻하지는 않는다. 그렇게 함으로써, 단지 자신이 자유민주주의를 믿지 않는다는 것을 증명한 것일 뿐이다. 이것은 주로 이념이 증명의 문제가 아니라 신념의 문제이기 때문이다. 바꾸어 말하면, 이념이 참이라는 것을 증명할 필요가 없다.
(a) 동정적인
(b) (정서적인) 지원을 제공하는
(c) 비판적인

해설 첫 번째 문장에 '이러한 주장'이 오해에 바탕을 두고 있다고 했고, 그 이유를 글 전체에 걸쳐 설명했으므로 저자가 비판적인 입장을 취함을 알 수 있다. (a)와 (b)는 비슷한 뜻을 나타내기 때문에 정답이 될 수 없다.

어구 argument 주장; 논거
misunderstanding 오해
liberal democracy 자유민주주의
deny 부인하다
believer 신봉자
proof 증명

based on ~에 바탕을 둔
nature 본성; 자연

principle 원칙, 원리
ideology 이념

정답 (c)

PRACTICE

1

해석 솔직히 말해서, 오사마 빈 라덴이 왜 그렇게 잔혹한 인물로 변했는지 모르겠다. 킹 압둘 아지즈 대학을 함께 다닐 때, 그는 종교에 대해, 심지어는 자선에 대해 관심을 가졌었다. 물론, 그가 이제까지 한 일은 완전히 잘못된 것이다. 그가 미국인들에게 저지른 일을 결코 용서하지 않을 것이다. 자기 자신의 종교를 배반한 것을 결코 용서하지 않을 것이다. 우리를 불명예스럽게 한 것을 결코 용서하지 않을 것이다.

Q. 글을 쓴 사람은 누구인가?
(a) 오사마 빈 라덴의 아버지
(b) 오사마 빈 라덴의 선생님
(c) 오사마 빈 라덴의 학생
(d) 오사마 빈 라덴의 친구

해설 첫 번째 문장과 두 번째 문장을 종합해 보면, 저자는 오사마 빈 라덴과 가까운 사이였음을 짐작할 수 있다. 특히 두 번째 문장에서 대학을 같이 다녔다고 했으므로 (d)와 같이 친구로 파악하는 것이 가장 자연스럽다.

어구 to be frank with you 솔직히 말해서
turn into ~로 변하다
charity 자선
betray 배반하다

monster 잔악한 인물; 괴물
forgive 용서하다
disgrace 불명예스럽게 하다

정답 (d)

2

해석 '재정 증명'과 관련하여, 저는 부모님에게서 관련 서류를 얻어야만 합니다. '부모 보증 서한'을 작성하기 위한 특별한 양식이 있습니까? 아니면 그냥 부모님이 저의 수업료와 생활비를 제공하겠다고 밝히는 서한을 쓰셔도 됩니까? '은행으로부터의 서한'과 관련하여, 한국의 은행들은 대개 '예금 증명서'를 발급합니다. 이것을 귀(貴)대학에서도 받아주시나요? 아니면 제 거래은행에 특별한 서한을 발급할 것을 요청해야 합니까?

Q. 글을 쓴 이는 누구에게 글을 쓰고 있나?
(a) 은행 창구 직원
(b) 대학 관계자
(c) 우체국
(d) 공인회계사

해설 '재정 증명'이나 '부모 보증 서한' 등에 대한 내용을 문의하고 있고, 분명하게 '귀(貴)대학'이라고 밝혔으므로, 입학과 관련된 사항을 대학 관계자에게 문의하는 서한임을 알 수 있다. 따라서 정답은 (b)다. 특히 (d)로 착각하지 않도록 유의해야 한다.

어구 with regard to ~에 관해
verification 증명; 확인
form (서류) 양식
state 진술하다; 상태
living expenses 생활비
issue 발급하다
deposit 예금
request 요청하다

financial 재정적인
relevant 관련된
guarantee 보증
tuition 수업료
regarding ~와 관련하여
certificate 증명서
acceptable 받아들일 수 있는

정답 (b)

UNIT 3 정오 유형 Ⅰ

EXERCISE
1 (c)   2 (a)

PRACTICE
1 (b)   2 (c)

유형 정리

1 내용과 반대되는 경우

해석 심지어 오늘날에도, 미국은 아주 많은 이들에게 약속의 땅으로 남아 있습니다. 이것은 우리나라가 시대의 시련을 이겨낸 나라이기 때문입니다. 우리나라는 희망과 사랑이 시작된 곳입니다. 우리나라는 모든 계층의 사람들을 껴안은 나라입니다. 따라서 새로운 시대의 우리의 지도력은 인류 역사의 진정한 시작을 나타낼 뿐만 아니라 새로운 세대의 인류가 시작됨을 의미합니다. 전 세계 모든 사람들을 겸허하게 섬김으로써 우리나라가 선도해 나갑시다.

어구 remain ~인 상태를 유지하다
stand 이겨내다, 참아내다
the home of ~의 발상지
embrace 껴안다; 채택하다
walk of life 계층
signify 의미하다; 상징하다
humanity 인류
serve 섬기다

nation 국가
trial 시련; 시험

era 시대
generation 세대
humbly 겸허하게
the globe 세계

2 내용에 언급되지 않은 경우

해석 혹시나 해서, 저는 2008년 8월 31일까지 계좌를 유지하고 싶다는 점을 언급해야 할 것 같습니다. 2008년 9월 1일에 계좌 해지 양식에 서명하여 귀(貴)은행에 팩스로 보내겠습니다. 덧붙여, 일부 거래의 내역을, 특히 보험 거래 내역을 저에게 이메일로 보내주셨으면 합니다. 제 딸의 학교가 일정 금액을 제 계좌에 입금할 것으로 생각됩니다. 그래서 그 모든 거래의 내역을 이메일로 보내주실 수 있으신지요?

어구 just in case 만일에 대비하여　mention 언급하다
account (은행) 계좌
sign 서명하다 cf. signature 서명
closure 폐점; 종결　　　detail 세부사항
transaction (상)거래　　insurance 보험
deposit 입금하다 (ant. withdraw 출금하다)

3 내용을 잘못 이해한 경우

해석 일반 상대성 이론을 공식으로 표현할 때, 아인슈타인은 우주에 관해 세 가지를 가정했다. 그 가운데 하나는 우주가 변화하지 않는다는 것이었다. 그렇지만 자신의 등식이 올바르다면 우주가 변화할 것이라는 것을 알아냈다. 문제를 다루기 위해, 아인슈타인은 우주 상수(常數)를 사용해서 자신의 등식을 바꾸었다. 유감스럽게도, 이것은 그의 끔찍한 실수였는데, 에드윈 허블이 우주가 변화하고 있다는 것을 밝혀냈기 때문이었다.

어구 formulate 공식으로 표현하다; 기획하다
theory of general relativity 일반 상대성 이론
assumption 가정　　　　equation 등식
address a problem 문제를 다루다
cosmological 우주론의　　constant 상수(常數)

EXERCISE

1

해석 인본주의 심리학은 행동주의와 정신분석학과는 상당히 다르다. 행동주의자들과 달리, 인본주의적 심리학자들은 사람이 '과학적' 연구의 피험자로가 아니라 독특한 개인으로 간주되어야 한다고 생각한다. 이들은 또한 정신분석학자들이 충동이 행동에 미치는 영향을 지나치게 강조한 것을 비판한다. 대신에, 이들은 심리학의 목적이 사람들로 하여금 잠재성을 실현하도록 돕는 것이라고 주장한다.
(a) 인본주의 심리학은 정신분석학과 유사하다.
(b) 인본주의 심리학은 사람들을 돕는 것과는 무관하다.
(c) 인본주의 심리학은 사람을 개인으로서 대우한다.

해설 행동주의와 정신분석학과 아주 다른 인본주의 심리학을 설명한 글이다. 이름에서 알 수 있듯이, 사람을 중심으로 여기는 심리학으로 이와 일치하는 설명은 (c)다. 참고로 아브라함 매슬로와 칼 로저스가 대표적인 학자에 속한다.

어구 humanistic 인본주의적인　　behaviorism 행동주의
psychoanalysis 정신분석학　　behaviorist 행동주의자
regard A as B A를 B로 간주하다　unique 독특한
individual 개인　　　　　subject 피실험자; 주제
psychoanalyst 정신분석학자
overemphasize 지나치게 강조하다
drive 충동, 동인(動因)
realize 실현하다; 깨닫다　　　potential 잠재성

정답 (c)

2

해석 물질적 부가 우리에게 행복을 가져다 줄 수 있는가? 너무도 많은 사람들이 그렇게 생각하는 것 같고, 이들은 많은 돈을 벌기 위해 어떤 일이라도 기꺼이 하려고 한다. 그들에게는 유감스럽게도, 물질적 부는 우리를 진정으로 행복하게 만들지 못한다. 이것은 주로 진정한 행복이 외부가 아니라 내면에서 비롯되는 것이기 때문이다. 더욱이, 진정한 행복은 내면의 평온을 요하는데, 내면의 평온은 물질적 부의 추구에 의해 부정적인 영향을 받을 수 있다.
(a) 내면의 평온은 행복에 있어 중요하다.
(b) 물질적 부는 행복을 보증한다.
(c) 진정한 행복은 외부에서 비롯된다.

해설 물질적 부의 추구와 진정한 행복 사이의 관계에 대한 글이다. 내면의 평온이 행복의 추구에 필요하다고 했으므로 정답은 (a)다. (b)와 (c)는 모두 글에서 밝힌 내용과 반대되기 때문에 정답이 될 수 없음에 유의하자.

어구 material 물질　　　　wealth 부(富)
willing to 기꺼이 ~하려고 하는　within 내면
without 외부　　　　　require 요구하다
inner 내면의　　　　　negatively 부정적으로
affect 영향을 미치다　　　pursuit 추구

정답 (a)

PRACTICE

1

해석 맥뉴어티의 작품의 여러 측면들이 내 눈을 사로잡았다. 무엇보다도, 그녀의 디자인은 그녀가 기존의 틀을 벗어나서 생각할 수 있다는 점을 말해준다. 사람들은 대개 티 테이블이 직사각형이어야 한다고 생각한다. 그러나 맥뉴어티는 이처럼 널리 퍼진 아이디어에 도전하여 삼각형 모양의 테이블을 생각해낸다. 이런 종류의 창의성은 미래를 위해 필수적이며, 양질의 교육에서만 비롯될 수 있다.

Q. 글에 따르면 다음 가운데 어느 것이 올바른가?
(a) 맥뉴어티의 작품은 전혀 창의적이지 않다.
(b) 맥뉴어티는 독창적으로 생각하는 사람이다.
(c) 맥뉴어티는 다른 사람들의 아이디어를 따른다.
(d) 맥뉴어티는 티 테이블이 직사각형 모양이어야 한다고 생각한다.

해설 티 테이블을 독창적으로 디자인한 맥뉴어티라는 사람에 대한 글이다. 맥뉴어티가 '기존의 틀을 벗어나서 생각'한다고 했으므로 정답은 (b)다. (a), (c), (d)는 모두 글의 내용과 반대되기 때문에 정답이 될 수 없다.

어구 more than anything else 무엇보다도
think outside the box 정형화된 틀에서 벗어나서 생각하다
supposed to ~하기로 되어 있는　rectangular 직사각형의
widespread 널리 퍼진
come up with ~를 생각해내다　triangular 삼각형의
creativity 창의성

정답 (b)

2

해석 흥미롭게도, 많은 사람들은 연역적 추론과 귀납적 추론 사이의 차이를 오해한다. 그들은 연역적 추론에서는 일반적인 가정으로부터 구체적인 결론이 유도된다고 생각한다. 또한 귀납적 추론에서는 개별적인 사실로부터 일반적인 결론이 유도된다고 생각한다. 그러나 그들의 생각은 잘못된 것이다. 연역적 추론에서는, 가정이 참이라면 결론은 단연코 참이다. 이와는 대조적으로, 귀납적 추론에서는, 가정이 참이라 하더라도 결론이 필연적으로 참이 아니다.

Q. 글에 따르면 다음 가운데 어느 것이 올바른가?

(a) 연역적 추론에서는, 일반적인 가정으로부터 구체적인 결론을 이끌어낸다.

(b) 귀납적 추론에서는, 개별적인 사실로부터 일반적인 결론을 이끌어낸다.

(c) 연역적 추론에서는, 가정이 참이라는 것이 결론이 참이라는 것을 보증한다.

(d) 귀납적 추론에서는, 가정이 참이라는 것이 결론이 참이라는 것을 보증한다.

해설 연역적 추론과 귀납적 추론의 차이를 설명한 글로 논리학과 관련되기 때문에 내용이 어렵게 느껴질 수 있다. 주어진 글에 따르면 정답은 (c)다. 중고등학교 과정에서는 대개 이 글에서 첫 번째에 제시된 것과 같이 학습했을 것으로 생각되는데, 실제로는 그렇지 않고 이 글에서 밝힌 것이 올바른 지식임을 참고하자. 특히, 귀납적 추론을 중고등학교 과정과 같이 이해하게 되면 얼마나 많은 개별적 사실이 일반적인 결론을 가능하게 하는가 하는 문제가 생긴다는 점에서, 그와 같은 잘못된 지식은 바로잡을 필요가 있다.

어구 interestingly 재미있게도   misunderstand 오해하다
deductive 연역적인   inductive 귀납적인
reasoning 추론   specific 구체적인, 특정한
conclusion 결론   assumption 가정
individual 개별적인   definitely 확실히
in contrast (이와는) 대조적으로
necessarily 필연적으로

정답 (c)

UNIT 4   정오 유형 Ⅱ

EXERCISE

1 (a)   **2** (c)

PRACTICE

1 (b)   **2** (c)

유형 정리

1   잘못된 Paraphrase

해석 장 뱁티스트 룰리는 최초의 지휘자로 널리 알려져 있었다. 그렇지만 지휘봉 대신에 그는 지휘하기 위해 긴 막대기를 사용했다. 이것은 그 당시에는 지휘봉이 없었기 때문이었다. 어느 날, 지휘를 하는 동안에, 그는 잘못하여 막대를 발에 밀어 넣었다. 그래서 그는 괴저에 걸려 사망했다. 최초의 지휘자의 비극적 죽음!

어구 widely 널리   conductor 지휘자
baton 지휘봉   stick 막대기
conduct 지휘하다   mistakenly 잘못하여
come down with (병에) 걸리다
gangrene 괴저   pass away 사망하다
tragic 비극적인

2   왜곡된 사실관계

해석 엔리코 페르미는 1938년도 노벨 물리학상을 수상했는데, 사람들이 그가 '새로운 방사성 원소'를 발견했다고 생각했기 때문이었다. 그렇지만 흥미롭게도, 페르미는 자신이 그런 원소를 발견했는지를 확신하지 못했다. 나중에, 세 명의 독일 과학자들은 페르미가 발견한 것이 핵분열로 인한 파편임을 증명했다. 페르미가 노벨상을 받을 때는 아무도 원자 핵분열이라는 현상에 대해 알지 못했는데, 원자 핵분열이 그 파편들을 초래했다. 어쩌면 페르미는 단지 운이 좋은 과학자일지도 모른다.

어구 physics 물리학   radioactive 방사성의
element 원소   fission 핵분열
fragment 파편, 조각   phenomenon 현상
atomic 원자의

3   지나친 추론

해석 나에게 큰 영향을 미쳐서 창의성의 강한 동인으로 남아 있는 것은 음악이 아름다울 뿐만 아니라 내용이 풍부하다는 것이다. 요한 파헬벨의 캐논 D 장조를 들을 때마다, 감미로운 선율에 감동을 받으면서, 동시에 많은 사람들의 평범하지만 아름다운 많은 이야기를 들을 수 있다. 사랑에 빠진 사람이 자신의 마음을 '노래하는' 것을 들을 수 있다. 야망이 있는 사람이 자신의 꿈에 대해 자랑스럽게 말하는 것을 들을 수 있다. 어머니가 애지중지하는 아들을 부르는 소리를 들을 수 있다. 이것은 아주 놀랍기만 하다.

어구 affect 영향을 미치다   motive 동인(動因), 동기
creativity 창의성   rich 풍부한
content 내용   major 장조
touch 감동시키다   sweet 감미로운
melody 선율   ambitious 야망이 있는
brag 자랑하다   beloved 애지중지하는

EXERCISE

1

해석 1994년 4월 28일, 북한은 기존의 정전협정을 새로운 평화 조약으로 대체하기 위해 백악관측이 (당시) 김일성 정권과 양자간 협상에 임해야 한다고 요구했다. 그 이후로 북한은 정전협정을 위반함으로써 기존의 정전 체제를 약화시키려 했다. 1995년 5월 3일, 김정일 정권은 북한으로부터 중립국감독위원회의 폴란드 임원을 추방함으로써 감독위원회를 폐쇄했다.

(a) 북한은 기존의 정전 체제를 좋아하지 않았다.

(b) 백악관측은 김정일 정권과 새로운 평화 조약을 체결하기 위한 협상을 하려고 했다.

(c) 북한은 중립국감독위원회를 지지했다.

해설 1994년과 1995년의 북한의 동향을 다룬 글로, 정전협정을 무력화시키기 위한 북한의 행동이 드러나 있다. 따라서 북한이 정전체제를 선호하지 않음을 알 수 있다. (b)는 주어진 글을 통해 알 수 없고, (c)는 주어진 내용에 어긋나기 때문에 정답이 될 수 없다.

어구 demand 강력히 요구하다   Washington 백악관측
enter into (협상 등에) 임하다   bilateral 양자간의
negotiation 협상   replace 대체하다
existing 기존의
armistice agreement 정전협정
treaty 조약
undermine (점차로) 약화시키다
regime 체제; 정권   violate 위반하다
expel 추방하다   commission 위원회

정답 (a)

2

해석 스티븐 호킹은 블랙홀에 대한 전문가이다. 그럼에도 불구하고, 한때 실수를 저질렀다. 1975년에 그는 백조자리 X-1에 블랙홀이

없다고 주장했다. 킵 톤이 반대 의견을 제시하여, 그들은 누가 옳은지를 두고 내기를 걸었다. 1990년에 호킹은 톤이 옳다는 것을 시인할 수밖에 없었다. 그렇지만 위대한 과학자로서의 명성에도 불구하고, 그는 자신의 패배를 인정하고 싶지 않았다. 심지어 친구를 시켜 톤의 사무실에서 내기의 기록을 훔치게까지 했다.

(a) 킵 톤이 블랙홀에 대한 전문가이다.
(b) 스티븐 호킹은 나쁜 과학자로서 악명이 높았다.
(c) 스티븐 호킹은 실수를 저질렀다.

해설 스티븐 호킹에 관한 일화를 다룬 글이다. (a)는 주어진 글을 통해 분명하게 판단할 수 없기 때문에 정답이 될 수 없다. (b)는 주어진 내용에 어긋나기 때문에 역시 정답이 될 수 없다. 따라서 정답은 (c)다. 특히 (a)를 정답으로 하지 않도록 유의해야 한다. 이 일화를 통해서 곧바로 킵 톤이 블랙홀에 대한 전문가라고 추론하는 것은 무리이기 때문이다.

어구 expert 전문가   nevertheless 그럼에도 불구하고
Cygnus 백조자리   make a bet 내기를 걸다
have no choice but to ~하지 않을 수 없다
admit 인정하다   reputation 명성, 평판
defeat 패배   record 기록

정답 (c)

PRACTICE

1

해석 힐러리 클린턴 상원의원이 오바마와 겨루는 데 대한 자신의 소회를 밝혔을 때, 많은 이들은 힐러리가 대통령 (경선) 선거운동을 그만둘 것이라고 생각했다. 그러나 힐러리는 그녀의 말이 단지 오바마와 자신이 '역사적 변화'에 직면해 있다는 것을 '인식'한 것이라고 말했다. 그렇지만 NBC에 따르면 힐러리가 끝까지 경선에 남을지는 확실하지 않다고 한다.

Q. 글에 따르면 다음 가운데 어느 것이 올바른가?
(a) 힐러리는 대통령 (경선) 선거 운동을 그만둘 것이다.
(b) 힐러리가 경선에 끝까지 남지 않을지도 모른다.
(c) 힐러리는 오바마를 증오한다.
(d) 오바마는 힐러리를 지지한다.

해설 힐러리와 오바마 사이의 대통령 경선에 관한 글이다. (a)는 힐러리가 반박한 내용이기 때문에 정답이 될 수 없다. 그리고 (c)와 (d)는 주어진 내용을 통해서 알 수 없기 때문에 정답이 아니다. 따라서 정답은 마지막 문장으로부터 알 수 있는 (b)다.

어구 senator 상원의원   express 표현하다
compete against ~와 경쟁하다
quit 그만두다   presidential 대통령의
campaign 선거운동remark 말, 논평
recognition 인식; 인정
on the verge of 막 ~하려고 하는 historic 역사적인

정답 (b)

2

해석 아시아의 직업윤리와 관련하여, 노고를 인정하지 않는 것이 그 요소 가운데 해 T인지는 확신하지 못한다. 전통적으로, 우리 한국인들은 노고를 높이 여기고, 그래서 참으로 성실한 사람을 찾는 것이 한국의 경영자들이 해야만 하는 가장 중요한 일들 가운데 하나이다. 더욱이, 가르치는 일이 단지 지식을 학생들에게 제공하는 것을 뜻하는 것이 아니라 주로 학생들의 마음에 감동을 주는 것이라고 굳게 믿는다. 참된 교육은 학생들의 영혼을 자유롭게 한다고 생각한다.

Q. 글에 따르면 다음 가운데 어느 것이 올바른가?
(a) 한국인들은 노고를 인정하지 않는다.
(b) 글쓴이는 참된 교육이 지식을 학생들에게 전하는 것을 뜻한다고 믿는다.
(c) 한국인들은 노고의 중요성을 인정한다.
(d) 참으로 성실한 사람을 찾는 것은 쉽다.

해설 한국인의 직업윤리와 관련된 내용이다. (a)와 (b)는 주어진 내용과 반대되기 때문에 정답이 될 수 없다. 반면 (d)는 내용으로 보아 올바르지 않다. 따라서 정답은 주어진 내용과 일치하는 (c)다.

어구 work ethic 직업윤리
appreciate 이해하다; 감사하다
element 요소   traditionally 전통적으로
think highly of ~를 높이 여기다
truly 참으로   earnest 성실한
knowledge 지식   primarily 주로
free 자유롭게 하다

정답 (c)

UNIT 5 세부사항 I

EXERCISE

1 (b)   2 (c)

PRACTICE

1 (c)   2 (b)

유형 정리

1 특정 인물 / 사물

해석 텍스트 투 스피치 소프트웨어닷컴(http://www.text-to-speech-software.com/)은 텍스트를 말로 전환하는 소프트웨어를 무료로 사용할 수 있는 기회를 드립니다. 이 소프트웨어를 사용하면 기사를 다양한 목소리로 들을 수 있어요. 기사를 화면에 복사해서 재생 버튼을 누르기만 하면 됩니다. 텍스트를 MP3 파일로 바꿀 수도 있습니다. 그러니 망설일 필요가 없죠? 한 번의 클릭으로 듣는 경험을 바꾸어 놓을 수 있습니다. (→ 실제로 이 사이트의 소프트웨어를 사용해 보면 알 수 있듯이, 텍스트를 음성으로 전환하는 소프트웨어는 아직 초기 단계이기 때문에 부자연스러움이 많이 느껴진다. 따라서 이 사이트에서 유료로 결제하지 않도록 주의하자. 그래도 궁금하면 시험판을 써보자.)

어구 chance 기회; 가능성   for free 공짜로
article 기사; 품목; 관사   copy 복사하다

2 인과 관계

해석 1971년에 필립 짐바르도가 한 유명한 실험에서, 그는 학생들로 하여금 감옥에서 교도관과 재소자의 역할을 하도록 했다. 시간이 흐르면서, 교도관들은 잔인해졌고 재소자들은 침울하게 되었다. 그는 이러한 변화가 학생들에게 부여된 역할을 통해 비롯되었다고 생각했다. 그에 따르면, 사람이 영향력 있는 역할을 맡게 되면 그 역할을 남용하여 잔악하게 될 가능성이 높다고 한다.

어구 experiment 실험   role 역할; 배역
guard 교도관   inmate 재소자
jail 감옥

depressed 침울한, 우울증에 걸린
powerful 강력한, 영향력이 있는
abuse 남용하다

3 비교 / 변화

해석 지적설계론은 진화론과는 매우 다르다. 무엇보다도 이 새 이론은 '지적인 설계자'가 모든 생물을 동시에 만들었다고 주장한다. 이런 의미에서 이 이론을 지지하는 이들은 복잡한 생물이 단순한 생물로부터 발달했다고 믿지 않는다. 그들에 따르면 그러한 변화는 불가능하다.

어구 theory 이론   evolution 진화
at the same time 동시에(=simultaneously)
supporter 지지자, 후원자   complex 복잡한

EXERCISE

1

해석 1998년에 에이미 리는 록 밴드를 만들었는데, 이 밴드는 에반에센스로 알려지게 되었다. 그녀가 고전음악과 헤비메탈 모두에 조예가 있어서 독특한 음악을 만들어 낼 수 있었다. 이것은 밴드의 첫 번째 앨범인 Fallen이 성공하는 데 도움을 주었다. 2006년에 두 번째 앨범인 The Open Door를 출시했는데, 이 앨범 또한 대단한 성공작이었다.
(a) 창시자가 여성이었기 때문에
(b) 밴드의 음악이 아주 독특했기 때문에
(c) 앨범이 아주 값쌌기 때문에

해설 이 밴드가 '독특한 음악'을 만들어 낼 수 있어서 크게 성공하게 된다는 내용으로 연결되므로 정답은 (b)다. (a)는 내용과 일치하긴 하지만 성공 이유가 아니다. (c)의 내용은 확인할 수 없다.

어구 create 창조하다   evanescence 헛됨, 덧없음
familiar with ~에 조예가 있는, ~에 익숙한
release 석방하다; 출시하다   turn out ~로 판명되다

정답 (b)

2

해석 1962년에 '침묵의 봄'을 출간했을 때 레이첼 칼슨은 엇갈린 반응을 받았다. 많은 이들은 부주의하게 살충제를 사용하는 데 따른 위험을 경고한 데 대해 그녀에게 감사했다. 반면 일부 살충제 제조 회사들은 그녀를 고소하겠다고 위협했다. 회사들은 그녀가 자신의 주장을 뒷받침하기 위해 거짓된 자료를 사용했다고 주장했다. 자신의 경고가 수년 동안의 과학적 연구에 바탕을 두고 있었기 때문에, 그녀는 자신의 입장을 지속적으로 옹호했다.
(a) 어떤 이들은 그녀의 저작에 관심을 가진 반면 다른 이들은 무관심했다.
(b) 어떤 이들은 그녀의 저작에 실망한 반면 다른 이들은 분노했다.
(c) 어떤 이들은 그녀의 저작을 환영한 반면 다른 이들은 불만을 토로했다.

해설 레이첼 칼슨에 대한 반응이 환영과 불만으로 나누어지기 때문에 정답은 (c)다. 특히 (b)로 답하지 않도록 주의해야 하는데, '분노'로 하나의 반응을 파악할 수는 있지만 다른 반응이 '실망'이 아니기 때문에 정답으로 볼 수 없다.

어구 mixed 혼합된   warn 경고하다
pesticide 살충제   threaten 위협하다, 협박하다
sue 고소하다   study 연구; 서재
defend 방어하다; 옹호하다   position 입장; 지위

정답 (c)

PRACTICE

1

해석 21세기가 시작되면서 사람들은 리더십에 대한 새로운 모델을 찾으려고 노력하고 있다. 많은 전문가들은 섬김의 리더십이 가장 유망한 모델이라고 생각한다. 섬김의 리더십의 개척자인 로버트 그린리프에 따르면, 진정한 지도자는 '자신이 이끄는 사람들을 섬기는 사람'이라고 했다. 그의 의견에 따르면, 지도자는 섬김을 받는 이들이 성장할 수 있도록 도와야 한다. 이것은 그들의 조직이 성장하는 데 도움이 되기도 한다.

Q. 그린리프의 견해에 의하면 다음 중 진정한 지도자는?
(a) 다른 이들을 통제하는 사람
(b) 다른 이들을 학대하는 사람
(c) 다른 이들을 발전시키는 사람
(d) 다른 이들을 관리하는 사람

해설 그린리프는 진정한 지도자가 다른 이들의 성장을 돕는 사람이라고 생각했으므로 정답은 (c)가 된다. 일반적인 견해로는 (d)도 지도자라고 파악될 수 있지만, 문제에서는 그린리프의 견해를 묻고 있으므로 정답이 될 수 없다.

어구 expert 전문가   servant 하인
promising 유망한   pioneer 개척자, 선구자

정답 (c)

2

해석 크리스마스에, 필리핀의 중심부에 소재한 쇼핑몰에서 화재가 발생하여 적어도 24명이 목숨을 잃었다. 경찰 관계자에 따르면, 화재는 폭죽 때문에 발생했다고 한다. 화재가 쇼핑몰의 입구를 덮쳐 많은 쇼핑객들이 건물 밖으로 나올 수가 없었다. 이후에 이들은 불에 타서 죽은 채로 발견되었다. 경찰은 이 지역에서 폭죽을 판매하는 것을 막으려 노력을 기울이고 있다.

Q. 화재가 무엇 때문에 발생했는가?
(a) 총기 때문에
(b) 불꽃 때문에
(c) 화실(火室) 때문에
(d) 반딧불 때문에

해설 보기 (b)에서 지문에 나온 '폭죽'을 '불꽃'으로 바꿔 표현하고 있으므로 정답은 (b)다. paraphrase로 제시된 다른 단어들이 '폭죽'과는 거리가 먼 다른 뜻을 나타낸다는 점도 기억해두자.

어구 claim (생명을) 앗아가다   central 중심의
break out (화재·전쟁 등이) 발생하다
firecracker 폭죽   entrance 입구; 입학, 입회

정답 (b)

EXERCISE
1 (b)   **2** (a)

PRACTICE
1 (b)   **2** (c)

유형 정리

1 특성

해석 '조국을 위해 바칠 생명이 하나밖에 없다는 것이 안타까울 뿐이다' 라고 미국 문화에서 국민적인 영웅인 네이단 헤일은 선언했다. 미국 독립전쟁 기간 동안에, 그는 교사로 위장함으로써 뉴욕시에서의 영국 군대의 동향에 대한 정보를 수집했다. 유감스럽게도, 영국의 한 소령이 헤일이 실제로 어떤 인물인지 알아내어 그를 붙잡았다. 그는 유언을 말하고 영국 병사들 앞에서 교수형에 처해졌다. 그의 말은 여전히 대다수 미국인들에게 감동을 주어서 그의 인기에 기여한다.

어구
regret 유감으로 여기다 　declare 선언하다
national 국민적인 　　　gather 수집하다
troop 군대 　　　　　　disguise 위장하다
major (육·공군의) 소령 　capture 포획하다
utter 말하다 　　　　　hang 교수형에 처하다
touch 감동시키다 　　　majority 대다수
contribute 기여하다
popularity 인기

2 이유

해석 2008년 2월 5일과 19일 사이에, 이매진컵 이노베이션 액셀러레이터가 실리콘밸리에서 개최되었다. 6개의 소프트웨어 디자인 팀이 그 경연대회에 참가했다. 대회 마지막 날에, 폴란드 팀은 '사업 준비성' 상을 수상했는데, 가상 달러 예산을 가장 많이 확보했기 때문이었다. 한국 팀은 '혁신' 상을 수상했는데, 비즈니스 전략을 적용하는 데 뛰어났기 때문이었다. 더욱이, 많은 심사관들은 한국 팀의 제품이 많은 이들의 삶을 바꾸어놓을 것이라고 느꼈다.

어구 take place (계획되어) 일어나다
take part in ~에 참가하다 　competition 경연대회; 경쟁
readiness 준비성 　　　　　award 상
virtual 가상의 　　　　　　budget 예산
innovation 혁신 　　　　　apply 적용하다
strategy 전략 　　　　　　judge 심사관

3 조건

해석 움직임이 너무도 느리기 때문에, 해우(海牛)는 종종 보트와 충돌하여 부상을 당하거나 죽음을 맞이한다. 슬프게도, 많은 해우들이 매년 목숨을 잃는다. 미국 지질조사소에 따르면, 적절한 조치를 취하지 않으면 '앞으로 100년 이내에 회복 기준'을 충족시키지 못할 가능성이 높다고 한다. 따라서 해우를 위험으로부터 보호해야 할 때이다.

어구 manatee 해우(海牛) 　　collide with ~와 부딪히다
lead to ~로 귀결되다 　　injury 부상
appropriate 적절한 　　　action 조치

possibility 가능성 　　　recovery 회복
criteria 기준, 규준 　　　protect 보호하다

EXERCISE

1

해석 해양 포유류 가운데 가장 빠른 동물은 무엇일까? 어떤 이들은 물속에서 시속 35마일로 움직일 수 있어서 큰돌고래가 가장 빠르다고 말한다. 그렇지만 카렌 번드박사에 따르면 범고래가 승자라고 한다. 빈번하게, 범고래는 물속에서 시속 35마일이 넘는 속도로 움직인다. 흥미롭게도 범고래는 돌고래과에 속한다. 짐작할 수 있듯이, 범고래는 돌고래과에서 가장 큰 성원이다.
(a) 범고래는 파충류이다.
(b) 범고래는 해양 포유류 가운데 가장 빠르다.
(c) 범고래는 해양 포유류 가운데 가장 크다.

해설 주어진 글에서 범고래가 포유류라고 했기 때문에 (a)는 정답이 아니다. 다음으로 (c)는 범고래가 돌고래과에서 가장 크다고 했기 때문에 정답이 될 수 없다. 따라서 정답은 (b)다.

어구 mammal 포유류
bottleneck dolphin 큰돌고래 　killer whale 범고래
belong to ~에 속하다 　　　family 과(科)

정답 (b)

2

해석 나는 늘 직원들뿐만 아니라 고객에게도 따스함과 희망의 메시지를 전하는 회사를 운영하는 것을 꿈꿔 왔다. 그런 회사가 진정으로 '회사'가 아니라고 생각할지도 모른다. 그러나 돈을 버는 것이 사업의 전부가 아니라고 생각한다. 사업은 아무런 감정도 없는 로봇이 아니라 사람들을 감동시키는 것과 필연적으로 관계된다. 현대인들이 가장 필요로 하는 것은 '고급' 제품이 아니라 자신들이 이해받고 있고 희망으로 가득하다고 느끼게 해주는 제품이다.
(a) 사람들을 감동시킬 수 있기 때문에
(b) 많은 돈을 벌 수 있기 때문에
(c) 편리한 로봇을 만들 수 있기 때문에

해설 글쓴이가 생각하는 진정한 회사에 관한 글이다. (b)는 글에서 배척하는 입장이기 때문에 정답이 아니다. 그리고 (c)는 내용과 전혀 관련이 없다. 따라서 정답은 글쓴이의 입장과 일치하는 (a)이다. 이것은 첫 번째 문장과 마지막 문장을 통해 충분히 확인할 수 있다.

어구 run (회사 등을) 운영하다 　customer 고객
employee 직원 　　　　　necessarily 필연적으로
concerned with ~와 관계된 　emotion 감정
contemporary 현대의; 동시대의
fancy 고급의
appreciate 이해하다; 감사하다

정답 (a)

PRACTICE

1

해석 짙은 도로를 유지하기 위한 수단으로서 미국 남부에 도입되었다. 널리 알려져 있듯이, 칡은 사람들로부터 어떤 도움도 필요로 하지 않는다. 게다가, 꽃과 잎이 아주 매력적이다. 그렇지만 유감스럽게도, 이 놀라운 식물은 다른 식물들을 죽여서 심각한 문제를 초래한다. 설상가상으로, 칡을 죽이는 것은 쉬운 일이 아니다.

Q. 왜 칡이 문제를 일으키고 있나?
- (a) 꽃이 매우 아름다워서
- (b) 다양한 식물들을 죽여서
- (c) 사람들이 돌볼 필요가 없어서
- (d) 미국에 도입되어서

해설 세부사항을 측정하는 유형이다. (a), (c), (d)는 모두 본문의 내용과 일치하지만 왜 칡이 문제를 일으키는가에 대한 답이 아니다. 마지막에서 두 번째 문장에서 확인할 수 있듯이 정답은 (b)다.

어구 kudzu 칡   introduce 도입하다; 소개하다
maintain 유지하다; 주장하다   human 사람
moreover 더욱이   attractive 매력적인
amazing 놀라운   serious 심각한; 진지한
to make matters worse 설상가상으로

정답 (b)

2

해석 한 번은 예수 그리스도가 원수를 사랑하라고 명령했다. 이 '명령'을 사업의 맥락에 적용할 수 있을까? 물론, 그렇게 할 수 있다. 이것은 주로 혹심한 경쟁이 사업체의 생존에 해롭기 때문이다. 따라서 전략적으로 사고하는 사업가들은 '원수'를 '사랑하는' 방법을 생각해내야 한다. 보다 중요한 사항으로, 예수의 명령은 사업체가 고객과 경쟁업체를 사랑으로 대함으로써 성공할 수 있음을 일깨워준다.

Q. 예수 그리스도의 명령이 왜 사업체에 중요한가?
- (a) 그 명령이 사업체에 해로울 수 있기 때문에
- (b) 그 명령이 사업의 맥락에 적용될 수 없기 때문에
- (c) 그 명령이 사업체의 성공을 도울 수 있기 때문에
- (d) 그 명령이 친구를 사랑하라고 일깨워주기 때문에

해설 종교적 명령을 사업의 맥락에 적용한 글이다. (a)는 '그 명령'이 아니라 '경쟁'이 사업체에 해로울 수 있다고 했으므로 주어진 내용과 어긋난다. (b)는 내용과 반대된다. 그리고 (d)는 주어진 내용을 잘못 해석한 것이기 때문에 정답이 아니다. 따라서 정답은 (c)다.

어구 Jesus Christ 예수 그리스도   enemy 적
apply 적용하다   context 맥락
mainly 주로   severe 모진
competition 경쟁   harmful 해로운
survival 생존   strategically 전략적으로
come up with 생각해내다   remind 상기시키다
deal with 다루다, 대우하다   competitor 경쟁자

정답 (c)

Chapter 4

UNIT 1 광고

EXERCISE

1 (b)   2 (c)

PRACTICE

1 (d)   2 (b)

유형 정리

1 제품

해석 프레쉬 노화방지 크림은 단순히 또 하나의 노화방지 크림이 아닙니다. 이 크림의 뛰어난 효과는 다양한 임상실험을 통해 입증되었습니다. 다른 크림과 달리, 이 제품은 얼굴에 있는 거의 모든 주름살을 제거할 수 있습니다. 게다가, 보톡스 주사와 달리, 이 크림을 사용하는 것은 고통이 전혀 없습니다. 그냥 이 크림을 바르고 더 젊어지십시오! 아무도 여러분의 실제 나이를 짐작할 수 없을 것입니다. 보다 많은 정보를 얻으시려면 1-800-555-2323으로 전화해 주십시오.

어구 anti-aging 노화 방지   extraordinary 뛰어난
effect 효과   various 다양한
clinical test 임상실험   remove 제거하다
wrinkle 주름살   botox injection 보톡스 주사
painless 고통이 없는
apply (크림 등을) 바르다   actual 실제의

2 교육 프로그램

해석 학습자 친화적 강좌는 학습자들에게 언어 학습에 대한 혁신적인 접근법을 제공합니다. SLA 전문가들이 크게 추천하는 이 강좌는 학생들이 네 가지 언어 능력을 가장 효율적인 방식으로 습득할 수 있게 합니다. 실생활에서 마주치는 과제와 비슷한 흥미로운 언어 활동을 제공함으로써, 이 프로그램은 여러분이 영어를 자신 있게 그리고 유창하게 구사할 수 있도록 해줍니다.

어구 -friendly ~친화적인   innovative 혁신적인
approach 접근법   recommend 추천하다
specialist 전문가   enable 가능하게 하다
master 완전히 습득하다   efficient 효율적인
engaging 흥미로운   real-life 실생활
task 과제, 과업
empower 자신감 있게 만들다; 권한을 부여하다
confidently 자신 있게   fluently 유창하게

3 서비스업

해석 Cozy Travel사(社)는 시골에 사는 행복을 경험하는 독특한 기회를 제공합니다. 아름다운 휴가용 별장에 머물면서, 숲속을 거닐고, 아주 멋진 석양을 지켜보고 친근한 사람들을 만나는 일을 즐길 수 있습니다. 그 곳에 영원히 머물고 싶어 하실지도 모릅니다. 가족 전체가 이 기회를 활용하신다면, 30% 할인을 해드립니다. 그러니 무엇을 망설이십니까?

어구 unique 독특한   opportunity 기회
cottage 별장   woods 숲
awesome 아주 멋진   sunset 석양, 일몰

friendly 친근한   forever 영원히
discount 할인

EXERCISE

1

해석 원스톱 인턴쉽 프로그램은 광고의 실세계를 탐험하는 굉장한 기회를 제공합니다. 3개월 동안 일급 광고사 가운데 한 곳에서 근무하도록 해드립니다. 지정된 카운슬러가 모든 면을 도와줍니다. 광고사를 고르고, 근무 일정을 계획하고, 아이디어에 대한 피드백을 제공하기 위해 여러분과 긴밀하게 협력합니다. 보다 많은 정보를 원하시면, 저희 웹사이트 www.one-stop-internship.com 을 방문해주세요.
(a) 카운슬러가 되다
(b) 광고의 실세계를 탐험하다
(c) 휴가를 즐기다

해설 두 번째 문장에서 '광고사에서 근무하도록' 해준다고 했으므로 광고의 실세계를 탐험한다는 내용의 (b)가 가장 적절하다. 이 인턴십 과정이 카운슬러가 되기 위한 것이나 휴가를 즐기기 위한 것이 아니므로 (a)와 (c)는 정답이 될 수 없다.

어구 opportunity 기회   arrange 마련하다
advertising agency 광고사   designated 지정된
counselor 카운슬러   closely 긴밀하게
feedback 피드백; 의견

정답 (b)

2

해석 Multilingual Translator는 진정으로 혁명적인 제품입니다. 다른 번역기와 달리, 이 제품은 단어나 문장을 그 맥락을 고려하여 번역합니다. 아시다시피, 맥락은 말의 의미를 정하는 데 있어 중요한 역할을 맡습니다. 그리고 Multilingual Translator는 말을 하는 맥락을 이해할 수 있는 유일한 번역 장치입니다. 그러니 무엇을 망설이십니까? 1-800-737-7878로 바로 전화 주세요.
(a) 아주 비싸다.
(b) 이용이 가능한 유일한 번역 장치이다.
(c) 번역을 할 때 맥락을 고려한다.

해설 맥락을 고려하여 번역하는 제품에 관한 광고이다. (a)는 주어진 내용을 통해서는 알 수 없기 때문에 정답이 아니다. (b)는 유일한 번역 장치가 아니라, 맥락을 고려하여 번역하는 유일한 장치가 되어야 올바른 설명이 된다. 따라서 정답은 (c)다. 참고로 아직 번역 장치는 맥락을 고려하여 번역하는 수준에는 이르지 못했다. 고려해야 하는 언어적 · 비(非)언어적 요소가 너무 많기 때문이다.

어구 revolutionary 혁명적인   product 제품
translation 번역   translate 번역하다
take into account 고려하다   play a role 역할을 하다
determine 결정하다   utterance 말, 발언
device 장치
capable of (최대 역량을 발휘하여) ~할 수 있는

정답 (c)

PRACTICE

1

해석 정말로 살을 빼고 싶나요? 정말로 아름다운 삶을 살아가고 싶나요? 그러면 저희의 놀라운 Fat-Free Pill을 드셔 보세요. 해야 할 일이라고는 이 약을 먹고 기다리는 것밖에 없습니다. 일 주일 후에, 여러분은 자신이 날씬하고 아름답게 변해 있는 것을 알게 될 것입니다. 믿을 수 있나요? 그러나 사실입니다. 저희의 혁신적인 약은 살을 빼는 가장 효과적인 방법으로 입증되었습니다. 보다 많은 정보를 원하시면, 저희 웹사이트 www.new-life.com을 방문해 주세요.

Q. 문장을 완성할 가장 적절한 선택지를 고르시오.
(a) 못생기고 뚱뚱하게
(b) 친근하고 친절하게
(c) 성실하고 정직하게
(d) 날씬하고 아름답게

해설 살을 빼게 하는 약에 대한 광고이다. 내용으로부터 (d)가 정답이라는 점을 쉽게 알 수 있다. (a)는 부정적인 특성이기 때문에 광고에 어울리지 않는다. 그리고 (b)와 (c)는 살을 빼는 것과는 무관하기 때문에 정답이 될 수 없다. 참고로 Exercise의 번역 장치와 마찬가지로 가상의 제품에 대한 광고이다.

어구 lose weight 체중을 줄이다   lead a life 삶을 영위하다
try 시도해보다   pill 약
slim 날씬한   innovative 혁신적인
effective 효과적인

정답 (d)

2

해석 TwinStar Hotel은 마닐라의 경제 구역의 중심으로부터 5분 거리에 편리하게 위치해 있습니다. 5성급 호텔의 편안함을 즐기면서, 고객들은 무료로 이메일을 읽거나 쓰고, 전화를 걸며, 팩스를 주고받을 수 있습니다! 저희는 24시간 내내 이용이 가능한 5개의 화상회의실도 갖추고 있습니다. 저희의 놀라운 호텔에서는 업무와 유희가 평화롭고 조화롭게 공존합니다. 보다 많은 정보를 원하시면, 1-800-323-2323으로 전화해 주십시오.

Q. 글로부터 추론할 수 있는 바는 무엇인가?
(a) 호텔은 매우 싸다.
(b) 호텔의 고객들은 업무를 처리할 수 있다.
(c) 호텔의 고객들은 무료로 팩스를 보낼 수 없다.
(d) 호텔에는 이용 가능한 객실이 5개밖에 없다.

해설 글에서 5성급 호텔이라고 했기 때문에 (a)는 정답이 될 수 없다. 그리고 (c)는 글의 내용과 반대되므로 정답이 아니다. (d)는 화상회의실의 수를 말해야 정답이 될 수 있다. 따라서 정답은 글의 내용으로부터 쉽게 추론할 수 있는 (b)다.

어구 conveniently 편리하게   located 위치한
heart 심장부   district 구역
comfort 편안함   for free 무료로
video conferencing 화상회의
around the clock 24시간 내내
peacefully 평화롭게   harmoniously 조화롭게

정답 (b)

UNIT 2 기사 I (사건·사고)

EXERCISE

1 (c)   2 (c)

PRACTICE

1 (d)   2 (b)

유형 정리

1 일반 사건

해석 2006년 8월 26일에 '온야'라는 이름의 늑대가 경찰에 의해 죽임을 당했다. 이 늑대는 코울 밸리의 니아비 동물원에서 탈출해 거리를 배회하면서 그렇게 이틀을 돌아다녔다. 이 사건은 동물원측의 부주의 때문에 발생했다. 동물원 관리자들이 온야에게 뛰어놀 수 있는 공간을 충분히 주었다면, 온야가 자신의 거주지에서 도망가는 일은 없었을 것이다. 동물원 관리자들은 동물 보호 법률을 위반한 혐의로 고발될 수도 있다.

어구 escape 탈출하다   walk the street 거리를 배회하다
incident 사건   space 공간; 우주
get away from ~를 떠나다
charge 고발하다; (벌금 등을) 부과하다

2 범죄

해석 1963년 8월 8일, 15명의 강도가 글래스고에서 런던으로 가는 우편 열차를 세웠다. 내부 인물의 도움으로 강도들은 이 열차가 수천 파운드의 돈을 운반하고 있다는 것을 알았다. 열차에 타고 나서, 강도들 가운데 한 명이 기관사를 때렸다. 그리고 나서, 그들은 돈이 들어 있는 120개의 자루를 탈취했다. 열차에서 내려 은신처로 간 다음에 그들은 돈을 나누었다. 나중에 그들 대부분은 경찰에 의해 체포되었다.

어구 mail train 우편 열차   robber 강도
insider 내부 인물   contain 포함하다

3 사고

해석 2003년 1월 8일, 터키 항공사의 비행기가 디아르 바키르 공항에 착륙을 시도하려다가 추락했다. 생존자 가운데 한 명인 알리에 일진(Aliye Ilgin)은 '비행기가 착륙할 때 거대한 소리와 함께 추락하여 불이 붙고 나서 부서졌다'라고 말했다. 비행기가 착륙을 시도할 때, 공항에는 짙은 안개가 끼었는데, 이 때문에 이 참담한 사고가 발생한 것으로 추정하고 있다. 5명이 이 비극적인 사건에서 살아 남았다.

어구 crash 심하게 부딪히다   land 땅; 착륙하다
survivor 생존자   horrible 끔찍한
survive ~에서 살아 남다   tragedy 비극, 비극적인 일

EXERCISE

1

해석 2007년 4월 16일, 버지니아 공대 캠퍼스에서 32명이 조승희에 의해 사살되었다. 그들 가운데 리비우 교수가 있었는데, 이 교수는 자신의 학생들 대부분이 창문을 통해 탈출하도록 도와주었다.

그들이 도망을 가는 동안 교수는 강의실의 문을 계속 잡고 있었다. 슬프게도, 여러 차례 총알을 맞은 후 교수는 숨을 거두었다. 비록 우리 곁에는 없지만, 그는 영원히 기억될 것이다.
(a) 어떤 정신이 나간 살인범
(b) 기억력을 향상시키는 방법
(c) 어떤 교수의 희생

해설 전체가 '교수의 희생'에 대한 내용이기 때문에 정답은 (c)다. 글의 초점이 살인범에 있지 않기 때문에 (a)가 정답이 될 수 없고 (b)는 글의 내용과 전혀 관련이 없지만 remember와 관련해 제시된 함정용 오답이라는 점도 기억해두자.

어구 be shot dead 사살되다   flee 도망가다
grab 붙잡다   pass away 사망하다

정답 (c)

2

해석 2002년 8월 26일, 크리스 토마스는 자선 행사의 일환으로 번지 점프를 했다. 그는 남부 웨일즈에 있는 모리스톤 병원을 위한 기금 모금에 자신의 힘을 보태기를 원했다. 수백 명의 사람들이 지켜보는 가운데, 그는 크레인에서 번지 점프를 했다. 갑자기 크레인과 그의 발을 연결한 끈이 끊어지면서 그는 땅바닥으로 떨어졌다. 심하게 부상을 입어 병원으로 후송되었다. 며칠 뒤에 그는 사망했다.
(a) 크리스 토마스는 많은 돈을 모았다.
(b) 그 행사에는 사람들이 거의 없었다.
(c) 크리스 토마스는 사망했다.

해설 세부사항을 측정하는 유형으로 정답은 (c)다. (a)는 글의 내용을 통해서는 확인할 수 없고 (b)는 글의 내용과 상반된다. 특히, 글의 내용을 통해 알 수 없는 보기가 오답으로 많이 나오는 것도 기억해두자.

어구 go bungee jumping 번지 점프를 하다
charity 자선   crane 크레인, 기중기
cord 끈   snap 끊어지다
fall to the ground 땅에 떨어지다
severely 심하게   injure 부상을 입다
pass away 사망하다

정답 (c)

PRACTICE

1

해석 1888년 8월과 11월 사이에, 자신을 '토막 살인자 잭'이라고 밝힌 한 남자가 런던에서 여러 명의 여성을 살해했다. 희생자를 살해할 때마다 이 연쇄 살인범은 희생자의 신체 일부를 잘라냈다. 심지어 그런 신체 일부를 경찰에 보내기까지 했다. 경찰의 많은 노력에도 불구하고 살인자의 신원을 밝히지도 못 했고 체포하지도 못 했다. 이 사건은 미해결인 채로 남았다.

Q. 글의 제목으로 가장 알맞은 것은?
(a) 런던의 침묵하는 희생자들
(b) 신원이 밝혀지지 않은 희생자들: 런던의 비밀
(c) 경찰관들의 좋았던 시절
(d) 토막 살인자 잭: 불가사의한 살인범

해설 글 전체의 내용이 '토막 살인자 잭'에 초점이 맞추어져 있기 때문에 정답은 (d)다. (a)와 (b)의 경우 범위가 너무 광범위하다. (c)는 글의 내용과는 전혀 관련이 없다. 이와 같은 보기의 구성 방식에 대해서도 익숙해지자.

어구 identify 신원을 밝히다   victim 희생자, 피해자
serial killer 연쇄 살인범   capture 체포하다

unsolved 미해결의

정답 (d)

2

해석 2007년 7월 23일, 영국의 워릭셔에서 약 100명의 사람들이 다섯 대의 UFO가 상공을 나는 것을 목격했다. 오후 10시 30분경에, 그 중 세 대가 밤하늘에서 삼각형 모양을 만들기 시작했다. 다른 두 대는 세 대 가까이에 위치했다. 항공 관제소에 따르면 밤하늘에는 특이한 활동이 없었다고 한다. 그렇지만 대부분의 관찰자들은 진짜 UFO를 봤다고 생각했다.

Q. 이 글에 따르면 다음 보기 중에서 올바른 설명은?
  (a) UFO 목격은 항공 관제소에서 일어났다.
  (b) 항공 관제소는 그 날 밤에 특이한 일은 발생하지 않았다고 밝혔다.
  (c) UFO들은 서로 싸웠다.
  (d) UFO의 목격은 아침에 일어났다.

해설 정답은 (b)다. 지문의 ~no extraordinary를 보기 (b)에서 nothing unusual로 바꿔 표현하고 있다.

어구 approximately 대략　　　　form 형성하다
triangular 삼각형 모양의　　position 위치에 놓다
air traffic control 항공 관제소　extraordinary 특이한

정답 (b)

UNIT 3　기사 Ⅱ (칼럼 · 독자 투고)

EXERCISE

1 (c)　　2 (a)

PRACTICE

1 (c)　　2 (d)

유형 정리

1　칼럼 유형1: 사회 현상

해석 우리 사회는 공공연한 애정 표현을 받아들일 수 있는가? 너무도 많은 커플들은 그렇게 생각하는 것 같고, 지하철이나 사무실 건물과 같은 공공장소에서 그들의 '사랑'을 감히 드러낸다. 그렇지만 이런 장소들은 다른 이들 앞에서 사랑을 보여주기 위해 있는 장소들이 아니다. 더욱이, 참된 사랑은 자신에게 남자친구나 여자친구가 있다는 것을 세상에 보여주기 위해 파트너를 이용하는 것이 아니라, 파트너를 존중하고 아끼는 것을 뜻한다.

어구 public 공공연한　　　　　display (감정의) 표시
acceptable 받아들일 수 있는　dare to 감히 ~하다
further 더욱이　　　　　　　care about ~를 아끼다

2　칼럼 유형2: 정책 비판

해석 우리의 영어 교육의 진짜 문제가 무엇인가? 어떤 이들은 수업 시간에 영어를 충분히 쓰지 않는 것이 주된 쟁점이라고 생각한다. 따라서 그들은 영어 교사들이 수업 시간에 영어만을 쓰도록 만들 계획이다. 유감스럽게도, 그들은 진짜 문제를 의식하지 못한다. 그들은 너무 많은 교사들이 영어를 효과적이고 효율적으로 가르치는 방법을 아예 알지 못한다는 사실을 인식하지 못한다.

어구 education 교육　　　　major 주된
issue 쟁점　　　　　　unaware of ~를 의식하지 못하는
simply 아예; 단지　　　effective 효과적인
efficient 효율적인

3　독자 투고

해석 요즘, 너무도 많은 중매 알선 업체들이 결혼의 경제적 측면을 강조한다. 예컨대, 그런 업체들 가운데 일부는 잠재적인 배우자를 끌어들이기 위해 부유한 젊은 여성을 '광고'한다. 문제는 돈이 성공적인 결혼을 보증할 수 없다는 것이다. 행복한 결혼은 돈이 아니라 상호 애정과 존중에 기반을 둔다. 따라서 중매 알선 업체들은 자신들의 '사업' 전략을 재고해야만 한다.

어구 matchmaking 중매　　　stress 강조하다
economic 경제적인　　　　aspect 측면
advertise 광고하다　　　　attract 끌어들이다
potential 잠재적인　　　　spouse 배우자
guarantee 보증하다　　　　based on ~에 바탕을 둔
mutual 서로간의　　　　　rethink 재고하다

EXERCISE

1

해석 많은 이들은 최고의 대학을 졸업하는 것이 자동적으로 삶의 성공으로 귀결될 것이라고 생각한다. 그러나 그렇지가 않다. 실제 세상에서 성공하기 위해서는, 대학이 가르쳐주지 않는 필수적인 능력을 개발해야만 한다. 무엇보다도, 문제를 창의적으로 해결할 줄 아는, 독립적으로 사고할 수 있는 사람이 되어야 한다. 덧붙여, 다른 사람들에게 동정심을 베풀어야 한다.
  (a) 돈을 많이 벌다
  (b) 전 세계에 걸쳐 유명해지다
  (c) 실제 세상에서 성공하다

해설 삶의 성공을 위한 조건을 다룬 글이다. (a)와 (b)도 성공으로 여겨질 수 있지만, 글에서 논의되는 특성들을 감안할 때 거리가 멀다. 무엇보다도 전체 글의 주제와 가장 자연스럽게 이어지는 (c)가 정답이 됨에 유의해야 한다.

어구 graduate from ~를 졸업하다　automatically 자동적으로
lead to ~로 귀결되다　　　develop 개발하다
essential 필수적인　　　　skill 능력
independent 독립적인　　　thinker 사색가, 사상가
creatively 창의적으로
compassionate 동정심이 있는

정답 (c)

2

해석 왜 아주 많은 스타들이 우울증을 겪는가? 물론, 여러 원인을 생각할 수 있다. 그 가운데 하나는 스타들에게 주어지는 큰 압박감이다. 어떤 의미에서, 스타들은 인기를 먹고 사는데, 인기는 아주 불안정하다. 사실, 유명 인사들은 하룻밤 사이에 인기를 잃을 수 있다. 따라서 그들은 끊임없이 인기에 대해 걱정하는데, 이와 같은 걱정은 낮은 자긍심과 극단적인 경우 우울증으로 귀결될 수 있다.
  (a) 스타들에게 주어지는 압박감이 우울증으로 귀결될 수 있다.
  (b) 왜 모든 여배우들이 아름다운가.
  (c) 인기는 보통 사람들의 건강을 해칠 수 있다.

해설 스타들이 우울증에 잘 걸리는 현상을 다룬 글이다. 따라서 정답은 (a)다. (b)는 글의 내용에 전혀 언급이 없기 때문에 정답이 될 수 없다. 그리고 (c)는 주어진 글이 보통 사람들의 건강에 관한 글이

아니기 때문에 정답이 아니다.

어구 suffer from (고통을) 겪다 　　depression 우울증; 공황
a number of 여러 (*동의어가 several임에 유의)
cause 원인; 대의명분 　　pressure 압박감; 압력
popularity 인기 　　unstable 불안정한
celebrity 유명인사 　　unpopular 인기가 없는
overnight 하룻밤 사이에 　　constantly 끊임없이
self-esteem 자긍심 　　extreme 극단적인

정답 (a)

PRACTICE

1

해석 어린이들과 그들의 행복에 대한 나의 열정 때문에 나는 인간공학에 각별한 관심을 갖게 되었다. 이 분야가 사무직 근로자들을 위한 보다 편안한 장비를 만드는 것과 주로 관련된다는 것은 잘 알고 있다. 그것은 매우 중요하다. 또한 인간공학을 장난감 디자인이나 어린이 이용 제품을 디자인하는 데 적용할 수 있다고 생각한다. 이것은 인간 공학이 우리가 일이나 놀이를 더 잘 할 수 있도록 사물을 디자인하는 가장 좋은 방법이 무엇인지를 보여주기 때문에 가능하다.

Q. 문장을 완성할 가장 적절한 선택지를 고르시오.
(a) 부유해지다
(b) 스포츠를 더 잘하다
(c) 일이나 놀이를 더 잘하다
(d) 훨씬 더 빨리 수영하다

해설 인간공학을 아동용 장난감이나 제품 디자인에 활용할 수 있음을 말한 글이다. 본래 사무직 근로자를 위한 편안한 장비의 개발과 관련이 있다는 점과 장난감 디자인에도 적용될 수 있음을 감안하면 정답은 (c)다.

어구 passion 열정 　　particular 특정한, 특별한
ergonomics 인간공학 　　field 분야
concerned with ~와 관련된 equipment 장비
apply 적용하다

정답 (c)

2

해석 유감스럽게도, 북한 정권은 북한 주민들의 생존이 아니라, 정권의 생존에만 관심이 있다. 이른바 김정일 정권에 대한 '햇볕정책'은 확실하게 실패할 것인데, 왜냐하면 이런 요소를 감안하지 않기 때문이다. 설상가상으로, 햇볕정책이 한국에 대한 적절한 안보 정책을 개발하는 데 장애가 될 가능성이 아주 높다.

Q. 글의 어조는 어떠한가?
(a) 낙관적인
(b) 후회하는
(c) 익살스러운
(d) 우려하는

해설 햇볕정책이 북한 정권의 특수성을 감안하지 않기 때문에 실패하게 되고, 또한 안보 정책의 개발에 장애가 될 것이라고 했으므로, 햇볕정책에 대한 우려를 나타냈음을 알 수 있다. 따라서 정답은 (d)다.

어구 regime 정권; 체제 　　survival 생존
so-called 이른바 　　take into account 고려하다
factor 요인, 요소
to make matters worse 설상가상으로
possibility 가능성 　　obstacle 장애
development 개발 　　appropriate 적합한
security 안보; 보안; 경비

정답 (d)

UNIT 4　기사 Ⅲ (일반 상식 기사)

EXERCISE

1 (c) 　　2 (b)

PRACTICE

1 (d) 　　2 (b)

유형 정리

1　경제 상식

해석 피싱은 정상적인 사용자로부터 기밀 정보를 얻어내려고 하는 것을 말한다. 피싱을 하는 이들은 빈번하게, 은행 계좌 내역에 대한 정보를 얻으려고 한다. 또는 신용카드 내역을 얻어내려고 한다. 어느 경우든, 피싱은 대개 진짜 금융 기관으로부터 온 것으로 생각하게 만드는 이메일을 보냄으로써 이루어진다. 따라서 이메일을 통해서 민감한 정보를 제공하는 데 극히 신중을 기해야 한다.

어구 phishing 피싱(Private data + Fishing)
obtain 획득하다 　　confidential 기밀의
normal 정상적인 　　attempt to ~하려고 시도하다
bank account 은행 계좌 　　detail 세부사항
financial 재정적인, 금융의 extremely 극히
provide 제공하다 　　sensitive 민감한

2　생활 상식

해석 다양한 방식으로 생선을 요리할 수 있다. 예컨대 오븐에서 생선을 요리할 수 있는데, 이렇게 하면 생선이 다른 재료와 섞이도록 할 수 있다. 또는 뜨거운 석쇠에서 생선을 요리할 수도 있다. 또한 다양한 종류의 생선을 찔 수도 있다. 생선을 훈제하는 것도 좋은 아이디어다. 어떤 방식을 택하든, 요리한 생선을 반드시 야채와 함께 접대하라.

어구 a variety of 다양한 　　oven 오븐
mix 섞다 　　ingredient (요리) 재료
grill 석쇠 　　steam (음식을) 찌다
smoke 훈제하다 　　serve (음식 등을) 내주다

3　건강 상식

해석 수면 결핍은 수면을 충분히 취하지 못한 것을 말한다. 수면 결핍이 생기면, 많은 점에서 건강에 부정적으로 영향을 미칠 수 있다. 피로를 느끼거나 일에 집중하는 데 어려움을 겪을지도 모른다. 극단적인 경우에는, 환시(幻視)나 환청을 겪을 수도 있다. 어떤 이들은 수면 결핍이 정신병으로 귀결될 수도 있다고 말하지만, 그런 주장을 뒷받침하기 위해서는 보다 많은 연구가 요구된다.

어구 deprivation 결핍 　　occur 발생하다
negatively 부정적으로 　　fatigued 노곤한
concentrate on ~에 집중하다
extreme 극단적인 　　illusion 환상, 환각
psychosis 정신병 　　require 요구하다
support 뒷받침하다

EXERCISE

1

해석 대략적으로 말해서, 공황장애 환자들은 일주일에 한 번 정도 공황발작을 경험한다. 공황발작이란 심하게 불안해하는 것을 말한다. 공황발작을 겪으면, 어지럽거나 떨리거나 기절하거나 땀을 흘리거나 메스꺼움을 느낀다. 공황발작은 예측할 수 없다. 공황발작이 스트레스가 심한 상황과 밀접하게 관련되는 것 같지도 않다. 많은 이들은 공황장애가 유전병이라고 생각한다.
(a) 부모를 자랑스러워하다
(b) 미래를 예측하다
(c) 심하게 불안해하다

해설 공황장애에 대한 글이다. 여러 증상으로부터 공황장애 환자가 심한 불안을 느낀다는 점을 쉽게 짐작할 수 있다. (a)나 (b)는 모두 주어진 글의 내용과 관계가 없기 때문에 정답이 될 수 없음에 유의해야 한다.

어구 roughly 대략적으로, 대충 · panic disorder 공황장애
panic attack 공황발작 · dizzy 현기증이 나는
tremble 떨다 · faint 기절하다
sweat 땀을 흘리다 · nausea 메스꺼움
unpredictable 예측할 수 없는
closely 밀접하게 · related to ~와 관련된
hereditary 유전되는

정답 (c)

2

해석 사실, 인터넷에서의 악플은 범죄로 간주될 수 있다. 이것은 주로 그런 말이 평판에 부정적인 영향을 미치기 때문이다. 예컨대 특정한 배우에 대해 계속해서 험담을 한다면 사람들이 그 배우가 재능이 없는 것으로 폄하할 가능성이 높다. 이런 일이 생기면 그 배우는 많이 괴로워해서 악플을 단 범죄자를 고소하고 싶어 할 수도 있다.
(a) 악플은 평판에 영향을 미치지 않는다.
(b) 악플은 범죄로 간주될 수 있다.
(c) 악플은 배우들이 성공하는 데 도움이 된다.

해설 심각한 사회적 문제로 대두된 악플에 관한 글이다. 첫 번째 문장에서 악플이 범죄로 간주될 수 있다고 했기 때문에 정답은 (b)다. 반면 (a)와 (c)는 주어진 내용과 반대되기 때문에 정답이 될 수 없다.

어구 malicious 악의적인
regard A as B A를 B로 간주하다
crime 범죄 · negatively 부정적으로
reputation 평판, 명성 · speak ill of ~를 험담하다
dismiss 진지하게 고려하지 않다; 해고하다
untalented 재능이 없는 · sue 고소하다
perpetrator 범죄자

정답 (b)

PRACTICE

1

해석 미국 국립보건원 대체의학사무국에 따르면, 대체의학은 '의학전문대학원에서 널리 가르치지 않는 치료법이나 보건 요법'을 가리킨다고 한다. 이런 치료법의 상당수는 질병이 일어나는 것을 예방하는 것을 목표로 한다. 덧붙여, 대체의학 종사자들은 환자의 건강의 모든 측면을 고려한다.

Q. 문장을 완성할 가장 적절한 선택지를 고르시오.
(a) 일반적으로 학습되는
(b) 널리 받아들여지는
(c) 일반적으로 다루어지는
(d) 널리 가르치지 않는

해설 대체의학에 관한 글이다. '대체'라는 말로부터 기존의 의학과 다르다는 점을 알 수 있고, 이와 같은 의학은 일반 의과전문대학원에서 가르치는 경우가 많지 않을 것이라는 점을 추론할 수 있다. 또한 질병 예방이 목적이 되는 경우가 많다고 했는데, 일반적으로 치료법은 일어난 질병을 고치는 것이기 때문에 차이가 있다. 이와 같은 점을 종합하면, 정답이 (d)라는 점을 알아낼 수 있다. 다소 까다로운 유형에 속한다.

어구 alternative medicine 대체의학
refer to ~를 지칭하다 · treatment 치료법
practice 관행; 연습
medical school 의학전문대학원
aimed at ~를 목표로 하는 · practitioner 종사자
take into account 고려하다 · aspect 측면

정답 (d)

2

해석 캐나다로 여행할 때, 많은 상점들이 여행자 수표를 받지 않는다는 사실을 고려할 필요가 있다. 이것은 주로 신용카드가 제품이나 서비스의 값을 치르는 보다 편리한 방법이기 때문이다. 이 사실을 감안하여, 일부 회사들은 여행자 체크카드를 발급하기 시작하는데, 여행자 체크카드는 신용카드와 아주 흡사하다. 그렇지만 그런 체크카드보다 신용카드를 사용할 것을 권한다.

Q. 글로부터 추론할 수 있는 바는 무엇인가?
(a) 캐나다의 상점들은 모두 여행자 수표를 받는다.
(b) 신용카드가 여행자 체크카드보다 더 편리하다.
(c) 여행자 체크카드가 신용카드보다 더 편리하다.
(d) 여행자 체크카드는 신용카드와 상당히 다르다.

해설 캐나다로 여행할 때 결제 수단으로서 여행자 수표가 불편할 수 있음을 밝힌 글이다. (a)는 글의 내용과 일치하지 않는다. (c)는 여행자 체크카드보다 신용카드를 쓰라고 했으므로 신용카드가 더 편리할 것으로 보는 것이 자연스럽다 (d)는 신용카드와 아주 흡사하다고 했으므로 정답이 될 수 없다. 따라서 정답은 (b)다.

어구 consider 고려하다 · accept 받아들이다
traveler's check 여행자 수표 · convenient 편리한
take into account 고려하다 · issue 발급하다
check card 체크카드 · similar to ~와 유사한
advisable 권할 만한

정답 (b)

UNIT 5 서한 I (일반 서한 · 이메일)

EXERCISE
1 (b)   2 (b)

PRACTICE
1 (c)   2 (d)

유형 정리

1 문의 / 감사 서한

해석 유감스럽게도, 제가 캐나다에 살고 있지 않고 신청 기한에 대한 시의적절한 통고를 받지도 못해서 어학 과정 신청 기한을 지키지 못했습니다. 어떻든, Canadian University에서는 2008년 9월부터 2009년 8월까지 제가 귀(貴)대학에서 어학 과정을 이수할 것을 요구합니다. 신청 기한을 놓쳤다는 점을 감안할 때, 어떻게 2008년도 영어 어학 과정을 신청하고 신청비를 지불할 수 있을지 궁금합니다.

어구 fail to ~하지 못하다
meet the deadline 기한을 지키다
application 지원, 신청   receive 받다
timely 시의적절한   notification 통고
at any rate 어쨌든   require 요구하다
application fee 신청비

2 항의 서한

해석 귀하의 서한에 감사드립니다. 그러나 교육 비디오나 사용자 설명서로부터 텍스트를 MP3 파일로 변환하는 데 대한 어떤 정보도 찾을 수 없습니다. 참고를 위해, 편지에 설명서의 사본을 동봉했습니다. 사본으로부터 아실 수 있듯이, MP3 파일을 만들어내는 것을 다루는 항목이 없습니다. 제가 아는 한 그것은 비디오에 대해서도 마찬가지인데, 제가 비디오를 봤기 때문에 이렇게 말씀드릴 수 있습니다. 제가 잘못된 프로그램을 받은 것인지 제 제품의 버전이 구(舊)버전인지는 모르겠습니다.

어구 convert 변환하다   reference 참고, 참조
enclose 동봉하다   copy 사본
entry (취급) 항목
as far as I know 내가 아는 한   version 버전

3 이메일

해석 헤더와 인코딩 체계의 문제로 지난 번 제 이메일을 열어보실 수 없었을 것으로 알고 있습니다. 두 가지를 모두 바꾸었으므로, 제 메일을 열고 읽으시는 데 아무런 어려움이 없으시기를 진정으로 바랍니다. 그리고 이 문제에 관해 귀하의 탁월한 서비스와 자상한 도움에 정말 감사드립니다. 제가 프랑스어를 유창하게 구사할 수 있다면 좋을 텐데요. 그렇지만, 현재로서는 제 상황을 양해해주실 것을 정중하게 요청하는 바입니다.

어구 due to ~로 인해   header 헤더
encoding 인코딩; 암호화, 부호화
appreciate 감사하다; 이해하다
generous 후하게 베푸는   excellent 뛰어난
fluent 유창한   matter 일
politely 정중하게   at present 현재는
                        circumstances 상황

EXERCISE

1

해석 물론, 저는 그처럼 자격을 갖춘 근로자를 찾는 것이 얼마나 어려운지 또한 그렇게 사람을 구하는 것이 얼마나 많은 일을 수반하는지를 잘 알고 있습니다. 그렇지만 저는 왜 가너 씨가 귀하에게 너무 많이 기대하는지를 이해할 수 있습니다. 어쨌든, 가너 씨가 우리 회사의 미래를 책임지고 있으니까요. 그렇지만 저는 귀하의 일에 대해 만족하고 또한 귀하의 뛰어난 서비스에 깊이 감사드립니다. 진심으로 고맙습니다.
(a) 괴롭히는
(b) 너무 많이 기대하는
(c) 고소하려고 하는

해설 바로 앞에서 아주 어려운 부탁을 하고 있음을 잘 알고 있다고 했고, 또한 회사의 장래까지 언급이 되었으므로, 가너 씨가 편지를 받는 사람에게 많이 기대를 하고 있음을 알 수 있다. 따라서 정답은 (b)다. (a)는 주어진 내용만으로는 알 수 없기 때문에 정답이 될 수 없음에 유의해야 한다.

어구 keenly 예리하게   aware 인식하는, 알고 있는
qualified 자격을 갖춘   entail 수반하다
responsible for ~를 책임지는
after all 어떻든, 결국엔   satisfied with ~에 만족한
grateful 고마움을 느끼는

정답 (b)

2

해석 그것은 아주 노고가 필요한 일처럼 들리겠지만 기쁜 소식이 있으니, 20년 동안 운영하면서 수십 명의 수석교사들의 지침서를 수집했다는 것입니다. 더욱이, 전임자가 모든 단계에서 지도하고 가르쳐줄 것입니다. 이행 기간이 약 3주 정도 될 것으로 생각되는데, 적응하고 배울 충분한 시간을 제공할 것입니다. 정말 중요한 것은 귀하의 태도입니다. 위험을 감수하여 몰라볼 정도로 발전하고 싶습니까?
(a) 이 편지를 쓴 사람은 경찰관이다.
(b) 이 편지는 수석교사 직책과 관련이 있다.
(c) 이 편지의 독자에게는 태도에 있어 심각한 문제가 있다.

해설 수석교사 직책에 대한 내용이 주가 되는 글이다. 따라서 정답은 (b)다. (a)는 이 글로부터 알 수 없기 때문에 정답이 아니다. 반면 (c)는 지나치게 추론을 한 것으로 마지막에서 두 번째 문장만으로 이렇게 추론할 수 없음에 특히 유의해야 한다.

어구 demanding 노고를 요하는   head teacher 수석교사
manual 지침서   operation 운영
moreover 더욱이   predecessor 전임자
every step of the way 모든 단계에서
transition 이행   adjust 적응하다, 조정하다
attitude 태도   recognition 인식, 인정

정답 (b)

PRACTICE

1

해석 저는 일본의 에리카 브레슬린입니다. 몇 가지 품목이 빠져 있는 것으로 알고 있습니다. 그러나 그것은 전혀 상관이 없으며, 그래서 주문을 하고 싶습니다. 전적으로 개인적인 이유로 주문한다는 점을 언급해야만 한다고 생각됩니다. 귀(貴)회사에서 제작한 DVD 타이틀을 즐겨 봅니다. 특히 Romance 시리즈의 높은 우

수성에 깊은 인상을 받았습니다.

Q. 문장을 완성할 가장 적절한 선택지를 고르시오.

(a) 전적으로 상업적인

(b) 절대적으로 낭만적인

(c) 전적으로 개인적인

(d) 전적으로 공식적인

해설 빈 칸 다음에 나오는 내용이 모두 편지를 쓴 본인에 대한 내용이고, 개인적으로 DVD 타이틀을 좋아하기 때문에 구입한다고 했으므로 정답은 (c)다. (b)의 경우에는 마지막 문장에서 Romance가 언급되었기 때문에 정답으로 생각할 수도 있지만, 그 앞에 문장과 관련하여 생각해야 하고, 또한 romantic이라는 말이 '사랑의 감정과 관련된'이란 뜻임을 감안할 때 정답이 될 수 없음에 유의해야 한다.

어구 item 품목   missing 빠져 있는

place an order 주문하다   mention 언급하다

produce 생산하다   particularly 특히

impressed 깊은 인상을 받은

정답 (c)

2

해석 이곳 서울은 약간 춥고, 그리고 맞아요, 이곳 하늘은 푸릅니다. 아, 동료들이 여전히 그리워하고 있고 저 또한 그렇다는 것을 말해야만 하겠네요. 그리고 혹시 매기 스미스가 누구인지 알고 있나요? 우리 회사의 새로운 직원인데, 일본에서 당신을 만났다고 하더군요. 정말 세상이 좁죠? 그리고 이곳 Faith House에서 탁월하게 일을 해준 데 대해 정말 고마워요. 당신의 헌신과 프로 정신을 아주 그리워하게 될 거예요.

Q. 글로부터 추론할 수 있는 바는 무엇인가?

(a) 이 편지를 읽는 이는 매기 스미스를 만나지 못했다.

(b) 이 편지를 쓴 사람은 일본에 살고 있다.

(c) 이 편지를 쓴 사람은 푸른 하늘을 전혀 못 본다.

(d) 이 편지를 읽는 이는 Faith House에서 일했다.

해설 글에서 매기 스미스가 글의 독자를 만난 적이 있다고 했으므로 (a)는 정답이 아니다. 그리고 첫 문장에서 '이곳 서울'이라고 했으므로 글을 쓴 사람이 한국에 살고 있음을 알 수 있다. (c)도 첫 문장의 내용에 어긋난다. 따라서 정답은 (d)다.

어구 colleague 동료   miss 그리워하다

happen to 우연히 ~하다   superb 탁월한

dedication 헌신   professionalism 프로 정신

정답 (d)

UNIT 6   서한 Ⅱ (추천서 · 지원서)

EXERCISE

1 (b)   **2** (a)

PRACTICE

1 (c)   **2** (d)

유형 정리

1   추천서

해석 탁월성을 추구하고자 하는 열정과 함께, 이 모든 특성들로 그녀는 단연코 귀국의 분자생물학의 발전에 기여하는 이상적인 과학자가 될 것입니다. 그리고 그녀를 귀(貴)명문대학에 추천하는 것을 큰 기쁨과 영광으로 생각합니다. 그녀가 귀 대학에 귀중한 자산이 될 것이라고 확신합니다.

어구 quality 특성; 품질   passion 열정

pursuit 추구   excellence 탁월함

definitely 확실히   ideal 이상적인

contribute to ~에 기여하다

molecular biology 분자생물학

honor 영광   prestigious 명문의

asset 자산

2   입사 지원서

해석 가족 친화적이면서 동시에 아주 성공적인 회사로서의 귀사의 명성에 대해 많이 들었습니다. 그 두 가지 요인 때문에 저는 귀사에 지원하게 되었습니다. 두 명의 사랑스러운 딸을 가진 어머니이기에, 제 가정생활이 존중되는 환경에서 일해야만 합니다. 그리고 물론, 어떤 '회사'이든 직원들이 행복하게 살게 하려면 살아남아서 번성해야만 합니다.

어구 reputation 명성, 평판   -friendly ~친화적인

factor 요인, 요소   compel 강요하다

firm 회사   lovely 사랑스러운

environment 환경   thrive 번창하다

3   입학 지원서

해석 이처럼 급속하게 변화하는 세상에서 성공하기 위해서, 회사는 국제적 요구와 지역적 요구를 깊이 이해하는 근로자를 필요로 합니다. 저는 Academic University가 그런 통찰력을 갖춘 학생을 양성하는, 세계에서 가장 좋은 곳이라고 믿습니다. 탄탄한 학문적 교과과정과 함께, Academic University는 제가 확실히 국제 경영에서 선도자가 될 수 있도록 하는 다양한 프로그램을 제공합니다. 그것이 제가 이 명문대학에 지원하는 주된 이유입니다.

어구 rapidly 급속히   global 국제적인

need 요구, 필요   insight 통찰력

a variety of 다양한   definitely 확실히

empower 권한을 부여하다

EXERCISE

1

해석 15년 이상의 교육 경력을 가진 오랜 언어 교사로서, 저는 아비게일 카펜터스가 재능이 뛰어난 언어 학습자라고 확언할 수 있습니다. 3년이 넘게 그녀를 가르쳐오면서 그녀가 '언어학자'로서 성장하는 것을 지켜봐왔습니다. 그녀는 언어가 본질적으로 우리 존재의 핵심을 다룬다는 것을 이해합니다. 따라서 그녀는 세상을 해석하는 다양한 방식을 탐구하기 위해 상당한 시간을 투자해왔습니다.
(a) 디자이너
(b) 언어학자
(c) 교사

해설 뛰어난 언어 학습자로서의 아비게일 카펜터스의 면모를 설명한 글이다. 따라서 이와 자연스럽게 이어질 수 있는 것은 (b)다. 디자인에 대한 언급이 전혀 없기 때문에 (a)가 정답이 될 수 없고 아비게일 카펜터스가 가르치는 사람이 아니기 때문에 (c)도 정답이 아니다.

어구 experience 경력; 경험 　　assure 확신시키다
gifted 재능이 뛰어난 　　observe 관찰하다
grow 성장하다 　　essentially 본질적으로
core 핵심 　　significant 상당한, 의미 있는
explore 탐구하다, 탐험하다 　　interpret 해석하다

정답 (b)

2

해석 훌륭한 디자인은 일상적인 것들의 본질에 대한 깊은 성찰에서만 비롯될 수 있는데, 일상적인 것들은 본질적으로 주위 환경과 조화를 이룹니다. 사물의 이와 같은 아름다운 본성을 예민하게 인식하고 있기 때문에, 저는 그것을 제 자신의 터치로 재해석하고 표현하고 싶습니다. 그렇게 하는 데 있어, 저는 '창의적으로 생각하는 사람으로서 성장'해야 한다는 데 대해 전적으로 동의합니다. 그래서 저는 Beauty College를 시각 예술가로서뿐만 아니라 사고(思考)하는 이로서 성장하는 장래의 모교로서 선택했습니다.
(a) 이 지원서를 쓴 이는 Beauty College에 지원한다.
(b) 이 지원서를 쓴 이는 창의적으로 생각하는 사람으로서 성장할 필요가 없다.
(c) 이 지원서를 쓴 이는 훌륭한 통역사가 되고 싶어한다.

해설 마지막 문장을 통해 글을 쓴 이가 Beauty College에 지원하고 있음을 알 수 있다. (b)는 주어진 글의 내용과 다르고, (c)는 글의 내용과 무관하다. interpret에 '통역하다'라는 뜻도 있는데, 이를 혼동하도록 유도한 선택지이다.

어구 insight 통찰력 　　nature 본성
harmony 조화 　　surroundings 주위 환경
keenly 예리하게 　　aware of ~를 의식하는
reinterpret 재해석하다 　　creative 창의적인
alma mater 모교 　　thinker 사색가, 사상가

정답 (a)

PRACTICE

1

해석 훌륭한 대학은 학생들에게 영성(靈性)을 심어주어야만 합니다. 그것이 제 확고부동한 신념이며 제가 Faith University에 지원하는 주된 이유입니다. 이것은 반학문적 태도처럼 들릴지도 모르지만, 그렇지가 않습니다. 이처럼 급속하게 변화하는 세계에서, 학생들은 학문적인 사안과 실제적인 사안을 자신감 있게 그리고 능숙하게 다룰 준비가 되어 있어야만 합니다. 그런 일은 보다 높은 정도의 영성을 요구합니다.

Q. 문장을 완성할 가장 적절한 선택지를 고르시오.
(a) ~에게 지식을 주다
(b) ~를 위해 보다 밝은 미래를 보장하다
(c) ~에게 영성을 심어주다
(d) ~에게 관심을 가지다

해설 마지막 문장을 통해 정답을 비교적 쉽게 찾을 수 있는 문제다. 정답은 (c)다. (a)는 글쓴이가 자신의 믿음이 반학문적인 것으로 생각될 수도 있다고 했으므로 정답이 아니다. (b)와 (d)는 마지막 문장에서 말한 영성과 연결되지 않기 때문에 정답이 될 수 없다.

어구 instill 심어주다 　　spirituality 영성(靈性)
main 주된 　　anti-academic 반(反)학문적인
practical 실제적인 　　concern (관련) 사안
confidence 자신감 　　require 요구하다

정답 (c)

2

해석 에릭 모리슨은 20년이 넘게 저와 일을 해왔습니다. 그럼에도 불구하고 저는 그의 헌신과 프로 정신에 계속해서 놀랍니다. 사실, 그가 얼마나 많은 밤을 프로젝트 수행에 보냈는지 기억할 수조차 없습니다. 덧붙여, 그는 계속해서 자신의 기량을 가다듬고 있는데, 그의 업무량을 감안하면 쉬운 일이 아닙니다. 이와 같은 것을 고려해서, 저는 그가 귀사에 큰 자산이 될 것으로 확신합니다.

Q. 글에 따르면 다음 가운데 어느 것이 올바른가?
(a) 이 추천서를 쓴 이는 에릭 모리슨을 잘 알지 못한다.
(b) 모리슨의 업무량은 작다.
(c) 에릭 모리슨은 아주 게으른 사람이다.
(d) 에릭 모리슨은 자신의 일에 헌신적이다.

해설 에릭 모리슨을 추천한 글이다. 20년 넘게 같이 일했다고 했으므로 (a)는 정답이 아니다. 그리고 에릭 모리슨의 업무량이 많음을 짐작할 수 있으므로 (b)도 정답이 아니다. 또한 에릭 모리슨의 헌신을 감안하면 (c)도 정답이 될 수 없다. 따라서 정답은 (d)다.

어구 continually 계속해서 　　amaze 깜짝 놀라게 하다
dedication 헌신 　　professionalism 프로 정신
project 프로젝트 　　sharpen 갈고닦다
workload 업무량 　　convinced 확신하는
asset 자산

정답 (d)

Chapter 5

UNIT 1 정치와 경제

EXERCISE
1 (a)　　2 (b)

PRACTICE
1 (d)　　2 (c)

유형 정리

1 정치

해석 대의민주주의에서, 정치가들은 독립적으로 판단하고 다양한 집단의 다양한 요구를 조정해야 하는 피(被)신탁인이 되어야 할 것으로 기대된다. 그렇지만 '협의 내용을 공표하는' 전략은 정치가들로 하여금 반대자들과 협상하는 어려운 과제를 피할 수 있게 한다. 그렇게 해서, 그들은 정책 입안 과정의 상충적인 속성을 무시할 수 있다.

어구 representative democracy 대의민주주의
politician 정치가　　trustee 피(被)신탁인
display 나타내다　　independent 독립적인
judgment 판단　　reconcile 조정하다
various 다양한　　strategy 전략
go pubic (비밀을) 공표하다　　avoid 피하다
negotiate 협상하다　　opponent 반대자, 적수
disregard 무시하다　　conflicting 상충하는
policy-making 정책 입안

2 경제

해석 많은 전문가들은 이명박 대통령이 한국의 경제를 일으켜 세우기 위해 다양한 조치를 취할 것이라고 예측한다. 그는 안전한 환경과 다양한 인센티브를 제공함으로써 외국인 투자를 유치할 것이다. 또한 새로운 대통령은 규제를 줄임으로써 대기업들이 보다 많이 투자할 수 있게 할 것이다. 끝으로, 그는 한국과 미국의 경제적 유대를 강화할 가능성이 높다.

어구 analyst 전문가　　predict 예측하다
measures 조치　　boost 향상시키다
attract 끌어들이다　　investment 투자
incentive 인센티브　　corporation (대)기업; 법인
reduce 감소시키다　　regulation 규제
strengthen 강화하다　　ties 유대 관계

3 경영

해석 이처럼 고도로 세계화된 시대에, 글로벌 경영은 선택이 아니라 필수이다. 세계 시장에서 살아남기 위해서 회사는 국가간 문화적 차이를 이해하고 이용하기 위해 모든 노력을 기울여야 한다. 역설적이게도, 이것은 위기가 아니라 기회인네, 왜냐하면 세계 시장에서 상업 활동이 급속히 팽창하고 있기 때문이다. 따라서 이 설호의 기회를 잡아서 전(全)세계에 중대한 영향을 끼쳐야 한다.

어구 globalized 세계화된　　option 선택
necessity 필수　　effort 노력
take advantage of ~를 이용하다
ironically 역설적이게도　　crisis 위기

business 상업 활동　　expand 확장하다
seize 잡다　　a golden opportunity 절호의 기회
make a difference 중대하게 영향을 미치다

EXERCISE

1

해석 찰스 앤더슨은 평등한 기회가 집단의 최상의 실적을 보장하기 위해 희생되어야 한다고 주장한다. 이 주장이 사회의 민간부문에 적용될 때 바람직하지 않은 결과를 초래하지는 않을 것이다. 그러나 이런 종류의 사고가 공공부문에 적용된다면 그 결과는 비극적일 것이다. 이것은 주로 공공부문의 목적이 민간부문의 목적과 아주 다르기 때문이다.
(a) 비극적인
(b) 바람직한
(c) 기쁜

해설 민간부문의 목적과 공공부문의 목적이 다르다고 말했기 때문에 공공부문에 적용되었을 때는 부정적인 결과가 나와야 한다. 따라서 정답은 (a)다. (b)와 (c)는 모두 긍정적인 특성이기 때문에 정답이 될 수 없다.

어구 argue 주장하다　　sacrifice 희생하다
ensure 확실하게 하다　　performance 실적; 수행
association 집단　　argument 주장; 논거
undesirable 바람직하지 못한　　apply 적용되다
private sector 민간부문　　public sector 공공부문

정답 (a)

2

해석 실업자 수치를 정말로 신뢰할 수 있는가? 사실, 많은 '잠재적' 근로자의 숫자가 그 수치에는 포함되어 있지 않다. 예컨대 일자리를 잃고서 다른 일자리를 구하지 않는다면 미국 노동부가 실업자로 간주하지 않는다. 더욱이, 많은 종류의 아르바이트 종사자들의 수가 실업자 수치에 포함되어 있지 않다. 이런 의미에서, 그 수치는 그다지 신뢰할 만한 것이 아니다.
(a) 미국 노동부는 실업자 수치와는 아무런 관계가 없다.
(b) 실업자 수치는 그리 신뢰할 만하지 않다.
(c) 실업자 수치는 잠재적 근로자의 수를 포함한다.

해설 미국 노동부는 실업자 수치를 산출하는 기관임을 알 수 있으므로 (a)는 정답이 아니다. 그리고 (c)는 잠재적 근로자의 수가 실업자 수치에 포함되지 않는다고 했으므로 정답이 될 수 없다. 따라서 정답은 (b)다. 이는 마지막 문장에서 바로 추론할 수 있다.

어구 trust 신뢰하다　　unemployment 실업
figure 수치　　potential 잠재적인
include 포함하다　　count 간주하다
reliable 신뢰할 만한

정답 (b)

PRACTICE

1

해석 1906년, 미국 정부는 셔먼 독점금지법에 따라 Standard Oil Company를 법정에 세웠다. 정부는 존 록펠러의 회사인 Standard Oil Company가 불공정한 경쟁 방법을 이용했다고 생각했다. 1911년, 미국 연방법원은 Standard Oil Company가 수십 개의 독립된 회사로 분리되도록 명했다. 역설적이게도, 그처럼 분리되고 나서, 록펠러는 세계에서 가장 부유한 사람이 되

었다.

Q. 문장을 완성할 가장 적절한 선택지를 고르시오.
(a) 구성하다
(b) 다루다
(c) 설명하다
(d) 분리되다

해설 빈 칸이 들어 있는 문장에 '수십 개의 독립된 회사로'라는 말이 있고, 반독점법이 적용되었으므로 회사를 분리할 것을 요구했음을 짐작할 수 있다. 나머지 선택지들은 모두 주어진 문장에 어울리지 않는다.

어구 take to court 소송을 제기하다　antitrust 반독점
make use of 이용하다　　　unfair 불공정한
competition 경쟁　　　　　break up 갈라지다
separate 별개의　　　　　　dissolution 분리

정답 (d)

2

해석 맥대니얼의 주장은 미국 사회의 본질을 설명하지 못한다. 널리 알려져 있듯이, 미국 사회는 백인이 주도하는 사회이다. 미국의 건국 이래로, 백인들은 정치적·경제적·사회적 활동 영역에서 우월함을 유지하기 위해 노력해왔다. 이런 의미에서 미국 사회는 흑인이 아닌 인종들과 흑인들끼리가 아니라, 백인과 백인이 아닌 인종들끼리 분열되어 있다.

Q. 글로부터 추론할 수 있는 바는 무엇인가?
(a) 흑인들은 아시아계 미국인들을 증오한다.
(b) 맥대니얼의 주장은 신뢰할 만하다.
(c) 백인들이 미국 사회를 지배한다.
(d) 흑인들은 백인들을 존중한다.

해설 (a)는 글의 내용을 통해 전혀 알 수 없기 때문에 정답이 될 수 없다. 그리고 (b)는 첫 번째 문장에서 맥대니얼의 주장을 반박했으므로 역시 정답이 아니다. 그리고 (d)는 글의 내용을 통해서 알 수 없으므로, 정답은 (c)다. (c)는 두 번째 문장을 통해 바로 추론할 수 있다. 이처럼 TEPS에서는 주어진 내용으로부터 바로 추론할 것을 요구하는 경우가 많다는 점을 특히 유념해야 한다.

어구 argument 주장; 논거　　　nature 본성, 본질
society 사회　　　　　　　dominant 지배적인
founding 건립, 건국　　　　maintain 유지하다; 주장하다
superiority 우월성　　　　arena 활동 영역
divide 분열시키다

정답 (c)

UNIT 2　사회와 역사

EXERCISE
1 (c)　　2 (c)

PRACTICE
1 (b)　　2 (d)

유형 정리

1　사회 현상

해석 요즘 너무도 많은 부모들이 자녀가 이른 나이에 영어를 배워야 한

다고 주장하고 있다. 국제 언어(영어)를 습득하는 것이 높은 사회적 지위로 이어질 수 있다는 점에서 이해할 만하다. 그렇지만, 유감스럽게도 일부 부모들은 심지어 자신의 자녀로 하여금 수백 개의 영어 문장을 외우게까지 하게 한다. 이들은 영어와 같은 외국어를 효과적으로 배우기 위해서는 정서적으로 준비가 되어 있어야 한다는 것을 이해할 필요가 있다.

어구 insist 주장하다, 고집하다　　understandable 이해할 만한
global 세계의　　　　　　　　lead to ~으로 귀결되다
go so far as to ~라는 극단적인 행동을 하다
effectively 효과적으로
emotionally 감정적으로, 정서적으로

2　사회 이슈

해석 한국국제무역협회에 따르면, 여성은 전체 국회의원의 13.4%만을 차지한다고 한다. 이 비율은 세계의 평균(수)치에 크게 미치지 못한다. 근본적으로, 사회생활의 모든 측면에서 여성의 권리를 옹호할 수 있도록 보다 많은 여성 정치인이 필요하다. 그러한 변화가 없다면, 한국에서의 양성 평등은 이루어지지 못할 것이다.

어구 make up 구성하다　　　percentage 비율
basically 근본적으로　　aspect 측면
gender equality 양성 평등　achieve 성취하다

3　역사

해석 맥아더의 인천 공격 이후에, 북한군은 남한에서 철수했다. 다시 한번, 민주주의 국가인 한국은 해방되었다. 완전한 승리를 원했기에, 미군은 공산주의자들인 북한군을 추적했다. 미군이 압록강에 도달할 무렵에, 매우 많은 수의 중공군이 개입했다. 맥아더는 미국이 핵미사일을 사용하여 중공을 공격해야 한다고 생각했다.

어구 offensive 공격　　　　withdraw 철수하다
democratic 민주적인　　free 해방시키다
chase 추적하다　　　　communist 공산주의자
intervene 개입하다

EXERCISE

1

해석 요즘, 너무나 많은 젊은 여성들이 충분히 날씬함에도 불구하고 다이어트를 하고 있다. 이것은 주로 매스미디어가 여성들로 하여금 날씬한 여성만이 아름답다고 믿도록 만들었기 때문이다. 이렇게 해서, 매스미디어는 우리들로 하여금 아름다움이 여성에게 가장 중요한 것이라고 또한 믿도록 만들었다. 그러나 그렇지가 않다. 여성에게 가장 중요한 것은 잠재력을 실현하는 것이다. 그렇게 하기 위해서 여성들은, 아름다움이 아닌 지성과 노력이 필요하다.
(a) 관계가
(b) 건강이
(c) 아름다움이

해설 글의 전체 흐름이 미(美)에 관한 것이므로 정답은 (c)다. 또한 다이어트(diet)가 나왔다고 해서 (b)를 답으로 선택하는 일이 없도록 해야 한다.

어구 go on a diet 다이어트하다　　matter 중요하다
realize 실현하다　　　　　　potential 잠재력
in order to ~하기 위해서　　intelligence 지성
effort 노력

정답 (c)

2

해석 9 · 11 테러 진상 (규명) 운동을 지지하는 이들은 미국 정부 내의 일단의 사람들이 9 · 11 테러가 발생하도록 허용했다고 주장한다. 지지자들 가운데 일부는 심지어 그 잔악한 집단이 9 · 11 테러 공격을 수행하도록 도와주기까지 했다고 말한다. 이들의 주장은 공식적인 해명의 부정확성에 토대를 두고 있다. 그렇지만 많은 전문가들은 그들의 주장이 틀렸다고 생각한다.

(a) 지지자들은 9 · 11 테러 공격이 아프가니스탄 정부의 탓이라고 비난한다.
(b) 이 운동의 주장은 전혀 근거가 없다.
(c) 이 운동의 주장은 일반적으로 받아들여지지 않는다.

해설 정오(true or false) 유형으로 글의 내용을 하나하나 확인해야 풀 수 있다. 정답은 (c)다. (a)에서 '아프가니스탄 정부'가 아니라 '미국 정부 내의 잔악한 집단'이 되어야 한다. (b)는 글에서 '공식적인 해명의 부정확성'이라는 부분 때문에 정답이 될 수 없다.

어구 supporter 지지자   attack 공격
cruel 잔인한   inaccuracy 부정확성
official 공식적인   expert 전문가
argument 주장; 논거

정답 (c)

PRACTICE

1

해석 요즘 우리는 너무나 많은 영화 속 폭력 장면에 노출되어 있다. 이것은 심각한 문제다. 많은 연구들은 '가짜' 폭력에 대한 노출이 진짜 폭력에 대한 무감각으로 귀결될 수 있다는 것을 입증했다. 영화에서 보게 되는 폭력은 '가짜' 폭력이다. 이 때문에 예견된 대로 많은 진짜 폭력의 사태를 초래하였다. 더 이상의 비극적 사태를 막기 위해서 영화 속 폭력을 금지시켜야 한다.

Q. 문장에 들어갈 가장 적절한 것을 고르시오.
(a) 폭력의 희생자에 대한 동정심
(b) 진짜 폭력에 대한 무감각
(c) 영화 속 폭력을 금지하려는 노력
(d) 미래를 예측하는 능력

해설 전체 글의 흐름을 통해 (b)가 정답임을 알 수 있다. 영화 속 '가짜' 폭력에 대한 노출이 '진짜' 폭력으로 귀결될 수 있다는 것은 '진짜' 폭력에 대한 무감각에서 비롯된다고 볼 수 있기 때문이다. (a)는 글의 내용과 어긋나고, (c)는 글의 내용과는 관련이 있지만 빈 칸에 들어갈 부분은 아니고 (d)는 지문의 predicted를 반복해 함정을 유도하고 있다.

어구 be exposed to ~에 노출되다   violent 폭력적인, 난폭한
study 연구   exposure 노출
insensitivity 무감각   instance 경우, 사례

정답 (b)

2

해석 1861년과 1865년 사이에, 북부 주들은 여러 이유로 남부 주들과 싸웠다. 쟁점 가운데 하나는 주의 권리였다. 남부 주들은 연방으로부터 탈퇴할 권리가 있다고 믿었다. 반면, 북부 주들은 그런 권리가 존재하지 않는다고 생각했다. 아브라함 링컨이 대통령으로 당선되자, 남부 주들은 자신들의 권리를 보호해야 한다고 느꼈다. 그들은 연방으로부터 탈퇴했다.

Q. 글을 통해 추론할 수 있는 것은 무엇인가?
(a) 북부 주들과 남부 주들은 모든 쟁점에 대해 동의했다.
(b) 아브라함 링컨은 남부 주 출신이었다.
(c) 아브라함 링컨은 어떤 주든지 연방으로부터 탈퇴할 수 있다고 믿었다.
(d) 남부 주들이 연방으로부터 탈퇴한 것이 전쟁 시작의 빌미가 되었다.

해설 추론문제는 다소 까다로운 문제 유형에 속한다. 지문은 전쟁이 시작된 배경에 대해 설명하고 있으므로 (d)를 정답으로 선택할 수 있다. (a)는 글의 내용과 상반되며 (b)와 (c)가 사실이라면 남부 주들이 '자신들의 권리를 보호해야 한다'고 느낄 이유가 없으므로 역시 정답이 될 수 없다.

어구 state 주; 상태   a number of 많은
withdraw 철수하다; 탈퇴하다   exist 존재하다

정답 (d)

UNIT 3   문화와 인물

EXERCISE
1 (c)   2 (a)

PRACTICE
1 (c)   2 (d)

유형 정리

1   문화 현상

해석 2004년 11월 25일, 배용준이 나리타 국제공항에 도착했다. 400여명의 경찰이 배치된 가운데, 약 4천 명의 일본 여성 팬들이 공항에 모여들었다. 무엇 때문에 그토록 많은 일본 여성들이 이 한국 배우에 열광할까? 이를 두고 많은 설명들이 제시됐는데, 그 가운데 하나는 배용준이 일본 여성으로 하여금 자신들의 이상형과 함께 있는 것을 상상하도록 해준다는 것이다.

어구 approximately 대략   present 존재하는
crazy about ~에 열광하는   enable 가능하게 하다
Prince Charming 이상형 (남자)

2   문화 정책

해석 1980년이래로, 많은 미국인들은 영어를 미국의 공용어로 제정하려고 노력했다. 이처럼 '영어만 사용하자'는 캠페인은 여러 언어 전문가들로부터 비판을 받아왔다. 전문가들은 영어가 미국 전역에서 널리 사용되고 있으며 영어의 지위가 다른 언어에 의해 위협을 받지 않는다고 지적한다. 그들의 생각에는, 이른바 '영어만 사용하자'는 운동은 이민자들에 대한 증오의 표현일 뿐이다.

어구 official 공식의, 공용의   criticize 비판하다
point out 지적하다   status 지위
threaten 위협하다   so-called 이른바
immigrant 이민자

3   인물

해석 많은 사람들의 생각과 달리, 패리스 힐튼은 영리한 광고인이다. 기본적으로, 힐튼은 제품을 파는 방법을 알고 있다. 그녀는 자신의 제품을 팔기 위해서는 사람들이 자신에게 관심을 가지도록 만들어야 한다고 이해하고 있다. 그래서 그녀는 사람들의 관심을 끄

는 일들을 감행한다. 일례로, 심지어 음주 운전까지 했는데, 이로 인해 많은 사람들이 그녀에 대한 기사를 읽게 되었다.

어구 unlike ~와 달리 advertiser 광고자
product 제품 dare to 감히 ~하다
attract (관심 등을) 끌다
drive under the influence of alcohol 음주 운전하다

EXERCISE

1

해석 힙합 문화에 매혹된 3세대의 비보이즈가 있다. 각 세대는 브레이크댄싱의 핵심적인 요소를 만들어 내는 데 일조했다. 1세대와 2세대는 젊은이들로 하여금 기본적인 동작을 개발하도록 했다. 3세대는 훨씬 더 많은 요소들을 개발했는데, 이 요소들이 오늘날의 브레이크댄싱 동작을 낳은 것으로 생각되는 것들이다. 요즘, 그런 요소들이 많은 나라에서 수천 명의 젊은이들을 매혹시키고 있다.
(a) 그들은 유럽의 전통 문화에 매혹되었다.
(b) 그들은 그림을 그리는 데 능숙했다.
(c) 그들은 브레이크댄싱 동작의 개발에 기여했다.

해설 정오 유형으로 글의 내용과 보기들을 하나하나 비교해야만 한다. 정답은 (c)인데 (a)는 '유럽의 전통 문화'가 아니라 '힙합 문화'여야 올바른 설명이다. (b)는 글의 내용을 통해서는 확인할 수 없다.

어구 generation 세대 fascinate 매혹시키다
essential 본질적인, 핵심적인
encourage 격려하다; 촉진하다
many more 훨씬 더 많은 charm 매혹시키다

정답 (c)

2

해석 아웅산 수지는 1988년 당시에 버마로 되돌아왔다. 병든 어머니를 보살피는 것이 그녀의 (방문) 목적이었다. 그렇지만 많은 이들이 군사 정부에 의해 죽임을 당하는 것을 보고 나서, 그녀의 삶은 극적으로 변했다. 군부 지배자들을 비판하면서 그들에 대한 비폭력 저항 운동을 이끌었다. 잔악한 정권은 그녀를 가택연금에 처하게 했다. 지배자들은 그녀가 그 나라(미얀마)를 떠나기를 원했지만 그녀는 그럴 생각이 없었다.
(a) 그녀는 민주 지도자였다.
(b) 그녀는 성격이 고약했다.
(c) 그녀는 남편과 살기 위해 당시 버마를 떠나고 싶어했다.

해설 추론 유형으로 다소 까다로운 문제다. (b)는 내용을 통해 알 수 없기 때문에 정답이 될 수 없고 (c)는 지문의 내용과 어긋난다. (a)는 군사 정부에 대항하여 저항 운동을 이끌었다는 내용으로부터 충분히 추론할 수 있으므로 정답이다.

어구 purpose 목적 military 군사의, 군사적인
dramatically 극적으로 opposition 저항
cruel 잔인한, 잔악한 regime 정권
house arrest 가택연금 unwilling 꺼리는

정답 (a)

PRACTICE

1

해석 뉴에이지운동의 기본적인 원칙 가운데 상당수는 데이비드 스팽글러에 의해 개발되었다. 엘리스 베일리와 달리, 그는 사랑과 희망의 새로운 시대를 이끌어오는 데 있어 인간의 노력의 중요성을 강조했다. 그는 사람들이 일정한 에너지를 사용하여 새로운 시대가 꽃피도록 할 수 있다고 믿었다. 1976년에 그는 첫 번째 책을 출간하면서 뉴에이지운동이 시작되는 데 도움을 주었다.

Q. 문장에 들어갈 가장 적절한 것을 고르시오.
(a) 외계인의 도래
(b) 환경 보호
(c) 인간의 노력
(d) 자신의 책을 출판하는 것

해설 글의 전반적인 흐름으로 보아 정답은 (c)다. 빈 칸이 포함된 문장 바로 다음의 문장에서 사람들의 노력을 말하는 부분이 나오기 때문이다. (a), (b), (d)는 이러한 전후 관계에 어울리지 않기 때문에 정답이 될 수 없음에 유의하자.

어구 principle 원칙, 원리 develop 개발하다
stress 강조하다
come to life 소생하다; 활기를 띠다

정답 (c)

2

해석 사실 힐러리 클린턴은 호락호락하지 않은 상대이다. 그녀는 원하는 것을 어떻게 얻는지 알고 있다. 바바라 올슨이 '후환'이라는 제목의 책에서 분명하게 지적했듯이, 힐러리의 방식은 솔 알린스키의 아이디어에 바탕을 두고 있다. 알린스키와 마찬가지로, 힐러리는 '바람직한' 사회적 변화를 가져오기 위해서 무슨 일이든 할 수 있다고 믿는다. 그래서 힐러리는 윤리나 전통을 존중하지 않는다. 힐러리는 심지어 자신의 결혼조차도 정치적 목적을 이루기 위한 도구로 사용했다.

Q. 글을 통해 추론할 수 있는 바는 무엇인가?
(a) 힐러리는 전통적인 사람이다.
(b) 힐러리의 생각은 알린스키의 생각과는 아주 다르다.
(c) 힐러리는 순수하게 사랑 때문에 결혼했다.
(d) 힐러리는 사회적 변화를 지지한다.

해설 추론 유형으로 내용을 통해 정확히 알 수 있는 사항을 정답으로 택해야 하는데, 정답은 (d)다. (a), (b), (c)는 모두 본문에서 언급한 사항과 어긋나기 때문에 정답이 될 수 없다. 반면 (d)는 네 번째 문장으로부터 자연스럽게 추론할 수 있는 내용임에 유의하자.

어구 smart cookie 호락호락하지 않은 상대
method 방법, 방식 based on ~에 기반한
bring about 초래하다 desirable 바람직한
ethics 윤리 realize 실현하다; 깨닫다

정답 (d)

UNIT 4 지구과학

EXERCISE

1 (c)   2 (b)

PRACTICE

1 (d)   2 (b)

유형 정리

1   지질학

해석 판구조론은 지구의 표층에 관한 이론이다. 이 이론에 따르면, 표층은 7개의 대형 판과 여러 소형 판으로 나누어져 있다고 한다. 놀랍게도, 이 판들은 1년에 대략 10cm의 속도로 움직인다. 더욱이, 판들은 서로에게 여러 방식으로 영향을 미친다. 판들은 합쳐지기도 하고 떨어지기도 하고 서로를 가로질러 갈 수도 있다. 부분적으로는 이런 운동으로 인해, 지진이 발생하고 화산이 폭발한다.

어구 plate tectonics 판구조론 theory 이론
outer layer 표층 divide 나누다
approximately 대략 unite 합쳐지다
separate 분리되다 earthquake 지진
volcano 화산 erupt (화산이) 폭발하다

2   지구의 역사

해석 한때는 큰 빙하들이 대빙하시대(홍적세)에 형성되었다고 생각했다. 게다가, 널리 퍼진 빙상들은 북아메리카와 유라시아에서 증감을 거듭했다. 그렇지만 현대의 연구에 따르면, 상당수의 빙하들이 대빙하시대 이전에 발달되었다고 한다. 현대의 연구는 또한 지구가 다른 빙하기에도 빙하로 뒤덮여 있었다는 것을 입증했다.

어구 glacier 빙하 Pleistocene Epoch 홍적세
widespread 널리 퍼진 ice sheet 빙상
wax and wane 증감하다 develop 발달하다

3   자연재해

해석 2004년 12월 26일, 강도 9.0의 지진이 인도양 남쪽에서 발생했다. 그 결과로 해일이 일어나서 인도와 스리랑카의 동쪽 연안을 강타했다. 몇 시간 후에, 이 해일로 225,000명이 넘는 사람들이 사망하고 대략 백만 명이 집을 잃었다. 이 파괴적인 해일은 해일에 대한 연구의 중요성을 상기시켰다.

어구 magnitude 강도 the Indian Ocean 인도양
tsunami 해일 (=tidal wave)
attack 공격하다 approximately 대략
homeless 집이 없는 destructive 파괴적인
remind 상기시키다

EXERCISE

1

해석 일출식(溢出式) 분화(噴火)와 폭발식 분화라는 두 가지 유형의 분화가 있다. 일출식 분화는 흘러내리는 것에 대해 저항이 덜 심한 마그마의 분출로 확인할 수 있다. 반면, 폭발식 분화는 흘러내리는 것에 대해 보다 저항이 심한 마그마에 의해 특징지워진다. 그

런 마그마에는 대개 많은 양의 기체가 들어 있다. 일반적으로 폭발식 분화가 일출식 분화에 비해 더 맹렬하다.

(a) 결과적으로

(b) 요컨대

(c) 반면

해설 일출식 분화와 폭발식 분화의 차이점을 설명한 글이다. 따라서 정답은 (c)다. 두 분화의 차이가 결과 관계가 아니기 때문에 (a)는 정답이 될 수 없다. 또한 요약 관계도 아니기 때문에 (b)도 정답이 아니다.

어구 eruption 분화(噴火) effusive 분출하는
explosive 파괴적인 identify 확인하다
outpouring 분출 resistant 저항력이 있는
characterize 특징짓다 quantity 양
violent 격렬한

정답 (c)

2

해석 해양지각은 대륙지각과는 아주 다르다. 우선 첫째로, 해양지각이 대륙지각에 비해 훨씬 더 생성시기가 짧다. 해양지각의 최대 생성 시기는 2억 년 전인데 반해, 대륙의 평균적인 생성 시기는 대략 20억 년 전이다. 둘째, 해양지각이 대륙지각에 비해 밀도가 더 높다. 해양지각의 평균 밀도가 약 3.3g/㎤인데 반해, 대륙지각의 평균 밀도는 대략 2.7g/㎤이다.

(a) 대륙지각이 해양지각에 비해 생성시기가 훨씬 더 짧다.

(b) 대륙지각이 해양지각에 비해 밀도가 덜 높다.

(c) 대륙지각이 해양지각에 비해 더 두껍다.

해설 (a)는 글의 내용과 반대가 되기 때문에 정답이 될 수 없다. 반면 (c)는 글을 통해 알 수 없기 때문에 정답이 아니다. 따라서 정답은 글의 내용과 일치하는 (b)다.

어구 oceanic 해양의 crust 지각
continental 대륙의 maximum 최대의
whereas ~한 반면 average 평균(의)
dense 밀도가 있는 density 밀도
mean 평균의

정답 (b)

PRACTICE

1

해석 지구과학자는 현재 지구가 어떻게 생겼는지를, 그리고 지구가 어떻게 발달했는가를 이해하려고 한다. 이 목적들을 이루기 위해, 지구과학자는 지구의 특징을 관찰하고 그런 다음에 그런 특징을 설명하는 가설을 내놓는다. 지구과학자는 또한 그런 가설을 검증하는 방법도 개발한다. 요컨대 지구과학자는 지구를 탐구하기 위해 과학적인 방법을 동원한다.

Q. 문장을 완성할 가장 적절한 선택지를 고르시오.

(a) 이와는 대조적으로

(b) 예컨대

(c) 그럼에도 불구하고

(d) 요긴대

해설 마지막 문장에서 전체 내용을 요약하고 있으므로 정답은 (d)다. (a)처럼 대조 관계이거나 (b)처럼 예시 관계이거나 (c)처럼 역접 관계로 연결되는 것이 아님에 유의하자.

어구 earth scientist 지구과학자 evolve 진화하다
achieve 성취하다 observe 관찰하다; 준수하다
characteristic 특징 advance 제안하다

hypothesis 가설
employ 이용하다; 채용하다

feature 특징
method 방법

정답 (d)

2

해석 제임스 러브록이 처음으로 가이아 가설을 제안했을 때, 과학자들은 대부분 그 가정을 터무니없는 것으로 치부했다. 이는 주로 그가 '지구의 자율성'이 '의도적인' 것이라고 암시했기 때문이다. 그의 가설에 따르면, 지구는 뚜렷한 목적을 가진 생명체로 간주될 수 있다. 이후에, 러브록은 자신의 입장을 바꾸어 자신이 '지구의 자율성이 생물상에 의한 계획을 수반한다'라고 암시한 적이 없다고 말했다.

Q. 글에 따르면 다음 가운데 어느 것이 올바른가?
(a) 제임스 러브록은 가이아 가설이 터무니없는 것이라고 치부했다.
(b) 한때 러브록은 지구가 생명체로 간주될 수 있다고 생각했다.
(c) 과학자들은 대부분 가이아 가설이 타당하다고 생각한다.
(d) 제임스 러브록은 지구가 기계로 간주될 수 있다고 시사했다.

해설 (a)는 제임스 러브록이 가이아 가설을 처음으로 제안한 과학자이기 때문에 정답이 될 수 없다. (c)도 글의 내용과 어긋난다. (d)는 글의 내용을 통해서 알 수 없기 때문에 정답이 아니다. 따라서 정답은 글의 내용과 일치하는 (b)다.

어구 propose 제안하다; 청혼하다   Gaia hypothesis 가이아 가설
dismiss 고려하지 않다   assumption 가정
ridiculous 터무니없는   planetary 지구의
purposeful 의도적인
regard A as B A를 B로 간주하다
imply 암시하다   involve 수반하다
biota 생물상

정답 (b)

UNIT 5 생물학

EXERCISE
1 (b)   2 (c)

PRACTICE
1 (c)   2 (b)

유형 정리

1   식물학

해석 피마자는 아프리카가 원산으로 12피트까지 자란다. 이 식물에는 리신이라고 불리는 유독물질이 들어 있는데, 유감스럽게도 그 유독물질은 독성이 아주 강하다. 그래서 동물이 피마자를 약간만 먹어도 죽을 가능성이 높다. 죽지 않는다 하더라도 그 동물은 설사, 복통, 또는 경련을 겪을 것이다. 그렇지만 흥미롭게도, 피마자는 중국과 인도에서 약품으로 쓰인다.

어구 castor bean 피마자   native 원산인
toxin 유독물질   ricin 리신
poisonous 독성이 강한   amount 양
diarrhea 설사   abdominal 복부의
convulsions 경련   medicine 약품

2   동물학

해석 너무도 많은 사람들이 거미가 곤충이라고 생각한다. 그러나 그렇지가 않다. 우선 첫째로, 거미는 다리가 여덟 개이다. 반면, 곤충은 모두 다리가 여섯 개이다. 둘째, 거미의 몸이 두 부분으로 되어 있는 데 반해, 곤충은 세 부분으로 되어 있다. 그러면 거미는 무엇인가? 거미는 거미류이다. 다른 거미류에는 전갈, 응애, 그리고 진드기가 포함된다. 거미들은 모두 곤충을 잡아먹는 포식동물이다.

어구 insect 곤충   arachnid 거미류
scorpion 전갈   mite 응애
tick 진드기   predator 포식동물

3   첨단 생물학 분야

해석 많은 사람들이 분자생물학과 미생물학을 혼동한다. 이것은 주로 두 분야가 모두 세포를 연구하는 것과 관련되기 때문이다. 그렇지만 그들은 서로와 아주 다르다. 분자생물학은 분자의 주요 유형인 단백질과 핵산을 탐구함으로써 유전의 과정을 설명하려고 한다. 이와는 대조적으로, 미생물학은 박테리아와 바이러스와 같은 단순한 생명체를 연구한다.

어구 confuse 혼동하다   molecular biology 분자생물학
microbiology 미생물학   concerned with ~와 관련된
genetic 유전의   protein 단백질
nucleic acid 핵산   molecule 분자

EXERCISE

1

해석 이제까지 알려진 것 가운데 가장 초기 형태의 조류인 시조새를 조사하면서 리차드 오웬은 두 가지 실수를 저질렀다. 첫째, 그는 앞부분을 뒷부분으로 착각했다. 둘째, 그는 두 가지 뚜렷한 특징을 간과했다. 그 가운데 하나는 시조새의 흉골이 평평하다는 점이었다. 만약 이 사실을 알아차렸다면, 시조새가 활공(滑空)밖에 하지 못했을 것이라고 짐작했을 것이다. 다른 하나는 시조새의 두개(頭蓋)가 파충류의 두개와 비슷하다는 것이었다.
(a) 중요한 발견을 이루어냈다
(b) 두 가지 실수를 저질렀다
(c) 그것을 파충류와 혼동했다

해설 리차드 오웬이 시조새를 조사하면서 실수를 한 일화에 관한 글이다. 전체 내용이 어떤 실수를 저질렀는가에 초점이 맞추어져 있기 때문에 정답이 (b)라는 점을 알 수 있다. (a)는 전체 글의 흐름에 어울리지 않는다. 그리고 (c)는 리차드 오웬이 시조새와 파충류의 두개골이 비슷하다는 점을 간과했다고 했기에 답이 될 수 없다.

어구 Archaeopteryx 시조새   mistake 착각하다
overlook 간과하다   distinguishing 뚜렷한
characteristic 특징   breastbone 흉골
glide 활공(滑空)하다; 미끄러지듯 움직이다
braincase 두개(頭蓋)   reptile 파충류

정답 (b)

2

해석 에너지를 이용해서, 세포는 화학물질을 만들어내고 자신을 복제한다. 그렇지만 자기 복제가 일어나기 위해서는, 세포가 그런 에너지를 활용하는 방법을 '알아야' 한다. 그런 지시사항은 세포에 포함되어 있다. 흥미롭게도, 이런 지시사항은 세포가 자기복제를 하기 전에 복사된다. 결과적으로, 각각의 딸세포는 자기복제를 위한 청사진을 갖게 된다.

(a) 화학물질을 생산하는 데 있어 세포는 에너지에 의존하지 않는다.
(b) 아무런 지시가 없어도, 세포는 자기복제를 할 줄 안다.
(c) 모든 딸세포는 자기복제를 하기 위해 에너지를 사용할 줄 안다.

해설 첫 번째 문장에 비추어볼 때 (a)는 내용과 어긋난다. 또한 (b)도 글의 내용과 반대로 설명되어 있다. 따라서 정답은 글의 내용으로부터 무리 없이 추론할 수 있는 (c)다. 이처럼 TEPS에서는 곧이곧대로 추론할 것이 요구된다는 점을 명심해야 한다.

어구 cell 세포   chemical 화학
substance 물질   reproduce 복제하다
self-reproduction 자기복제
utilize 이용하다   instruction 지시
contain 함유하다   copy 복사하다
daughter cell 딸세포   blueprint 청사진

정답 (c)

PRACTICE

1

해석 카렌 번드 교수에 따르면, 키티돼지코박쥐가 세계에서 가장 작은 포유류라고 한다. 태국이 원산지인 이 박쥐는 길이가 3-4센티미터이고 무게가 약 2그램이다. 그렇지만 일부 전문가들은 동의하지 않는다. 그들은 작은뒤쥐가 세계에서 가장 작은 동물이라고 주장한다. 그들의 주장은 작은뒤쥐가 키티돼지코박쥐보다 <u>더 가볍다</u>는 사실에 근거한다. 그러면 어느 쪽이 진실을 말하는 것일까?

Q. 문장을 완성할 가장 적절한 선택지를 고르시오.
(a) 더 빨리 움직인다
(b) 더 크다
(c) 더 가볍다
(d) 물속에서 더 잘 움직인다

해설 가장 작은 포유류를 둘러싼 논란을 설명한 글이다. 따라서 '작다'라는 개념과 연결될 수 있는 말이 빈 칸에 와야만 한다. 정답은 (c)다. (b)는 '작다'라는 말의 반의어이기 때문에 정답이 될 수 없고, (a)와 (d)는 관련이 없는 내용이다.

어구 bumblebee bat 키티돼지코박쥐
mammal 포유류   native 원산인
pygmy shrew 작은뒤쥐   argument 주장; 논거

정답 (c)

2

해석 사이언스 2005년 6월 17일호에서, 황우석과 그의 팀은 인간의 배아로부터 줄기세포를 추출했다고 알렸다. 그들에 따르면 그 줄기세포는 어떤 기관이나 조직으로든지 자랄 수 있다고 한다. 그렇지만 여러 사람들의 그들의 성과에 의문을 제기하자, 황우석과 공동 저자인 제럴드 쉐튼은 사이언스지에 그들의 논문을 철회해 줄 것을 요청했다. 한국인 과학자인 황우석은 그들의 보고에서 실수가 있었다고 언급했다. 그럼에도 불구하고, 그는 그 실수가 무엇인지를 명확하게 밝히지 않았다.

Q. 글로부터 추론할 수 있는 것은 무엇인가?
(a) 황우석은 사람들에게 자신의 실수가 무엇인지 알렸다.
(b) 황우석과 쉐튼은 그들이 논문에 오류가 있다고 생각했다
(c) 모든 과학자들은 황우석의 성과가 완벽하다는 데 동의했다.
(d) 황우석의 줄기세포는 간으로 자라날 수 없다.

해설 (a)는 본문의 내용과 어긋나므로 정답이 아니다. (c)는 성과에 의문이 제기되었다고 했으므로 역시 정답이 될 수 없다. (d)는 결과 발표로 짐작해 볼 때 정답이 아니다. 따라서 정답은 글의 내용으로부터 바로 추론할 수 있는 (b)다.

어구 extract 추출하다   stem cell 줄기세포
embryo 배아   organ 기관
tissue 조직   question 의문을 제기하다
withdraw 철회하다   paper 논문
clarify 명확히 밝히다

정답 (b)

UNIT 6   환경과학

EXERCISE
1 (c)   **2** (b)

PRACTICE
1 (d)   **2** (b)

유형 정리

1   생태계

해석 생물다양성이란 특정한 생태계에 존재하는 다양한 생명체를 가리킨다. 생물다양성을 객관적으로 측정하는 다양한 방법들이 있다. 그것들 가운데 하나는 일정한 생태계에 있는 유전자의 다양성을 조사하는 것이다. 환경 보호론자들은 가능하면 많은 유전자를 유지하려는 경향이 있다. 반면, 생태학자들은 그런 접근법으로는 목적을 성취하지 못할 것이라고 우려한다.

어구 biodiversity 생물다양성   refer to 지칭하다
variety 다양성   ecosystem 생태계
objectively 객관적으로   measure 측정하다
gene 유전자
conservationist 환경 보호론자
maintain 유지하다   ecologist 생태학자

2   오염

해석 광공해(光公害)란 사람들이 방해가 되는 빛을 만들어내는 것을 가리킨다. 산업화의 부작용인 광공해는 인간의 건강에 부정적으로 영향을 미치고 다양한 생태계를 어지럽힐 수 있다.. 예컨대, 과도한 빛에 노출되는 것은 피로와 스트레스로 귀결될 수 있다. 마찬가지로, 방해가 되는 빛은 밤에 개화하는 꽃들이 씨를 만들어내지 못하게 할 수 있는데, 이로 인해 그런 식물들이 감소할지도 모른다.

어구 light pollution 광공해(光公害)   intrude 방해하다
side effect 부작용   industrialization 산업화
negatively 부정적으로   disturb 어지럽히다
ecosystem 생태계   exposure 노출
excessive 과도한   fatigue 피로
bloom 개화하다   produce 생산하다
result in ~으로 귀결되다   decrease 감소

3   기상 이변

해석 지구온난화와 관련하여, 과학자들은 많은 것을 밝혀냈지만, 여전히 그 현상을 이해하는 데 어려움을 겪고 있다. 과학자들은 기후가 인간의 활동에 의해 크게 영향을 받는다는 사실을 입증했다. 문제는 기후의 일정한 변화의 정확한 원인을 특정하지 못한다는 것이다. 따라서 과학자들은 기후 패턴에 영향을 미치는 다양한 요

인을 검사하는 과학적인 방법을 개발하기 위해 노력하고 있다.

어구 regarding ~와 관련하여 　global warming 지구온난화
phenomenon 현상 　　　　　affect 영향을 미치다
specify 특정하다 　　　　　certain 일정한; 확실한
factor 요인

EXERCISE

1

해석 사막화가 발생하면, 그 영향을 받는 땅은 다양한 생명체를 지지하
는 능력을 잃기 시작한다. 땅의 지하수면이 내려가고, 표토가 소
금으로 뒤덮이며, 토착 식물들이 사라지기 시작한다. 과학자들에
따르면, 인간의 활동이 사막의 확장에 기여하며, <u>과감한 조치가
취해지지 않는</u> 한, 사막화는 계속해서 우리의 환경을 해칠 것이다.
(a) 사람들이 계속해서 숲에 산다
(b) 보다 많은 나무를 베어내다
(c) 과감한 조치가 취해지다

해설 인간의 활동이 사막화와 관련이 있다는 점을 감안하면, 근본적인
대책이 필요하다는 점을 알 수 있다. 따라서 이와 연결될 수 있는
(c)가 정답이다. (a)나 (b)는 주어진 글을 통해서는 사막화와의 관
계가 분명하지 않기 때문에 정답이 될 수 없다.

어구 desertification 사막화
groundwater table 지하수면
topsoil 표토 　　　　　　　native 토착의
contribute to ~에 기여하다
radical 과감한; 근본적인 　　measures 조치

정답 (c)

2

해석 생태계에는 두 가지 요소가 있다. 하나는 햇빛, 물, 그리고 토양
과 같은 물질적 환경이다. 다른 하나는 생태계 내의 유기생명체이
다. 에너지가 생태계 전체에 걸쳐 흐르면서 구성요소들 사이에 영
양분을 나누어준다. 널리 알려져 있듯이, 그 에너지는 태양에서
비롯되는데, 태양은 지구의 모든 생태계에 영양분을 공급한다.
(a) 생태계에는 세 가지 요소가 있다.
(b) 생태계는 에너지를 태양에 의존한다.
(c) 생태계에는 유기생명체가 포함되지 않는다.

해설 (a)는 두 가지 요소가 되어야 올바른 설명이 된다. (c)는 유기생명
체가 포함된다고 했으므로 정답이 될 수 없다. 따라서 정답은 글
의 내용과 일치하는 (b)다.

어구 element 요소 　　　　　　ecosystem 생태계
physical 물질적 　　　　　　soil 토양
organism 유기체 　　　　　　distribute 분배하다
nutrient 영양분 　　　　　　constituent 구성요소
nurture 영양분을 공급하다

정답 (b)

PRACTICE

1

해석 2007년 12월 7일, 홍콩 선적 유조선인 허베이스피리트호가 삼성
중공업 크레인바지선에 부딪혔다. 유조선은 서해상에 약 10,500
톤의 석유를 유출했다. 이 석유 유출은 유명한 태안 지역에 <u>상당한
정도로</u> 영향을 미쳤다. 이 지역을 찾는 관광객이 거의 없고 지역 해
산물업계도 그 파괴적인 석유 유출 사고에 심한 타격을 입었다.

Q. 문장을 완성할 가장 적절한 선택지를 고르시오.
(a) 긍정적으로
(b) 작은 정도로
(c) 건설적으로
(d) 상당한 정도로

해설 관광객의 급감과 해산물업계의 타격을 고려할 때 '상당한 정도로'
영향을 받았다고 보는 것이 올바르다. 따라서 정답은 (d)다. (a)
와 (c)는 영향이 부정적이었음을 감안할 때 정답이 아니다. 그리
고 (b)는 영향이 작았다고 할 수 없기 때문에 정답이 될 수 없다.

어구 register 등록하다 　　　　　oil tanker 유조선
crane barge 크레인바지선 　　leak 유출하다
affect 영향을 미치다 　　　　　seafood 해산물
be hard hit 타격을 크게 입다 　destructive 파괴적인

정답 (d)

2

해석 탈삼림화는 삼림이 다른 용도로 쓰이는 땅으로 대체되는 것을 가
리킨다. 탈삼림화가 발생하면, 환경에 부정적으로 영향을 미칠 수
있다. 우선 첫째로, 탈삼림화는 온실효과를 악화시키는데, 이는
대기로부터 탄소를 제거할 수 있는 나무나 식물이 더 이상 존재하
지 않기 때문이다. 둘째, 탈삼림화는 나무와 식물과 같은 중요한
구성요소가 사라진다는 점에서 생물 다양성을 감소시킨다.

Q. 글에 따르면 다음 가운데 어느 것이 올바른가?
(a) 탈삼림화는 다양한 방식으로 환경을 돕는다.
(b) 생물 다양성은 탈삼림화에 의해 부정적으로 영향을 받을 수
　있다.
(c) 탈삼림화는 온실효과와 무관하다.
(d) 탈삼림화는 나무와 식물이 급속하게 자라는 것을 돕는다.

해설 (a)와 (c)는 주어진 내용에 어긋나기 때문에 정답이 아니다. 그리
고 (d)는 나무와 식물이 사라지게 만드는 것이기 때문에 정답이
될 수 없다. 따라서 정답은 글의 내용과 일치하는 (b)다.

어구 deforestation 탈삼림화 　　　replace 대체하다
negatively 부정적으로 　　　　worsen 악화시키다
greenhouse effect 온실효과 　　eliminate 제거하다
carbon 탄소 　　　　　　　　reduce 감소시키다
biodiversity 생물 다양성 　　　constituent 구성요소

정답 (b)

UNIT 7　생활과학

EXERCISE

1 (b)	2 (c)

PRACTICE

1 (b)	2 (d)

유형 정리

1　의학

해석 많은 전문가들은 비만이 건강에 해로운 생활방식에서 비롯된다고
생각한다. 예컨대 많은 사람들은 다양한 이유로 과식하는 경향이
있다. 어떤 이들은 스트레스를 해소하기 위해 음식에 의존한다.
다른 이들은 음식이 즉각적으로 이용이 가능해서 많은 양을 먹기

도 한다. 설상가상으로, 너무도 많은 사람들이 운동을 충분히 하지 않는다. 이렇게 건강에 해로운 생활방식이 대부분의 비만 사례의 원인이다.

어구 expert 전문가 　　　 obesity 비만
unhealthy 건강에 해로운 　　　 lifestyle 생활방식
tend to ～하는 경향이 있다 　　　 overeat 과식하다
various 다양한 　　　 release 해소
readily 손쉽게
to make matters worse 설상가상으로
account for 원인이다

2 기술

해석 PR-GB.com에 따르면, NovelMaker.com이 NextUp의 TextAloud(http://www.MextUp.com)를 교정 도구를 찾는 회원들에게 권장한다고 한다. 이것은 주로 상을 수상한 그 프로그램이 작가들로 하여금 작품의 리듬을 포착할 수 있도록 해주기 때문이다. 물론, 텍스트를 말로 바꾸어 주는 이 도구는 오타를 쉽게 찾도록 해준다. 게다가, TextAloud는 어떤 연령이나, 성별, 말투든지 다양한 목소리를 제공한다.

어구 recommend 추천하다 　　　 proofread 교정하다
catch 포착하다 　　　 typo 오타
variety 다양성 　　　 gender 성별
accent 말투

3 첨단 과학

해석 인공지능의 한 분야로서, 감성적 컴퓨팅은 인간의 감정을 다룰 줄 아는 기계와 장치를 고안하려고 한다. 오랫동안, 과학자들은 감정이 인간의 삶에서 주된 역할을 하지 않는다고 생각했다. 이런 이유로, 과학자들은 감정을 처리할 수 있는 기계를 개발하려고 하지 않았다. 근래에 과학자들은 감정이 인간의 삶의 모든 측면에 영향을 미친다는 사실을 알아냈다. 그래서 과학자들은 기계가 인간의 감정을 처리할 수 있도록 하는 다양한 방법을 탐구하기 시작했다.

어구 artificial intelligence 인공지능 　 affective 감성적
computing 컴퓨팅 　　　 device 장치
deal with 다루다 　　　 play a role 역할을 하다
process 처리하다 　　　 aspect 측면
empower 권한을 부여하다

EXERCISE

1

해석 미국심장학회에 따르면, 적포도주를 소비하는 것과 심장질환의 감소 사이에는 직접적인 관계가 없다고 한다. 학회는 연구자들이 현재 적포도주의 플라보노이드가 인간의 건강에 미치는 영향을 연구하고 있다고 지적한다. 현재까지, 어떤 연구도 적포도주가 직접적으로 심장질환 발병의 위험을 감소시킨다는 것을 입증하지 못했다.
(a) 인과의
(b) 직접적인 관계가 없는
(c) 관계가 멀지 않은

해설 마지막 문장을 통해서 적포도주를 마시는 것이 직접적으로 심장질환의 발병을 감소시키지는 않는다는 사실을 확인할 수 있으므로 정답은 (b)다. 계속 논란이 되고 있는 사안인데, 주어진 글이 취하는 입장을 정확히 파악해야 한다.

어구 direct 직접적인 　　　 consumption 소비
red wine 적포도주 　　　 currently 현재

flavonoid 플라보노이드 　　　 directly 직접적으로
develop 발병하다

정답 (b)

2

해석 현재는 나노로봇공학이 발달 초기 단계에 있기 때문에 충분히 활용할 수 없다. 그렇지만 완전히 개발된다면, 이 기술은 우리의 삶을 혁명적으로 바꾸어놓을 수 있다. 예컨대, 극도로 작은 로봇을 이용하여 의사들은 미세수술을 할 수 있다. 이것이 가능해지면, 해로운 박테리아나 바이러스를 훨씬 더 쉽게 제거하여 거의 모든 질병을 치료할 수 있다. 또한 고도로 향상된 제품을 효과적으로 제작할 수도 있게 된다.
(a) 나노로봇공학은 일상생활에 영향을 미치지 못한다.
(b) 나노로봇공학은 의학과는 무관하다.
(c) 나노로봇공학은 충분히 개발되지 못했다.

해설 (a)와 (b)는 모두 주어진 내용과 어긋난다. 따라서 정답은 글의 내용을 통해 정확히 알 수 있는 (c)다. 참고로 독해 부분에서 제시된 지문 가운데, 전문적인 내용에 관한 지문은 모두 현재 최신의 내용을 충실히 반영한 지문이기 때문에, 내용을 숙지해둘 필요가 있다.

어구 utilize 이용하다 　　 nanorobotics 나노로봇공학
initial 초기의 　　 stage 단계
revolutionize 혁명을 일으키다
microsurgery 미세수술 　　 destroy 파괴하다
manufacture 제조하다 　　 advanced 향상된
effective 효과적인

정답 (c)

PRACTICE

1

해석 국립 폐암 파트너쉽에 따르면, 여성들은 많은 방식으로 폐암 발병 위험을 줄일 수 있다고 한다. 우선 첫째로, 담배를 끊는 것은 언제나 좋은 아이디어이다. 1-800-QUIT-NOW로 전화하거나 www.naquitline.org 사이트를 방문하라. 둘째, 집안의 라돈 수치가 너무 높으면, 라돈 수치를 줄일 수 있는 장치를 설치하는 편이 낫다. 마지막으로, 건강에 좋은 다양한 음식을 먹고 규칙적으로 운동을 하라.

Q. 문장을 완성할 가장 적절한 선택지를 고르시오.
(a) 흡연을 계속하다
(b) 담배를 끊다
(c) 음주를 계속하다
(d) 도박을 끊다

해설 글의 내용이 폐암의 발병 위험을 줄이는 것이므로 금연과 관련이 있을 것으로 쉽게 짐작할 수 있다. 따라서 정답은 (b)다. (a)는 정반대의 내용이기 때문에 정답이 아니다. 그리고 (c)와 (d)는 일단 폐암과는 관련성이 낮다.

어구 reduce 감소시키다 　　　 risk 위험
lung cancer 폐암 　　　 radon 라돈
install 설치하다 　　　 a variety of 다양한
regularly 정기적으로

정답 (b)

2

해석 팟캐스팅에 관한 전문가로서, 팟캐스트 수신프로그램인 Juice가 아주 유용하다고 생각한다. http://juicereceiver.

sourceforge.net/을 방문함으로써 프로그램을 내려받을 수 있다. 이 수신프로그램을 설치하고 나면, 두 가지 방식으로 팟캐스트를 정기적으로 수신할 수 있다. Selection 버튼을 클릭함으로써 이용 가능한 모든 팟캐스트를 볼 수 있다. 또는 특정한 팟캐스트의 URL을 알고 있다면, 수신프로그램에 URL을 입력하면 된다. 이제, 여러분은 팟캐스트를 즐기기 위한 가장 편리한 도구 가운데 하나를 가진 셈이다.

Q. 글로부터 추론할 수 있는 것은 무엇인가?
　(a) 글쓴이는 팟캐스팅에 대해 아는 것이 거의 없다.
　(b) Juice는 팟캐스트를 전세계로 송신하는 도구이다.
　(c) Juice는 우편으로 구입해야만 한다.
　(d) Juice는 팟캐스트를 사용하기 위한 아주 편리한 도구이다.

해설 (a)는 글쓴이가 전문가라고 밝혔기 때문에 정답이 아니다. 그리고 (b)는 수신하는 도구가 되어야 올바른 설명이 된다. (c)는 내용에 나와 있지 않고 웹사이트를 방문해서 다운로드받는 것으로 설명되어 있으므로 정답이 될 수 없다. 따라서 정답은 (d)다.

어구 expert 전문가　　　　　　podcasting 팟캐스팅
　receiver 수신장치　　　　　download 다운로드하다
　install 설치하다　　　　　　subscribe to 구독하다
　available 이용할 수 있는　　 enter 입력하다

정답 (d)

UNIT 8　철학과 예술

EXERCISE
1 (a)　　**2** (c)

PRACTICE
1 (d)　　**2** (a)

유형 정리

1　철학

해석 쇠렌 키에르케고르에 따르면, 삶에는 심미적 단계, 윤리적 단계, 그리고 신앙적 단계의 세 '단계'가 있다고 한다. 이전 단계가 자동적으로 이후 단계로 귀결되지는 않는다. 그렇지만 이후 단계는 이전 단계들의 목표이다. 이후 단계들은 또한 이전 단계를 중요한 요소로서 포함한다. 키에르케고르는 특히 신앙적 단계를 탐구하는 데 관심이 있었으면, 그의 저작을 통해 그 중요성을 강조했다.

어구 stage 단계　　　　aesthetic 심미적인
　ethical 윤리적인　　religious 종교적인
　automatically 자동적으로　　lead to ~으로 귀결되다
　goal 목적　　　　　　element 요소
　particularly 특히　　　stress 강조하다

2　예술

해석 대략 백 년 전에, 이사도라 덩컨은 예술이 본질적으로 실용적이어서, 자유로운 영혼을 표현하려고 하는, 가장 원초적인 인간의 요구를 충족시킨다고 갈파했다. 영혼은 아주 순수하고, 아주 아름다우며, 아주 강하다. 자유로운 영혼을 표현하는 데 있어, 예술은 인간이라는 조건을 조명하고 자유에 이르는 길을 보여주는 데 있어 주도적인 역할을 할 수 있다. 이 점을 고려하여, 덩컨은 보통

사람들을 자유롭게 할 목적으로 예술을 '세속화'하려고 노력했다.

어구 approximately 대략
　observe 알아차린 바를 말하다; 관찰하다
　essentially 본질적으로　　satisfy 충족시키다
　pure 순수한　　　　　　　play a role 역할을 하다
　shed light on ~를 조명하다　liberty 자유
　secularize 세속화하다

3　대중문화

해석 잉그마르 베르히만의 영화는 인간이라는 조건을 독특하게 개성적인 스타일로 탐구한다. 그의 영화는 사람의 다른 사람과의 관계와 같은 문제를 다룬다. 보다 중요한 사항으로, 그의 뛰어난 영화들은 진정한 자아를 찾기 위한 시도들이다. 베르히만은 그 목적을 성취하는 데 있어 거짓된 외양을 없애는 것이 필요하다고 생각했다. 그는 그 과제가 성취할 수 있으면서도 이룰 수 없는 것이라고 느꼈던 것 같다.

어구 explore 탐구하다　　　　uniquely 독특하게
　deal with 다루다　　　　　extraordinary 뛰어난
　attempt 시도　　　　　　　achieve 성취하다
　get rid of 없애다　　　　　appearance 외양
　achievable 성취할 수 있는　unattainable 이룰 수 없는

EXERCISE

1

해석 이탈리아를 방문하는 동안, 르누아르는 고전주의의 뚜렷한 특징들에 깊은 인상을 받았다. 고전주의에서는 선이 형태의 참된 아름다움을 나타내기 위해 분명하고 아름답게 그려졌다. 덧붙여, 부드럽게 그리는 것이 인체의 우아함을 표현하는 강력한 방법이라고 인식되었다. 이런 특징들에 깊이 영향을 받아서, 르누아르는 인상주의와 결별하기로 결심한다.
　(a) 결별하다
　(b) 계속해서 지지하다
　(c) 배우다

해설 르누아르가 고전주의의 영향을 받아 인상주의와 갈라서게 되는 계기를 맞이했음을 설명한 글이다. 따라서 정답은 (a)다. 인상주의와 고전주의가 다른 화풍이라는 점을 감안하고 주어진 내용을 종합해 보면 (a)가 정답이라는 점을 알 수 있다.

어구 impress 강한 인상을 남기다　distinguishing 뚜렷한
　characteristic 특징　　　　　classicism 고전주의
　clearly 분명하게　　　　　　smooth 부드러운
　recognize 인식하다　　　　　grace 우아함
　influence 영향을 미치다　　　break with ~와 갈라서다
　Impressionism 인상주의

정답 (a)

2

해석 칼 야스퍼스의 '일반 정신병리학'은 실존주의가 정신의학에 영향을 미쳤음을 증명했다. 이 책에서 야스퍼스는 정신과 의사가 정신병 환자의 세계를, 그 환자의 경험 속에 동정적으로 참가함으로써 이해해야 한다는 점을 시사했다. 마찬가지로, 루트비히 빈스방거의 '사상의 도약에 관해서는' 정신의학에 대한 실존주의 영향을 보여주었다. 빈스방거는 환자가 실존적인 가능성을 실현하지 못하기 때문에 정신병이 발생한다고 생각했다.
　(a) 칼 야스퍼스는 실존주의가 정신의학에 도움을 주지 않을 것이라고 생각했다.

(b) 루트비히 빈스방거는 실존주의를 지지하지 않는다.

(c) 실존주의는 여러 점에서 정신의학에 영향을 미쳤다.

해설 실존주의가 정신의학에 미친 영향을 설명한 글이다. (a)와 (b)는 모두 주어진 글의 내용에 어긋난다. 따라서 정답은 글의 내용과 일치하는 (c)다. 다소 까다롭게 느껴질 수 있지만, 글의 중심 내용 파악에 초점을 맞추면 문제를 푸는 데 크게 지장은 없다.

어구 psychopathology 정신병리학

existentialism 실존주의   psychiatry 정신의학

suggest 시사하다; 제안하다   psychiatrist 정신과의사

sympathetically 동정하여   likewise 마찬가지로

mental illness 정신병   existential 실존적인

정답 (c)

PRACTICE

1

해석 흥미롭게도, 도교와 유교 사이에는 유사한 점이 많다. 이것은 주로 사람, 사회, 그리고 우주에 대한 도교와 유교의 사고가 공통된 전통에 바탕을 두고 있기 때문이다. 그 전통은 공자와 노자가 등장하기 이전에 정립되었다. 그렇지만 이런 공통 요소에도 불구하고, 도교는 물질세계를 초월하려고 한다는 점에서 유교와 다르다.

Q. 문장을 완성할 가장 적절한 선택지를 고르시오.

(a) 똑같은

(b) 유사한

(c) 관계가 있는

(d) 다른

해설 주어진 문장에서 '공통 요소에도 불구하고'라고 했으므로 그 다음에는 서로 '다르다'는 말이 오는 것이 자연스럽다. 따라서 정답은 (d)다. 참고로 (a)와 (b)는 비슷한 내용이기 때문에 정답이 될 수 없다.

어구 Taoism 도교   Confucianism 유교

common 공통의   establish 확립하다

Confucius 공자   Lao-tzu 노자

transcend 초월하다

정답 (d)

2

해석 놀랍게도, 영화 'Clueless'는 제인 오스틴의 'Emma'에 바탕을 두고 있다. 짐작할지도 모르지만, 엠마 우드하우스가 쉐어 호로위츠가 '된다'. 둘은 모두 응석받이로 자란 젊은 여성들이다. 덧붙여, 그들은 따돌림을 받는 이를 친구로 사귀고 중매도 선다. 엠마가 마차에서 모험을 하는 데 반해, 쉐어는 운전면허 시험에 떨어진다. 이런 식으로, 닮은 점들이 끝이 없다.

Q. 글에 따르면 다음 가운데 어느 것이 올바른가?

(a) 제인 오스틴의 'Emma'는 영화 'Clueless'에 많은 점에서 영향을 미쳤다.

(b) 쉐어 호로위츠는 교양 있는 젊은 여성이다.

(c) 수줍음을 많이 타서, 엠마 우드하우스는 중매를 서지 않는다.

(d) 제인 오스틴의 'Emma'는 영화 'Clueless'와는 무관하다.

해설 (b)는 글의 내용을 통해서 성확히 알 수가 없기 때문에 정답이 아니다. '교양 있는' 여성인지 아닌지를 판단할 수 있는 단서가 없기 때문이다. 다음으로 (c)와 (d)는 글의 내용에 어긋난다. 따라서 정답은 (a)다.

어구 clueless 무능한   based on ~에 바탕을 둔

spoiled 응석받이로 자란   outsider 따돌림을 받는 사람

play matchmaker 중매 서다   carriage 마차

parallel 닮은 점   endless 끝없는

정답 (a)

독해 모의고사

PART I

1 (c)	**2** (b)	**3** (d)	**4** (d)	**5** (a)
6 (c)	**7** (a)	**8** (c)	**9** (c)	**10** (b)
11 (a)	**12** (b)	**13** (d)	**14** (b)	**15** (c)
16 (d)				

PART II

17 (a)	**18** (b)	**19** (d)	**20** (a)	**21** (b)
22 (c)	**23** (b)	**24** (d)	**25** (a)	**26** (d)
27 (a)	**28** (c)	**29** (d)	**30** (b)	**31** (c)
32 (b)	**33** (a)	**34** (d)	**35** (b)	**36** (a)
37 (a)				

PART III

38 (c)	**39** (c)	**40** (d)

PART I

1

해석 국립암연구소에 따르면, 차(茶)가 암의 발병 위험을 실제로 감소시킬 수 있는지는 확실하지 않다고 한다. 어떤 연구들은 차를 소비하는 것이 암의 위험을 줄인다는 주장을 뒷받침한다. 반면, 다른 연구들은 그 주장을 뒷받침하지 않는다. 이것은 주로 개인의 식단과 생활방식과 같은 다른 요인이 암의 위험을 감소시키는 데 도움이 되기 때문이다.

(a) 절대적으로 맞는

(b) 확실한

(c) 확실하지 않은

(d) 결심이 확고한

해설 차(茶)의 소비와 암의 발병 위험 감소 사이에 상반되는 연구 결과가 존재한다는 점을 감안하면 정답은 (c)다. 대개 차가 암의 예방에 도움이 된다고 생각하는 경우가 많은데, 이처럼 반대되는 연구 결과도 있음을 알아두자.

어구 actually 실제로   reduce 감소시키다

develop 발병하다   consumption 소비

factor 요인, 요소   diet 식단; 다이어트

lifestyle 생활방식

정답 (c)

2

해석 2008년 2월 26일, 뉴욕 필하모닉 오케스트라가 북한의 평양에 있는 동평양대극장에서 공연했다. 이것은 김정일 정권이 최초로 미국 오케스트라가 그 '공산주의' 국가에서 콘서트를 개최하도록 허용한 것이었다. 그렇지만 이 행사가 전말로 평범한 북한 사람들을 감동시켰는지 그렇지 않은지는 분명하지 않다. 이것은 그들이 대개 자유롭게 행동하도록 허용되지 않기 때문이다.

(a) 비판했다
(b) 공연했다
(c) 한국인들을 맞이했다
(d) 미국인들을 흥겹게 했다

해설 두 번째 문장에서 콘서트를 개최했다고 했으므로 정답은 이와 연결되는 (b)이다. 나머지 선택지들은 무엇보다도 주어진 글을 통해서 분명하게 알 수 없기 때문에 정답이 될 수 없음에 유의해야 한다. 이처럼 글을 통해 분명하게 알 수 있는 것만이 정답이 될 수 있음을 명심하자.

어구 perform 공연하다　　　　permit 허용하다
communist 공산주의의　　　touch 감동시키다

정답 (b)

3

해석 AP통신사에 따르면, 부시 대통령의 특별보좌관인 티모시 고글리가 표절했다는 것을 인정하고 나서 금요일에 사임했다고 한다. 그의 표절 사실은 〈더 뉴스센티널〉의 전(前) 칼럼니스트인 낸시 놀이 발견했다. 놀은 고글리의 공로를 인정하지 않고 제프리 하트의 글을 베꼈다고 지적했다. 그녀의 보도에 대응하여, 백악관측은 이 문제를 즉각적으로 다루었다.
(a) 화가 났다
(b) 자화자찬했다
(c) 우쭐해졌다
(d) 사임했다

해설 마지막 문장에서 백악관측이 즉각적으로 처리했음과 표절 사실을 시인한 것을 종합해 보면, 정답은 (d)다. 자신의 잘못에 대한 감정으로 (b)나 (c)는 자연스럽지 못하다. 그리고 만약 화를 낼 정도라면 잘못을 시인하지 않았을 것이므로 (a)도 정답이 아니다.

어구 assistant 보좌관　　　　resign 사임하다
acknowledge 인정하다　　　plagiarism 표절
credit 공로의 인정
address a problem 문제를 다루다

정답 (d)

4

해석 브레슬린 씨 귀하
Faith Corporation에서의 상무 직책에 대해 이야기를 나눌 수 있어서 아주 기뻤습니다. 면접에서 말씀드렸듯이, 저는 대기업의 관리직 경력이 10년이 넘습니다. 그리고 제 모든 동료들은 관리자로서, 보다 정확하게는 업무 처리를 촉진해주는 이로서 저의 능력에 깊은 인상을 받았습니다. 따라서 제가 귀사(貴社)에 큰 자산이 될 것으로 확신합니다.
(a) 골칫거리
(b) 아주 쉬운 일
(c) 악한(惡漢)
(d) 큰 자산

해설 경력과 동료들의 인정을 감안할 때 정답은 (d)다. 인터뷰에 대한 감사 서한이다. 기본적인 양식이 주어진 글과 같음을 참고하자. 그리고 나머지 선택지들의 뜻도 정확히 익혀두자.

어구 managing director 상무, 전무　　position 직책
mention 언급하다　　　　　managerial 관리직의
corporation 기업; 법인　　　colleague 동료
facilitator 일의 성취를 촉진해주는 사람
convinced 확신하는

정답 (d)

5

해석 ABC 뉴스 기술 관련 기고가인 베키 월리에 따르면, 바이오디젤은 일반 디젤과 식물성 기름의 혼합물이라고 한다. 흥미롭게도, 바이오디젤은 현재의 모든 디젤 엔진에서 이용할 수 있다. 따라서 바이오디젤을 쓰거나 쓰지 않는 것을 선택할 수 있다. 바이오디젤 사용과 관련하여 알아야 할 한 가지 사항은 오일 필터를 보다 빈번하게 교체해야 한다는 것이다.
(a) 현재의 모든
(b) 새로운 (것만)
(c) 구형의 (것만)
(d) 일제만

해설 바로 다음 문장에서 사용 여부를 선택할 수 있다고 했고, 마지막 문장에서 바이오디젤을 쓰게 되면 발생하는 일을 말했으므로, 모든 디젤 엔진에 쓸 수 있음을 짐작할 수 있다. 따라서 정답은 (a)다. 나머지는 모두 주어진 맥락에 자연스럽게 어울리지 않는다.

어구 contributor 기고가　　　　biodiesel 바이오디젤
mixture 혼합물　　　　　regular 일반의
utilize 이용하다　　　　　oil filter 오일 필터

정답 (a)

6

해석 많은 한국인들은 2차 세계대전 당시 잔악하게 행동한 데 대해 일본을 비판한다. 이들은 섬나라 일본이 윤리적으로 올바르지 못한 일을 했다고 생각한다. 이러한 판단은 윤리적 개념이 국제 정치에서 중요한 역할을 맡는다는 믿음에 바탕을 두고 있다. '이상주의'의 관점에서는 그러한 생각이 사리에 완전히 부합한다. 반면, 그런 판단은 '현실주의'의 관점에서는 말이 되지 않는다. 이것은 현실주의자들이 윤리적 개념이 국제 정치에서 설 자리가 없다고 생각하기 때문이다.
(a) 이타적인 행동
(b) 긍정적인 태도
(c) 잔악한 행동
(d) 낙관적인 태도

해설 비판하는 대상이 나와야 하고, '윤리적으로 올바르지 못한'이라는 말과 연결되어야 하므로 정답은 (c)다. 물론 상식적으로 답을 할 수도 있지만, 언제나 주어진 글을 정확하게 이해한 바탕 위에서 문제를 풀어나가야 함을 잊어서는 안 된다.

어구 criticize 비판하다　　　　ethically 윤리적으로
ethical 윤리적인　　　　　concept 개념
play a part 역할을 하다　　　perspective 관점
idealism 이상주의
make sense 사리에 맞다　　　realism 현실주의
realist 현실주의자　　　　　altruistic 이타적인

정답 (c)

7

해석 제게, 축구는 단지 일종의 스포츠가 아니라 삶의 방식입니다. 축구는 제 열정입니다. 이것은 단지 제가 그 활발한 스포츠를 하는 것을 즐기기 때문만이 아닙니다. 그리고 제가 승리에 대한 무자비한 욕망에 사로잡혀 있기 때문이지도 않습니다. 그것은 주로 축구가 우리가 누구인지 알게 해주기 때문입니다. 축구는 우리가 성공을 얻으려고 애쓰는 연약한 존재라는 사실을 가르쳐줍니다. 축구는 또한 성공이 성취하기가 어렵다는 점도 일깨워줍니다. 역설적이게도, 축구는 성공이 전부가 아니라는 것을 분명하게 의식하도록 만들어줍니다. 가장 중요한 것은 우리가 꿈을 실현하기 위해 노력하는 데 있어 얼마나 성실한가 하는 것입니다.

(a) 가장 중요하다
(b) 중요하지 않다
(c) 중요성이 거의 없다
(d) 우리를 성가시게 하다

해설 전체적인 글의 흐름, 그리고 바로 앞에서 성공이 전부가 아니라고 말한 점 등을 종합하면 (a)가 정답이다. (b)와 (c)는 근본적으로 같은 의미이기 때문에 정답이 될 수 없다. 그리고 (d)는 글의 흐름에 적합하지 않다.

어구 passion 열정　　　　　merely 단지
enslave 사로잡히다　　　ruthless 무자비한
desire 욕망　　　　　　feeble 나약한
strive for ~을 얻으려고 애쓰다　　sincere 성실한

정답 (a)

8

해석 1990년대 후반에, 많은 인터넷 기업들이 미국에 설립되었다. 문제는 그들 대부분이 <u>수익을 얻지</u> 못했다는 것이었다. 그럼에도 불구하고, 그 회사들의 주가는 급속하게 증가했다. 그래서 2000년 3월 무렵에 나스닥 (종합 주가) 지수는 5,048에 이르렀다. 결국엔 인터넷 거품이 터져서, 2002년 10월 무렵에 나스닥 지수는 1,114로 떨어졌다.
(a) 인터넷을 사용하다
(b) 로봇을 만들다
(c) 수익을 얻다
(d) 많은 사람들을 고용하다

해설 인터넷 버블이 터지게 된 경위를 설명한 글이다. 주가가 오르는 것과 관련된 내용이 나와야 하므로 정답은 (c)다. 나머지 선택지들은 주가 상승과는 크게 관계가 없다.

어구 found 설립하다　　　　　stock price 주가
rapidly 급속하게　　　　　composite index 종합 지수

정답 (c)

9

해석 기원전 600년대 후반에, 드라콘이라는 이름의 입법가가 아테네에 대한 새로운 일련의 법률을 기초했다. 놀랍게도, 그의 법률은 극히 잔악했다. 어떤 이들은 그 법률들이 피로 쓰여졌다고 말하기도 했다. 예컨대 어떤 사람이 빚을 갚지 못하면, 노예가 될 수도 있었다. 심지어 사소한 범죄조차도 사형으로 처벌할 수 있었다. 드라콘의 법률은 draconian이라는 단어를 낳았는데, 이 단어는 '<u>극히 가혹한</u>'이란 뜻이다.
(a) 각별히 친절한
(b) 아주 자비로운
(c) 극히 가혹한
(d) 극히 유용한

해설 글의 전체 흐름에 비추어 보면, 드라콘이 제정한 법률이 아주 가혹했음을 알 수 있다. 이와 연결되는 것은 (c)로 정답이다. (a)와 (b)는 비슷한 내용이기 때문에 정답이 될 수 없다. 그리고 (d)는 글의 흐름에 적합하지 않으므로 정답이 될 수 없다.

어구 legislator 입법가　　　　draft 기안하다
cruel 산혹한　　　　　　pelly 사소한
death penalty 사형　　　draconian 극히 가혹한

정답 (c)

10

해석 진정한 영웅은 공동체를 위해서 올바른 일을 하기로 결정한, 단지 평범한 사람들이다. 인간으로서, 우리는 가족, 이웃, 그리고 국가

에 대해 책임이 있다. 그런 책임을 <u>무시하거나 소홀히 할</u> 수도 없고 해서도 안 된다. 그것이 인간이라는 것의 참된 의미이며 우리는 일상생활과 인간으로서의 삶에서 의무감의 중요성을 늘 인식해야 한다.
(a) 주의를 기울이다
(b) 무시하거나 소홀히 하다
(c) 찬사를 바치다
(d) 신경을 쓰거나 다루다

해설 전반적으로 책임과 의무를 강조하는 글이다. 따라서 책임과 의무를 저버려서는 안 된다는 말이 되어야 하므로 빈 칸에는 부정적인 말이 와야 한다. 정답은 (b)이다. 나머지는 긍정적이거나 중립적인 말이므로 정답이 될 수 없다.

어구 ordinary 평범한　　　　community 공동체
responsibility 책임　　　aware of ~을 의식하는
sense of duty 의무감　　everyday 일상적인

정답 (b)

11

해석 저는 진화론을 검토하는 것이 제 종교에 어긋나지 않는다고 굳게 믿습니다. 그 '이론'이 아직 과학 법칙이 아니라는 점을 언급해야만 합니다. 그래서 진화론은 보다 많은 연구를 요합니다. 더욱이, 전향적으로 사고하는 많은 학자들이 지적하듯이, 진화론은 과학적으로 <u>일관성이나 설득력이 떨어질</u> 수도 있습니다. 그런 문제를 탐구하는 데 있어, 우리는 열린 마음의 중요성을 의식해야만 합니다.
(a) 일관되거나 설득력이 있는
(b) 잘못되거나 타당성이 없는
(c) 신뢰할 만하거나 받아들일 수 없는
(d) 불법적이거나 적법한

해설 진화론이 과학 법칙이 아니라 이론일 뿐이라는 점과 종교적인 입장이 강조되고 있다는 점을 종합할 때, 진화론을 부정적으로 생각하고 있음을 알 수 있다. 따라서 정답은 (a)다. 빈 칸 앞에 not이 있기 때문에 빈 칸에는 모두 긍정적인 말이 들어가야만 한다. 나머지 선택지들은 이에서 어긋나기 때문에 정답이 될 수 없다.

어구 firmly 확고하게　　theory of evolution 진화론
forward-thinking 전향적으로 사고하는
scholar 학자　　matter 문제

정답 (a)

12

해석 농구팀 주장으로서의 제 경험으로부터 팀원들을 감동시키기 위해서는 그들의 마음에 닿아야 한다는 것을 배웠습니다. 자신의 진정한 자아를 먼저 알지 못하는 한, 다른 사람들에게 의미 있는 방식으로 영향을 미칠 수 없습니다. 진정한 자아를 찾는 것은 자신에게 <u>온전히 진솔할 것</u>을 요합니다. 자신이 진정으로 바라는 것은 무엇인가? 정말로 자신을 행복하게 하는 것은 무엇인가? 자신을 울게 만드는 것은 무엇인가?
(a) 전혀 알지 못하는
(b) 온전히 진솔한
(c) 온전히 만족한
(d) 극도로 시샘하는

해설 다른 사람에게 의미 있게 영향을 미치기 위해서는 자신을 먼저 알아야 한다는 점을 강조한 글이다. 다음에 이어지는 내용이 모두 진실성을 요구하는 질문들이므로 정답은 (b)이다.

어구 captain 주장　　　　move 감동시키다
touch 감동시키다　　　unless ~하지 않는 한
influence 영향을 미치다　meaningful 의미 있는

이란 뜻을 나타낸다.

정답 (b)

13

해석 마틴 루이스 박사에 따르면, 소말리아는 '국가'가 아니라고 한다. 이것은 주로 1991년 이래로 안정적인 정부가 없었기 때문이다. 소말리아는 과도연방정부에 의해 부분적으로 지배를 받고 있다. 이 정부는 국제 사회로부터 인정을 받았다. 그럼에도 불구하고, 그 정부가 너무도 나약해서 많은 이들이 그 정부가 급속히 붕괴되지 않을까 우려한다.
(a) 전적으로 지배되는
(b) 끊임없이 공격당하는
(c) 심하게 비판을 받는
(d) 부분적으로 지배받는

해설 안정적인 정부가 없다는 점, 그리고 현재 과도정부가 약하다는 점을 감안하면, 나라 전체에 대한 지배가 불가능하다는 것을 알 수 있다. 따라서 정답은 (d)다. 특히 (a)가 정답이 아니라는 점에 유의해야 한다. 만약 (a)라면 국가라고 할 수 있기 때문이다.

어구 stable 안정적인   government 정부
recognize 인정하다   concerned 우려하는
collapse 붕괴하다   in no time 급속히, 곧

정답 (d)

14

해석 18세였을 때, 말콤 엑스는 뉴욕시에 살면서 일했다. 그의 일은 나이트클럽의 구두닦이였다. 운 좋게도, 그는 일부 유명한 흑인 음악가들을 만날 수 있었다. 그렇지만 유감스럽게도, 그는 마약을 팔고 사람들의 돈을 빼앗는 범죄 활동에 관여하게 되었다.
(a) 단속을 강화했다
(b) 관여하게 되었다
(c) 관여하지 않게 되었다
(d) 그만두기로 결심했다

해설 '유감스럽게도'라는 말로 시작했고, however가 있어서 바로 앞의 내용과 상반되어야 하므로 정답은 (b)이다. 말콤 엑스의 당시 직업을 감안할 때 (a)는 정답이 될 수 없다. 그리고 (c)와 (d)는 근본적으로 같은 말이므로 정답이 될 수 없다. 이와 같은 선택지는 실전에서도 바로 포착하여 정답에서 제외해야 한다.

어구 shoeshiner 구두닦이   criminal 범죄의
deal in 판매하다   rob (사람에게서) 빼앗다

정답 (b)

15

해석 Catch-22는 미국 작가 조셉 헬러가 쓴 소설이다. 이 소설은 주로 존 요사리안이 2차 세계대전의 시련에서 살아남으려고 하는 시도에 초점을 맞추고 있다. 제목에 들어 있는 'catch(예기치 않은 어려움)'는 자기모순인 공군의 규정을 가리킨다. 이 규정에 따르면, 위험한 비행 작전을 계속하면 정신이 이상한 것으로 간주된다. 반면, 정신 이상 때문에 그런 비행 작전을 피하고 싶다고 공식적으로 말하면 정신이 정상인 것으로 간주된다. 따라서 위험한 (전투) 비행 작전을 피할 방법이 없다.
(a) 예컨대
(b) 따라서
(c) 반면
(d) 요컨대

해설 공군의 모순된 규정을 설명하는 부분인데, 앞뒤로 상반되는 내용이므로 정답은 (c)다. 참고로 이 소설의 제목으로부터 Catch-22라는 숙어가 생겨났는데, '벗어날 수 없는 모순된 상황'

어구 focus on ~에 초점을 맞추다   ordeal 시련
catch (숨어 있는) 어려움   contradict 모순되다
regulation 규정, 규제   deem 판단하다, 간주하다
mission 비행 작전   sane 제정신의
madness 정신 이상

정답 (c)

16

해석 '200파운드짜리 미녀 [원문대로]'는 미녀인 것의 고뇌를 묘사한, 아주 놀라운 영화이다. 이 영화는 강한나가 점쟁이를 찾아가는 것으로 시작한다. 본래 그녀는 못생기고 뚱뚱했다. 성형수술을 받고 나서, 강한나는 날씬하고 예쁘게 변했다. 그러나 그녀는 그런 미녀가 자신이 정말로 원하던 것이 아니라는 것을 깨닫는다. 그래서 콘서트에서 팬들에게 진실을 밝히고는 처음부터 다시 자신의 일을 시작했다.
(a) 그럼에도 불구하고
(b) 말이 나와서 하는 말인데
(c) 예컨대
(d) 그래서

해설 성형수술 이후에 자신이 바라던 모습이 아님을 깨닫고 진실을 밝혔다고 했으므로 결과 관계를 나타내야 한다. 따라서 정답은 (d)다. 참고로 이 영화의 우리나라 제목은 '미녀는 괴로워'이다. 주어진 글에서 [sic]이라고 한 것은 200 Pounds Beauty가 틀린 표현인데, 원문 그대로 옮겼음을 밝히기 위해서이다. 올바른 표현은 'The 200-Pound Beauty' 또는 'A Beauty in Agony'이다.

어구 depict 묘사하다   agony 고뇌   fortune-teller 점쟁이
originally 본래   undergo 겪다   plastic surgery 성형수술
slender 날씬한   realize 깨닫다

정답 (d)

PART II

17

해석 (2008년 3월 2일자) Naples Daily News에 따르면, 플로리다 상공회의소는 플로리다 주(州)의회에서 자신들의 목소리가 반영되도록 하기 위해 열심히 노력할 것이라고 한다. 그 재계 조직은 이 주(州)의회가 주(州)의 교육을 향상시키고 경제 성장을 촉진하기를 희망한다. 덧붙여, 상공회의소는 주(州)의회가 헌법을 수호하고 개인의 재산권을 보호하기 위해 더 많은 일을 해야 한다고 생각한다.

Q. 글의 제목으로 가장 적절한 것은 무엇인가?
(a) 정치적 · 경제적 향상을 요구하는 재계 지도자들
(b) 잔혹한 기관으로 변한 플로리다 상공회의소
(c) 플로리다 주(州)의회에서 논의될 다양한 문제들
(d) 비판을 받고 있는 미국 헌법

해설 전반적으로 상공회의소가 주(州)의회에서 자신들의 주장을 관철시키기 위해 노력할 것이라는 내용이므로 정답은 (a)이다. (b)는 지나치게 비약한 것으로 이 글만으로는 그렇게 판단할 수가 없다. (c)와 (d)는 관계가 되지만 중심 내용이 아니기 때문에 정답이 아니다.

어구 chamber of commerce 상공회의소
legislature (특히 주의) 의회   improve 향상시키다
promote 증진하다; 승진시키다   Constitution 헌법
safeguard 보호하다   property right 재산권

정답 (a)

18

해석 귀하와 저 사이의 전화 통화와 관련하여, 몇 가지 사안을 설명하고 제 입장을 양해해 주십사 하고 진지하게 부탁드릴 필요가 있습니다. 저희 Faith International School은 20년이 넘게 학생들에게 양질의 교육을 제공해 왔으며, 경험으로부터 자격을 갖춘 교사를 선발하는 것이 학생들에게 제공할 수 있는 교육의 수준에 결정적이라는 사실을 배웠습니다. 이 때문에, 저희는 새로운 교사를 채용하는 일을 극히 신중하게 처리해 왔습니다.

Q. 글의 주제가 무엇인가?
(a) 글을 읽는 이의 무지를 비판하는 것
(b) 학교의 채용 정책을 설명하는 것
(c) 글을 읽는 이를 중요한 행사에 초대하는 것
(d) 답장이 늦어진 데 대해 글을 읽는 이에게 사과하는 것

해설 높은 수준의 교육을 위해 교사를 아주 신중하게 선발하는 정책을 택하고 있음을 설명한 글이다. 따라서 정답은 (b)이다. (a)는 언급되지 않았고, (c)와 (d) 역시 글의 내용과 거리가 멀다.

어구 regarding ~에 관해　　matter 사안
quality 양질의　　qualified 자격을 갖춘
vital 결정적인, 극히 중대한　　cautious 조심하는
hire 고용하다

정답 (b)

19

해석 2008년 3월 7일과 9일 사이에, Juggle This!가 뉴욕시에서 개최됩니다. 이 행사는 뉴욕시의 제7회 연례 저글링 축제이며, 모든 저글러들을 이 유명한 행사에 정중하게 초대합니다. 참가자들은 다양한 게임과 워크숍을 즐길 것입니다. 이 축제는 Pratt Institute에서 열립니다. 보다 많은 정보를 원하시면 http://www.jugglenyc.com/fests.html을 방문해 주세요.

Q. 글의 주된 내용은 무엇인가?
(a) 뉴욕시
(b) Pratt Institute의 명성
(c) 웹사이트 방문하기
(d) 저글링 축제

해설 전반적으로 저글링 축제의 시기와 장소, 그리고 행사 등을 안내한 글이다. 따라서 정답은 (d)다. (b)의 경우에는 Pratt Institute의 명성이 언급되지 않았고, 또한 이 글에서 단순히 축제 장소로서의 의미만 가지므로 정답이 아니다.

어구 annual 연례의　　juggling 저글링
juggler 저글러　　cordially 정중하게

정답 (d)

20

해석 제 이름은 에리카 스미스이며 저는 한국의 Hope Academy의 교사입니다. 저희 학생 가운데 한 명인 캐서린 킴이 명문인 귀교에 진학을 원합니다. 그래서 저희는 어떻게 $50의 응시료를 지불해야 하는지 궁금합니다. 수표를 보내야 합니까, 아니면 신용카드로 지불할 수도 있습니까? 또는 우편환을 보내야 합니까? 이 가운데 어떤 방식으로든 지불할 용의가 있습니다.

Q. 지문의 주된 목적은 무엇인가?
(a) 응시료를 지불하는 방법을 문의하기 위해
(b) 학생을 도와준 데 대해 글을 읽는 이에게 감사를 표하기 위해
(c) 글을 읽는 이가 학교에 지원하지 못한 것을 비판하기 위해
(d) 지원 절차가 너무 복잡하다는 불만을 토로하기 위해

해설 전반적으로 응시료 납부 방법을 몰라서 문의하는 글이다. (b)는 아직 일어나지 않은 일이고, (c)와 (d)는 글의 취지에 부합하지 않기 때문에 정답이 아니다. 따라서 정답은 (a)다.

어구 attend (학교에) 다니다　　prestigious 명문의
application fee 신청비, 응시료
check 수표　　credit card 신용카드
money order 우편환　　method 방법

정답 (a)

21

해석 저희의 SuperMemory Chip은 혁명적인 제품입니다. 이 아주 작은 칩으로, 기억력을 900%만큼이나 늘릴 수 있습니다. 그래서 사업에 필요한 중요한 자료를 모두 암기할 수 있습니다. 또한 한 달 이내에 외국어를 완전히 습득할 수 있습니다. 덧붙여, 저의 메모리칩은 나쁜 기억을 영구적으로 제거할 수 있게 합니다. 보다 많은 정보를 원하시면, http://www.supermemory.com을 방문해 주세요.

Q. 글의 제목으로 가장 적절한 것은 무엇인가?
(a) 혁명이 가까이 왔다
(b) SuperMemory Chip이 기억력을 향상시킨다
(c) 외국어를 마스터하는 효율적인 방법
(d) 나쁜 기억이 일상생활에 미치는 영향

해설 SuperMemory Chip을 통해 기억력을 향상시킬 수 있음을 말하고 있으므로 정답은 (b)이다. (a)는 revolutionary에 이끌리는 것을 유도하는 오답이다. 그리고 (c)와 (d)는 글의 중심 내용이 아니라는 점에 유의해야 한다.

어구 revolutionary 혁명적인　　tiny 아주 작은
increase 증가시키다　　memorize 암기하다
master 완전히 습득하다　　enable 가능하게 하다
get rid of 없애다
once and for all 영구적으로

정답 (b)

22

해석 텔레파시가 정말로 존재하는가? 많은 전문가들은 그런 과학적으로 설명이 불가능한 능력이 존재하는 것을 뒷받침하는 과학적 증거가 없다고 주장한다. 그럼에도 불구하고, 텔레파시를 수반한 일부 사례는 실제인 것 같아서, 네바다대학교 의식연구소 소장인 딘 라딘은 텔레파시와 같은 심령현상이 실제라고 주장한다.

Q. 글의 주제는 무엇인가?
(a) 과학적 증거를 수집하는 방법
(b) 딘 라딘의 개인적인 삶
(c) 텔레파시의 존재
(d) 네바다대학교 의식연구소

해설 첫 번째 문장과 마지막 문장을 통해 분명하게 확인할 수 있듯이 텔레파시의 존재 여부에 대한 논란을 다룬 글이다. 따라서 정답은 (c)다. (a)와 (b)는 지문의 내용과 거리가 멀고 (d)는 부분적인 내용일 뿐이다.

어구 telepathy 텔레파시　　exist 존재하다
expert 전문가　　argue 주장하다
evidcnc 증거
paranormal 과학적으로 설명이 안 되는
invovle 수반하다　　psychic 심령의
phenomenon 현상

정답 (c)

23

해석 보스턴 대학교의 졸업생인 마틴 루터 킹 주니어는 '내게는 꿈이 있습니다'라고 선언했습니다. 그의 꿈은 모든 사람들이 존중받고 자신의 행복을 추구할 수 있도록 하는 것입니다. 저는 인류 전체에 대한 그의 비전이 보스턴 대학교에서 제공하는 양질의 교육의 산물이라고 확신합니다. 따라서 저는 그를 본받고 넓은 시야를 개발하며 보스턴 대학교에서의 제 삶의 모든 측면에서 탁월성을 추구하는 데 전념하고자 합니다.

Q. 글에 따르면 다음 가운데 어느 것이 올바른가?
(a) 글쓴이는 보스턴 대학교에 지원하고 있지 않다.
(b) 마틴 루터 킹 주니어는 보스턴 대학교를 졸업했다.
(c) 글쓴이는 마틴 루터 킹 주니어를 보스턴에서 만났다.
(d) 마틴 루터 킹 주니어는 보스턴 대학교에서 가르쳤다.

해설 보스턴 대학교에 지원하면서 쓴 글이므로 (a)는 정답이 아니다. 그리고 (c)와 (d)는 이 글을 통해서는 알 수가 없다. 따라서 이 글을 통해 분명하게 확인할 수 있는 (b)가 정답이다.

어구 graduate 졸업생　　　　　pursue 추구하다
convinced 확신하는　　　　vision 비전
human race 인류　　　　　product 산물; 제품
follow suit 따라하다　　　　perspective 관점

정답 (b)

24

해석 한 나라의 국내총생산(GDP)을 살펴봄으로써, 그 나라 경제가 잘되고 있는지 그렇지 않은지를 알아낼 수 있다. 이것은 주로 그 수치가 그 나라 내에서 경제적 자원이 어떻게 이용되는지를 분명하게 보여주기 때문이다. 흥미롭게도, GDP는 일정한 재화나 서비스가 그 나라에 있는 외국인들에 의해 생산되는지에 대해서는 나타내지 않는다.

Q. 글에 따르면 다음 가운데 어느 것이 올바른가?
(a) GDP는 경제의 규모를 나타내지 않는다.
(b) GDP는 GNP와 똑같다.
(c) GDP는 더 이상 널리 쓰이지 않는다.
(d) GDP는 경제지표이다.

해설 우선 (b)와 (c)는 본문에서 말하지 않았기 때문에 알 수 없다. 따라서 정답이 될 수 없다. 반면 (a)는 주어진 내용을 바탕으로 추론해 보면 GDP가 한 나라의 경제규모를 나타낸다는 것을 알 수 있다. 따라서 정답은 (d)다. (a)와 혼동하지 않도록 유의해야 하는데, 이와 같은 경우에 언제나 본문을 통해 분명하게 알 수 있는 것이 정답이 된다는 점을 명심해야 한다.

어구 gross domestic product 국내총생산
perform 수행하다　　　　figure 수치
economic 경제의　　　　resources 자원
utilize 이용하다　　　　　indicate 나타내다
certain 일정한; 확실한　　goods 재화

정답 (d)

25

해석 널리 알려져 있듯이, 한국 선생님들은 매우 엄하시고 많은 노력을 요구하시는데, 제 선생님들도 예외가 아니었습니다. 그분들은 제가 최고의 첼로 연주가가 되기를 원하셨습니다. 그것이 제게는 너무 큰 부담이었을지도 모르지만, 저는 선생님들이 저를 그처럼 높이 평가해주셔서 정말로 기쁩니다. 그래서 저는 최선을 다했고 점차로 모든 능력을 마스터했습니다. 어떻든, 우리는 우리 자신을 충분히 믿고서 충분히 실패하면 어떤 일이든 해낼 수 있으니까요.

저는 또한 어떤 상황에서도 희망이 있다고 생각합니다.

Q. 글에 따르면 다음 가운데 어느 것이 올바른가?
(a) 글쓴이는 낙관적이다.
(b) 글쓴이는 피아니스트가 되고 싶어 한다.
(c) 글쓴이의 선생님들은 엄하지 않았다.
(d) 글쓴이는 최선을 다하는 것의 가치를 믿지 않는다.

해설 특히 마지막의 두 문장을 통해 글쓴이의 낙관적인 태도를 엿볼 수 있다. 따라서 정답은 (a)다. 나머지 선택지들은 모두 본문의 내용에 어긋난다. 따라서 정답이 될 수 없다.

어구 strict 엄한　　　　　　demanding 많은 노력을 요하는
exception 예외　　　　　cellist 첼로 연주자
think highly of ~를 높이 평가하다
gradually 점차로　　　　master 완전히 습득하다

정답 (a)

26

해석 감수성과 상상력이라는 두 가지 주요 특성이 새로운 시대를 특징짓습니다. 첫째로, 인터넷의 광범위한 사용은 사람들로 하여금 이성이 아니라 감정에 보다 민감해지도록 만들었습니다. 역설적이게도, 반미감정은 그에 대한 고통스런 증거입니다. 사람들은 미국에 대해 감정적으로 반응합니다. 둘째, 상상력은 우리 삶의 많은 측면에서 점점 더 영향력이 커져가고 있습니다.

Q. 새로운 시대의 특징은 무엇인가?
(a) 이성과 지식
(b) 반미감정
(c) 인터넷과 기술
(d) 감정과 창의성

해설 첫 번째 문장에서 밝힌 sensitivity와 imagination의 적절한 paraphrase를 찾으면 된다. 따라서 정답은 (d)다. 특히, 본문의 일부 내용에 이끌려 (b)나 (c)를 정답으로 생각하지 않도록 유의해야 한다.

어구 era 시대　　　　　　　characterize 특징짓다
sensitivity 감수성　　　　imagination 상상력
widespread 광범위한　　compel 강요하다
sensitive 민감한　　　　reason 이성
ironically 아이러니하게도　emotional 감정적인
influential 영향력이 있는

정답 (d)

27

해석 메리 케이 애쉬는 원칙에 기반을 둔 회사를 세웠기 때문에 제 역할 모델 가운데 한 명입니다. 그녀는 늘 '우리는 올바른 일을 한다.'라고 말했습니다. 이 원칙을 고수함으로써, 그녀는 미국에서 가장 성공적인 회사들 가운데 하나를 설립하는 데 성공했습니다. 덧붙여, 그녀의 회사는 다양한 나라의 다양한 사람들에게 희망과 사랑을 주는 국제적인 기업입니다.

Q. 다음 가운데 어느 것이 글에서 언급되지 않았는가?
(a) 메리 케이 애쉬는 백만장자였다.
(b) 메리 케이 애쉬는 성공적인 회사를 설립했다.
(c) 메리 케이 애쉬는 원칙을 존중했다.
(d) 메리 케이 애쉬는 많은 외국인들에게 희망을 주었다.

해설 (b), (c), (d)는 모두 본문에서 확인할 수 있다. 그렇지만 (a)에 대해서는 본문에서 전혀 언급이 없기 때문에 정답이다. 이처럼 문제를 풀어나갈 때, 본문을 통해 정확히 알 수 있는 사항만을 생각해야 한다는 점을 명심하자.

어구 role model 역할 모델
principle-based 원칙에 기초한
adhere to ~를 고수하다　　　establish 설립하다
global 국제적인　　　　　　　various 다양한

정답 (a)

28

해석 '니코마코스 윤리학'에서 아리스토텔레스는 플라톤의 형상 이론을 비판한다. 아리스토텔레스는 플라톤이 형상이 다른 세계에 속한다고 단언한다는 점에서 틀렸다고 지적한다. 플라톤은 우리가 사물과 사물의 추상적인 형태를 구별할 수 있기 때문에 각각이 서로다른 세계에 속한다고 생각한다. 아리스토텔레스의 견해로는, 플라톤의 결론이 논리적으로 옳지 않다.

Q. 글에 따르면 다음 가운데 어느 것이 올바른가?
(a) 아리스토텔레스는 플라톤에게 논리학을 가르쳤다.
(b) 아리스토텔레스의 결론은 옳지 않다.
(c) 아리스토텔레스는 플라톤과 생각이 달랐다.
(d) 플라톤은 아리스토텔레스에게 윤리학을 가르쳤다.

해설 주어진 글에서 아리스토텔레스와 플라톤의 사상 차이를 확인할 수 있으므로 정답은 (c)다. 나머지 선택지들은 주어진 글에서 분명하게 밝히지 않았기 때문에 정답이 될 수 없음에 유의해야 한다. 언제나 주어진 글에 충실해야 함을 명심하자.

어구 ethics 윤리학　　　　　　criticize 비판하다
form 형상　　　　　　　　assert 단언하다
belong to ~에 속하다　　　distinguish 구별하다
conclusion 결론　　　　　logically 논리적으로
logic 논리학

정답 (c)

29

해석 대륙 이동이란 지구의 대륙이 서로에게서 멀어지는 현상을 가리킨다. 이 개념은 알프레드 베게너에 의해 도입되었다. 많은 자료에 바탕을 두어, 베게너는 본래는 오직 하나의 대륙이 존재했다고 생각했다. 그는 그 대륙을 '판게아'라고 불렀다. 대략 2억년 전에, 판게아는 여러 부분으로 갈라졌고 그 부분들은 서로에게서 멀어져갔다.

Q. 글에 따르면 다음 가운데 어느 것이 올바른가?
(a) 알프레드 베게너는 대륙 이동이라는 개념을 받아들이지 않았다.
(b) 베게너에 따르면 판게아는 20억 년 전에 여러 부분으로 갈라졌다.
(c) 알프레드 베게너는 본래 여러 대륙이 존재했다고 생각했다.
(d) 베게너의 이론은 많은 양의 자료에 바탕을 두고 있다.

해설 세 번째 문장을 통해 정답을 분명하게 확인할 수 있는데, 정답은 (d)다. 나머지 선택지들은 모두 주어진 글의 내용에 어긋난다. 판구조론과 함께 대륙이동설도 정확히 그 내용을 익혀두는 것이 바람직하다.

어구 continental drift 대륙 이동　　concept 개념
introduce 도입하다; 소개하다　　based on ~에 바탕을 둔
originally 본래　　　　　　　　drift ~를 떠내려 보내다

정답 (d)

30

해석 1919년 3월 1일, 한국인들은 삼일운동을 전개했다. 서울의 태화관에서 한국의 '독립선언문'이 낭독되었다. 수천 명의 한국인들이 거리로 뛰쳐나와 일본으로부터의 독립을 요구했다. 대략 2백만 명의 한국인들이 이 평화적인 운동에 참가했다. 그러나 이 운동은 일본인들에 의해 잔혹하게 진압을 당했다.

Q. 글에 따르면 다음 가운데 어느 것이 올바른가?
(a) 일본인들은 삼일운동을 환영했다.
(b) 삼일운동은 평화적인 운동이었다.
(c) 한국인들은 중국으로부터의 독립을 요구했다.
(d) 대략 2천 명의 한국인들이 삼일운동에 참가했다.

해설 삼일운동에 대한 설명으로 정답은 (b)이다. 물론 삼일운동에 대한 상식만 갖추고 있어도 문제를 쉽게 풀 수 있긴 하다. 그렇지만 그렇다 하더라도 주어진 예문을 꼼꼼하게 확인하는 습관을 잊어서는 안 된다. 이 지문에서도 참가인원의 수와 같은 사항이 대부분이 망각하고 있을 것으로 생각되기 때문이다. 어떻든 언제나 판단의 기준이 주어진 글이라는 점을 명심해야만 한다.

어구 launch 착수하다; 출시하다
declaration of independence 독립선언문
take to the streets 거리로 뛰쳐나오다
participate in ~에 참가하다
peaceful 평화적인　　　　　cruelly 잔혹하게
suppress 탄압하다

정답 (b)

31

해석 니콜이 충분히 의식하고 있듯이, 예술은 본질적으로 자기표현입니다. 그런 것으로서, 예술은 일정 정도로 자기 수양할 것을 요구하는데, 저는 니콜이 자기 수양이 아주 뛰어난 예술가라고 확인할 수 있습니다. 이것은 주로 그녀가 전통적인 방식으로 양육되었기 때문이라고 생각됩니다. 예술은 또한 자유를 뜻하는데, 니콜은 이 점도 또한 이해하고 있습니다. 더욱이 니콜은 결코 예술의 실용적인 측면을 망각한 적이 없는데, 그래서 패션 디자인에서의 경력을 추구하게 되었습니다.

Q. 니콜은 어떤 학생인가?
(a) 오만하고 시샘이 많은 (학생)
(b) 전통적이고 상상력이 부족한 (학생)
(c) 예술적이고 실용적인 (학생)
(d) 게으르고 수줍음이 많은 (학생)

해설 주어진 내용을 통해 니콜이 '예술적이고 실용적인' 학생이라는 점을 알 수 있으므로 정답은 (c)다. 나머지는 주어진 내용을 통해 알 수 없기 때문에 정답이 아니다. 언제나 전체적인 글의 흐름에 유의해야 함을 명심하자.

어구 aware 인식하고 있는　　self-expression 자기 표현
require 요구하다
self-discipline 자기 도야, 자기 훈련
assure 확신시키다　　　　upbringing 양육된 방식
practical 실용적인　　　　aspect 측면
pursue 추구하다

정답 (c)

32

해석 Newsweek과의 전화 인터뷰에서, 수아드 레이자는 왜 그녀가 미국 이민·세관 집행국에 협조하기로 결심했는지를 설명했다. 레이자는 그녀의 가족이 만든 위조 서류가 미국에 대한 또 다른 테러공격을 돕는 데 쓰일지도 모른다고 우려했다. 그녀는 가족에 대한 충실함보다도 나라에 대한 충성심이 더 중요하다고 생각했다. http://www.newsweek.com/id/117121를 방문하여 이 놀라운 이야기를 읽어 보라.

Q. 글에 따르면 다음 가운데 어느 것이 올바른가?
(a) 수아드 레이자는 미국 이민·세관 집행국에 협조하지 않았다.
(b) 수아드 레이자는 나라가 가족보다 더 중요하다고 생각했다.

(c) 수아드 레이자는 멕시코에서 양육되었다.
(d) 수아드 레이자는 미국에 대한 또 다른 테러공격에 협조할 심산이었다.

해설 마지막에서 두 번째 문장을 통해 (b)가 정답임을 알 수 있다. (a)와 (d)는 주어진 내용에 어긋난다. 반면 (c)는 주어진 내용을 통해서 알 수 없기 때문에 결코 정답이 될 수 없음에 유의하자.

어구 concerned 우려하는   document 서류
attack 공격   loyalty 충성(심)

정답 (b)

33

해석 사람들이 생각하는 바와 달리, DontDateHimGirl.com은 나쁜 남자들에 대한 불만을 토로하기 위한 웹사이트가 아니다. 실제로, 이 사이트는 여성의 삶을 향상시킬 수 있는 '사회적 네트워킹 사이트'이다. 예컨대, 자긍심을 높이는 방법에 대한 정보마저도 찾을 수 있다. 덧붙여, 이 웹사이트는 이성 관계에 문제가 있는 남성들에게도 좋은 곳이다.

Q. DontDateHimGirl.com은 어떤 웹사이트인가?
(a) 여성들이 더 나은 삶을 살도록 도와주는 웹사이트
(b) 여성들이 남성을 증오하도록 만드는 웹사이트
(c) 정치 활동에 대한 정보를 제공하는 웹사이트
(d) 남성들이 서로를 증오하도록 만드는 웹사이트

해설 두 번째 문장으로부터 (a)가 정답임을 알 수 있다. 특히 (b)를 정답으로 착각해서는 안 된다. 첫 번째 문장에 not이 포함되어 있음에 유의해야 한다. 그리고 (c)와 (d)는 주어진 글만으로는 알 수 없기 때문에 정답이 아니다.

어구 complaint 불평   actually 실제로는
improve 향상시키다   self-esteem 자긍심
relationship (이성) 관계

정답 (a)

34

해석 죠 슈와쯔 박사에 따르면, 숙취는 술에 들어 있는 메탄올 때문에 생긴다고 한다. 효소가 메탄올을 포름알데히드로 바꾸는데, 포름알데히드는 심한 두통과 피로를 초래한다. 그렇지만 위키피디아에 따르면, 숙취는 에탄올에 의해 초래되는데, 에탄올은 신체가 물을 손실하도록 만든다. 그러면 죠 슈와쯔 박사와 위키피디아 가운데 어느 쪽이 진실을 말하는 것일까?

Q. 글로부터 추론할 수 있는 바는 무엇인가?
(a) 위키피디아는 숙취가 메탄올 때문에 생긴다고 설명한다.
(b) 위키피디아에 따르면, 메탄올은 신체가 물을 손실하도록 만든다.
(c) 슈와쯔 박사와 위키피디아가 둘 다 옳다.
(d) 슈와쯔 박사는 숙취가 메탄올에 의해 초래된다고 생각한다.

해설 숙취의 원인에 대한 대립되는 의견을 다룬 글이다. 첫 번째 문장으로부터 (d)가 정답임을 확인할 수 있다. (a)와 (b)에서는 메탄올을 에탄올로 바꾸면 정답이 된다. 그리고 메탄올과 에탄올이 서로 다르다는 점을 감안할 때, 또한 마지막 문장에서 어느 쪽이 옳은지를 생각해 보도록 하고 있으므로 (c)는 정답이 될 수 없다.

어구 hangover 숙취   methanol 메탄올
contain 함유하다   alcoholic drink 알콜 음료
enzyme 효소   formaldehyde 포름알데히드
ethanol 에탄올

정답 (d)

35

해석 안네 프랑크 박물관의 대변인인 에리카 프린스는 피터 쉬프에 대한 보다 많은 정보를 찾고 있는데, 쉬프는 안네 프랑크의 '하나의 진실한 사랑'이다. 그의 사진은 그의 친구인 언스트 미켈리스에 의해 박물관에 주어졌다. 쉬프와 미켈리스는 베를린에 있는 홀드하임 슐에 같이 다녔다. 1942년, 두 친구가 헤어질 때, 사진을 서로 교환했다. 피터 쉬프에 대한 보다 많은 정보를 갖고 있다면, http://www.annefrank.org을 방문함으로써 그 대변인에게 연락을 취하라.

Q. 글로부터 추론할 수 있는 바는 무엇인가?
(a) 안네 프랑크는 언스트 미켈리스를 사랑했다.
(b) 피트 쉬프에 대한 정보가 충분하지 않다.
(c) 안네 프랑크와 언스트 미켈리스는 같은 학교를 다녔다.
(d) 언스트 미켈리스와 피터 쉬프는 1945년에 헤어졌다.

해설 첫 번째 문장과 마지막 문장을 통해 피터 쉬프에 대한 정보가 충분하지 않음을 알 수 있으므로 정답은 (b)이다. 나머지 선택지들은 주어진 내용과 어긋나기 때문에 정답이 될 수 없다. 이처럼 주어진 문장으로부터 바로 알아낼 수 있는 형태의 추론이 TEPS 독해 영역 추론 유형의 대표적인 특성이다.

어구 spokeswoman (여성) 대변인
Holdheim Schule 베를린에 있는 유태인 학교
part 헤어지다   exchange 교환하다

정답 (b)

36

해석 해리성 둔주 환자들은 자신들이 누구인지 완전히 잊어버린다. 그래서 집을 떠나 전혀 다른 곳에서 살아가기 시작한다. 자신들이 다른 사람이라고 생각할 수도 있다. 이 질병은 몇 시간, 며칠, 또는 몇 달 동안 지속될 수 있다. 많은 정신과의사들은 이 장애가 이혼을 당하거나 실직과 같은 충격적인 경험에서 비롯된다고 생각한다.

Q. 글로부터 추론할 수 있는 바는 무엇인가?
(a) 해리성 둔주 환자들은 때때로 정체성을 잊어버린다.
(b) 해리성 둔주는 대개 몇 년 동안 지속된다.
(c) 해리성 둔주 환자들은 유명인사가 자신들을 사랑한다고 생각한다.
(d) 해리성 둔주 환자들은 자신들이 지극히 뚱뚱하다고 생각한다.

해설 첫 번째 문장을 통해 정답이 (a)임을 알 수 있다. 주어진 글에서 이 질병이 몇 달 정도까지 지속될 수 있다고 했으므로, 그 이후에는 정상으로 돌아와서 정체성을 찾게 되리라고 추론할 수 있다. 그리고 (b)는 주어진 내용에 어긋나며, (c)와 (d)는 다른 정신질환과 관련된 설명으로 주어진 내용과는 거리가 멀다.

어구 dissociative fugue 해리성 둔주
entirely 전적으로   last 지속되다
psychiatrist 정신과의사   disorder 장애
result from ~으로부터 비롯되다

정답 (a)

37

해석 앞으로의 진로를 선택한 다음에 나는 예기치 않은 장애에 직면했는데, 그 장애는 바로 영어였다. 역설적이게도, 나는 이 사랑스러운 언어를 사랑한다. 미국 영화를 아주 많이 봤고, 미국 노래를 아주 많이 들었고, 미국 책들을 아주 많이 읽었다. 그들 모두 다양한 방식으로 내 마음에 와 닿았다. 문제는 TEPS 시험에서 높은 점수를 받아야 한다는 것이었다. 뭐라고? TEPS 시험? 도대체 그

게 무엇인가?

Q. 글로부터 추론할 수 있는 바는 무엇인가?
(a) 글쓴이는 영어를 아주 좋아한다.
(b) 글쓴이는 미국 영화를 즐기지 않는다.
(c) 글쓴이는 TEPS 시험에서 높은 점수를 받았다.
(d) 글쓴이는 미국 노래들을 많이 작곡했다.

해설 두 번째 문장으로부터 정답이 (a)임을 알 수 있다. (b)는 주어진 내용에 어긋난다. 반면 (c)와 (d)에 대해서는 주어진 글만으로는 알 수가 없기 때문에 정답이 될 수 없다. 이처럼 TEPS에서는 추론의 허용 폭이 상대적으로 좁다는 점을 명심해야 한다. 반드시 주어진 글의 구체적인 문장으로부터 바로 추론할 수 있는 내용을 선택하는 습관을 들이자.

어구 decide on (숙고하여) 선택하다 career path 진로
be faced with ~에 직면하다 unexpected 예기치 않은
obstacle 장애 ironically 역설적이게도
lovely 사랑스러운 touch 감동시키다

정답 (a)

PART III

38

해석 2004년 민주당 전당 대회에서, 버락 오바마는 기조연설을 했다. (a) 그 연설에서 오바마는 모든 미국 아동들이 만족할 만한 삶을 살아갈 수 있도록 하는 데 있어 정부의 중요성을 강조했다. (b) 그 목적을 이루는 데 있어 정부가 우선순위를 바로잡아야 한다고 오바마는 생각했다. (c) 덧붙여, 그는 미국이 이라크와 전쟁을 벌여서는 안 된다고 언급했다. (d) 그는 또한 정부가 모든 미국인들에게 평등한 기회를 제공해야 한다고 생각했다.

해설 글 전체의 흐름이 미국 정부와 미국인들 사이의 관계라는 점을 감안할 때 정답은 (c)다. (c)는 미국과 이라크의 관계라는 다른 내용이기 때문이다. 비교적 난이도가 낮다고 하더라도 꼼꼼하게 따져보는 습관을 잊어서는 안 된다.

어구 keynote address 기조연설 stress 강조하다
decent 만족할 만한 achieve 성취하다
priority 우선권 equal 평등한

정답 (c)

39

해석 NASA의 에임스 연구 센터의 수석연구원인 토니 콜라프릿트는 2대의 우주선을 달로 보내는 계획을 발표했다. (a) 놀랍게도 두 우주선은 달의 남극에 충돌할 예정이다. (b) 콜라프릿트는 많은 이들이 그 프로젝트에 대해 우려하고 있다는 것을 알고 있다. (c) 그들은 NASA가 외계에서 우주인을 찾아주기를 희망한다. (d) 그러나 그는 그런 프로젝트가 '매우 경제적'이라는 사실을 강조한다.

해설 우주선의 달 충돌 프로젝트를 설명한 글이기 때문에 외계인의 발견을 다룬 (c)가 정답이다. 일단 프로젝트의 범위가 달이고, 달과 충돌시키는 것이기 때문에 (c)처럼 지나치게 비약해서 생각해서는 안 된다는 점을 명심하자.

어구 principal 주된 investigator 연구관
announce 발표하다 spacecraft 우주선
clash into ~와 충돌하다
concerned about ~에 대해 우려하는
alien 외계인

정답 (c)

40

해석 유감스럽게도, 너무도 많은 언어교사들은 언어를 기계와 같은 부품의 혼합으로 간주한다. (a) 그래서 그들은 무의미한 반복과 끝없는 연습이 학습자로 하여금 특정 언어를 구사할 수 있게 할 것이라고 생각한다. (b) 그렇지가 않다. (c) 언어를 성공적으로 익힌 학습자가 되려면 목표 언어의 핵심, 또는 정신에, 닿아야만 한다. (d) 많은 능숙한 학습자들은 의미에서의 미묘한 차이를 본능적으로 지각한다.

해설 언어에 대한 잘못된 생각을 지적하고 올바른 언어 학습법의 핵심을 밝힌 글이다. 이와 같은 주제에 비추어 볼 때, (d)는 전혀 다른 내용이므로 정답이다. 이처럼 무관한 문장 고르기가 대체로 보아 난이도가 낮은 편이기는 하지만, 글 전체의 흐름에 비추어 각 문장의 적합성을 판단하는 능력을 측정한다는 점을 감안하여, 꼼꼼하게 따져보는 습관을 평소에 길러야 한다. 언제나 글의 일관성을 염두에 두고, 영어식 사고를 배양하여 실전 TEPS 준비에 만전을 기하자.

어구 regard A as B A를 B로 간주하다
mixture 혼합(물) meaningless 무의미한
repetition 반복 endless 끝없는
command (언어를) 구사하다 target 목표
skillful 능숙한 instinctively 본능적으로
perceive 지각하다 subtle 미묘한

정답 (d)

TEPS

Test of English Proficiency
developed by
Seoul National University

청해 Listening Comprehension

문법 Grammar

어휘 Vocabulary

독해 Reading Comprehension

수험번호 Registration No.

성명 Name / 한글 / 한자

문제지번호 Test Booklet No.

감독관확인란

주민등록번호 National ID No.

수험번호 Registration No.

비밀번호 Password

좌석번호 Seat No.

고사실란 Room No.

서약

본인은 필기구 및 기재오류와 답안지 훼손으로 인한 책임을 지고, 부정행위 처리규정을 준수할 것을 서약합니다.

답안 작성시 유의사항

1. 답안 작성은 반드시 컴퓨터용 싸인펜을 사용해야 합니다.
2. 답안을 정정할 경우 수정테이프(수정액은 불가)를 사용해야 합니다.
3. 본 답안지는 컴퓨터로 처리되므로 훼손해서는 안되며, 답안지 하단의 타이밍마크(▮▮▮)를 찢거나 낙서 등으로 인한 해손시 본인에게 불이익이 발생할 수 있습니다.
4. 답안은 문항당 정답을 1개만 골라 ▮와 같이 정확히 기재해야 하며, 필기구 오류나 본인의 부주의로 잘못 표기한 경우에는 답 관리위원회의 OMR판독기의 판독결과에 따르며, 그 결과는 본인이 책임집니다.

Good ▮ Bad ⦶ ⦷ ⦵ ⊗ Ⓨ

뒷면(Side2)

TEPS
Test of English Proficiency
developed by
Seoul National University

응시일자 : 20 　 년 　 월 　 일

성명	영문
	서명

<부정행위 및 규정위반 처리규정>

1. 모든 부정행위 및 규정위반 적발 및 이에 대한 조치는 TEPS관리위원 회의 처리규정에 따라 이루어집니다.

2. 부정행위 및 규정위반 행위는 현장 적발 뿐만 아니라 사후에도 적발될 수 있으며 모두 동일한 조치가 취해 집니다.

3. 부정행위 및 규정위반 적발 시 당해 성적은 무효 처리되며 사안에 따라 최대 5년까지 TEPS관리위원회에서 주관하는 모든 시험의 응시자격이 제한됩니다.

4. 문제지 이외에 메모를 하는 행위와 시험 문제의 일부 또는 전부를 유출 하거나 공개하는 경우 부정행위로 처리됩니다.

5. 각 파트별 시간을 준수하지 않거나, 시험 종료 후 답안 작성을 계속할 경우 규정위반으로 처리됩니다.

단체 구분
학생 ⃝ 　 일반 ⃝

질문란

1. 귀하의 TEPS 응시목적은?
ⓐ 입사지원 ⓑ 인사정책 ⓒ 입시
ⓓ 개인실력측정 ⓔ 국가고시지원 ⓕ 기타

2. 귀하의 영어권 체류 경험은?
ⓐ 없다 ⓑ 6개월 미만 ⓒ 1년 미만
ⓓ 1년이상 3년 미만 ⓔ 3년 이상

3. 귀하께서 응시하고 계신 고사장에 대한 만족도는?
ⓐ 0점 ⓑ 1점 ⓒ 3점
ⓓ 4점 ⓔ 5점

4. 최근 2년내 TEPS 응시하셨는?
ⓐ 없다 ⓑ 1회 ⓒ 2회
ⓓ 3회 ⓔ 4회 ⓕ 5회 이상

성명 (성·이름순으로 기재)

학력		전공	직업
	졸업 / 재학·휴학		
초등학교		인문	공무원
중학교		사회과학·법학	교사·교수
고등학교		경제학·경영학	군인
전문대학		자연과학	의료인
대학교		의학·약학·간호학	자영업
대학원		공학	회사원
		교육학	주부
		음악·미술·체육	자원
		기타	기타

직종	직책
고위임직원	임원
전문직(과학·공학)	부장
전문직 (교육)	과장
전문직(법률·회계·금융)	대리
기술·준전문직	계장
사무·보조	사원
서비스·판매	인턴
생산관련	기타
기타	기타

TEPS

Test of English Proficiency
developed by
Seoul National University

| 수험번호 Registration No. | 성명 Name | 한글 | 한자 |

| 문제지번호 Test Booklet No. | 감독관확인란 |

청해 Listening Comprehension

(문항 1~60)

문법 Grammar

(문항 1~50)

어휘 Vocabulary

(문항 1~50)

독해 Reading Comprehension

(문항 1~40)

주민등록번호 National ID No.

수험번호 Registration No.

비밀번호 Password

좌석번호 Seat No.

고사실란 Room No.

유의사항

서약

본인은 필기구 및 기재오류와 답안지 훼손으로 인한 책임을 지고, 부정행위 처리규정을 준수할 것을 서약합니다.

답안작성시 유의사항

1. 답안 작성은 반드시 **컴퓨터용 싸인펜**을 사용해야 합니다.
2. 답안을 정정할 경우 수정테이프(수정액)를 사용해야 합니다.
3. 본 답안지는 컴퓨터로 처리되므로 훼손해서는 안되며, 답안지 하단의 타이밍마크(▮▮▮)를 찢거나, 낙서 등으로 이를 더럽히지 않도록 주의해야 합니다.
4. 답안은 문항당 정답을 1개만 골라 ● 와 같이 정확히 기재해야 하며, 필기구 오류나 본인의 부주의로 잘못 표기한 경우에는 답 관리위원회의 OMR판독기의 판독결과에 따르며, 그 결과는 본인이 책임집니다.

Good ●
Bad ◐ ◑ ◓ ⊗ ◍

TEPS

Test of English Proficiency
developed by
Seoul National University

응시일자 : 20　　　년　　　월　　　일

〈부정행위 및 규정위반 처리규정〉

1. 모든 부정행위 및 규정위반 적발 및 이에 대한 조치는 TEPS관리위원 회의 처리규정에 따라 이루어집니다.

2. 부정행위 및 규정위반 행위는 현장 적발 뿐만 아니라 사후에도 적발될 수 있으며 모두 동일한 조치가 취해 집니다.

3. 부정행위 적발 시 당해 성적은 무효 화되며 사안에 따라 최대 5년까지 TEPS관리위원회에서 주관하는 모든 시험의 응시자격이 제한됩니다.

4. 문제지 이외에 메모를 하는 행위와 시험 문제의 일부 또는 전부를 유출 하거나 공개하는 경우 부정행위로 처리됩니다.

5. 각 파트별 시간을 준수하지 않거나, 시험 종료 후 답안 작성을 계속할 경우 규정위반으로 처리됩니다.

성 명 (성·이름순으로 기재)

성 HONG GIL DONG
명 (성·이름순으로 기재)

	EX	A	B	C	D	E	F	G	H	I	J	K	L	M	N	O	P	Q	R	S	T	U	V	W	X	Y	Z
	H																										

성 명

단체구분

학생	일반
○	○

질문란

1. 귀하의 TEPS 응시목적은?
   (a) 입사지원　(b) 인사정책
   (c) 개인실력측정　(d) 입시
   (e) 국가고시 지원　(f) 기타

2. 귀하의 영어권 체류 경험은?
   (a) 없다　(b) 6개월 미만
   (c) 6개월 이상 1년 미만　(d) 1년 이상 2년 미만
   (e) 2년 이상 3년 미만　(f) 3년 이상

3. 귀하께서 응시하고 계신 교사정에 대한 만족도는?
   (a) 0점　(b) 1점
   (c) 2점　(d) 3점
   (e) 4점　(f) 5점

4. 최근 2년내 TEPS 응시횟수는?
   (a) 없다　(b) 1회
   (c) 2회　(d) 3회
   (e) 4회　(f) 5회 이상

성 명 : 영문
서명

학력

학력	재학 졸업 중퇴
초등학교	
중학교	
고등학교	
전문대학	
대학교	
대학원	

전공

인문
사회과학·법학
경제학·경영학
자연과학
의학·약학·간호학
공학
예·체능
음악·미술·체육
기타

직업

공무원
교사준비
교사
군인
의료인
자영업
학생
회사원
무직
기타

직종

고위 임원 / 관리
전문직 (과학·공학)
전문직 (교·육)
전문직(법률·회계·금융)
기술공
사무
영업
판매
보호서비스
생산
단순노무
농어업
운전
기능직
비서
기타

직책

임원
부장
차장
과장
대리
사원
계
기타

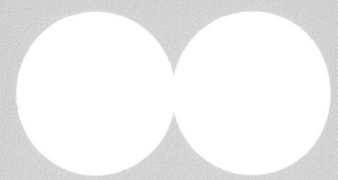

1 TEPS가 보인다!
실제 TEPS와 같은, 엄선된 양질의 문제를 실었다.

2 초보자도 알기 쉽게 충실한 해설을 담았다!
알찬 내용과 충실한 해설로 영어 초보자들도 TEPS를 만만하게 시작할 수 있다.

3 모든 영역을 골고루 다룬 기초 종합서다!
균형 있는 학습이 되도록 모든 영역을 28개 UNIT으로 구성했다.

TEPS 첫걸음 R/C는...

▶ UNIT별로 특화된 EXERCISE를 통해 해당 UNIT의 내용을 효율적으로 학습하도록 했다.

▶ "독해"의 경우 UNIT별로 "Tips"를 제공해 유형별 또는 전반적으로 독해에 필요한 관련 정보를 제공했다.

▶ "어휘"의 경우 UNIT별로 핵심이 되는 대표 어휘들을 충실한 해설을 담아 제시했다.

▶ "문법"의 경우 TEPS에 필요한 핵심 문법사항을 알기 쉽게 정리했다.

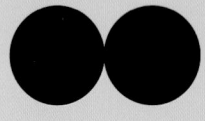

독해 · 청해 · 문법

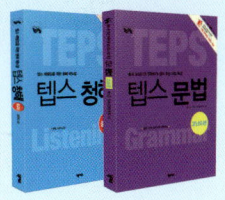

서울대 텝스 관리위원회 최신기출 Listening | 서울대학교 TEPS관리위원회 문제 제공 · 넥서스 TEPS연구소 해설 | 320쪽 | 19,800원
서울대 텝스 관리위원회 최신기출 Reading | 서울대학교 TEPS관리위원회 문제 제공 · 넥서스 TEPS연구소 해설 | 568쪽 | 24,800원
서울대 텝스 관리위원회 최신기출 스피킹·라이팅 | 서울대학교 TEPS관리위원회 문제 제공 · 유경하 해설 | 340쪽 | 28,000원
서울대 텝스 관리위원회 최신기출 i-TEPS | 서울대학교 TEPS관리위원회 문제 제공 · 넥서스 TEPS연구소 해설 | 296쪽 | 19,800원

How to 텝스 독해 기본편 | 양준희 · 넥서스 TEPS연구소 지음 | 312쪽 | 17,500원
How to 텝스 독해 중급편 | 장우리 지음 | 360쪽 | 17,500원
How to 텝스 독해 고난도편 | 넥서스 TEPS연구소 지음 | 324쪽 | 17,500원
How to 텝스 청해 중급편 | 양준희 지음 | 276쪽 | 18,500원
How to 텝스 문법 고난도편 | 테스 김 · 넥서스 TEPS연구소 지음 | 160쪽 | 12,500원

어휘

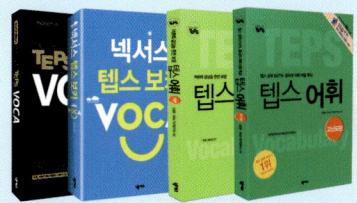

텝스 기출모의 1200 | 넥서스 TEPS연구소 지음 | 456쪽 | 18,500원
How to TEPS 실전력 500 · 600 · 700 · 800 · 900 | 넥서스 TEPS연구소 지음 | 308쪽 | 실전력 500~800: 16,500원, 실전력 900: 18,000원
서울대 텝스 관리위원회 텝스 실전 연습 5회+1회 | 서울대학교 TEPS관리위원회 문제 제공 | 200쪽 | 9,800원
텝스 기출모의 5회분 | 넥서스 TEPS연구소 지음 | 364쪽 | 14,500원

서울대 최신기출 TEPS VOCA | 넥서스 TEPS연구소 · 문덕 지음 | 544쪽 | 15,000원
How to TEPS VOCA | 김무룡 · 넥서스 TEPS연구소 지음 | 320쪽 | 12,800원
How to 텝스 넥서스 텝스 보카 | 이기헌 지음 | 536쪽 | 15,000원
How to 텝스 어휘 기본편 | 고명희 · 넥서스 TEPS연구소 지음 | 304쪽 | 15,500원
How to 텝스 어휘 고난도편 | 김무룡 · 넥서스 TEPS연구소 지음 | 296쪽 | 17,000원

고급 (800점 이상)

How to TEPS 시크릿 청해편 · 독해편 | 유니스 정(청해), 정성수(독해) 지음 | 청해: 22,500원, 독해: 14,500원
텝스, 어려운 파트만 콕콕 찍어 점수 따기(청해 PART 4 · 문법 PART 3,4) | 이성희 · 전종삼 지음 | 176쪽 | 13,000원

How to TEPS 실전 800 어휘편 · 청해편 · 문법편 · 독해편 | 넥서스 TEPS연구소(어휘, 청해, 독해), 테스 김(문법) 지음 | 어휘: 12,800원, 청해: 19,000원, 문법: 16,000원, 독해: 19,000원
How to TEPS 실전 900 청해편 · 문법편 · 독해편 | 김철용(청해), 이용재(문법), 김철용(독해) 지음 | 청해: 17,000원, 문법: 16,500원, 독해: 17,500원

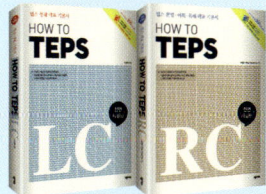

How to TEPS L/C | 이성희 지음 | 400쪽 | 19,800원
How to TEPS R/C | 이정은 · 넥서스 TEPS연구소 지음 | 396쪽 | 19,800원

How to TEPS Expert L | 박영주 지음 | 340쪽 | 21,000원
How to TEPS Expert GVR | 박영주 지음 | 520쪽 | 28,000원
How to TEPS Expert 고난도 실전 모의고사 | 넥서스 TEPS연구소 지음 | 388쪽 | 21,500원

넥서스

"모두가 인정한 **그들이** 만들었다!"

서울대 공식
2015~2016
최신기출!

〈서울대 텝스 최신기출 1200제〉 문제집/해설집

1 현재 공개된 공식 기출
1,200문항 독점 수록

2 수험생들의 필살기 **TEPS 만점 전략**

3 문제집과 해설집 별도 제작

4 실제 고사장에서 듣던 **청해 음성**